The Perfect Child

How To Raise A Perfect Child, Who Always Loves You And Never Does Anything Wrong.

Nathan Guy Hatch

Second Edition, September 2024

© 2025 Nathan Hatch

for
S. N. S. M. A. O. M. J. D. J. G.
C. B. C. C. K. M. K. M. E. G.

ABOUT THIS BOOK

This is a stand-alone companion to *Fuck Portion Control*. While this book talks about some health and nutritional issues, the other more thoroughly explores themes of health, nutrition, illness, and problems related to metabolic wellness including conditions such as depression, anxiety, cancer, thyroid disease, insomnia, erectile dysfunction, and alcoholism and addiction, and strategies for the resolution of those problems and the standards of a healthful diet, good nutrition, and healthy eating habits. This book encompasses psychological, social, and emotional wellbeing of human beings, especially as it relates to our development as children and effectiveness as adults and parents.

Content

The Perfect Parent	11
Intergenerational Trauma	19
Basics of Parenting	30
Intermediate Parenting	43
Advanced Parenting	55
Misconceptions About Parenting	67
The Self-Defeating Ego	77
Learning and Development	86
Abuse	96
Discipline	109
Self Care	121
Self Compassion	146
Inventory Therapy	162
Amending Relationships	208
Pseudoempathy and the Duality of Control Mechanisms	222
No	232
Teenagers	244
Replicating Tribal Structures	252
Education	269
Systems of Failure	281
Nutrition, Growth, and Maturation	304
Sexuality	318
Friendship, Bullying, and Other Social Challenges	335
Problem Children	354
Our Other Half	368
The End	392

A Public Service Announcement,
From Your Sink

You may think you know your sink,
But your use does rather stink.
I am not your bin for dishes,
Please don't fill me to the brink.
A sink is not for storage of
Uneaten bowls of porridge,
Or that oil that was too hot,
Please, sir! Leave it in the pot!
You'd think a dirty shoe would be
Washed outside, but eww,
It's here all gross and grimy
On my surface once so shiny.
There are some other uses,
Are approved that I, amuses—
You may strain your mashed potatoes,
You may mix your chocolate mousses.
You may water pretty flowers,
You may cry with me for hours.
But the best use I am used for,
The one that's always fun,
Is filling me with soapy water
To wash a newborn baby bum.

1

The Perfect Parent

In the Summer of 1998 when I was seventeen I finally found some friends with whom I could be rebellious. It wasn't my intent to be rebellious, but for most of my teenage years I had associated with a crowd of well-behaved kids from religiously conservative families, because that was expected of me, and they were some of the worst people I have ever met—constantly gossiping, rarely warm, and as a closeted gay boy people with whom I felt in constant danger for my wellbeing should they really get to know me. My new friends were two boys my age whom I had observed at a distance and greatly longed to be companions until I eventually gathered enough courage to approach them (one of whom is still a best friend to this day and possessed of not an ounce of malice). But they were inclined toward slightly more mischief than the others with whom I associated, and so when my new friends first proposed we go "pool-hopping," I was immediately gripped both by a thrill of excitement and an arresting sense of hesitation. Pool-hopping is just the act of trespassing on (in?) public or private swimming pools after hours and under cover of darkness so as not to get caught. Our first target was the local recreation center which had only a low fence surrounding the enormous complex. During the day I practiced there with my swimming team, so when we pulled up to the street outside I feigned a bit more excitement than I actually felt, since to me this was a familiar and comfortable place but which also made it perfect for my first brazen attempt at lawbreaking. But when we ran up and over the fence I suddenly realized we were all going swimming in our underwear. Being raised in a prudish, body-shaming culture this aspect of my unexpected rebellion was suddenly a far greater taboo than trespassing.

Making the situation more heated was the invitation of several other high school boys, one for whom I had an enormous crush. The surge of teenage testosterone drove me to blind indulgence as we stripped off our shirts and pants and slipped into the dark, cool water. Well, I slipped into the pool because I was smart. The others (including my crush) chose to cannonball.

"Hey, idiot!" my friend Tanner whispered angrily to the boy after he came up for air. "Be quiet!"

The warm, dry Summer air was perfect for a night swim, and we all cruised around low in the water, laughing quietly, splashing, and wrestling each other and having some of the most fun I ever had in my childhood. Suddenly a light nearly as bright as the sun shone across the pool and illuminated the fences closing us in, making them appear like the perimeter of an incarceration center. "Shhhh!" said Tanner, though all of us were already frozen by instinct, keeping our heads just above water and below the lip of the pool deck. The light moved back and forth across the complex. It was originating from the street, and clearly from that of a police car. Luckily for us the pool was on the top of a small hill, which made looking down into it impossible unless one were to walk right up to it. An inaudible sound of a police radio crackled for a moment, then the light went off and the sound of the car faded into the distance.

Emboldened by our success we lingered a great while longer, then when our fingers were pruny and cold we slipped back out of the water, put on our clothes over soaking wet skin and retreated back to our respective homes to sneak in late after curfew.

Several weeks and pools later the end of Summer fast approached, and the looming threat of our final year in High School began to burden us with a vague but impending sense of urgency. All of us boys came from unstable homes, and being together was cathartic and escapist, but not yet adults had no sense of what the real world was really like, nor how to remove ourselves from the kinds of turmoil each of us was subjected on a daily basis. The usual neighborhood pool-hopping and toilet papering was no longer a sufficient counterbalance to the fast approaching end of our childhood. One Saturday night when Tanner was feeling especially restless, he proposed something truly epic. "How about we jump the fence at *Seven Peaks?*"

Seven Peaks was a giant water park near our town. The only one in our region, actually. It was huge, with towering water slides, a lazy river, and an enormous wave pool. It was a sweltering night, and our teenage restlessness demanded an outlet this daring, this risky. Like common criminals our complacency of getting away with our earlier misdeeds had deluded us into an errant sense of impunity that not a single moment was spent considering the ill-conceived nature of this plan, and off we went to the water park.

The complex sprawled for acres and acres surrounded by a very tall fence beyond which was open space and treeless lawn. Finding an acceptably secluded and shaded spot to begin our assault was tricky, but eventually we happened on a place where we could scale the fence in darkness. "What if they have security cameras?" I asked as we walked up to the complex. "There's not any," confidently replied my friend Will. The long drive to the park had given my brain enough time to suggest some second thoughts, and now that we had arrived and seeing it in person, I knew that this was a bad idea. But I had never before had such a bond with friends, nor felt like I truly belonged with anyone, and I would do anything to keep myself in their lives. Including put myself into danger. So when they began to scale the fence, I followed.

Leaping over the top of the fence I landed on the other side where there was no turning back—Well, technically I *could* have turned back, but I was committed now and decided to enjoy without any reservation the last remaining moments of my childhood. We scattered across the park, some of us going directly for the wave pool, leaving a trail of clothes behind us as we went. The water was very cold, which felt refreshing in the heated night air, but the complex was so open, so exposed that there was none of the relaxation or joy that came with our previous experiences. The wave pool, closest to the fence and set low by the pool deck felt the safest. But my adventurous friends and the others we'd invited along couldn't resist the sight of the empty water slides and after only a few moments in the wave pool took off toward the tower, laughing with even more carelessness than we had trespassing a small neighborhood pool.

Reluctantly, I pulled myself out of the water and followed. As our bare feet plodded up the steps, their middling attempts to muffle laughter was amplified by the empty, hollow slides. "There's no water in them!" said one of the others suddenly. Their bare feet began squeaking loudly against the dry fiberglass shell as they tried to descend, the tube acting as a megaphone for their hollering and the banging of feet, knees, and elbows. Any pretense to be clandestine was totally abandoned. Of course, they also had to go to the very tallest of the corkscrew slides, so by the time I finally reached the top some had already emerged at the other end and splashed out into the landing pools.

The tube was completely dark, and the silence of the night seemed to somehow echo back at me as I stared down its throat. Only once had I ever been in such a tight space, a pair of caves outside our small town we regularly explored which were later sealed up for good after someone got stuck in them and died. There was a little bit of water in the queue trough. I splashed some of the water into the slide to lubricate it, and jumped inside.

I only slid for a few feet, as the water rushed quickly away from me and as soon as it was gone the slide was suddenly as dry as if water had never been in it. Stuck to the shell I proceeded to crab walk down the rest of the way, wishing now the experience had been thrilling enough to justify all of this trouble when suddenly I heard the voices of grown men outside, down below me.

"What's going on?" one of them said. Will's reply was inaudible, but his sheepish tone which meant he was in trouble was unmistakable. For a moment I considered hiding in the slide and waiting for them all to leave. But then I would be alone, in my underwear, trapped in a giant water park in another town without a ride home.

I was not surprised to see the police when I emerged from the other end. It just seemed like a natural consequence to our stupidity, so I smiled a bit when they directed their combat-grade flashlights in my face, feeling only a little ridiculous at being caught in such a compromising position. The cops were nice enough, actually, especially because we didn't resist at all (and probably because we were all teenagers in our underwear). After we had retrieved our clothes and settled obediently on the curb they told us of the time they were called to the park to apprehend adults who were naked and one they had to chase up the side of the nearby mountain with a helicopter as he tried to flee. One by one they called each of our parents, but when they got to me, my parents were at a resort in the mountains for the weekend with the rest of my family. I had purposefully protested going with them because things with my parents were going so badly. Being around them did nothing but fuel my overwhelming depression, which would soon culminate in trying to take my own life, and any reprieve from them was becoming a necessity and not simple teenage discontent. In truth I was suddenly proud of myself for having done something daring, something fun, something that would make a great story when enough time had passed. But now this meant that there was no one to collect me. One of the officers drove me to a nearby juvenile detention center. It was dark, as if not a single other person was in the building. He opened a door to a dorm with two small beds wrapped with coarse, brown blankets. My father would be there to collect me in the morning, he said.

    I slept fast and heavy, exhausted from the night's antics, but early in the morning, before the sun had even rose over the mountains, my angry father appeared at the door to my little prison, the noise of which woke me immediately. He was silent most of our drive home. There was some lecture, but I didn't pay attention because it was the same kind of bullshit they flung at me when I didn't want to wear my hair a certain way or asked to take a foreign language class instead of seminary. But then he said I had to accompany him back up to the resort. I had been on many of these family trips to hotels for a few days, sleeping on the floor in a sleeping bag because my parents couldn't or wouldn't pay for extra rooms, herded from activity to activity because my restless parents could never just sit poolside or take a picnic on the hike and take in the view. I was also now six-foot-six and two hundred twenty-five pounds, and riding in the back of his Porsche was like riding in a carnival bumper car. A few months earlier my father had also caught me looking at gay porn on the computers at his office building. He had forced me against my will to tell my mother, and both had promptly rejected me. Constant lectures, condemnation, and pressure to engage our bishop and other religious leaders about my sexuality (which I did not understand, since I was only seventeen) was driving me unawares toward irreparable despair, and being in their presence only served to intensify the pain of my torment. The anxiety made me snap. Angry, I refused to go. Then my father began to berate me for all of it, and every insult, every harsh word uttered in my direction across my entire childhood suddenly broke me. I shouted that I hated him and slammed the plate of food I was carrying onto the ground and it shattered across the clean wood floor. Never in my life had I lashed out in anger. Not even once had I ever punched or hit my brother, or broken something in a fit of rage. In that moment both I and my father realized that I was becoming a man and was large enough to stand up for myself, not physically but emotionally and intellectually. Frightened of my new power, I fled the house and into the surrounding woods.

The sun was bright and blazing, and the dry scrub oaks were thick and comforting. Far enough from the house, that I could still see it but not risk being seen, I sat down against a rock. The buzz of cicadas rang loud against the apparent stillness. Even though I was emotionally exhausted I could not cry very much. Instead of sadness or anger or hatred there simply seemed to be a whole lot of nothing. I knew that trespassing was both stupid and wrong, and I knew that my Dad didn't really care that I had gone there. He drank alcohol as a teenager, smoked pot, had *Playboys*, engaged in recreational arson, and engaged in all sorts of premarital sex, and also looked at pornography even as an adult, in his marriage. I got the best grades in my family, was captain of my swim team, and was on student council. I had never even kissed another person, drank, smoked, or once gotten in any other trouble. He would later admit to me that he thought my stunt was funny at the time, but thought he needed to be mean and calloused to teach me a lesson, which meant showing no compassion, no camaraderie, no pity for his oldest child.

Despair threatened to overwhelm me. Why did I have to suffer this burden? What had I done to deserve the hatred and shame which threatened to swallow me up before I had even made it out of childhood? Why even with all my obedience and spiritual wrestling and pleading couldn't I draw redemption to myself? I could not understand why I felt the way I did, why I did not want to live, why my family didn't love me, why I couldn't be straight. I finally cried there until there were no more tears left to cry and the sun began to burn my skin, reluctantly picked myself up and headed back toward the house.

It must have only been an hour or so since I ran off, and when I got home I thought I was seeing things again at the sight of another police cruiser parked out front of our house. Immediately I thought something was wrong with my father and hurried inside.

Two policemen stood talking with my dad in the dining room. They all scowled at me when I showed up, and suddenly I realized they were there about me. "Son," said one of them. "We have to respond to calls about domestic violence. You're lucky you didn't do anything worse. Next time we'll have to arrest you."

The blood drained from my face. I had just been arrested, and now my own father had called the police on me because I broke a plate? *Did he tell you about all the horrific things he said to me?* I wanted to say. But I knew if I caused a scene that things would get worse for me, so I remained quiet. The police finished talking to my father, strutting around the house as if their belts and their guns and their uniform gave them power over all of humanity, and I finally realized that my father didn't actually care about me. It all made sense—how they responded to finding out I was gay, how they encouraged me to lie, the constant disparagement, never coming to any of my swimming meets or school events, never engaging with academics, not helping me prepare for college, making me work for him instead of letting me have a normal summer job. Why he'd forced me to play basketball when I started growing tall and then began telling me I wasn't athletic or driven when I didn't do well or show the requisite amount of enthusiasm for his constant criticism and harassment. It was all about them. About control. It was all justified as concern for me, but I was *dying*. It couldn't be for me. It seemed I was nothing more than a constant reminder of everything he hated in himself. All his own personal disappointments and regrets and failures. I understood that there, standing before him and the two police officers in my own home. It was *never* about me.

I completely shut down after that, surrendering to my fate, understanding that I only had to endure the last year or so of my time with them. My Senior Year was an empty blur filled with remorse, fear, and loss. My body began to buckle under my depression. I became tired and lethargic, distant, distracted. The year before I was in three advanced placement classes and done exceptionally. I could barely handle normal classes and so I dropped all but advanced placement art class, which was a rare respite and opportunity to release some of my pain and frustration through creativity. But unable still to reconcile my struggle I grew ever resistant to my parent's abuse and neglect, and as soon as graduation passed they wasted no more than a few weeks before asking me to leave. Then, lost in the world of men and ill prepared for adulthood I would struggle valiantly for a couple more years before finally trying to kill myself.

I have often been rebuffed by parents when attempting to intervene on the behalf of their children as if my advice is criticism rather than attempts to empower them, as if I could not possibly comprehend the realities of parenthood, and the mere suggestion that they are not shining pillars of success is somehow morally offensive. Toward the end of my twenties during a family reunion my brother and his new young daughter, the first of many nieces and nephews, had a total meltdown when she didn't want to get in the car to go somewhere. She was particularly good at grabbing anything at all she could hold onto, and after visiting with my dogs had crawled into their kennel and when her parents tried to extract her clung screaming, hilariously, to the bars from inside the cage with both hands. But, frustrated by her fit he began to hurl insults at her, telling her how terrible she was. Empathetic to the feelings that children have which cause such disparities between adult needs or wants and the child's I tried to intervene for both their sakes—to help my lovely niece feel safe and to empower my brother with effective strategies which would help him get what he needed and help spare her from the kind of pain I had gone through. Instead, he quickly cut me off with a curt reply, "It's different when you're actually a parent," he said. "You'll know if you ever have your own," and forcibly hauled her off, tears streaming down her pudgy little cheeks.

But in reality my brother had no more comprehension of parenthood than I did. Less even, considering his approach to parenting which showed the same kind of callous, detached, and ineffective authoritarian behavior he learned from my own parents which in the end required the brutish leveraging of his size advantage to force his will on a little, thirty-pound child. A total, abject inability to understand the motivations of children and the reasons they act and react as they do, without any compassion or patience for their newness and innocence and ignorance. *Yes, I'm the one that doesn't know how to parent even though it's your child sprawled out on the floor screaming at the top of her lungs just because she has to get into the car.*

The insistence by parents that they remain uncriticized for their mistakes or even praised for simply showing up is a uniquely arrogant position that would not be tolerated in any other capacity of human life. If a young man walked onto a baseball field with no prior experience expecting to be a starter he would be roundly chastised and rightly harangued for his naivety and sense of entitlement. Nobody would be expected to even attempt Chopin let alone well if they had never practiced piano. Yet for some inexplicable reason parents are expected to be good at parenting even though they've never done it before, and expect other people to keep their mouth shut when they are clearly failing at best and at worst actively committing abuse and clearly being stressed out to all hell by the experience. Worst of all, parents themselves expect that they should be good at something they've never done before and in all likelihood had very poor instruction. Several studies have shown (what is already obvious) that intergenerational parenting (meaning that grandparents participate in the active, daily rearing of children) produces more successful and healthy adults. Most societies which still practice intergenerational parenting are those which tend to be more economically challenged (or not yet seduced away by conveniences of monetary success), because the younger adults of reproducing age are also those which generally provide for the family, so the children are then incidentally left with grandparents as caretakers and thus benefit from a wider group of adults, some of whom also possess more knowledge, wisdom, and experience whom are thus more effective. In our Western and more economically prosperous societies our wealth and opportunity interrupts this natural tribal structure of human existence, with more experienced grandparents being far less involved in the direct responsibilities of parenting, and as such thrusts new parents into their role without adequate preparation or resources, while also burdened with the virility and distractions of youth, which in turn further strains their emotional, social, and intellectual resources, their marriages, and then their connection with their own children. Especially when previous generations are also inadequate and ineffective at parenting this problem compounds itself as successive generations become more and more self-centered due to instincts for self-preservation which are caused by abuse at the hands of the previous generation.

I was absolutely one of the best possible children any parent could have hoped for—talented, ambitious, handsome, creative, helpful, loving, kind, and extremely intelligent, and yet because of the shit job their own parents did, and the scars and trauma they carried into their adulthoods they could not even see the reality of their own family, that of one which most parents in the history of mankind would be envious, and instead used it as a stage on which to reenact over and over their own unresolved and psychologically stunted development and childhood trauma, causing the very problems with their children they wanted to avoid and making their lives a miserable nightmare of hatred, anger, and pain. Parenting is often much harder than it needs to be, only becoming difficult largely due to our own experiences and unresolved pain and trauma which color our perception of life, our sense of self-worth, what it means to be a parent, our children, ignorance, the effectiveness of our behavior, our relationships with other people including our spouse or significant other, and misunderstandings about life in general. Many parents believe they must be perfect in order to be good parents or even a good person, but this misses entirely the point of parenthood, which is to empower your children with the skills, strengths, and wisdom they will need not just to lead a successful life, but even to survive it. Tumbling through parenthood we become alarmed when our experiences cause us to realize that maybe we don't actually know what we're doing, which only further emboldens us to try harder but which also makes our mistakes that much more painful and setbacks that much more infuriating, as the clock counts down faster and faster.

It is entirely possible for parents to be perfect parents. Not in the sense of never making mistakes, but to instead wholly fulfill the role and function we are meant to, which is a role that most of us are also wholly ignorant, you know, because of our own parents, and their parents, and their parents before them and so on. When we do discover what it means to be a good parent, not only can we be more effective in our role and more efficient with our time, energy, and resources, the responsibility becomes as easy and even more satisfying than our lives when we were single, because being a perfect parent, for instance, *requires* that we make mistakes that our children learn how to handle the mistakes that they will make. But most of us want to believe we can avoid mistakes or should not make them in the first place, and so model for our children willful ignorance and self-destructive behaviors and then act surprised when they get knocked up or we find them smoking cigarettes behind the church or when they try to commit suicide. Trying to be perfect is exactly the opposite of being a good parent. This world is not perfect and we fail our children only when we fail to recognize our own self-worth and the realities of life and, as would be expected, parenting then becomes impossibly stressful. Every parent has the capacity to succeed, even to heights we never thought possible and even when our own pasts seem too difficult to bear. We can discover bliss not only in our role as parents but also ourselves, and actually live the kinds of lives promised by all those other books on parenting.

2

Intergenerational Trauma

When I was only a few months old my parents went on a trip to Europe even though they had also only been there a month before I was born and wasn't a once-in-a-lifetime reason to leave their very first, very young child. I was left in the care of my Nana, and when they returned a few weeks later I forgot who they were and refused to go to them, and it seems that before I could even roll over I knew what was in store for my life with them and wanted nothing to do with it.
 For all I knew my Nana was a wonderful person. Though not very personable or trusting she was always brightly cheerful and welcoming, her bright eyes shining even until her final years, the tone in her voice always as warm as a Summer's day, and her generosity had no bounds, in truth it was difficult after receiving fifty-dollars every birthday from them even when they lived only on social security not to feel some resentment for my other, wealthier Grandmother who gave us only five. But now as an adult I realize my Nana's incessant pleasantness was every bit as artificial as her jet-black, perfectly coiffed hair. Pricilla Joyce, as she was named, came from a time when parents didn't really spend the luxury of acting on emotions, and she was composed and reserved and never suffered fools. She was of the generation which endured the terrors of the Second World War, a time when humanity very nearly ate itself and committed unspeakable atrocities the world never even knew was possible. Her parents too were those who saw the First World War, when for the first time in human history untold thousands of human beings could be exploded apart by bombs or extinguished by chemical agents. The

trauma of living through those kinds of events is not something the human mind can manage, at all, and even for those who survived or never directly saw combat it takes from them the meaning of being human and everything we have ever believed about life and God.

One day when seeing a picture of my Nana's father in his own military uniform I asked her about him, having never been told about our great-grandparents long passed and thinking how handsome he was. He had fought in the First World War and she still had his hat, which to my excitement she extracted from a closet and gifted to me. To know that I was related to someone so brave and strong was indescribably affirming.

Both my Nana and my Granddad were always quick to make us feel welcome and loved, but never broached anything even remotely vulnerable. When I was in eighth grade I received an assignment to interview a family member about their life, and after much deliberation decided to choose my Granddad even though I also felt extremely intimidated by him. They lived in Arizona, a ten-hour drive once or twice every summer which seemed like a week itself to little children, and grew up hearing stories of how tough and mean my Granddad was, which were justified when we saw him bark at his mules or dogs but rebuffed when he made us pie and whipped cream or tricked us into believing he could inflate his bicep by blowing into his thumb.

I probably started our conversation with some awkward formality about interviewing him about his life. "I have to interview you," I think I said.

"Oh?" he replied, sounding surprised but also open. "What should we talk about?"

"What was life like when you were a teenager?" I asked. I knew he had served in the war, but at that age really had no idea what that really meant nor that there were so many which occurred in the twentieth century let alone the difference between any of them. "Well," he said. "I was too young to be drafted until it was nearly over. But when I turned eighteen they sent me off to basic training in San Diego. I made a buddy when I got there, and our nights on leave we went out looking for girls and to get a drink. One night we went out and found this bar, but when we went inside we realized we had gotten into a bar for homosexuals—"

I froze immediately, waiting for the stinging words to come from his mouth which would add to all the other horrible things I had heard about gay men, knowing well by that time I was one of them and understanding now that my secret would cost me the love of my family should it ever get out. In a moment which stretched out far longer than it was, I secretly hoped he would be the one to show me the love I had not yet found from my own flesh and blood, not from my religion, and not even from God.

"We didn't mind," he laughed. "We had a drink and a guy hit on my buddy and we had a great time."

I couldn't believe my ears. All my life I had only ever heard of homosexuals in the context of visceral animus, of hatred and condemnation, not deserving of love but certainly disease. Here was my Granddad, the tough guy, the patriarch, the rancher and horse breeder, the man feared by every one of my uncles talking admirably about a time he went to a gay bar. In the 1940's. Clearly Granddad knew I was gay and meant in that moment to help me. It did, though not to the degree I would require to avoid the despair which would savage me as a young man, but without which I would nonetheless have believed life to be *utterly* without love. Later, throughout my teenage years whenever we visited my Grandparents he would joke incessantly about when I was going to bring home a girlfriend, like the time when he first taught me how to drive stick-shift through the dry Arizona mountains in his twenty-year-old Dodge Ram pickup. "So when you gonna get yourself a girlfriend, Nathan?" He would say while elbowing me strongly, the pearl buttons of his cowboy shirt sleeves pressing sharply into my skin. I would smile to hide my embarrassment and secretly wish I could run away and hide. This continued even into my twenties, after my suicide attempt, long after I had come out but which I now realize too late was probably his attempt to get me to come out to him, but because they and my own parents' collective religious conservatism, bigotry, and habit of taking life too seriously I sadly mistook it for harassment and never did give him a chance to show if he accepted me or not. I found out later that Granddad had a niece who was lesbian who came out many, many years before whom I met later when my great uncle Gary was dying, and my Granddad's generosity of spirit made more and more sense as I got to know more of his own extended family.

Though my parents have many striking and admirable qualities as people, parenting is something at which they really failed (unless the bar being set is that they didn't kill us, but is that really the standard we're trying to meet?). But their particular failure is not at all unique to their generation, with emotional trauma, discontent, and destructive and contentious interpersonal relationships being the norm rather than the exception with the majority of their generation. I have twenty-four aunts and uncles and only one single pair of them are not angry, divisive, bigoted, hateful, fearful, suspicious, entitled, contemptuous, and utterly failed at parenting. Nearly all of them are child abusers, some even drugged their children, and most of them rejected me and my other homosexual cousins when we came out. Several years after recovering from cancer and a failed relationship and not having been home to see my family for several years (because the stress of being around them was the last thing I could handle) my father during a nice weekend afternoon in which I had been trying to get him to stop working and spend time with me to watch a show about the history of food and cooking since we are both skilled chefs suddenly turned on me after an innocuous comment about the economy probably going under in the next year or two (which it did) and excoriated me as if I were an actual geopolitical adversary and not his son whom he hadn't seen in person for almost three years who was trying to lighten the mood. He was so incensed that for a moment I actually feared for my physical safety, which I had not even on that day when I broke the plate. He left and I was shaking so badly I had to sit down for fear of my legs giving out (I had just been recovering from cancer and was still pretty weak). Having had enough of my mother's dissociation and obsessively compulsive cleaning to avoid any sort of meaningful interaction with me too I cut my trip short and cried the entire twelve-hour drive back to Los Angeles. Anguished and cursing my stupidity for falling back into expecting them to be any different than they were I tried to channel my remorse into something useful and began to ponder why it was that nearly every one of my parent's generation were so angry, so resentful, so ungrateful and discontent even as they gorge themselves on obscene amounts of wealth and prosperity that no other generation throughout the entire history of mankind has even dreamed. The immoral accumulation of junk and crap and excess simply for the sake of it, presented with an abundance of opportunity while obliterating any chance at making real and lasting changes to the human race, money and privilege hoarded by a generation who whine like pigs while possessed of such incongruent and unimaginable prosperity equalled only by their contempt.

The mass murder of High School students in Parkland, Florida by gun violence had also just occurred, and my thoughts drifted to the murdered children and their friends who will be forever traumatized by what they went through. I thought of the children who will never experience a school shooting but whom are regularly subjected to active shooter drills, hiding under their desks as practice alarms suggest their own impending, violent deaths and suddenly the image merged with that of my own parents' generation hiding under *their* desks during preparatory nuclear drills during the Cold War Era. Suddenly I saw the kids at Parkland and Newtown and Red Lake all the way back to Columbine the year I graduated High School and the mass terror being perpetrated on children not just from actual shootings but the entire system focused pathologically to the systemic torment of children and understood that the very same mass fear of violence and imminent threat of bodily harm was also done to the baby-boom generation. For decades my parents' generation were surrounded not just by war but also the threat of war, and their parents having been through actual war, robbed of naivety and happiness became scarred and detached, unable to comfort themselves for the horrors they had seen were unable to save their own children from nebulous and omnipotent psychological threat of an unstoppable and omniscient foreign government raining down total nuclear holocaust, threats which continued for decades through the tumultuous conflicts into the Sixties and Seventies. I cannot imagine how terrible my childhood would have been with regular indoctrination and fear of imminent death by nuclear immolation, and yet my parent's generation lived it.

There is a black and white cartoon from 1951 called *"Duck and Cover"* which begins with a cutesy, Disney-style animated turtle walking down the road on a beautiful sunny day to a stupid jingle, minding his own business, wearing a comically small hard hat, when out of nowhere a mischievous monkey lowers a firecracker near his head. The firecracker explodes, but the turtle is spared from having his head split open and suffering a gruesome death because he "ducked for cover." This cartoon was an attempt to gently introduce the threat of nuclear holocaust to children, and goes on to tell them about atomic bombs and how it will absolutely kill you if someone drops it on us, which they will do, and that dying from an atomic bomb is a lot like burning to death, but you wouldn't know what that's like so they then show video of enormous flames engulfing the screen so they could vividly imagine it. Before long the film segues into images of children, without any parental support, fleeing a playground while the banshee-wails of a nuclear warning siren play ominously in the distance, describing the exact horrific events of a nuclear explosion through animated images of homes being knocked over and burned and trees being stripped of their foliage, just in case your nightmare tonight lacks any details. The purpose of those films, and of active shooter drills being practiced today, was never to get children prepared for actual catastrophe, which in all reality they would die anyway and such films would do nothing to save them. Children can be prepared for emergencies of any type without being told how they will actually die, or the frightening particulars of why the threat exists in the first place. The film's discussion of evil actors possessing cruel and violent means to end your life stemmed from an authoritarian government and fear-mongering culture of the time, lead from the Eisenhower Presidency which helped catalyze and feed post-war tensions and thus a role for him in which to feel effective, he and his enablers seeking to extend the controversy, fear, and anxiety of military conflict in order to maintain control and power, which is accomplished exactly through such kinds of propaganda and fear-mongering, especially toward and exploiting children. Even if it was imperative for children to practice such drills, such as we do today for active shooters, such information can be non-specific and generalized for any emergency, to avoid traumatizing them. But it does not accomplish this because the point is not preparation, but indoctrination, with fear and distrust, which in turn creates more reactionary and fearful adults whom then subject themselves to control and authoritarianism but which in turn damages an entire generation. The anger of my parent's generation is that which has its origins in mass childhood trauma. Pain and fear which has never been named, let alone healed, which has resurfaced as their lifelines wane and their visit from the angel of death fast approaches, forcing out the unresolved trauma and fear of their past as they desperately search for salvation. All their lives they were told if they just believed certain ways or achieved certain success or bought certain things they would be happy. Their marriages in ruins and their children mentally ill they are realizing too late the mistakes of their past. They have run out of time and only at the very end have they realized they have never been happy, and lash out in resentment and anger and hatred. It makes sense that their generation should be restless and unfulfilled in spite of their prosperity. The prosperity was always just a distraction from the trauma of their youths which resides at the back of the mind, the driving force behind their restless ambition and calloused disregard for others, the Earth, and even their own wellbeing and that of their children. It is this way with anyone who has experienced overwhelming pain and heartache in their childhoods—unable to heal the memory of such horrors and conditioned to believe that life is so invaluable and dispensable creates people who can never recognize peace, even when it holds them tight.

    Though robbed of the financial windfall of the preceding generation, my *Millennial* generation is quite lucky in terms of history—The prospect of imminent death by nuclear annihilation ceased being inflicted on children just as we were born, and the trauma of mass school shootings had not yet begun.

We existed in a brief and relatively blissful world of He-Man, Pogs, Nintendo, and Tamagotchi, where the only real danger to our eventual adulthood was whether or not we would get into a prestigious university or a regular one. While many of us might have individual trauma from localized origins such as parental abuse which, at the hands of affected Baby-Boomers is quite widespread, we have had a general luxury of being blessed with a prosperous and optimistic worldview, having come of age under the advent of the internet and the unprecedented economic boom and relative peace of the 1990s. It's no wonder that while Millennials struggle in the current economic climate we are more able to let go of such ambitions and the pathological pursuit of money because we have no strong motivation to distract ourselves from the kinds of existential crises which other generations have suffered. Making matters worse, my parents' generation are often religious, even those who were Hippies in their younger years, but because their religious beliefs do nothing to resolve the internal conflict of trauma within the subconscious they are left believing they should feel wonderful when they do not, further frustrating their struggle to find happiness and satisfaction, and as their time runs out they grow ever more angry at the world, believing their entire lives that wealth and strong religious convictions and entitlement would bring the kind of enlightenment they so desperately crave to realize only at the very end the consequence of the deception and no time left to course correct.

But of course there is always time to change, to repair the past, to find healing. Those who don't are only stuck because of the nature of the ego, which believes itself trapped in imaginary cement, and the lack of skills which are required to do it. Relief from trauma is sweet no matter what time of life it is achieved. When it happens it is as if all that ever hurt no longer matters, making the past no longer matter, and since we are only ever what we are at the present moment it becomes our entire life.

Worrisome is the threat of school shootings, or more appropriately the hysteria and misplaced policies and practices which burden children with fears which should be borne instead by adults, and the effect these policies will have upon the young when they enter their own adulthoods will result in the very same kinds of anxiety, fear, anger, and pursuit of insubstantial distractions as currently plagues the Boomer generation if they are not careful to overcome their own collective trauma and find resolution to the internal conflicts of pain and loss which will surely result. One of my sisters purposefully torments her children by telling them all the horrible things that are happening in the world. When she was a child my parents watched local news every night, and the sensationalist framing of crime, tragedy, and war (the Iraq war) brought nightmares and trauma to several of my siblings. Without tools to heal this trauma in herself she believes that also traumatizing her own children will prepare them for the future, instead of handicapping them with debilitating fear and anxiety, and they already as little children display behaviors of extreme trauma like biting all the skin around their fingernails.

We all have trauma to some degree or another from our pasts, and this kind of work as outlined throughout this book is required by anyone who wishes to find resolution to themes with which we struggle during our lives, even if it is not as grandiose as geopolitical and intergenerational conflict. But larger, intergenerational trauma such as occurred to the Boomer generation and to those experiencing mass-shootings alters the course of man and history itself, and can render entire generations ineffective and destructive if we do not help each other toward healing. Awareness at least can be some kind of salve, but many of us try to handle our trauma by wrestling with our psyche or resolving to have a better attitude or discipline and thus persist with trauma even the entirety of our lives, because trauma resides in the unconscious mind and cannot be accessed by our will, and purposeful trauma therapy is the only way to overcome the burdens of the past which imprison happiness and satisfaction.

These themes also illustrate the first and foremost requirement for becoming a good or effective parent, which is that we must first resolve within ourselves the tumult of emotional conflict which resulted from our own childhood. *Oh, is that all?* you might ask. Yes it seems like an overwhelming prospect, especially since most of us choose to deal with our unresolved pain and trauma in the same way that previous generations always have—by ignoring it or distracting ourselves from it. Often parents are thrust into the role of parenting before any kind of healing can occur, and though adults appear as adults, when they first become one they have not yet actually lived as an adult, in an adult body, doing adult things, and as such are actually a child residing in an adult's body. It is no wonder that parents are bad at being parents, because they are often still children when they become parents themselves, not yet having had the experiences from which they will eventually gain wisdom. While many people are resistant to change or to self-analysis, which can come off or appear as self-centeredness, it is not actually self-centeredness which motivates us to resist but simply the lack of effective means which help us feel empowered to change and to heal. Most of us feel helpless and at the mercy of our past and our trauma and unresolved pain, because in reality we are helpless to it. Being unable to understand even how to make a change let alone make one we then feel inadequate, and fear others discovering this inadequacy and insecurity, and so like my brother lash out in resentment and anger when confronted with criticism or offers for help, as it seems to confirm our fear of being helpless. Willingness to learn and then willingness to make changes are first required before actually attempting to make the change, and the fact that you have opened this book and reached this point demonstrates those qualities! In fact, this is one of the hallmarks of good parenting, which is simply a willingness to grow and do better. Harms can almost always be repaired, if done properly, so even making mistakes is not really a problem so much as the refusal to fix them, and this too results from feeling unable to fix wrongs when it is required of us, never having been taught how to do so and thus possessing no confidence or familiarity for it. If at any time my parents had come to me voluntarily and said they were sorry for the way they treated me, in spite of all the abuse and neglect and pain and suffering I would still have gladly forgiven all of it without hesitation or question, even after forty years of it. The reality is that children always love their parents—but sadly it is not true the other way around. There are far too many abusers and murderers of children to demonstrate the falsity of that idea—but that children do always love their parents with undying affection is built into our very biology, and it is only through serious neglect, abuse, and the corruption of love that it can ever be otherwise. Even to this day I still acquiesce to my parents though they have done almost nothing to amend the pain and suffering they caused and continue to cause, because from the time that I could see and even after they drove me to try and take my own life I wanted nothing more than to have them near me and to love me in return.

Because of the work I have done on my own life I have achieved the ability to see into people's minds and hearts, to understand their long histories of pain and trauma, the events which have preceded their lives to the point in which I engage with them and the fears and insecurities that originate the actions they take and the things they say. My disappointment in my parents and the way they treated me is not gone, but it is enlightened by an understanding of why they, as human animals, do not possess the magnanimous qualities I was raised to believe they did, and without excusing their behavior understand and have compassion for the pain which drives them. This is the skill which parents can learn in order to become effective toward their own children and role as parent—removing the trauma and pain of our own past we become empowered with the ability to understand why people do what they do (i.e. our children) and what they really want, which is not always what they are able to communicate.

One Christmas when I was home visiting my family and we were all congregating at a condominium in Park City, Utah one of my new nephews suddenly broke down and fell completely to pieces. His mother, embarrassed at his behavior and lacking compassion for herself and her child, immediately became belligerent, refused to entertain his tantrum, and hauled him off to the pantry and shut him in the dark. The screams that little boy released still haunt me. But my sister was treated exactly the same way during her own childhood. When she refused to go to bed my father would take her and put her into the garage, alone, in the dark and cold, and her screams would shake the entire house, filling me with fear and hatred for him and my mother who encouraged it. Because this trauma happened to my sister it was the only reality which she knew to deal with noncompliant children. Another approach had never been demonstrated to her. We also as humans typically deal with this kind of childhood trauma by trying to ignore it, or move on from it which is in practice just ignoring it. This actually means that we shut down our sense of compassion, for ourselves, our minds engaging in all kinds of acrobatics to either justify, excuse, or ignore those things which we have very little power in resolving, such as trauma caused by those on whom we were utterly reliant as children. Because my sister both didn't understand that what she had gone through as a child was in fact child abuse, and had tried all her life to move past and deal with this abuse by putting it aside, it in turn meant cutting off compassion for the little girl she once was, and since that little girl went through horrifying trauma then could not feel compassion for someone else going through the exact same thing, which in this moment was her own son. Horrified by what was occurring but not seeking to enflame the situation I quickly stood up and put my body between her and the pantry without saying a word, opened the door, and got down on my knees to look into my nephew's tear-stained face. "What's wrong?" I asked. "I want my shorts," he eventually managed to choke out. Apparently he had a favorite pair of orange shorts which were at my parents' house and not at the condo where we were. But for some reason my sister was unable to communicate this to him in a way which satisfied both his desire for them and her desire that he stop asking. Being unburdened by both the responsibilities and stress of parenthood but also the particular traumas unique to her own life experience, I was able to understand exactly what he wanted and how the situation could be resolved. "Oh, I'm sorry," I said to him while giving him a hug. "I know you want those, and we would give them to you but they're at Grandma's right now, so we can't actually get them until we go there. But when we do go back there you'll have them."

His impulse was at first to continue crying for them, but what I said made so much plain sense that even a toddler in the midst of a meltdown understood the logic. He wiped his eyes and we stood up but not before my sister tried to lob another threat his way which I promptly stopped with an angry wave of my hand. The episode was then entirely over in less than a minute and never even needed to be a problem in the first place.

In reality, this episode was only ever a problem because of my sister's own abuse as a child and unresolved pain and trauma triggered by stimuli of the situation, which recreated the very same conditions under which she had also been abused as a child, because a child wanting a favorite pair of shorts is demonstrably *not* a problem. But unable to summon the kind of patience and compassion that would have otherwise diffused the situation, since those were not shown to her as a child and as such did not possess them for herself, was instead controlled by the heightened emotions and the way in which her child's behavior touched the sensitive and painful memories it triggered within herself.

Years later my sister would come around to realize that the trauma and pain from her childhood was getting in the way of her adult life and her relationship with her husband and children, and learned how to find compassion for herself and resolve childhood trauma as is discussed throughout this book. Seeing how it benefited my life she also wanted to experience the same relief and empowerment it brought. Clouded by her own trauma, her perception of her children was burdensome, frustrating, constantly strained by conflict, and was actually causing her to see her own children as a loathsome burden, which she did not want to be experiencing.

Many parents think that confident adults came from childhoods which instilled discipline and bravery. This is an utter falsehood espoused by abusive adults to cover their own heinous treatment of children. Confident and happy children come from homes where they could absolutely rely on their parents as a safe harbor, knowing that no matter how they tried or failed in the real world always had the protection and guidance of loving and committed adults to come home to. Children are utterly and in every way incapable of providing for themselves, both materialistically and developmentally but also emotionally and intellectually, and although they have never yet lived are usually treated as manipulative masterminds with as much life experience and wiles as an adult, little schemers who purposefully coerce and inconvenience to attain selfish and self-centered ends rather than the entirely helpless, reactionary, instinctual, naive, and innocent creatures they are. Children who must grow up in the homes of abusive adults grow in an environment of fear and volatility, and as adults are every bit as insecure and afraid as those who raised them. A child only acts the way they do because they are utterly helpless and unable to care or provide for themselves. Without parents children will die, so they are designed by nature to be loud, obnoxious, and demanding by instinct, to draw the attention of neglectful and abusive parents, to force adequate rearing if the parents are not otherwise naturally able to do it well. A baby doesn't cry because it's a brat. A baby cries because if it didn't, adults would have no idea when it needs something and they would all die and so would we as a species. Younger children don't crave sugar because they are undisciplined hedonists addicted to happiness but because sugar is a biochemical method of energy storage which helps their bodies to feel good (especially when they are stressed). When adults are unable to resolve their own emotional trauma and it impairs their effectiveness as parents, survival instincts within the child kick in to try to attain the things they need for their own survival that the adult is otherwise unable or unwilling to provide, even if it causes the child to become the recipient of abuse or neglect, because that is still better than death. But this in turn stresses out the adult even more, whose behavior is no less instinctual or mature than that of the children, and then the entire family unit is left operating on base, animalistic, survival instincts. When she was able to resolve the pain and trauma of her past, my sister finally saw that her children's combative, disagreeable behavior was simply a reaction to her own reactions to her own insecurities which had the effect of withholding love, tenderness, and compassion from them, because she also withheld it from herself, and when this was resolved her children very rapidly became calmer, happier, more productive, nearly like they were different people altogether, though they weren't in reality any different, only the situation was different because of the work she was willing to do.

 We are met by the unfortunate reality that although it is our parents' fault that we are traumatized and abused it is our responsibility to heal from it, and to not pass on the same mistakes and pain to the next generation as they did to us. Life works this way to teach us the reality of existence, that we are both alone and together, that there is sadness as well as happiness, that life and death exist together. Balance is the word to describe this, though most people errantly and arrogantly consider balance to mean perfection in one thing, which is not at all what balance is. We are affected and we also affect. Those who are ineffectual parents refuse to recognize the former while dwelling excessively on the latter, because the dearth of interpersonal skills and emotional self-care makes us feel keenly our ineffectiveness and inadequacies. When we empower ourselves to first resolve our own trauma, by exercising self-compassion by undertaking this work to care for ourselves, only then can we operate effectively to empower our own children to do the same and pass down the kinds of knowledge, skills, and self-compassion which is the true point of parenting.

Intergenerational trauma is the only real impediment to good parenting. Failing to have compassion for ourselves in turn prevents us from having compassion for our children. Trying to be a good parent without ever having taken care of yourself in this way is like trying to play Chopin when you have never sat at a piano while suffering from unresolved Cold War trauma. You will fail. But failure is not the problem—when we have tools to accomplish the resolution of our unresolved pain and experiences of trauma there is no such thing as failure, because everything can be resolved, mistakes can be fixed, and that is the most important skill that any person can learn. Especially parents, because it not only helps ourselves but will help our children help themselves in return, thus empowering children to live successful lives on their own, which is the entire point of parenting in the first place, and thus also resolve the cycle of intergenerational trauma.

3

Basics of Parenting

The summer when I was thirty-two-years old was the first time in my entire life I was ever allowed to bring home a romantic partner to meet my family. The last of my siblings was getting married and I had initially refused the invitation based on my previous experience with my parents and siblings who practice exclusionary religious rituals which preclude from participating those who do not conform to their religious beliefs (even other family members and members of their own religion) at special occasions such as marriage which is traditionally supposed to affirm family relationships, not divide them. When my only brother got married I was not asked to be his best man, since I was gay and would not be allowed at the ceremony, and the only friend I have known my entire life got married without me. My sisters too all spent their joyful day hidden in a secret church building rather than walking the aisle before family and friends in a beautiful wedding dress and allowing us to witness and participate in what should be a happy and momentous occasion to strengthen the legitimacy, social support, and bonds of a marriage. Rather than be humiliated and isolated, this time I had planned simply to stay home, especially since I now had a man at my side whom I loved deeply and felt offense at being required to choose between him and their callous religious ideology.

"Oh, I was looking forward to meeting him," replied my mother when I told her of my decision. "But I understand if you don't want to come."

It was not the response I expected, and I was suddenly surprised. "Really?" I asked. "That changes things. If you are inviting both of us I will come." "Yes," she replied. But there were more issues, so I continued. "I'm worried about other people." I said. "Like Grandma. Does she know I'm gay?"

"I already talked to her," said my Mom. "I told her that Nathan was going to bring his partner and that she wasn't allowed to say anything inappropriate but she said, *'I've known Nathan was that way since he was a little kid, and I would NEVER say anything to hurt him.'*"

Hearing this put a big smile on my face. For the first time it seemed like I had an actual family, and one who actually loved me for who I was. Everything was going to turn out okay in the end, it seemed, even if we did have our differences.

Most of my siblings had already met my partner via webcam, so his introduction was not an enormous affair, but the warmth which they showed in welcoming both him and me quickly undid nearly all the decades of pain and rejection I had endured. My parents had rented us a very large vacation home to house everyone for the wedding, and I had not anticipated how cathartic it would be to see my brand new nieces and nephews all clamoring around my partner. I cried quietly in our bedroom when the emotions became overwhelming. *This is what it's like to get married and grow a family*, I thought.

My partner and I were put straight to work helping with the wedding preparations. He helped the bride construct her bouquet which had been driving her nuts. Then we started helping to construct a favorite dish of our family's (and that of the bride to be) called *Kalua Pig* which, as you might have guessed, originates from the Hawaiian Islands where we lived for several years and requires ungodly amounts of meat even when it's *not* made for several hundred wedding guests. Suddenly my family were all dressed in their Sunday clothes and departing for the wedding while my partner and I were still shredding pork. They just assumed that since we weren't allowed in the ceremony that we could just take care of nearly two-hundred pounds of meat-shredding by ourselves. Suddenly I couldn't help but feel like I had been overly quixotic in my earlier reevaluation of people who had no qualms about cutting their own child out of their lives in the first place, and when the last person shut the front door to the big, empty, unfamiliar home, I had to fight not to let the lump in my throat win out. "I'm sorry," I said to him as our fingers began cramping. "I probably should have expected this."

"It's okay," he said. "I love your family, and at least we're together."

"Yeah," I agreed.

During the reception I introduced many of my cousins to my partner. One of my little cousins was not so little anymore, now nearly looking at me at eye level spent a long time in enthusiastic conversation with both my partner and I. We knew that look—the realization that you are not actually alone in this world. Since I was the only out gay boy in our whole family it was very exciting to know that someone else in our family was on my side (although I also immediately felt sorry for him, knowing that he would have a similar experience in his family as I did in mine). Driving back home in my parent's car, alone with my Mom and Dad and my partner, I mentioned that my little cousin was also gay. "Don't say that," said my mother tersely. My father didn't say anything, and suddenly all four of us were frozen in the awkward realization that my partner and I were not being embraced, but simply tolerated. After the wedding they all went back to the tradition of keeping their distance, even though I constantly tried to reach out to them, show interest in their lives, their children, help in their pursuits and struggles, buy expensive presents for their birthdays and holidays even when I couldn't afford it, and spent much time and energy helping them and their children with their health problems.

Several years after getting cancer and the tragic end of that relationship, after finally putting my life back together, my brother one day unsolicitedly lectured me on my relationship with our parents. He'd had a particularly wonderful moment of love for his own children and couldn't possibly understand how parents could not love their children and decided to cope with that horrible realization by insisting that our parents loved me. "Sure, they *think* they love me," I said, "but that's not love. They *like* me. They want me in their lives because I'm fun, I'm charming, smart, and handsome. I care about them and help them with their health. I make them feel good, and they are proud of being the parent of someone so talented and admirable. But that is not *love*. They think only of me in terms of what I can do for them. When your child comes out as gay and you throw them out of the house or when he nearly completes suicide and you respond by comparing him to pedophiles and murderers, or spend the last twenty years only talking to him a few minutes once or twice a month, refusing to ever meet any of his friends and lovers or include him in important family events, and with their time and money support institutions and governments which actively work to harm his safety, and prejudice his own siblings against him that is the very *antithesis* of love. They don't let me into their lives. They never ask how I am or what I'm doing because they don't want to know. If I talk about meeting someone they avert their eyes and change the subject. Or when I tell them about me or my cousin being attacked with homophobic slurs by those with whom they are ostensibly allied and warn them that the same thing is going to happen to their grandchildren they respond either by ignoring it or actually defending those people. *They don't know what love is.*"

It was a hard pill to swallow. But my parents' generation were not shown the kind of love which children need and deserve because of their own parents' collective trauma and inability to give it to them, and since they never experienced love do not have any to give.

This absence of familial love is also no coincidence of circumstance. Although our parents and grandparents and great grandparents going all the way back to the American Civil War have endured much trauma throughout their lives, the psychology and psychiatry profession for most of contemporary history promoted detachment from children as the supposedly healthy approach to parenting. This was always extremely suspicious because detachment from children causes trauma as children try to navigate life feeling alone and unsupported, and in response develop destructive coping mechanisms and mental health disorders like attention seeking, depression, bullying, thieving, lying, fear of intimacy, substance abuse, and suicidal ideation which then later requires the services of mental health professionals. The accepted practice of detachment eventually culminated in the psychotic conclusion of the poorly attributed "Attachment Therapy" model in which children are outright abused, restrained, and broken until they ultimately submit. Submission is not love, it is giving up, and creates of its own more extreme mental health problems, especially addiction behaviors as an adult, and this so-called therapy even resulted in the deaths of several children.

Love is the most basic tenet of parenting, but it is also unfortunately one of the most elusive and difficult to accomplish since many of us do not even know what love really looks like. Love is *not* a feeling. Love is action. The feeling we mistake as love is really only our selfish sense of *want* and the desire to fulfill our own needs, where love recognizes the value of another through demonstrable action. I took the occasion with my brother to also point out the disparity of claiming to love me while raising his children in a religion which teaches them to despise me. Unlike my parents, my brother does love me and has demonstrated it many times over the years, but he immediately became defensive and accused me of hating his children, leveraging my obvious affection for them and my vulnerability as a single, childless gay man as ammunition to win an argument and subvert his own personal responsibility. But his reticence to consider the effect of his choices on my life and our relationship is also rooted in our childhood and the things I did as a child in response to the environment in which we were raised which created an adversarial rather than brotherly relationship between us. Because they were not empowered with more effective and healthy parenting skills, my mother and father engendered a sense of competition between us in order to dominate us. This is an extremely common tactic parents use to feel more in control, using their children against each other to subordinate them. This is also almost never a conscious parenting strategy, but occurs simply because of the dependence relationship between parents and children and competition for scarce emotional and material resources between children and their siblings. Around the time that I was eight-years old we lived in a small suburban rambler in Norther Utah, and my brother and I shared a room at the far end of an unfinished basement. The walls were sheet-rocked and painted but the floor was bare, cold concrete littered with a few randomly placed carpet scraps. Even the laundry room was closer to the stairs than we were. One Sunday after returning home and dinner was being prepared my mother commanded us all to spit out our gum, which was used during long and boring religious services as a way to keep us quiet. Being the overachieving and eager-to-please gay boy I was, this command was obeyed promptly and without question. Gay boys are often the best at everything, including obedience, as a way to overcompensate for debilitating fears of rejection. But a little while later in the basement I noticed my brother still chewing his gum. Eager for any opportunity to justify my existence and prove my indispensability to our parents and thus receive the majority of the love and attention which was in short supply I immediately bounded up the stairs to report him. I felt great pride and cunning at finding a way to trumpet my own obedience while exploiting his mistake and demonstrating myself a responsible and willing participant in the authoritarian system, thus increasing my position within the ranks, and followed my mother eagerly back down to the basement to enact merciless vengeance upon my little brother.

"Why didn't you spit out your gum?" she said angrily. "I did," he protested, opening his mouth to reveal it completely empty. My mother looked inside and was satisfied.

But it was too convenient, too fast for my brother to have gotten rid of his gum in a responsible way. I knew he had been disobedient and, robbed of my chance to dominate and win the approval of my mother, I was determined to exploit his error. Quickly looking around for a possible hiding spot for the illicit chewing gum I saw there were very few places which could have served as an improvised receptacle. Under the carpets it would have stuck and eventually been discovered. There was a couch at the far end by the stairs but that would have risked getting caught as my mother came from upstairs. Then there was the dark and empty laundry room immediately near where he had been standing. Suddenly I saw the abyssal gap between the dryer and washer—the only possible place that gum could have gone so quickly without risk of being discovered. I walked to the gap and sure enough there was a little green wad of chewing gum in the back on the floor between the machines. "Mom!" I shouted excitedly. "It's here!" My mother's indignation at being disobeyed came swiftly to his bottom, and though I was filled even then with a sense of guilt for my failure to protect my own brother I had, at least temporarily, greatly improved my own chances for survival.

This kind of exploitative competition continued throughout our childhood, our brotherly relationship regularly interrupted with opportunistic occasions to subjugate the other. But since I was always bigger and more experienced it more often resulted in his disparagement and my promotion at his expense. Gay boys typically go through puberty on the same timeline as girls (where straight boys do not until a bit later), so even though I was only a year older than him I was always far taller and more mature, and there was a period of years where I had discovered my penis while my little brother was still naively stuck in childhood. Having to share a room with someone who was both immature and given to competition with me for approval from our parents by tattling proved truly frustrating. It reached an apex when, after inheriting my parents' old, discarded television I one day saw a preview for the movie of the week called *The Blue Lagoon* airing on television, which is a famous film about two teenagers coming of age while marooned on a desert island. Any straight boy who saw this movie during their youth was forever enchained to Brooke Shields. But as a twelve-year-old gay boy the teenage Christopher Atkins with his incredible head of blonde curls and pouty lips, wearing nothing but a loin cloth was a fantasy I had never even dreamed. The preview also teased an incredibly erotic, romantic sex scene. It was my first chance to ever see another boy naked, and I was not about to let my nosy little brother ruin it. Abhorrently, I resorted to extreme harassment and ridicule to purposefully make him cry so much that my parents would finally relent and give us separate rooms, which they unfortunately did. I got to see that movie and Christopher's naked butt as he made love under a canopy of flowers and have one of my own incredible coming-of-age experiences, but my behavior toward my brother effectively castrated what little relationship we had remaining, which has never closed even as we matured into kinder and more caring adults and even in spite of my efforts to make amends for my behavior, because some wounds can never, in truth, be healed, which is a hard lesson that many of us never learn until it is too late.

Baby birds of many species will actively peck and kill their siblings and toss their lifeless bodies out of the nest in competition for the parents' undivided support and attention. Many baby mammals get crowded out of access to mother's teat if they are not big enough to wrestle their siblings out of the way. Human instincts to survive are no less vicious, and when children are not provided with sufficient access to emotional intimacy (or in other words, love) instinctive drives to fight for sparing resources inspire competitive behaviors every bit as wild and animalistic as any other creature on this earth. The gum incident was about so much more than gum. Because children are absolutely incapable of providing for themselves, both materially but also emotionally, they are wholly reliant on parents for the things required to survive in life, and if parents are unable or unwilling to provide sufficiently for their children, the desperate desire to survive typically overcomes higher emotions and children then engage in cutthroat and desperate conflicts. Competition for love is also not simply an esoteric concept, but is practically relevant for actual survival since a parent's love directly results in tangible resources needed for survival like food, clothing, shelter, and skills and knowledge which may empower offspring to survive. When a child feels the need to compete with their siblings something maleficent has occurred which sets the children in fear for their own survival which thus triggers competitive instincts within them at the expense of others, since children are far more naturally inclined toward cooperation and love than adults.

Of course, this often happens because parents are selfish and desire more resources or time for ourselves, but parents only feel this way in the first place because we do not understand how to take care of both our own needs and that of our children at the same time, feeling that "me time" only exists if our children are not physically present, and since children are always present means as a parent we are never caring for our own needs.

The parent who cannot care for their own needs while also caring for children is also one who then withdraws emotionally from their children, because the inability to take care of their own needs engenders resentment toward their children which in turn prejudices how the parent interacts with a child. This then interrupts access to other areas necessary for a child's wellbeing like time, food, energy, opportunity, and even emotional and physical safety. This reduced access to resources required for survival then triggers insecurity and reactive survival instincts in children like competition and attention seeking. These behaviors place further demands upon a parent with already limited capacity to handle parenthood and thus results in further frustration, resentment, anger, and resultant deprivation of emotional support and material access for children. For example if as a parent, we feel the only time we can take care of ourselves is at night when children are asleep we then anticipate and desire bedtime as a break from parenting responsibilities so that we can take care of our own needs. When a child then has problems getting to bed, frustrated and tired and looking forward to our break will then attack or punish a child for not going to bed, because in so doing they have deprived us of our own needs. This in turn communicates to a child that we are not emotionally available which then triggers crying and other emotional conflict in order to force our attention upon them, but because our goal for bedtime is not the wellbeing of our child but instead that we can have a break from parenting we grow even more frustrated and angry which even further deprives our child of emotional support which causes even more emotional turmoil until a struggle for control eventually culminates with the parent asserting our dominance at the expense of our child's mental and emotional wellbeing.

Most parents think that the opposite of punishment is indulgence, but this isn't even close to how reality works and is only a result of previous inadequate and abusive parenting we experienced from our own parents. Indulging children is just another method of manipulation and control, which in turn results from parents and adults who do not understand their own life experiences, trauma, and pain nor how to be effective in life. Giving children what they need in terms of love and affection, hugs and kisses, close physical contact, eye contact and personal intimacy, food and nutrition, clothes, toys, time, friends, shelter, opportunity, and education only ever seems indulgent if we were also raised by calloused, cruel, and harsh parents who themselves were raised this way and thus use our needs and wants against us, to manipulate and control, and so on and so on. But parents who employ such strategies of deprivation and reward find themselves then dealing with the headache of warring, dissatisfied children, constantly at odds with each other, having to put out the very fires we started and unable to see the fruits of our own malicious behavior as if these little humans who came out of our bodies and raised and reared solely by ourselves are a product of their machinations and not *ours*, the adult. I can be among as many as ten or twelve of my nieces and nephews and feel less stressed than I do around just one of my siblings, because children are easy to control but adults trenchant and obtuse. Children can be satisfied with a kind smile, a hug, and a little eye contact even when we don't give them what they want. But because parenting for most parents is an exercise in control and domination we regard providing that which is necessary for children as the very act of ceding power and control rather than good, effective parenting. A niece who had a reputation for being "difficult" and "out of control" became putty in my hands in about five minutes after throwing a tantrum because I demonstrated to her that I cared for how she felt and how she was being taken care of, instead of threatening her with punishment, which only reinforces the problem of scarce emotional support and access to resources which triggers such behavior in the first place. She had fallen apart at the sight of her cousins' car pulling away from the parking lot to go home and nearly dashed after them into the road even though it was a wintry, bitterly cold day. Thankfully my arms were long enough to catch her coat before she ran into traffic. But she fought my hold and screamed to be taken with them. Other parents view this kind of behavior as willfulness and defiance, but in reality she just wanted to be part of our family and to not miss out on being together, since those needs were not met with her own family. Sympathetic to her needs I refused to let her down at all until she listened to me, never threatening punishment but instead exercising persistence. "I am not going to let you down until you listen to me," I repeated until she realized that resistance was futile. I then explained to her (even though she was pouting and not looking at me) that the day was ending and our cousins were going home to their own house, not back to hers as she thought, and that if she went with them it would mean driving all the way to their house just to go to bed once they got there. "Do you want to go home to their house?" I asked. "No," she admitted. "I know you want to be with them, and I'm sorry you felt left out. But they're coming back tomorrow too, so the sooner we get home and go to bed the sooner you will see them again." My willingness to be patient with her supported through action my proclamation of love, and my ability to communicate an understanding of exactly why she was disappointed and hurt showed empathy, which is the manifestation of love. Though not once during the encounter did I give her what she demanded nor allow her to control the situation, she was so completely satisfied that she stopped crying and sat in the wagon willingly, and even began laughing as we continued home and rolled over the bumps in the uneven sidewalk (and also never again gave me trouble that entire trip).

I was effective in that moment with my niece in being her surrogate parent because I gave her the things she needed (which in that moment she identified as only available from the things she was asking for) which were unconditional love and a sense of belonging. Knowing they are loved provides so much emotional stability it also helps prevent many of the consequences of other mistakes, since children are naturally inclined toward unconditional love themselves, and love in return helps them know that at the end of the day they are always going to be cared for, even if they don't get the things they want.

But the inability or failure to provide sufficiently for love and affection for children is in reality an inability for the adult to acquire these things for themselves. Raised by people who did as bad or worse a job at parenting as we are doing means we too were not given the skills required to achieve these things for ourselves and is the primary reason why parenting becomes so difficult, so how can we be expected to provide such things for children when we do not even have them in the first place? Just as my own parents' generation was denied access to love and thus have no idea what it is, we too cannot give love until we have found it for ourselves. Single, childless adults like myself are able to ignore such shortcomings of self-care, but by the very presence of children parents are forced to confront their own inadequacies and shortcomings, and this in turn causes much more dismay, resentment, pain, frustration, and perhaps failure and feelings of inadequacy, because we *are* inadequate, because no one ever taught us the skills we need to take care of ourselves as adults, and since we can't even take care of ourselves how in the world are we to care for children?

As a parent we are hardly ever alone, and if we require alone time to take care of ourself we will be woefully uncared for. The definition of adulthood is the ability to provide for our own needs, whether that be securing food or shelter or seeking out companionship, but also (and perhaps most importantly) our own emotional support. When our ability to care for ourselves is retarded, because of inadequate parenting, we are in reality adults who are still children, and like children we blame the world and our circumstances for our own problems since we have never moved beyond childhood into the self-sufficient nature of adulthood, which is not the shallow facades of earning money or having things and material success or even having sex and partying but the ability to provide for one's own emotional and personal wellbeing. This is one of the reasons why rich people are so often poor in character, because their resources and the resultant permissiveness it facilitates provides an opportunity to never be confronted by the consequences of childish behavior. The same happens in any adult who is raised by another which does not also possess skills and abilities of self-awareness, self-care, self-compassion, and self-determination. As a parent with responsibilities it is not only possible that we achieve self-care while also caring for children, but required.

Our responsibility to ourselves and to our families are not mutually exclusive, but only seem to be when we have never been shown how this is accomplished. Essentially, parents who fail to care for themselves while caring for children fail to differentiate themselves from their child and the responsibilities of parenthood, feeling obligated to indulge every whim and need of a child or to oppositely react in frustration and exhaustion from this obligation through rejection and punishment when neglect of our own self-care becomes too great to bear. Because parents do not differentiate themselves from their children or their responsibility as a parent we confuse acts of parenting and childcare as acts of caring for ourselves, when in fact they are not. If we were to go to a spa and get lunch with several friends, the presence of our friends does not distract from enjoyment of our time, and even adds to our enjoyment, even if they talk on and on about their relationship troubles or how much they hate their parents or are frustrated by work. When we take our children to a pool we are also at the pool, an activity that for many people would be otherwise relaxing and enjoyable. We would even be playing in the water and having a good time, but suddenly add children into the dynamic and all relaxation and recreation vanishes, because we are no longer having a good time but instead have intertwined our identities with our children and then spend the entire time experiencing the occasion through their experience and not our own. If this can be separated, everything we do with and for our children can also be for ourselves and thus also accomplish self care without neglecting our responsibilities as a parent. If we were single, most of the activities required in parenting are things we would be doing anyway— Cleaning, cooking, reading, working, going to the park, taking care of the dog, paying bills, earning money, going to school, waking up early, staying up late, eating healthy, etc. Parenting most often only requires that we make a little more food, read a little more books, spend a little more money, and clean a little more mess (okay—sometimes it is *a lot* more mess, but you're deluding yourself if you think you wouldn't also be cleaning up your own messes anyway). There is no reason why an adult cannot enjoy every moment of every day even with children around. But because as adults we are now the ones responsible for our own emotional and material wellbeing it is we who must find love for ourselves in order that we may give it to others. Failure to understand that we are worthy of self-care, self-compassion, and self-determination is what stands in our way of having that. Children are only a reminder of it.

Even if we are not parents, the same psychological barriers which prevent effective parenting also prevent effective self-realization, because the problems of parenting have almost nothing to do with being a parent, but a traumatized adult with inherited prejudices and biases about how life works, our sense of self, and a lack of skills required to successfully navigate adulthood. Many of us as adults wait for love to come to us, believing that we are reliant on others to obtain it. But because other adults are also too often burdened with unresolved pain and trauma from their own childhoods, this proves difficult, if not impossible. Since the definition of adulthood is also not other people's responsibility to us but instead our own capacity to provide for ourselves, reliance on others for love as an adult is actually the *opposite* of love. This too is not an esoteric concept, but one rooted in practicality and demonstrable behavior. Just as I demonstrated love to my niece by being patient and showing empathy, finding love for ourselves lies in action, choices, and behavior. Having patience for ourselves, empathy for our experiences, and compassion for our needs and desires are behaviors which care for our own wellbeing. Because love is the demonstration of these behaviors, the very act of practicing these towards ourselves *is* the act of having love for ourselves, and the more it is practiced the more familiar and easy and cathartic it can become. Since we then provide love for ourselves we can then increase our supply of it, and in turn have enough to share with others.

When I was a young child my mother one day threatened that if I slipped off my new shoes by stepping on the heels instead of unlacing them she would never buy me another pair of shoes again. We hadn't yet gone to get my new shoes and I don't remember ever stepping on the heels anyway (I do all the time now though), and they certainly were not damaged. I suppose my mother thought if she preemptively threatened me she wouldn't have to potentially deal with ruined shoes and yet greater financial stress than what they were already experiencing, but what I distinctly remember from the experience is not that I should carefully take off my shoes to make them last longer but that I had a mother who would not take care of my needs if she felt it justified, as I certainly was not in any position to acquire my own shoes. As adults we often believe our wisdom and life experience justifies the means of parenting, forgetting that children have no reference for anything that happens to them or what we do to them. I suppose if my mother was a hyperbolic person given to exaggeration but whom also showered us with affection this threat would have been received more metaphorically, but in reality we were not the recipient of hugs and kisses, but emotional volatility, threats, and even physical violence occurred often along with plenty of screaming and emotional manipulation. Because children do not have the ability to separate themselves or effectively protest against mistreatment we often navigate mentally and emotionally around our parents whom then take this involuntary submission as evidence of validity in their behavior, since many people do not even analyze their own behavior unless they meet obvious consequences of it. In reality every time we deliver threats and demonstrate ourselves to be unreliable or unpredictable to our children we destroy our relationship with them, and to this day nearly every time I put on my shoes I am reminded not that I should treat my belongings with care but that of my mother's rage and threat to not care for me.

While abstaining from demonstrations which are antagonistic to love (such as threatening children) is very important for our effectiveness as a parent, the active demonstration of love through physical affection is an important affirmation of love and is the outlet through which emotional availability is facilitated since, remember, love is *not* a feeling, but action. But with children it is commonly difficult for parents to show physical affection, especially when demonstrable affection was also withheld from us, never having had an example of what that looks like and even feeling threatened by it. But a lack of physical affection is guaranteed to cause children stress, depression, or even more severe emotional problems which can later in life lead to things like eating disorders, choosing harmful friends and associates, and engaging in self-destructive behaviors such promiscuity as the child seeks to find acceptance and intimacy from other sources. When a young child does not receive enough physical closeness and emotional availability from a parent one of the first visible signs of this stress is prolonged finger or object sucking. Denied the intimacy of closeness with a parent the child feels unsafe, and as such seeks to provide reassurance which would otherwise come from the touch of a parent. Finger sucking or blankey or toy sucking is actually a form of self-care, providing for themselves what is not forthcoming from their environment, but because of our moralistic and calloused ideologies is typically viewed as a weakness and vulnerability to which parents react with anger, shame, and punishment. As fully-grown adults, a child who was deprived of physical closeness with their parent will participate in excessive obsession with relationships and sex in attempts to soothe the stress created by the physical absence of the parent. This is actually a natural, instinctual and biological reaction for a human animal in response to deprivation of physical closeness since such deprivation in evolutionary terms would have more often been caused by a high mortality rate among adults and not simply emotional retardation on the part of parents. The stress caused by emotional absence of a parent (whether or not they are physically absent) promotes violence, antisocial mental trauma, and an increase in promiscuity as a counter measure to the loss of adult members by increasing chances for procreation by stimulating behavior more likely to result in a correction of population deficiency. There is a psychiatric concept called *Attachment Theory* which very nearly gets this right, recognizing that children are hardwired by nature to need close proximity to an adult, but it entirely misses the evolutionary reason for this aspect of human nature, which is literal physical safety and thus an increased chance of living to adulthood. Being apart from the safety of parents literally induces fear because fear increases vigilance, and a child relegated to a life of hypervigilance will always grow up with trauma. Withholding physical affection from children may spare us the discomfort of drawing close to others and confronting our emotional pain and disappointment, but it will doom children to an emotionally volatile future and burden us with the headaches and frustration of rebellious and promiscuous teenagers, early pregnancy, broken families, violence, drug and alcohol addiction, emotional turmoil, and other effects caused by the stress of emotional isolation.

Since love is an act, not a feeling, taking every opportunity to hold our children, cuddle them, and make direct eye contact will fulfill this need. If children do things like fight you off when you want to hold them that is a great indication that you are doing a good job, because they are getting enough physical affection they feel emboldened and safe. Many parents resent children for this kind of behavior because they are demonstrating independence, and even grown adults will then engage in manipulative and abusive behavior to destroy independence, break their spirit, and engender dependence for our own selfish emotional needs and control mechanisms. Selfishness is not love, but for many of us it is all we know, so it can be confusing and difficult to understand exactly what is appropriate or useful. Whenever we have uncomfortable feelings it is usually our own unresolved trauma being triggered by some stimuli such as rejection, for which instead of trying to make others responsible (including our own children) we should instead take a moment to have compassion for ourselves, our own feelings, and the trauma we have been through which these moments remind us. Later in this book the trauma inventory therapy will help to clarify and resolve such trauma and will make it much easier to practice healthy behaviors.

It is stereotypically considered that mothers have greater emotional bonds with their children, and fathers are often relegated to a more detached role in family life, often overcompensating for this deficit by trying to be the authority figure. This is a control mechanism meant to help men feel better when we feel vulnerable and marginalized but mostly also enflames insecurity and emotional turmoil and detachment from family. The reason that mothers have closer relationships to children has nothing to do with being female, but is literally a function of the closeness, time, and eye contact spent during breast feeding and rearing that usually occurs between mother and children. Mothers breastfeeding their babies usually spend the entirety of that time gazing into the baby's eyes, and because eye contact is the most powerful way to develop intimacy between persons babies then become indefatigably enamored with their mothers, especially because they are also getting fed and associate food and nurture with the mother. Fathers can also achieve this level of love and intimacy with their own children if they do the same, taking turns to bottle feed their children and make loving eye contact with their babies, and holding them instead of leaving them in their cribs or on the floor all the time. This eye contact however can even be cultivated with older children, as it is never too late to show up for family relationships, and only requires subversion of our own hesitance and ego to achieve.

Once in California after I put my life back together and benefited from an increase in the kind of awareness such as has led me to write about my experiences, one of my sisters came to visit, and after a nice dinner as we walked back to the car which was several blocks away I instinctually put my arm around her. Suddenly, she stiffened so rigidly that it became difficult for us to even walk, such was her aversion to touch, even from close family members. When I was a teenager one of my beautiful cousins got pregnant when she was seventeen, in spite of her parents strict adherence to their religious institution. Her parents then not only forced her and the father to get married, they did so in their basement, in a hasty, tiny, quiet ceremony without the typical joy and celebration of a marriage, even though my cousin was so in love with her incredible boyfriend (to whom she is still married) and the fact that they were bringing a new life into this world. Similarly traumatized from their childhood as my own parents, my cousin's parents also used their access to pharmaceuticals since the father was a drug rep to drug their children and avoid the immediate consequences which came from withholding affection from their children, and in turn caused severe emotional and physical damage to their children which led to much greater heartache in the future, including rampant depression, alcoholism, and even infertility in some of them.

It is so difficult to explore and correct these deficiencies we suffer from our childhoods that parents would rather harm their own children than confront their own pain and trauma. But as parents we often fail to see how our indulgence of emotional sensitivities and pain in the present sets in motion later events which are even worse, and the reluctance then to acknowledge how our problems are of our own making impairs us from ever correcting the past and thus engenders yet more suffering in the future as we fail to learn and to take care of ourselves. In terms of cause and consequence, it does not matter that it is difficult to show or receive displays of emotional affection as an adult. It may be true that this aversion comes from very painful events in our past. But our failure to provide this for ourselves and thus our children will also damage them the way it damaged us, and will always create more suffering for ourselves in the future and sustain the cycles of pain and abuse which are passed from generation to generation. Once when visiting my parents, one of my older nephews out of the blue ran up to his mother and threw his arms around her and declared, unsolicited, "I love you, Mom," melting my sister's heart and then running off again to play. I was touched by the affection she had so deftly earned from her own children and the closeness engendered in spite of also having come from our family which never did that kind of thing, and told her how much I appreciated getting to see it and how proud I was of her as a mother. I think her experience as a surrogate parent along with me in the care and rearing of our own siblings gave both of us valuable insight which for her paid off well and helped to avoid the same abuse and harm we suffered, and many generations can be spared from the cycles of abuse and trauma if only one parent makes the effort to heal themselves from it.

The most basic provision a parent needs to provide for children is love. All other failures of parenting can be resolved, but not the absence of love. Providing love for children is done through demonstrable acts of affection—touch, hugs, kisses, and play, but also giving our time, energy, attention, and care. Empathy is love in action, without which it is not love but *want*. Love is the recognition of value in another, which the act of empathy demonstrates, and if accomplishing these things is difficult it only means that we first need to practice showing love to ourselves. Doing so will give us the resources to in turn share love with others.

4

Intermediate Parenting

During the second grade my parents got us a set of books called *Childcraft*. It was an incredible, colorfully illustrated collection of fifteen volumes of encyclopedic information and activities for children and was my favorite as a child second only to an enormous tome on animals that weighed as much as both of my youngest sisters combined. One day when at home I saw a craft project in one of the *Childcraft* books (I think the one on animals) that I wanted to do, and thought it might be a nice idea to bring it to school so my entire class could also take part.
"Yeah we can probably do that," said my teacher when I showed her the book. "Leave it on my desk and we'll see."
I waited excitedly for the chance to do the project, thinking I had also been of help to my teacher in providing some educational material. But days quickly turned into weeks and still she had not introduced it to the class. Then one day my book disappeared from off her desk.
"Where's that book I gave you?" I asked her one day.
"What book?" she said tersely.
I tried to explain but she grew impatient and told me to go sit down. It was nearing the end of the year, and I was afraid that school would be over and not only would we never get to do the craft project but that I would also lose one of those precious books and the set would then be incomplete. After I sat down, another student got up and approached her desk to ask something inaudible. Her face suddenly grew furious. "I'm sick of you guys asking to use the bathroom!" she screamed. "No more asking to use the bathroom today!"

My embarrassed classmate turned and went to sit down, but it was only just then that I realized I also had to go. *Urgently*. But terrified, I daren't get up from my seat, and was unable to hold it before class was over.

The feeling of peeing yourself is a uniquely disturbing experience, because it doesn't end when the peeing stops. Your clothes and the seat of your chair get soaked in urine, and you have to sit in it, and it also starts to get cold after a little while, and your pants stick to every part of your lower half as you walk, constantly reminding you of the fact that you peed yourself. I could see the bathroom door from inside the classroom, and yet I was so terrified of this abusive adult that I sat there and willingly pissed myself rather than risk angering her further. Nobody saw my wet clothes, though, and in second grade children are still inclined toward unconditional empathy that it would not have been been much of a big deal. But my mother didn't care that my teacher had prevented me from going to the bathroom, but I also didn't tell her about the book because now I thought it was my fault that my teacher had stolen it and I might get in even more trouble than I was for being forced to piss myself. The year ended and I never saw that book again.

Unfortunately, this was not the limit of my uncomfortable experiences with my own pee as child, and as I approached the ages of nine and ten peeing the bed was still a nightly occurrence for myself. I would wake in the middle of the night or in the morning in a wet puddle of my own urine. The older I got the more embarrassing and stressful it was. But even when I was still a young child one of my sisters told a cousin of ours that I wet the bed, and it was a mortifying experience I fervently denied.

It is far more common than most of us know for children to wet the bed into the later years of their childhood, since the experience is taboo and used as fodder for ridicule nobody then readily admits or discusses, and parents and children alike are left to feel like it is a problem only they must endure when in fact *everybody* does to some degree or another. I crack up laughing every time I hear of children going poop in random places as if they are a domesticated animal. But the misunderstandings about such problems motivate parents to actually do more harm to children while also increasing their own stress. My father eventually began to act on his embarrassed about my condition one day when I was eleven by making it his responsibility to cure me. My first thought was that he might take me to doctor, since that was the natural way to handle medical conditions, so I was absolutely horrified when he insisted that I begin drinking excessive quantities of water during the day to "expand my bladder," and then to not drink *any* water after dinnertime. I tried to argue with him about why this wouldn't work, but he threatened to take away our *Super Nintendo* if I didn't comply. So for several weeks I was water intoxicated throughout the day and then completely parched every single night (water intoxication is a real thing and children do die after being forced to drink excessive amounts of water). Unsurprisingly, this didn't do anything at all to change my problem. Frustrated, he gave up for awhile, but then at twelve-years of age he thought that setting an alarm for midnight and waking to pee would fix the problem. I couldn't understand how a medical condition could be cured by setting an alarm and waking up during the night, but again he threatened me with consequences if I failed. He thought I was doing it wrong or lying to him, so then he set his alarm for several nights to make sure I was waking up (thankfully that didn't last very long). At fourteen my father decided that I had to hold my pee and not urinate during the day after again drinking more water. This was obviously never going to happen—I mean, seriously a person cannot hold their pee beyond a reasonable time—so I only pretended to comply. Finally around the age of fifteen my parents relented and finally took me to the doctor. I was prescribed some medication and my problem stopped, permanently, overnight.

The embarrassment of having a medical problem that is so ridiculously tied to shame and personal worth also kept me from receiving the kind of medical care that could have fixed it. Because bed-wetting is such a universal occurrence for all children, it would instead be helpful to know that bedwetting is caused by both nutritional and environmental stress, and children who experience enuresis (nocturnal involuntary urination) beyond the age of five such as occurred in my case are very likely on the autism spectrum or experiencing some other neurological stress. My other book, *Fuck Portion Control*, covers the dietary, pathogenic, scientific basis in more detail but excess urine production is caused by the presence of inflammatory foods and chemicals in the diet as well as excessive ammonia production by pathogenic, opportunistic microbes, because the body must work diligently to rescue itself from inflammation and ammonia excess. Inflammation is actually water influx into cells, and inflammation does serve valuable purposes in cellular processes of growth and healing, but because inflammation is a chemical process the introduction of inflammatory substances such as gluten from common wheat, polyunsaturated fats as are abundant in soy, corn, and canola oils, or the endocrine disrupting properties of toxic agrochemical dioxins, pesticides, and glyphosate, produces catastrophic and systemic inflammation to which the body has no choice but to continue producing urine in order to eliminate inflammation, otherwise it would quite literally die. The same processes which cause inflammation also promote an increase uptake of water in the first place, and my parent's unwillingness to feed us healthful food and to instead save money buying cheap, mass-produced and processed food items was the main reason that I even had this problem in the first place. Parents often feed their children cheap and inferior foods, as if children are somehow immune to poor diets, as if food is inconsequential to growth and its only purpose is to shut them up about being hungry, when in fact it is from the very food we eat that our bodies are made and from which they function, the whole fucking point of eating, and if you pay less for food and feed children cheap shit now the cost will become catastrophic later in healthcare bills and behavioral problems. Most consequentially, a bad diet exposes children to colonization by pathogens of opportunity which cause disease and metabolic stress. Ammonia is also extremely toxic to the nervous system, and a major product of opportunistic bacteria and parasites which impairs development and must be rapidly detoxified, which occurs primarily through urine, and pathogens which produce ammonia can be prevented by eating a good diet, high in fruit, and other specific strategies as discussed in my other work.

Emotional stress can also do the same thing as a poor diet. When children exist in emotionally stressful and unfulfilling environments they naturally generate more stress-associated hormones like adrenaline and cortisol and less healthful hormones like dopamine and thyroid, and stress hormones are also increased by processes of inflammation in order to assist a body to overcome nutritional and environmental insults, so the addition of a poor diet to a poor home environment such as where I was raised prevents a child from developing normally, in mind *and* body. While eating crappy food can save us money and ostensibly the reason parents do feed their kids terrible food, this mindset and lack of access to better nutritional resources is actually more a consequence of the isolation that many parents experience as individuals and as couples, from other families and even from their own immediate family members. When I was a young man, probably around my late-teens, I one day received a letter from my Grandfather (not Granddad) which was several pages long and implored me to live my life with respect to his religious beliefs. It was more or less the same letter he sent to all of his male grandchildren, but it demonstrated not a single bit of awareness for me as an individual. I don't specifically remember the content nor where it even is because I wasn't even sure that my grandfather even knew my name. My Grandma on my mother's side was a different story, visiting us at least once a year, if not more, and after we were no longer small children really was not ashamed in showering us with love and attention. But our Grandfather, for some reason, never once in his entire life ever came to visit us, and even when we visited him hardly ever even said hello and I don't think I had a single conversation with him in all my life until the day he died. Even though my Granddad was a great cook, we only ever ate with them during our once-yearly visit, and likewise almost never saw the family members who lived near us even when they were no more than thirty-minutes away. In fact, we only ever rarely ate with other families at all, and a good 95% of our food culture was isolated and contained only to our own family, not only preventing access to a broader range of foods and food culture but also to emotional and social support and resources. Humans are social creatures, and it's no wonder that so many generations of disaffected people suffer depression, insomnia, worry, anger, frustration, and premature aging in their lives when we are taught and then willfully adopt erroneous ideas about dependence, independence, self-sufficiency, self-reliance, self-worth, and society's perception of us. A clouded leopard is designed to and can live in isolation. But the idea of such a creature's independence and isolation is more of an illusion than fact, since humans are largely given to illogical and subjective observational fallacies, thinking that just because we don't see something means it's not there. A male clouded leopard's territory ranges over many square miles of land, and all cat species scent mark, which is a social behavior which facilitates communication between individuals, and the time they don't spend hunting and sleeping is still spent guarding their territory and interacting with other individuals even if only though scent communication. Because we are *more* social than other animals doesn't mean that other animals aren't also social creatures. Crocodiles are regarded with animus and prejudice as violent, calloused, emotionless killing machines even though they congregate in large groups, display very complex social behaviors and adaptations of social animals, care aggressively for their young, and only kill when they have to eat, which is only about fifty times in an entire year.

But indeed we are far more social than many other species, and this social aspect of our existence is also *not* optional. There is no scenario where a human being isolates, lives apart from other humans either physically or emotionally, and thrives. We have biological instincts and requirements for human interaction which when deficient come at a deficit to our wellbeing. When I was writing my other book I had written a passage talking about my depression setting in around the age of fifteen, not really remembering exactly when it started and assuming there was no way that younger children could or should be depressed. But to my horror I found journal entries written when I was twelve-years old talking about how I didn't want to live anymore. Some instances of abuse or trauma will make an individual inclined toward isolation, and in fact there are some biological instincts which stimulate this behavior, but those are not indications of an ability to thrive on our own but instead a testament to the harm we are capable of causing each other and when our access to social connection is impaired.

Parenting is one of those aspects of human society which is especially dependent on a multitude of participants as what is accomplished by social animal groups. It is absolutely impossible for a single person or even a couple to raise children successfully without the help of other adult members of society. At the very least, children require interaction with a variety of adults to learn and incorporate life lessons, aspects of personality, and survival information and resources, a need that one or two people cannot even remotely begin fulfill on their own such as when my father tried to cure me of a medical condition without any knowledge or training or even attempting to seek outside support. Luckily we benefit from many modern advancements which reduce some of the most painful aspects of parenting, such as child mortality, which was so common in generations past that nearly every parent which previously lived experienced the death of at least one child, if not several. Now it is every bit as uncommon to lose a child as what used to be common. But that doesn't make the other aspects of parenting easier, or more successful, and without the assistance of other adults the job of parenting as a human becomes so incredibly stressful that parents cannot actually accomplish the job at all, let alone well, not because we are not capable of being good parents ourselves but because the job itself absolutely requires the involvement of many more adults than simply one or two. Many studies examine the role which other adults such as grandparents and extended family play in the successful rearing of offspring. A study in 2010, for instance, found that when grandparents were involved in a child's upbringing the mistakes of a parent such as overly negative or harsh parenting had measurably less of a detrimental outcome for the child. Any rational observer can also see that parents who have the assistance of their own parents in the rearing of offspring are simply less stressed since the responsibility is shared, but they also benefit from the wisdom and assistance of their more experienced family members. Many societies which are less developed still benefit from a natural family structure which retains aging parents in the home of their children, which in turn relieves some of the direct responsibilities of parenting from the actual parents while also improving the experience for both parents and children through their accumulated wisdom and knowledge.

Because parents are really just newly grown children and haven't actually parented before, it's insane for parents to think they should be or could be good at parenting (or even adulting) without assistance. We never stop requiring help no matter old we get, and for some reason we expect new parents to be good at parenting even though they've never done it before which in turn causes them to become defensive when receiving advice (especially the unsolicited type!), and then remain incapable of solving certain parenting challenges. This happens because many parents themselves deliver parenting advice in the form of criticism and shame to which we naturally respond with defensiveness. Shame is also used as a parenting tool because it is so powerful. But it is equally powerful in destroying both a child's sense of self-esteem as well as our emotional bond with them, since we then become the very source of that pain and self-hatred, as well as impair our children's ability to function as a healthy adult once they are grown. It does not matter the reason, as failing to ask for help or to build the social structures required for successful parenting is also an example of failing to care for ourselves. Self-care does not mean going about doing things alone. Self-care is providing for our own needs, and this includes the asking for and receiving of assistance, and parenting is a responsibility that needs all the help it can get. Most of the time grandparents, even if quirky or dedicated to odd beliefs and practices, can still help bring very effective doting and love to the lives of children while also helping to share some of the time and energy required to parent. For instance, even the simple ability to go take a shower while a grandparent watches over a child can help invigorate and refresh a tired parent who can then return with renewed energy to finish out the day. But when this is extended to involve more family and chosen family more frequently and more intimately it fulfills the real responsibilities of parenting, which is not to do it all by ourselves but instead to facilitate our children's access to the safety, support, and opportunity provided by groups of tightly connected social animals.

Parenting should not be done alone as a person nor alone as a couple, and while many parents do engage some degree of assistance, mostly the role of parenting is done individually and separate from other adults and other families, and recruitment into sharing responsibilities of parenthood is incidental, such as planning a night out at the movies or having not seen your own parents for a while, which results in the exchange of some parenting responsibilities or favors which may or may not have much of an impact on child-rearing. Many parents think they have friends but in reality simply have other parents with whom they exchange babysitting and driving responsibilities, which is absolutely *not* friendship. Just as caring for ourselves may take the form of making what we want to eat or taking some time for ourselves, actively integrating family life with other adults needs to be a proactive effort that does not simply and superficially include other adults merely for logistical and mundane purposes. Asking someone to come babysit for you constantly will simply engender resentment and they will avoid having a relationship with you because you only use them for their presence and do not give anything in return. A family is defined by the demonstration of love, and using other people is *not* a demonstration of love. Our inability or hesitance to ask others to be part of our family comes from deep personal insecurities and wounds caused by the past and the fears of rejection engendered by such experiences, then we treat people as objects for our own fulfillment in order to communicate our independence from them. These fears can often be so powerful that couples cling only to each other, even when their relationship is terrible, relying only on themselves for emotional support and never inviting outside adults to participate in their family. But the problem remains that modern family life is burdened by insufficient social support even though we reside among thousands of other parents, friends, and neighbors, and parents who attempt to parent on their own will always fail because it cannot be done in that way.

Sometimes we hesitate to make new friends and establish new bonds because we are afraid of other people, and in reality there are many people in the world who do not make good friends and can even be a danger to our welfare and that of our children. Having the involvement of other adults too invites criticism, and many of us who are intensely bothered by criticism would rather remain isolated and overburdened than willingly expose ourselves to it. But our inability to recognize dangerous people, the inability to set healthy boundaries, or a tendency to self-destructively choose harmful, disloyal, and or dangerous associates comes also from our inability to care for ourselves and to resolve the pain and trauma which burden us with particular coping mechanisms which in turn make us vulnerable to such mistakes or individuals. The remainder of this book functions to relieve these kinds of vulnerabilities, and in turn empower ourselves to better recognize candidates to invite into our families, how to steer clear of those who are not, to set healthy boundaries rather than just boundaries, and to empower us to strengthen and foster the kinds of emotional bonds that define a family, even to those whom we are not biologically related.

Sometimes we move away from already established family and friends, or other times they pass away or leave us. In this case the need for societal and familial support does not diminish, and we are still required to make our own family wherever we live rather than waiting for one to come to us. Most people crave the same kind of inclusion that we and our children crave as well, because we are all humans and all humans need connection and family, and this makes it much easier to establish new families whatever our circumstances. A sibling of mine who has a son whom is gay once had to move across the country, and part of her fear came from the unknown place they were moving and whether their son would be as safe as he was in the place they were leaving. Specifically, my nephew had a friend who was every bit as effeminate, creative, and wonderful as he was but this boy was twice the size of every other child in school. I myself was always a head taller than other kids, and this kept any teasing or bullying to a bare minimum. My sibling was, in this sense, already benefitting from community in the rearing of her children, finding also commonality and support and from a great group of friends, other mothers, and locally residing family whom at various times and in various functions all assisted in the mutual care and rearing of my nieces and nephew. Moving to their new home did not immediately provide the same communal parenting support, and they felt alone and isolated and parenting became a far more stressful responsibility. Part of establishing the kinds of social support groups which facilitate successful parenting does require at least some degree of stability, and it is understandable that new opportunities and new experiences can draw people away from their established family groups. Most often, the instability is really just a distraction to keep us from having to confront our own pain and trauma, and in making decisions to uproot our families we really just lose valuable relationships, time, and access to social resources while increasing our stress as parents, damaging our own social and emotional welfare, and even damaging our children in the process.

In the middle of seventh-grade our parents decided to move us yet again, this time to a small town after living in the relative metropolis of Salt Lake City for a couple years. I had finally begun to establish a small group of good friends and was almost recovered from our last move, and experience convinced me that life was never going to be stable and that having friends was a useless exercise in pain and loss. My new Junior High was cliche in its small-town love of football, cheerleaders, and religion and far less diverse, and while I have always attracted friends my newly dissociative personality prevented me from recognizing opportunities for friendship even when people literally asked me to be theirs. As a result, I was left to retreat even further into my own insecurities and neuroses. At my school in Salt Lake City we weren't allowed to actually shower after physical education classes, and were instead instructed just to remove our shirts and bend over to rinse our torsos in the water. It was perhaps an overly cautious attempt to protect children from harassment, and served simply to delay my intense and growing insecurity about my own body and sexuality. Suddenly at this new school, after my first day of Physical Education class and entering the locker room my eyes just about fell out of my head at the sight of dozens and dozens of completely naked young men parading around the locker room like it was no more uncommon than a day at the beach. Not one or two of about forty boys were wearing clothes, not even the ones after whom I had been secretly lusting, and I was suddenly so aroused that I daren't take off my own clothes for fear of sprouting a boner in front of my new classmates and being rejected by my new schoolmates before I even had a chance to ingratiate myself among them.

Alone and without any real friends to feel a sense of safety, this fear of the locker room dominated my experience in my new school and persisted for the rest of that year. When eighth-grade began I had finally started to make some friends and begun to feel a bit more comfortable, but I still could not gather the courage to strip down and shower even though I was constantly sticky after class, and with all of my being wished I was brave enough to experience the thrill of being naked in public and empowered by the self-confidence such freedom required. To make matters worse, the most popular student in ninth-grade was now in my P.E. class—A beautiful boy named Mike with light brown hair, blue eyes, who was an intimidating six-foot-two, and every day I got to see him undress and walk around the showers completely naked, his beautiful dick swinging around from brand new growth of manly body hair made the terror of getting an erection while defenseless and exposed more and more a real possibility. One morning early in the year after we ran onto the field during P.E. to play a game of touch football (which I absolutely hated), I was suddenly slammed into the ground and the wind knocked out of me, only to turn around after recovering to see Mike trotting off from my broken body, strutting back to his friends on the opposing team as if he had successfully proven himself an alpha-male by taking out his only (apparent) rival, since I was probably also as tall or taller than he was. His confusion when I neither retaliated nor retreated but stared back at him with longing was apparent. I suppose he expected confrontation, but I was breathless with desire, unable to move or even smile or sneer at him for my complete and total infatuation and disbelief that he had even noticed me let alone felt his entire body against mine. To my dismay Mike never tackled me again, although I liked to dream that he also had a secret crush on me and still thinks about that day and the love-struck boy he tackled.

But even at the beginning of ninth-grade, when my hormones and maturation were finally becoming familiar rather than frightening and I had finally established some more consistent friendships, I had grown so accustomed to my fear that I still could not gather enough courage to take off my clothes. One day my father approached me after school. "Nathan," he said as he closed the door to his office behind him. "I got a call from your coach today. He says you aren't showering after gym class."

Oh. My embarrassment though was rapidly forgotten realizing I could finally be relieved of this unending perturbation and insecurity. "I'm afraid that I'll get an erection in the showers," I admitted honestly. My Dad was so taken aback by my response it was comical even at the time, and I would have laughed if it hadn't also been so awkward. "Oh," he said. "Well, it's really difficult to get an erection after exercise. Your body is tired. You'll be fine."

Unlike much of the supposed advice which came from his mouth, this seemed entirely logical, but finally talking about my fear and not being thrown out of the house for it made me realize how ridiculous I was being, and I made a plan to finally strip completely naked next time we ran the mile at school. The fateful day came and my fear and excitement turned gym into something far more erotic than it really needed to be. Dripping with sweat I stepped into the locker room and breathed in the smell of sweat and boys, but for fear of hesitating and the risk of talking myself out of it I stripped everything down at once in a single motion, peeled off my shirt and put everything in the locker. My cock flopped around freely in front of the entire locker room as I walked proudly into the showers, as if I had done this every day of my life, and suddenly I was no longer just a boy. I could feel myself engorge slightly with the thrill of my newfound freedom, but my body was sufficiently tired that I knew it not only wouldn't betray me but also gave me the impression of being just a bit bigger than I normally was. To my horror *and* amusement several of the younger guys suddenly took to racing across the shower room to slip and slide on the tile, buck naked, as if we weren't all completely naked. The other boys laughed, and so did I, at them but also myself.

As a child I was unable to recognize that this experience of profound insecurity originated not at all about being naked among other boys or getting an erection, but the simple fact that I felt alone in the world and if bad things happened to me I had no wherewithal to find safety, and as such was far more burdened by fear than children who do grow up supported by familiar friends and family members. This absence of strong social connections would prove truly dangerous to my wellbeing when I did finally come out as a young man. Not a single adult in my life was available to save me when debilitating suicidal depression and ostracization from my own family drove me from my own home and community, and not one of my friends whom I'd only known for several years at an emotional distance reached out to maintain our friendships after the revelation that I was homosexual. This also probably says a lot about the effect of religion on the wellbeing of children, but it also illustrates the irony of having many adult members of a religious community and none of whom are able to help children truly in need, whom are rather gate-keepers and wardens than resources for healthy childhood development, and while their presence in our lives can seem to fulfill the role required of other adults in the rearing of children, in reality it tends to do the opposite, even exposing children to dangers of predatory and mentally unwell adults. From a selfish perspective, integrating other adults into family structures at the very least relieves some of the stress of the responsibility, but the fact that it also improves a child's experience by increasing their access to emotional support, experience, insight, counselors, skills, wisdom, and protection and safety makes it an indispensable strategy to parent well and effectively.

Inviting other adult members into a family can seem like a daunting undertaking, however, especially if we were not shown how or even that we can because of the example set by our own parents. But, like the previous chapter of practicing self-care and self-love, inviting other adults into our family life should not be something we do simply to improve the job of parenting or even because we think our children need adults in their lives, but to instead choose other adults with whom we share common interests, goals, tastes, hobbies, and traditions. You know, friends. When the only other adults in a child's life are those who also serve a function for those children, such as teachers, parents, doctors, therapists, etc., they are never exposed to what real adult interpersonal relationships can or should look like. Though including our friends in our family life may provide a selfish purpose for us, it also models for children the dynamics of interpersonal adult relationships, and we can teach them through example how to acquire, maintain, and foster healthy adult relationships as discussed in the upcoming chapter on friendship while also relieving us of the stress of emotional isolation. Friends can be family members too, like our children's aunts or uncles, or they can be completely biologically unrelated. One of the pitfalls we often undertake when making friends, though, is to choose them out of convenience and proximity. Supposed friendships which result from religious groups are typically these, where people associate simply because they know each other rather than actually having anything in common. These are relationships of convenience and by definition are not candidates for the kinds of emotional bonds required to establish chosen family. They also exist typically to embolden and empower religious beliefs, and as such have a utility of purpose which by definition subverts the nature of friendship. Friends can come from such likeminded groups, but real friendships should always be made because we like who they are and not because we like their money, status, religious beliefs, politics, or security. In making those kinds of relationships of utility, parents, again, seek to provide for their needs *apart* from that of children rather than while also caring for children. Similarly, making play-dates as an excuse to associate with other adults concerns only the children and not the adults, where relief from the stress of parenting comes only when we learn to take care of ourselves while also caring for our children.

We also cannot expect to establish familial bonds with others when we remain emotionally distant from them. Even though I lived just a few blocks from one of my sisters for two years I was not once invited over for dinner with their family, even though I invited her and her husband to my house once or twice a week when they lived near me in Los Angeles. One of the problems with trauma is that it can disconnect us from those we love without even realizing we are doing this, and by extension depriving our children of relationships with others as well. Fostering family relationships, even if only with chosen family (people whom we are not related to by blood but invite into our family structures) is extremely important not only for our children's wellbeing but also ours as well. We would not ask our husband to make an appointment to show up at your house for dinner—that's the entire point of having a husband, and as it should be with our chosen family, fostering the kinds of bonds which achieve emotional intimacy of family. Regarding other adults with indifference and formality is a defensive mechanism meant to prevent the very kinds of emotional bonds which are required to create a family but which also open us up to possible pain and disappointment, so we protect ourselves from vulnerability but which also keeps us from finding the kind of connections which enrich our lives and empower us in our endeavors. Thinking that our friends are annoying or people we would not want to stop by uninvited is a symptom of unresolved trauma and the very manifestation of those defensive walls which imprison us. While including other adults in the parenting experience benefits children, it is primarily and just like the oxygen mask analogy meant for our own wellbeing, which in turn happens to benefit our children, and not the other way around.

Many families around the world do practice the integration of other adults into family structures, with children growing up knowing their parents' friends and extended family members as well as or better than they know their own parents, and these relationships also facilitate healthier and more fulfilled parents which in turn provide a richer experience and access to broader resources for children as a side-effect. That most of us are already possessed of family which can serve this function makes accomplishing it simply a matter of engaging in more connection, cooperation, empathy, and kindness. While sometimes we do need to relocate for important reasons, stability greatly facilitates the maintenance of emotional bonds simply through familiarity and consistency. But for those of us who have a hard time making friends there is a secret to making friends, which is that familiarity begets friendship. This is why making friends as a child can be so effortless but sometimes difficult as an adult—kids are often thrust into environments in which they consistently encounter the same other children. But because we are not aware of this reality this principle never dawns on us as adults, and since we tend to participate less and less in novel and diverse social functions we also find it far more difficult to make friends. When nearing forty I realized I had never made any substantial relationships in Los Angeles, even after living there for the last fifteen years, because I was insecure as a young adult and beset by emotional and mental health problems I typically chose friends who were more compatible with my insecurities and trauma, which included other alcoholics and emotionally damaged people who were not good friends nor romantic partners. Then, when I got sober and healthy and healed my alcoholism thought erroneously I might find friends among the recovery community. Other damaged, codependent, addicts do not make great friends even when sober, because the trauma which besets addiction and alcoholism is not effectively addressed in the recovery community, and even though I had found some great experiences in Los Angeles realized how much better off my life would have been if instead of excitement and opportunity sought stability and community, and chosen a few loyal friends and created family relationships, which would have been far more valuable now as an adult than any success or wealth I had dreamt as a young man. Consistently finding ourselves in the same places can acclimate others to our presence and give them an opportunity to observe us at a distance just as we do them, and then facilitate friendship through familiarity just as it did when we were children. Work often substitutes as the environment for this function, but if we have sufficient trauma surrounding authority, responsibility, failure, or rejection we may not be emotionally available for friendship with coworkers and supervisors, and so it is very important to practice trauma therapy as discussed later in this book to resolve those barriers.

Attempting to parent on our own or alone as a couple is just not a successful parenting strategy. It not only deprives us of the logistical support of other adults, it is emotionally harder and less demonstrably effective for the success of parenting, and we only isolate as a protective mechanism to shield ourselves from the kind of intimacy with other adults which would in fact enrich our own lives and provide for our own emotional wellbeing anyway. That other adults also want family and deep connections and relationships means there is no real reason we cannot have this other than our own insecurities, hesitation, and lack of empathy both for ourselves and for others. Include other adults in your lives in more aspects than formal invitations to associate. Hang out with friends and involve chosen family in moments that are normally reserved only for family, because that's what they are. If you treat them as family they will be family. If you want to be a great parent, tear down walls of indifference, bring people together, and foster bonds of love with all the important people in your life.

5

Advanced Parenting

In the middle of third grade one day my teacher was reading to us from *Scary Stories to Tell in the Dark* (the original version before they censored the incredible art of Stephen Gammell). It was October, after my eighth birthday, and I had settled into a small group of friends with whom at recess we we would run around pinching each other's butts for some reason. My teacher was really nice, a great relief after my horrifying experience in second grade, and the story she was reading was so delightfully terrifying and gross that I was genuinely disappointed when a strange woman walked in the room to interrupt us.

"Nathan Hatch?" said the stranger. I looked first to my teacher, then to the woman who motioned me to follow her. Why I would be called from class was a mystery. I was sure that I was in some kind of trouble, and the woman escorted me to a small office near the Principal's and shut the door behind us.

I was directed to sit across from the desk, where there was a collection of small plastic animals scattered across the side on which I was seated. "We're going to work on your speech," said the woman. "My speech?" I said. "Yes. Your lisp. You don't pronounce your s's correctly."

I was not aware before then that anything was very wrong with my speech, and suddenly here I was getting special treatment for it. Looking back on old videos, my lisp was very heavy and adorable. But I suppose my parents thought it was finally time that I get over it.

"Say, 'snake,'" said the lady as she took the tiny, plastic rattlesnake and moved it out front toward me. I knew what a snake was.

"Th-nake," I replied.
"No, sssssnake," she said, as if I didn't know the word.
"Thhhhhnake."
"Try saying S."
"Sth."
"S."
"Sth."
"Let's move on. Can you read this sentence for me?"

She placed a small piece of paper in front of me that was a worksheet of sorts written in large letters. "Sthally sthells stheasthellths by the stheasthore."

"Let's have you say it a few more times."

I did as asked, and after a few more minutes of repeating s-words she said I had done a great job and could go back to class which, to my disappointment, had finished that day's *Scary Story*. Even though I had been quietly removed from class, I was now aware that I was different, and that there was apparently something wrong with me that I required special help in a special room with a special lady.

This supposed speech therapy went on for one day a week for several months, her placing little animals whose names included an s and I telling her the name of that animal and repeating tired lines and phrases full of s. Apparently speech therapy consists of nothing but repeating words over and over until the child is painfully aware that adults think they are messed up.

One day at home my mother heard me say a word with an s and looked at me funny. "Show me where you are putting your tongue when you say your s's?" she asked. I walked up to her and made an *s* sound. "Oh," she said. "No, you are placing your tongue at the roof of your mouth. When you make an s, your tongue goes behind your lower teeth. Try it."

I put my tongue behind my lower teeth. "S."

In literally thirty-seconds my mother did what a trained speech therapist could not do for months, and my lisp only ever again came out when I would get drunk (as an adult). If I said I was grateful for this, though, I would be lying because my lisp made me different, and it was cute, and there is nothing wrong with lisps. I probably would have grown out of it, or not, but in that moment my mother was uncharacteristically helpful and kind, and didn't characterize my lisp as a personal failing the way they did so many of my other problems in life.

But the lesson I learned that day was not that I needed to speak differently, or even how to say s's properly. Instead I learned that my mother *cared* about me, but also that she cared about how I was perceived, understanding that they knew of and signed on to my therapy during school, and that it was important for *them* to be assuaged of the embarrassment of having a child with a lisp. This led to the logical conclusion that having a lisp was not really okay, which in turn meant that I was not really okay for having a lisp, and wondering what else about me was a potential liability for my own wellbeing and ability to survive in the world.

As parents we often think that our successes and failures as a parent reflect whether or not we are a good parent. The most insecure of us sees evidence of our failures as evidence of having failed, but rather than fixing our mistakes then try to fight evidence of it and thus end up harming our children even more. Those of us who think we are good parents also often tend to ignore evidence of our shortcomings out of a sense of powerlessness, believing that we are the only ones responsible for the very life we brought into the world and feeling so overwhelmed by our responsibility it is easier to pretend that we're doing well and the problem lies elsewhere. Those parents who have a good experience in their role will also think that they are the ones responsible for it going well even though they probably have not had to face many problems themselves.

But the process of parenting is far and beyond a much more unconscious, biological process than any of us are even aware. As children we are completely helpless from the moment we are born until maybe our late-middle teenage years. We have no ability to care for ourselves until we have had time to grow a sizable body and gained sufficient life experience to recognize dangers and become able to navigate them. If parents were allowed to actually decide or devise how parenting works, no children would actually survive, even those of good parents, and we would not be a species on this earth. In the course of parenting most of us never even consider the true nature of parenting and how the actual biological dynamics of human physiology function to facilitate the creation and maturation of new generations of human animals, in spite of parenting and not because of it. In reality, parenting is an entirely unconscious act, one in which children absorb our perceptions of life and everything in it.

For instance, the damage caused by religionist parents towards a child's perception of sex and their bodies would, if left up to our machinations, entirely stop reproduction due to fear of sex and intimacy. If this kind of parenting was practiced in enough of the population the entire human race would simply cease to exist in a generation. But biology is, for better or worse, far more powerful than social constructs, and even when adults are driven insane by harmful conceptions of morality and incapacitated by shame and self-hatred they cannot deny the biological instinct to mate and will thus engage in reproduction in spite of themselves. This is the reason why those who fervently espouse sexual modesty, restraint, and abstinence are also often those with the most deviant sexual behaviors, as preoccupation with such themes belies their struggle with heightened sexual compulsion which is in truth a species-centric adaptation which occurs during emotional, nutritional, and environmental stress to increase the chances of fertilization before the expiry of the animal those stresses portend. Biology facilitates but does not actually care if we are a good parent, nor if we produce well-developed children. Like every animal on this planet, humans are possessed of biological instincts and survival strategies which ensure our survival as a species and not necessarily as individuals (which is why there are more than seven billion of us on the planet now), and this occurs regardless of how well we parent. Anti-social behaviors like murder, theft, abuse, violence, subjugation, oppression, and even rape are all evolutionary survival mechanisms which expend the individual to promote the species when parents fail to successfully empower their offspring with more effective survival skills and resources, which is why most other species of animals on this planet also commit these atrocities. Ducks commit rape and zebras commit infanticide, but the individual being sacrificed for the perpetuation of the species is not the victim but the perpetrator, tormented by pain and trauma and driven to madness and antisocial behaviors by biological instincts, never getting to experience the peace and love and joy which comes to healthy, luckier generations.

In opposition to how religious institutions so pessimistically regard the human condition, as social animals we are actually more naturally inclined toward civility, cooperation, love, harmony, collaboration, sharing, and kindness, because these strategies are more effective in promoting our success as a species than those which harm social structures, and it is only when our higher instincts are damaged that our baser ones are revealed. Rather than the need to mould and shape children away from less desirable instincts, in reality a parent need only *avoid* damaging their children's natural instincts in order to raise successful and well-developed adults. Of course, this is often hard to do because of the damage suffered at the hands of our own parents, which in turn make it difficult not to repeat in the lives of our children unless we are empowered with skills and knowledge to repair the past and heal our wounds. But unfortunately we are the only ones responsible for our healing. Because our formative years occurred as children, this also informs our very perception of life itself, and uncovering the damage which is done to us as children requires a fundamental change in our very idea of what it means to be human, to live, because the very formation of our identity and understanding of life is an unconscious biological process entirely separate and unknown to our conscious mind as we grow and experience life through the mechanisms built into our unconscious biology which guarantees growth and learning regardless of our individual experience with parents and children.

Because of the risk to our survival should parents fail, children are programmed with various survival strategies which become more obvious when parents fail to sufficiently support a child. When children feel that their parents' love and attention is earned and not freely given, for instance, this results in instinctual competition between children such as I demonstrated toward my brother, which are not taught nor observed but are as much a biological instinct as is a dog's inclination to sniff other dog butts, or a bear's instinct to find a den at the approach of winter. We don't consciously recognize instincts because that is exactly the point of instinct! If we had conscious control of these kinds of biological functions, *they would not be instinct*. One interesting human instinct is the motivation for men to stop thrusting during intercourse once they've orgasmed. No man has ever been told—*hey, you should stop fucking after you come*. But all men do. The reason we do this is because the penis becomes extremely sensitive after orgasm. This is how instinct in animals is facilitated—though sensation information and hormonal and reactive responses to our environment. The reason that human males do this is because the glans of the human penis is shaped like a shovel, and continuing to fuck after orgasm actually *removes* semen from a vagina. This shape of the glans is an adaptation to compete with the sperm of other males, because humans evolved to have multiple sexual partners simultaneously, which is a common occurrence in human sexuality in spite of religious dogmatic protestations toward sexual behavior. Unhealthy males suffer a condition called *soft glans* (also discussed in my other book, along with sexual health) during which the glans does not tumesce fully and thus does not form an effective shovel-shape, and a healthy male glans being more engorged than less healthy males is thus more efficient at removing semen from a vagina and thus improving his chances of passing on genetic material (as well as bringing his partner to orgasm), so long as he stops fucking after orgasm. The size of human male reproductive organs is also a function of our propensity for promiscuity throughout our evolutionary history, with longer and larger male penises being able to reach further inside and thus outcompete other penises.

The reality of our ancestors' sexual life is not so lascivious as this might imply, where rather than being a species comprised of slutty, disloyal men and women fucking like animals with no regard to feelings or love we instead lived in cohesive family groups in which the adult males more or less shared sexual partners rather than fight for mates the way males of most other species do, in a system of polyamory, where all adults were the parents for all the created offspring and each of us would have had several adults who functioned in the role of fathers and mothers rather than only one of each. Fathers loved mothers every bit as they did their offspring, but they also loved their friends who hunted and died alongside them and fought to protect and provide for the entire family, because love is leveraged by biology to promote the success of reproduction and parenting in social animals. Human families are often described as monogamous family groups, even by scientific researchers and even though monogamy is not even remotely the predominant practice among humans, who are by nature driven in spite of our ideologies by instincts to mate with multiple partners. Because monogamy is possible does not mean that we are a monogamous species, which we absolutely are not. This unique sexual structure of human evolution and behavior enabled human males to more effectively protect and provide for family groups, being emotionally bonded and allied to their friends and male relatives through such intimate relationships rather than in competition with each other. Humans are uniquely polyandrous and polygamous—not actively in social practice, but biologically inclined toward it, and very few other species in nature do this. Though crass, this human behavior is even reflected in pornography in group sexual reenactments and male-dominated scenarios consumed largely by heterosexual men. Sexual activity and interests shared between adult heterosexual males creates a fraternity among adult males because our biological evolution was achieved through such fraternal instincts, and to this day is still a common experience for most men at some point in their lives, which you will be familiar with if you have ever spent any time in a men's locker room or in the military. It is actually this uniquely cohesive and fraternal intimacy between adult human males what perpetuated our species across the face of the earth, not our technological innovations or intellect, because those would never have happened had our closeness not first facilitated a space for discovery, creative problem solving, and collaboration which is otherwise inhibited in species whose males compete with each other for mating.

For this reason, young men are more instinctually inclined to prioritize their friends rather than their fathers and family, as young women are oppositely more inclined toward prioritizing their mothers and family over friends, because the fraternity between human male peers is one of the evolutionary instincts we have which perpetuated the survival of our species separately from the function of parenting. While gossiping is an unsavory behavior it too is part of our evolutionary toolkit. While individuals may suffer from gossip, in reality it makes us aware of problems faced by others and thus in a position to help them should we be inclined or to also avoid the same kinds of liabilities which befell them, not because there is any dignity or justification for the topics of gossip but because of the danger we ourselves might face while living amongst hateful or spiteful other humans and, if we are equally as shallow and fearful, adjust our behavior to align with those interests instead of risking our safety to stand up for what is right. But in fact, all our emotions are instincts, from fear to love to shame and hatred, facilitated by hormones and neurology and instincts are why children who have no life experience, wisdom, or barely any communication skills can sometimes appear to be wily and scheming creatures but whom in truth are simply following our biological, instinctual programming meant to ensure our survival in spite of however well we may or may not succeed as parents, programming which will empower them to secure resources and grow into an adult and pass on their genes when, not if, we fail to do our job. The ability of a newborn infant to recognize smiles and laughter while having absolutely no ability to communicate through language is the precise demonstration of just how much instinct we possess as human beings, and the willful ignorance to our own instincts and how they drive our choices and behaviors does nothing but imperil our own wellbeing and effectiveness in life.

When children are under direct threat of active abuse by parents, a child will instinctually respond by shutting down, as an adaptive survival mechanism completely originating from biology and not learned behavior, to avoid drawing unnecessary attention to themselves which might increase their chances of expiration through direct competition with more powerful adults. These adaptive behaviors cause a person to become shy, nervous, anxious, or sensitive to criticism and teasing which can be attitudes inherited from parents but which are in reality activation of primal human instincts which facilitate navigation and survival among other human beings. This also often results in debilitating psychological coping mechanisms such as dissociation, where the mind of a child dissociates from reality and personal relationships in order to survive the pain of abuse. This is what occurred to me and greatly impaired my ability to make friends and form close relationships with others, and as an adult dissociation prevents us from being present or even staying on task since our mind is conditioned to dissociate from our experiences whenever we are stressed or anxious. Children who are at risk of neglect or indifference oppositely present with loud, demanding, disobedient refusal to comply and instinctually to resist a parent's suffocating neuroses in order to draw attention to themselves and thus an increase in access to needed resources, and since we as a species are possessed of various personality types our response individually to each type of abuse can be relative and run the entire spectrum of human personality. Typically, some combination of abuse occurs and evolves in dysfunctional homes as children instinctually navigate the complexities of being dependent on adults who are also potential liabilities, and it is these instinctual survival mechanisms formed in childhood which are responsible for our personal identity and conception of the world and *not* the superficial content of a parent's parenting. In this regard, parenting is entirely and without exception a function of the subconscious, both from the adult and to the child, in which children's minds absorb and observe unconscious attitudes, strategies, and skills of the adults in their orbit that they may actually survive and succeed in life in spite of and not because of parenting. Misunderstanding human development, most parents then believe that getting children into the best schools, pushing them to excel, and moulding them into respectable adults are the keys to success, when in reality their fevered persecution of their own children driven by their own personal fears and insecurities instead triggers reflexive, instinctual, adaptive coping mechanisms to subvert the stress caused by a parent like lying, cheating, defiance, and even promiscuity, because children's minds do not see or hear the value in your words but the fear and insecurity which motivates your behavior and thence see the world as something they too should fear, and then we are somehow surprised when our children become an alcoholic or addict as if we hadn't spent the first two decades of their life threatening them with hell if they masturbate or try cigarettes. Instincts facilitate our development in life, without which we would simply be ciphers and evolutionary failures, and parents who fight instinct and nature rather than harmonizing with it are doomed to failure because we are in truth fighting millions of years of biological evolution which cannot be subverted.

Parenting instincts are also no less a biological adaptation to rearing offspring when we are unable to do this consciously and in healthy ways. For instance, a child who grows up in an abusive environment is likely, from the point of evolutionary biology, to be living in a world which is harsh and merciless, and as a result will themselves develop strategies to survive in that world which are equally harsh and cruel, even if it means depriving the child of a fulfilling life. Such parents through their abuse will empower their child to develop hyperawareness for other potential dangers to their own wellbeing. Or, children whose realities are so violent and traumatizing might develop coping mechanisms of detachment and avoidance in order to mentally cope with things which the human mind is unable, and this in turn will produce children who are themselves more detached from the higher emotions of human experience and thus more ruthless and conniving toward the acquisition of resources and thus their own survival, long enough at least to themselves create another generation. Essentially, each human person is not designed simply to live our own life, but instead to serve as a facilitator for the lives of both the generation before us and several more after, at the behest and mercy of biology, completely unaware of how our selfishness, mistakes, and successes are actually a collective biology survival strategy which is not even a little bit concerned with our individuality. We think that because we can speak and write and make art and design rocketships that we are not beholden to the very same biological instincts as every other creature on this planet, when in fact we are almost nothing but instinct and driven every bit as ignorantly by biological design.

This does not mean we are incapable of rising above our biological instincts. In fact, we are uniquely endowed with the ability to communicate, to consume information, to explore the depths of biology, science, the universe, and spirituality to improve our condition and also that of others in our lives. The reality of biology is not one limited by base instincts and mundane and mechanical systems of tissue and death, but that all of us are connected and biology facilitates life and spirituality and is not separate from it, and only requires the resolution of trauma in order to find easy happiness and satisfaction.

One weekend my brother and I went to stay at our cousins' who lived just a short drive from us. Their oldest was exactly my age, and basically a heterosexual version of myself. Their second was about my brother's age too, so the four of us were often paired up when we went to visit them. But my cousins' parents told them never to divulge that their parents drank alcohol or ate out at restaurants on Sundays (which was not allowed in their religion), implying that my family didn't like or approve of them and in the process prejudicing our ability to relate with each other. My own parents didn't much regard them at all, and so even though we lived only a town away we never saw them but two or three times a year. During this particular trip my brother and I were rudely woken early one morning to the sounds of my uncle beating his youngest son, who screamed and cried in protest while my aunt insisted he stop, not because it was, you know, wrong, but because my brother and I were in the other room. The tone in my uncle's voice as he hit his child and berated him for leaving a bowl of chocolate chips on the floor made it clear that he enjoyed what he was doing, as if it were some kind of sport. No surprise, he was also one of the uncles whom when I was thirteen, in front of my whole family, expressed a desire to kill a gay man who had hit on him once when he was traveling.

I was always afraid of my cousin—not fearful but just in awe of his power as a young man, his athleticism, confidence, and raw heterosexuality. He once defended me against a group of other young men walking on the other side of a road who shouted out in a jeering tone if I was a girl or a boy. He told me not to listen to them in a way which made me feel safe with him. Sadly, my cousins also now struggle with abusing their own children, depression, and substance abuse as what occurs when children are raised in a house of horrors and the psychological damage of living in a world as a helpless child when the parents who gave birth to you are also a threat to your very safety. My cousin and I needed each other. Both friendless, sad, and lost, we were told by our parents that the other didn't care for us, even though the reality was that we loved each other deeply, unknowingly, and much intergenerational pain and heartache could have been avoided if even one of our parents had done just a small amount of self-care for their own emotional wellbeing instead of burdening it upon their little children.

The most important thing that parents don't understand about parenting is that, while your child was born of you, they are not actually part of you. Each child is their very own person with their own personality traits, likes and dislikes, and various quirks of personality and spirit which are every bit as independent of you as you are from your own parents, friends, and your partner. It is surprising when children come into the world and are at the same time very much alike *and unlike* either of their parents. The antagonism of the presence of an *other* then hurls parents into a crisis of identity as we struggle to make sense of our own pasts, beliefs, and prejudices, using their own children as a receptacle for their fears and frustrations. When we as parents confuse our identity with that of a child it becomes incredibly difficult for us to accomplish our role successfully. Because the mind of such a parent mistakes a child as part of themselves we react in ways which only consider ourselves and our experience and not that of the child, in our reaction to various stimuli, which too often is anger and frustration, even in situations which would normally induce pride and joy since in reality our child is *not* us but an entirely separate and independent human being (independent meaning separate, not self-sufficient), and the actions of our child reveal to us the conditions of reality which we as the parent wish to actively reject, often violently. If for instance we as a parent believe we are worthless we also consider our children to be worthless no matter how well they actually do, because we do not believe in ourselves and feel like failures in spite of our own accomplishments we also see our children as failures in spite of theirs. If a parent is insecure we regard our children as insecure, and instead of letting kids tease each other and have a good time will teach them to be offended at everything just as we are. If we are promiscuous or given to preoccupation with sex and ashamed of it we project this attitude onto our children and expose them too to sex and body shame even when they haven't even reached adolescence. This is what happens when parents try to live vicariously through children, cliche as it may seem, does happen in nearly every family, parents mistaking the accomplishments and failures of children as our own, wishing and hoping for them to do what we could not and in so doing somehow atone for our weaknesses when we would abjectly resent the same being done to us when we were children, and become parents who lack the skills to accomplish our own needs and desires and believe that others should do it for us. Growing up under the care of such parents is heartbreakingly lonely because our parents are so concerned with how we fail to fix their own problems that they in turn withdraw from emotional intimacy with us, and then we grow to adults with debilitating fear, neuroses, and loneliness even when others are just an arm's length from our hearts. But then we repeat this cycle when we become parents, and after years and years of projecting our negativity and shame onto our children we come to completely misunderstand who they are, mistaking the shadow of our deepest fears and insecurities for the very children who once fed at our breast and reject those whom we would otherwise have given our lives.

One weekend when I was twelve my parents had allowed us to rent the brand new game *Super Mario World*, for the *Nintendo Entertainment System*, because it was summer and the weekend. And since rentals only lasted several days my brother and I decided it would be a good idea to wake up early on a Saturday morning to play before my Dad forced us off to work at his construction site. The game was incredible, and my brother and I were having a really great time playing Mario in his frog suit when suddenly my father charged into the living room, bleary-eyed and raging. Without saying a word he ripped the Nintendo out of the wall, furiously yanking at the cords, then retreated back into the darkness with Nintendo in hand. We never saw it again. Well, I did actually see it a few years later—it was hidden on the dirt shelf of the cellar under our house behind the furnace. But I daren't speak about it. But at no point had my father said we couldn't play the game. Nor were we in violation of time constraints, or other responsibilities required to play. His frustration simply came out of the blue. Unexplained and without recourse. In fact, we thought that playing it before the day started and not trying to play when we were obligated to work was considerate of them and the rest of the family. My father was always awake early every day, even weekends, and in fact berated us if we ever tried to sleep in, so waking him up was also not why he raged at us and took away one of the only joys of our childhood. At the time we assumed it was some self-righteous hatred for video games and being cranky early on a weekend morning. When I was a grown man I finally asked him about that day, and he revealed a deep hatred for my brother and I being better than him at video games. He once played with us as children for about five minutes, and never picked it up again. But would stay up at night playing after we went to bed to try and get better at it. Hearing this made my heart sink. All the years lost, never having fun with him even though he *was* playing video games simply because he was embarrassed at his sons being better than him at something he shouldn't even be good at anyway. Confusing our joy as his personal failure.

For a parent who doesn't understand that their children are separate and unique persons, no matter what their children do, it is like watching themselves in a magic mirror that forces the parent to peer unflinchingly at themselves, so even when children do things that are good, like being talented at video games, or especially when they make mistakes, the reaction of the parent is toward their own insecurity, which is often great, rather than the child's reality. This is why childhood is so often confusing for children, who try their best to do everything a parent wants, and even when they do what is right and expected are still treated as if we have not. Instead of admiring my father as a disciplined and responsible person, I saw him as an emotionally unstable, irrational, and sophomoric brat possessing a total lack of self awareness and self-control, without a single trait I wished to emulate in my own life. As a teenager, I resolved that I would not be like him one bit when I was an adult. But the reality was that my biological programming learned from these occasions to react with volatility when my insecurities were threatened, because the function and effect of parenting is not at all a conscious process, and as an adult I often behaved in exactly the same way he did, though I thought it otherwise simply because the context for my behavior was different.

Anger as an emotion is good and can serve a valuable purpose for dealing with the realities of life. Many things can make us angry, and anger is simply an instinct which enables us to survive life. If we did not get angry we would never set boundaries, and would be exploited and likely perish from abuse or neglect, or fail to take action when it is required. But the emotion of anger is not the same thing as *acting* on anger. This is what ineffective parents misunderstand in general, is that having a feeling does not mean we can or even should act on it, and certainly not without consequences. Intellectually, people may say, '*sure, that's obvious.*' But the next time someone insults us or cuts us off in traffic we return the behavior without a second thought. I did not realize there was a difference between feelings and action until I was thirty-four, when I first set foot into a twelve-step program. Like me, many of us were never taught how to properly handle or manage our feelings, being demonstrated for us instead that actions were the same as feelings. You get hurt, cry. You get insulted, insult back. Someone takes issue with something you've done, defend yourself. Feelings were simply the logical precursor to action, and justify as adults and parents everything that we are inclined to do because to our parents there was no difference between them and us. This is, in reality, exactly how *children* behave, moving instantly from emotion to action without any self-awareness or being conscious of the process inbetween and our complete and total control over whether we do actually act on emotions or not. Feeling entitled to our emotions we believe that others are in turn obliged to indulge and even respect our behavior and excuses every bit as a whiny, tantrum throwing child. I once tried to explain to my mother that crying every time she hurt someone instead of saying sorry was a form of manipulation, and then she proceeded to lecture me saying women are different and entitled to cry whenever they wanted.

But we also behave like this as adults because we do not feel worthy or otherwise empowered to get what we want or need as a human being, and in truth our reaction to feelings comes from feeling powerless in our own lives, then use the limited set of tools in our arsenal of survival strategies which is usually a set of ineffective instinctual coping mechanism and few actual, productive, and healthy life skills because our parents did not possess them either and so our view of the world and how we operate within it is a product wrought almost entirely from instinct and unconscious human coping behavior. Then these insecurities and control behaviors get passed onto our children because it is impossible to be consciously aware of instinct. When that instinct is born of trauma it is especially destructive. A parent who insists on always demonstrating intelligence is actually communicating an insecurity of being stupid and instructing children to be afraid of being perceived as such. A parent who reacts poorly to inconvenience or criticism is actually communicating fear of others to their children. Whenever I had a romantic partner who was unfaithful (which was unfortunately common in my choice of men) I deigned to educate them to the severity of their mistake, my pain, and justify why I was hurt, but also why I should be treated well. On the face of it such responses seem rational, except that I felt insecure and powerless to find men who would actually treat me well in the first place because I had learned from my experience growing up that all men must be controlled and dominated and made to do what I wished, and that romance was a thing of which to be afraid and thus manipulated. This incorrect lesson about life taught me that I was worthless and unlovable and thus was incapable of finding someone who would actually treat me with love and kindness and justified my own controlling behavior because of the intensity of fear and trauma which motivated such harmful conceptions of life and my own worth as a person. This is why parents and children, and also spouses and partners, siblings, and friends don't get along—because everyone thinks their emotions justify their actions and choices and so nobody ever changes because instinct is a more powerful driver of human behavior than any of us can be consciously cognizant. The same thoughts you have for shouting at your child to go to bed because it's your time is the same sense of entitlement that serial killers have when they murder their victims. *I am entitled to act on my feelings.*

In order to be in control as a parent and not have the role of parenting in control of us we must refrain from reacting to our emotions, disappointment, and trauma and confusing our children as the embodiment of everything we love or hate about ourselves and our own lives. Children are their own persons, they are not projections of us no matter how real it may seem, and acting on our unconscious fears, trauma, and insecurity will transmit them to the psyche of our children because of the entirely subconscious function of the parent-child relationship engineered by our human biology. When we make such mistakes it is because we have not resolved the pain and trauma from our own childhoods, and our subconscious mind drives us to try to resolve our problems with instinctual coping mechanisms, using our children as receptacles for our pain and disappointment, in the fulfillment of biological design meant to ensure the survival of our species at our expense (and that of our children) and which perpetuates the same kind of abuse which was committed against us. Taking time to care for ourselves by resolving our own experiences of pain and trauma from our pasts can instead empower us to separate our actions from instinct, our identities from that of our children, and in turn find more fulfillment and success as a parent, as a spouse, and as an individual, and to inactivate the most harmful subconscious biological systems which take over during our failure to parent well.

6

Misconceptions About Parenting

Some of the most wonderful experiences I had as a child were camping with my family. My dad loved camping and when we went into the mountains he packed days of good food like steaks or pork for campfire barbecue, and pancake breakfasts with sausages and egg. Campfire food takes on a smokey flavor that's not possible to replicate, sitting in the woods as the sun pierces through the cold, damp morning surrounded by the sweet scent of pines. My dad built a large hutch just for camping that could be placed at the back of the truck which organized all the salt and pepper, herbs and spices, and array of utensils required for real cheffery. One location frequented for our camping trips was a kid's sleep-away camp after the season was done, an entire rustic staff cabin all to ourselves on the edge of a beautiful lake. Near the cabin there was also a woodpile home of dozens of chipmunks, and I spent most of the time seated near them frozen in anticipation with a little cookie or bread in my hand as the brave little beasts would scamper on my legs or climb my shoulders to get a view of the cookie before grabbing bites and running off to their woodpile. I think I loved camping because it was something my dad loved, and he freely and unconditionally shared his love of food and the outdoors with us. It was impossible to have a bad time in the woods because my parents were always having a good time. I don't remember a single argument ever occurring during any camping trip, not even the rare times we got lost, or had car troubles.

The amount of love I had for camping was matched only by my intense hatred of skiing. On the face of it, a father taking his children to the slopes is usually something to be lauded. But where camping was something fun for my father, skiing was instead an exercise in what poor skiers his sons truly were, and instead of helping him chop wood for a roaring campfire, preparing dutch-oven cobbler, or taking a walk by a mountain stream, skiing was mostly my dad criticizing me on almost every run about how I was not skiing right and what I should be doing to be better, or taunting me for not being brave enough to tackle more difficult slopes or for being tired and done with the day when my feet were soggy and achy and my underclothes soaked with sweat and I began to shiver from the cold. My little sisters, too young and too female to attract his pedagogy, picked up skiing on their own time and in their own way and ended up becoming very talented at it in their own right (or with snowboarding when that became a thing). One ski trip when I was a very young teenager I remember finally getting frustrated with my dad at his constant criticism and finally complained about the way he was treating me. Like a bratty child he skied away, leaving me alone on the slope. The difference between camping and skiing could have many different causes, but the thing that changed my father's behavior from benevolent caregiver in the woods to pissy disciplinarian at a ski resort was the presence of other people. In the woods it was just us. On the slopes, it was the world.

For my tenth birthday my parents threw a small family party at our restaurant. I didn't have any friends, because of how often my parents moved us, so the only attendees were my siblings, our grandparents who at the time lived near us to help with the restaurant, and our newly married Aunt and her anti-social husband. I opened my few, small presents in the largest dining room of the English-style manor my father had built several years earlier to house the restaurant, the culmination of a long held dream of his. The ceiling was vaulted with beautiful wood beams, and tall, leaded glass windows flanked both sides of the long room. A taxidermy moose head trophy watched the occasion from one end, at the other a large stage which would host musicians on busy weekend nights. The floor was stamped to resemble cobblestone, decorated with enormous oriental rugs atop which sat the antique chairs and tables marked by decades of wear and ruin. When my parents first were building this restaurant and received the shipment of furnishings acquired overseas my brother and I excitedly scrambled onto the authentic pump organ and promptly broke the ancient, decayed fabric belts which facilitated the pump action then pretended it was already broken when asked what happened to it.

The last present on the table was a small box that jingled when I shook it. Unwrapping and opening the small white box I was surprised to find a leather collar and leash. Confused, thinking for a moment I was supposed to wear it, I looked to my parents who in turn pointed to Granddad who stood in the doorway holding the littlest, most precious, tan cocker spaniel puppy.

I had not even asked for a puppy, as our unstable and constant moving probably seemed to just imply the impossibility of having a pet. I ran excitedly to Granddad but he had put the puppy down and it had immediately scampered under the tables to sniff everything. I followed him on my hands and knees around the chairs, "Hi puppy!"

"What are you going to name him?" asked my mother. I thought for a second, but we were standing in the perfect name. "Dudley!" I announced proudly (it was the name of our restaurant).

Dudley would come to live with us, but unfortunately my father made him sleep outside in a hastily constructed dog house. Alone, in the harsh Utah climate. He went crazy from not being included in the family and one day bit my little sister when we were camping. I felt sorry for Dudley, being powerless to improve his quality of life. Never being allowed to have him in my bed or run and play with him in the warm house during cold winters. Ice chunks would grow on his curly fur when he ran in the snow, and would melt into his fur when he curled up in the doghouse alone at night. One weekend when we were at our cousin's house my parents informed me they had given Dudley away to someone else, because he had bitten my sister. I was devastated, but I knew he was probably going to a better home, so I did not protest.

When I was in High School my family gathered to read scriptures each morning. As a teenager who was already not getting sufficient sleep, over-training on the swimming team, and socially stressed due to rampant homophobia and bigotry in my family and community our early waking to read archaic texts which promoted incest, murder, child abuse, genocide, xenophobia, racism, homophobia, and the absolution of responsibility for one's own transgressions was a lot of things, but certainly not cathartic. One day during one of these family scripture gatherings my father was inexplicably inspired to suddenly and preemptively threaten my brother and I, in front of the whole family, about our sex life, even though none of us had yet to secure a girlfriend (or that I was obviously homosexual). "If either of you ever get a girl pregnant," he said angrily, "don't even bother coming home."

Shocked and embarrassed we all sat there in silence. He had said it with as much animosity as if we had actually already done it or even anything like it, as if we were not the obedient, well-behaved, academically committed and sexless Boy Scouts we actually were (literal Boy Scouts, but also metaphorical ones as well). And never mind the fact that he had engaged in rampant and unbridled sexual activity as a teenager and drank alcohol underage. Of all the things my father felt responsibility for, sure, responsible procreation by his own children should be on that list. But was it so dire as to warrant the kind of anger and frustration a random morning before school toward children who were some of the absolutely best behaved in the entire town and school?

In retrospect my father probably regretted saying it, especially when it was confirmed that I would never actually get a woman pregnant. But that day I learned not to practice responsible sexual behavior, but that my own father would not take care of me if I made a mistake of that magnitude, because that is what he said he would do, because children learn by perceiving a parent's perceptions of life, and in that moment I learned that my father was not only emotionally volatile and unreliable, but completely unaware of who his children actually were and what their lives were really like. I *also* did not want to get pregnant and become a teenage father. It was very high up on my list of things *not* to do. Even if I was straight and it happened to me, such mistakes are clearly not something children plan to do or are even aware of, and to know that my only father would kick me out on the street for it only demonstrated how little love he actually had for us. Of course, I didn't believe that he would actually do that to us, but not more than a year later they would ask me to move out because I was gay, and cut off all familial support, and I didn't believe he would actually do something like that because I didn't want to believe that my life could be in such actual danger and mean so little to my own parents.

Such displays of indifference over time increased my unwillingness to obey them at all, because I understood that nothing I ever did actually mattered to them, that they would treat me poorly whether I behaved or not, whether I succeeded or failed, so there was really no point in trying to please them in the first place. As parents we behave irrationally and ineffectively because fears are amplified by the stresses and responsibilities of parenthood. A single person can effectively ignore or suppress many of the fears which linger at the back of our psyche. But parenting brings these fears to the front of our consciousness, demanding they be addressed and confronted, because of the unconscious biological systems designed by nature to prepare children through our unconscious behavior. At the time of his outburst my father could have been burdened by any of a number of problems and the fears to which they relate—financial problems, a failing marriage, or his own self worth and effectiveness, and his insecurity led in turn to entertain yet more fears, perhaps the fantasy of dealing with an unexpected teenage pregnancy and how much more stress would come from yet another mouth to feed, and it became too great for him to bear in silence and so chose to explode his frustration at us on what could have been a otherwise quiet and beautiful morning. Getting me Dudley was probably done as an act of feeling obligated to give me a good childhood which, by definition, must include a dog (adopt shelter animals!), but without considering the real responsibilities which it would require for him and then later also still misunderstanding how much more difficult he made the situation by refusing to allow Dudley inside where I could take better responsibility for my own dog and thus relieve him of it.

One day before school when I was fifteen my mother implored me not to put on my muddy shoes, which were in the garage, and walk through the house (that she even knew they were muddy was beyond me). Obediently, I carried them and put them on at the front porch, then gaily strode across the street and up the grassy hill across from our house excited to see my friends at the bus stop. When I reached the top of the hill my mother suddenly opened the large front door to our house. "Dammit you piece of shit, Nathan!" she screamed angrily, her voice echoing through the neighborhood. "You tracked mud over my clean floor after I told you not to!" Then slammed the heavy wood door and the bang echoed through the neighborhood. The experience would have been less demoralizing if my mother swore regularly and not only the second time in my life I had ever heard her say such words. But because of her own unresolved pain and trauma my mother was unable to extricate herself from the coping mechanisms developed from her own experiences of abuse. Cleaning was one of the ways in which my mother felt she could exercise some control over her life. As a child she and her siblings were actually used by their own mother as the cleaning crew. My grandmother would not clean much herself, and used manipulation and abuse to convince my mother that her very self-worth depended on the house being clean. But cleaning was also a way that my mother could in turn control her mother, since when she cleaned her life was more pleasant, her mother less manipulative. So when my mother is presented by messes she doesn't just see a mess, she sees the very world coming down around her. This does not excuse her bad choices any more than my alcoholism excused me from driving my car drunk into a concrete wall, but it does provide insight into why we behave the way we do and where our self-defeating perceptions of life originate. Many of us have other such control mechanisms we use to help us feel safe in a world where death or misfortune can come at any time from any direction. Some of us are germaphobes, believing that we can prevent disease if we are excessively clean. But good microbes are also destroyed by being excessively cleanly, and because good microbes protect us against disease we inadvertently cause our own illnesses. Some of us think we can control life by having lots of money, but still continue to feel out of control even when we are well off, feeling that our financial security could be taken away at any moment or spend ourselves into financial straits in neurotic attempts to make ourselves *feel* rich. Others of us work out constantly, exhaustively, attempting to subvert weakness, aging, and even death, but because the body cannot indefinitely sustain such physical stress our body ends up giving out prematurely and we develop insomnia, erectile dysfunction, depression and even cancer. The morning that my father thought to threaten us in regard to our sexual behavior was a day that my father felt out of control of things which he thought he should be in control, and sought then to wrest that control for himself but in the process hurt his own children and increased his own stress and future problems.

We behave this way because we believe that we alone are responsible for a lot more of life than what actually falls within the limits of our mortal responsibility. My father felt that he was the only one responsible not only for feeding and housing his own children, but also preventing their getting pregnant randomly when they are out in the world, preventing birth and reproduction, that if it happened he would then be responsible for also feeding and caring for the new baby in addition to his other responsibilities, having a wife, six children, and living through an economy which was currently imploding while having leveraged his financial resources, and the thought of an additional mouth to feed was probably just more than he could bear. In truth, most of our frustrations as parents come because we do feel like we are alone, even when our spouse is by our side and doing their part, even when things are going well, and that all of it is only up to us. My father ironically belonged to a religion which taught socialism, communal welfare, and the redistribution of wealth, and were taught that God is always watching out for them. But in practice, the contrary ideology of self-sufficiency, shame in weakness, emotional isolation, and hyperfixation on wealth and capitalism ironically practiced by adherents in opposition of its socialist welfare origins cut him off from the support of the very community to which he belonged, as it does most men in such societies, as well as that from parents and brothers and sisters and children who should all be involved in the lives of their family members, to support and protect each other, to share experience, love, and resources. Belief in the God of his religion also did nothing to assuage his fears, because belief is really just want, and his version of God required obedience to receive support, the parameters of which are also kind of sketchy and undefined, and in truth those who profess a belief in God do not actually understand the nature of God else they would not be afraid, nor inclined to proselytize since it is a very personal, not public experience, and why such persons require the protection of religious institutions, to help them feel safe in a world in which they in truth feel unsafe and out of control.

Our ideas for what we are responsible in life are not only burdensome, they are misguided and in turn cause us to be ineffective in those areas which we are actually responsible, since we are ill-informed and our energies diluted. When we go for employment, for instance, many of us believe it is our responsibility to convince someone to hire us. We get an eduction, learn skills, type up a snazzy resume, dress our best, do our hair, check our nostrils for boogers, deliver a smile and a warm handshake, and say everything we think they want to hear. But in spite of our best efforts we may very well not get the job. We become despondent, deflated, especially when we fail over and over, believing that we have not succeeded in our goal. In reality, when we fail to secure employment we are only failing because we misunderstand the scope of our responsibility. When trying to land a job it is not our job to get a job. We are not actually capable of deciding whether or not we are hired. It is not in our control, no matter how much we try to act like it is. During a job search we are *only* responsible for showing up for opportunity and doing our best. In that sense, even when we cannot find a job we are succeeding *every* time we send off a resume or application or go in for an interview. More primitive humans as well as those alive today worship ideas of divine in the belief that the divine can alter fate for us, even to the subversion, sacrificing, or murder of other human beings, and yet our fate remains the very same as is everyone else's, because we actually cannot control most things in life, and the Universe does not engage in favoritism. The pseudo-religious idea that God can be entreated to our cause is a wholly self-centered delusion which completely misunderstands the nature of God, meant in truth to comfort and exploit fearful human beings. The very definition of God is that we cannot control life, the divine, the Universe. This does not mean we are alone, it means that we are powerless to bend fate or subvert cause and consequence. Sometimes we can make better choices which do improve our chances, but this is also simply an effect of cause and consequence and not because we have any real power in life, which is why we still collide with fate and misfortune even when we make good choices.

It is a mistake to think we are responsible for outcomes rather than our own behavior, and when it comes to children we can really only control a very limited aspect of our existence and our role as parents. Sometimes we cannot even choose what we can feed our kids, if we are limited by poverty, inequality, or disaster, or conversely burdened by prosperity and the ability to shield our children from immediate consequences of their bad choices. Often we cannot even control our own child, and attempts to do so typically result in more severe rebellion or dysfunction, and yet we continue insisting that we can control life even though generation after generation has made the same mistakes, thinking for some reason we will yet be them who exert control without consequences, even when life is yelling at us *'no, you can't.'*

In his fear my father also did not consider all the ways in which he was *not* solely responsible for his children, nor actually alone. His wife whom in reality was a very capable and helpful person herself, nor the society in which they lived and the civic and religious leaders tasked with supporting their communities, nor the actual children nearly grown, talented and capable and helpful who could continue their academic pursuits even as parents, nor extended family, nor the joy a new baby would bring to the family.

In reality, the responsibilities of parenting are limited only to showing up for opportunity and doing our best. This means responsibility for our choices but not necessarily outcome and certainly not fate, which is actually beyond our ability to do. Many parents go to extraordinary lengths to protect their children from death and disease, only to still have their child catch the flu or respiratory syncytial virus, or get shot at school. Or parents give up responsibility for children entirely because they feel powerless to affect the outcome, when in reality we are still required to show up and to do our best regardless of our ability to affect the outcome. Very often we act in opposition to our own interests and actually promote our child's demise, such as when parents feed their children foods they believe to be healthy which actually increases the risk of death and disease, or when my parents rejected me for being gay because my parents thought it was their responsibility to determine my sexuality, and I ended up trying to commit suicide. In fact, the cultivation of depression, suicide, and substance abuse in children is one of the most dire consequences of parenting beliefs that take responsibility for things we cannot control as it pertains to raising children. Believing we are responsible not only for every success and every failure but every potential success and every potential failure we thus spend every moment of our lives obsessed with every single thing a child does, delivering manipulative and patronizing praise or swift and merciless punishment, endlessly stressed by the impossibility of the responsibility we have taken upon ourselves.

Practically, misunderstanding the scope of our responsibilities as parents causes us to waste the entirety of our lives concerned about things that don't actually concern us, and miss out on the joy and fulfillment of having a family in the first place. Many parents, especially mothers, feel that they are not only responsible for the things that happen to our children but even the very feelings our children feel. We may see a child crying and think we must stop them from feeling sad, or our child may be angry, even at us, and the powerlessness their emotions makes us feel in turn makes us seek to extinguish that powerlessness by dominating and controlling their very emotional state. But since it is impossible to control another person's feelings, when presented with the evidence of our true powerless over life such as when a child is sad or angry or even happy we lash out and instead of consoling our children try to dominate them to force their very emotions to conform to our will. Once when a sibling told my mother they needed help with depression my mother responded, "Do you want to be like Rachel?" who was a girl that had depression who was on medication. Though Rachel was actually getting help with her condition and doing pretty well my sister not only did not get help, she experienced an increase in loneliness and suffering because my mother felt it was her responsibility to control even the emotions of her own children which, feeling powerless to actually help, instead tried to deny and invalidate those feelings, as if doing so would make the problem go away. My childhood could have been filled with love, good food, video games, family, and learning valuable professional skills from my talented father and effective interpersonal skills from my charming mother. Instead, it was spent simply trying to survive my parents' neurotic obsession with my personality, sexuality, emotions, and independence. Several of my siblings have intuitively realized through their own experience how exhausting, painful, and simply unproductive it is to take responsibility for life itself, and through their access to my experience were able to make changes, to heal their unresolved pain and childhood trauma which now provides them the space to actually enjoy their children, and to their surprise found lovely and amazing little humans who are not even remotely the terrible or out of control children they previously thought. Obsessive, fearful parenting does not even accomplish what it sets out to do and even invents more problems than we had in the first place, there is no benefit to persisting with the insistence that we control and dominate life, other than to selfishly acquiesce to fear.

One day in the summer before fourth-grade I saw a horde of boys running up and down the field at school kicking a ball. I don't think I even knew it was called soccer, but I really wanted to play. "No," said my mother every time I asked. But I could not get the idea of running under the sun with other boys my age out of my head. It looked like so much fun and something I could do. I kept asking and eventually she relented. Earlier in my life I had played T-ball and one season of baseball. My parents had signed me up for these but not being even old enough to have real opinions I went along without objection. Because every game ended with us gathering around for the traditional end-of-game treat, usually some kind of popsicle, I quickly decided that I really liked baseball. During one game while playing short stop the ball was hit in my direction. I scooped it up with my glove and hurled it to the first-baseman who instantly tagged out the hitter. I felt a sense of pride knowing I had played well, and to my surprise the ball came my way again on two other hits. I didn't miss a single throw to first-base. He and I got into a grove, a little team within a team, effectively neutralizing the other side and getting our team up to bat.

I looked forward to more baseball, but we moved towns and I was so distracted by being uprooted again that I completely forgot about it. Likewise, only a few weeks into playing soccer I fell off the monkey bars at school and broke my arm. Then we moved again before the next summer, to the city, and I forgot about my interest in soccer.

When I was thirteen and expressed disinterest in joining a basketball league, my father put his foot down. "You're going to play," he said. The thing was, I hated basketball and had never really played, and all of sudden my father was driven by this merciless need to make me into nothing less than a basketball star even though I had not for the last several years shown any interest or skill for it. Now that I was fully into adolescence and dealing with so much insecurity and strange feelings, jumping into an aggressive and unfamiliar sport was terrifying. I also knew my father well by this point and his efforts to teach me would only make these feelings worse, not better. Still, he forced me into a league and weekend practices with him in which he berated and insulted me when I didn't do well. Failing to show even an ounce of aggression drove him insane, and made any bond between us that might have remained quickly evaporate.

As I began to resist playing basketball and this incessant pressure to succeed he began to resort to more malicious and manipulative control tactics. "You're not athletic," he would say. "You're not fast. You're not good. You have no gumption. You're lazy. You're undisciplined." And I began to believe him, and to hate sports and him even more. In ninth-grade while trying out for the basketball team (ironically finally starting to get good and to enjoy playing with my friends) I was knocked over during tryouts by someone playing dirty and my kneecap hit the ground first and popped off, ending my miserable basketball career for good (I still made cuts, but couldn't run for more than a year afterward). Because this ruined my father's plans for me, which were rooted in his perception of life and misunderstanding his role as parent, I was from there out regarded with utter disappointment and indifference, and having no more reason to be interested in my life since he could not exercise his perceived responsibilities he completely checked out of it, even though I segued effortlessly of my own interest into competitive swimming and began to excel, winning races, and was even voted team captain one year, all the while believing I was not athletic even while being one of the fastest swimmers in my State and even though I had shown no less interest in sports throughout my entire childhood, only because of the way my father characterized me through manipulative attempts to turn me into something he felt was within his ability and responsibility to achieve.

Every person, even children, have their own life, their own choices, their own talents, and their own responsibilities. When a parent assumes those things for their children they effectively rob children of the opportunity to develop and grow themselves and in effect prevent the very thing they purportedly want for their child. If instead of coaching and berating me into becoming a basketball star my father had just turned me loose in a group of boys who were friendly and accepting with whom to play basketball I would probably have found a love of it on my own, not for the sport but for the friends I made through playing it (and isn't that the point of sport—to make friends?). Besides, I played Center because of my height, but though I was tall was only as tall as the smallest Forwards and Point Guards in the NBA, and not nearly as fast or driven enough to compete, which made his aspirations for me ridiculously unrealistic. A parent of one of my nephews who is also homosexual expressed a dilemma at getting their son to play at least one sport (strangely not considering his dancing a sport, even though dance is far more physical and demanding). I mentioned that they could introduce sport to him not as something he needed to do or was good for him, but to communicate to him the real point to sport or having these skills which is for the making of friends and associating with other people, and that whether we are good or not isn't the point. It wasn't until I was in my early thirties that I realized how athletic I actually was as a child, and that my father's perception of me was based only on his own personal fears and attempts to manipulate me, and how his characterization damaged my self-worth and personal identity, and that if he had instead nurtured my self-esteem and provided a more stable home life I would probably have naturally become a more accomplished athlete. Or not. Either would have been fine, and it was fine that I was not inclined to play basketball, which is kind of a stupid sport anyway. One-hundred-plus points a game? Please. Just a bunch of overpaid babies constantly whining about how someone just pushed them. If instead of trying to fulfill himself through me my father had joined a league of his own, for his own fulfillment and self-care, and excelled, progressed, and found accomplishment of his own he would have found the actual validation he had erroneously been expecting me, a shy, young, autistic teenager to do for him.

We are not responsible for making our children a success. They will do that themselves. The scope of responsibility in parenting is far narrower than we assume as parents. We only must show up and do our best. Provide access to wisdom and experience, feed them, protect them, provide opportunity and a supportive family. If you can. Children are every bit as capable of succeeding as you were when you were a child. They are their own person, and the more we recognize that reality the more effective a parent we can be.

We are also not alone as parents, even when we feel like it. We may have friends, neighbors, parents, siblings, and even government and other institutions and programs to provide us help. Believing we are alone is a self-centered control mechanism borne out of the pain and manipulation of our childhoods. It is a lie. Believing it robs us of the empowerment we may gain otherwise. It also demonstrates ignorance to the true nature of God and our purpose on this Earth, the point of which is not to control others or receive stuff but to recognize our proper place in the cosmos, the truth of which is immensely comforting and empowering. Rather than listening to opportunistic and exploitive religious institutions and burdening our children with our personal fears and insecurities, strength is found through self-reflection, meditation, and self-care as discussed in these remaining chapters.

7

The Self-Defeating Ego

After my suicide attempt I escaped to Hawaii for a misguided desire to reconcile with my family and to recuperate, but was subjected to the same if not worse moralistic denigration and harassment as what led to my suicidal depression in the first place. Because I no longer had a job, money, social support, or possessions, I was stuck there unless I somehow got a job and saved up enough to pay my way out (which would take a very long time), or found some other way to get myself out of there. Sick of being treated like a criminal and tired of sleeping on a cot behind my parent's living room couch I began looking for a way to plan my escape and chart a course to begin my life again. I began to search for friends on the island. One day I met a boy and two girls who were on Maui after completing their massage therapy training, and their friendship kept me from completely collapsing into my depression.

But it was quickly apparent that moving back in with my family was a mistake. In spite of my depression and knowing about my suicide attempt they treated me with even more contempt than ever, comparing me to pedophiles and murders, threatening me if I revealed my being gay to our youngest, teenage siblings, and shaming me for being unambitious. Since I had quit my job and given away my belongings in order to get to Hawaii in the first place I was also trapped there. During a desperate attempt to get some distance between me and my abusers I met a handsome man in a bar on Honolulu with whom I had a brief romantic affair. He offered to let me stay with him in Los Angeles, a dream I never thought could come true, and after saving up enough money for a plane ticket finally made my way back to the mainland.

Unfortunately I had no idea how to make it in a big city, and my romantic interest was emotional volatile, one day screaming at me for leaving a clean plate in his sink I gave up and found a job back in Utah and made the long, lonely drive from Los Angeles back to the hellhole from which most of my life's problems had sprung. I had arranged to stay with a friend to whom I had lent my furniture while away in Hawaii whom had recently purchased a condo but couldn't afford to furnish it, and it had been a very useful arrangement for the both of us. But I was sidelined after arriving and my potential new employer said they couldn't actually hire me yet, so I had to find a new job. I did, in less than a week, but my friend berated me for not having started work and lectured me about his own virtuous history of employment as if working in construction with my Dad since the age of thirteen didn't count, disbelieving I would be hired and kicked me out of the apartment furnished entirely with my furniture.

I did get offered the job the next day, but with nowhere to go I found myself facing homelessness. I called my Dad crying and explained my situation, that with my new job I could pay him back within a month if he helped me secure an apartment. Instead, he angrily refused to lend me any money and again took the opportunity to lecture me and blame me for my problems. For several days I slept in my car, and used my little remaining money for a gym membership to take a shower, but at least I knew I had money coming in. After repeatedly waking up cramped and pained from sleeping in a tiny Jetta I spent a few nights at the home of a trick or two found in the local bars, but eventually got my first paycheck and eventually a new place to live.

Many years later, after experiencing their own similar misfortunes, my parents were trying to put their own lives back together, but extended themselves beyond their means and found themselves in a tight spot and asked some of my married siblings for help. But instead of grateful children who didn't hesitate to lend a hand, my siblings acted exactly as calloused, condescending, and miserly as my parents had demonstrated by their own behavior, and gossiped about and lectured my parents on their mistakes and poor financial habits, shaming their audacity to ask for help exactly as they had me when I was homeless in spite of my pained efforts to establish myself amid debilitating suicidal depression. Even when I was a child we were shamed about our lack of material success, constantly being told what failures we were because we had not saved up and purchased our own vehicles as our father had done at our age (no accounting for inflation) or homes as young adults, or failed to climb corporate ladders which neither of my parents had done either.

No doubt my parents thought they were trying to teach us the value of self sufficiency and force ambition in anticipation of raising possible human failures. In reality they were demonstrating contempt for those in need, who ask for help, who make mistakes, who are vulnerable. Indeed my parents often went out of their way to help people, but they were just as quick to level condemnation at those they helped as well, regarding the homeless or the downtrod as if they had invited their situation, as if they were better than those we helped and thus converting opportunities of service into an exercise of condescension. We were also led to resent those with money, wealth, and status, equating a person or family's career and material success to their value as human beings, because their religious beliefs tied material wealth to spiritual worth, which itself implied superiority, also something to be condemned. Clearly my parents had not considered how parenting their children to despise those who asked for help would come right back around and hurt them when they were aged, nearing retirement, finding themselves also up a creek because life is cyclical and no one endures unending success, their children acting exactly the way they were instructed.

Even good parents are actually doomed to be betrayed by their own children to some degree or another because we see in the mirror of our children the reflection of everything we love and hate about *ourselves*. This in turn forces us to confront things we would rather deny, and denying those insecurities in turn motivates us to act in opposition to them, and because we are those in possession of the insecurities we are fighting, thus not only inform our children exactly how to hurt us but teach them to actively do so.

One summer when I was thirty-two and on vacation with a partner in the Hamptons of New York State I got an unexpected call from my mother. The weather was humid and hot, and every day we were wearing shorts and unbuttoned linen shirts, having cocktails poolside at enormous homes, jaunting about roadside cafes and farmstands. But my mother was distraught, "You need to talk to your father," she said. Suddenly I was alarmed, ready to pack up my bags and head to the airport immediately if my Nana was dying or had an accident. "No," I said. "You can't say something like that and not tell me what's wrong."

"Your father wants to divorce me."

Oh. *About time*, I thought.

"Mom I'm so sorry. What are you doing about it? Are you guys going to go to therapy or anything?"

"We're already divorced," she said.

"WHAT?"

"We signed the papers last night."

This was sounding a lot less like he wanted a divorce and more like they *both* wanted it. "Why didn't you put up a fight?" I asked.

"There's no point," she said.

She was right, and I was only surprised that this was happening now instead of ten years ago. My Dad apparently told her he was just waiting until the last of our siblings was married because, you know, that's considerate to waste a decade of someone else's life? That same partner would also go on to also leave me, after asking me to marry him even when he knew he didn't want to be with me, using the engagement as a manipulation.

But my parents' divorce only lasted three months. They got married again without telling anyone, surprising us on webcam one day and shaking their ring fingers as if we should be excited for them. But my mother had spent the last three months talking about how cruel and unkind my father was in leaving her. How devastated and hurt. In fact, she had spent most of my life telling me what a terrible husband he was. "You get the partner you are worthy of," she would say during moments of overwhelming self-pity, imploring us to be good so we could avoid marrying someone like our father. The divorce was simply a validation of all the years disparaging him to us, and not one of us was happy for their reunion. My sisters, especially endeared to their mother and conditioned to consider divorce a violation of their religious beliefs resented my father even after they got remarried, refusing for years to forgive him and causing no small amount of pain in return, but all the while he unaware of the irony of teaching his children to despise divorce and separation, sex and lust, decades spent upholding religious beliefs that a marriage is valid only if it remained forever, and those who failed to comply be rejected.

Not so much of our self-defeating behaviors as parents is so based in religion. Many parents teach their children to reject people who are fat, weak, or ill. They revere strength, discipline, and health. But because we eventually grow old and our bodies fail us, children who have been taught to reject the infirm and unwell are repulsed by the presence of our aging bodies, and will stick us in retirement homes and rarely call or visit because they cannot stand the sight of us violating those standards we taught them. Some parents teach children that liars are evil, because they are painfully aware of their own inclinations for dishonesty, seeking to obfuscate their deception with protestations of honor and truth, then when children mature and discover the truth of our misdeeds turn on us in furious indignation, since it's exactly how they were raised to regard such people who made mistakes. Others revere intelligence and knowledge, and disparage those who are stupid and dim, and then our children grow to be leaps and bounds more educated and brilliant than we could ever be and treat us with the disdain we taught them for those who are stupid, who now is us. Some parents teach their children to be severely pious, moral, and to judge sexuality and relationships with harshness and condemnation, because they are insecure about their own desires of the flesh and embarrassment for fantasies lascivious and deviant. Then when they can no longer stand to look at their spouse and file for divorce are treated as a pariah for the many years they spent conditioning their children to hate who we were afraid we were all along.

This entire problem can be summed up by the simple word *hypocrisy*. But for a parent it is a very real danger which can imperil our later years as our own progeny turn against us or complicate our relationship with them or our spouses or friends in the very way we have unconsciously prepared them to do, leaving us suffering more pain and heartache during a time when our age and mortality are also robbing us of our prior independence. But the solution to this particular problem is a very simple one, though many humans, and especially parents, are loathe to do it—which is learning and teaching the ability to apologize and make amends. Not simply saying the words sorry, but earnestly understanding how to repair wrongs and strengthen bonds of intimacy through restitution shows children that instead of condemning and judging people for their mistakes and weaknesses, we should desire, give, and seek reconciliation and compassion. But our tendency to tell our children exactly how to hurt us is still a very subtle and insidious hazard of being a parent, and one which originates from our lack of self-compassion and operates on principles of Karma and cause and consequence. The present is always rooted in the past, and though we make mistakes we do not deserve the painful experiences which accompany them, even when our actions cause them—they are simply the natural course of fate which is inextricable from life, and until we learn how to show ourselves the love and compassion we do deserve we will never be able to teach it to our children. After all, we cannot give what we do not have, and as such it can be helpful to understand why and where these impulses for self-sabotage originate, the ego's role in sustaining them, and how we can better subvert our negative instincts.

The biological origin of the ego is not actually to cause interpersonal problems, arrogance and obstinance, get in the way of our best intentions, or even to make us ambitious. The role of the ego in nature is simply to help protect an animal against potential threats to their person. When we are young children (or young animals, as it were) we begin to experience life with a clean slate. We do not directly inherit our parents' experiences like some hive-mind organism but instead experience their memories and life lessons through their behavior and perception of their own environment as discussed in previous chapters. A parent who was poor and destitute growing up who was taught by their own parents that money is the ultimate salvation may show patterns of behavior such as miserliness or obsession with never wasting things. Having lived through the great depression, my generation's grandparents learned with much difficulty the value of having resources, especially food. To their own children whom had never experienced a famine they obsessively insisted that plates be emptied entirely before being excused from the table. At a time when Western countries also began to experience the greatest excess of consumption and food production ever seen in the history of humankind this had the unintended consequence of promoting overconsumption, not just of food but of *everything*, since much was available but attitudes were also biased toward the totality of consumption, and the generation after accumulated more junk and shit than what was probably ever possessed by the entirety of human history. Intergenerationally, a population of humans who experience real threats to their survival and wellbeing were able, because of the role of the ego, to react instinctively to their experience and through facilitation of the ego pass on those lessons to their offspring. Even though they are not our biological parents, gay men who lived during the AIDS crisis were subjected to extreme prejudice of bodies and illness and fears of death and through the function of the ego pass on lessons of strength and health to shape the next generation into body-conscious and fitness-obsessed fanatics. A more healthy example of the function of the ego is when we are abused or taken advantage of and respond in kind by erecting boundaries to protect ourselves in the future. If we had no ego there would be no visceral, biological reaction to threats, perceived or those which are real, and as such would not respond effectively not only to our own detriment but that of the generation to come.

The ego of course wreaks havoc on our lives as well, but even the origins of harmful personality disorders which result from the expression of the ego are rooted in past, real dangers and harms. Because of my size and height I am often set upon unexpectedly by insecure straight men who are antagonized merely by my presence. For many years this was inexplicable and alarming, and often even dangerous to my own wellbeing. My ego responded by regarding straight men as potential threats to my safety in order to increase my awareness of this potential threat and thus increase preparedness. This same response is triggered in women also who, after reaching adolescence (or even before) find themselves the target of sexual predation and harassment, and are themselves then served by the ego in ways which help to train their attention to potential threats to their further survival. But even in the men who act in this manner the ego is also participating—those who react offensively to my size are reminded instinctually of their smallness and helplessness as a child, when perhaps they were abused by their own towering, powerful fathers, and without realizing it they identify a kind, harmless, autistic, gay man as a potential threat, not because I displayed any behavior or indication that I would beat them up but simply because the ego is alerting them of the similarity to their earlier suffering and trauma. It's just like if we were wild human animals and saw one of our friends get eaten by a sabretooth cat. Our ego would thereon out identify sabretooth cats as a danger to their wellbeing. For sexual predators the very same fear of helplessness experienced as children drives them to assert control and dominance over those who are now weaker than them, because feelings of being helpless trigger the ego to demand the neutralizing of that fear but at the cost of their very humanity.

This individual defensive psychology can also influence and precipitate global socioeconomic and political instability and conflict, such as is seen in war. There is a lot of focus on Germany and Nazis as perpetrators of past wars, but in reality that entire region of Europe was at the time gripped by widespread racism and ethnic nationalism, and one of the reasons Germany marched first into Poland at the onset of World War II was because Poland at the time had every bit as much ethnic nationalistic antagonism as Germany, and each country saw the other as an enemy instead of a neighbor. People who suffer from myopic stresses of racism and xenophobia naturally fear others (literally the definition of both terms) and in turn see others as adversaries and obstacles with whom they must contend rather than humans with whom they could cooperate and collaborate, and this is even more intense if a perceived adversary is not just passive and disinterested but also actively antagonizing your own personal bigoted beliefs and convictions of ethnic exceptionalism, then war breaks out more easily between these groups because of the intensity of egotistical defensiveness, even when they are in reality extremely homogenous groups, especially when you consider that there is in fact no such thing as race, as if that could ever be an excuse for heinous behavior anyway, and that every single human being on the planet is in fact also a human being.

It is often mentioned that many positive experiences are required to counterbalance even one negative one. This is sometimes leveraged in other parenting books or self-help advice to assist grasping a more positive outlook on life, or to affect positive outcomes in children. But this naively misstates why this occurs within us at all—which is the very same self-preservation instincts that exists within each of us as a human animal. Our lives are simply never under threat from butterflies, hugs, or rainbows. Kisses, kindness, and friendship do not bring death, injury, or starvation. To survive as a mortal creature we are greater attuned to potential threats to our wellbeing that we may better survive. This attunement is developed in childhood, through our experiences but also facilitated intergenerationally through our parents and grandparents by demonstrating their own conditioning through those subconscious actions demonstrating their perceptions of life, and we thus become more aware of the threats which may occur to rob us of what we want or need to survive. That is also why the effect of parenting upon a child is an unconscious process, because if we were required to make and remember a list of everything we should teach a child we would utterly fail, so biological instincts kick in through the function of fear, insecurity, and the ego to instead decide what it is a child should learn.

One of the most harmful of egotistical, intergenerational survival mechanisms is the controlling or manipulation of other humans. Mothers and fathers having experienced or learned abuse and abandonment from their own parents or romantic partners develop strategies and skills in reaction to the protective nature of the ego to mitigate their own misfortune with regard to other humans as an adult. Instead of giving love freely and unconditionally to those in whom we are interested we challenge them, press them, demand of them demonstrations of affection and commitment, to satisfy the needs of the ego in identifying and neutralizing possible threats to our happiness paramount to and at the expense of actual harmony, peace, and love. Throughout the entirety of my young adulthood I was insecure and demanding in relationships, because I had seen it confirmed in my own experiences that love was fleeting, conditional, and unreliable, taught by my own parents and siblings and friends that affection could only be got by wresting it from others, a perception of life seemingly confirmed in adulthood meeting individuals whom would participate in this dynamic. This in turn limited my success and experience as an adult because the only partners available to me were then those willing to submit to this kind of demanding treatment who were themselves possessed of complimentary ideas about love and self-worth which fit together like a jigsaw puzzle with my coping mechanisms, and as such all of these relationships were doomed from the very start since the only relationships I could achieve needed to be facilitated through these perceptions of life and the function of my individual ego.

My mother one day was watching one of my nieces while getting ready for the day. She hadn't yet put on her makeup or done her hair. "Nana, you're ugly," said my niece.

Children can be so blunt that in the moment of their unrestrained expression they can seem intentionally cruel. My mother was devastated when relating to me the experience, but in turn I was perplexed why she did not immediately identify herself as the very source of the incident. "You always told us we were ugly growing up," I said. "As a way to manipulate and control us."

"I did not," she said, immediately defensive.

"Yes you did—" I insisted. "Whenever we were sad or angry you would tell us to smile because we looked ugly when we frowned. Once, when I was a teenager you literally said 'I wish I had a camera right now so I could record how ugly you look.'"

My mother was speechless at the clarity of my memory and the realization that her experience was in fact a Karmic cycle in which she had long been trapped. Her own mother probably used appearance and self-worth as a tool to also manipulate her children and feel a sense of control as a parent. My mother's emphasis on physical appearance growing up conditioned all of my sisters to evaluate their self worth based on their physical appearance and to similarly use appearance manipulatively. Being a parent can be frustrating and exhausting, and since most parents do not have the tools to effectively deal with the challenges it presents we reach for instincts and lessons learned from our own childhood to feel empowered as adults. My great-grandmother, the renowned beautician, and my grandmother also beset with fake hair extensions, tattooed makeup, all concerned with the excessive and superficial trappings common among the War generations by which they defined their self worth. My own mother a beauty queen and model in her youth was no doubt deeply familiar with the effectiveness of using self-esteem and appearance as a weapon, being herself subjected to the same stinging remarks and comments in her youth then in her desperation of caring for six children while suffering depression, metabolic illness, and an unkind husband reached into her limited bag of tools to pull out the only one which she had been empowered to use when the responsibilities of parenting became too stressful passed down to her own child and grandchild now found herself a victim of her own behavior.

After forty years of abuse I was finally forced to end my relationship with my parents whom, unrelentingly, insisted still on treating me with same derision and disdain as a grown man as they had in my teens. Then, without the buffer of me taking most of the abuse and shielding my siblings they in turn became increasingly targeted, and then also began to withdraw from a relationship with our parents as well (although that had been occurring for many years already, with all but one literally moving as far away from our parents as they could get). Because parents have such a size and age advantage over our young children we can easily get our way and become used to imposing our worldviews, ideology, beliefs, and opinions in our own families, deluding ourselves in an entirely self-constructed facade of reality, and run an incredible risk of believing our own bullshit. Many older parents become ostracized from their children because children eventually grow up and gain in size, wisdom, and autonomy and recognize that what we did to them as children was, in fact, abuse. Lacking also the skills to mend relationships and repair our wrongs such parents cling the more obstinately to our anti-social, destructive, and self-centered behavior because we have trained ourselves to do just that for decades, never learning how to empathize with others (or ourselves) or to learn from our mistakes, then lose the very relationships on which we have come so much to depend, the very authors of our own misery. Above all it profits a parent to be self-honest and liberate ourselves from the restrictions of the ego, else we find ourselves angry, resentful, and alone in our twilight years.

Though it causes many unpleasant and even frightening and painful experiences, the ego structure is ultimately a good thing. It provides us with a necessary tool for the human animal to survive and succeed in life. It is daily and moment to moment protecting us against very real threats to our very existence, even if some or most of them are in truth just perceptions and fears. It is only when we operate in reaction to instinct, when unresolved pain and trauma from our past guide our ideas about life that the ego will get in the way of what we truly want and sabotage our best interests, but which only happens because the body wants to take care of us, and will do anything to make sure this happens even if it means robbing us of the love and happiness that we so desperately desire. Because of her unresolved trauma my mother could not see her granddaughter's apparent insult for what it really was, a realization by an innocent and naive child that people grow old communicated through a limited set of tools, and if my mother had instead known compassion for herself and the condition of mortality would instead have shared wisdom with my niece that growing old is a normal and wonderful part of life. Even in those who desperately desire love the ego can see love as a source of danger, and as such can keep us from it. We as parents cannot then help ourselves from teaching our own children exactly the ways in which they can and should betray us, if we so operate in life without learning how to amend our wrongs and demonstrate compassion for our own weaknesses and shortcomings, because it is our biology at work, the unconscious purpose of passing down knowledge through example and reaction that our children too might survive, our life lessons to that of our offspring delivered at our expense should we fail to learn this skill.

This is why the mitigation of much parenting difficulty can be accomplished through self-reflective practices and resolving the pain and trauma of our past. By gaining a deeper, richer understanding of the reality of these experiences, what caused them and what they did for us we attain more enlightened knowledge of how life works and how it works for us, thus acquiring an increase in compassion for ourselves, which in turn teaches us new skills for achieving true success, which in turn engenders an increase in confidence which then mitigates the need for the ego—at least the need for it to step in and take over when we are not living consciously. It is impossible to subjugate the ego entirely. After all, it is part of our biology and doing so would render us incapable of living and is not in fact even possible. But its role in our lives can be leveraged for much more success and happiness than is our typical experience, especially when it comes to the rearing of children, when its role in our lives is understood not just through intellectual enlightenment but also lived experiences. While there are many difficult parts of parenting, parenting need not be difficult, and it is only ever difficult because we are willfully blind to the function of our own ego and the pain and self-hatred which complicates our responsibilities as parents.

8

Learning and Development

You have to understand that we did not even know what a video game console was when we opened the *Nintendo Entertainment System* Christmas 1987. A gift from my maternal grandparents, it had to be explained and demonstrated before we really understood what an amazing, miracle of a present and technology it actually was, especially considering the swift and resentful disapproval of my parents. There seemed a wide disparity between the fact that my parents' parents were the ones with the wisdom to purchase for us such a gift while my own parents, much younger and less wise, were the ones condemning it as a thing of indolence and waste.

Yet the *Nintendo's* position in our household made it a useful tool for our manipulation—not because we weren't absolutely the best children than any parent could have ever wished for, which we absolutely were, but because my parents' fears and insecurities as individuals and parents was entirely based on the anticipation of problems, even when there was no justification or rationale, so we were constantly treated as terrible children in anticipation of being terrible children even though we were never terrible children. So the *NES* proved a useful tool to facilitate my parents' control and domination and as such retained a place in our home for several years.

Parenting from this perspective is exhausting and comes with little effective tools since it is not at all based in reality, and so parents operating from a handicap must devise machinations by which to force the outcomes they desire. Throughout the years of my childhood I would often conflict with my parents about video games and computer use, because they wanted me to be the embodiment of a disciplined, self-deprived, and morally rigid refutation of their subconscious fears and insecurities, while I was interested instead in developing as a person and experiencing my life on my terms. My parents never offered anything that was as mind-expanding or developmentally effective as playing video games. Not only could I escape the bleak and meaningless torment of our religionist and self-hating prison, I could learn and grow both mentally and physically in ways which were not possible otherwise. Video games, television, and electronic devices are often derided as a dopamine-inducing distraction from real life, as if dopamine is a hormone of vice rather than the the hormone which promotes the successful behaviors of social animals, but when real life is nothing but a meaningless expression of unresolved trauma, unrestrained bigotry, and endless interpersonal conflict the appeal of such escapist and superior methods of experiencing life become a necessity.

As a young man embarking into the world without many skills to survive it was my insistence on playing video games and using and learning computer software that gave me the only skills by which I was able to persist in the world, without which I would surely have plunged headlong into poverty and real failure (which would only have been a problem at the time due to my lack of perspective on what money and material possessions really mean). Able to teach myself complicated technical and artistic skills for which most other people attain four-year degrees and rack up tens of thousands of dollars of debt I was immediately able to enter the workforce and rise to a position of some prominence in my field without a day of higher education (but let me be clear it is far better to go to college and this is not an example to live by). My parents at many turns failed to empower me with skills that could enable a successful life, none more glaring than those needed within interpersonal relationships, which are arguably far more valuable than any trade or degree or pedigree. Moving from home to home, never learning how to make friends or establish a secure social foundation I found myself a desperate loner without the ability to connect to others and often skipping from one or two convenient friendships or relationships to the next. The skills of creativity and technical fluency I developed by defiantly pursuing video game technology developed my hand-eye coordination and capacity for conceptualizing 3D space, which in turn helped me become an accomplished 3D artist which in turn paid more than twice as much compensation as traditional 2D graphic animation. My success in turn gave me a satisfying outlet to find pride, accomplishment, interest, and entertainment, but also some interconnectedness with other people. My spatial awareness and intuitive problem solving skills developed in youth through such creative activities also afforded me the ability to think in ways which facilitated my accomplishments in discerning the origins of disease and to cure myself and others now of alcoholism and addiction, hair loss, thyroid disease, depression, and cancer as discussed in my book *Fuck Portion Control*, which absolutely would never would have occurred otherwise.

Many parents approach learning and development as if children are purposefully uncurious, willfully lazy, and resistant to progress and success, even when those children already actively and voluntarily express desires to help in the kitchen, home improvement projects, the use of tools, or insist on reading and practicing skills which emulate their parents. Because my parents treated me with contempt whenever I wanted to help or made mistakes I grew up thinking I was stupid, lazy, and talentless, even when there was ample evidence to the contrary. One day at our restaurant, also when I was ten years old (which has since been paved over by a parking lot for a shopping center), I was in the back lot feeding our pigeons and pheasants which were in a large coop next to the pig pen and heard some baby birds chirping from inside the pen's cinderblock wall. Curious, I climbed on top of the coop roof and grabbed the wall to hoist myself up, but the cinder blocks had not been securely mortared together and immediately came loose, causing me to fall backwards on top of the coop, crashing through the roof (thankfully injuring none of the birds), the blocks falling on top of me and bruising and cutting my skin. I stumbled back to the restaurant feeling ashamed and embarrassed at having made such a dumb mistake, which my father reinforced by scolding me for the damage I had caused and telling me how stupid I was for having done it. Though I got better grades and achieved more academically than my parents ever did I always thought I was stupid growing up because my father communicated his own insecurity about his own intelligence by consistently berating us whenever we made mistakes, were naive, or wanted to help out with the cooking or other household projects. As parents we are often resistant to the natural learning instincts of children because our own past traumas and biases against those qualities of childhood vulnerability are mistaken as the source of our trauma rather than abuse of opportunistic, cruel, and insecure adults, then passing this trauma onto our own children which disrupts their natural inclination for learning through participation which would otherwise make parenting far more simple. Likewise, playing video games as a child was a big reason for my own increased intelligence and skills as an adult, and children do not want to play video games because they are lazy, fun-seeking hedonists but because video games are an extremely stimulating developmental activity which builds neurological dexterity and heightened cognitive development, and games help enrich the lives of children while also occupying their attention and giving parents some free time. But parents like my father oppose such activities because they are threatened by them, not because they are actually concerned with their child's wellbeing, and the same kind of resistance to child development is repeated in every generation with parents attempting to control access to information, books, music, or social and academic opportunities, using the novelty or prejudice against one medium or another as pretext for asserting control when in fact such experiences not only enrich and enlighten children but also alleviate some of the responsibilities of parenting if parents would only let go of their iron grip and instincts to dominate.

One of my sisters is proactive in creating experiences for her children to specifically engage in scientific experimentation and play. One day a week she sets up interesting inquiries on the workings of physics, biology, chemistry, or nature, with hands on interaction with chemicals, devices, bugs and animals, or day trips to amazing and wonderful institutions. On the face of it this seems like a proactive and successful parent who works tirelessly to give her children the best life they can and expose them to experiences she never got as a child. In reality she is a controlling and manipulative parent who actively sabotages her children's natural curiosity. When her children don't want to participate she berates them and punishes them for not sitting still or for being interested in other things which are not actually the thing she prepared for them, because she put in all this time and effort into creating the experience. When she's exhausted by the planning and execution and all these demanding activities she is quick to lose her temper and emotionally abuses and manipulates them into compliance, or simply to vent her excessive emotions for no good reason because she has no other outlet through which to express them. If they are not actively grateful she lectures them on how ungrateful and disappointing they are. So experiences of this nature become associated with pain and heartache rather than inspiring curiosity.

She was, as a child, severely neglected by my parents who, for instance, chose to go on a vacation to Europe instead of taking her to her very first day of school. The pain of her experience motivates within her a desire to do better for her own children, but because it originates from unresolved trauma and insecurity actually perpetuates the cycle of intergenerational abuse and is in truth the same thing done to her own children as was done to her, just in a different context, since the purpose is in truth a self-centered desire to subvert her own pain and trauma.

Likewise another sister is psychotically in denial over the origin of her own children's pathological chewing and peeling of fingernails and skin, which they do as an outlet for the unrelenting stress they experience under her and her husband's similar antagonism and harassment of children who are absolutely wonderful, thoughtful, talented, obedient, and amazing, who incidentally also demonstrate the same exaggerated interests in escapist video game participation as I did, not because escapism is bad but because their parents think nothing of making their children into receptacles for their own tempers, psychoses, and anxieties.

Because as parents we often feel like we have to do more for our children than we actually need to, we often undertake more than we perhaps desire or have energy to do, out of a sense of obligation coupled with a poor estimation of our children's natural propensity for success. Nowhere is this more evident than when it comes to learning, education, and development. A parent fatigued and exhausted by their own behavior and '*doing it for their children*' then begin to identify the children as the source of their fatigue and frustration rather than our own prejudices and ineptitude, and so begin to resent the children for not responding the way in which we selfishly demand, which in turn creates a vicious cycle of trying too hard, taking on too much, doing too much, and then becoming exhausted because of our own voluntary and excessive complicating situations, or abandoning our responsibilities altogether because it's too much, then making our family pay the price for our inability to care for our emotional welfare and the resultant dearth of patience, empathy, and wisdom.

Children are naturally inclined to explore, learn, develop, and grow. They do not even *need* outside motivation to do so. It is built into our very biology to discover and seek out knowledge and information because to fail at this would also mean perishing altogether. Learning is the only way that children can actually survive, and as such children are literally born with strong internal motivation to seek out new knowledge. That is why children are especially equipped to learn even multiple languages as small children, something grown adults find frustratingly difficult. Parents who overwork themselves and expend tremendous emotional energy trying to get their kids to do schoolwork, perform well, and pick up enriching hobbies are also those who got bored when their children repeatedly questioned them about mundane things when they were even younger, who tuned them down when a child asked to be read to, or denied them when wanting to be taken to the library, play video games, or help with the dishes.

When I was very young I loved coloring on pictures that my mother drew for me. She was so talented and could draw horses and mermaids and other things I dearly loved. I would approach her and ask if she could draw this, or that, and because children rush through drawings this was probably aggravatingly incessant. Eventually when more of my five siblings had arrived my mother one day lost her patience indulging me in this favor. "Nathan," she said in exasperation while breastfeeding my newest sibling, "just do it yourself."

"I can't—"

"Yes, you can. Just think about what a horse looks like in your head and then draw it on the paper."

I reluctantly went to draw it myself, but quickly learned that I *could* draw myself and that it was immensely rewarding and empowering. Out of necessity for her sanity my mother inadvertently showed me that I could do something on my own where, if she had not otherwise been overly burdened, may have gone on indefinitely doing it for me. In reality, children often ask these kinds of indulgences of their parents not because they actually want us to do it for them, but because they don't yet know they can do it themselves. They are not asking us to do things for them. They've only been on this goddamned earth for very short period of time and are ignorant to the possibilities of human life. But as parents we just hear what is coming out of their mouths and then overburden ourselves with demands and busy work which in reality are demands for education and *empowerment*. My mother inadvertently gave me one of the only skills I developed well as a child, to be an artist, which in turn brought me much self-esteem and developed my personal identity, because she finally reached a breaking point where doing it for me finally became literally impossible.

During a visit from my brother my beautiful young niece kept pestering him with incessant prompts, "Dad?" "Dad?" "Dad?" she said over and over, even while he ignored her and talked to me about her as if she wasn't sitting right there next to us. By this point he had three more children and no longer the luxury of pretending to be a perfect parent, and instead of answering her he turned to me and asked in exasperation, "how would you deal with that?"

At first I was overjoyed at finally being asked to help. As an older brother I knew no other way to find value for myself if not being of use to others, and no other way to ingratiate myself into the lives of those whom I loved. But, *deal with that?* I thought angrily, though I refrained from betraying my contempt. *'That' is your daughter, whom you are neglecting.* "She wants to be acknowledged," I said instead. "She keeps repeating herself because you are ignoring her. The only way to 'deal' with her is to actually communicate with her."

It was no coincidence that my sibling and his partner later began to talk about my niece as if she was slow in learning, for which I was completely surprised because she was actually more intelligent than even I was at her age. The only reason her parents thought she had any deficiency was because they spoke to her in condescending, exaggerated baby talk and failed to connect directly with her due to their own considerations of childhood and biases informed from their own experiences, completely unaware of her natural brilliance and motivation for learning for never having given her the opportunity to communicate in ways that weren't patronizingly dumb, who now that they've had enough children to be distracted from interfering in her development now easily demonstrates remarkable intellect and interests in programming, building, making, and creating for someone of her age which, like my propensity for art, she developed all on her own once her parents were unable to persist in pressuring her to achieve.

We respond as parents to our children's capacity for learning because our own remembered experiences as a child was also one of powerlessness and humiliation. Grown into adults we remember the vulnerability of childhood which came from our helplessness and inexperience, and this in turn triggers uncomfortable vulnerabilities we would rather not acknowledge and in so doing withhold compassion for the child that was ourselves. We then react to our children as if they are as powerless and helpless as we remember ourselves to have been, believing that vulnerability to be the reason for our pain and trauma rather than the maleficent and exploitive behavior of others. But children are not yet adults. They have no concept of adulthood, merely living in naivety and ignorance, driven by natural instincts to survive and develop as best we can. They do not consciously know how powerless they really are, and are ignorant to the limitations of life since they have not yet encountered them (which are far too often also our own parents). So children act out of naivety in good ways as much as bad, and seek out self-improvement as readily as they do food and sleep and play. A parent needs to spend exactly ZERO energy getting their children to learn. Often we don't even need to facilitate learning, though it is helpful, as children intuitively find all sorts of ways to glean information themselves. Plop a stack of books in front of a child, even one who cannot read, and they will consume them voraciously. A new strategy which has become quite popular is to turn on the closed captions while the television is on, which basically becomes a reading and spelling tool while children watch their favorite shows and you get to make yourself a sandwich and coffee. Other children are also a source of learning, which is why play and friends are so important, gleaning rules of kindness, sharing, and the consequences of self-centered behaviors to develop the most valuable interpersonal skills that can help a child prepare for their future far more effectively than any formal education. But other children are also potent motivators for learning, which is why many children look forward to and love attending school, but also why social ostracization can oppositely impair a child's natural inclination for learning since social inclusion is far more consequential to a child's wellbeing.

The greatest harm we do our children when it comes to learning and development is doing everything for them—or even just a lot for them—instead of empowering them with skills they require to live successfully. Obviously children are incapable of cooking all their meals, going shopping, and securing shelter and protection. But I watch in frustration as my siblings and other parents settle rivalries and conflicts amongst cousins and friends without empowering their child to try it themselves at all, reprimanding the offenders or coddling the offended without giving them tools to do it themselves because, again, they are supposedly helpless children. During one family visit a lovely niece of mine was actively rejecting her younger sister while playing with the cousins her age, feeling perhaps for the first time truly included in a group but being raised by conservative, traumatized adults also feeling that inclusion to be tenuous and fragile. On more than several occasions she selfishly guarded that membership by cajoling and offending her younger sister, to keep her out of the group, who came upstairs crying about what they had said or done to her and my heart broke remembering how I similarly treated my brother when we were children. Her parents are one of the more skilled pair in my family, but would simply reprimand the older girl and send them all back, and it would happen over and over again. One day when there was not tension and we had time between activities I quietly invited my niece to sit with me on the patio outside, and I related to her my behavior toward my brother when we were children, how I hurt him and how it permanently scarred my relationship with him even though I tried to repair it, because sometimes you can't fix things that are broken and how much I deeply regret having done it. I then charged her with the protection of her younger sister since she was the oldest, her responsibility of caring for those who are vulnerable, and to prevent the same thing from happening to their relationship. She listened earnestly the whole time and her behavior changed immediately.

Likewise, parents start making their children do the dishes as soon as they are able to avoid dropping plates, but they never teach children teamwork by having *everyone* clean up the after dinner mess until it is done, because the point is not to teach children skills they require but to use them for labor so we can have a break from our responsibilities, so a child learns how to load the dishwasher but never how to be part of a team nor to effectively maintain their own environment without being overcome by stress and trauma. All too late parents are only interested in letting kids do things for themselves when they are eighteen and ready to leave home and do not demonstrate any successful self-care skills or responsibilities because we spent their entire childhood taking on all the responsibilities of parenthood instead of sharing them or alternatively berating children for harm we have caused by our own behavior, failing entirely to empower our children and without any wherewithal to fix our mistake simply kick them out of the house to learn hard life lessons on their own. This problem is most especially exhibited too by poor and middle class families which have been deluded into believing there is some morally admirable aspect of failing to adequately prepare children for the future or providing them a financial and material safety net. Rich people and rich families are rich because they pass down wealth and accomplishment, which has its own pitfalls and arguably also more disadvantages due to the delusions which wealth facilitates, but their children succeed in the material world because their parents have often successfully prepared their children in ways which facilitate learning and development rather than doing it for them, ironically, since they are well provided for materially which in turn facilitates a more detached approach to parenting, for better and worse. There is nothing admirable about kicking children out of the house unprepared. This is a total failure as a parent and an intergenerational problem that can take entire additional generations to rectify, since the ensuring generations are raised by inadequate and unskilled parents who don't learn valuable life lessons until after their children are also grown, which perpetuates and amplifies the problem since reproduction is exponential, and before anything can be done about it entire populations collapse or are burdened by widespread psychological illnesses, unrest, and economic inequality.

My Granddad loved to tell a story about me when I was eight. He was visiting us and all the adults were watching a nature program. It was about whales, and they didn't even think I was listening—playing behind the couch with some toys by myself—but then David Attenborough said that the humpback whale's penis was ten feet in length. "Whoa!" I shouted. "That's a big *penis!*"

We often consider children naive and incapable, but this is far from the truth and again originates from our unresolved traumatic experiences when we were children, and children are far more aware and intelligent even in ignorance than we like to admit. Once when conversing with one of my sisters her four-year-old daughter was listening to our conversation and realized that I had not understood the context of my sister's story and interrupted us to provide astute clarification. The impulse to 'do it for them' or to instead abandon and neglect children because we feel incapable of succeeding originate from our negative evaluation of our own experiences as children and thus a negative evaluation of childhood, our insecurities over powerlessness so uncomfortable we either want to fix it or to ignore it altogether. Doing either will permanently damage our child the way we were damaged by our own parents, who were in turn by theirs, who were in turn by theirs, and so on and so on.

The key to facilitating healthy intellectual development in children is to have not just compassion for the powerlessness of a child, but to be grateful for it. To love their naivety and ignorance as a strength which empowers them to try things that we would not even attempt. The fear of disappointment or frustration or pain which will come from their mistakes is really our own fear of disappointment, frustration, and pain. We cannot take theirs from them, and in trying to do so will cause them harm. Such experiences are an important part of life from which we not only learn lessons to help ourselves live better in the future, but which are required to experience the full breadth of living, without which our experience would be dull and meaningless anyway. The lack of faith in our children is a lack of faith in ourself. Because of our extensive failures and our conditioning as children we carry this self-defeating attitude into parenthood and then force it in turn upon our own children. If we don't have faith in ourself or don't have faith in our children then just shut up and keep quiet about it until they can prove you wrong (and not just until they fail).

The biggest motivator for treating children like they are more dependent on us than they really are, and one which is also extremely insidious, is that we as parents find self-worth and value in our role as parent. If we are someone who has little self-worth and a poor estimation of our own value this then becomes a psychosis in which we seek (even if subconsciously) to condemn our children to permanent dependence on us and thus secure indefinitely our usefulness as a parent. Indeed, most failed childhoods are the result of this pathological need for parents to feel needed at any cost, which parades as concern for our children but in reality is a total absence of it, instead only desiring to facilitate our own indispensability at the expense of our children. My parents refrained from ever teaching us about finances, taxes, money management, frugality, and responsibility to in part handicap our success as adults, and then when we failed financially became emotionally and intellectually reliant on them, but through which they could then also withhold aid and further indenture our dependence and thus secure one of the only effective methods of developing self worth they know. Of course, none of this is conscious or even intentional. We are not born into this world devising machinations for the demise of our loved ones. Such responses are those innate biological instincts which facilitate the perpetuation of our species, engineering social structures and interdependencies when they are not made consciously, strategies which evolved over millions of years in response to the demands of the environment and our evolution as human primates, mammals, and animals. We react in such a way because we too were denied healthy and fulfilling experiences by our own parents, so instead of just giving up and laying at the roadside to die we have built-in, nefarious, and even ruthless instincts that go beyond learned behavior and consciousness which cannot be identified by those it controls without the conscious resolution of the origination trauma which catalyzed its genesis in the first place. This starts first by having compassion for the child that we once were, the child that is still you, and then we can find compassion for the ones we brought here.

 The first rule when it comes to learning and development is that we must facilitate opportunities for growth and development and empower our children in these opportunities by teaching and showing them useful skills, but we absolutely cannot and should not do it for them. Reading is absolutely the most important and probably the only important practical skill that any child really needs, because if a person can not only read but also *desires* to read they can and will teach themselves any and all skills which are required to live and to succeed. I taught myself my career which normally requires four years of higher learning and crippling debt simply by reading the help menu of all the software needed for my discipline. Once a child knows the alphabet and starts to read, if we facilitate access to books they will naturally devour them. Just as I was forcefully abandoned to art and learned to do it for myself, much of a parent's reluctance to read to their children is simply because we have not enlightened a child to the fact that they can also read on their own! It's okay to not want to read to our children constantly. We have things to do and we should be taking care of ourselves in addition to our children, and we cannot well take care of children if we do not also take care of ourselves. After a child gets to a place where they can read sufficiently, change reading to *group* reading, where everyone in the family chooses a book to read on their own together can increase child empowerment without depriving them of access to parental support and family while we are also empowered to care for our own interests. Unlike my father who would abandon my brother and I at work and task us with cleaning up the sawdust and debris instead of working alongside him, this is not an excuse to abandon parenting responsibilities but instead a strategy which cares for our own wellbeing while at the same time empowering our children, not neglecting them. This can familiarize children with reading on their own without making them feel unwanted or excluded, and will rapidly and naturally lead to self-sufficiency in reading. To also employ other methods of learning like turning on the closed captioning for TV shows or supplying children with games and other reading activities, even encourage reading on play dates so that friendship is also associated with reading, extending this to other life lessons like interpersonal conflict resolution and personal responsibility, the learning and development of children will essentially progress on its own. Then, instead of resenting children for their reliance on us this will in turn free more emotional energy and availability to support, encourage, and champion our children in more effective ways. Access to safe social media also facilitates high rates of literacy and emotional intelligence since children need to be able to spell, read, and interact successfully with a diverse group of people in order to participate in those platforms. Video games teach valuable creative problem solving skills, rational thought exercises, and develops motor neural and cognitive pathways which can promote physical and mental development, coordination, cognitive capacity, creativity, and socialization. Learning and development can be one of the most fun and rewarding aspects of parenting, if we relent control and have compassion for our own childhood experiences and facilitate rather than control our own children's access to opportunity.

Because learning in children is most strongly inspired by the behavior of adults and parents, exposing children to demonstrations of skills and talents is the best way to motivate introduction to learning avenues. Parents who play no musical instruments will have a difficult time convincing children to learn. But a parent who can sit down and play a wonderful song on a guitar or piano will fast see their children clambering on their lap to do the same. This also is true of all pursuits such as reading, academics, cooking, art, and athletics. I once took my guitar on a trip to see my siblings and every single one of my nieces and nephews wanted to try playing it. If we as parents do not have skills that we think our children should have, or should at least be familiar with, it is most easy to inspire their involvement by exposing them to other adults who do. This phenomena of children wanting to be like their parents or other adults they admire means that all a parent has to do to inspire learning and development is simply practice their own interests, skills, and self-care, and children will naturally follow without requiring any special exertion or effort.

9

Abuse

The summer when I was fifteen my father, growing increasingly frustrated and annoyed with my brother and I (mostly I), sent us for the first and only time alone to our grandparent's cabin in the mountains of Arizona to spend a few weeks learning discipline and hard work. Naturally nervous and completely terrified of life, I was beyond stressed at being forced out of my home to go live with people who would hardly talk to us during a family visit, let alone during continual and isolated residence for several weeks without any books, television, or video games to fill the silence. Our arrival was, however, no less warm and loving that those which we had grown accustomed. The first day all we did was cook, and before we even started dinner my Granddad stuck a fork in the middle of each of several *whole* pumpkin pies he had made, topped each with generous amounts of whipped cream, and plopped an entire pie in from of each of us. "Tonight," he said, "we're having ROUND pieces!"

But wracked with the anxiety of knowing that my Granddad would insist on horseback riding, chores, or even—God forbid—learning to hunt, I could hardly relax for even a moment. The next day was not just fun and games but I did quickly take to enjoying being in his barns, brushing the horses, and shoveling manure. Though they made me nervous, I loved horses and there was a freeing, primal, quiet connection to and love of nature my Granddad had which nobody else in my family shared. But later that day I was then assigned to mow the lawn.

"With what?" I asked, having never seen a lawnmower at their house and assuming perhaps that the horses or deer kept their grass short. Granddad huffed and directed me to a strange contraption with a handle that looked like a giant, heavy whisk turned on its side. It was a push-mower. At one point we owned a riding lawnmower, but nobody had ever thought to bring my grandparents into the modern era. "That?" I whined. "You can do it," he snapped impatiently, leaving me alone with the old, decaying contraption.

Pulling the mower away from the faded board and batten cabin, I lined it up with the lawn and began to push. The wheels barely moved and the gears screamed as metal scraped on metal as the blades protested. I was tall but not so tall nor heavy that I could get any leverage on the mower at all. The damn thing was rusted beyond belief and there was no way in hell I could push it even a few feet let alone a single pass on the lawn.

Embarrassed about my weakness because of my conditioning by my father and being constantly shamed and derided for being skinny and small and frightened of disappointing my Granddad whom I assumed would be even worse than my own father, I went inside and hid in the living room and turned on the TV to watch a movie. My Granddad saw the lonely mower and unfinished lawn and came in to find me. "What are you doing?" He said.

"I can't push it," I replied. He glared at me, huffed, and went out to mow the lawn while I watched sadly from the living room while the television played in the background.

Thankfully his disappointment didn't last long though, and the next day we were up early with his brother, Uncle Gary (the father of my lesbian great aunt) and our Uncle to saddle horses and set out for a long ride. Growing braver, but also enamoured by her beauty, I asked to ride the thoroughbred racing horse, Dances for Dollars he had been raising for the last several years. If I had known how spirited she actually was, I would probably never have actually gotten on her. But my Granddad was a good horse man and his animals well cared for and trained, and my naivety was indulged and we set off across town and up into the dense forest outside of Pinedale.

Even for someone who loved and rode horses, it always takes a little time to settle in and relax after having not ridden in awhile, but even though as a racing horse Dances was naturally competitive and strove every step to be in front of all the others I soon grew pacified by her spirited, rhythmic trot and confident effortlessness in which she carried me.

Soon we were deep in the forest, and the trail began to rise steeply. At a dip in the road traversed by a rivulet and crowded on all sides by dense forest my Granddad navigated his mule first through the water and out the other side. It was my turn to cross. I prodded her forward over the creek but she was not at all interested in walking in the water, nor listening to me. "No! Whoa!" I shouted as she began to plough under the low-hanging trees instead. Dances was several hands taller than all the other animals, and I myself a lanky teenager meant there was no room for both of us to pass under the unforgiving branches of the ponderosa pines. The lowest branches were at my waist, and though I clung to Dances as her powerful body drove us through the trees the branches pushed me off the saddle. I leaned far to the side trying to get out of the way of the thickest branches because it was a long ways down from her back, but my tight grip on the reins merely made her even more determined to push through. A thick branch stuck into my torso, ripping into my shirt and cutting my skin. As Dances pushed forward the tree took my shirt and tore it slowly from the top right shoulder across my chest and off my back like a male stripper removing his shirt during a show, left with nothing but the collar and one sleeve and the rest dangling from my back.

My Granddad laughed uproariously, "Are you okay?" he asked. I laughed and nodded. "You gotta show her who's in charge!" Dances never did kick me off, though she did kick my Dad and other adults who rode her at other times, and after seeing her buck never dared get on again. But I like to think we bonded that day when she dragged me through the trees.

My Granddad took my brother and I out every day on horseback to collect discarded Elk antlers, which sold for about fifty to a hundred bucks a set, depending on their size. He would lead us directly to them and act as if he never saw them until we were right on top and impossible for I or my brother to miss, and sent us a check for our "share" of the proceeds, which was all of it, when we returned to Utah after he supposedly sold them. On another ride (this time on a mule) I somehow stopped my animal right over a rattlesnake which my Granddad spotted and calmly got me to walk my horse forward without any incident, and killed the snake and cooked it for dinner (I tried it but was so weirded-out that I don't remember how it tasted).

The contrast between how my Grandparents treated me and my brother, even when we were misbehaved or disappointing, was inexplicably incongruent with the shame and derision their children used in raising us. Not once did Granddad call me names or insulted me for being weak, or harassed me when I felt insecure or failed to meet his expectations. But I knew from the stories told by my father that he had not at all been a gentle or benevolent father himself. But I could not help but wonder how the disparity of my parents' behavior and their own parents' behavior was so starkly disparate, and at the end of my visit felt the same reservation at the thought of returning home that I had at my arrival.

Throughout the early Nineties one of my sisters was absolutely tormented by my parents. She demonstrated several behaviors which parents often find aggravating—finger sucking, afraid to go to bed, and enthusiastic, probing questions, boisterous singing, and incessant requests to play. My parents went about dealing with these behaviors using some common methods—threatening to withhold toys, food, or even beloved possessions like her 'blankey' if she did not stop sucking her fingers, telling her to stop singing when they grew tired of it, and threatening punishment if she did not go to bed. Attempts at reasoning and warning of permanently crooked teeth entirely failed to convince my sister to stop finger sucking. Growing frustrated and lacking any effective means to produce the outcome they desired, they began to resort to more desperate and inhumane strategies including duct-taping mittens around her hands or using deterrent anti-finger sucking products which contain intensely bitter chemicals. They even used hot sauce, which didn't just burn her mouth but also her delicate skin, the threat of which alone was enough to send her into a maelstrom of fear and crying. When my sister wouldn't go to sleep at night, my exhausted and desperate parents began locking her in the dark garage, her screams as she begged to be let back in the house as clear in my head today as they were when I was a teenager.

All of us were absolute delights as children, each with our own magnificent individualities, talents, and quirks. I had a lisp and was effervescent and intelligent and creative, and being the first born a natural leader of my compatriots. My brother was technically brilliant and very kind, and more adventurous and brave than any of us. His twin was lovely and shy, sweet and soft-spoken and always a ready participant in my machinations and ready to care for the rest of us and make sure we felt special and loved. My second sister was a spitfire who let no one get away with any bullshit and kept everybody on their toes with her wry jokes and probing intellect. The finger sucker was a magnificent songstress never out of costume whose spontaneity as a child still cracks us up whenever we watch home movies and whose jubilant personality brought light and joy into a home often burdened with sorrow. The last of us was a total tom-boy to the point where I suspected her also of also being homosexual like me when we were younger, in opposition to my femininity she paraded around for years in her famous cowboy-pirate getup—cowboy hat, pistols and holsters, an eyepatch, hook, and boots. But my sister who was often shut in the garage brought the most love to our family. Entirely lacking in selfishness she never thought twice about talking to us or engaging in fun or helping out, or serenading us with one of her brilliant original songs or a particular selection from *The Little Mermaid*.

Yet my parents' frustration with this completely heartbreaking little girl was leagues beyond what any of the rest of us endured, their obsession with her finger-sucking as obstinate as her refusal to stop, their will to silence her at night as unrelenting as her demand to be freed. The struggle over her behavior was truly one of dominance and submission, and greatly exceeded the normal, rational tug-of-war which accompanies all parent-child dynamics. Many years later when my sister had her own children she was confronted by the very same "problems" with her own daughter, a nearly identical copy of herself who delighted in the same kinds of theatrics, singing, and joy in performance (but also a bit more mischief). My sister, wise to the effects the abuse had on her life, turned to me for insight on how to address these issues, because her initial response was to also wrest control from her daughter and coerce her into obedience. We explored the origins of her attitudes toward these childhood behaviors and why the approach taken by my parents not only failed to resolve the situation but inflicted severe and lasting psychological damage upon a child far worse than the consequences of finger sucking and not going to sleep on time.

Children suck their fingers as a self-soothing behavior that brings them comfort. Knowing this, the act of finger sucking indicates a need to be soothed, not for mittens to be duct-taped around their tiny hands or doused in hot sauce. Because the suckling reflex is associated with closeness and physical contact with a parent, the act of sucking on toys, fingers, or blankets or other objects of comfort mimic or replicate the comfort normally afforded by the protection and intimacy of being physically close to parents. Parents readily avoid physical intimacy with their children, not only because our lives are busy and our minds preoccupied but because our lifestyles also conveniently excuse our discomfort with emotional vulnerability. Being deprived of close physical touch of a parent then stimulates stress in an infant which results in crying and protestation as an adaptive response which forces a parent to pay attention and to draw them near, the mechanisms of biological parent-child relationships kicking in when parents fail at their job, since being near a parent is safe and being far from them in evolutionary terms is unsafe and increases the risk of predation and death.

When children suckle their fingers or other objects of comfort they are doing so to alleviate the stress of physical separation, to duplicate the soothing and consoling experience which is normally provided by the touch of a loving parent, since love in this sense also means the satisfaction of primal desires for safety and protection through proximity to large adults. It is common for children to suck their fingers well beyond infancy, but when it continues longer than a parent thinks appropriate, if the parent is insecure it begins to trigger unsettling feelings of helplessness and insecurity in us. Feeling powerless to resolve the situation because of our own trauma and lack of empowerment and sensing the situation as a failure on our part but ignorant of how to resolve it then seek to neutralize our discomfort by neutralizing the evidence of our failure through dominance and subordination. Such feelings are the reason that abuse even happens at all—because children are part of us and a mirror which forces us to see things in ourselves for which we are ashamed or embarrassed and wish to ignore, which remind us of our own experiences of helplessness in childhood, crippled by unresolved trauma and lacking skills to care for our own wellbeing effectively respond to our fears and insecurities by fighting the sources which trigger them, which in this case is our children. Because finger sucking especially demonstrates helplessness and insecure adults loathe feeling helpless, parents then pathologically obsess over finger sucking behavior as if it is a serious behavioral problem, which it absolutely is not. Finger sucking does not actually cause teeth misalignment. Such deformities of dentition occur because a child's dietary health is insufficient, lacking sufficient dietary carotenes, vitamin K, E, and sunlight for vitamin D which nutrients participate in the proper formation of dentition and facial structures as demonstrated by the famous dentist Weston A. Price and his survey of indigenous populations and the effects of industrialized diets. An insufficient diet makes teeth unable to resist the gentle pressures of finger sucking, which itself is not forceful enough to misalign healthy teeth, not to mention that children lose their baby teeth anyway and concern for their dental health is merely a distraction from a parent's obsessive preoccupation and to justify their abuse. Then, because the parent's ego is what is truly at stake in the situation and not the actual wellbeing of the child, no effort is spared until the child is fully dominated into submission.

There is a horrific German folktale about a little boy who gets his thumbs cut off by a demonic tailor because he sucked them, and I believe a direct line could be traced from this very kind of intentionally inflicted childhood trauma and the rise of the murderous Nazi regime, who were pathologically obsessed with weakness and dominating everyone around them. Because finger sucking in reality serves as a proxy for closeness to the parent, prolonged finger sucking is a sign of insufficient physical and emotional affection and closeness with a child, and so the solution to address it is to provide generous attention, especially physical contact in the form of hugs, kisses, play, and cuddling, which are required of parents anyway. Especially by the time the third or fourth or fifth child comes into a family, parents who are ill-equipped to provide sufficient attention for even one or two children have almost no time or attention to spare for the others, even if unintentional, but it does not mitigate the biological need for children to have this kind of access to their parent, and in reality our limitations of time or resources are just used as excuses for parents to avoid the discomfort we feel from such vulnerability. The same stress caused by an absence of connection and contact also catalyzes other behavioral problems like fear of sleeping or the dark, increased attention seeking, or increased interpersonal conflict with siblings and friends. In nature a human child would be in near constant physical contact with their parent, and it is unnatural for us to be separated so formally as we so often are, burdened by unhealthy ideas of dependence and separation. A child sucks their fingers because their own mother or father does not love them, resents their vulnerability, and keeps an emotional distance from them. A child's biological programming for survival then kicks in and overpowers the parent-child relationship when parents fail to provide, for which the only option is to correct these deficiencies. Literally just doubling or tripling the amount of hugs, kisses, and cuddling directed at children will reverse these problems.

Likewise, when children display excessively needy behaviors such as constantly annoying the parents or other adult caretakers, insisting on continuous contact and engagement and persistent interference and lax compliance a child is responding to insufficient emotional availability from the parent. The warning signals of stress which begin to rise in response to a dearth of demonstrative love causes a child to instinctually draw attention to themselves, purposefully and with force. Most parents treat this behavior and regard such children as being willful, as if they have all the relevant experience and wisdom as a fully grown adult, treating children as if they are maliciously and purposefully manipulative rather than operating on instinct and the naive and helpless little creatures they actually are. Annoyed and insecure, parents then respond to these demands for attention by fighting the child, coercing, hitting, shaming, or engaging in other types of abusive behavior as if they are justified by their own emotional motivation and excused of heinous behavior simply by virtue of being a parent. Most parents are selfish, self-centered animals who don't think much of others and aren't good at being parents. Because a child is abjectly helpless and wholly dependent on parents, and parents are not by virtue of their position at all dependent on the children, when neglect occurs, even if it is unintentional, a child's biology is designed as such to draw attention to themselves, no matter the cause and even if it does catalyze abuse, because as far as biology is concerned, at least the parent is aware of the child's presence. As I said before, if children were quiet, insular, and passive very few of them would actually survive and we would swiftly cease to be a species upon this earth. It is for the survival of the human race in its entirety that children respond to neglect in the manner they do, and parents who fall behind or are hampered by their own remnant childhood trauma also find themselves at the mercy of biology.

When as a parent we are confronted by the very same behaviors in our own children which were used as an excuse to abuse and subjugate us as a child and thus the apparent source of unspeakable pain and torment, such as was my sister's experience, the feelings we experienced as a child resurface as fresh as if we were still a child, and compounds the helplessness and vulnerability of our experience. Because such feelings of helplessness accompanied the abuse and traumatic experiences we respond to our child as if we are again in the position of experiencing those feelings and pain, rather than now the adult who is in charge and no longer actually helpless, and act out just as we did when we were a child, motivated by emotion and self-preservation. This is how abuse is perpetuated from generation to generation, by parents who are still children on the inside feeling their emotions justify their actions. When confronted by the vulnerability and dependence of myself and my siblings as children my own parents were forced to relive the traumas from their own childhood, and acted out on those feelings of terror and pain in desperate self-preservation but now upon new, vulnerable little children now also doomed to repeat the cycle when they are grown.

Parents who abuse do not understand that our feelings of pain, frustration, and helplessness were valid when we were a child. Being abused and tormented is wrong, and we are right to react to such malign and calloused behavior defensively and painfully. But, growing up and becoming an adult, with means and power and autonomy we experience the same feelings and mistakenly believe that we are as much justified in them as an adult as we were when we were young, since the quality and intensity of our feelings does not change simply because our bodies grow, and because our identity as a person forms when we are children, not adults. This is often made worse by our parents using our helplessness and dependence as a child to convince us that we are the ones responsible for the abuse we receive, which is an effective abuse technique which seeks to absolve a parent for the pain we cause children. My parents so harassed my sister about her finger sucking, insisting that it was because she sucked her fingers that she was subjected to such painful experiences that in her adulthood with several children she had never actually considered that the entire ordeal was the fault of our parents and in fact had nothing to do with her sucking her fingers. Because they had convinced her so effectively that it was her fault because she sucked her fingers she in turn also considered it her own daughter's fault that her daughter sucked her fingers. Without skills to understand why we become abusive and hurtful, the only option left to traumatized adults is to place blame elsewhere and to in turn visit trauma upon others. Children being as naive and dependent as they are then have no choice but to submit to the abuse and agree with parents that yes, they are at fault and deserve the abuse. Because this is not actuality true, when the child reaches adulthood the reality is so alarming that the human mind chooses instead to continue believing that we can control what happened to us by our own behavior and thus perpetuates abuse on our own children, blaming them in turn for the abuse we choose to act upon them. Children, instinctively understanding that they still require the love and affection they need and deserve, continue to persist as long as they can sustain until they are finally beaten into submission and their light and unbridled enthusiasm for life is finally and fully snuffed out.

In healthy homes, children have space to explore who they are as a person. They develop their own tastes in toys, music, clothing, activities, and personal interests like particular academic pursuits, playing certain musical instruments, or what kind of friends and people they enjoy and who they want to be when they grow up. When as children we are instead brought up in an abusive home, we do not have much space to figure out who we are as individuals, and instead spend all of our time and energy simply trying to navigate and survive our own parents, so everything a child does is oriented toward the parent, adopting their tastes in music, clothing, and personal identity for our own, never learning what makes us special nor what we want for our own lives. In my youth I listened to my parents' music, wore the clothes they chose for me, and even had the same haircut until I was seventeen when I finally realized what a cypher I actually was. When we grow up in such a home we fail to develop our own personalities and interests, then as adults we often turn to alcohol or drugs as a shortcut to enjoying ourselves, never having found our own interests and strengths beyond what our immediate environment and responsibilities required. Often when I help people recovering from addiction and alcoholism much of our time is spent trying to figure out what it means for the person to actually enjoy themselves, having never been able to spend time learning what things in life they truly enjoy, having never experienced satisfaction and fulfillment, because of the psychological block caused by their abusive childhood which did not allow space for them to explore who they were as an individual, because of the excessive emotional domination of our parents. Because finger sucking, acting out, annoying and persistent demands for attention are in reality caused by deficits of physical and emotional affection, the only way to truly resolve these so-called "problems" is to provide the actual physical and emotional love children both deserve and require, so that our children do not have to spend their childhoods trying to survive us. Like my sister whom recoiled from my embrace on the walk back to our car from dinner, the damage done to children in childhood which manifests itself as displays of self-soothing behavior and what originates from the withholding of affection is deep and permanent, and parents only risk making it more traumatic if we attempt to extinguish it though denial and discipline and not to instead admit our role in its development and make changes to our behavior to correct the deficiency and restore emotional bonds.

Our inability to provide children with altruistic, earnest, and sustained emotional availability, intimacy, and connection in the first place is because we find such emotional vulnerability very difficult and uncomfortable due to our own experiences of rejection. Exposing ourselves emotionally and physically as children opened us to opportunities to be hurt by those who were supposed to protect and love us. As a defensive mechanism facilitated by the ego we then, as adults, parents, and spouses cut ourselves off from emotional and close physical contact which would again open us up to be hurt. But this is the entire point of life, and the only way in which we may experience the depths of living and love, by willingly offering ourselves to be hurt by those we love, by making the bonds which are later rent through death and loss. Clinging to our pain and disappointment will only cause our own children to suffer the same at our hand. Having a child is an opportunity to heal all of the wounds of our past, but since we have largely been taught to ignore our wounds in misguided efforts to move forward we do not otherwise possess the skills required to address them, and thence the presence of this little, vulnerable child forces us to reflect and in horror and revulsion lash out at them, now every bit as culpable and guilty as our own abusers. We must open ourselves to vulnerability, to act in spite of our wounds, to learn compassion for the little child still inside us who was denied the love and affection we needed and deserved.

I once dated a boy who was a victim of sexual abuse by a relative throughout his youth, and when he finally got the courage to ask for help his own mother told him never to talk about it, refusing to help him and in turn causing him even more pain and heartache in addition to his horrifying experience at the hands of a predator. Perhaps my love interest's mother was also sexually assaulted as a child, and she reacted to her own child's similar helplessness and failure to protect him the way her parents failed to protect her, revisited with vivid and horrifying memories of her own trauma which was greater than her love for her son. But this is the very problem which perpetuates abuse! As a parent we cannot turn away from pain and trauma as we wished to do in childhood if we desire to protect our children from the a similar fate. No matter how much we may feel like it, we are no longer a helpless child, and our reticence to face the past simply originates from both underestimating of what we are now capable and a lack of compassion for our experience, our heartache, our pain. Those who are sexually assaulted as children are often also told by adults, explicitly or otherwise, that they are complicit in the abuse the same way we are for other abuse. It is a lie used by the adult to avoid consequence for actions they know are wrong—especially because they know exactly the kind of pain they are causing and become every bit as terrible as their abusers. Because we try or want to believe we have some control in life over the terrible things that happen to us this also means that we had some control over the terrible things that happened to us, but the truth is we do not. Even when we try our best and do everything right, bad things still happen. That is the very point of life. If we had control over those kinds of things we would not even be here. We must experience the full breadth of life, which means its pain and horrors as well as its joys. The first step in overcoming the kinds of trauma which cause us to condemn and shun our own children with callous disregard for their pain is above all to have compassion for ourself. The things we went through as a child truly were horrifying, sad, and painful. We were abused by our parents or other adults responsible for our wellbeing, who exploited our weakness and vulnerability for their own benefit, though we tried our best and to be good and to love our family unconditionally. Unlike parents, children are naturally inclined toward unconditional love, and even after decades of abuse children continue to forgive and permit their parents, even when maybe they shouldn't. We were an innocent and entirely helpless child, incapable of protecting and providing for ourself, and without the support of adults we would certainly have perished.

Female children are also often more abused than their male counterparts, even by their own mothers, because of unconscious consequences of the patriarchal systems in which most of us live, where men are told that their only value comes from being the head of a home and ability to provide for a family, and to protect women and children because of their status as a male. A patriarchal system does not mean that men are bad, nor are they alone to blame for the institution because women and mothers are every bit evangelists for the patriarchy as men and fathers. The mother of one of my old boyfriends once told him in a fit of homophobic rage that only women brought love into a relationship, not men, reinforcing through her own behavior and choices one of the fundamental harms of patriarchy which is to condition men not to have nor express their own feelings. My own mother visiting me on a rare occasion when I was young saw a white carnation given to me by a friend for my birthday, and instead of admiring its beauty and the loving gesture in which it was given declared that "men do not give each other flowers." She was right, in a way, that yes men are more likely to give each other bullets, a direct consequence of patriarchal oppression, wherein abused and traumatized egomaniacs and dictators exploit the desires and needs of young men to commit heinous crimes and engage in fear and war mongering and crime and the abuse of women and children, to exploit the vulnerable because they are taught that being male means denying compassion and empathy and exploiting whom you are able. In a patriarchal system women are taught that they are inferior and that men are superior, even and often by mothers who believe and sustain those systems, and resenting their own vulnerability and fearing the same in their little girls then treat their daughters with increased harshness, inadvertently perpetuating the same negative conception of femaleness which caused their own pain and suffering.

Most women and mothers are not even aware how their behavior supports patriarchal abuse. For instance teaching girls and young women to dress modestly in order to control the desires of men, which denies the personal responsibility men have for their own behavior and puts that burden instead onto girls and young women. Or sexual assault victims who are conditioned to submit to male authority and continue to do so even when they have been violated and the systems proven to be dangerous to their own wellbeing. A woman I know was raped during college, but instead of reporting it to the police went to her religious institution as she had been conditioned which, run by men, then blamed her for the attack and then subsequently was further groomed by a religious superior who demanded she visit his home and place of work to constantly report on her sexual activity. The indoctrination which was used to condition her to submit to and be a willing participant in her own abuse and exploitation was not her fault at all, nor the fact that she was raped, but her willing and continued participation in the very institution responsible for her exploitation even as an adult realizing fully the cause and source of her experience is a perfect example of how women also actively support the very ideas and institution of patriarchal abuse and one of the reasons why it does not end, because it is not a system only made nor sustained by men, and feeling powerless to challenge our oppressors instead submit to and thereby perpetuate and sustain it. As a gay man most of the abuse in my life which I suffered under the system of patriarchy came directly from women, because I did not fit into the patriarchal expectations of the system which give women some sense of control and power through their sexuality, and this made those women, who are also victims of it, feel thusly uncomfortable and powerless toward me, because patriarchy forces women to consider their personal worth as a function of their body.

Nearly the entirety of the abuse directed by mothers towards their daughters is targeted specifically at their first born daughter, being the first to show up in the family immediately becomes the target of all a mother's anxieties, frustrations, disappointment, and resentments for being a women under systems of patriarchy, since that anger and pain cannot be directed at men and those who uphold oppression is more virulently channeled toward young women than the first born sons. Young girls often valiantly resist such unfair treatment, which makes for especially spectacular fireworks of emotion and saddles promising young girls with debilitating trauma, self-hatred, and fear to which no young person should be subjected and leads later in life to things like eating disorders, depression, and alcoholism and addiction. Fathers and boys make the resolution of this struggle impossible as they willingly follow the cues of their wife and mother, who have far more power in a family than any other member. It was with no small amount of frustration that I watched such trauma play out out in the lives of many of my relatives, my young nieces and cousins cruelly and unjustly characterized as wild or willful, even by their own mothers who were exactly the same when they were children and when nothing they did could ever justify such abuse, not even their very struggle to fight it.

But many men are all too willing to uphold patriarchy and subject themselves, their wives, and their young children to oppressive systems of conformity which ruin the courageous and imprison the innocent simply to uphold fear and anxious misconceptions of manhood. For all his strengths my Granddad was also somewhat misogynist, and often treated women as if they were put on this earth for his satisfaction and thereby inferior, as did my own father, which included his own daughters whom he more readily regarded with contempt and condescension than his sons, as if they were stupid and so undeserving of dignity and respect, their mothers actively endorsing this abuse instead of refusing it, even (or especially) when my sisters demonstrated intelligence and wit which exceeded his own.

No doubt my Granddad also learned this behavior from his own parents, being a member of a misogynistic and patriarchal religion. With my siblings, my mother reinforced these roles when my Dad abused and harassed my sisters even for his own mistakes, refusing to take care of her own needs, conditioned also by abuse to submit to such cruel and inhuman behavior and to regard men as superior, and actively sustained and supported the systems which helped perpetuate both hers and our abuse every bit as much as my father. As a result many of my sisters became unconsciously frightened of men, believing themselves to be powerless and confined, and they too failed to care for their own needs, unconsciously resent being women and so disadvantaged, then unable to care for themselves turned their frustration out on husbands and children when the stress of powerlessness became too great.

Worse, unconsciously fearing our female children will be vulnerable to the same harm and exploitation which caused their pain, mothers and fathers instinctually treat them more harshly than boys in a misguided attempt to toughen them up and prepare them for such vulnerability (or simply for resentment of this perceived vulnerability), which in turn places blame for violation and exploitation on them rather than on those who commit harms and exploit the vulnerable and thus sustains the system of patriarchal abuse, each generation convincing their daughters (and gay sons) that it's their own fault they are abused simply because of who they are.

Many of us turn to religion for answers to problems which in truth rise from abuse, especially since members of religion often advertise relief as a feature of the institution, for instance my friend who was raped and then stalked by her church leaders still searching that religion for answers to the pain she suffered in it. But religions do not possess tools to resolve experiences of abuse, that is why we struggle in them for years and decades without ever solving our problems. They are only ever coping tools which try to make us feel better about things over which we have little or not control, such as death, loss, and disappointment, and we are left to struggle with pain and trauma in spite of conviction because although God may care about our wellbeing simply subscribing to religion is not how trauma is resolved.

Our past may not have sufficiently prepared us for the responsibility of adulthood, but life does not care one lick about that, and many adults make terrible mistakes before we have set even two feet into adulthood, and being abused does not in the least prevent us from also being an abuser, which is the very mechanism by which abuse is perpetuated, our misery, pain, and trauma being the source of emotional instability, control mechanism, and frustration used as excuses for the way we act in order to cope with those experiences. Once when I was young and thought I was still justified in losing my temper (because that was what was modeled for me) I hurt my dog and had to take him to the hospital. In that moment I realized through my mistake that I am responsible for my behavior—not in an abstract, ideological concept but in the very real consequence of having to live with my choices and actions. I became every bit as terrible a person as my own parents, an a abuser and offender even though I identified as someone who was abused, which did not actually prevent me from also being an abuser and sustaining the systems responsible for the perpetuation of the very abuse through which I had suffered. The sadness and horror of my mistake still haunts me to this day, even though it has been twenty years. I am still ashamed and hope for his forgiveness regularly.

Because our mothers like Mary Wollstonecraft, Susan B. Anthony, Sojourner Truth, Betty Friedan, Coretta Scott King, Gloria Steinem, Jane Fonda, Gloria Allred, Anita Hill, Carrie Fisher, Betty White, Susan Harris, Madonna, Mae West, and Bea Arthur fought for the rights of women we are no longer really subject to the patriarchy except what we consciously or unconsciously allow. Trauma and abuse can convince both women and men to submit to oppression and to operate as if we are not individually powerful, and to do horrible things to one another and in our frustration turn our anger out upon helpless children as if it be their fault and not ours that they are abused by us, because we first and foremost do not know how to care for our own needs, to set healthy boundaries and actually act like an adult. Misery loves company, but it's not because we want others to be miserable—quite the opposite we simply want compatriots, togetherness, to not be alone in this dark world. Abusers pass on abuse because we cannot make sense of our experiences, why the adults responsible for our love and care did none such for us. Lacking then the skills and opportunity to resolve such issues since our own caretakers did not empower us we instinctively act upon the only tools at our disposal, which are instinct and learned behavior of control mechanisms. Having been abused as a child and then rejected by his family my love interest could only then reject me, as well as every other person who tried to draw near to him, having no skills to resolve the trauma of his experience to allow an emotionally fulfilling relationship and the vulnerability such a relationship requires. But he was also now an adult, not actually a helpless child, but because we form our identity when we are a child most of us grow into adults believing our actions and choices are still justified by our feelings, which they are not. Many young adults entering college for the first time and living with other humans who are not their intimate relations continue behaving in their new environments as if they are spoilt children fed and clothed and attended daily by caretakers. Volatile emotional conflict then erupts as we are rudely awakened to the presence of other children and the realization that the world does not, in fact, revolve around us.

Continuing to act on our feelings as if they justify our behavior is what enables abuse. We are no longer children. *As adults, we are not entitled to indulge our emotional whims and instability*. It is the very source of abuse. Adults for instance who cry when we hurt others or make mistakes to manipulate and avoid consequences for our behavior might think we are avoiding consequences. In reality we are undermining and destroying the integrity and bonds of our relationships, compromising our own position rather than securing it. Cajoling, ridiculing, and criticizing partners and children for perceived weaknesses that make *us* feel uncomfortable only makes them hate us and to withdraw from the relationship, since we have demonstrated that we are not a person to be trusted. If we feel uncomfortable when our children suck their fingers, ask for attention, sing silly songs, get angry, hit their siblings and friends, are female, gay, or different in some way, or exhibit emotional instability, stop acting like a child and look inward at the feelings which impair your ability to be a good parent, acknowledge the pain and trauma from your own experiences which their behavior reminds us. Having made mistakes in the past is no excuse for continuing to make them, and the resolution of our fear, pain, and trauma as discussed in upcoming chapters can and does teach new tools by which to live effectively and leave behind the burdens of the past. Each of us is individually powerful, as equally able to uplift, help, and heal as we are to hurt and destroy. Power is always an illusion, a psychological trick of our human mind meant to perpetuate our survival as a species and not our individual wellbeing. To resolve the trauma and pain of the past and stop systems and cycles of abuse requires above all to find compassion for the little child we once were, the one we still are, and in turn will find it for those whom we are tasked to care.

10

Discipline

I don't remember exactly what I had done to incur my mother's wrath this time, since she lost her temper at even the most trivial of offenses, but it must have been especially egregious because instead of spanking me herself with the belt she said, "Your father is going to spank you when he gets home."

I was seven or eight and my dad had never yet in my young life laid a hand on me, so I was exceptionally terrified by the anticipation of a new kind of pain at the hands of someone so strong and powerful. The time I had to also anticipate my impending doom was more than enough to produce extreme remorse for whatever it was that I did (notice I don't remember). Repeated pleas for mercy and fervent apology did not sway my mother's resolve. So, as a backup plan I snuck into my room and put on three extra pair of underwear.

My Dad came home later that night and I was summoned to his room and the door closed unceremoniously behind me. He talked to me about what I had done. It became clear that he too thought my mother was over-reacting, but because she demanded it he still had to spank me. He laid me over his knee. I braced for impact and prepared myself to act more injured than I might be if I wasn't wearing extra underwear. *SMACK!* came a loud sound from behind but without any impact to my bottom. I looked up at him fearfully, thinking something had gone wrong and that I was still going to get a beating. But he had merely slapped his own hand, and I was free to go with the warning that next time he would not be so generous.

There are only two lessons of positivity I have ever learned from my father. One was to employ patience when dealing with combative strangers, the other was to restrain oneself from acting in violence, and though I do not at all remember what it was that I had done that day, engrained in my memory is the example he set in responsible discipline and the restraint he showed in dealing with me. Of course, there are many other examples where my parents absolutely failed, but I was in truth extremely lucky to have not been born to, say, most of my aunts and uncles who beat and abused my cousins mercilessly.

Discipline is the first taboo of parenting, and every parent has their own self-righteousness ideas of what is right and permissible when it comes to the disciplining of children. My heart breaks whenever I am around my siblings who torment their children with emotional volatility and manipulation, knowing the only thing that prevents me from saving them from a life doomed to the same overwhelming despair, depression, and mental trauma we endured is also their very problem parent, whom I was also powerless to save from their trauma. Many adults feel justified in using emotional and physical abuse and punishment to correct children, excused and even encouraged by tradition and influential religious institutions. My younger siblings without the ability to empathize don't understand my refusal to engage with my parents, because they did not grow up homosexual in a bigoted household, constantly fearing for their safety, and also as the first born child bearing the full weight of parents' collective anxieties, beaten with a belt or thumped on the head any time I so much as frowned, since my mother also finally abandoned physical punishment around the birth of our fourth sibling. As a consequence, they live their lives and parent as if the reasons for my problems as a child and as an adult (and thus their own children) was my own fault because they, like most of us, believe the lies we were told as children about our culpability in our own abuse, and cope with the pain and trauma from their own childhoods as if we actually had control over the things which were done to us rather than what was perpetuated by abusive parents. Making our experience even more obfuscated is that homosexual or otherwise differently gendered children often overcompensate for fears of rejection by being even more obedient and excellent which in my case as the oldest child set a tone of compliant behavior which is atypical of families where older children are duly more inclined toward rebellion and permissiveness if parents are at all unreasonable and unstable. Instead of viewing the failures of my parents' generation as a warning, my siblings forge on repeating the very same mistakes and behavior as if their generation will be the first in history to squeeze positive results from the same tired mistakes, pretending that the mental illness and emotional instability of generations past was not a result of the very same abuses and mistakes they continue to perpetuate from generation to generation.

Myself and many of my cousins, despite growing up in staunchly conservative homes, developed debilitating depression, mental illness, and common substance abuse problems because chemicals like alcohol, marijuana, and cocaine medicate the neurological disease which result from abuse and environmental and dietary stress as discussed in my book *Fuck Portion Control*. Even after witnessing my abuse and experience dealing with suicidal depression and recovering from alcoholism one of my sisters claimed in a conversation that she was glad to have chosen not to become an alcoholic or experimented with any substances. She actually smoked pot three times in high school, which is three more times than I ever did until I was twenty-six, and I immediately reprimanded her for the glaring ignorance and callousness of her position. Claiming that substance abuse is a choice when a person knows full-well that they did not endure half the torment and pain as a person with the disease speaks more about humanity's desire to ignore realities which confirm our mortality and powerlessness in life. If a person lives in a world where alcoholism is a choice that means they can choose not to have it. It's as simple as that. They are empowered to determine their own safety. This also translates to other morally self-righteous and maleficent ideology such as that sexual assault results from slutty behavior or that violent racism can be avoided simply by obeying the law. We want to believe that we can protect ourselves from things which otherwise are meaningless and terrifying. The prospect that terrible things happen to us *just because* and not that we can control and invite them is the driving force behind prejudice and indifference, ironically even and especially (but not surprising) from people who are asked by their religious ideals to demonstrate empathy and compassion. But this attitude as it persists within the role of parenting causes parents to be sorely ineffective as parents, especially when it comes to discipline because, like our original abusers, discipline is regarded as something which is actually controlled by the child rather than the autonomous parent. Most insidious are those parents who use religion as an excuse for terrorizing their children, which in turn robs children of their relationship with God, since God becomes associated with the source of their pain and trauma.

Discipline is not punishment, but it is often mislabeled as such. Discipline is the ability to exercise self control, and losing your shit with a belt in hand across the bottom of a small helpless child is exactly the opposite of discipline. Because of contemporary attitudes on punishment parents are, thankfully, far less likely to beat their children than generations past. But emotional manipulation and punishment is still widespread and accepted because parents are the only ones who regulate or have a say in such matters, not children, who would without a doubt protest such treatment if they were possessed of the autonomy, life experience, and intellect of an adult. This occurs because our motivations for disciplining children is usually not because they've actually done anything wrong but because they have in some way, even if by their simple presence, set off or triggered fears and insecurities we as parents have never resolved, and as such our motivation for punishment is to neutralize that which triggered our fears and not actually to parent. Because of these unconscious and subversive psychological dynamics, most of us live entire lives separate from the one of which we are actually conscious.

The condition of *narcissism* has sometimes been regarded as an effect of physical abuse. But there are many narcissistic adults who were not also beaten as children, and the psychology profession often treats narcissists as if they are choosing to be narcissists and are inherently villainous and without redemption rather than severely traumatized human beings. The problem of narcissism arises from a profound absence of affection for a child, and this can be demonstrated either by physical violence, which demonstrates extreme resentment and lack of love, or also by severe indifference and emotional disconnection in an adult and without any replacement figure to provide the emotional connection from adults that children require. Having been given no love a child must then provide it for themselves, but because they are children and have no real coping skills this becomes excessive self-preoccupation and self-love and thus emotional separation from others. Also not knowing themselves, the only concept a child has is of their physical self and their body, and never having a chance to develop emotionally connect extreme value and concern for the physical body, since that is how they perceive their own self worth. Because the trauma of war impaired our parents' parents ability to express affection, narcissism became widespread amongst the baby-boom generation, even in families who did not engage in physical abuse, but especially if they did, simply because parents were too traumatized to provide love and affection for their children. Punishment which replicates either of these deprivations of affection has the very same effect upon the psyche of a child, which is to communicate an absence of worth. This in turn disrupts a child's sense of belonging, identity, and personal worth and engenders isolation and pathological self-reliance. When a child is deprived of the safety and love through aggressive and severe punishments, the family itself becomes a source of danger, and feeling alone in the world a child must then rely on self-preservation behaviors like dishonesty, theft, sociopathy, promiscuity, disloyalty, narcissism, etc., in order that they may survive. Very often, these punishments are unjust, excessive, and opportunistic, so the child also learns the skill of lying and dishonesty in order to survive the experience. By demonstrating for a child that control is achieved by force and domination, this in turn shows a child that force and domination are how ends are achieved in life, and narcissists also grow up to become abusers, cheats, rapists, emotional leaches, and generally ineffective and incapable adults burdened with mania, egoism, depression, dishonesty, anxiety, and desperation.

As my father showed me that fateful day when I got a "spanking," discipline is as much about the parent's behavior as it the child's. We all make mistakes, and the purpose of discipline and punishment should be the demonstration of how to responsibly and effectively resolve our mistakes. If as a parent we demonstrate emotional volatility and inconsistent retribution all we do for the child (and for ourselves) is to perpetuate an inability to behave effectively. Because punishment then does not empower a child to resolve and repair their mistakes, even more mistakes and misbehavior result, which in turn results in more domination by the parent and in turn more resistance from the child. Of course, a parent's instinct to punish originates too from our own conceptions of self-worth and effectiveness, modeled for us by our own ineffective parents, and as such we likely lack skills required to discipline in a way which is effective.

A child should never be made to feel that membership in the family is dependent on their behavior. Many parents use membership and inclusion in the family as a tool to leverage compliance. For instance, we will say something like '*if you do that again you're going to your room.*' Most parents treat trivial incursions as if the entire stability of the family is at stake, when in fact the child probably just did something you don't like and not even something which is inherently wrong. I once told my mother I wasn't interested in seeing her because she supported and engaged in consumption of homophobic, bigoted, and racist institutions which made her act toward me with extreme indifference and she responded saying, "you people" are responsible for the destruction of our family and the demise of the country. THE COUNTRY. Obviously this was a ridiculous indulging of her own personal insecurities, and it was also a perfect demonstration about how every whap on the head or beating with a belt we received as a child was fueled not by concern for the wellbeing of her children but an excuse to vent unresolved fears and frustrations with life itself, and since children are a persistent responsibility which can trigger fears and insecurities become a receptacle for those frustrations, and it is no wonder we grow into deranged and mentally ill adults without tools to come to terms with such horrors. I have no idea how my own parents were disciplined as children, but the fact that they have never even broached such topics and refuse to talk about those things in addition to their own behavior toward their own children hints at the same if not worse kinds of child abuse.

In her later years my mother became obsessed with child sexual abuse, and I think it very likely she, like many young girls, was a victim of rape or other sexual assault as a child which set the foundation for her mental instability as an adult, especially since the patriarchal system under which we live and the religionist community from which she came actively fosters sexual abuse and refuses to provide assistance for victims. But this is why discipline is also not only usually ineffective but actually adds to the stress of parenting is because it is most often arbitrary to our personal insecurities, fears, and trauma and dependent only upon our particular mood, and because our offense is of a personal nature we in turn make it personal to the child, and in the process impair their access to the love and affection they require to be helpful members of the family in the first place. One of my ex boyfriends was frequently abused by his father who displayed a particularly psychotic detachment while physically abusing his son, pretending it was impersonal and simply structured discipline, but spanking like this is explicitly a sexual act, abusing the sensitive and sexual areas of a child and using the guise of punishment to openly sexually abuse a child. His father later related to him having been sexually abused as a child himself, and this is exactly how abuse is passed from generation to generation, children as adults passing on their unresolved trauma to their own children. While these are extreme examples there is far more widespread examples of mediocrity, abuse being passed through seemingly trivial control and manipulation behaviors which are far less likely to be addressed because such behavior is far easier to ignore or excuse, such as using constant threats to control children, especially in anticipation of conflict or misbehavior, passing on our fear and insecurity and psychotic desires for control, and because children are abjectly dependent on the family for their survival, threatening their membership in the family as a tool to force obedience communicates to a child the precariousness of their safety which in turn motivates the development of self-protective and manipulative behaviors to provide themselves with resources we now refuse them. A child's paramount desire and goal is inclusion and acceptance, and threatening that does not increase their desire to comply but instead their fear of loss, which in turn only increases their emotional instability and thus inability to comply.

To be obedient, children need a set of consistent rules by which they can inform and judge their own behavior. This is not a printed list to be taped on the wall, and if you do that you are not doing well at all as a parent, because you are asking your children to adhere to rules that you yourself are not following and thereby demonstrating hypocrisy and unreliability as acceptable personality traits. It is our own behavior and our consistency which is the standard children need, for the satisfaction of our unconscious biological survival mechanisms at the root of development, which is not aware of conscious inputs such as a stupid list pinned to a cork board. Once when visiting a sister for the holidays my beautiful nieces and nephew were having a great time playing with LEGOS in their dining room. My sister answered a phone call, but instead of leaving the room or even asking her children to be quiet she stood in the middle of the chaos trying to talk. When that started to become burdensome she stepped away from her kids. One of them deigned ask a question which my distracted sister ignored and stepped further away from into a nearby laundry room, closing the door partway behind her. Not having received an answer her son followed and continued asking. Finally finishing the call and hanging up the phone she flew into a rage and eviscerated her young children for daring to make noise and bother her while on the phone. But not once had she asked them to be quiet or to give her distance or otherwise instructed them how she expected them to behave while one the phone call, using the opportunity instead as an excuse to vent her mounting frustrations. Even if she had set clear standards for their behavior in such a moment this kind of offense hardly warrants the level of cruelty and unrestrained volatility which followed. They were just being loud. Not a single one broke something or fought with another or hit or called anyone names. Nobody died. Nobody got hurt. They were just having fun. Asking a parent a question is also not an offense, though many parents do treat their children as if it is, when the real problem is that parents have failed to set the kinds of boundaries which communicate to children that domination of social encounters is not acceptable. Erupting from the laundry room my sister's only goal was to exploit the situation and vent her emotional frustration at the expense of her children. Having never established the rules for receiving such punishment (which in reality was merely their existence) she can hardly be expected to have children which honor those expectations to which they are actually ignorant. Then, delivering punishment without clear and consistent rules causes children to become frightened, confused, and incapable of satisfying the whims of an adult. They begin to develop coping mechanisms of fear, mind-reading, pessimism, anxiety, hyper-awareness, agitation, and volatility themselves and the cycle of abuse and supposed misbehavior never ceases.

Rules for behavior are established by our considered response to behavior. If a child wants to get down from the dinner table and we launch into a lengthy admonishment and justification for our decision such as, *"you haven't eaten hardly any of your food and you didn't eat your lunch this afternoon and you were hungry and threw a fit and missed your nap…"* the child we are talking to will not be able to discern the rule by which they are to abide, because of the sheer vomit of information, and will as a result simply continue to ask for permission to get down (even if they are crying or throwing a fit, they are still asking for permission). If instead we simply say "no," a child easily understands that they are not allowed down from the dinner table. Once while visiting my parents one of my nieces refused to comply with her mother's demand to join us at the table. Anticipating a fight, I reached out my arm to my niece and invited her to sit with me and she *immediately* ran to the table and climbed on my lap and ate her entire dinner. Her parent's use of discipline and punishment is so inconsistent, so entirely dictated by the tenor of their emotions that there is no set of rules by which my niece can effectively judge what she should do, to the degree that it doesn't even benefit her to try and behave. If she doesn't behave they explode. If she does behave her parent still explodes. So what point is there in behaving?

Likewise, response to offenses also dictate rules for behavior, but most parents try to explain to children what they have done wrong as if children don't already know it. For instance, a child older than four or five hitting another child is fully aware that their actions are wrong, that is why they are doing it—to get a reaction and force their will upon another person, and even though the child has been repeatedly taught that hitting is wrong a parent will still sit there and explain, *"we don't do that in this family. Hitting is wrong. You shouldn't do that. Your sister was only trying to do this or that. Etc."* rather than providing immediate consequences for their behavior through which they would in turn immediately understand our rule set rather than having to discern it through lengthy admonitions and diatribes. What's actually occurring in this moment is again a parent feeling helpless and frustrated in turn trying to justify our role and authority, to little children. This then fails or then we try to correct our perceived ineffectiveness by then asserting even more dominance, anger, and willfulness at our children which is actually the very same behavior only delivered in a different tone, giving our children power to unmoor our emotional stability and thus becoming children ourselves.

Instead of punishment, a parent need only *insist* that a child obey. Without threat, coercion, or retribution since these only encourage a child to resort to more novel machinations of navigating instability, a parent can and should simply persist in the admonition of children until compliance is achieved. In practice this is simply repeating yourself without emotional volatility nor justification until the child obeys. Hilariously, one of my sisters who used to become frustrated and angry when children didn't immediately obey her took the demeanor when trying this for the first time of an annoying and spoiled middle-schooler saying, *"go to bed go to bed go to bed,"* like an annoyed and broken alarm clock, but it still worked because children above all cannot stand monotony. The effect of this approach is *not* domination or control, nor is it an opportunity to indulge our emotional volatility, which weakens our position by communicating to children that they have power over our emotions. Nor is its usefulness in the exact words chosen, though it should be brief and without justification or excuses for our decision. When a child fails to obey, negotiating and arguing with them *immediately* undermines the authority of the parent for the simple fact that the child is privileged to participate in decision-making processes, which at moments such as bedtime or whether they are not allowed to hit another child, they should not. This is also not the same as withholding empathy, such as if a child wants something which the parent cannot actually give them, nor is it again an exercise in domination and subordination. The usefulness of this method comes from such confidence, even if pretended, that a parent has such absolute authority that no displays of insecurity or self-doubt is required to justify our position, that there is absolutely zero other options for the child than to make for themselves the only choice presented by the parent—*also being allowed rather than forced to make that choice.*

Many years ago I learned very effective methods of dog-training from watching Caesar Milan on the *Animal Planet Channel*. One of the most useful methods he taught was how to teach a dog to swim, especially when a dog is frightened of water. Throwing a dog in water when it's not willing to swim only serves to traumatize them, and will remain frightened of water. Oppositely, lovingly and patronizingly cooing also only reinforces their fear since the human's attempt at consoling them implies there is actually something to be afraid of. Instead, the most helpful method was to use a leash and gently but insistently lead them to the water, then when the dog resisted going in the leash was used not to drag them in but simply to prevent turning away from the pool. The human then neither forced them in nor allowed them to retreat, and this left only one choice for the dog, to move forward. But because the human would not force them to make the choice and only allowed the possibility for one choice, the dog would make the choice on their own and thus be empowered by their decision. Because the person controlling the lead did not force them into the pool, the dog then further trusted the human, which led to further cooperation and success.

Our words are the lead which choses the direction for a child without forcefully pulling them into the pool. Instead of saying, *"Go get ready for bed or I won't read you a story,"* we say *"Go get ready for bed."* If the child complains, we don't again follow it up with threats or punishment, *"or I won't read you story,"* we simply say again, *"Go get ready for bed."* This is also not a countdown to explosion, or tinged with an unspoken emotional threat. It is said with confidence, not derision, scorn, or frustration, or even feigned calmness which are all attempts at emotional manipulation, but just whatever mood we're in and with impartiality repeating it as many times as is required until the child obeys. Children seriously cannot stand to be told the same thing over and over and to your amazement will relent very quickly. When this behavior is the norm children will understand that there's no point in negotiating but also trust that you aren't out to harm them and as such will even more quickly and willingly obey in the future. Calm insistence that the next step set forth by the parent is the only option for them but also actually *allowing* the child to make the choice can near effortlessly control children because they are made to feel empowered, which is the entire point of parenting in the first place, not only to do what is good for themselves but to effectively interact with us, now provided with a clear set of rules and

expectations which are no longer arbitrary to our particular mood.
Emotional punishment is also unfortunately a ubiquitous and insidious parenting strategy, and leads to conceptions of low self-worth, depression, and insecurity. *"You don't want people to dislike you, do you?"* a parent might say when a child does something wrong, implying that their self-worth is tied to obedience. *"People don't like liars. You won't succeed if you don't do your homework. Children in Africa are going hungry but you won't eat your food (implying they are ungrateful)."* Emotional manipulation is effective because a parent's estimation of a child can threaten their feeling of safety within the family, because why would a parent care for a child they don't respect or even dislike, and as such engenders fear, which is a powerful motivator. Feeling threatened, a child will comply, but only because they are scared of abandonment. This in turn communicates still that we are a threat to their wellbeing, and the precariousness of their situation, and in turn makes them feel unstable and vulnerable, stimulating yet more disagreeable behavior and instincts for self-preservation which are at odds with our needs as parents.

It is actually quite rare that a child should ever warrant punishment at all. More commonly, behaviors which are typically punished are usually things which simply frustrate a parent's personal insecurities, and being unable to coerce their children to behave in certain ways but which are not, in fact, actual infractions of behavioral standards nor even disobedience. A child not wanting to go to bed is not actually disobeying, but asking for relief from the stress of emotional separation from a parent. A child who does not eat their food is not infracting rules but simply isn't hungry, or is distracted or stressed. A parent's insistence that children obey us is in truth a struggle for dominance, which is an unhelpful interpersonal struggle entirely separate and distinct from parenting, though the two are often confused. This is most strongly demonstrated by the punishing of children even for their feelings and not because any actions which warranted it. A child having a meltdown at the table should not be punished for being angry or sad but because they hit someone or threw something. But because as parents we are often unnerved by our own children's feelings and thus made aware of our own which we also dislike we often punish because of our distaste for our own emotions and not actually what the child has done, which if we are truly honest with ourselves is most often not a big deal whatsoever.

When I was five or six we lived in Hawaii, on the island of Honolulu in the town of Kailua. It was a literal paradise and the only time in my young life I was actually happy, although that was not a function of living in a literal heaven but that my parents had the assistance of my aunt, who came to live with us and work as our nanny, and thus relieve a great portion of stress from the responsibilities of parenting which in turn afforded us much more access to love and emotional fulfillment to them and to other adults like my aunt. We spent most of our days going down to the beach and playing in the gentle surf, and eating papaya and mango as daily snacks.

One day when I was sitting near the water and building a sandcastle the tide reversed direction and began to advance up the shore. Eventually the waves began to cover my castle, but I was determined not to let nature wipe out my hard work. I began to build a moat around my creation to keep the water from washing it away. The moat was deep enough that the water entirely covered my legs as I sat. One particularly large wave washed all the way over me. Suddenly I felt a sharp pain on my leg, as if someone had stabbed me with a hot knife. It was more pain than I had ever felt, but because I couldn't see anything there I was at a loss for what was happening. When the wave retreated, however, there was a small blue blob of a jellyfish on my thigh. I screamed and knocked it off, and my Aunt came running to my rescue. She saw to my medical treatment and emotional care which, if my mother had been alone, would have had that responsibility on top of all the other things she needed to do for the day.

Later that year I was rummaging through my parent's bathroom drawers during a moment of boredom and came upon a tiny pair of silver scissors. They were so cute, and fit comfortably around my small fingers. I wanted something to cut with them, but having no paper nearby decided that my hair was a good second option. It was long, after all, having lived in Hawaii for so long now had begun to adopt the laissez-faire lifestyle of a surfer. I took one length of hair and cut it at the base. The sweet sensation of the blades gliding through each individual strand was exactly the thing I had wanted to feel. But then I looked at myself in the mirror. There was a glaring spot of sheared hair right on the front of my forehead. I had made a mistake.

I went out of the bathroom to get help. My mother was not nice about it. "What did you do?" she cried. But her response was probably a lot more subdued and censored on account of the presence of my aunt, her sister in law, considering her behavior during such offenses when other adults were not around. She reprimanded me for my carelessness, but it would not be the end of her vengeance. My head was shaved completely bald as a manipulative and emotional punishment meant to shame me for what I'd done, which itself was not actually wrong in the least and in no way deserved such humiliating treatment. I remember feeling at the time how mortifying it was, but believing those feelings to just be my sensitivity and my parents in the right I accepted my sentence bravely. In fact it was simply a punishment meant to assert dominance, that my mother, and not myself, was in charge of how my hair and appearance looked, and that I was never, ever allowed to make those kinds of decisions.

Children do sometimes try to get their way when it is not appropriate, although many parents respond to every attempt at negotiation with force and anger, which again is the act of dominance, not parenting. But when children do fall apart at being denied or told to comply to things which are reasonable and necessary, such as bedtime, using *reassurance* rather than justification or excuses or trying to subdue them with domination and subjugation can demonstrate empathy for their frustration and further empower us to obtain the result we desire, and works extremely well with insistence because both behaviors demonstrate emotional stability and empathy for the child without actually giving them what they want. An example of justification or excuses for our position might occur when a child tries to use pity as a strategy to get their way, *"but I still want to play,"* and we may reply, *"but you played all day long,"* or *"it's late,"* or *"I let you play yesterday, and your friend has to go home too, and you were tired all day because you didn't have a nap, and I don't want you to be tired tomorrow…"* These attempts to justify our position as a parent do not work because justification and excuses are arbitrary and thus debatable, which is exactly what a child then tries to do. *"No I didn't get to,"* or *"but they got to stay out late!"* or *"But I'm not tired!"* Rather than justifying our position, reassurance can demonstrate empathy for their feelings without giving any ground on our position, *"I know you don't want to, but it's bedtime"* or *"you will get to play with your friends tomorrow."* Neither statement is debatable, and the latter is actually an incentive, and as such there isn't much a child can actually debate with us, and because we haven't created the space for a debate we have in turn not delegated any role of parenting to the child. Using reassurance without contempt or frustration also communicates to a child that we hold them in a position of esteem and are thus reinforcing their sense of safety and belonging within the family structure, further increasing our effectiveness since it is insecurity which does motivate disobedience.

Responding also to children's bad behavior with humor and admiration or love for their individual quirks and vulnerabilities can also turn these experiences from something which frustrates our ego and engenders distrust and resentment to that which fills us with love and gratitude for even having a child in the first place, valuing their naive joy and innocent vulnerability instead of trying to squash it, and taking power away from tantrums and acting out since they no longer elicit an emotional reaction in us. Because really a child's refusal to go to bed is sweet and funny and indicative of their innocence and desire to be with us at all times because of how desperately they love us. It is only a parent's self-centered egoism and unresolved personal insecurities which turns such lovely moments into conflict, because there is in truth no conflict but what we ourselves engineer, and as are most problems in parenting (and life in general) simply our *perception* of things rather than reality. Of course, pretending to be happy or enjoy these moments is not the same as genuinely appreciating them, and pretending to have feelings we do not have is actually an act of manipulation and should be avoided always, and genuine love and appreciation for our children's fallibility and innocence comes instead from finding that same love and appreciation for ourselves and our own fallibility as discussed in the upcoming chapter on inventory therapy, for in reality it is impossible to change many of our behaviors through conscious effort, which is why it is so often difficult, because it is actually motivated by the subconscious, over which the conscious mind has no control (that's why it's called the subconscious).

To implement the use of *insistence* in preference of punishment and coercion in our parenting toolkit we can practice it alone or with our partner first, roleplaying typical scenarios to help us be more familiar with how we might use it. But we will also improve the more we use it in our relationship with our children which can further inform, reinforce, and embolden our own confidence in its effective use, and even if we don't do it right at the start it will still likely be more effective than what we were doing before, and will improve the more familiar it becomes. When children's disobedience does need to be addressed it is then appropriate to use leverage against them appropriate to the degree of their offense. If for instance a child has hit another in spite of being told not to, it might then be appropriate to send them to their room or separate them from the family, but not in a way which characterizes their self worth *"you are bad"* but instead their actions *"what you did was bad,"* which can also be helped by being frank rather than patronizing. When preemptively threatening to do this to a child we communicate that they are not welcome in the family and that we expect them to be badly behaved, and so they will be, but when it occurs in response to something they have actually done and in the context of their actions and not who they are as a person, the personal responsibility for consequences is then inextricably connected to their behavior, and as such this kind of punishment empowers a child to behave better in the future without damaging their development, since it is something they can control, like choices, not something they cannot control, such as self-worth, since our set of rules is now consistent and not subject to the changeable and inconsistent emotional whims and attitudes of adults.

Children hardly ever do anything which requires punishment. Instead, our goal should be to empower our children to repair their mistakes through discipline, not punishment, and take compassion for our own sensitivities, practicing the kind of self-care which will subvert the need to make children responsible for our unresolved pain and trauma from which punishment originates in the first place.

11

Self Care

"I bet you're fed up with all these kids," my mother quipped after several days of family gatherings during Christmastime one year when I was a grown man and still single. I knew she didn't intend to prejudicially suggest that a single, childless, gay man didn't like children, but I was angry anyway. "No, *I love them.*" I replied, trying to veil the contempt I so badly wanted to loose. "It's their parents that annoy me."

My nieces and nephews are the most darling things in the entire world. I would do anything for them, least of all put up with some fervent enthusiasm for LEGOs, food, or Star Wars, which also happen to be my interests as well. Unable to have my own children, I watch my siblings with no small amount of jealousy, and yet am regarded with contempt in spite of my constant enthusiasm for their children and attempts to be involved in their lives rebuffed. I wrote the poem at the beginning of this book for the birth of one of my nieces, and not more than a year later my sibling didn't remember even hearing it, let alone keep it.

Several adults in my family, including my parents, do not like children, and my mother that day was projecting her own attitudes on me, perhaps envious at my apparent youth and supposed freedom. The reality is that the loneliness of having no family of my own while watching my own siblings ungratefully torment and harass their precious children was at times overwhelming and deeply depressing. Knowing these children were also being raised in a religion which teaches them to keep their emotional distance from other family members and judge me for being gay made me wonder at times if trying to maintain a relationship with any of them was even worth it. A particularly egregious conflict with some of my siblings resulted in one lying to the rest of our family that I had said I hated their children, which to people who are already prejudiced against me only further served to destroy what little connection to my own siblings remained, when in reality they had tried to use their children to manipulate me instead of taking responsibility for their harmful behavior.

From the time I was asked to leave home my younger siblings were prejudiced against me by my own parents who in my absence constantly discussed me in terms of being deviant and in violation of their standards and against their family rather than a frightened and lonely child struggling to hang on to them. Although I exhausted much energy trying to ingratiate myself with my siblings by taking interest in their lives, helping them with their problems, giving gifts, and making myself available to support them in spite of my own overwhelming burdens with cancer, alcoholism, a failed relationship, loneliness, and other problems of my own their collective reluctance to remain close with me, and with each other, and even develop and maintain other healthy adult relationships as they cling to coping and control mechanisms meant to prevent emotional intimacy in the first place, my efforts only seemed to increase their resentment and rejection, excused and obfuscated through obsessive preoccupation with their new families as if the old ones are no longer valuable, even though this same pattern of familial abandonment and loneliness has repeated itself through the previous several generations, splitting apart our own parent's families and kept our cousins at a distance, isolating adult children from the emotional and material support normally provided by the family structure which, sadly, also pretends the same sorry fate is not destined for their own children.

Excessive preoccupation with children is not actually about the wellbeing of children, but is instead a distraction from our own emotional and psychological trauma, and parents who are or believe they are overly self-sacrificing are actually some of the *worst* parents and the *worst* abusers because our preoccupation originates from an absence of self-compassion, and when we do not have compassion for ourselves we cannot in turn show it to others, most of all our own children. Good parenting is in reality a more selfish practice than selfless parenting achieves. Not in the sense of self-centeredness but that of self-care and personal responsibility for our own wellbeing, the requirement for which does not actually vanish when children begin to appear on the scene. My desire to help my siblings and thus justify my value as a family member was mistaken, and even counterintuitive, because those who will not even help themselves cannot actually be helped, and I shouldn't have had to justify membership in my own family anyway. The truth is we cannot be good parents if we do not first care for ourselves, because our ability to care for our children requires the material, physical, environmental, and emotional resources which are achieved only by self-care and taking responsibility for our own lives and our own personal wellbeing. If we are not happy and calm how can we care for our children who are not? If we are not physically healthy how can we spend the energy and physical effort required to provide for and protect children? If we do not have the talents and resources to earn sufficient income how can we provide the material resources required? The failure to care for oneself as a parent thus leads to *incredible* amounts of emotional, physical, and material distress, added to the stress of ideological preconceptions of self-worth and failure, altogether results in overwhelming resentment and anger too great for even two people to bear which is then distributed across the entirety of the family and even extended relations and friends, in addition to the inability to be an effective parent results in such destruction of the family and mental, emotional, and even physical trauma in children that it impairs their own ability to parent when they are grown that the cycle can never be broken without serious self-care.

One day when I was eight and my father came home from work and was sitting on the couch with my mother I excitedly ran in from the garage and asked him to shoot baskets with me. Considering how much in the future he would want me to be a basketball star it was especially odd when he turned me down (as we did not often play together). "I'll pay you fifty-cents for every basked you make," he said in an effort to appease me. I was especially demoralized because it was my first time realizing that my own dad did not like playing with me, but I didn't protest and instead went out to try and shoot baskets, which didn't last every long on account of feeling so lonely.

In reality my dad, being an architect and general contractor, was probably and rightfully tired after a long day on a job site and just wanted to sit and relax instead of having to stand around shooting baskets. What most parents don'trealize is there is never anything wrong with what we need or want, but in how we go about getting our needs met, and not being possessed of effective self-care skills, having not been taught them himself, my dad felt insecure about communicating his need for self-care at that moment, disappointing his son, and so resorted to manipulation to avoid demonstrating vulnerability and the obligation he felt interfered with his current needs, in the process communicating a lack of care for my wellbeing and setting the stage for years of interfamilial conflict.

The kind of self-care required to undo the suffering of our past which is at the root of our problems does not mean abandoning children for a day at the spa (although that can occasionally be helpful). Behavior which abandons our responsibilities as a parent is merely self-centeredness and indulges desires for avoidance of responsibilities and neglect which are no different than the indulgence of emotional instability and over-parenting, both simply strategies which seek to control our environment when we feel out of control. A day at the spa, a night at the movies, or a long vacation in the tropics is not actually a break from the responsibilities of parenting or other daily life, but is instead a break from our psychological burdens which are triggered by those responsibilities. It is entirely possible to find the kind of relief in every day life normally afforded by taking time away from our responsibilities, we only lack the empowerment and insight to accomplish care for ourselves while also caring for others.

Healthy self-care which must be practiced as a parent is the kind which carves out space for ourselves amongst our family members, not apart from them. My father, believing he could only care for his needs or mine and not both at once used the only self-care tools at his disposal—dishonesty and manipulation—which then undermined our ability to bond as father and son, me unaware of his needs since he did not communicate them and resenting him for not helping me fulfill my needs as a child unable to do it myself. Oppositely, a parent who believes the presence of their children requires excessive self-sacrifice is a parent who fails to take care of their own needs. Most of us don't actually know how to care for ourselves since our own parents did not either, so we find ourselves frustrated and annoyed simply by the presence of our families and children and responsibilities and deal with it by increasingly treating them, and our spouses, and our siblings who write books about parenting even though they don't have children, with contempt and resentment since we do not possess effective skills through which we can resolve our psychological problems, and yet we must still spend the majority of our time with our families, which in turn leaves very little room for actualizing self-care unless we learn how to practice self-care without also requiring separation from our responsibilities.

Taking care of ourselves while also caring for children in such a way which produces the outcome of creating love and providing emotional availably looks in practice like doing things for yourself while you are also doing them for children, not instead of. A parent who cannot give their children hugs and kisses without feeling uncomfortable is only considering the act as one of giving. But giving hugs and kisses to your children can also be the act of getting hugs and kisses for yourself. Giving physical affection to children is also getting it for yourself. Instead of being a short-order chef for your children, make something for breakfast, lunch, or dinner that you want to eat. Sure, children will not and should not eat some things like shellfish or raw, bitter greens, but that does not also mean you have to be their personal chef and make macaroni and cheese when you're also making other food. I was once horrified when visiting a sister to see her walk around at lunch time and ask every child what they wanted for lunch, then proceed to make three separate dishes which took about forty-five minutes to prepare and then did not eat anything herself. No. Even if this provides you a sense of purpose, this is not good parenting. It engenders entitlement, ingratitude, and teaches children that your time is not worth much to you. Later, it came as no surprise when their children whined at having to eat certain foods, and even turned their nose up at what was provided for dessert, which then frustrated my sister and her husband, but she had earlier shown her children that she was willing to wait on them, so why shouldn't they expect that? Such parenting demonstrates behaviors of people-pleasing and failure to practice self-care and set boundaries, and children whose parents do everything for them grow up to be adults who do not know how to take care of themselves, not because they are spoiled but because their parent was too busy doing things for other people and never demonstrated how to practice self-care. To practice self-care, make what you want for lunch, because you are the adult and children are along for the ride (while making reasonable accommodations for the needs and limitations of children). If you require a bacon, lettuce, and tomato sandwich every day for lunch to feel satisfied and happy then make yourself a bacon, lettuce, and tomato sandwich every day for lunch. Making them a peanut butter and jelly sandwich is then not much more effort since you already have to get out the bread and utensils, and spreading some peanut butter or jelly requires very little effort. After hearing me talk about self-care in a similar way, a sister of mine told me that she didn't realize she was neglecting herself in the mornings, always rushing to get her children breakfast before herself. But self-care is important because we must care for ourselves so that we can then have the energy and resources to care for others. It's a lot like the pre-flight safety briefing—put on your own oxygen mask before attempting to help others. When our first goal as a parent is to neutralize any possible unpleasantness, punish disobedience, and maintain order you are putting the mask on the other passengers before yourself. First you must learn how to practice self care and then actually practice self care. Once you have done this you can then help others and actually be effective. My sister now makes something for herself first (or what she is making for everyone), and it gives her more energy and emotional strength to take care of her kids.

Another example of self-care is not waiting until children go to bed before enjoying yourself for the evening. If you like to end the day with some dessert, make it for your children too. If you like to end the day reading, include them in a book you will also enjoy or, if they are too young, you can set them near you with books of their own, to read together as a family but separate with your own interests. If you need to practice therapies such as those contained within this book to resolve emotional pain and trauma—set aside time during the day when children are expected to play with their toys, read books, or entreat your spouse or other family members to care for them while you take the time to take care of yourself. When your children trigger emotions in you that cause you to react with resentment, anger, and frustration, first ask yourself why you feel this way and examine that answer before you respond. This is the act of practicing empathy and patience for yourself, by recognizing or understanding why you feel the way you do, rather than jumping right into reaction which oppositely ignores why you feel that way and as such practices indifference and apathy to your own experience.

Those of us who are single or childless have much more time, energy, and resources to devote to self-care, but even identifying what self-care actually is can be confusing or misleading. Most of us think we are practicing self-care when we go to the gym or eat a healthy diet. But our idea of what makes a diet healthy can actually be self-destructive and harmful habits like eating too few calories or avoiding sugar. Most of us with trauma actually consider true self-care habits like eating delicious foods, playing video games, or relaxing in the sun with a good book to be unproductive or distracting, and we may in fact spend all of our time and energy obsessively fixated on what we think we need to be or need to be doing and how we aren't measuring up to our own or others' expectations and actually hurting or depriving ourselves of real care and attention that we need, not even realizing we repeat the same patterns of self-harm and self-hatred demonstrated by our own parents. If my father had known better self-care skills at a moment such as when I asked him to shoot baskets with me he might have responded with something that both cared for his needs and my own at the same time. "I'm exhausted from working all day," he could have said. "Come sit with me, or we can play later when I'm rested." Such a response would have communicated that he trusted me to value his needs as much as my own, and given me the opportunity to demonstrate it without manipulating the response he desired. Even if I had protested, a parent is the adult and can insist they recognize what the child wants or needs but are unable in the moment to fulfill it, but still inviting a child to be part of our lives since in that moment I didn't want to play basketball, I wanted to be with my dad, and in doing so also demonstrate to children healthy self-care behavior and how to set healthy boundaries with others (not just boundaries).

The impulse to do everything for our children is another way we fail to engage in proper self-care. Becoming accustomed to providing every single waking need for infants and toddlers we continue this behavior into early childhood even when children are older and well-capable of doing things on their own, out of habit but also because we tend to ignore our own wellbeing when we are burdened with unresolved psychological trauma, being unable to resolve them look to our environment for ways which we can distract ourselves, and children provide a convenient and potent distraction. Parenthood then becomes an all-encompassing identity, especially for people who might not have very good opinions of their self worth in the first place, since what more value could we want than in being the guardian of little children? But then we spend many years in this identity, and forget who we are as individuals, and when parenthood is one of the only sources of self-esteem it then feeds into a demoralizing cycle of dissatisfaction, restlessness, frustration, and eventually resentment.

One day while sitting on the porch of my sister's house while several of my other siblings and their families were visiting, my sister whose house it was emerged with a tall glass of water and plopped herself down on an armchair next to me. She had spent many hours cooking and cleaning and herding hoards of children, and a moment of sweet respite brought the release of a much deserved sigh. But no more than ten seconds after sitting one of my darling nieces came running up to her excitedly. "Mom!" she shouted, "Come throw me in the air!" My sister's expression descended into what could only be described as restrained horror. She clearly did not want to fill this request and had certainly deserved a moment to herself, but she shifted as if she meant to accommodate the request. "Nope!" I interjected sternly but with a smile and shaking my head. "Your mom deserves a break. You can go play with everyone else for a while." My niece looked at me with surprise, but she laughed and said, "okay," and ran off to play while my sister sank back gratefully into her chair. Another time when we were camping a nephew ran up to his mother and requested assistance in finding a toy or something as if it was the most important thing ever in his entire life, even though they had not yet spent *any* time looking themselves and we were surrounded by so many cousins and other people who could assist. Similarly, my sister had just spent the better part of two hours planning and running a scavenger hunt for all of the children, after helping with breakfast and lunch and hauling around a toddler and taking many of them on four-wheeler rides up the dirt roads. "Uh-uh," I interjected. "Let your mom have a break. You can find it yourself—or ask your cousins." He too went off on his own without so much as a word of protest and easily found what he was looking for while my sister got to sit by the fire and drink a soda and chat with me.

This problem is worst in parents who feel they must be overly-self sacrificing to be a good parent, and lack the kind of self-compassion required to care for ourselves which is absolutely required first in order to succeed as a parent, least of all to demonstrate healthy self-care behaviors to our own children! Feeling ashamed, guilty, or insecure we take every measure of the day to please others, most of all our children, and willingly or ignorantly neglect our own needs. But because we are neglecting our own needs we in turn become resentful, annoyed, and frustrated, and eventually (or regularly) lash out at our children when the frustration becomes too much to bear as we would any imbalanced relationship and thus cause everyone harm and become abusive even though our original intent was to be self-sacrificing. It does not matter that you view yourself a dedicated and self-sacrificing parent. If you run out of energy because of the choices you make to neglect your own wellbeing and end up lashing out at children, you are abusing them and not, in fact, acting self-sacrificially but entirely self-centeredly.

Many parents are overly dedicated to their children believing their commitment will endear children to the parent and thus engender reciprocal obligation and appreciation. But the motivation for acting this way is entirely selfish and self-centered and not actually about the wellbeing of the child, and as such it does nothing but engender resentment, distrust, and ingratitude in children even if the parent is in fact doing a great deal for the child and exhausting their own emotional, physical, and material resources. When I was younger my parents kept the company of some friends and business partners whom my sister and I loathed. We could tell that they were horrible people even though we were small children. My parents frequently accompanied these people on trips and dinners and put up with their poor behavior in order to maintain the financial arrangement, bringing us along under the guise of us having a good time, but which was in reality only meant to leverage our involvement to promote the security of the relationship. These people later turned out to be drug addicts and committed crimes which negatively affected my parents business. Exhaustive overtures of parents often fail to achieve the ends which parents desire because the parent is exhausting themselves for reasons which actually have nothing to do with the child, using children as an excuse to avoid understandably uncomfortable psychological realties, and children, being sensitive and as yet unencumbered by such psychological barriers, keenly sense these disparities and respond in kind. Burdening a child also with a sense of obligation in return for parental contributions such as the cost of raising children or the emotional toll parenting requires is a blatant manipulation placing responsibly for the decisions and choices of an adult upon a helpless and defenseless child who is entirely incapable not only of making such decisions but also defending themselves against such manipulation, and being highly perceptive to the incongruity and dishonest motivation causes a child to be less appreciative, not more, even if they give us the answers and words we demand, just as we might if a romantic partner or friend—or our own mother—tried to make us responsible for their life choices and responsibilities.

Failure also to discipline children is a failure to practice self-care. Many of us feel insecure about disciplining a child for doing something which is unacceptable because we know that we will overreact and cause them more harm. So we will refrain from correcting when it is required and instead persist through the stress of a child screaming or slamming doors, holding in our frustration until it finally explodes in an adult tantrum equally destabilizing and harmful, where the effective and mature correction of unacceptable behavior would instead create calmness, demonstrate leadership, and set healthy boundaries that care for our own needs without hurting others.

As are all problems in parenting this tendency to avoid responsibility for our own wellbeing occurs because of the example set by our own parents, but many parents persist with behaviors which are unproductive and exhausting even when the uselessness is plainly obvious, because we simply don't have other tools or options at our disposal. New skills and behaviors are required to find resolution just as we might for any other skill we desired. Hardly anyone would succeed in a law career simply from watching their parent practice law, and any candidate for a job would be required to attain a degree in order to practice and spend many years in internship and training. But when we parent we are thrust into the position without this kind of preparation, even when our own parents were clearly terrible, and then somehow expect ourselves to do well? It's fucking ridiculous. Once when I was a young adult, after my suicide attempt, I got into a heated argument with my parents about the way they treated me as a child and the plainly destructive consequences it had on my life and ability to succeed as an adult and avoid such serious problems such as suicidal depression. "What did you want us to do?" my mother shouted at me instead of taking responsibility for their abuse and neglect or even showing a bit of empathy— "you didn't come with an instruction manual!"

I couldn't believe she actually said something so cliché, especially since she hated reading and had probably never picked up another book besides scripture in the last twenty years of her life (which, by the way, is *supposed* to be an instruction manual). To say nothing of the obvious impropriety of treating a gay child with prejudice and bigotry. "There are literally hundreds of books on parenting at the library!" I screamed.

A lot of parents do read books on parenting, and while many of them do contain some useful information they are mostly focused on the child, rather than the parent, which is the entire problem with parenting in the first place. Parenting is not actually about the child. *It is entirely about the parent.*

Most self-help books also make things worse by functioning merely to make us feel good about what we are already doing, and do little to actually affect real change. One of my siblings regularly reads self-help books but won't read a page of mine because they instinctively know that mine will make them actually confront their problems, which is understandably uncomfortable to do. Flowery, masturbatory language about our purpose in life and motivation and willpower which do not actually have any meaning entrench already widely accepted ideas at the root of our problems and support rather than challenge the ignoring of unresolved trauma and failure to amend personal failings, simply repackaging the same tired and problematic human institutions which over and over have failed us and failed our parents and their parents, functioning only to make us *feel* better about our problems since we don't actually have the skills or strength to change them.

Most parents cherish the nighttime routine because it heralds the time of day when they finally get a break. If we have these feelings—we would be a normal human—but it also shows us how we are not caring for ourselves during the day, and are in essence actually doing too much for children, or at least not doing enough to care for ourselves.

It is entirely possible to care for ourself at the same time as our children, our spouse, and not separate from, to meet all our responsibilities and thus avoid the feelings of frustration, fatigue, and resentment which come from failing to care for our own needs. Part of the reason we fail to also care for ourselves is the practice of certain control behaviors masquerading as parenting which are ineffective and produce the opposite results from that which create space to also care for ourselves. If, for instance, a parent fears children falling apart and shouting and fighting they probably spend much of the day trying to prevent or subvert those events which lead to these unfortunate episodes. Such strategies may be things like letting children watch their favorite shows in order to keep them calm, or indulge them when they demand certain foods and treats, or to practice restraint or patience when children hit or take things from other children in order to avoid the possible tantrum which may follow. Further at the root of this behavior is the discomfort we feel when our children are loud and crying or displaying other emotional behavior which either aggravates or embarrasses us. These experiences trigger deep feelings of vulnerability and insecurity, the shame of failure, and weaknesses such as poor estimates of our self-worth demonstrated through the act of parenting we would rather not admit, which then motivates us to avoid such triggers as we go about our day to day lives trying to avoid experiences that frustrate and hurt us. As such, the purpose of controlling our children is not about what the children do but how their behavior and presence make us feel. Since the entire thrust of a parents' day is then spent intending to avoid these uncomfortable emotional triggers, the entire day is also spent oriented toward the child and never in conscious consideration of our own needs. As such, when the little shits are finally in their bed and you can finally go fuck your husband as the only time of the day available to take care of ourself, but we're too tired anyway so we probably just fight with our spouse or watch a show and pass out from sheer exhaustion, but all the while haunted by the real likelihood a child wakes in the night and needs to pee or get a glass of water or cry about a nightmare, so even during our brief reprieve we continue to anticipate anxiety and frustration anyway and never actually take the time to care for ourselves. Trying to sustain this unsustainable situation causes stress to build and build until we are no longer humanly capable of handling the responsibilities of parenting, and explode at our partners and children to release our frustration caused by not meeting our needs, and start the cycle over.

Self care requires that we also take care of our needs, which go neglected both in relationships and as parents. Our self-neglect is not just because we are preoccupied with our children, however, or that our time doesn't allow for taking care of our needs, but is instead a symptom of not knowing exactly *how* to ask for what we need or even that we need to ask in the first place. Feelings of low-self worth naturally lead to behaviors in which we minimize, ignore, or neglect things we need from relationships, our environment, our schedules and jobs because we do not feel that our needs are worth prioritizing in the first place. Once, a sibling asked if I would help them decide on colors for their new house. We had been spending time browsing websites and talking about furnishings and finishes, so I assumed we would spend another delightful afternoon online shopping. But they sent me a picture of their house and instructions on what colors to photoshop over the shutters and exterior trim. Because they did not know how to ask for a favor, they purposefully misled me to the nature of their need, to extract a commitment from me while being deceived to the time commitment it really required. Because I was no longer burdened by the insecurities of my past and associated control mechanisms, I was not offended and talked with them instead about why they didn't feel like they could just ask for help honestly instead of resorting to control mechanisms, especially since I would have been delighted to help in that capacity anyway (and did).

A parent can always care for their children and themselves at the same time. It is only because our own parents taught us that they are separate that we even think it's not possible, having never seen how it is done. But because we are now adults we can teach ourselves new skills and provide for our own needs without neglecting those of whom we are responsible. Abandoning one responsibility for the other is simply a result of coping and control mechanisms acquired in youth which distort our perception of our own self worth, and first discovering what that means for us and resolving the issues of our past can then make space for us to hug our children and view both their mistakes and ours with compassion and pity rather than the resentment which impairs emotional availability. Worse, when we fail to practice self-care we model for our children that they also do not need to practice self-care, and that they should neglect their needs and deprive themselves of personal responsibility and accountability, since we are doing for them what they should be doing themselves, then later condemn them for these very defects as if we haven't all along been teaching them to behave this way. For instance, always cleaning up our children's messes communicates to them that someone will do those things for them, and then they move into adulthood not knowing how to actually clean up their own homes and messes (literal *and* metaphorical), but also leaving them to do it alone and refusing to help also communicates that they are alone and that no one will ever help them and that they should also not ask nor expect to have help. If we cannot successfully build the proper resources of energy, time, material, and social support for ourselves, set healthy boundaries, and take care of our own needs how can we possibly hope to take on the monumental task of parenting with all its responsibilities and requirements nor succeed in parenting our children to meet their own responsibilities when they are grown?

When we neglect our own needs by not asking for what we need we bottle up our frustrations, disappointments, burdens, and obstacles to performance due to misguided intentions of being nice, agreeable, and amenable, feeling maybe that it's not so important that we listen to Celine Dion while vacuuming the house and so relent when our children beg for *KidsBop* or the fucking *Frozen* soundtrack for the hundred-billionth time. Maybe we acquiesce to our partner's plea to go on a trip this weekend even though we went on one last weekend and we are feeling a cold coming on but which isn't really that bad. Or maybe we fear the repercussions of asking for help, such as from a husband who is irritable, self-centered, and exhausted or a wife who is emotionally volatile and overly-sensitive, or siblings with whom we grew up in an abusive home and fear the emotions we feel when engaging with them. We may also get down and clean up all those legos and race car tracks even though our children are every bit as capable of putting them back in the box as they were taking them out. But regardless of our reasons, what always happens is that our failure to care for our needs eventually leads to us blowing up and releasing all of the accumulated frustration when it becomes too much to bear, and results in pain, heartache, hurt feelings and egos, and turns our family members into adversaries and objects for resentment even though we are the ones not asking for what we need.

Being unable to provide for our own needs, many of us require significant others or children to mind-read our needs without actually communicating to them what we need in the first place, then we use their failure to be telepathic as the pretense for an argument to release our anger and frustration. This is absolutely a cruel and wholly self-centered exploitation of our loved ones and is the definition of abusive behavior. People do not know what we need unless we tell them, and even then we can fail to communicate properly because of the nuances of language and each person's unique experiences with language and ability to understand. Once when I was younger my first boyfriend and I were discussing something I don't remember, but he mentioned having a '*car-note.*' Having not grown up in the Southern United States I had never heard of a car-note. Asking what it was provided no more clarity than before, and I had some fun at his expense watching him try to get me to understand by simply repeating *car-note* over and over as if I was just too stupid to understand. Personal experience colors our perception of language as much as it does every other life experience, and then expecting our partner or children not only to anticipate our needs but also to accommodate our personal sensitivities and retaliatory offense is just arrogant.

But, like all coping mechanisms, this kind of behavior originates simply from our lack of better interpersonal and self-care skills and the absence of compassion for ourselves, being so ill equipped to handle life, replaced with shame and insecurity. Asking for what we want takes the form of speaking up, making decisions, and taking action to get ourselves those things we need in order to lead healthy, productive, and successful lives. Neglecting those needs fails to accomplish this, and succeeds only in validating the ego and deepening personal insecurities. Asking for what we need is also not the same thing as shaming others for not giving it to us. If we say to a husband, *"it would be great if the trash got taken out,"* this implies a subtle but unmistakeable insult that things are not in fact great and that it's also their fault that the trash is not taken out. Or when we are afraid or unable to ask for what we need we might say, *"sure, we can go eat there,"* when really you don't want to and then end up being sour about it the rest of the night because *you* fucking *lied*. Dishonesty is not actually truth just because you want to keep the peace or don't feel like you can ask for what you want and need. I once worked with a woman who felt anxiety every time she had to make a purchase, and constantly talked about her husband in a way which made me believe he made her feel bad about spending too much money. So I was later surprised to find out that he had never actually had a problem with her spending habits, and that she was just in truth insecure about spending his money and even gotten upset at him on several occasions for her own sense of insecurity even though he had never given her any reason to feel that way, and in reality was instead from her personal childhood experiences of unmet material needs and conditioning toward money and self-care. Dishonesty is still dishonesty, no matter our intensions, and when we lie to partners or children out of a sense of self-sacrifice, *we are still lying*. Of course, there are fun lies like Santa Claus, or that parents love each child equally, but when the lie also prevents us from getting what we need to function and to succeed, the only person then to blame is ourselves.

Failing to ask for what we need is in truth caused by unresolved trauma and incorrect ideas of our own self-worth, feeling we are not even worthy of asking for what we need in the first place. Confronting this trauma can be very uncomfortable to do, and there is truly much pain and heartache in life, so much that many of us find it easier to escape into the soothing embrace of drugs, alcohol, or emotional volatility and interpersonal conflict rather than revisit the horrors of the past. But this too is only because we do not feel empowered to effectively deal with such despair. On a practical level, the failure to care for ourselves originates in the absence of *self-compassion*. It is actually okay to feel anger and hatred for kids. You're not a bad person for having these feelings. It's okay to regret getting pregnant and having to give all of our free time and spending money to a family. Parenting is hard. Life is hard. Feeling that we are not allowed to have these feelings in the first place also originates from the same abuse and trauma of our childhoods, when our parents convinced us that our feelings were responsible for the bad things that happened to us (i.e. what they did to us). Feelings are *not* actions. You must act on feelings in order to become a bad person. Feelings are the result of trauma, pain, and insecurities which we did not ask for nor deserve, but which are a necessary part of life in order that we may feel the sting of mortality and the vulnerability which accompanies it. Feelings in response to pain, frustration, and disappointment occur on purpose and are part of our evolutionary biology meant to draw the attention of an animal to the sources of stress in their environment. It is what we do in response to that stress which determines our effectiveness, and not possessing skills to effectively respond to that stress, we as parents tend inadvertently to increase it. Then, unable to face the depths of emotion which accompany the shame of resenting the burden of children we detach ourselves from our children and count down the minutes until we are rid of them. Sensing our detachment, children then try even harder to get our attention, to protect their chances of survival since they depend on our attention to achieve it. This increases our frustration to the point where we become even psychopathic under the stress, then in reality we become the very same abusers, since we are not caring for ourselves and thus have no capacity to care for others.

Practicing self-care *while* parenting and not only during breaks from parenting is actually some of the most effective parenting that can be practiced. Demonstrating self-care practices actively teaches children how to also practice self-care, empowering them with skills for setting boundaries which will protect them from exploitation and manipulation as adults, but also protects them from the burdens of unresolved pain and trauma, since they will be empowered with skills to care for themselves by learning from our example. I learned from my self-sacrificing mother to be self-sacrificing, and thus when predatory men approached me for relationships I was exploited and abused and taken advantage of, where if she had instead demonstrated for me (and her mother for her, and so on) skills to care for myself first I would never have placed myself in such situations. Other life skills like paying taxes and being financially responsible are skills of self-care that many adults lack, which is a direct consequence of the excessive focus on children and insufficient self-care for the parent. Because the parent ends up doing so much for the child the child never develops or gains experience actually caring for themselves and thus is immobilized as an adult or experiences great stress and ineffectiveness doing even mundane tasks required in adulthood like running a household. Children who are forced to be clean and responsible through emotional assaults and the manipulative use of insults and valuations of self-worth do not become an adult who cares for themselves by cleaning their environment and caring for their belongings but instead associate cleaning with negative self-esteem and find the responsibilities of being clean to be burdensome rather than empowering. A stereotypical caricature of a child failing to care for themselves is a young man living in his parent's basement playing video games all day—which is in fact one manifestation of a disease called *learned hopelessness* which is caused by neurological damage to the serotonergic center of the brain (discussed in my other book), and must be addressed with emotional empowerment as well as nutritional, medical, and environmental factors. By modeling the kind of behavior of self-care and healthy boundaries, since again children learn by example and not through instruction, we are actually better parents since we model for them healthy behaviors which in turn empower them to do the same.

An unwillingness to practice self-care also usually results in the tendency to ask children for permission to parent. Because the focus of the adult is on placating children to avoid moments of emotional volatility and discomfort parents resort to interacting with their children in ways which allow the child to decide the outcome of events and not the parent. An example might be when a child takes something from another and the parent then negotiates with either of them to discuss the event. *"We don't do that,"* is a prime example of a parent negotiating with a child and asking for permission to parent. The use of the word *"we"* betrays a parent's excessive identification with the role of parent, confusing the line between adult and child and enmeshing the identity of the child with the parent and parent with child. On the face of it this kind of language appears diplomatic and democratic, and is often inspired by a parent's wish for their children to understand their reasoning and beliefs. But in such an instant the parent is not the one who took something, nor is the other child, and the use of *"we"* fails to communicate the individual responsibility a child has for their own behavior by distributing that responsibility across multiple parties. The phrase also passively suggests that membership among the *"we"* also requires certain behavior, which it absolutely should not. *"No. Give that back,"* or *"Uh-uh, do not take things from other people. Ask first. And if they say no, you still don't get to take it,"* or *"that is unacceptable,"* delvers unambiguous instruction on personal responsibility and accountability. A parent who negotiates with their children and finds it ineffective will typically then resort to spanking or other accelerated emotional wrestling to achieve their goal, but which only further obfuscates clarity and causes much pain and heartache, and it is never required nor acceptable to hurt family members. Negotiating parental responsibility with children also makes children responsible for the responsibilities of parenting, which they cannot do. When a parent fails to lead and does not demonstrate responsible, kind, empathetic behavior and personal responsibility children become acutely aware of the absence of leadership, and because they cannot function as a parent become highly insecure, fearful, clingy, needy, volatile, and even attempt to assume the absence of parenting and act out in ways which are disruptive, annoying, and antagonistic. When a child is forced to do something through emotional manipulation such as what passive phrases like *"we don't do that,"* which implies lessons of self-worth and acceptance, they are also denied the autonomy they are entitled to and respond by reacting more defiantly in order to reclaim some autonomy, which if the parent is at all motivated by egoism then results in more dramatic struggles of will until one is finally victorious. Though we have authority, being a parent is *not* about being an authority figure. Our job is *not* to dominate children. It is only guardian and guide. The impulse to dominate results from those feelings of insecurity caused by the pain and trauma and helplessness of our own childhood, now using parenthood as an opportunity to assert control inappropriately, and the consequences of doing so lie only upon our head and manifest as less control as children grow and rebel. When we misunderstand our purpose as a parent and attempt to use parenthood as an exercise in control and dominance is when we cause abuse and impair a child's normal development, and doom our relationship with them and in turn the strength of our own future position in life.

    Because negotiating with children for permission to parent is ineffective, this often leaves the parent feeling frustrated and without tools by which to effect the outcomes we need. Reaching into our limited toolbox of parenting strategies the act of then threatening children with consequences typically follows. If a child tends to fall apart at dinnertime or complain about meal options or refuses to eat, being unable to get a desired outcome from our first attempt the parent will threaten the child if they don't comply, with consequences such as early bedtime, going hungry, or going without dessert. But the act of threatening a child directly communicates to them that their own parents are a danger to their safety and the fulfillment of the things on which they depend and are utterly hopeless to get for themselves. Faced with the prospect of losing the things they need for their actual survival, the child's instinctual, biological response is to react with alarm and even greater antagonism in order to increase pressure on the adult to provide what they require which, superficially yes is not more time watching *Dora the Explorer*, but the child's mind does not understand psychological, biological survival instincts and the reaction is not about exactly whatever the child is expressing but more deep, subconscious reaction to large themes of dominance, control, and deprivation. Many parents, growing frustrated by and anticipating a continued pattern of noncompliance and emotional outbursts will also preemptively threaten their child with consequences even when the child has not yet actually misbehaved. This is even more catastrophic for the parent-child relationship and the successful outcome of our efforts because not only are you communicating to the child an implied precariousness of their position in your home and esteem, you are characterizing the child as one who is by default to be mistrusted and antagonized, undermining their sense of self-esteem which will only further engender animosity and resentment. Using threats to control children a parent actively deprives a child's of access to resources required for survival (even if it is only perception of access) and becomes by their own behavior an active threat to the child's survival, and the only response available to the child is not compliance but even greater conflict as they instinctually seek to secure access to the things the parent is not willing or able to give.

Threatening children also originates from a parent's unwillingness to practice self-care. Depriving ourselves of the fulfillment and satisfaction which results from self-care, parents are then adversely affected by misbehavior and emotional outbursts instead of being immune or empathetic because the only access we have to self-fulfillment is during the absence of children, which is rare, especially when misbehavior derails scheduling expectations, and parents, looking forward to the only time during which we feel we can practice self-care then react by becoming angry and hurtful in return. It doesn't actually matter in the moment that a child won't eat their dinner. There's nothing wrong with it except what is relevant to the personal fears, sensitivities, and expectations of the parent and interruption of bedtime and thus intrusion into their cherished alone time. If as a parent we no longer require alone time for our own fulfillment, since it occurs throughout the day because we have been actively caring for ourselves as well as our children, then the overwhelming emotional response which leads to emotional conflicts and desperation of threats no longer occurs, and thus no reason to react in an unconsidered and threatening manner toward misbehaving children, and so such moments are also neutralized before they even begin since children no longer feel the sense of threat to their wellbeing and are more likely to feel satisfied and not act out in the first place, since acting out is merely and always simply a response to perceptions of instability and imposition on required resources. Additionally, because self-care originates and is enabled by self-compassion, a parent who practices self-care also practices self-compassion and thus has compassion to share with family members who dislike mushrooms. This compassion enables us to communicate with children in such a way as to assist in solving problems without the need for threats, which thus empowers both the child and the parent to resolve problems easily and without much conflict, and profoundly reduces all incidents of antagonism and stress in the family, and most importantly assisting the parent in feeling effective and empowered in our role as parent.

An adult who is insecure in our position as a parent and unable to practice self-care may react by forcing boundaries on children by withholding help and emotional involvement to varying degrees. A great example of this is the trend of letting children cry themselves to sleep. Ostensibly this practice is designed to prevent excessive attachment as the child grows, but in reality the excessive attachment is caused by insufficient emotional and physical availability of the parents in the first place, and is an instinctive reaction to the deficiency which is further compounded by the parent further removing the emotional and physical connection and thus committing abuse and developmental trauma to a child. Human beings are not designed to be separated from each other, in fact. We need each other to be happy and fulfilled, and when this is forced upon children by our own family members more pain and trauma is caused, not less, as we detach ourselves from the child to create the indifference required to practice it and in turn the children from us to survive the pain of rejection.

In the summer when I was twelve and still a scared little gay boy our scout group was going to scout camp for a week. I had never been away from home and I had not yet made any good friends since we had only moved to the area several months earlier. When I expressed my fear of going my father, no doubt uncomfortable with my insecurity and his apparent failure to empower his son, simply refused to listen or show any empathy and forced me to go. I tried to be brave but because I was so uncomfortable and none of the other boys were inclined toward befriending me I spent the entire week alone, crying in my bunk at night, and a day before the end discovered that a scout-leader was returning to the city early and asked if he would take me back. My father's "tough-love" not only failed to provide me with an opportunity for growth, but actively and further undermined my trust and love for him, since he had clearly demonstrated himself to be an active participant in causing harm and cared more for how he felt than what happened to me. Human infants are designed by nature to be constantly near other adults, especially the parents. It's perfectly fine to let them sleep alone as long as it doesn't cause stress. But frenzied crying at being left alone is a child's biological response to being abandoned, and if this is the case it is evidence that you have not adequately communicated to the child that they are protected, and further insisting on this position only serves to further undermine our position as a parent and increase our stress and frustration as they grow. The opposite of abandonment is to manipulatively indulge a child's every whim in order to prevent moments of acting out, which is still the self-centered desire on the part of the parent to avoid moments of discomfort. There is nothing wrong with children falling sleep for the night on or near their parents, then being transferred to bed.

My parents used to have a sound system which the volume dial was broken, and turning it too far in the opposite direction would cause it to go from completely silent to the peak volume of which it was capable. Once when visiting for the holidays my brother (who had kids of his own) accidentally turned the dial the wrong way and nearly blew the ear drums out of everyone present, but my sister's first child was sleeping in a nearby room and she rushed into the living room and eviscerated my brother mercilessly, even though it had clearly been an accident and even though her kid didn't even wake up. The pathological obsession with children's sleep is likewise rooted in an inability for parents to care for themselves, their only reprieve thence during children's sleep, which is why parents fail to recognize that children can and often do sleep through almost anything and in any environment. Some friends I knew in Palm Springs oppositely threw parties and allowed their young son to be up regularly until midnight or even later, which even though the child was present was still separating self-care from parenting since the child's needs were also being ignored, while success lies in doing *both*, not one or the other. When a parent is able to find the ability to care for their own needs while also parenting and not only apart from it, a parent feels fulfilled and is thus less dependent on the small and impermanent moments of freedom such as when children are asleep, and as such stop being hurtful to others as well as their own children surrounding matters such as bedtime since unavoidable interruptions will always occur to derail such plainly unreasonable expectations anyway.

In order to care for oneself we must indulge ourselves *while also* caring for children and not separately from them. Children are along for the ride, and though we often give them the wheel, they are not actually the drivers. A practical application of the kind of self-care while also caring for children can be things such as making what *we* want for breakfast or lunch, not what children want (within reason—it's not okay for instance to feed children mimosas for breakfast). Children can eat what we make or they can go hungry, or they can just have fruit or cereal. Being a short-order chef for our children *does not make you a good parent*. It only communicates to children that we do not value our own time and energy, so why should they? Make one lunch for everyone. If they don't want it, they can go without. But then again parents do this because when a child goes hungry they also get cranky, and scream, and cry, and so the parent is doing this in order to avoid or prevent such behavior as previously discussed. But in reality this behavior is occurring because we have demonstrated for our child that we don't know how to care for ourselves or set boundaries, and they can in turn exploit our inability to practice self-care since they have become accustomed to us waiting on their every need, and the problem is not in fact that we refused to be a short-order chef nor that our children are self-centered and opportunistic but that we by your very own behavior have instructed our children *to* take advantage of our time and energy. Other examples of self care can be napping also when our children do. Most parents (especially mothers) may take this time to accomplish more chores or work, especially in relation to the family such as laundry or cleaning, but we were also up late, and are also tired, and if we nap we will actually have *more* energy to continue the day or to wake up at night with the baby. Parents will put their child in a room to nap, but if we take a nap with our kid this can happen anywhere—the living room, our bedroom in our own bed, sleeping near each other as would occur more naturally for our human ancestors. When children are older we can let them read their own books and stories of their choosing while we also read our favorite book instead of always reading to them, which is more helpful anyway since reading and wanting to read on their own is one of the most valuable skills a human can learn. Simple too are also activities like putting away the laundry—children can and should help take care of their belongings as they are able, and the whole family (including the Dad!) can sit down and fold laundry together. It's okay if the children's clothes aren't folded right—doing it yourself is, again, trying to prevent emotionally uncomfortable triggers for yourself such as a child wearing a wrinkled shirt, which is in reality not a problem at all except for our own personal insecurities which it triggers, which unaddressed is another example of the stress of our past and perception of reality as the primary source of stress in parenting and not the actual responsibility itself. Having help folding clothes (which is now also an instructional and skill-building activity for children) the chores now get done quicker which in turn creates more time for other activities. If a child wants you to play with them but you have chores or don't love playing with kids' toys, instead of turning them down or lying and suffering through another Princess role-play you can invite them to come help you or to come sit on the couch or do something *with you* that you like, since really they are just asking to be with you. When we have guests over and a child attempts to dominate conversation or insist that visitors focus on them instead of us, inviting children to sit and listen and instead allow us time with our friend sets a healthy boundary and facilitates our own personal fulfillment while also allowing a child to participate without deferring to them, where a frustrated parent who is incapable of self-care will either permit children to dominate social occasions and guests (thus making guests less likely to return, not because the child is unpleasant but because domination is), or oppositely banish the children from participating altogether, which again is attempting to make time for ourselves by separating family away rather than finding our own space alongside them.

    The language used when putting boundaries between us and our children is also somewhat important and, if it originates from a place of frustration and contempt, we will automatically choose the wrong words even when we try not to and spend much deliberation devising the best approach. I desperately love my nieces and nephews, but I am also not stressed out or triggered by their behavior, in fact finding their antics and emotions to be entertaining and sweet, so when I talk to them I instinctively and unconsciously use language which communicates my esteem for them. When interrupting them to advocate for my sisters one of the phrases I used was *"You can do it yourself..."* This is a very empowering phrase when spoken sincerely by an adult even though it was in effect a rebuke, because it implies several other important and empowering statements—one, that they are actually more capable of achieving their goal than they realize and thus more personally effective and empowered in their life than they were aware or even considered. Two, that I believe in them since I am stating they can achieve something and not disparaging them or anticipating failure. Lastly, the assurance that we are still there to assist should they fail in turn makes them feel more secure in taking chances since failure can be assisted by a strong and confident adult ally. Telling a child to just go away or saying *do it yourself* instead of *you can do it yourself* is absolutely not the same thing. That kind of language implies that they are annoying to us or that we can't be bothered, which does exactly all the opposite that my phrasing accomplished. This kind of language originates from the subconscious, which always betrays our true underlying attitudes, but most especially toward children who are incomparably and uniquely perceptive, which is why deliberating on what to say or consciously choosing words does not always find success. If you have ever deliberated about how to phrase something you know will start an argument, and in spite of your long wrestling and best intent still caused an argument, you have encountered this impossibility of separating our subconscious from conscious expression. Without addressing the emotional roots and lifelong trauma from which our attitudes originate it can be difficult or even impossible to set effective, healthy boundaries and to instead only set boundaries. Subconscious emotional content of communication is far more powerful than any words we can chose. But consciously considering what words and language we use to communicate our position or even better to be conscious of our motivation for speaking in the first place can be helpful, always remembering that how we feel is also how we are going to sound, no matter the words chosen, and paying attention to and analyzing our feelings will make this far more effective.

Many people think that self-care takes the form of going the gym and working out, or dieting or reading self-help books. While enjoyment activities can be self-care, these kinds are usually self-improvement, which is not at all the same as self-care. Self-care is always and simply things which reduce stress. But if we have to get our children ready, pack up everything, and exhaust ourselves on a treadmill because we don't want to be fat we are actively increasing stress and not, in fact, practicing self-care. Dieting is by definition starving ourselves, which is the antithesis of self-care. Many people attend the gym or exercise classes because it also provides opportunity to interact with friends and get out of the house. This part *is* self care, since interaction with others brings us a sense of belonging, safety, and fulfillment, and getting sunshine and fresh air and moving our bodies can be stress-relieving if done for fun and recreation. Play dates are often arranged as an excuse for parents to find their own friends, since as adults we tend to be unwilling to show the kind of vulnerability required to simply ask someone to be our friend, but because such gatherings are ostensibly for the satisfaction of children and not the adults the entire occasion tends to center around and concerns children, and adults in turn miss out on excellent opportunities to satisfy their own connection and friendship needs, using children as defense mechanisms which in turn prevent intimacy and bonding. Instead, arranging social engagements for adults to gather and meet and children happening to come along for the occasion can shift the focus toward our personal care and satisfaction. Once when talking to a sister of mine I mentioned talking to another who also has more children for several hours on the phone a few times a week. She was shocked. "How?" she asked in amazement. "Isn't she busy?" For a moment I was confused, but then I realized that this sister could not separate her identity from the role of parent. "It's not like she stops parenting when we're talking," I said. "I'm there talking with her while she's parenting. She reprimands them if needed, makes food, and I'm there with her and sometimes even helping by chatting with one of the kids if they need some attention." This is how healthy families work, but when parents don't understand how to care for themselves as well as their children we ironically separate ourselves from other relationships and activities which would improve our experience and assist with parenting. My siblings who cannot find a way to integrate me and other siblings and other adults into their own lives aside from the function of parenting and a marriage not only make their own responsibilities more stressful, but also deprive their children of relationships with other adults which would expand and broaden their emotional and material development. It's exactly why even though my siblings and I have twenty-six aunts and uncles not a single one of us has a relationship with any of them nor even one of my hundred-plus cousins a relationship with my parents. This greatly increases the stress for a parent, since logistically the involvement of other adults lessens and distributes the stress and responsibilities of parenting. It's why my siblings get so excited when my abusive and neglectful parents visit them, because even though they are often unpleasant and also stressful, for a moment they get to experience the relief of shared parenting duties they would otherwise have commonly if they were able to find a way to care for themselves by developing real adults relationships. Depriving ourselves of the same kind of social support, friendship, and opportunity we desire for our children is not self-sacrifice, and only increases the stress of parenting and burdens children with the same problems when they grow up. So the opposite, establishing friendships and social connections, though perhaps difficult and emotionally uncomfortable for those of us who don't know how to, is also an example of self-care. In addition to the playdates and friends made for children, also make a friend with the old lady across the street, or that chill single girl at your job, or the couple with grown children in college. Plan on being friends with them simply for your benefit (and theirs). Our children will be incidentally enriched by the experience anyway was they watch and learn from your ability to establish and maintain relationships, exposed to a broader range of adults and healthy friendship and self-care behaviors.

  We can clue ourselves into whether or not we are asking for and making our needs known by the emotion which motivates us to take action. If we feel resentful, fearful, or contemptuous when asking for our needs we have waited far too long to ask and need to do a better job taking care of needs *before* they are needed and not *after* they have been neglected. If we need help with the chores or getting errands done, instead of quietly doing it all yourself and secretly resenting your partner and parenthood or saying something vague and manipulative we must ask directly and without implicit valuations of the subject of our request and our relationship with them. For instance, *"hey will you help me with something?"* is actually a blatant attempt to manipulate and control. Purposely withholding useful information the other person could use to gauge the scope of commitment which the request might require is a demand that they demonstrate the degree of their commitment to us rather than whether or not they will just do us a favor. Are you going to ask them to take out the trash or to go slay a dragon? By the way, this kind of passive-aggressive behavior can also be neutralized by the same practice of self-care of setting boundaries by asking for what we need with something like *"I need to hear what it is first,"* which communicates to the requester that your personal identity and self-worth is not tied to this exercise in control and thus reclaims our power. Instead of trying to get what we need through indirectness and control mechanisms, say it directly—*"I need help getting the kids to school tomorrow, can you help me?"* The phrases such as *I need help* or *can you help me* display vulnerability by opening ourselves to be refused, which is why we avoid asking this way in the first place, but in turn communicates to another person that we *trust* them not necessarily to help, but to be on our side and to care for that trust. It also provides the opportunity for our partners (or friends, family, coworkers, bosses, etc.) to voluntarily demonstrate their commitment to us instead of forcibly extracting the response we want. Most importantly, this allows us to admit that we cannot do everything ourselves and thus relieves us of the stress of believing we should, while also actively strengthening social bonds and security through the distribution of responsibility.

More subtle are failures to ask for what we need during interpersonal conflict. If a partner makes us feel neglected or hurt, in communicating that we are hurt decide to say something like *"you're a terrible husband,"* or *"you're so selfish,"* or *"why would you do that?"* does not actually communicate what we need. It merely seeks to hurt them in return and to then manipulate others into submission, purposefully failing to deliver useful information by which they could better act in the future which would also rob us of the opportunity to further manipulate them. Such behavior also prevents us from getting what we really need to be happy, healthy, and effective since they don't fucking know exactly what we are asking. Of course, if we actively seek to engage in conflict, calling someone an asshole or a bigot is an effective strategy to spite people for their harmful behavior, but within the bounds of an intimate relationship such as a marriage which requires cooperation and companionship, spiting others will only engineer the destruction of our relationships.

Often when we are trying to set boundaries for ourselves but without possessing healthy and effective tools to do so we will lie in order to save ourselves from obligations or commitments which are burdensome. An example of this may be when someone asks if we want to do something but we are tired and the last thing we want to do is go put on clothes and be social, so we make up some excuse of a prior commitment or family obligation. Ostensibly we make up these lies to spare the other person's feelings, but typically the other person knows we are not being honest, even if it's just a feeling, and our unwillingness to trust them communicates our lack of esteem for them and thus harms the integrity of our relationship anyway, because we do not know how to properly take care of our own needs. Family members may sometimes ask us for help with something and we feel terrible for turning them down so we say yes but then fail to follow through on our commitment, passively ignoring or missing whatever it was we agreed to do. Or we may call in sick to work and pretend we have an illness when in truth we are just so stressed out that we need a mental health break. All of these problems of deception and the failure to ask for what we need come because we lack self-compassion for our own limitations and devalue our own needs and wants, and thus feeling unable to ask for what we need by responding in a way which takes care of our own needs as well as those of others we resort to deception and dishonesty as if they are acceptable behaviors. Then, having lied to people who love us begin to accumulate guilt and shame for our behavior when in fact there was never any reason to be ashamed of setting healthy boundaries nor saying no nor asking for what we need. There is never any reason not to tell the truth when we cannot or do not want to do things which interfere with our own wellbeing, and failing to tell the truth actively reduces our position and damages our emotional security. If we feel too tired or depressed to go out with friends, instead of lying we can say *I'm sorry, I really don't feel like going out tonight.* With such a response we not only ask for what we need, we also allow our friends and loved ones to demonstrate supportive behavior for us which will further strengthen emotional bonds. Or, if a family member asks us to help out with something we just don't have the time and energy to do, instead of lying that we will help them and potentially damaging the relationship and our integrity when we later fail to do it say, *I should help you but things are so busy, I'm stressed out, and if I commit to that I'm just going to be angry and resentful.* Some of us who are insecure will also try to set these kinds of boundaries but in a way which in turn causes conflict, such as accusing another person of something or criticizing their behavior as a defensive reaction to disguise our guilt we feel for saying no. For instance, if a family member asks us for money and we berate them for being irresponsible instead of simply saying *no, sorry* or making long excuses about our own financial situation or history with disappointment, feeling the need to explain ourselves and justify our own needs. When we fail to care for our needs by not asking for what we need or using lying, dishonesty, or conflict to set boundaries we actively fail to practice self-care and must learn why our lack of self-esteem causes us to care for our needs only through deceptive and evasive behaviors which in the long run only serves to add to our stress and worsen our conception of ourselves, where learning to care for our needs proactively and honestly can free us emotionally and materially to better care for ourselves and thus those who rely on us.

    One of my biggest pet-peeves about mainstream therapy and people trying to sound diplomatic during interpersonal conflict is to advocate the use of *"I statements."* This is just utterly asinine because *"I think you're a bitch,"* is no less hurtful than *"you're a bitch."* The *'I'* is silent. Or *"I think you're lazy"* or *"I think we don't have enough sex."* The addition of *'I'* doesn't communicate anything we didn't already know nor alter selfish intent. Instead, the healthy and effective way to ask for what we need in relationships and during interpersonal conflict means to stop focusing and phrasing our needs in terms of other people and instead in terms of our own behavior. Instead of saying something like *"I think you're annoying"* say *"I need some time to myself, please go away,"* or instead of saying *"why can't you be nicer?"* say *"that doesn't make me feel very good."* *"You never take out the trash,"* should be *"this trash can is full and if I have to take it out one more time I'm going to scream."* *"It would be great if you helped out around the house sometimes,"* should be *"the kids are driving me crazy, can you take them from me on a regular basis so I can have a break so that I don't go absolutely bonkers?"* You'll notice that my alternative examples are not nice, kind, or even lacking in disappointment or frustration. That's because the idea that we need to censor such feelings originates from the psychological trauma caused by our parents punishing and shaming us for feelings as children to absolve themselves of the consequences of their abuse or mistakes. But this personal censorship also prevents us from asking for what we need by pretending or minimizing feelings which result from not getting what we need. We fail to care for our needs because when we tried to do that as children we were reprimanded for trying. There's actually nothing wrong with being disappointed, hurt, frustrated, or even angry. But there is a *big* difference between making someone (or someones) feel like they are bad for doing things that cause us those feelings. When we responsibly ask for what we need instead of blaming others for failing us we also communicate these normally offensive feelings in ways which are actually not threatening, since we are merely expressing our anger but not making the other person's self-worth and personal identity the target of that anger, and it can even endear us further to our partners since we are being open and transparent and providing them with information about us rather than trying to manipulate or control them, leaving it up to them to decide what they will do with the information and allowing them to make their own choices instead of trying to make it for them. Interpersonal conflict is always stimulating, but when it actually becomes personally offensive is the line where we begin to do damage to our relationships and thus our position and security. Getting mad at someone because you are frustrated can be fun and funny if you don't characterize your anger as a result of their personal weaknesses. Taking responsibility for our own failure to anticipate and ask for our needs allows our family, friends, coworkers, bosses, etc., to be part of the solution and thus helpful to us, which in turn gives them a sense of usefulness which only increases the strength of our relationships while also solving our problems and taking care of our needs in the process.

Because we often only resort to setting boundaries after we become frustrated and fed up, we do so in ways which cause pain to those whom we are charged to care and in so doing fail to practice self-care, which requires that we set boundaries in anticipation of our needs and not after they have been neglected. One of my darling nephews was obsessed with a television series and the singing, dancing, and characters. What I thought was just a passing obsession spanned two years of fevered proselytizing. His parents unquestioningly relent to every request to play the songs from this show, every single day, unless it's bedtime or dinnertime (although we once had to sit through it during dinner too). I quickly became annoyed by this behavior, not because the song is unpleasant but because such behavior is an imbalance in the give-and-take required of all relationships and was in truth an attempt to dominate and control relationships as learned from his mother, testing those around him to gauge how much he can press us. I quickly put a stop to it when I realized what was going on. But where an annoyed, frustrated and permissive parent (or other adult) might finally set boundaries in such a situation only after they become so angry as to shout or berate a child and make them feel bad once their patience is worn, as if it's the child's fault and not in fact the adult's failure to set boundaries, I acted to care for my own sanity when asked if I would put on the song yet again that I had heard already a half-dozen times by saying, "Nope!"

That was it. No explanation. No justification. He was very confused by an adult setting boundaries without making him feel bad, and looked at me with puzzlement as I put on my own song. He didn't ask me to play that damn fucking song again when I was already listening to music, but he did ask me who the artist was we were now listening to (it was Carley Rae Jepson) and we talked about our favorite songs and movies which did *not actually include the one which he had been obsessed*, because that obsession was actually a control mechanism which served the purpose of carving out a space for himself which was not readily forthcoming from his environment. When some of my nieces asked me to chase them after I had just made myself coffee, I replied by laughing that they were mistaken if they thought I was going to chase them after having just made coffee, but promised that I would do so later, when I was finished (which I also kept). Because I enjoy coffee for quite a while, twice they came to ask if I was done yet, and I simply replied with a "Nope!" This light-hearted establishment of immutable boundaries both lets children know that they are seen and heard and cared for but reserves for the adult our needs which must be respected reciprocally. This communicates to children that they are safe, so there is therefore no reason to increase attention seeking, because their needs are met also by the adult's needs being met. Because the adult is the adult it is the adult's responsibility to establish boundaries and care for ourselves, and not the child's, which is why parenting books or approaches which focus on strategies to control or shape a child fail because it is in truth the adult who must be addressed, and focusing with such single-mindedness on the child in turn neglects our own self-care and development.

Other ways to practice self-care can come at moments like reading time. Of course, it's good and necessary for parents to read to their children, but as children grow and improve in reading ability parents can transition reading time to an activity in which everyone chooses their *own* book to read to themselves but in proximity to and with parents, allowing parents to indulge and satisfy their own interests while also demonstrating self-care for their children, and simultaneously encouraging children to develop their own interests and ability and desire to read on their own (browsing your iPhone while they read will *not* accomplish this).

When I was a child it was a common practice for one of us to assume dish duty after dinner. Since my parents cooked the meal we were expected to take turns cleaning up. But though my parents got a break from cleaning they inadvertently demonstrated the opposite of self-care. The ability to practice self-care means caring for our needs *while* we are also parenting. This policy of taking turns with dishes was simply my parents engineering more breaks from parenting, checking out of their responsibilities after laboring. A single person who lives on their own must also do the dishes after cooking, and my parents, thinking they were teaching self-sufficiency by making us do the dishes, were in reality demonstrating laziness and reluctance to meet responsibilities and practice self-care in keeping one's environment clean. Making the matter worse, the division of responsibility between kids communicated a sense of disconnect between family members rather than teamwork and cooperation, and engendered isolation and loneliness, each of us despondent when our turn came do the dishes because everyone else would flee the kitchen and leave us to labor alone. Instead, a parent practicing self-care participates in every family chore and duty until it's finished, demonstrating responsibility for one's own care through responsible and thorough commitment, and in turn models the behavior that everyone participate in cleanup as well as cooking, laundry, and other chores *with* the rest of the family and not apart from them. A small demonstration of this concept did occur for a short while in my childhood, when my mother devised cleaning days where we all cleaned our rooms at the same time. Because we were all engaged in the same activity at the same time it became fun and empowering. By demonstrating the healthy behaviors an adult requires to function on their own (which does not actually involve the delegation of tasks to children) while also insisting that everyone assist and participate the parent simultaneously practices and demonstrates self-care and the setting of healthy boundaries and expectations, parenting and practicing self-care at the same time.

Self-care also takes the form of going to the dentist, buying new clothes (but not shopping as a distraction from emotions or responsibilities), financial responsibility, enjoying hobbies, gardening, saving money, making friends, maintaining relationships, not allowing liars or abusive people to take advantage of us, showing compassion for those who do us harm (since forgiveness is self-care), journaling, civic engagement, pursuing a career independent of parenting (even if it's just part time), keeping the pantry organized, reading books, listening to music and watching movies and television we enjoy, going to therapy, sorting through accumulated possessions, making good food, appointing and finishing our home (within our means and not from a place of materialism), keeping our home clean, or practicing inventory therapy. When we as parents first and foremost make sure our needs are met and take care of ourselves we then find strength and emotional and mental resources to care for our children. Oppositely, if we break ourselves and deny our needs within the role as parent we will only end up abusing and destroying our children. Finding compassion for ourself and the things we have been through will give us the permission to actually practice the self-care we need, and further empower us to be an effective parent rather than one grasping desperately for any sense of relief. We deserve to be parented too, but since we are now an adult and likely the child of parents who lack such skills, we are the one who can and should provide this for ourselves.

12

Self Compassion

One day in fourth grade I was on the playground during recess playing with my friends. It was a hot, Utah spring day and the sun was blazing, turning the surface of the playground equipment into warming irons. The heat did nothing to slow down my enthusiasm for tag, and while fleeing one of my friends I decided to go across the monkey bars. My hands were already sweaty an by the time I got to the end it was clear I was going to slip. I quickly put my feet on the wooden landing platform at the end, but my hands slipped off while my body was still at an angle. I fell backward, feet trapped on the landing a good 18 inches off the ground. Instinctually my arms went back to catch myself, and my body hit the ground with a crack as my elbow snapped in two.
 It didn't really hurt because my body immediately went into shock, but I knew something was wrong and, feeling lightheaded, walked slowly up to the teacher on recess duty at the top of the hill who had seen me fall and holding my arm and didn't even bother getting up.
 Taken to the Principal's office, my parents were called, but nobody came to get me for over an hour, covered in sand from the playground, my arm throbbing and aching, head swimming. Eventually my Granddad showed up at the door. He and my Nana had moved to Utah to help my Dad with his restaurant, and while I confused why neither of my parents had come I was at least very relieved to see him.
 Granddad loaded me into the car and took me right to the restaurant. But my dad said he couldn't take me to the hospital yet, and I had to sit on the lawn, holding my broken arm, while he kept working. I don't know how much

time passed on the grass, but it was long enough that I fell asleep, arm still broken, with the sun getting low in the sky by the time my Dad finally took me to the hospital. It was a clean break, requiring surgery and two pins to set the bone, though I did get to play Nintendo while in my hospital bed.

It is extremely difficult as a an adult to know compassion for ourselves when none was shown to us as children. We simply do not know what is or how to do it. Self compassion is not an emotion, it is a skill that is taught (or not taught) to children by the example of their parents. When our own parents do not have the skills to practice self care or self compassion they cannot teach them to us, then we grow up without them as well, our lives become extremely stressful as a result, and then we in turn fail to empower our own children and doom them to the same fate.

I found out some time after an ex of mine broke up with me that he had been saying terrible things about me both after and during our relationship, even though he had been constantly cheating on me from the beginning and did other harmful things to me while we were together and when we broke up. To my horror, the heartache continued beyond losing someone I loved, knowing that after causing me such harm as he already did was willing to add to it by destroying my reputation among our friends and acquaintances for no real reason other than to cover for his own sense of guilt and shame. I felt helpless and extremely sad, and the pain triggered a fervent, intellectual onslaught of self-defense schemes and intellectual role-playing should I ever get the opportunity to defend myself to those being poisoned against me. '*No, I would say to my imaginary antagonists, that was not true! He said this or that, lied to me, and over the years the situation devolved into a much more complicated struggle to survive.*' Etc., etc.

It is very common and instinctual for us as humans to engage in such imagined scenarios and conflicts to help us cope with uncomfortable and painful events in our lives, that endless stream of defensive dialogue that can be the mind and conscious, and we are right to feel offended when people hurt us, and both the desire to defend ourselves, stand up for what is right, and up to those people who hurt us is not just understandable, but part of our innate instincts to survive. Above all we long to be loved, to belong, and the actions of such actors directly damage and impair our ability to fulfill this need, because we, as a human animal, would likely die when alone that impediments to this requirement for our survival affect us strongly. The danger of being rejected by the group, being tossed out into the cold to be consumed by wild animals or die from starvation is a primal biological fear which all of us possess. Today the risk in practice is less primal but no less frightening. Being alone in the world often means reduced ability to provide for oneself, including medical care, quality of nutrition, and shelter, clothes, economic opportunities, etc. It also means the kind of loneliness that can be devastating, a paucity of friends and mates. That is why when people ridicule us, coalesce into cliques and gang up on us, or kick us out of our families, or even simply criticize or antagonize us it is so painful and frightening and inspires an equally strong, instinctual reaction to fight back, because in evolutionary terms our very existence could be at risk.

One of the most eruptive arguments of my teenage life happened the Summer I was eighteen, and I escaped to my room and slammed the door. I don't even remember what the argument was about. Probably me not going on a mission or having no life plan, since I had been expected to go on a mission but was not allowed since I was gay and thus stuck in a catch-22 within my own family. The next day my mother asked to speak with me, alone, and in a very somber tone asked me to move out. My father didn't even bother showing up for my exiling. I had completely had it with their abuse and neglect anyway, constantly shaming me and harassing me with increasingly frantic confrontations. My mother resented me for growing up, for not being straight, for failing to go on a mission like a good Mormon and hated who I was, constantly criticizing everything I did and showing no interest in helping me advance through the next steps of my life.

I was going to be nineteen-years old in several months. I had only just graduated High School and all my friends had moved off to college or were waiting to serve their own missions. Wishing still to obey my parents I had fervently entreated the support of my bishop by confiding in him my sexuality whom after months and months of moving goal posts finally said he just didn't think I was ready even though many other boys were approved who had even already engaged in full sexual intercourse with women and I had not yet even kissed another person. There was no backup plan. I had not applied to any colleges because that would have been a sign of not wanting to serve a mission. Now it was too late to apply to colleges, and my parents didn't want me living at home. They refused to help me get into college unless I went to the Mormon University, but that also had the same requirements as serving a mission—Not being gay.

Living on my own without many skills to do so in a community which didn't only reject me but actively persecuted me was exceptionally harrowing, and it wasn't until I was a grown man that I realized just how insane this period of my life actually was. My first roommates were fervent adherents to the church who, despite my continued association, did not have a single conversation with me even though I tried to befriend them. Apartments in the city surrounding the university were not autonomous residences but all abided by inappropriate and strict influence of segregation of sexes and religionist behavior. Lonely and listless I moved apartments frequently, at each one finding members who even called me names when I finally stopped going to church and refused to allow me into their circles when they learned I was nineteen (which meant I was not on a mission). During the time of this my desperate loneliness I discovered Erasure, Annie Lennox, and other heroes of gay pop culture whose art brought me deep feelings of belonging and solace when I most needed it. I managed to get a good job as a graphic artist at a screen printing company. Exceptionally talented for my age I increased my pay from the starting wage of thirteen-dollars an hour to eighteen in just six months.

One day my dad invited me to his offices. "I want you to come work for me," he said. "I want to eventually leave my business to you and your brother, and we need to stick together as family." My heart jumped. I was so used to being rejected by my family that an active invitation to be involved in their lives was more than I could have ever hoped for. "Okay," I agreed, and without a second thought quit my well-paying job and showed up to my first day of work at his offices.

I didn't want to work in Real Estate. I had unrealized creative abilities and dreams of being a filmmaker or artist. But I also didn't want to be alone in the world, without those with whom I was raised, and walking into his offices as an actual employee instead of a convenient janitor held its own excitement. If I did stay here and worked to earn enough money I could probably pursue my other ambitions on the side.

I sat down on the couch in his office and waited for him to finish a phone call.

"You can't work for me if you're going to be gay," he said after he hung up. The blood drained from my face. I felt sick. It had been a trap the entire time. My own father tricked me into quitting a well-paying job in order to try and force me to change my sexuality, which I had already been trying to do for the last four years without any progress. "What?" I gasped. He repeated the line along with some justification about clients, reputation, and a bunch of other bigoted stuff. Pain turned to rage. I yelled at him in his office for being so conniving, for putting me in this position, for deceiving me. "You're changing," he offered as an excuse for his behavior. "I am not," I insisted. "You're already becoming more feminine."

In that moment I realized that my own father didn't know who I was. I was not *becoming* feminine. I was dropping the protective facade I had adopted the entirety of my adolescence, the vigilant, tiring, moment to moment editing of my behavior to avoid being found out, which any intelligent adult paying attention would have easily seen through anyway.

In our desperation to belong, to secure our position among the groups on which we depend for our survival and to reduce the risk of being tossed into the abyss, many of us develop skills and traits meant to increase our attachment to these groups. We become funny, or rich, or wise, or a good friend, or a prolific chef, edit our mannerisms and personality, or workout desperately and become ripped and chiseled. Many of us preemptively reject groups, isolate, or maintain only those relationships which are necessary or stressless. Others employ deviant behaviors to manipulate those around us in attempts to engineer their advocacy, by lying, exaggerating, boasting, or ridiculing others believing that by reducing their position we thus increase our own. Even though behaviors to denigrate in attempts to improve one's own image is detestable, the reality is that it does work to some extent, at least among certain deplorable populations and groups of people who enjoy social fireworks and gossip, which is what nearly every popular clique in school consists. The fear of rejection is sometimes so intense that people are willing to sacrifice their own humanity and reject others to prevent the same thing from happening to them.

When we were children my parents got caught up in a contentious lawsuit with a husband and wife whom had purchased one of our homes and then tried to force my dad to carry the costs of replacing the kitchen cabinets and finishes to their tastes. The wife had my dad coming by their house even to change lightbulbs. When it became clear that my dad could not be taken advantage of to the degree they desired, they launched a lawsuit to extort the entire value of the home from us. My father has his flaws, but his architectural and construction skills are as good as they come, and the family ended up losing the lawsuit. But because they had bought the home in which we lived these people had moved into our neighborhood (we moved a few streets away). They began attending our church and making friends with our family's friends, and when their behavior became acrimonious they immediately set out disparaging my parents to our community and friends. I had to sit and listen to this woman teach church classes on God and forgiving your neighbor knowing full well she and her husband were *bearing false witness* for their own financial gain at our expense and trying to ruin my parent's reputation in order to improve their own. Imploring our religious leader for help he refused, claiming to stay out of civic issues (except, of course, when gays and lesbians want to get married) and even though this family was vicious with their gossiping and hatred. Even though we had also known many of the families in this community for many years, none of them stood up to these people even though their behavior was reprehensible, and eventually we moved away for good. The lawsuit was immensely stressful on our family. I was called to testify that the basement in which we lived was not, in fact, ice-cold during the winter. The judge was an amazing psychopath who later lost his judgeship when he was busted for cocaine use. The lawyer for the other family was also their own brother. Unsurprisingly, the couple divorced years later, and my parents don't maintain any relationships with any of the people we used to go on vacations with, who all still live in that miserable little town.

Nobody in the community in which we lived were willing to stand up to these supposedly powerful people, because fear of being rejected by the group is even stronger among religious communities, and the family themselves, some of the most fearful and insane people I've ever met, sought to strike out at others and take in order to strengthen their material position, to unjustly destroy my parent's reputation, with no consideration of how their behavior affected the many other lives in orbit of their gluttony, including their own poor children. Neither was my own father willing to defend his son and instead chose to destroy our relationship rather than confront bigotry and stand up for his own family, and do what is right. So strong is the fear of rejection that many of us ruin our own lives pursuing the subversion of fear.

All of us have varying degrees of uncomfortable and painful encounters with other humans. Many women suffer sexual assault and are expected to move on and function like a whole and unaffected person. Some men are wrongly accused and imprisoned, for years and years, for things they never did and in spite of being a good person while the rest of us go about our lives as if such atrocities don't happen regularly. Many of us have unpleasant encounters with dating and romance, the victims of abuse and harassment from exploitive and opportunistic predators. Friends can turn on us and feed us to the wolves, and parents can turn their backs on their own children in favor of authoritarian institutions. At these crossroads, when our hearts are broken, our bonds cut by razors, and life seems like one heartache after another, the act and instinct to plunge into self-defense which comes so naturally to us is in truth the very opposite of self-compassion. We think that defending ourselves, our reputations, and our feelings is self-care, and the actual act of defending ourselves is, but the thoughts and feelings which swirl in a vortex of pain, anger, and resentment which motivate the impulse to defend ourselves is, in actuality, denying the effect that others have upon our lives. Seeking to resolve the pain or disappointment which overwhelms us we immediately begin entertaining self-pitying revisions of how we might have avoided the problem in the first place, regret how we made a mistake, or lament how terrible the people are who did this to us or what we would do if given the chance to defend ourselves. This instinct forgets about the little child within us who is crying in the corner, who more than anything needs a good, lingering hug to envelop them, to shield out the world and protect them from the pain and heartache. In moments when we are hurt by the world we are that little child, due all of the love and protection deserved by children, even if we somehow participated or played a role in the problem.

When the thought of someone who has done us harm pops into our mind and our reaction is to ruminate on the event we are in reality focusing on that person and in so doing actually ignoring ourselves, tormenting the child within us, and actively practicing the opposite of self-care. *I can't believe he did this to me,* we think. *They're such an asshole. She's such a terrible person. If only I had done this. If only that hadn't happened.* Or we run through the series of events with them and edit it in our minds to find what might have been a less painful outcome or a more effective response, the dialogue of the mind playing out the script of our lives in an endless loop of regret and resentment.

When we rush into action in response to painful events we are running away from ourselves, that little child in the corner, leaving them exposed and abandoned to face the darkness alone. Because as adults we have no one to provide us this protection we must instead do it for ourselves. If we don't, the problem compounds itself and can in turn become unbearable. If we are charged with the care and protection of actual children, it becomes nearly impossible to parent since we cannot even parent the little child that is us, as the role of parent is not authoritarian but guide and guardian. If we abandon the child inside us, we also abandon the ones to whom we gave birth.

Self-compassion takes the form of giving up the intellectual fight to defend ourselves. Stop making plans and schemes to justify our hurt and pain and experiences, to confront those who have done us wrong and defend our position, and instead give the little child that is you a hug by sitting with yourself and the pain we feel rather than from where it came, recognizing that harm has occurred, that people have hurt us and stop at that. Yes, it's very awful that they did this to us, and it hurts. But stop there. Moving from us to focus on them, though it happens in our mind, is also literally moving away from ourselves and thus withholding compassion from ourselves. Pain does not, in fact, need to be justified, and people do not need to be managed. Let them boil in their anger, let their families fall apart under the weight of their lies and hatred, let them wallow in their money and their shallow victory. We will go care for ourselves and emerge from the experience a stronger, more compassionate and confident person because of it.

As a grown man, while experimenting with infectious bacteria to understand how the immune system works at one point I got so ill it prevented me from bending over or expending much energy, and I left an apartment in shambles after moving out. I knew it was in poor condition, I was embarrassed, and offered preemptively to forfeit as much of my deposit as was required to clean it and repair things. But the landlord instead fabricated additional charges and fees which far exceeded the amount of the deposit. I had been an entirely responsible tenant, paid rent several days early every single month for the two years I resided there (except when he lost my rent). I was even amenable and patient when we discovered that I had been paying the electricity of the adjacent unit, communal laundry room, and exterior security lights (no wonder my bill was so high!). I was not well off by any means, and for him to take advantage of me in a time of weakness was nothing short of criminal. He sent me a screenshot of a webpage to purchase a refrigerator as if it was a receipt. He refused to acknowledge the photos I took of the apartment when I moved in and the preexisting conditions of his cheap and shoddy construction job, and blamed some small damage on me for having to redo all the sheetrock of an entire wall which in reality was to install the sound-proofing he had not put in and which caused an incredible amount of stress from a loud and obnoxious neighbor. I did not get any of my refund back even though I confronted him about his lies, and without any legal recourse had to let this criminal win and keep my money unlawfully and unethically. My younger self would have been devastated by this setback. I would have spent hours, days, and weeks ruminating on how I was wronged, taken advantage of, and how I could get justice and protect myself. But, overcome by feelings of helplessness and anger in the moment I instead knew that I had escaped a horrible living situation. I had put more effort into vetting my new apartment and moved to a beautiful mountain town, paying less money for a more wonderful place to live. I sat with the pain of being used and hurt, but I stopped ruminating on what a terrible person the landlord was, because in doing so I was forgetting myself and how I needed to be comforted. The landlord has to live with who he is—a dishonest fuck who nobody respects or even likes, who lied and stole from a kind and helpful person recovering from cancer and debilitating metabolic illness. It did suck, but I had so much more than I did before, even if I was out some money, and I no longer had to live in his shitty apartment or put up with such a terrible person. I also didn't do anything wrong, and I could sleep knowing that, though he to this day cannot say the same. It was okay that this happened, and it was okay that I felt sad about it. I slept peacefully every night afterward and woke up every morning overcome with joy living in my new apartment, making scones and watching the morning sunlight light up the snow-peaked mountains as I sipped coffee and worked on this book.

Especially after a devastating breakup I always thought I needed others to help me get well. A friend, a therapist, or perhaps a parent. I felt powerless and helpless in a world that didn't make much sense and no tools to help me cope with the unpredictability of life. Growing up we were taught that if we were good and made the right choices that things would work out. But life still did not work out, and so we were left without recourse. Often horrible things happen to those who are good and good things happen for those who are evil. I though that my loneliness and heartbreak needed another adult to overcome it, which is why I got into a relationship with the person who later hurt me in the first place. Even narcissists and sociopaths who insist on the virtue of autonomy cannot bear even a few minutes apart from other human beings. Many of us walk through life thinking that other people are mature, that they can help, and we seek their power and presence to save us from our sorrow and helplessness only to find that in spite of their protestations they are every bit as lonely, scared, and lost as we.

Such despair is simply the void left by the absence of our own parents, not the physical, real parents which we may or may not still have, but the symbolic role their person filled in our experience. Now grown, we cannot get back that protection, that assurance which, even if they were abusive meant we were aligned with power. But it is an illusion anyway, an illusion which protects us as children from understanding the frightening truth that all life is impermanent, the realization of which is compounded by the terror of no longer having the protection of god-like parents. Now truly helpless and terrified, the fear of being lost, rejected, tossed out of humanity for most is unbearable, so we devise all sorts of ways in which we try to stay alive, desperately trying to avoid the pain and heartache which may come and so portend our demise. Conditioned by our childhood to believe we are invisible, disposable, insignificant, or revolting we seek outside ourselves for any distraction which can turn our head and our attention. Most people spend their entire lives never turning inward, forever chasing money, status, success, religion, sex, love, conflict, or security just so we never have to peak beneath the funeral mask of our childhood. In reality the ability to enjoy one's own company and to be unmoored by disharmony comes from introspection and the healing of childhood trauma, to bravely reconsider all those awful experiences we had as vulnerable children and recognize that our pain did not come from being helpless or powerless but because we were raised by yet other children who also do not recognize their inherent self worth.

When as parents we feel insecure or uncomfortable about our own children's feelings say, if our child were to get mad at us for something, such feelings are an excellent indicator of our failure to feel compassion for ourselves. Since we do not have compassion for our own feelings of embarrassment, anger, peevishness, sadness, shame, etc. we also do not in turn have compassion for those same feelings in our children. This is the genesis of our tendency to try to control even our children's emotions, because their emotions make us aware of our own and since we have no compassion for ourselves act out in turn to try and remove the stimulus which has evoked them, which are our own children's feelings and thus cause them abuse and to adopt the very same absence of compassion for themselves that we are demonstrating for ourself.

Little children are often happy, bright, and delightful even when they are raised by abusive parents. I have heard too often parents talk about a child in preference for their earlier years, when they were nothing but a little ball of joy and thus less of a burden upon the parents. The confidence, unconditional love, and unbridled joy of infancy is a result of pure naivety, an unblemished conception of life starting on a clean slate, and it is heartless and lacking of compassion to expect growing children to stay as blissfully naive and joyful for our own self-centered fulfillment, especially since much of their frustration and pain has come from our own behavior which affects them. It is natural that children should become marred by the world as they grow, and resenting the change in them is also resenting the same which occurred in us, which is understandable, but not the projection of that disappointment onto them. Doing so withholds compassion both from them and from ourselves, the little child we once were and the one we still are.

Pity and self-pity are often mistaken as compassion, but they are in fact quite different. Pity focuses on others. The abuser. The thief. The disobedient child or the hateful parent and the things they have done to hurt or disappoint us rather than the pain and hurt itself. This is often the case because feelings are not easily described, and words fail to fully encompass that which is ethereal and intangible, especially if we have never been taught how, or worse, taught to deny as a coping mechanism. Very often when coaching someone on inventory therapy I will ask them why it hurt them when their boyfriend left or their wife berated them or their children threw a fit. They will respond, 'because it hurt.' Yes, but why? Why does it hurt? If a stranger came up to us and did the same thing to us it would not hurt even half as much. But they are often perplexed and unable to say the words out loud which would make them vulnerable, simply admitting that we are hurt because we love them.

While self-pity is often vilified by abusive and self-centered narcissists to attack others, there is nothing inherently wrong with self-pity. It is an invaluable, adaptive survival tool we naturally adopt when sources of self-esteem are not forthcoming from our environment, or when we lack the ability to be effective in our lives because of our lack of tools to provide for our own needs and wellbeing, feeling powerless and at the mercy of life and other people. Children from healthy homes have an abundance of attention and validation and as such do not need self-pity as tool to find self-worth and self-esteem, but having been raised in a home where parents were neglectful or abusive we were never shown that we were valuable and wanted and as such failed to develop a true sense of self-worth and personal identity, so of course we have self-pity. Self-pity was a way for us to create value for ourselves where none before existed, and there is nothing wrong with the motivations which underlie self-pity. Wanting attention from the people in your lives, to be loved and to be seen is entirely honest, rational, and valid.

But because pity is anchored to our relationship with external events and actors it continues to perpetuate an absence of self-worth and self-compassion, distracting us from who we really are, which is entirely separate from what happens to us and around us. Having compassion for our emotional needs, our desire to be seen, to be loved, or to be wanted is a more cathartic replacement for self-pity, because for self-pity to thrive it requires denial of our needs.

The reasons we want others to pay us attention or use misfortune as a vehicle for engagement is borne simply from the idea that such needs and desires in the first place are invalid, that we should not have them, because such needs were used in our youth as vectors for harm and neglect when our parents did not have the capacity to show us the love and attention we deserve. Compassion and self-compassion instead focuses on our inner experiences and real needs, the inherent self-identity which is separate from others and the events which affect our lives, and recognizes our emotions and the *effects* those events and people had on us rather than those events and people directly. If instead as a teenager I had known compassion for myself and how much it hurt and how messed up it was to be rejected by my family rather than expecting myself to deal with it I was overwhelmed by the rejection and did not realize I could build a new family and new relationships with people who actually cared about my wellbeing. The only tools I had were to focus on dangers like rejection, to try and protect myself from more disappointment, but doing so is never actually possible and it only prevented me from finding true self worth and finding connection with others. A person with self-pity will feel ashamed at not getting a job, while a person with compassion will appreciate their effort in trying to get one. Someone with self-pity will think that getting fat is shameful and people will hate us, while a person with self-compassion will realize that our body is mortal and that we cannot truly control biology. Someone who is alone or lonely will, if they are dominated by self-pity, be preoccupied with being alone, where someone who has compassion for themselves being alone will recognize it is painful only if we do not like being with ourself.

Many of us love pets like dogs and cats and might even prefer their company to that of humans. Unlike children a pet also does not prevent singles or couples from going out on the weekends or having a day job, and pets are always excited to see us and cuddle up on the couch when we get home without demanding anything but food and love. While dogs and cats can be wonderful companions the primary reason we love them more than children or other humans in truth is that over them we hold absolute power. A pet dog or cat cannot really feed themselves without our support, and if we are abusive can shut them away if we desire. In truth our deep love of pets is in part because of their helplessness which predisposes them to total dependence on us and thus makes us feel secure, knowing we can never really lose them no matter how we behave. Dogs and cats are every bit as emotionally complex as humans, and can get in arguments with other dogs or cats and act selfish, controlling, or fearful. Humans likewise can be every bit as sweet, loving, and kind as other animals. Unless it is traumatized out of us, children, friends, and lovers can absolutely adore us and just like dogs and cats desire to spend their every waking moment with us or thinking of us. Boyfriends and girlfriends become enamoured by our presence and dream of us even when separated but for an hour, and friends will sacrifice their dignity and self respect just to be in our presence, but those very characteristics we adore in pets instead inspires contempt for humans because these are also what make us vulnerable and dependent like the animals over which we lord, and lacking that power and control over humans we have over pets makes us uncomfortable instead of comforted because in reality we do not desire the love of pets but the comfort of control, and in so doing deny ourselves the opportunity for love and companionship we so crave.

Pity is likewise anchored to our fear of vulnerability, knowing we cannot control other humans the way we can helpless dogs and cats seek to engineer control through manipulation, even when that pity is turned inward to justify legitimate needs for love and companionship because we do not feel worthy of them. Instead, having compassion for our emotional needs the way we might a pet is cathartic to self-pity, respecting our desire to be seen, to be loved, or to be wanted. Self-pity is oppositely a denial of our needs, instead of asking for help and being vulnerable we erect walls of control using emotions and emotional obligation as control mechanisms. The reasons we want others to pay us attention or use misfortune as a vehicle for engagement is borne simply from the idea that our needs and desires in the first place are invalid and make us weak and vulnerable because such needs were used in our youth as vectors for harm, neglect, and control when our parents did not have the capacity to show us the love and attention we deserved. Compassion and self-compassion instead focuses on our inner experiences and needs. the inherent self-identity which is separate from others and the events which affect our lives, and recognizes our emotions and the *effects* of external events and trauma rather than those events and people directly. If instead as a teenager I had known compassion for myself and how much it hurt and how messed up it was to be rejected by my family rather than expecting myself to deal with it and trying to fight for validation I could have built a new life and my own family with people who actually cared about my wellbeing. Instead, the only tools I had were to focus on potential threats to my wellbeing, such as rejection or financial stress, to try and protect myself from even more disappointment, but doing so is never actually possible and it only prevented me from finding real self worth and real connection with others because all relationships inherently risk loss and rejection. A person with self-pity will feel ashamed at not getting a job while a person with compassion will appreciate their own effort and gain confidence just from trying. Someone with self-pity will think that getting fat is shameful and people will hate us while a person with self-compassion will realize our body is mortal and that we cannot truly control biology. Someone who is alone or lonely will, if they are dominated by self-pity, be preoccupied with being alone where someone with self compassion will recognize it is painful only if we do not like ourselves.

Because parents become practiced in giving to and helping their children it tends to become second nature, becoming a deep and important factor in our identity as a person, finding usefulness and purpose in acting as a nearly full time giving machine. So when a person uses giving and helping as a manipulative behavior which comes with a debt they practice over and over and over a behavior which undermines trust, love, and intimate bonds. Presented with obstacles as we age and life progresses this behavior can in turn backfire spectacularly as children grow and begin to understand the manipulation behind our actions, and suddenly all of our years of hard work are regarded with spite and resentment since it was never altruistic, intended always from the beginning to improve our own position, even sometimes at the expense of the child's wellbeing. This behavior extends to other relationships too, both within a marriage and without, where we feel entitled to a response or benefit simply because we do things for others. This a blatant power game which will only cause us further pain and heartache, because it too is an attempt to control life, which we cannot actually do, so when our ambitions for giving are thwarted we are met with frustration and disappointment since the goal was never only to give in the first place. Giving with intent to receive is deceit. It is an adulteration. It is an unwillingness to face the pain and disappointment of our pasts and to instead control life in ways which we have absolutely no control. We cannot prevent pain and heartache, and attempts to do so will only cause us more pain and even deeper heartache as loved ones respond to our manipulation by keeping their distance, emotionally as well as physically, even when we do it ostensibly because we love them.

Like my response to harm at the hands of predatory men and the impulse to justify and defend my experience and pain, seeking to control or gain through the act of giving is also the opposite of having compassion for ourselves. The act of giving with intent to receive is one of self-preservation, which is not the same as compassion, and originates from the unconscious belief that we are not worthy of or cannot get for ourselves the things we require for a fulfilling life. This misconception of our self-worth originates from abusive denial or deprivation in childhood, and as adults without compassion for ourselves or a proper estimation of our own self-worth now go about obtaining those through subterfuge and deceit. Self-preservation is based in fear, and fear comes because we do not feel empowered or even worthy of the things we are trying to attain for ourselves in the first place, which we would feel if we had compassion for ourselves and thus empowered not to resort to such manipulative strategies to get what we could simply ask for. Many parents use complex and exhausting methods to get from their spouses and children what only requires a simple, brief conversation. If my father wanted me in his life all he had to do was ask me to dinner and take an interest in me. Instead, he concocted a deceitful and hurtful plan to swindle me out of a secure job and then use my dependence on him to force compliance. Wives sometimes get their husbands gifts or get their hair done or buy new clothes (to excite their husband, which is also a gift) in the anticipation that it will win his attention, but then he may be distracted by work or harboring struggles he has not yet revealed to her and when our supposedly "selfless" gift fails to get the result we wanted, in turn break down crying as a way to elicit the response we wanted from the beginning and what motivated the scheme in the first place. Husbands may do the same, working hard and plying gifts on their spouses then growing angry when it does not lead to sex, or if they gain weight or otherwise fail to meet our selfish, self-centered intentions giving a partner a gift of weight-loss tools or a gym membership. Even getting pregnant and expecting our partner to celebrate even though they become obviously frightened by the unexpected responsibility and instead of showing compassion to the person we supposedly love react with hostility and anger, because we in fact do not have compassion for ourselves and so have none we can give.

Every Christmas holiday my parents would expend a great deal of time and energy making mountains of banana bread and Christmas cookies. It might have been a cherished childhood memory except that the majority of these were for neighbors and business. We were allowed hardly any for ourselves, even though we were the family of the people making them. This sounds like it was a generous gesture on the part of my parents, but remember that they moved on average every year or two, and did not maintain friendships with the people for which they were slaving away in the kitchen. My parents continue to make cookies and undertake other exhausting projects for neighbors they also openly deride and complain about. This supposedly generous giving is in reality a tool to achieve a desired outcome in their lives, which is to endear themselves to their community in a preemptive attempt to obfuscate personal insecurities. Since I don't care what my neighbors think of me I am not driven by a desire to flatter them and thus not beholden to the exhaustion of my time and energy baking for people I don't even know. When I do spend time giving, helping, or serving people it comes from a genuine sense of concern or love and not a deceitful attempt to engender myself to them, because I no longer have patience for prostrating myself to people who don't care for me.

Growing up in the kind of self-righteous communities I did, we were occasionally obliged to participate in token acts of service. Because nobody was actually interested in the betterment or uplifting of the downtrodden and destitute, cliche service activities like feeding the homeless on Thanksgiving or Christmas or giving to coat drives were standard events, dripping with moralistic preaching about the value of service from people whose only act of serving were these such pretentious demonstrations of moral superiority. Real acts of service are not motivated by a sense of obligation, storing pennies in heaven for fear of not getting what's owed when we die. The tainting of generosity for the subversion of comeuppance is itself a plague upon humanity, because of the deceitful pretense of affection which accompanies it which undermines and destroys social bonds. If the service-minded truly cared about retirees in retirement homes they would visit often instead of performing a song at the holidays, or champion and campaign for improved standards of elderly care. If the people feeding homeless at the holidays actually cared for them they would vote and organize to eliminate barriers which promote homelessness and increase the function of social programs to assist and care for those in need. Taking seriously concepts of integrity and accountability, the absolute absence of morality from these hollow shows of piety and condescension were part of the fuel which helped me understand the true mindless institutionalism that was the religion of my youth, and the pretended happiness, hidden struggles, and miserable desperation of its adherents finally made sense. We cannot live a life infected with lies, pretenses, ulterior motives and manipulative posturing and expect happiness, even or especially in matters of spirituality. Such expectations are wholly incompatible with human nature, which is naturally inclined to serve, to love, and to find community. When the human mind perceives deceit it becomes unreliable, always in danger of being discovered, forever juggling the excuses and indifferences and justification for human frailty which all of us share equally. There is no shame in making mistakes, in being subject to pain and disappointment. These experiences bring us richness in life from which we may taste the power of living and grow as a person. Attempting to distract ourselves from uncomfortable realities causes psychological illness, broken families, and abject sadness. The function of pretended service is to distract, to justify our wrongs and mistakes and put off responsibility for the pain we cause others, and as such it does not have the intended effect of healing us nor those onto whom we foist our neuroses, and the mind feels keenly the inconsistency of unamended wrongs and pretended demonstrations of service.

For human beings, giving and serving is in reality a biological need as social creatures to engage in cooperation and assist each other in our collective survival. That is why true, non-ulterior service can be so satisfying, and why such displays of service do not take the performative form of helping the most destitute only when it is convenient and forgetting them the rest of the year. Real service means giving our time and attention to our family members instead of overworking or passing the days on our phone and social media. Real service means teaching children to cook and how to pay bills so that they may navigate the world of adults successfully. Service means campaigning and voting for those who are disenfranchised, even those who appear to be our opponent and antagonist, standing up for those who are oppressed and challenging those who exploit and oppress.

Giving, serving, and helping others must always come from a genuine place of love or care for those on whom we bestow these behaviors, especially children. When we act from a place of fear and insecurity to use our giving and contribution to shore up our needs rather than motivated by love it makes our efforts ineffective, even compounding our problems, where truly selfless acts of giving which are not concerned about outcome make us more efficient with our time, more discerning about whom we spend it on, and since our energies are more narrowly directed thus ironically more effective. When I was younger and more successful than my siblings I was generous with my money, a prolific gift-giver, spending much time and money for occasions such as birthdays and holidays believing that in so doing I was strengthening bonds of intimacy. But even those on whom I lavished presents betrayed me, aligning themselves with bigoted and homophobic ideals and institutions, keeping me out of the emotional entanglement of their families. I give now only when I feel like it, when my love and affection for someone or concern for others is so great that I wish to give simply for the act itself. This not only saves a lot of money but also time and emotional energy, and it also engenders or perhaps originates from a sense of self compassion, because I now know that I am worth caring for and empowered to get that which I need from life, and no longer need to use petty coping strategies to supplement an absence of self-worth.

Opportunities to show ourselves compassion occur daily, and often consist of simply being kind and patient to ourselves, our emotions, and our bodies, waiting a little while to act on feelings and problems so that we do not react reflexively to how we feel, since this often involves instinctual control mechanisms, which will be removed by the trauma therapy in the upcoming chapter. There is nothing wrong with being frustrated by a mess, afraid of a partner leaving, or sad about being financially constrained. Problems arise instead when we *act* on those feelings. Many times too our own biology is working just as it should but we mistake personal problems for those of a moral or discipline problem. For instance, when we are metabolically ill and aging our biology naturally downregulates motivation through reduced production of dopamine in order to motivate reduced physical activity, since expending calories is an evolutionary liability for any animal that is metabolically sick or chronically infected by bacteria, parasites, and viruses, which most people are. The apparent laziness or inability to rouse ourselves to clean the house or pick up clutter is literally the body trying to save us from dying from nutrient exhaustion caused by our mortal susceptibility to disease. I once worked with a young man who, as a child, got infected by lyme disease, which is both a parasitic and bacterial infection caught from tick bites, which causes debilitating fatigue and chronic immune exhaustion, but his parents constantly shamed him to be more active and ambitious, showing little compassion for his medical condition, and he developed a severe eating disorder, anxiety, depression, premature hair loss, and total loss of erectile dysfunction at the age of twenty until finding my work and asking me for help. I myself had cystic fibrosis my entire life, which I didn't even know about until I was forty-one years old, and much of the muted aspects of my personality which did not meet my father's neurotic expectations for me to fulfill his unrealized dreams and anxieties was due to being chronically ill and more susceptible to stress, infection, and later cancer and diabetes. Many people are not kind, but we are also unkind to ourselves, usually because we were taught to be so, and practicing self-care through showing ourselves the compassion we both desire and deserve can ironically help us be more productive and effective in our lives since we then stop wasting emotional energy being so hard on ourselves. The motivation to clean often occurs after other accomplishments such as having a great day at work or a nice social interaction because the rise in dopamine from those stimuli reverses the biological instinct to preserve energy. Being wise to the biological factors which affect the endocrine system and thus behavior such as is explored in *Fuck Portion Control* can help us be more effective in our own lives by having compassion for our mortality and limitations, and as a parent if we have children by empowering them in similar ways with these tools we teach ourselves.

    We can and should first be a parent to the little child within us, the one who is wounded and fearful. They have not been reassured nor comforted after stepping into the void of adulthood. With no more parent to guide and protect us, we look everywhere but within. The truth is that we are now adults, and every one of us has the power to be that parent for ourselves that we have always needed and wanted. That is what it means to be an adult. This does not mean simply material provisions, but also those which are emotional and spiritual and social as well. Self-compassion is parenting yourself. Not in authority or discipline, but compassion, love, and comfort. Charging off to defend our ego, our person, turns away from the child within that needs to hear it's okay to feel sad, to feel hurt, and to have been hurt. Stay with the child within you. Stop reacting to life defensively. Practice the self-care that shows compassion for what you have gone through and how difficult life can be.

Self-pity is ignorant of compassion, and compassion is found through practicing self-care. Through action. Doing that which is needed to care for ourselves and our wellbeing. Self-pity entertains misfortune and ignores culpability. Compassion moves through it, and the act of moving through is doing, practicing, sharing, learning, and accepting. By understanding that it is okay that we make mistakes, that we are vulnerable to predators, that our mortal condition is limited, and having compassion for our weaknesses I was empowered to lift others also out of cycles of despair and recrimination. This also occurs when we do the same as a parent. By lifting ourself out of the depths of self-pity and discovering self-compassion and self-care we in turn gain an enormous reservoir of compassion which we can then share with others, namely our own children, and this empowerment not only makes the role of parent far less stressful, it makes it more successful, since by sharing this empowerment we enable our own children to become their own parents (as adults) and thus better able to navigate the darkness which life can sometimes bring, now full of light for the vantage to which we have lifted ourselves and in the process, them.

13

Inventory Therapy

In the beginning of the 1950's a psychiatrist by the name of Dr. Murray Bowen began properly describing the psychological dynamic between parents and children which facilitated conflict and abuse. For the first time it was explained that when two people are in conflict (such as within a marriage) each of them cannot alone bear the stress between them and in turn require a third party with whom to share the stress. This process was called *triangulation*, and within a marriage the target third party is most often children whom by their proximity and absence of interpersonal boundaries cannot help but become receptacles for this stress. Though Bowen had overtly misogynistic attitudes about women and was bigoted and ignorant toward homosexuals (he was a 1950's psychiatrist, after all), he did understand the dynamics of interpersonal conflict and how abuse is perpetuated from parent to child and from generation to generation.

But conflict between two individuals does not even need to be animus to cause conflict triangulation. The stress which occurs in normal relationships from financial stress, personal tastes, errors in translation, or even that which occurs with extended family members is enough that we as individuals cannot bear it alone and thus require outlets to express that stress. Very often it is animus, though, as husbands harass their partners about their appearance or domestic responsibilities or wives shame their partners about work ethic or manhood. Manipulative behavior is rife within relationships, which in turn creates a tremendous amount of stress for both parties. Then children become unwilling participants in this dynamic since we are conveniently nearby and helpless, and are thusly harmed in our development without any skills or abilities to protect ourselves from it. When I was younger my mother always told me how horrible my father was to her. This was a blatant and abusive manipulation meant to engender pity for herself and to undermine my affection for my own father in retribution for his misdeeds. Children have no business being involved in the dynamics of adult relationships, but that is not a reality most of us are lucky to have lived. The result then is psychological and developmental damage to a child which affects how we in turn operate as a grown adult, and the cycle is repeated again within the next generation. My mother probably witnessed a same or similar dynamic in her own parent's relationship, being coerced into the drama which occurs between adults, having no life experience, maturity, or physical ability to set personal boundaries by which to protect her own innocent state of childhood from such manipulation, and because it was the standard modeled for her simply repeated it. My great grandmother Rose was an absolutely fabulous woman and ran her own beauty school and salon in Arizona when she was a young mother, but she was also very opinionated and ambitious and I can easily see how my grandmother was also neglected and burdened by the same kinds of dynamics which in turn created the situation which hurt my own mother which in turn hurt me as a child. We are incapable as adults of living life on our own, and we require other human beings with which to form bonds and relationships, to spread the burden of living between us all, and when those relationships we need also become sources of frustration and pain and without tools to properly handle such encounters become hurtful in turn as we try to protect ourselves. When individuals are also cut off from the healthy support of intimate friendships and other adult relationships due to an inability of ourselves and others to be emotionally available and cooperative, the stress between partners increases proportional to the decrease in access to support and lack of interpersonal tools, and then the pressure has only a few directions in which it can release, which is unfortunately toward us as little children who are incapable of withstanding it.

Specifically, the effect of abuse triangulation creates one of three personality types or functional identities which form out of necessity within these triangulation dynamics. This specificity of effect was described later by Dr. Stephen Karpman who established the *Karpman Drama Triangles* model of abuse triangulation, and all of us who have lived through the dynamics of abuse, regardless of severity (remember that abuse can happen even by accident), end up adapting to the dynamic of the environment by forming an identity which helps us to navigate within that dynamic. Because as children we are entirely incapable of caring for ourselves, we are designed by nature to adapt to the needs of the parent, to endear ourselves to them, to draw attention to ourselves though affection, curiosity, persistence, or even conflict. It would not very well profit a child to tell his mother that she should not be involving him in such matters when she sits down to cry after being told she is fat by the man who is supposed to love her. If children were somehow able to protect themselves from an abusive father they might risk also losing his support and be abandoned to the wild. So children are naturally possessed of unconditional love in order that we not by our own behavior interfere with our chances of survival, which in turn places us in direct involvement in the very dynamics which cause abuse. Growing up in this dynamic and through instinct and observation devising the tools we require to survive childhood (not necessarily life in general), we graduate into adulthood ill prepared to be effective adults, since we were never taught the healthy skills required to successfully navigate adulthood, and are ineffective in turn, which then makes us frustrated, insecure, resentful, and further compounds our ineffectiveness as we cause or worsen problems because of our ineffectiveness which again compounds our pain and frustration and so on, as our specific identity developed within the confines of a dysfunctional parent-child relationship in turn impairs our ability to relate with and form relationships with other adults. These identities are so elemental to our existence that we do not even see their function in our lives until we are perhaps much older and have accumulated much life experience as to finally enlighten us, and we instead see our version of reality which, filtered through the perception of our particular identity, is so undeniable as to appear as truth, when it in fact is as much a facade as the Matrix was to Neo.

Our development of one of these fractured personality types occurs because our experience as a child is limited to adult humans with whom we must devise methods to survival, to cope with the specific manipulation and behavior they in turn use to navigate their own lives. It is a survival strategy which develops instinctually to the inconsistencies and volatility of our environment in assumption that life as an adult will be equally unstable. There are three specific identities or personality types which result from the fracturing of self caused by such abuse. Type one and most obvious and potent is the identity Dr. Karpman identified as the *Persecutor*. This is typically an "alpha male" or "alpha female" type of persona who is aggressive, dominant, authoritative, critical, overtly demeaning, and often narcissistic. This personality develops in response to parents who are overly passive, neglectful, and self-pitying to empower a child to achieve needs unmet by the adult. They typically appear as strong personalities who dominate everyone around them, but most especially family members, and to the general public appear as charismatic and bold individuals. The persecutor blames, shames, attacks, and generally sees others as impediments to the realization of their wants and needs. A wife who is fat is actively robbing the husband of his entitlement to someone fit and lean. Or a mother whose son is financially irresponsible finds him as an impediment to her own financial security as she bails him out time and again and expends her own financial resources. Persecutors also trumpet their own fitness and health (or in reality lack of sickness which is not really the same thing) in terms of self-worth as a person and apparent imperviousness to mortality. They are also unlikely to offer compassion for those who encounter misfortune, are ill, out of work, who make mistakes, who reveal weakness, blaming everyone else for their problems and never taking responsibility for their own. A Karpman type one feels or believes they could have anything or achieve anything if only people did not stand in their way, and take what is rightfully theirs, and entitlement is a strong theme throughout their daily lives.

Persecutor type personalities are also very susceptible to scams, fraud, and bad business deals because the dynamics of deceit flatter the ego of a persecutor personality and exploit the very delusions of entitlement and infallibility they want to believe about themselves. When we have a persecutor personality we invariably also attract to us weaker personality types who believe they need a strong person to help protect them, and by our own behavior manufacture the very scenario we believe impedes us from realizing our own potential, because other adults who are actually strong and capable don't want anything to do with an aggressive, dominant asshole. Subconsciously, a persecutor personality will always actively seek out weaker personality types because such persons are the only ones who can also affirm and validate our identity and perception of life as one who would succeed if only others didn't stand in our way. Because our identity as a persecutor also depends on being not only strong but also impervious and auspicious, any symptoms of mortality such as acne, fat, illness, age, impotence, financial stress, failure, weakness, rejection, or consequence causes extreme psychological stress and motivates aggressive and obsessive actions aimed solely at neutralizing those apparent weakness. They also display immense amounts of arrogance which is widely mistaken as confidence, as confidence is the strength to accept weaknesses, not deny them, something the persecutor ironically cannot do, where arrogance is the attempt to dominate and subjugate reality. The persecutor, dependent on the domination of others and the indulging of arrogance fall apart when faced with inconvenience or failure, especially when romance is concerned since we are reliant on others to fulfill our romantic needs, where those possessed truly of confidence understand that failure is a valuable resource and of itself does not limit our future or potential as a human being.

Type two is the *Victim* (me!), the polar opposite of the persecutor and one who believes themselves to be weak and ineffectual and thus in need of someone or someones who are dominant and strong in order to compensate for our ineptitude and paucity of self-confidence, to facilitate the successes we believe ourselves incapable. As a timid and insecure young man I believed that I needed encounters with privileged, talented, strong, confident, outgoing, successful, or powerful people in order to find the success both professionally and personally I thought was necessary and desirable to lift myself up to a position of strength. I was often afraid of others, and thought myself elementally incapable of networking, teamwork, and friendships I saw happening all around me. Where the persecutor believes that others stand in their way, the victim identity intrinsically believes they are helpless without the assistance of others in achieving their goals. A persecutor blames victims and a victim blames themselves. Instead of being the aggressor in a relationship and approaching boys and men who drew my attention I usually waited for others to come to me, but because I was shy and timid this always resulted in the aforementioned persecutor personality drawn to my permissiveness, and I would tumble headlong into an interdependent drama of offense and recrimination which served only to reinforce our respective fractured identities. I could not attract the attention of a healthy, stable adult because none such adults desire the burden of caring for an insecure and imbalanced adult. To be clear, those who blame or shame a victim for believing themselves helpless *are the persecutor type*—blaming others for their problems instead of displaying compassion. It is actually compassion which motivates healthy adults to reject such dependent persons, where persecutors instead seek them, because indulging dependence serves only to sustain it as facilitated by a complimentary persecutor type which lacks compassion for the victim. A persecutor identifying and shaming victims is in fact fulfilling their own delusions of being powerful and independent. The victim personality actively attracts to themselves the persecutor type for the apparent strength and dominance they desire, and I was likewise perplexed to constantly find myself paired with men whom I thought strong and confident but who demonstrated only an absence of compassion for myself and others and extreme emotional volatility, blaming me for their problems and actively schemed and acted against both my interests and theirs within the relationship and without, engaging in infidelity, blame, dishonesty, and abundant resentment and animosity, since they perceived my weaknesses as impediments to the realization of their desires.

In truth the victim type is every bit as capable *and culpable* in our actions and decisions as the persecutor. Neither type is any more or less powerful or effective in their life choices than the other, but merely burdened by biases wrought from our life experiences which color our perception of life and our own personal worth and effectiveness. I viewed my situations as a chance of fate and something which happened to me instead of my own personal choices to enter into relationships with abusive and narcissistic people so obviously volatile and self-centered in the first place, and to also put up with and persist in such relationships even after they demonstrated behaviors which were harmful. But there was nothing but perception and unresolved childhood pain and trauma and lack of empowerment which impaired me from actually achieving the things I wanted and taking care of myself in the way I supposed came from others. Many victim personalities can also be just as aggressive and dominant as a persecutor, however, ironically dominating a relationship through excessive preoccupation with their perceived helplessness. As all of these psychological products of trauma revolve around control, taking ourselves way to seriously is an enormous burden characteristic of all three types and precludes the ability to relax, have fun, and enjoy relationships for what they are.

Because these psychological orientations originate from our biology as a human animal they are widespread and participate in the destiny of all humanity. Many contributors to public dialogue and leadership are exasperated at the eagerness of the destitute and downtrod to support those who actually hoard money, enrich themselves, and scheme and lobby government to further impoverish the very people who support them. Those with the victim personality desire strength and power from those they perceive as such, the persecutor identity, who must therefore be someone who is powerful and successful and arrogant, even criminal. Other persecutor types also support this behavior because it validates their own actions and worldview. As such, both types actively promote rather than resist such actors even when it actually disadvantages or endangers them. Likewise, those in power who are professional criminals, power-hungry, and merciless view others as impediments to the satisfaction of domination and control, and thus actively exploit, abuse, and literally persecute those whom their worldview defines as victims, by definition incapable of success and unworthy of enrichment on their own. Because leaders who distribute wealth, provide opportunity, and care for everyone invalidate the perceptions of these identities, many of us fight against mutually beneficial systems with every ounce of our being even though such systems would benefit us materially, economically, and politically, actively rejecting our own enrichment and empowerment in order to reinforce and validate our personal identities.

Type three and last of the identities which form from abuse triangles is described as the *Helper*, which actually makes it sound more innocuous and altruistic than it really is, and should probably be called the underminer because we who are the helper type are not interested in truly helping, because just like the persecutor and the victim, it is a way for us to feel a sense of purpose and to be validated, for our own benefit and not that of others, and if nobody needs help then we don't feel seen or useful. Karpman helper types are often middle children, although not always, and found their function within dysfunctional family groups as a mediator or inbetween. Watching conflict between parents and other siblings (or parent to parent if they were only children), the helper felt unseen and unloved unless they inserted themselves into the conflict surrounding them, and thus grow up being conditioned to see themselves without value unless they are somehow intervening on others' behalf. Then, because this function requires conflict a person who is a helper unconsciously enflames and perpetuates conflict and insecurity in those around them in order to generate the source of their self-esteem. People with this personality type are often those who interject themselves in conflict which is not directed to them personally, and often gives undermining and unhelpful advice. For instance, a helper I know suggested locking me and my father in a room until we resolved our differences. But my father is my abuser whom, by his very relationship to me and my siblings is an authority figure and thus has more power than I do. It would be like suggesting a rapist and his victim get locked in a room together until they resolve their problems. It's completely insane. But it's also exactly the kind of behavior that is hallmark of the helper type, who needs conflict in order to feel purpose. Both Karpman the persecutor and helper types are those who insist that offenders should be forgiven for their offenses even while they have not asked for forgiveness and continue to offend, because persecutors do not want to face the consequences of their behavior and helpers want a supply of conflict to manage their feelings of insecurity. Helpers also might subtly or not so subtly suggest that the victim (in this case an actual victim but also the victim personality) bears some responsibility for harm which is done to them and will say things like, *"maybe you antagonized them,"* implying that we brought abuse or harm upon ourselves. *"Your dress was too revealing,"* or *"you're too angry,"* attempting to appear helpful but all the while trying to destroy the self-esteem and boundaries of others so they may be all the more reliant upon us. If as a helper we were to truly empower and assist another person they might actually resolve their problem and then they will no longer be vulnerable to our manipulations. This is perhaps the most destructive and malicious of these personality types because it is so duplicitous, even to the person who suffers it, because it actively seeks to enable and empower abuse, but we may truly feel like others need us or that what we are doing isn't harmful, even though it is very harmful. Because it is self-serving, the helper personality also often supports a persecutor type and takes advantage of victims, opportunistically bridging divides during conflict to exploit it for our own benefit.

Another great example of the helper type are those on the internet and social media who leap on others for honest mistakes, missteps, or errors in translation to enflame mistakes into controversies, then playing the part of intermediary in the very conflicts we create. We might also be the type to tell a partner, friend, or family member that nobody loves them or will love them as much as we do, or that we love them more than anyone else in the world which is both absurd and indemonstrable and in reality only designed to engender dependence. Or we might use someone's outward vulnerabilities like weight, acne, appearance, body type, illness, or exploit personal information they share with us as an excuse to interject ourselves through pretended concern and fulfill our own emotional satisfaction at their expense. This personality type is very common in families where parents are blatantly abusive but whom are defended by some of the siblings in an attempt to "keep the peace," which is in reality a manipulation to engineer our own usefulness, securing our position in an insecure family, but in effect only contributes to conflict and helps sustain abuse and thus our purpose as intermediary or arbiter. Having grown up as the peacemaker or intermediary we know no other way to function in life, our value being derived from this role since our personality never had room to explore its own inherent value, and as such require constant conflict in order to justify our very existence, and as such true resolution or assistance is not really offered or even intended since it would completely invalidate what we perceive to be the source of our value.

The psychology profession is actually stocked with helper personalities, which is why people can spend so much time and money engaged in therapy and never resolve our problems. The issue is more insidious because therapists are genuinely unaware of how they fulfill rather than solve conflict triangles through their own actions and profession and in so doing actively engender conflict and self-pity in patients. Motivated by feelings of low-self worth or a need to find value through others, helpers find the mental health profession to be a prime hunting ground to sustain their fractured perception of self. I was more often assisted in my years of mental illness by psychiatrists rather than psychologists because this ulterior motive is more easily disguised and facilitated by the esoterically conceptual nature inherent to psychology, where psychiatry integrates more biology, hormones, physical health, and actual human physiology into their education and profession, which in turn provides less space for psychological manipulation (though the past horrors of psychiatry in the experimentation and harm caused to people like Rosemary Kennedy are crimes against humanity, and the mistaken use and abuse of antipsychotic medications which continues today is also unhelpful and even dangerously harmful). One doctor who really did impact my life was a psychiatrist who didn't even prescribe me medication. Instead, she was the first to teach me methods of relaxation and how to detach my feelings from my actions and to begin exploring hormonal and environmental contributions to my condition. Of all the half-dozen psychologists I saw and the many with whom I am acquainted or friends all practice the same unconscious motivation of sustaining a client's problems in order to also sustain their own self-worth. One psychologist I worked with was Vice President of a school of psychology at a prestigious university, and after my twelfth session with him where I once again was crying about my failed relationship of many months prior over which I had expressed a desire to heal I realized I was not being given *any* skills or knowledge which might empower me and would only find an empty bank account from my experience. Instead of validating my pain and empowering me with encouragement, a friend in the psychology profession once told me when anguishing over a painful breakup which occurred just a few days prior that my ex didn't owe me anything, admonishing *me* for the harm his actions had wrought in my life and compounding my inability to extract myself from the episode. Likewise, the several counselors I saw with an ex during the waning and tumultuous years of our companionship all not only failed to assist us but further entrenched feelings of entitlement and resentment between us both.

One of the ways in which this subversion of progress is practiced is the withholding of emotional involvement and compassion from clients, in maintaining a detached distance in order to not become involved in their lives. But it is through compassion and empathy that we understand the experience of another to thus become empowered to help them. The therapy industry mistakes empathy for codependence because helpers, just like the other two personality types, cannot actually experience empathy due to their own trauma and thus think the codependence and pseudoempathy they feel is empathy. Real empathy does not give away our own emotional power nor cause us to literally feel the feelings of others as what occurs in pseudoempathy, it only makes us emotionally aware of what others are feeling and experiencing. The very fact that detachment from clients is even taught in the profession is evidence of and facilitates the presence of the helper personality, since true empathy would neuter a helper's ability to operate since they would then become aware and ashamed of the effect their behavior has on their targets. The concept of triangulation and Karpman Drama Triangles has also been around for decades, and yet its use by most mental health professionals to treat their patients is rare since gate-keepers of these institutions are themselves likely the helper type and thus motivated by self-interest, since it is extremely effective in empowering patients and clients to understand the origins of our own psychological stress.

The way couple's therapy works is also highly inappropriate and unproductive because who in their fucking mind thinks its a good idea to put two warring egomaniacs in a room to talk about how much they despise the other? Couple's therapy is a naked and blatant strategy by therapists (albeit unconscious) to cultivate and engender conflict. There is always a greater aggressor in conflicts, and no therapist can fully disguise their preference for one client over another anyway, and making people express their frustrations with another person while that person is present does nothing but shame them and enflame tensions, which is completely the opposite of compassion which is required to empower those people to change their behavior. But couple's therapy done individually and to teach each person tools to find compassion for themselves so they may change their own behavior would be too empowering and thus is not practiced in order to sustain the industry. But this problem is also coupled with a willful ignorance to the biological origination of conditions like anxiety, depression, irritability, sexual dissatisfaction, anger, etc., and the role of hormones, nutrition, and neurological health which can never be addressed only by psychotherapy, since such knowledge would actually produce results and thus supposedly engineer the uselessness of their profession which itself is a fear which originates from the same insufficient estimation of self-worth rather than reality since, you know, there are seven-billion fucking people on this planet and new ones being born every day to abusive environments and thus a bottomless supply of potential clients.

The purpose of these different responses to trauma described by the Karpman model are meant to cause a variety of responses to conditions of life so that organisms have a greater breadth of survival skills for a similar breadth of circumstances (and yes they are not limited to humans only), with some animals being more timid and afraid which helps to keep them out of danger while others are bold sometimes even to the point of endangerment, and the third type observes both to opportunistically copy and support the behavior of the one who is more successful. In terms of survival these adaptations empower a species—but not the individual—for instance those who are more bold and entitled may take ignorant risks to acquire more resources while those who are more timid will better avoid danger. I once watched a video of two wild chickadees being fed where one would take only one seed at a time and quickly fly away to eat on a branch by themselves but the other would happily perch on the man's finger and always tried to take two seeds at a time which could not fit in its mouth. I was struck by how uncannily those two reminded me exactly of myself and my old boyfriend, and how lucky was the bold bird that this man had altruistic and not predatory intentions. While these strategies help a species they do not help us as we are driven by instincts informed by fear and act like animals in the desire to control that fear. So it is instead helpful to understand this biological psychology and its impacts on our person and wellbeing as an individual. While this can seem difficult I find it helpful to summarize the different fractions of personality which originate from abusive triangulation as *"I don't need you"* for the persecutor, *"I need you"* for the victim, and *"you need me"* for the helper.

The shared deficiency with all these fractions of self is that other people are the source of our problems, and as such we entirely orient the focus of our energies toward others while conveniently ignoring or marginalizing our own culpability and, more importantly, ability and responsibility in providing for ourselves not just materially but also emotionally, ambitiously, and our own sense of self-worth. We perceive life through these fractured identities because we have not been taught effective skills with which to otherwise handle life, having been parented by children who also suffer and thus present these insufficient toolsets, and without a means to effectively resolve our situation find ourselves tumbling around and around within it for years and years and years, experience the same kinds of problems time and time again and never finding resolution to hurdles from which we would otherwise learn and grow. Many of us may only have a somewhat fractured sense of self worth which doesn't present such glaring obstacles to satisfaction and fulfillment as those with more severe trauma and instability, but our situation in this case is more dire since we have no compulsory motivation to eventually force us to fix our lives, and there is the danger of living the entirety without ever practicing the kind of self-reflection which may resolve our pain and trauma and the deficiencies of character which permeate our family relationships and ability to parent. A man, for instance, who is married to a beautiful woman, has a great sex life, children, money, and success may still harbor feelings of resentment and frustration which originate from attitudes of either the persecutor or victim personality which in turn limit how emotionally entwined he is with his wife or children, how much he appreciates the success he has found, and the satisfaction which would otherwise be forthcoming from such accomplishment, and thus spends yet more time at work and with colleagues and business associates to avoid the vague and subconscious burden he feels in the presence of his family, then only when his children are fully grown and having families of their own in his loneliness does he finally realize this mistake when it is too late, but which it actually isn't but only seems that way for the very same unresolved pain and trauma which colors our perception of life, and will just continue being distant until the event of his death because of an unwillingness to face our past, our insecurities, and admit vulnerability and responsibility for our actions, as children in truth never really grow up and always desperately love their parents even after decades of traumatic abuse and neglect.

The reason most people do not succeed in breaking out of these psychological constraints is because we also only have the tools which are associated with each, and our efforts to reform or improve are based in fear, insecurity, and self shame where instead compassion and introspection are required to let go of the trauma which caused this, not self will and discipline. Recognizing exactly how and that we are damaged by our pasts and our childhoods through the practice of inventory helps empower us to understand the mechanisms not only by which we were harmed but also how we cause harm to ourselves and to those around us. But to heal these wounds and to restore a wholeness and singular identity of self requires the kind of introspection and reflection that few are willing to do. We all invariably occupy each separate identity at one time or another, with one being predominant, because we do not understand what prevents us from taking care of our own needs. Another psychologist, Dr. Margalis Fjelstad, further developed resolutions to these roles and unlike most mental health therapy provides a way out of these kinds of psychological cages in which she suggested the resolution of our fractured personal identities as described in the Karpman model requires "taking a center position" between all three, as a whole individual, practicing the opposite strengths of each identity's weaknesses. But we cannot identify what those are without also identifying how we have been affected by our environment throughout the course of our lives which created the trauma and fracturing in the first place. Even though most self-help books may impart superficially new information, their effect is really only to make us feel good about ourselves and the way we already are, since we feel powerless to otherwise change our lives wish instead to feel comforted in our powerlessness. But we make mistakes. We hurt others, and we must face our fears and unresolved trauma if we wish to stop the cycles of pain and recrimination which dominate our lives. Those of us who are fearful and weak insist that we bear no responsibly when we hurt others *"because that was not our intention,"* because in truth we feel powerless to avoid hurting others. When we have this mindset it is because our weakness and vulnerability as a child was used in turn as an excuse for our torment. Parents wielding pain and punishment and the threat of expulsion from the bonds of love and the safety of family excused their abuse also with justification through our own actions. In reality our parents acted selfishly, with hatred and anger and resentment and ineptitude at our presence in their lives. It was blindingly painful and horrifyingly sad to us as children who were in truth the ones trying our best. My nieces and nephews who followed their mother around the house while she was on the phone simply wanted to take part in her adult life, to participate in the joy and the novelty of a phone call and the emotional connection of conversation with another adult, to observe how they interact with one another and thus learn by example skills with which they could improve their position as they grew and developed. Instead of love and togetherness they were instead met with furious resentment and malicious wrath, learning instead to temper their curiosity and desire to belong, to fear their own mother and scheme in the future how to avoid her inconsistent and opportunistic volatility. Reluctance to admit to our culpability was learned in such an environment of our upbringing, our subconscious mind still terrified of the ramifications of admitting our faults, my sister unable to find love and compassion for her children because none was shown to her when she was a child.

Specific psychological disorders like dissociation, narcissism, anxiety, histrionic disorder, eating disorders, and anger management problems are all control and coping mechanisms learned or adopted in childhood in order to navigate the turbulent world we think we live in. My experience as a child which led to development of a dissociative personality was one of constant and relentless heartache, but it is natural for the human mind to dissociate from reality as a defensive mechanism in order to cope with such trauma. While this was a defensive behavior it later did not serve me as an adult, and in truth it impaired my ability to make friends and choose quality romantic partners, not to mention the debilitating loneliness and anxiety which came with it. No parent wants such a future for their child, but we certainly parent as if we do, and the only way to prevent that from happening to our own children is to resolve such deep psychological trauma which causes us to literally disconnect from life around us through purposeful introspective therapy such as this practice accomplishes, because this kind of therapy communicates directly with the subconscious, which we cannot do with our conscious mind (that's why it's called the subconscious), and through the act of doing finally find the compassion for ourselves we have so long desired from others.

Any defensiveness of any is a sign that trauma therapy is mandatory. Defensiveness is a protective survival mechanism learned in childhood, but not only does it not serve us as adults—it actively imperils our wellbeing as we become susceptible to the manipulations and control behaviors of others. We do not actually need to justify ourselves to other people, and we all make mistakes and hurt people, even if by accident. Other people also can hurt us for fun or for power and we can become their unwitting pawns because of our own insecurities and reflex to defend our position or interests, believing such people need only be reasoned with or resisted sufficiently to solve our conflicts, never recognizing their very intent is duplicitous and manipulative and thrives on our reactionary engagement.

Our resistance to self-reflection occurs because of those defensive mechanisms of the ego, whose purpose it is to protect us from harm and from threat. But in reality these instinctual reactions to life open us up to exploitation and cause us to be self-defeating as biology works against our own interests to perpetuate our species at our individual expense. In reality we are empowered against the laws of nature by admitting fault and taking responsibility for our mistakes. It protects us both from the influence of other people and the consequences of being hurtful ourselves. But more than that, by practicing trauma therapy we also, happily, learn that we are actually not so reprehensible as we may fear, which is only a byproduct of our experiences meant to engender hyperawareness and self-preservation. The reluctance to delve into the pain of our pasts is a fear that we really are responsible for all the pain and abuse which has come our way, but the reality is that we are all actually quite wonderful, good, and special people and are simply not aware of it, at least up until the point where we started behaving badly as an adult, but for which we can actually learn to find compassion for ourselves and the mistakes we have made, by learning why we did it and thus being empowered in the future to avoid getting in our own way. Suffering great abuses no adult would be expected to endure we instead carry a great burden with us assuming our culpability for something over which we never had control. The justification and excuses used by our abusers to cause our pain and suffering are only our reality so long as we continue to carry them with us, and this practice teaches our subconscious the reality of our self-worth and enlightens us to what tools we developed to survive childhood which no longer serve us as adults, to improve our effectiveness through empowerment. In practicing inventory therapy we learn how old behaviors act in opposition to what we want, then when we are presented with the same situations which would otherwise trigger self-defeating coping mechanism our brain says, *"Oh—last time we did this and it got us the opposite of what we really wanted. Maybe this time we try something different."* Then, no longer motivated from a place of pain and psychological trauma our brains automatically come up with solutions and choices which are rooted in a new sense of self-worth and self-compassion, and in turn compassion also for others where before there was only reactionary resentment and defensiveness, we then act on that new position and have a markedly different experience which in turn generates confidence and ability to better navigate life.

Inventory trauma therapy consists of two parts—the *personal inventory* and the *fear inventory*. I first learned a version of this from the program *Alcoholics Anonymous*, and found it to be one of the most effective psychological therapies I've ever come across and repurposed it through my own experience to this form which is more neutral for those who are not also suffering from substance abuse. In reality this is a therapy for dealing with life and the problems that unresolved pain and trauma cause us. While the original practice is heavily centered around individual accountability and burdened also by poor conceptions of individual worth, I recognized within the framework of human psychology the coping mechanisms developed in childhood which reveal themselves as character problems in adulthood, and as such have been able to author this version of the therapy which more effectively empowers people to more fully and effectively resolve the pain and trauma of our pasts which motivate control and coping mechanisms in the first place. Missing from the original therapy and most mental health therapy is compassion for the origins of anti-social and self-defeating behavior as a separate concept from the actual behavior itself. While it may seem a bit hyperbolic, no person intends to actually commit harm to others, even when they are aware that their actions cause harm. One of the reasons that evil persists in this world is because evil people do not at all think they are evil. Crimes and abuse all originate from coping mechanisms developed instinctually in childhood, and those who wrong others do so because they advance into adulthood still operating from the perspective of individual survival engendered in them during their formative years, knowing no other way in which they may succeed in life, no opportunity to change course, and no skills by which they may resolve and heal the traumatic experiences which motivate their behavior. This practice is empowerment in action, learning through the simple act of writing how to be more effective, self-compassionate, and efficient in our own lives and thus become more satisfied and, ironically, better in control of our lives by letting go of control. Becoming empowered we become calmer, more confident, replacing insecurity with strength having now learned how life really works. It is absolutely the best way that anyone can become an excellent parent, since the role of parent is at its core the preparation of a new generation to effectively navigate life, and there is no more effective way to navigate life than to resolve the personal trauma and pain of our pasts and empower ourselves to meet life on life's terms.

This practice is best performed in a notebook, but any scrap of paper can do and it doesn't really matter how it's executed—the mere act of writing *is* the therapy. Beyond that it requires no extraneous exercise of willpower or supplemental therapy, although it can be helpful to discuss insight and experiences with neutral and helpful third parties if desired. But writing is how we communicate with our subconscious, the very act of putting pen to paper is the conscious mind conversing with the subconscious. Resolution of problems suddenly vanish after sitting and writing about them in this manner and we find ourselves renewed and refreshed almost immediately since our subconscious mind becomes satisfied and empowered by the information this practice illuminates. Total resolution of frustration, regret, and self-defeating practices does require that this practice be completed, however, not just as is convenient for our ego, and while it can be apportioned to a limited amount per day to allow for other uses of our time, failing to prioritize and complete this practice is itself a coping and control mechanism meant to protect our ego at the expense of our best interests. This resistance is very common in people attempting to try this practice, and I have had more than a few people in my life and work actually check out of our relationship simply to avoid the reminder when seeing me that they need to do inventory. Once begun, it nags at the mind because for the first time in perhaps our entire lives real relief from our problems is in sight, and this persistent nagging of the conscience cannot be quieted. The ego prizes above all its control and coping mechanisms because these ostensibly provide ammunition to fight painful experiences of loss, abuse, disappointment, and failure, and hyperawareness of threats to our person in an attempt to *feel* safe.

But therein lies the problem—that such tools of the ego only make us *feel* safe. They do not, in practice, often provide real safety and in fact can make us more vulnerable to the very things which we fear by undermining our relationships and self confidence. They can also prevent us from enjoying life and our successes. A classic example of this is how most of us feel dissatisfied by our achievements even when we do get to realize our hopes and dreams, and after they have occurred are no more happy than we were before, and look pathologically forward to the next great thing and the one after that and the one after that, never actually finding the fulfillment we thought would come from success. Failure to understand our fears can also bring us the very heartache we wish to avoid. As I have often related, my fear of rejection and placing myself in a situations to be rejected caused me to accept partners who were abusive and beneath my standards, because how could I actually love anyone like that in the first place and thus be hurt? But I discovered that I could, in fact, love them deeply and only be more hurt by people who had an increased propensity to hurt in the first place. Family members accustomed to the disappointing dynamics borne out of abusive homes seek the security of control and manipulation in their new families only to find those also infected with the same resentment and pain and frustration of their old families because such problems come from the same control and coping mechanisms born of fear and pain. It is natural to feel resistance to self-reflection because of these instinctual parts of human psychology and are not, in fact, a deficit of character or weakness of human spirit. But they do prevent transcendence to a higher state of consciousness free of the restraints of regret and refusal of responsibility, to understand the purpose of life and suffering and joy which tempers the suffering of mortality and makes even the most mundane parts of life wildly fulfilling. There is a reason why so few on this earth have ever achieved transcendence—unlike religion and society and living on instinct, fear, animosity, and prejudice, achieving enlightenment requires subversion of the ego such as this practice demands, and for some it is too great a barrier to pass. But if you do it promises the kind of spirituality and magnanimity which is told in fantasy and myth, the ability to peer into the cosmos and converse with eternity, which is not some magical ride on the backs of angels into the heavens but something in which we live every day of our lives and entirely perceptible if only we make the space to perceive it.

Subverting the ego may seem like a daunting task, but that is only because we also believe we must use willpower, which in truth is never stronger than the ego. In reality, all that is required for the success of this practice is to sit down and write! The first part of this trauma therapy is the *Personal Inventory*. Fear above all motivates our actions, but to understand fear we must first understand how we act on fear and what form it presents in our lives. This is best accomplished by inventorying our life experiences so that we may become familiar with the events which have shaped our identity and worldview. As I discuss in the chapter on such, this practice is self-care in action, taking the time to sit with our experiences, hard as they may be to revisit, to care for our needs and begin the resolution of our pain and trauma through action, not willpower. When we resist this we fail to practice self-care, choosing instead to ignore that which we find uncomfortable and failing to exercise compassion for ourselves. But this practice also gets really easy the more it is practiced because the mind naturally begins to associate it as a source of joy, relief, and empowerment, and we will within a short period of time find ourselves looking forward to it with as much anticipation as a night in watching a movie or a good, stiff cocktail.

The first column in the personal inventory practice is titled *Resentment*. Here we write the name of a person, institution, idea, obligation, concept, event, problem, trauma, etc. which causes us any kind of consternation. Resentments are poison to life. They make us hate people, fear others, lose sleep, become hurtful, and sabotage our own self-interests. Resentments are typically the things in life which cause us pain and disappointment and, unlike what our mother might have told us, it is okay and natural that we have resentments. Resentment, regret, and remembered trauma is the function of the ego in making us more aware of future potential threats to our personal safety and satisfaction, of the things which can impair our ability to live a successful life and contribute individually to humanity. Becoming aware of and learning from our surroundings attunes us to potential dangers and frustration, the function of instinct in empowering us to protect ourselves by increasing awareness of the horrible kinds of things which can happen to us. But in reality resentments pile up and burden our mind and our soul and make us fearful, frustrated, and anxious as they sit in our mind, taking up valuable space which is better used for enlightened purposes, and an animal operating from a place of so much fear is reactive and ineffective as it makes decisions which are not informed by reality and burdened by instincts for self-preservation. So we begin this practice by identifying exactly those people, institutions, ideas, events, and other experiences in our lives which cause us the suffering and pain and disappointment we have endured, and write them on paper to be inventoried.

Sometimes we might think we have no resentments, such as a wonderful young man I once coached who, after signing up for inventory coaching could not think of a single thing to write in resentments. He stated that he had no resentments because he thought ill of no one in his life, desiring to be a good person mistook the act of forgiveness as an absence of resentment and perceived the word resentment to mean an absence of forgiveness and associated with negativity. I invited him to instead start telling me about his childhood and his personal life and within five minutes he broke down in tears about his struggles with a mentally ill parent who subjected him to unbearable sadness and painful events no child should ever have to endure. Resentment is a bit of a distasteful word, but the function of it here is simply to identify the source from which our suffering originated, be that parents, a friend, church, government, children, God, some jerk at the market, the Universe, life in general, or sometimes even ourselves. Sometimes we have resentments for concepts like obligation, being a parent, being married, being poor, being rich, being a minority. We can have resentments for accidents, breaking bones, surgery, illness, doctors, lawyers, police, clergy, teachers, students. We can have resentments for money, financial institutions, financial obligation, financial losses, thieves, mistakes, or bad business deals. We can resent having to cook or to eat or sleep, or for sadness and misery and even death. In reality we all have a long list of resentment, unless we have literally lived our entire life locked in a basement, in which case we would still have a list which could fill a few pages. *Anything* which causes us to ruminate, stew, obsess, regret, feel sadness, remorse, pain, heartache, frustration, disappointment, disillusionment, anxiety, or fear is, for the purpose of this practice, a resentment.

In the next column under *Cause* we write a brief phrase or phrases about the event and the reason for the resentment. It is helpful to split up repeat offenders into each separate cause, rather than lumping many causes into one resentment. For example, most people's inventory will be dominated by their parents, but we do not write "Dad" and then the entire list of offenses he has ever committed against us. Doing this is entertaining our resentment of him and focusing on his behavior rather than how or even that his behavior affected *us*. Instead, we write "Dad" in the resentment column each time we enter each new offense, which places emphasis on the action of the person rather than the person themselves (or idea or institution), which are not themselves inherently offensive but their actions or choices by which we are hurt. If a repeat offender should offend after we have already done inventory on our experiences with them, we make a new entry to understand and heal the fresh frustration. This is a *practice*, meant to be done repeatedly and often, a tool with which to improve our life and experience. At the outset there is a bulk of writing and entry which may take up much of our time, but it can in truth be completed in less than a week or two with commitment and dedication and has enlightenment ever come so quickly or effortlessly to any human on this earth? At the outset I recognized and so desired the relief this practice would bring that I did not stop writing except to sleep and work until I was done. The tools this practice teaches us then empowers us in our lives moving forward, and the insight helps us better navigate life, also then reducing (but by no means eliminating) the occurrence of such encounters in the first place, but which also empowers us to handle and resolve those which do occur more effectively and satisfactorily, since we can never actually control life or prevent bad things from happening. *Cause* is as simple as the simple fact that something happened. For instance if our bank charged us an exorbitant and exploitive amount of money for an overdraft, or the I.R.S. forcibly collected a reassessment of taxes from our bank account during the coronavirus outbreak four years after we filed them and we could hardly afford rent that month. Parents or children often do things that hurt us, so in addition to the action they took which was the source of the problem we also can write other causes which are related to the event and how it affected our life. For instance, if a child does something like throw tantrums or refuses to eat at the dinner table and it reminds us of our own experience as a child in which we subject to abuse ostensibly for doing the very same thing, we can write under *cause* its connection to our past and the vulnerability, frustration, and even hatred it makes us feel. If a boss or coworker undermines our performance at work, in addition to their action we can also write that it threatens our sense of self-worth and accomplishment, or maybe even our ability to earn money and feel secure in our employment.

We typically also in our experiences with pain, frustration, and disappointment attempt to minimize our experience by considering such events as *maybe not that bad* or *perhaps we overreacted or are being too sensitive or unreasonable*, and as such fail to properly recognize the extent to which such events cause us harm. If a wife berates us and our attitude about something there may be an unconscious instinct to tough it out, but which ignores how we are being truly affected by such treatment at the hands of someone we love and, being personally dishonest out of a sense of misplaced machismo or incorrect definition of personal strength, and never actually resolve the problem since we actively choose to minimize our experience. Accurately inventorying exactly what caused the harm done to us better helps us understand why and how we are hurt by life, where typically we choose to ignore or move on from such events in hope of more positive experiences in the future, which is nice in concept but in practice is actually avoidance and neglect of our own wellbeing and self-compassion, having previously no tools with which to address such experiences other than just ignoring them.

Emotions also go in the cause column, though most of us misunderstand that we cannot actually control our emotions, no matter how hard we try or wish to do so. We very well can control how we act *in response* to emotions, but over emotions themselves we have no control. Many mothers and fathers will feel hatred of their children, even the littlest, cutest infants when they bite, knock their skull against yours, pull our hair, spit up on our nice clothes, cry at all hours of the night or in public or on an airplane and then some asshole cusses us out for it. It's perfectly fine to feel our feelings in those moments. Life is difficult, and parenting is difficult, and it's okay and expected to feel badly in response to inconvenient, painful, or frustrating events. There is never anything wrong with how we feel, even to hate our children in the moments they cause us pain and frustration. Feeling this way means we are a human with biological instincts to help guide us through life and does not at all mean we do not actually love our children. Many of us feel ashamed of feelings like jealousy, helplessness, fear, spite, sexual desire, and control and try to hide or ignore those feelings which in turn gives them greater power over us

Personal Inventory

Resentment	Cause	Part(s) Hurt	My Part	Character Weaknesses
a person, idea, institution, event, obligation, problem, limitation, trauma, etc.	a brief description of every and all possible causes	(self-esteem, pride, emotional security, financial security, personal relations, sex relations, ambitions)	our role in contributing or continuing to contribute	various character weaknesses revealed by the resentment

Samples

Resentment	Cause	Part(s) Hurt	My Part	Character Weaknesses
Dad	did not accept me when I came out.	self-esteem pride emotional security personal relations	I lied about being straight, chose to come out, continue to hold resentment against him	fearful resentful unforgiving timid cowardly dishonest self-pity overly-serious self-hatred shame unrealistic
being sick	I hate being sick, it's been years since I've been healthy and I can't figure out how to get well. reduces my options for romance and activities. taught as a child that being ill is bad. microbes like parasites and viruses are everywhere and hard to resolve	self-esteem pride emotional security personal relations sex relations ambitions	dieted and starved myself for years, ate what I thought was healthy but wasn't, took bad medications and supplements. now I'm taking care of myself properly though	insecure fearful resentful overly-serious self-pity self-hatred shame unrealistic delusional judgemental harsh
work	not getting paid what I'm worth. boss is a jerk. I have to work to earn money. boring.	self-esteem pride financial security ambitions	took this job in the first place. not finding something new. trying to appease an unreasonable boss.	resentful ungrateful overly-serious unrealistic servile fake timid entitled materialistic

and motivates destructive behaviors as we try to control and manipulate our environment. Instead it is how we act on feelings that is the problem and what actually brings us the recrimination, pain, loss, frustration, and other problems or saves us from them, and having compassion for how we feel and what we want by writing it under the *cause* column can actually improve our effectiveness and behavior and minimize harm and pain to ourselves and others by acknowledging our feelings and desires. As I discuss in my other book, feelings are also hormones such as cortisol and adrenaline in order to heighten our perception and response to threats to our person, be they from wild animals or the wild animal in diapers who sinks their surprisingly sharp, brand new teeth into the fat rolls of our stomach or the tender nipple of our breast. Of course we will feel bad when this happens. Inventorying how it made us feel in addition to the actual mundane details of the event itself is written under *cause* so that we may fully understand the effect our experiences have upon our lives.

During the span of a human life we require certain things in order to live a successful, happy, and fulfilled life and frankly to also avoid dying. These are basic necessities such as food, shelter, clothes, companionship, safety, love both platonic and erotic, community, opportunity, accomplishment, and perhaps even children. Whenever unpleasant or painful things happen to us (the things we write under *cause* and *resentment*) they are painful because they endanger any one of these needs which are required for life. If, as a child, a parent threatened to withhold dinner, we fell apart and became hysterical because as children we literally cannot provide food for ourselves. This is one of the reasons why threatening children is so absolutely traumatic for us and in so doing actively destroys our bond with parents. Instead of threatening we can say—*this is what we are having for dinner and you can eat it or go hungry*. By no means does this allow a child to misbehave without consequences, but it invites the child to be part of the family and avoids impairing their development because we are still providing them food and not threatening their very life by withholding it, and also allowing them the autonomy to choose whether they will participate with the family or go hungry (and the consequences of going hungry are too great for them to insist very much). When terrible things happen like losing a job or being collected on by the I.R.S. when we don't have any money to spare our ability to provide food, shelter, clothing, medicine, and even for companionship or social opportunity is suddenly impaired. Money can also be a shallow pursuit which is identified with ego, pride, self-esteem, and ambition, but the threat against our very ability to not die from hunger or want of shelter is a very real and primal need for sustenance and our reaction to such frightening and painful events of financial loss or insufficiency, even if only imagined but very much when it is real is part of the warning system which our biological psychology means to communicate and enlighten us to threats to our very survival and thus the reason for intensity of pain and frustration which accompanies it. If instead we were animals which smiled under adversity and shrugged our shoulders at loss and hardship we would not have survived the last several millions of years of our evolution. The purpose of pain is to make us aware of danger. Though we dislike pain, without it we would not be here, which is the entire reason it is uncomfortable and unbearable, to cause awareness of the limitations to our existence and thus to stay as clear of them as we are able.

But our past experiences of pain can weigh heavily upon the mind and soul, and as such we can become mired in overly pessimistic, negative, resentful episodes of our past. This also serves the purpose of motivating reflection and hopefully understanding of the event, since if we do not learn from our past we are far more likely to reencounter or succumb to the very same kinds of dangers. But, having ineffective skills with which to practice introspection these events are never resolved psychologically since no satisfying understanding of them is ever reached. We are abused because we deserved it. We were attacked because we didn't see it coming. We were taken advantage of because all people are terrible and dishonest. None of these are true, and so the event persists in our psyche until we finally learn the true nature of reality and are thus actually empowered. Finally learning from our experience as this practice facilitates then brings us confidence to meet the same or similar encounters in the future now armed with tools which actually help us to cope with them effectively, or even to confidently avoid them altogether now that we understand why or how they actually occur. But this still does not change the fact that we are hurt and that many times we cannot do anything to prevent pain and disappointment, and so we must identify how we are hurt if we at all expect to be able to come to terms with that pain. So, under the next column titled *Part(s) Hurt* we identify the parts of self which are damaged by these events and resentments. These parts are the elements which make up our identity as a person and the construction of self which, when damaged, cause the pain and suffering we experience. But these parts of self are not arbitrary, chosen from our own conceptions because we do not get to decide the parameters of life. These instead are chosen from a list of options which categorize the various human needs we have: *self-esteem, pride, emotional security, financial security, personal relations, sex relations, and ambitions*. Choosing any or all of these parts of self affected by the experience we write them down in this column. This column helps us identify exactly how we are affected by the events and encounters in our lives which in turn establishes compassion for our mortality and experiences rather than seeking to deny them.

Clues to what we write in each column lie in what we wrote in the one which preceded it. So, if determining what part of self was damaged by a particular event seems difficult we can revisit our entry in the preceding column to better identify those parts. For example, the I.R.S. taking our money definitely affects our financial security. But it may also affect our pride and self esteem, or our ambitions if we were planning on paying last years taxes with that money or buying a new washer and dryer. Or if a romantic partner says we are fat that might affect our sexual relations, personal relations, and emotional security since they have proven themselves to be an adversary and more concerned with their selfish desires than our wellbeing. If friends talk about us behind our back that could affect our personal relations and emotional security, since their presence in our lives provided us with a group with which to associate which now appears in jeopardy. If a husband or wife cheats on us that could damage our pride and self-esteem (which can sometimes be the same thing but I consider pride as being more about personal accomplishment whereas self-esteem being inherent worth as an individual).

Sometimes we are unaware of which parts are hurt. For instance, many people try to compensate for past events which made them feel insecure about themselves or their value as a person by adopting confidence as a way to cope with the pain and insecurity, and so will not choose pride or self-esteem because they now view themselves as impervious to such disappointment. But this very act of adopting confidence is a defensive mechanism which shows deep wounds to pride and self esteem (and is actually arrogance, not confidence, since confidence accepts weaknesses and arrogance denies them), and of course we are wounded in such ways since none of us is completely unfeeling. Again, if identifying the parts of self which are hurt seems difficult, revisiting our entry in the column before can identify which parts of ourselves have been damaged. Even though we only write from a limited list of options this column is extremely important because we must admit that we have even been hurt in the first place in order to find compassion for our experiences. We can hardly expect to be relieved of our burdens when we pretend they don't exist in the first place, which is why obstinate adults who refuse to acknowledge our painful pasts accelerate into senility and antagonism in old age as our waning lifeline and fear of death exaggerates the role of the ego in trying to protect us from the pain and disappointment of life. The things identified in *parts hurt* are those we fail to realize when unpleasant things happen to us and we in turn ruminate about how mean or cruel or what an asshole other people are for hurting us or how our loss or disappointment will cause us other problems and inconveniences, in so doing fail to actually find compassion for ourselves by focusing on other people or things we cannot control rather than our own experience and the pain we experience. We often feel empowered by our anger, our pain and resentment, but as the saying goes—resentment is like drinking poison and waiting for the other person to die. Resentment is the manifestation of fear, and fear causes immense amounts of suffering, unrest, and further pain of which we can only be rid by facing our past and honoring our experiences through the kind of self-reflection and self-compassion realized through the *parts hurt* column.

Most of our problems as a human being come simply from being deluded to our ability to control life and how we can be effective as a mortal animal, which is why when bad things happen to us we instinctually focus on the source of our troubles rather than the effect they have on our lives. The first three columns of the personal inventory are meant to illuminate for us the parts of life over which we actually have *no* control. Because life can be so painful and so frustrating we adapt to it by trying to assert control over many parts of it, and being powerless try to make ourselves feel better by adopting beliefs, attitudes, and coping mechanisms which delude us into a sense of control. This is why we do things like believe in religion, because the fear of things like death is so profound and so absolute that we can spend most of our life, waking and otherwise, obsessed and frightened of something which can be so overwhelming and terrifying, but though we have no actual control over it participate in complicated and time consuming behaviors and commitments which help distract us from fear, even sacrificing family relationships, marriages, friendships, opportunity, and material resources. Trying to control things we cannot control not only makes us ineffective in our lives, it also wastes precious emotional, physical, and spiritual energy, and no wonder that parents burdened with the trauma of their own childhoods attempting to parent brand new children while also struggling with jobs and relationships and mortality fall apart and lose their shit when things don't go well, or even have absolute nervous breakdowns or become alcoholic or completely abandon their responsibility. This practice is a worksheet which teaches us how we can narrow, empower, and embolden our efforts to actually affect our own lives, by first identifying the things which we cannot control in the first place and thus redirecting our energies to those we can. As such, the last two columns instead identify those things we can actually control—which when writing down empowers our subconscious by illuminating for it the limited scope of what we actually can affect in our own lives and thus making our energies more effective while also relieving us of the responsibly for such impossible things as *death*. The inventory practice is in fact *The Serenity Prayer* in action: "God, grant me the serenity to accept the things I cannot change, courage to change the things I can, and wisdom to know the difference." It shows us on paper what we can control and what we cannot control and thus empowers us to be more effective in our lives, but because writing communicates with our subconscious it more importantly empowers and changes our psyche and heals unresolved pain and trauma in ways we might never have thought possible.

The last two columns are meant to show how we affect our own experience and how we are effective in our lives rather than how our lives are effected. Knowing how the events of our lives have shaped us helps us to finally find resolution and wholeness, but knowing how we actually exert power and control in our lives helps us to actually affect change. Having previously no real skills to be effective we instead focused our efforts on things we cannot really control anyway, such as wether we get sick and die, how much money we have, or whether other people love us or not. Learning from this practice the ways in which we are actually effective firstly relieves us of the burden of controlling things we cannot control (everything in the first three columns). This in turn frees up enormous amounts of time and energy which can be applied to areas in which we are actually effective. If, for instance, we are someone who spends a great deal of time worried about and trying to prevent a partner from cheating, leaving us, looking at porn, or forcing them to behave in ways which demonstrate their commitment to us which in truth turns a relationship from something exciting and transcendent into a metaphorical prison we instead learn to accept through this practice the reality that we cannot actually control whether our partner would choose to leave or cheat on us. They are entirely an autonomous individual, and if they want to cheat or leave, they will. In fact, we actively increase that possibility by acting on control behaviors because through our own actions we engender resentment and animosity instead of love and acceptance. No longer feeling obligated to control another person since the inventory therapy helps make us aware of our responsibilities, all that time and emotional energy spent fighting and despising each other is suddenly freed to be used in the pursuit of anything else. Turn it into time having fun, or pursuing healthy interests and hobbies, or increasing our effectiveness in parenting. The last two columns are the most empowering, because they help us identify the ways in which we are actually effective in our lives and thus help us stop wasting time and energy trying to bend life to our will, which can never be done anyway.

As such, under the fourth column, *My Part*, we list our actions which we took which contributed to the resentment or *continue* to contribute to it. Not every event included our actions, especially those which happened to us as children. Emotions are also not our part—many times I will see people write things in *my part* such as *I let them make me angry*, or *I choose to be sad*. This is not how life works, nor our emotions, which are, you will remember, hormones. We want to believe we have power over our emotions because that means we are empowered to choose those we feel. But in reality this is impossible. We cannot will our hormones to behave, and those who try to control their emotions often tend to be those who are most emotionally volatile, and our lack of control makes us try to take ownership for emotions and the lack of control which is frightening. We do not choose to be in pain when someone hurts us. Insults make us feel shame, theft or betrayal make us feel angry, disruption to our plans and ambitions make us feel frustrated or disappointed. Abandonment causes loneliness and loss causes sadness and despair. Feelings are entirely not within the scope of the *my part* column and instead go under *cause*. *My part* is always actions—*I shouted at them, I stole that item, I hit them, I cheated, I lied, I withheld affection, I demanded sex, I harassed her, I hid the last piece of cake, I drove drunk, I talked behind their back, was defensive, reacted poorly, ducked my responsibility, antagonized him, wrote that nasty email, said those hurtful things, flirted with that handsome coworker, left my wife*, or *made that purchase, didn't monitor my bank account* or, *didn't pay my taxes*.

But *my part* is never a criticism of ourselves nor judgment of our value as a person. In fact, many things we write under *my part* can also be positive actions—*I stood up for them, I chose to have children, I married her, I didn't cheat, I asked for a raise, I accepted this job, woke up early, went on that flight, or paid for dinner*. It wasn't until I wrote this book and inventoried my loss of Dudley at ten years old that I realized I hadn't actually played a role in his misery as I have thought for the last thirty years of my life, and I in fact tried to help him, nor that he also probably went to a really good home where he might have been happy for the rest of his life, which I had never even considered. Our propensity for self-criticism in response to our mistakes and actions is part of the reason why we avoid doing introspective therapy such as this, but which also condemns us to suffer even when we needn't, and originates also from the opportunistic exploitation of our mistakes by parents, friends, bosses, or romantic partners who characterize our value as a person in order to manipulate and coerce us into doing what they want, and the fear of validating the very excuses used to justify our abuse we then resist analyzing our own behavior in fear of validating our abusers, but what in reality is never valid and has nothing to do with our inherent self-worth but instead the desire to exert control over our environment. While many of our actions written in my part may be offenses against others and may indeed have caused harm, the true function of this column is to help our subconscious mind identify exactly the ways in which we affect our own life experience in opposition to those things we we cannot control which affect it. When a boss comes into our office and yells at us, that experience is not something we do to affect our own life. That is why it goes under *cause*. But we do in turn affect our experience in how we choose to react or respond to our boss, or if we did precede the event by stealing from them or by not showing up for work. Losing an account is not something we choose and so goes into *cause*, but talking bad about a client *is* something we did. Having employees quit on us is something that goes in *cause* but refusing to pay them well or using our position of authority to abuse them is *my part*. Being hit by a husband is not something we can control but choosing to stay in the relationship is. Sometimes we make choices which are good but which nonetheless bring us unpleasant experiences, such as confess to a lie, but inventorying our experience helps us feel more empowered, not less, understanding how we can take ownership for our own wellbeing. The sole purpose of *my part* is simply a sober analysis of how we are able to affect our own experiences in opposition to those things which affect us which have heretofore occupied a disproportionate amount of our time and energy, and by so doing empower our brain to narrow its focus and that of our energy and efforts and become more effective and efficient in how we live our lives and deal with our problems.

One of the most common coping mechanisms we have which belongs in *my part* that many fail to recognize because it is so instinctual is the act of mind reading. Trying to anticipate what others are or will be feeling, thinking, or their reactions is a very common defensive and control mechanism developed in response to unpredictable parents or especially volatile environments (for instance being bullied). It is part of the trauma which prevents us from getting to know ourselves and feeling calm and satisfied by life because we are always fixated on others in anticipation of their behavior, rather than our own. Fearing reprisal, conflict, rejection, animosity, or humiliation we try to divine the very inner thoughts of others so that we might in turn protect ourselves. Our only job in life is to show up for opportunity and do our best. We are not responsible for outcomes, only our behavior, and we certainly cannot control the behavior of others which is the entire point of this coping mechanism, thinking that if we can anticipate it we can then do something about it. But that is not our job, nor within our control. Mind reading is not something we can actually do, and it often works against our best interests, as a control mechanism is based on negative expectations and will prejudice our perception of others, especially our spouses, siblings, and children, and then we react negatively to conflict or criticism as if justified by supposedly having anticipated it. This is a symptom of taking life way too seriously, deeply rooted insecurity borne from a volatile childhood in which we were often abused or neglected. But the act of mind reading is a control mechanism which attempts to prevent unpleasant experiences and thus goes in *my part* if it is relevant for each particular resentment.

Often we are too cerebral when trying to identify *my part*, because we are raised to be hyperaware and manipulative to avoid encountering heartache we tend to overthink and look far into things to try to protect ourselves. *My part* is often very simple choices such as choosing to take part such as in a marriage, a date, or even continuing to be part of a relationship. To get pregnant and have kids. To put them in school or football. To make dinner. To not make dinner. To withhold truth. Often *my part* is also the act of *not* doing something, like failing to care for ourselves, stand up for our needs, or to even simply failing to eat enough and stay ahead of our blood sugar. *My part* is the most important section of the personal inventory and many people end up using the inventory to unconsciously entertain self-pity and will only identify negative behaviors in *my part* and entirely fail to identify positive behaviors which then leads to a constantly negative experience and thus avoidance of the inventory therapy. It is required to be entirely self honest and identify all the ways in which we take part in our experiences, not only those which are more complex and certainly not limited only to those which are "bad," and remembering the difference between *cause* and *my part*, for instance falling in love is an emotion and not, in fact, under our control and thus goes under cause, but choosing to be in a relationship with someone whom we are in love (or pursue them, or stalk them, etc.) belongs under *my part*.

When we are children, we play no role in *my part*, being entirely incapable of providing the things for ourselves which are required to survive life we then do not bear responsibly for our actions. Because our parents are the ones who provide for us on whom we are solely and wholly and utterly dependent they are in fact the originators of the choices and actions we take as children. I have seen many grown men and women break down when finally realizing when asked what part they played in their abuse coming up with the answer *"none,"* having lived their entire lives believing at least on a subconscious level that they somehow invited or participated in the abuse which brought them so much unbearable pain and anguish. In some cases our part played in the events of our childhood may be continuing to hold on to the resentment somehow, such as how I continued to resent my father for only ever coming to one-half of one of my swim meets. Being especially self-honest during *my part* is very important so that we can actually enlighten ourselves to the reality of our own existence and effectiveness in our own lives. Many of us prefer not to acknowledge the mistakes or wrongs we have committed, nor our powerless over certain things, and sometimes we are also dishonest about our positive actions and effectiveness as well as that which is unhelpful. I once tried to assist someone who was a total kleptomaniac and stole from many businesses over a span of many years. When we got to *my part* and began inventorying everything he stole he began to grow increasingly uncomfortable with the practice and eventually quit it altogether. His instinctual reaction to ignore and avoid consequences appeared to him (his ego) perhaps as protecting his own wellbeing from the consequences of his actions, but in reality he simply continued being insecure and paranoid about his thievery and the potential consequences which might result—not only the retribution of his victims but also his own opinion of himself and relationships with friends, family, or love interests or employers. The refusal to acknowledge his part also demonstrated a lack of compassion for *why* he did it in the first place, which was to engineer a sense of self-worth and excitement while suffering through a heartbreakingly neglectful and despairing childhood. Refusal to acknowledge his part was also refusal to acknowledge the pain he went through, and he descended once again into serious substance abuse in order to escape this unbearable burden. The reality was that *none* of his thievery was very egregious. AT ALL. It was all stupid stuff like chapsticks from *Hot Topic* or T-shirts from the *Gap* or used jewelry from second hand shops. Making reparations for his crimes would not have even landed him a sideways look, let alone legal consequences, especially because he had been a minor, but would have relieved him of an unbearable amount of personal suffering due to his inaccurate estimate of his own self-worth and value as a person, which would have been resolved completely by bravely finishing the inventory and being totally self-honest in the inventory of his actions under *my part*. In truth he was more afraid of facing his own existential fears about his self-worth and value as a person than the external consequences of his actions, afraid that admitting to his thievery would prove him to be the terrible person he feared he might be rather than the delightful and handsome young man I knew him to be, to which he is still ignorant and fearful. Likewise, I was terrified to account for my own part in my life and the harms I had committed against others, the list of which in my mind seemed long and egregious and justified the many abuses I suffered from my family, community, and religious institutions. In reality I only had to apologize for a handful of arguments and mostly telling people to fuck off, LOL, and to pay some back taxes. For most of us, our mistakes are compounded by the psychological harm of abusive and opportunistic parents or life experiences which have convinced us that we are the sum of our weaknesses and thus deserving of the cruel and callous abuse we suffered in the first place. The only way to liberate ourselves from this burden is to honestly identify *my part* when practicing the inventory, even when our ego demands otherwise. Practicing *my part* is the act of showing compassion for ourselves and thus building stores of it which we in turn can share with others.

In the last column, *Character Weakness* we list character traits which we possess which motivate our actions and choices listed under *my part*. This too is not a judgment of our character or value as a person, which is itself simply the residue of shame and self-hatred at the hands of abusive and neglectful people in our lives, but instead a way to identify exactly how the events of our past have caused damage to us as a person which thus cause us to adopt coping mechanisms which we use to survive life. My favorite example to use in the illustration of this reality are pathological liars, since everyone hates liars. But the talent of lying is actually an instinctual coping mechanism adopted to survive childhood when parents are especially and opportunistically vindictive, using any mistake no matter how trivial as an excuse to abuse and who use the child as an outlet for their overflowing anger and hatred. We might have naturally adopted lying and dishonesty as a way to avoid this heinous abuse just to survive our own childhood. Since childhood is the time which also forms our personal identity and survival strategies to use in adulthood, a child from such a home erroneously (and unconsciously) believes that lying is the only effective life tool to avoid pain and heartache and even death. But of course, lying in adulthood more often causes us immense amounts of stress and isolation as we deal with mistakes and insecurities through dishonesty, and build for ourselves unnecessary consequences and complicated, unmanageable lives.

A recent example of the unnecessary use of dishonesty concerns the political climate of this era, when majority leaders concocted ridiculous justifications for refusing to consider an oppositional nominee for the Supreme Court, where their position as the party in power would have been more than sufficient justification and were later presented with events which exposed their poorly disguised deceit, putting themselves in a completely unnecessary situation simply because of the their self-hatred and absence of self-compassion. Liars go out of their way to cause themselves more problems because true power in life comes from taking responsibility for our behavior. Shirking responsibility instead delegates that power to fate and happenstance. But because the identity of those who are dishonest is also accompanied by deeply held insecurities of self-worth and the perception that our very dishonesty further devalues it we become controlled by our fears and insecurities which actively work to undermine our personal power and effectiveness. Partners who lie about cheating could just be single and slutty and have a great time and build multiple beneficial friendships and intimate relationships which value independence and exploration, but acting instead on insecurities deprive themselves of what they need or want in life unnecessarily while also hurting others in the process. Thieving can originate from childhood fears either of being deprived that which is necessary to survive life such as food and clothing or as a means to achieve attention and self-worth because of a neglectful childhood short on love and emotional security.

Most debilitatingly, coping mechanisms such as fear and insecurity which result from very traumatic experiences of assault, rejection, abuse, exploitation, etc., serve to make us hyperaware of more potential threats to our person, since it is through such threats that our very ability to survive life can be subverted. But then as an adult we spend every waking minute fearing other people and repeat the trauma of our past, peering around every proverbial corner with anxiety, avoid opportunities for personal and professional advancement, or even preemptively destroy romantic affairs even when we have never again actually experienced the things of which we are afraid. Many adults unconsciously react to fears and insecurities surrounding money and material wealth and its influence on our social status by buying everything we can with our money, because the instinct to prove that we are financially secure causes us to accumulate tangible evidence to prove it, but which thus causes the very financial insecurity of which we are afraid and subverts monetary frugality and responsibility which would actually provide us the stability we crave, living paycheck to paycheck and constantly finding ourselves in the red even when we have actually made more than sufficient income to thrive. Other coping mechanisms such as perfectionism also disrupt our lives by commandeering our minds and preventing satisfaction from our accomplishments even when we are very successful, never actually being satisfied and always believing we need more and more to justify our self-worth which as a child was characterized by what we did, not who we are. Laziness is a preemptive coping mechanism to avoid perfectionist failure and thus the belief that we are incapable as a human being because we cannot be perfect which was probably communicated to us by parents who anticipated failure and took it upon themselves to do the things we needed to be allowed to do as children. Being vain, narcissistic, or having self-pity is the mind's attempt to provide a sense of self-worth which was not forthcoming from our environment as children. Timidity and shyness is an attempt to cope with fears of rejection by avoiding attention in the first place. Being defensive or confrontational is a sense that we must protect ourselves from opportunistic devaluations of our worth as a person which probably occurred in our childhood from parents who insulted and humiliated us, and so on and so on.

Sometimes the *character weaknesses* we identify are only those which support self-pity which, remember, is a replacement for love and self-worth which is absent from our environment, and as such indulge our own selfish desire to hold others responsible for behavior that is in fact our own. As in *my part*, it is required that we be thorough and completely self-honest when evaluating our character weaknesses. Once when helping someone whose family performed an intervention to address their substance abuse, in addition to character weaknesses of combativeness, insecurity, poor self-worth, fearfulness, etc., the person failed to recognize *selfishness* even though selfishness is the very hallmark of alcoholic and addictive behavior, focusing only on the inconvenience of being sent to rehab rather than the effect of their reckless and destructive use of drugs and alcohol on others (though they had properly identified *my part*). Everything written under *character weakness* is a coping mechanism devised in childhood to survive or mitigate pain and disappointment. But an adult should be capable of supporting ourselves emotionally and materially, as such these behaviors no longer serve us since we are no longer dependent on parents to fulfill our needs, and because our identity was formed in childhood and because we were not given skills to care for ourselves in healthier and more effective ways we are unaware of how these coping mechanisms *prevent* fulfillment of our needs as an adult. This is resolved by identifying them under *character weakness*, which then makes our subconscious aware of them which in turn allows us the space to act differently when presented by the same stimuli which trigger our reactions and emotions.

There are no wrong answers in any of these columns, and what should be written down should be relevant to our own experience, but there is also no limit on how many character weaknesses can be written down. Many of my own entires have more words in the character weakness lists than the rest of the entry. The unwillingness to identify character weaknesses is itself a character weakness of being *overly-serious*. It's not actually a big deal that we are liars or cheats or vain or sad or egoistic. These are common failings of humanity which make us who we are, coping mechanisms which helped us survive as children, and doing inventory therapy can empower us with a sense of humor to our weaknesses rather than being controlled by them. Before doing this practice I would have become angry if anyone suggested that I wasn't nice. I was expected to be nice, raised as a nice person, and so I thought I was nice. The reality was that I was not nice at all. To the point of being comical. Recognizing this coping mechanism as a strategy to survive abusive and opportunistic people gave me compassion for myself and my experiences, and to laugh at just how deluded I was in my personal identity and how mean I actually was. Becoming unconsciously aware of our character weaknesses as this practice accomplishes in turn causes us to naturally adopt the opposite strengths. Becoming aware that we are dishonest, fearful, controlling, or possessed of other coping mechanisms which actually work against our best interests causes the subconscious mind to instead choose new behaviors and new strategies when we are faced with those situations, people, or insecurities which triggered our coping mechanisms, acting on these new behaviors we then find ourselves more successful in our efforts which in turn cements our new character strengths the more we encounter success and the more aware we become of our true effectiveness in our own lives.

Most of us spend much of our time and emotional energy trying to justify our existence and experiences to ourselves and to other people in our lives. But in reality we do not need to justify our experience. We only feel the need to do this because we in turn do not have compassion for ourselves and the things which happen to us. Oppositely we might also minimize what has happened to us in an attempt to cope. In the first three columns we see exactly how we have been effected by our experiences, and properly recognizing the weight and impact by which they have shaped our lives. Completing this practice then removes the need or reflex to justify ourselves to other people which in turn gives us the power of real confidence. Acknowledging how or even that we were hurt in turn instills a true sense of self-worth, since we are now evaluating how our self-worth was damaged by our past. If we don't value something we don't care what happens to it. That's exactly what happens when we try to ignore our pasts and "move on" from unpleasant experiences, and this practice actively reverses our self-neglect, valuing ourselves and thus spending time assessing damage and in the process learning self-compassion. Because of our tendency to minimize our own experiences we sometimes don't even think to inventory common life events or problems because they are so broad, not immediately consuming, or even seemingly trivial or common, and even those like myself who use this practice on a daily basis may not even consider that we can and should inventory things like hating the end of a weekend and an approaching Monday, the end of a vacation, fear of missing out, physical injury, being an alcoholic or addict, paying taxes, being married, getting old, bearing children, impotence, authoritarianism, going for a job interview, self-reliance, math, needing an education, having to cook food, baking, mortality, needing friends, that murder exists or that nature seems cruel, politics, or having our enthusiasm deflated when we stubbed our toe when we were feeling really good before that happened, or any other general life theme, and doing so can help us understand why our reaction to these problems causes us distress and disappointment and thus resolve its influence over our lives. Even the very desire for seeming good and healthy things like success or making progress in business, profession, or personal life can be and usually is in truth desire for control over life and thus the illusory comfort such control imparts, for which inventory therapy can illuminate our subconscious coping mechanisms and free us of the limitations these inauthentic needs impose upon our experience and effectiveness.

Examples of Character Weakness

selfish	*manipulative*	*envious*	*submissive*
contempt	*distrusting*	*vindictive*	*self-centered*
dishonest	*overly-trusting*	*hubris*	*harsh*
defensive	*overly-serious*	*greedy*	*arrogant*
unrealistic	*combative*	*insincere*	*insensitive*
irresponsible	*anxious*	*deceitful*	*undisciplined*
self-pity	*frustrated*	*impatient*	*rage*
short-tempered	*pessimistic*	*mean*	*gullible*
fearful	*liar*	*sycophant*	*procrastination*
controlling	*unkind*	*coward*	*bigoted*
apathetic	*rude*	*jealous*	*perfectionist*
hypocrite	*boastful*	*unreliable*	*immoral*
histrionic	*shy*	*cruel*	*self-righteous*
intolerant	*conceited*	*miserly*	*posessive*
reckless	*abusive*	*egoistic*	*spiteful*
fake	*judgemental*	*irritable*	*willful*
narrow-minded	*petty*	*braggart*	*cheater*
uncaring	*dogmatic*	*gossiping*	*conniving*
critical	*thieving*	*slothful*	*servile*
self-critical	*prejudiced*	*inconsistent*	*covetous*
codependent	*confrontational*	*unforgiving*	*violent*
vain	*entitled*	*cynical*	*naive*
envy	*boorish*	*low self-worth*	*restless*
uptight	*messy*	*shallow*	*prudish*
compulsive	*materialistic*	*self-defeating*	*demanding*
quarrelsome	*slovenly*	*callous*	*withdrawn*
agoraphobic	*ignorant*	*dissociative*	*distracted*
paranoid	*nosy*	*needy*	*stubborn*
discontent	*isolating*	*avoidant*	*disorganized*
bossy	*inescure*	*ungrateful*	*pretentious*
shame	*resentful*	*mind-reading*	*careless*
untrustworthy	*narcissistic*	*lazy*	*disloyal*

The beauty of this therapy is that healing comes simply from the act of writing, and does not otherwise require much effort beyond the actual act of sitting down and spending time in inventory. Trying to bend our life and control emotions is the opposite of what we do in this therapy. Writing is the only thing which must be accomplished, and the results will reveal themselves automatically after doing so. When our subconscious is made aware of the real parameters of our lives—what we actually control and not what we have previously believed, our mind automatically tries new behaviors based on the new information we have learned. Becoming aware that we punish and harass our children not because they are bad but because their presence triggers certain insecurities, the next time they hit someone or cry at the dinner table our subconscious, now aware of our coping mechanisms and how they compound our problems rather than relieve them thinks, "*oh, last time we did [this] and it actually made the problem worse. Maybe let's try something new—*" and we instinctually try new behaviors and approaches. Even if these new approaches don't work immediately, our awareness enabled by the therapy facilitates experimentation informed by experience, so we begin to become more effective than we used to be, being able to use information from our environment to improve our effectiveness rather than ignoring it. The successes we begin to experience then engenders confidence and feelings of empowerment, because we are actually able to control our life in the ways we have always desired but were unable. It requires no willpower or change in mindset and attitude, which also change simply through the act of writing. We do need to be willing to give up our coping mechanisms, but this also happens intuitively as we continue practicing and become more and more aware of how little they actually profit us. The only thing required for the success of the therapy is the act of doing it. *Resistance or unwillingness to practicing inventory therapy should itself be inventoried!* This practice does not require self-discipline. It requires self-compassion. Believing we must be disciplined to practice is the opposite of self-compassion, doing it because we have to, not because we *can*, and understanding why we resent or resist doing the practice instead of trying to make ourselves do it replaces ideas of poor self-worth with the compassion found through making an entry, and can help us get over emotional and mental hurdles to practice. Nearly always when working with alcoholics or addicts they fail to realize that they can and should inventory a resentment for having the disease in the first place! Because our identities are so unconscious and so familiar our tendency to marginalize our experiences is so instinctual we don't even think to care for ourselves or prioritize our experiences, heartache, and pain. Those who struggle with substance abuse also ironically have no idea how to enjoy themselves, being unable to understand what things in life truly bring satisfaction and so must resort to chemical intervention to achieve that which would otherwise come from the development of real friendships, tastes, hobbies, interests, and indulging one's own wellbeing which instead are inhibited by such experiences of trauma and an absence of self-compassion. To resolve such issues in anyone, inventory should thus be made of absolutely *everything* that causes us disappointment, frustration, pain, resentment, regret, remorse, hurt, etc., no matter how small or seemingly insignificant or marginalized.

The second part of this practice is the *Fear Inventory* (yes, there is more). Fears are preconceptions about life which prevent us from living fully. Fears cause us to avoid situations, people, challenges, and opportunity. Often they motivate animus, resentment, pain, and actively undermine our own wellbeing and work against our self-interests even though they ostensibly exist to do the opposite. Coping mechanisms and character weakness all actually originate from a specific fear or set of fears. For instance, people who fear financial insecurity may lie, cheat, steal, or coerce, agitate, or belittle their significant others, children, and friends in dealing with that fear. They may be miserly or selfish with their prosperity. They may also spend egregiously or irresponsibly and constantly live in a state of financial insecurity in order to subvert the fear by exercising the active use of their money. The fear of financial insecurity is itself a more primal fear of death caused from lack of resources, which can also include the social and emotional security which comes from attracting other humans to us through material wealth. This fear also comes from being afraid that no one is watching out for us, or not believing in some kind of higher power or purpose, that life is left only up to us. Fear of imperfection drives us to obsess over our personal effectiveness and robs us of satisfaction in our achievements. Some fears are more visceral, like fear of the dark, of violence, of men, of our mother, of natural disasters, impending doom or wild animals. Fears are created in our childhood in response to unpleasant experiences, pain, and abuse. In reality, fear is a biological mechanism used to make us aware of potential threats to our person.

If we had no fears we would not even be on this earth as a species. Fear of the dark, of heights, of wild animals, of disease, and of competition are all fears which have kept our species alive throughout the ages. If a bird did not have a fear of cats it would simply succumb to predation. If humans did not have a fear of water if they can't swim they might drown. As such, the development of our fears originate in our biology and the instincts we have for self-preservation. But since they are also reactionary and instinctual, and also develop when we are small children when we are more helpless, they are also often misunderstood and more severe than what is useful as an adult, and as such can get in the way of things we really want. For instance, if as a child we were the frequent recipient of rejection by family or friends we may, as adults, simply avoid friendships or romantic engagements due to our fears of rejection, and thus by our own behavior engineer the very loneliness and isolation we regret. If we get attacked by a dog as a child we might grow up into an adult which fears them, and then never actually get to experience the joy of animal companionship. If our parent used threats and deprivation as a parenting tool we may develop fears of financial insecurity and spend all our money as adults buying things to subvert our fear but which in turn drains our bank account and prevents the actual financial health which would give us peace of mind. Fears of being unlovable may motivate us to spend energy within relationships coercing partners to demonstrate their commitment for the subversion of our fear and thus turn relationships into an exercise of dominance and willfulness rather than the free expression of love. This latter example was one which plagued my own life, having been rejected by my own family as a child I developed fears that people and relationships were unreliable and that I was unworthy of love, and not taught healthy skills to resolve such internal and interpersonal conflicts instead reactively coerced demonstrations of commitment from my partners, and did not give them the chance to give love on their own and in their own time, which in turn added stress to being in a relationship with me and thus less motivation to remain and an increased likelihood of actually being alone (not to mention the effect of motivating me to choose unreliable partners in the first place). Fear can be debilitating and overwhelming, driving us even into insanity, because it is such a primal and biological survival mechanism which is more concerned with the survival of our entire species rather than us as an individual. When we fail to understand our fears we are instead operating simply as a human animal which comes with all the limitations imposed by instinct and ignorance.

Our response to fear and indeed even the very purpose of fear are also largely attempts to neutralize the thing of which we are afraid rather than fear itself, since fear is an esoteric and intangible construct of the human psyche. The human mind is designed to address fear by addressing the subject of our fear and not fear directly. Fearing competition and danger from other humans we buy guns and engage in arms races. Fearing crime we empower armed and aggressive law enforcement institutions to suppress our communities and stifle economic prosperity. Fearing our own self-worth we waste the entirety of our lives and relationships pursuing money and status. In fact, it is this very dynamic of our response to fear which carves us up into disparate political, regional, and ideological alliances. Those whose lives are dominated by fear and the desire to subvert that which they are afraid are those drawn to power simply for the sake of it, who sacrifice their morality and humanity merely to feel protected and empowered against that which they are afraid. This is the purpose which religion serves in the lives of man, to bring feelings of reassurance and power over things which are frightening whether or not it actually does. It is why people willingly bankrupt themselves in support of institutions and persons who exploit them. Why voters choose leaders who rig political systems against their best interests. They are not ignorant to the consequences of their actions nor the debilitating effect it has on their lives—It is the price they are willing to pay for protection from fear. The justification for their actions is simply that. Their belief is in the power to subvert that which they are afraid, rather than fear itself.

The fear inventory transforms esoteric, intangible fears into something which is tangible, allowing that we can in turn confront and resolve them, which is entirely possible, rather than that which we are afraid, which is impossible. Those who more naturally understand that our problem is fear and not that of which we are afraid are more happy, hopeful, creative, accomplished, capable, unifying, fun, and successful. Unencumbered by the inhibitory limitations of fear we are able to expand beyond the bounds which limit our counterparts which in turn opens opportunity for success and effectiveness in our lives we could never realize while encumbered by fear. The only reason I was even able to write these books was because inventory therapy helped me see how I previously acted on my fears and got in my own way, because the effect of fear is subversive and unconscious. In truth it is impossible to subvert the things of which we are afraid. We cannot stop death. We cannot stop pain, or disappointment, or inconvenience. Sure, we can improve our life and position by acting with wisdom, but fear immobilizes and distracts us and makes us stupid. Fear of death causes people to spend their energy dieting, destroying and abusing their bodies, having disfiguring plastic surgery and losing physical functions like arousal and the ability to have sex from the use of debilitating medications and products and abuse. Fear of losing children causes parents to impair children's development and produce inept and dysfunctional adults, or destroy a relationship with their spouse (or ex spouse) which in turn undermines their access to children anyway. Parents afraid of death and the unknown of the afterlife choose religious bigotry and hatred instead of their own children. Acting on fear causes us the very pain and heartache we experience in life. It makes us miserable, despondent, and ineffective.

Inventorying our fears flips the biological function of fear on its head, helping our mind to identify and address the fear directly rather that that of which we are afraid. This neutralizes fear altogether and thus the very inspiration to have our control mechanisms and insecurities in the first place. This also relieves us of a great deal of suffering, since fear can be all-encompassing and obsessive, keeping us in a state of constant hyper-vigilance for threats to our person, and frees an enormous amount of emotional energy, time, and resources. No longer afraid of our bank account we actually manage it properly and accumulate wealth. No longer afraid of losing our children we actually spend time interacting with them and developing real emotional intimacy. No longer afraid of rejection we actually have fun dating and take chances on healthy and inspiring adults of whom we were once afraid.

Fear also has a direct consequence on our physical health, because the mechanisms of fear are accomplished through the action of stress hormones like adrenaline, cortisol, and the torporific hormones which reduce metabolic health, and if we have other metabolic illnesses our fear can make our physical health immeasurably worse. This is what happens when people absolutely lose their minds and become psychologically ill, or when people feel overwhelming terror at certain fears which lead to phobias such as of flying, groups of people, germs, etc. It's also why marijuana, ironically, can make people become paranoid and agitated when they use it, when their cortisol expression is already elevated due to metabolic disease, since marijuana increases cortisol expression (which is also why it can be used medically, since it's basically like injecting steroids, but which is also why it can come with unhelpful side effects). Addressing metabolic health as discussed in *Fuck Portion Control* can resolve the effect that excessive stress hormones have in promoting the exaggeration of our fear response. But the actual fear itself and the trigger for stress hormone expression comes from the psyche and our perception of our lives, our safety, and effectiveness in life. Believing ourselves required but unable to neutralize death, those of us who are driven by a fear of death plead to the divine to spare us from it, make excuses for sin, and foment fear and self-pity, concocting magnificent schemes which seek to facilitate the subversion of fear but in so doing simply serve to empower our fears and increase

Fear Inventory

Fear	Cause	Effect	A Better Way?
a person, idea, institution, event, obligation, limitation, trauma, or problem of which we are afraid	a brief description of what caused this fear.	what effect does having this fear have on our life?	how might we differently consider that which we are afraid?

Samples

Fear	Cause	Effect	A Better Way?
failure	I do fail, sometimes often. Failure is hard. People have taken advantage of my failures or shamed me for them. Taught in my youth that failure is wrong. Can compromise my wellbeing.	Keeps me from trying. Don't enjoy my successes. Stressed and anxious. Feel alone and ashamed. Sometimes also makes me more likely to fail because I'm so worried about failing. Judge others for their own failures. No compassion for myself. Afraid and fearful.	It's okay to fail! Even necessary for growth. I am not actually alone even when I feel that way. The Universe is watching out for me and things are going to happen the way they are going to happen. I don't need to be in control all the time. I can recover even when I do fail, as I have repeatedly demonstrated in the past. Everything will be okay. If it's not, that's okay too.
conflict	arguments and fights are stressful and sometimes even scary. was taught to fear them and avoid them, to not let others control me, not empowered with effective conflict resolution skills	I avoid conflict all the time, even by lying or misleading people and can't handle when it does happen. I also don't share myself with others which creates a wall between us.	conflict is actually good! It helps people meet needs and needn't be so serious. conflict also doesn't mean there needs to be a loser—both sides can win and most conflict is just poor communication

our mental, spiritual, and physical suffering. A person who is truly unafraid instead recognizes that it is *okay* that we die. That it is okay that we don't know what happens after death. That the likelihood is death will care for us every bit as life has done brings us new and amazing comfort we never though possible. Ironically, those who fear do not in fact understand the nature of God, which is why they fear so desperately in the first place and seek evidence to assuage our fears, because knowledge of God is found through acceptance of mortal realities rather than efforts to subvert them.

All resentments are associated with one or more underlying fears which is what motivates our control mechanisms revealed in how we respond to those resentments, and by inventorying these fears we can understand and resolve them, because all fears are simply caused by ignorance and this practice provides us with answers for why we have such fears in the first place. A fear of death is not actually a fear of death, which you will come to understand through the successful practice of inventory, but instead a fear of dying with yet unamended wrongs, expiring while still burdened with the guilt and shame of our mistakes and thus no more chance to repair them. We are also taught to fear death, to consider it as bad or scary, as punishment for our natural weaknesses as a human being, associated with pain and terror, or that there is only one life or that life is a test which determines your eternal fate, or that there is nothing to look forward to after death and we simply cease to exist (which though perpetuated by supposed atheist intellectuals demonstrates an embarrassing failure to understand the immutable nature of energy in the universe). Rather than removing the thing of which we are afraid, which is impossible, the knowledge of *why* we fear is the key to removing that fear, which is done by this practice.

When resentments are inventoried so too should we inventory the fears associated with each resentment, and like the Personal Inventory fears should always be inventoried separately from each other, never lumped into groups of multiple fears because that entertains our fear rather than helping us come to accept the things of which we are afraid. Sometimes it takes many entries of the same fear to fully understand it, so it should not be assumed that inventorying a fear once will relieve us of it. Only after sufficient time and effort have been applied to fully understanding each fear will we be relieved of its burden. To take a fear inventory we begin by copying the *fear inventory* form to paper. Under the first column titled *Fear* we write the name of any fear which causes us any and all kinds of suffering. Some of us try to cope with fears by pretending we aren't afraid. For instance, some people might have a fear of insecurity or that they aren't worth much as a person and will compensate again by adopting confidence. But the very fact that we do this belies the existence of fear. Confidence is not a choice. It is not something we choose. It originates naturally from empowerment and knowledge of our own, inherent worth. What most people believe is confidence is in reality arrogance, the denial of our weaknesses, where confidence willingly acknowledges them. Fears can be anything, and fears can even be nested within other fears. For instance, a fear of death is also a fear of not having control or a fear that we are all alone. Fears of losing a romantic partner may also be fears of low-self worth, fear of failure, fear of our own ineffectiveness, fear of loss, fear of disappointment, fear of pain, etc. Sometimes we might not be able to consciously identify fears. The coping mechanisms written in *character weakness* can reveal specific underlying fears and can inform us to what fears control our lives. For instance, the character weakness arrogance is based on fears of low self-worth. Thieving can originate from fear of financial insecurity. Dishonesty is a fear of recrimination or conflict. Perfectionism is a fear of failure. Being irresponsible is a fear of accountability. Timidity and combativeness both originate from a fear of confrontation. Insecurity is fear of rejection. Self-destructive is a fear of love and attachment.

Remember, that we cannot neutralize fear by neutralizing the thing of which we are afraid. When we do that we destroy relationships, opportunities, and become self-defeating. The rules of life do not change simply because we resent them. So instead, accepting those limitations by inventorying our fears, like the personal inventory frees us of the burden caused by fears and thus enormous amounts of emotional energy, time, and resources. Suddenly we are no longer angry at rejection and resentful of the person who rejected us but compassionate to our experience and empathetic to the person who caused us pain which really has very little to actually do with us but we don't know that because we have not practiced self-compassion until now. When raising children we no longer fear they're going to be a failure when they grow up and as such are empowered to actually engage in positive reinforcement and engender emotional intimacy and strengthen our bonds and help grow their skills and talents. No longer afraid of what our partner might do to us we actually begin to enjoy our relationship. No longer afraid of being fired at work become more effective and fulfilled by responsibility. Identifying every *fear* which controls our lives is the first step in practicing the fear inventory.

Next, under *Cause* we write from where this fear originated. Fear of financial insecurity perhaps originates because we are, in fact, reliant in many ways on money to survive, and a lack of money causes stress and impairs our access to other things we need to survive like food, clothing, and shelter. As this illustrates, the cause of a fear is often because the existence of the thing of which we are afraid is something that actually does exist or does happen to us. A fear of failure often exists because we do in fact fail, even often. Even worse, people will often actively exploit our failures and use it as ammunition against us. Death actually is a thing, and we all must die, so that is one cause of the fear of death, but choosing to ignore reality or pretend death is a long way off or delude ourselves into acrobatic religious beliefs to distract us from this fear instead gives the fear of death immense power over our lives because we do not truly understand what causes the fear in the first place. Death is often used as a cudgel by parents and religious leaders to make us feel terrible about ourselves and thus easier to coerce and control (in turn to give themselves a feeling of control). Death is also often unpleasant such as during disease or accidents or violence, all of which are also fears to inventory. But it is largely through societal attitudes and our past experiences that we have these fears to begin with, and identifying their origins empowers us to begin accepting the fear, since we begin to understand why we have it, which is usually because of

Examples of Fear
(fear of...)

- death
- failure
- imperfection
- conflict
- confrontation
- loss
- heartache
- other people
- love
- relationships
- parents
- mom
- dad
- ineffectiveness
- disappointment
- not having control
- mortality
- illness
- injury
- doctors
- hospitals
- weakness
- sadness
- emotions
- intimacy
- sex
- touch
- mistakes
- pain
- rejection
- loneliness
- authority
- going outside
- aging
- responsibility
- crowds (agoraphobia)
- public speaking
- recrimination
- gangs
- guns
- violence
- men
- women
- having children
- being a bad parent
- going into labor
- marriage
- commitment
- insecurity
- embarrassment
- financial insecurity
- the law
- government
- institutions
- taxes
- money
- work
- police
- getting in trouble
- being found out
- imprisonment
- shame
- success
- vulnerability
- crime
- burglary
- home invasion
- snakes
- spiders
- water
- heights
- flying
- bugs
- germs
- needles
- cars
- driving
- night
- sleep
- nightmares
- animals
- blood
- disease
- weather
- thunder
- loud noises
- the dead
- choking
- exploitation
- being worthless
- ineptitude
- being socially awkward
- incompetence
- incontinence
- bodily functions
- accidents
- awkwardness
- monogamy
- mental illness
- relapse
- unemployment
- showing emotion
- sobriety
- hurting others
- wealthy people
- science
- religion
- demons
- destruction
- damnation
- the I.R.S.
- terrorists
- abandonment
- being stupid
- intelligent people
- God
- being unattractive
- being undesirable
- creditors
- the future
- the end
- friends
- not having friends
- inventory therapy
- the past
- assault
- claustrophobia
- cancer
- happiness
- clowns
- computers
- technology
- progress
- traveling
- gaining weight
- ridicule
- change
- apology
- making amends
- test results
- specific people or places
- specific outcomes or events
- waking up in the morning
- starting the day
- missing out

our prejudices surrounding the thing of which we are afraid and ignorance to reality rather than any real need to fear these things. Clues to the *cause* of our fears can also be found in the resentment and cause columns of the personal inventory, since it is often our past experiences which inform and catalyze the fear response. For instance, fear of authority may have originated from experiences of abuse or recrimination suffered by opportunistic and self-righteous parents, religious leaders, or employers who exploit our vulnerability for their own personal gain and control. Or fear of helplessness, violence, or even sex may be caused by experiences of sexual assault, violence, and abuse. Fear of being powerless may simply result from having been a child and at one point powerless. A fear of rejection may have been caused by past failures or painful experiences with family or ineffective and inexperienced romantic behaviors, or being taught that rejection defines our self-worth or should be considered with severity (rather than levity). Identifying the cause of our fears is the opposite of making other people or life in general responsible for them, and redirects our energies from controlling life and other people to instead having compassion for our mortal condition and understanding and operating within the natural bounds and limitations of our effectiveness which in turn empowers us to actually be effective in our lives.

Under *Effect* we then write what effect our particular fear has on our lives. Not the effect of the thing of which we are afraid—but possession of the fear and what that fear does to us. This is important because when we try to live in spite of our fears we are in fact ignoring or suppressing our fears and in turn ignore how they also control and disrupt our lives. Recognizing that a fear of intimacy prevents us from growing close to others helps us see how we actually engineer the very self-defeating behaviors which get in our own way. Like, seriously, the degree to which we fuck up our lives in response to fear is about ninety-percent of our day to day problems, and life in reality is a very lovely and amazing experience of which most of us are wholly ignorant, because we perceive it through the psychological interpretation of our ego and fear. The effect of a fear of death is not to actually die, although it may actually increase our chances of it, but instead to spend our entire lives always fearing the end, never actually enjoying our life in the present. Fears of our children being failures may have the effect of stressing them out, aggravating interpersonal conflict, engendering animosity, resentment, stressing *us* out, preventing enjoyment of and feeling pride for our children, and even catalyzing through our behavior the very problems that we fear. Fear of authority may cause us to avoid or even antagonize authority figures, or miss out on opportunities altogether, or become ineffective when presented by challenges from authority figures. For instance, people who are sensitive to criticism and fear authority might mistake a bosses' criticism at work as a personal attack rather than something which really doesn't matter and in many cases is actually appropriate, and become repeatedly hurt, frustrated, or antagonistic in a work environment. They do not enjoy their employment, and are then stressed and dissatisfied by each day, fail to see coworkers as friends and companions, and perhaps jump from job to job to deal with the consequences of acting on fear. Fear of conflict may keep us on edge and even trigger or exaggerate conflict which does occur. I once joked to a romantic partner after he yelled at me over a conflict setting up a television that I wasn't going to give him the blowjob I had planned. It was a sardonic, erotic joke but he immediately launched into a tirade accusing me of using sex as a weapon, when in fact I had just been trying to turn him on by teasing (so he missed out on it after all), and our entire relationship was a macrocosm of this inability to enjoy life because of very consequential personal fears. Fear of accountability may prevent us from amending relationships when we have offended others, for instance when we do things to hurt friends or family and then distance ourselves from them because their very presence reminds us of our failure. Fear of failure may keep us from taking chances and acting on opportunity, or at the very least keep us from enjoying the success we have earned, such as we who find wild professional success for whom our accomplishments are never enough. Fear of illness keeps us not only from enjoying the health we have but very often actually doing things which cause illness in the first place, resenting our body which is in truth only trying to take care of us and facilitate life in the first place. Fear of others prevents us from engaging in civics or prejudices us against people who would otherwise be neighbors, friends, and brothers and sisters and exaggerating rather than solving political conflict and animosity, self-sabotaging our own success because we characterized our countrymen as "deplorable" instead of having compassion for and engaging them as a true leader would do. The effect of fear on our lives is often in stark contrast for what we truly want for ourselves, so it is only in facing our fears by practicing this therapy that we can truly get what we want from life. If the purpose of sacrificing relationships, morality, and personal dignity to belong to institutions or political movements is for the security they bring wouldn't the security of no fear in the first place be a better option? Which requires no compromise of morality, relationships, or our own wellbeing? This is accomplished by identifying exactly how fears effect our lives.

Effect is not the effect that thing of which we are afraid has on our lives. It is the effect of having the fear. It is very important to understand this point because it is an exploration of the influence fear has over our behavior and conception of life, not the effect of those things we fear, because fear is the primary cause of ineffective action and choices which result in consequences which disrupt our lives and cause frustration and pain. Identifying how fear controls our lives by writing it under effect empowers us to see how we submit to fear and perpetuate it in our lives. Another example is a *fear of conflict* might be that conflict is unpleasant. That might be an effect of conflict but it is not an effect of the fear of conflict. Of course conflict can be unpleasant. Instead, the effect that this fear has on our lives that we may be constantly in a state of anticipating potential conflict, running scenarios and dialogue in our mind to explore every possible unpleasant encounter even when there is none, or we may be excessively affected by conflict when it does occur and even when there really isn't much at stake. Maybe we overreact, or take ourselves too seriously, or avoid interactions or relationships because of this fear. Such a fear can also make us ineffective in confrontation, because we overreact or fail to consider any legitimacy of our opponent's position. We may be defensive, or oppositely hesitate to ask for what we need, to neglect our wellbeing, to neglect our relationships, our spouse, our children, to avoid human interaction, to isolate, to be anxious, fearful, and resentful, to control others, to be unforgiving, to end relationships, to self-destruct, or miss out on opportunity. Even behaviors such as nail-biting, being restless, stressed, dissatisfied, judgmental, unkind, etc., is an effect of having many types of fear. The *effect* is what effect having this fear has upon our lives, not the effect of that thing of which we are afraid, which would instead be part of the *cause*.

The last column is *A Better Way*, in which we write an opposite way to consider that which we are afraid, especially as it pertains to trusting life to carry us through, not on our own limited mortality, but in terms of a personal concept of a higher power, the nature of the Universe, or our powerlessness over fate. Since most of our fears originate from trying to control and navigate fate with our own pitiful abilities and obstinate self-reliance, and being unable to actually control that which we are afraid, the opposite is to consider these things in the context of those powers which do actually control our fate and the workings of the Universe. It is not a conception of what our life would be like without this fear, nor the things we could do to control that of which we are afraid, but is a different way of thinking about that which we are afraid. For instance, we never consider that there is actually such a thing as good conflict, or that both sides can often in fact be right at the same time, that everyone's needs are legitimate. Conflict does not inherently require one person winning and the other losing, and we can ask for what we need without making another person feel bad about theirs. In trying to control our fear of death we may diet, starve, exhaust our physical energy, fight with family, adopt destructive religious beliefs, destroy relationships, cheat on our aging spouses, chase inappropriately younger sexual targets, seek superficial distractions like plastic surgery, or find comfort in financial or social status to delude ourselves into a state of denial, and yet none of this actually improves or changes the fact that we will die, so the fear thus lingers in spite of our most strained and frenetic efforts because at no time have we actually accepted death as a reality of our existence. So rather than doing more things which try to control death a better way than fearing death might be to realize *that it's okay that we die*. That all people die, or that it's okay not to know what happens afterward. I mean seriously, it really does not matter if we know what happens or not. What's going to happen is what's going to happen—The same forces which placed us on this earth are also those responsible for taking us out, so they have as much interest in our death as they did our birth, neither of which were up to us. Because of how biology works and the end of our sensory abilities you may also be surprised and relieved to realize that death is not actually something we experience. Or we can trust life or our higher power to carry us through to the next stage of existence just as it brought us into this one, that life will play out regardless of our conception or concern with death. That rather than all the negativity we have been taught death is natural and good, because it makes room for new life and new people and carries us forward to the next stage of existence. That energy is immutable and that we simply change form upon death.

Another example might be a fear of losing a job or the process of moving, the abandonment of everything we have built and starting over somewhere new and unfamiliar. Instead of fearing everything that could go wrong or deluding ourselves into believing nothing will go wrong a better way would be to realize that we are probably being given an exciting opportunity for change, that God or the Universe is watching out for us and helping us along our life path as it always has, that life is ever changing and there is probably a reason greater than what we can see in the moment, that we are in fact not alone, and that we will most likely meet this challenge just fine the way we have others throughout the course of our life. If things do go wrong we can always ask for help or solve problems as they may occur without needing to constantly worry about what might happen. Maybe we will also meet new friends or have new opportunities to realize our hopes or dreams. Or maybe it will go just as badly as we thought, but it will actually be okay because we are capable of a lot more than we give ourselves credit. Plus we may be surrounded by others who are coming with us or on whom we can rely for help should things be difficult. The point in resolving our fears by exploring a different way to think about fear is not to pretend that things will be okay when they aren't. We often fear death because it does happen. People die and we can die in painful ways. Delusion to reality is part of the problem, and the key to accepting reality is to explore reasons why we don't need to fear it. This is a sober analysis of reality rather than what our coping mechanisms, delusions, and biases have heretofore allowed us to comprehend, how ignoring or minimizing fears has actually given them power and why we do not need to ignore nor minimize them. Nothing is as finite or dogmatic or hopeless as it appeared. Life is far more wonderful and amazing that we ever knew. We are far more capable and okay than we feared. Disappointments, frustration, and pain are never permanent. To speak the name of fear and identify exactly what we are afraid of, and what it means to our lives is to take power away from fear, which is really the only reason it controls our life in the first place.

    Another example of doing the fear inventory incorrectly which is quite common are fears related to health and illness. We may write down a fear of aging, or getting sick, or fat, then write that the cause is getting a certain disease or putting on extra pounds or not going to the gym. The effect we may write then is that this fear makes us not take care of our health and avoid the gym, or that we may not get on that diet that we need to do. The better way may then be written as needing to do that diet, eat healthy, workout, and take care of our bodies. *This is all entirely wrong*, and continues to demonstrate a desire to control life and those things which we fear, which is impossible to do and exactly what drives our misery and ineffectiveness. The correct way to inventory a fear of aging, of getting sick, or getting fat is that they are caused by our past negative experiences with these issues, by hearing, seeing, and being taught that being sick, fat, or old is a bad thing. Or in fact being rejected by people for these very perceived failings. It also occurs because we *do* get old, sick, and fat. These things exist, and they do cause us pain, frustration, and heartache, which is exactly why we are afraid of them. But then the effect this fear has on our lives (not the effect of those things of which we are afraid but the fact of having the fear in the first place) is to never enjoy the health we *do* have, never appreciating our mortal body, always anticipating misfortune, and living in a constant state of anxiety. The *effect* causes us to diet, to exhaust ourselves, to abuse and starve our body and take it for granted. It may even cause us to reject or destroy relationships with other people as we project our fear onto others, to offend our wives and our husbands and our children because of their own mortal limitations over which they are equally powerless, to resent God and life and hate ourselves. *A better way* would then be not to diet or "take care of our body" (which is usually not at all taking care of our body), but to understand that we are mortal, that there are limitations to what we can achieve physically, that it is okay that we are mortal. That in truth our body is *always* taking care of us because it too wants to live and to thrive. That even if people reject us because of our physical health we are still valuable to ourselves and to our concept of a higher power, that their behavior is not a reflection of us but instead their own personal fears, insecurities, unresolved trauma, and poor estimation of their own self-worth. To understand that we will be okay, and that we can enjoy and appreciate our body no matter the struggles which befall us, and that we can care for our body in truly healthy ways by eating well and not abusing it.

Inventory should take up *many* pages. Mine took five hours to share with another person. Someone took eleven hours to share theirs with me (sharing is not required, though, and should be done with discretion, and is not appropriate, say, to make an inventory about our spouse and then share our list of disappointments in them, which is in fact a contrived manipulation). The clutter in a well-lived life is abundant, and all that toil shoved to the back of the mind takes up a *lot* of space. It is no wonder this therapy is so healing. As the first entries are gotten rid of older memories will pop into our head as we're vacuuming or driving to work, or even while writing down other thoughts. Write them down and get them out. Fears also never occur singularly, and entering one fear will always reveal yet other connected fears which must also be inventoried to fully experience resolution. For instance a fear of death is also a fear of loss, of pain, disappointment, punishment, the unknown, losing control, aging, illness, etc.

After finishing our entire life inventory we then use this tool daily to help us cope with experiences we continue to have, to constantly help us grow and discover new strengths and talents, since life never stops happening (until it does). This will further improve our confidence and quality of life as we learn more and greater lessons of personal worth and effectiveness, finding strengths we never knew we could have and joys in experiences which we used to think small and insignificant. Again, if we feel any resistance to practice inventory, writing that as an entry can help us understand why we feel resistance or make excuses not to do it and thence make the practice easier to accomplish. Because all resentments are driven by fear, the most important part of this practice is the fear inventory, so make sure to always identify and write down related fears whenever writing resentments.

Do not use the inventory to entertain self-pity. Self-pity is a useful tool to provide self-worth when it is not forthcoming from the environment, but it also strengthens coping mechanisms and deludes us to our true effectiveness and self-worth and, like the young alcoholic who refused to let go of self pity will only serve to impair our life and effectiveness even though in the moment it may feel cathartic. Ironically, the inventory therapy is all about ourselves, which might seem like an exercise in self-pity, but in reality it forces us to acknowledge and confront control and coping mechanisms, and since denial is fuel for self-pity those who overly rely on it and lack compassion for themselves find inventory threatening, because at first it appears to deny one of the only tools we have to effect our experience and feel empowered. The act of entertaining self-pity in the inventory practice takes the form of inventorying ourselves rather than others or events which have happened to us, trying to enter emotions into *my part*, or dishonestly ignoring or trivializing our own behavior in *my part*. For instance, when I first learned the version of inventory from alcoholics anonymous I was tempted to inventory my own personal failures or destructive behaviors, but this very act denies that those things result from experiences of trauma from my past and lack of effective life skills, while also pretending I had no choice in those mistakes or failures as if they were something that happened to me and not something I chose. The young alcoholic who rejected my help and entertained substantial self-pity would even change the tone of her voice when sharing the *my part* of the very few inventories she did to make herself sound even more small and helpless, as if she couldn't have possibly been responsible for the things she said or chose to do, or had no choice or was forced by people or circumstances against her will. The prospect of taking responsibility for our actions is only daunting because we have never been taught how to do it, but it must be done and this skill can only be learned by practice, and it is indeed a very valuable and empowering skill. Sometimes we are also tempted to identify only those character weaknesses which support self-pity or write things that are not even character weaknesses, like being weak or being sad, which are not character weaknesses at all but are instead effects of trauma. Rather, use the inventory therapy to enlighten the mind to the ways in which we are or are not effective in our own life and be especially self-honest in writing. Being self-honest is the act of having compassion for ourselves, and self-compassion and self-pity never exist in the same place at once. It is either one or the other and if the choice be self-pity then self-compassion will always remain to you a stranger.

  Finally, communicate to the Universe, God, or your concept of a Higher Power your intention to let go of character weaknesses and fears we have written down after every practice. Denying the presence of God or insisting God exists is an ego and coping mechanism designed to help us handle themes and fears that are greater than ourselves and our ability to comprehend. God did not offend us as children or disappoint us as adults, other people and life did that, and trying to cope with trauma, pain, and heartache by conceptualizing God or the absence of God is no different than any other mundane coping or control mechanism. The truth is we can never know such things, but communicating with our concept of a higher power is the act of submitting to the reality that in fact control very little as a mortal human being, and this entire process is about accepting reality, not denying it, which means accepting our limited capacity to understand that which we can never actually understand, our past, our fallibility, and to make room for personal growth, and does not really matter how we do it, only that we do. Being willing to let go of control mechanisms and let go of those things over which we have no control empowers this practice to change weakness into strength. The ego does put up resistance to practicing trauma therapy, and very few people in truth will even attempt these practices because the fear of not having control can be extremely intimidating. Others still will practice only so much as is required to resolve the most egregious and stressful behaviors and situations and so will stop once things are good enough to endure. But that also is a trap of the ego which will entomb us into a state of mediocrity in which we will still continue to experience irritating and frustrating consequences of our own behavior and failure to understand our psyche and the true extent of our pain and trauma. Again, trying to force ourselves to do self-improvement is the opposite of self-care which requires empathy for ourselves and not self-will, and resistance to practicing inventory should instead be inventoried so that we may enlighten our subconscious to understand the reasons why we continue engaging in self-defeating behavior. Inventory the inventory, or inventory that introspective therapy is even required to find resolution of our problems and that life can be difficult and frustrating.

Another coping mechanism which may get in the way is a vague feeling that we have no time to actually do inventory therapy, being busy and preoccupied with so much else going on in our lives. But in truth we can find time for anything we prioritize, and people will often make excuses for being busy even though we have time to go to the gym, attend church, watch television, browse social media, or socialize with friends. To overcome this hurdle stop managing your schedule through vagary and actually look at the times of day in which there is time to practice inventory. Many mothers feel overwhelmed by children and schedules when in truth there are often as many as several hours in the day when little children can be sat in front of the television while we practice this important therapy, or a friend or relative can come watch them so we can practice self-care through inventory. Putting off inventory or only doing small amounts infrequently is in truth a coping mechanism to avoid doing that which makes us uncomfortable, which should also be inventoried so that we begin to understand how we get in our own way and fail to care for our own wellbeing.

Refusing to address trauma, facing life on our own, and forcing our will on others while refusing to confront and accept our past is also the antithesis of belief in God or a higher power. To many of us God was used as an excuse to hurt us by people who, in reality, know nothing about God, when in fact God is merely the indefatigable forces of Nature and the Universe, over which we are all powerless. Believers and atheists alike try to control fate by concocting fantastical answers to questions we absolutely cannot know, which are really only meant to make them feel better about their own fears and are no different than fictional entertainment, telling God what they are as if we dictate to them and not them to us. It can help to discuss the inventory with your personal concept of a higher power, to pray that our character weaknesses be taken as we are willing to let go. Whenever we pray it should never be for our own selfish means, to get things and stuff, for ends to work in our favor, for our will to become reality. Instead pray for understanding, and to know the nature of God and what God would have us do.

Sometimes it may also seem like we need to inventory the same thing many times without coming to a satisfying conclusion, and everyone will have several themes over which we must wrestle frequently. When this happens it is because there are very subtle, as yet imperceptible issues underlying those themes which we have not yet discovered, which involve other events or psychological trauma we are not yet aware. If repetition presents itself during inventory it is a sign that deeper, subconscious themes are at play which remain to be discovered, which through repetition and meditation will eventually come to light. Persistence is key, and satisfactory conclusions will come if effort is applied.

Across the ages in books, fairytales, mythology, and religious institution we have heard of those rare few who achieve enlightenment and move to a new plane of existence through which they find incredible happiness and perceive the bounds of the Universe and the throne of the divine. Though millions practice devotion to ritual, tradition, and dogma, such enlightenment has eluded us because the reality is that Heaven exists not above us nor Hell below—both are here, at once, and we reside in them according to our life experience and choices, as we yet live and not after we die. Some live in Hell though they have not yet died, and others live in Heaven though hey have not yet been redeemed. Those who foment anger, cheat, lie, steal, rape, abuse, manipulate, condemn, hate, and control are even now living the consequences of their crimes in Hell on Earth, being removed from humanity and the knowledge of satisfaction, friendship, love, and peace because of our selfishness and failure to find compassion for our mortal condition and thus that of those around us. Those who embrace family and friends, stand up for the downtrod, take joy in the small things of life, serve mankind, and perceive the sun through dark clouds are those already living in Heaven, here and now on Earth, not having to wait until the end to reap our reward. There is no difference between the beyond and the now. They are one and the same, the very energies of the Universe are not reserved for another life but flow through us as the energy of life itself which makes all of creation. The consequences of our choices are met upon us the moment we take action. Resolving our trauma through inventory therapy is the means by which we all can find this enlightenment, to sweep away the pain of the past and the burden of our mistakes to make room for a higher plane of existence. With such tools we can free ourselves from self-defeating behaviors and peer beyond the superficial veil which obscures most human life, and in so doing find the answers to questions which really matter. This insight in turn helps us to become our own parents, the kind we deserved as children, to do for ourselves which others could not, and in turn empower our own children to experience joy and happiness, *because* of life and not in spite of it, and all that this incredible experience requires is willingness, pen, and paper.

14

Amending Relationships

The bravest thing a human being can do is utter the words, "I'm sorry." And because most human beings are cowards, we usually corrupt it by adding a qualifier like *"but,"* or *"you're too sensitive,"* or *"you feel that way,"* and refuse to take responsibility for our behavior.

Many of us will not even say sorry even when we have caused much offense, clinging more tightly to our sense of entitlement than a spoiled child to a prized toy. But the ability to say sorry and make a proper amends is also one of the most empowering skill sets we can learn for ourselves. Saying sorry and rectifying our mistakes endears us to others, strengthens emotional bonds, and builds a deep sense of trust and admiration. It can also remove the burdensome threat of jeopardy, such as if you have committed a crime or heinous act or cheated on a partner. Tax cheats or dishonest landlords who steal from their tenants are forever burdened by their conscience but without better skills by which to live will doggedly cling to their greed and dishonesty as if these are acceptable business practices without any moral or social consequences. It is a miserable prospect to spend an entire life drowning in guilt, looking around every proverbial corner anticipating possible discovery or consequence when we can simply admit mistakes, take responsibility for our shortcomings, and fix the harm we have caused.

There is one simple reason we as humans do not readily make amends for the wrongs we have done which is that our parents punished us unjustly and harshly when we made mistakes instead of teaching us how to properly handle making mistakes. Having been a vulnerable and naive child our experiences of punishment, retaliation, and consequence were paired with opportunistic exploitation and demoralizing humiliation, experiences which took from us our dignity, sense of self, and effectiveness as an individual from which we then learned defensive mechanisms to protect our ego (and that we should protect our ego). A parent's reaction to a child who has caused offense is typically to lash out and punish which fails to actually teach any empowering skill or tool by which a child can take responsibility for their own behavior, care for their own relationships, and fix the problems they might cause. Now grown into an adult we are thus unempowered and ineffective in the management of our mistakes and personal relationships and lack the confidence to effectively repair damage we cause and thus driven by insecurity, fear, and egoism when confronted by consequences we do not feel empowered to handle.

Worse than this are the many parents who are emotionally volatile, opportunistic, and abusively use opportunities to vent their emotions onto children because we were receptacles without boundaries into which they could dump their own pain and frustration with life, even when we did not actually make real mistakes or caused real offense. This kind of abuse is that which directly results in psychological fracturing described by the Karpman model, and because those of us with narcissism often endured excessive and exploitative punishment and neglect as children we also had to learn how to lie effectively in order to take care of ourselves and survive the abuse. Trained to deal with life through dishonesty and fear only possess these tools and a mistrustful worldview in adulthood, only to find it ineffective for protecting our interests and needs since lying among adults breeds suspicion, distrust, and destroys relationships, but having never been taught effective interpersonal skills to repair mistakes and cultivate trust and intimacy find ourselves at odds with everyone, accumulating a mountain of resentment, hurt, and mistrust and feeling frustrated by our inability to meet our needs and desires without hurting others.

To an adult who does not know how to make an effective amends the prospect of apologizing is truly frightening, because it was the vulnerability of having made a mistake as a child which was exploited by powerful and calloused adults who hurt us, learning that making mistakes is an opportunity others can and do exploit and manipulate. So intense is this fear we sometimes prefer to eliminate important relationships and hurt people we ostensibly care about rather than admit we made a mistake.

People do, in fact, exploit our weaknesses for their own benefit, which seems to justify harsh defense mechanisms. But if we need others to be fulfilled and experience love it is contradictory to refuse the same to others and expect to receive from them what we ourselves will not give. Many of us want leniency for our mistakes and understanding for our insecurities, but turn around and blame our partners, friends, and children when they purposefully or by accident reveal their own to us. Other humans desire the same respect, trust, security, and empathy as we do and by refusing to give security, trust, respect, and empathy we actively engineer our own instability and undermine our own interests as those people in our lives react to our behavior the same way we would if the same was done to us. This is why being able to say sorry and repair mistakes is one of the most empowering tools a person can learn because the cultivation of skills which build and secure relationships in turn provides us security, opportunity, and fulfillment, whereas undermining those brings instability, loss, and separation, either from emotional relationships or those which provide income and other material resources, thus actively working against our own best interests and perpetuating our own fear, instability, and restlessness by our behavior, not that of others.

But the refusal to make amends for our mistakes is also an incredibly selfish and self-centered adult behavior meant to squeeze as much control over our environment and its inhabitants as we possibly can, and refusing to apologize and make amends (often using other people's behavior as a poor excuse) is indeed a significant control mechanism. One of the reasons we tend to revere vile murderers such as Alexander "the Great," Napoleon, or even fictional characters like Darth Vader or the Targaryens is that we desire power to make the world in our image, to control fear by control of others, to conquer our seeming helplessness and vulnerability to pain and heartache by…causing it to others? Those regions of the world whom Alexander invaded do not call him Great because he was a coward, murderer, and warmonger as are all such whom inflict violence on other people.

While the ego may desire power, the conscience which is offended by wrongdoing wants instead to live in harmony with family, friends, and neighbors, to help them and be part of life, not in opposition to it, and so a person who refuses to make right that which we have done wrong lives in constant agitation, always fearful, and rarely fulfilled no matter how much success we may achieve. Those of us who have the most difficult time practicing inventory therapy are also those who refuse to let go of control, and the fear of making an apology is the fear of losing control we think we have of people, circumstances, reputation, relationships, experiences, freedom, money, love, pride, etc. But making mistakes and hurting others is the greatest liability of all as it not only costs us parts of life we actually need but also our very humanity as we make amoral choices at the cost of another's wellbeing and suppress our higher emotions like empathy and shame in order to handle living while knowing we have caused others such awful harm.

Honestly saying sorry is one of the easiest things we can do in life (if our wrongs are not especially egregious), and the only reason it seems so serious and so jeopardizing is because we also learned from our experiences as children to underestimate our self worth and effectiveness. It is not very easy to control a child who is aware of their self worth, so parents who use control as a parenting tool beat down our self esteem and fail to empower us with skills that would defend our peace and develop esteem, learning in the process to take ourselves and life much, much too seriously and distrust others and refuse to let them be themselves. Excessive seriousness is the greatest poison in any life. None of us is so great as to warrant the absence of humor and levity. *"I totally acted like a dick to you, you didn't deserve that, it was really rude and I'm sorry I hurt you,"* is the easiest and most disarming sentence a person could say and yet people will literally destroy important relationships or risk legal prosecution than risk letting go of the ego, because to our traumatized minds the ego is the only thing protecting us from further harm, when in reality it is usually the greatest liability. The idea that saying sorry jeopardizes our relationship but saying *"you've gained weight"* does not is fucking idiotic, yet we repeatedly behave this way.

To those of us who carry an abundance of trauma life is often a jigsaw puzzle of confusion, and many things of which we are afraid or perceive in a negative light are actually not only nothing to be afraid of but can be wonderful experiences. For instance, many of us have been raised in religious, insane homes and being possessed of more rational minds mistook our natural, instinctual mistrust of zealotry, stupidity, and cruelty as being noncompliant or deviant when in fact these instincts to heal wounds and separate ourselves from insanity are the most admirable traits a human can possess. Likewise the prospect of apology can seem extremely upsetting, but that is only because this too has been corrupted and neglected by our traumatized childhoods and apology in fact is very spiritual and peaceful when done correctly without regard for protecting our ego.

Oftentimes when we want to resolve conflicts in relationships we spend a lot of time setting up the script inside our head beforehand, trying to anticipate how to say what we want to say without causing yet another fight, anxious about the other person's reaction and how we can best avoid uncomfortable confrontation. But this very act and behavior IS CONTROL, a blatant attempt to manipulate and design the feelings and responses of other people, which is something we can never actually do, and so these encounters always descend into conflict because in reality our intent is never to make things better but to save face, exert control, and pretend to have feelings we do not. It never matters how we say things in this context because there is no way to kindly or respectfully manipulate others, and it is often difficult to see this behavior as control because we feel entitled to act on our feelings. Control is what other people do. I don't control. I just want you to listen to me and do my bidding.

An especially profound misunderstanding we all have during interpersonal conflict is that there is nothing wrong with what we want. We all have desires and needs and even those which might seem harmful come from real problems with our emotional, physical, and material wellness which need to be addressed, and it is how we go about acting on those feelings and needs and trying to get what we desire that is the problem. I once knew an incredibly handsome, kind, and talented young man who was constantly suspicious about what his girlfriend was up to and was having a hard time not acting on his desire to stalk her. Because of his lack of self care and relationship skills he did not recognize that refraining from doing so was actually very admirable, nor that he could just text her and ask her what she was up to. Realizing he could actually just engage with his girlfriend rather than wonder what she may or may not be doing was something that had never crossed his mind because he fundamentally did not understand that there is nothing wrong with wanting security in a relationship because his own parents destroyed those instincts for self preservation as part of their abuse strategy (which was also used on them by their parents and so on). Lacking skills to recognize the difference between thought and action as well as effective skills and self-care behaviors which provide our needs without harming others we reach only for the ones we have, those control and coping mechanisms learned in youth during duress and borne of basic human survival instincts. Knowing these are inefficient due to our long histories of failure we become even more insecure and manipulative when acting out, such as planning out how our manipulation will proceed, but we either signal to others we are insecure, self-doubting, or duplicitous or actively harm and take from others and thus incur the consequences we desired to avoid. Even when our control behaviors do bring results they are usually pitiful or painful, with great cost to our emotional, mental, and spiritual wellbeing and are hardly worth the cost. But our psyches are traumatized and we lack higher mental and emotional skills and do not even recognize when we are fighting over meaningless trophies in egoism, mistaking pieces of paper for riches, submission for love, and gratification for satisfaction.

In reality we can and should be frank about our needs. "We haven't been dating very long and I don't trust you yet," communicates our position where remaining silent and pretending we don't have needs allows people to take advantage of us or prevents real intimacy from occurring. If a person responds poorly to the revelation of our needs that is a way out of potential relationships with abusive people, a life skill we often did not acquire since our parents did not have it to teach. But sometimes people use needs as a manipulative tool too, such as when apologizing for how *we* are affected by our poor behavior. *I've felt so bad since our fight*, instead of *I'm sorry I hurt you*, or *I miss our conversations and getting to hang out with you*, instead of *I'm sorry I hurt you*, or *things have been so rough* instead of *I'm sorry I hurt you*. This is a blatant control mechanisms meant to engender pity from a victim, to manipulate their emotional attachment to us and win back engagement without actually apologizing. It was not until well after the dissolution of a long relationship with an abusive boyfriend that I realized he never actually told me he was sorry for what he did and would never do it again. Instead he purposefully chose words like *I feel so bad*, or *I'm sorry you found out* which are not actually apologies. While this strategy is often effective against others who also have unresolved trauma, even if it does work to win conflict resolution it destabilizes the relationship because the unconscious mind of both partners understand that there is a disparity between our words and actions and a preference for our own benefit at the expense of theirs. But we should value our partner's wellbeing as much as our own, and if we do not this is a fundamental sign of unresolved childhood trauma and control mechanisms which prevent real intimacy, and extends also to non erotic relationships such as with friends, business partners, and family members. Even if someone accepts this manipulation there will exist an imbalance in the power dynamics of the relationship and thus an inability to find fulfillment.

The desire to control others is what drives the fear of making an apology because that would mean letting go of control of others, as well as outcomes, which we are often not willing to do because of our unresolved experiences of abuse and the coping and control mechanisms which give us a sense of control over our lives. After all, how can we make our husband or wife stay if we can't control them? The answer is *it is not your job to make them stay.* We cannot control others, no matter how much we wish, and trying to make anyone do what we want, including to love us or give us the things we want or need is a control behavior no matter how valid our need or desire. There is never anything wrong with wanting your loved one to stay with you, to not lose our children, to have friendships and professional relationships, to have sex, to feel comforted, safe, or to be recognized or loved or respected, but so many of us take those desires and act on them in ways which cause harm and manipulate, and that is where abuse occurs because we can never make people do what we wish, we cannot make them feel what they will not, and we cannot prevent fate from taking its course and when it does it is all the more painful as the delusion of control we have constructed is mercilessly torn apart, misunderstanding the nature of nature and the parameters which bookend our mortal lives.

The dynamics of control, its undesirable consequences, and behavioral peculiarities as characterized by the Karpman model are well demonstrated in the so-called *'paradox of tolerance'* where supposed philosophers put forward the question of whether tolerance can ever be absolute. They explain that absolute tolerance eventually leads to intolerant behavior by those who are intolerant and so tolerance cannot be absolute without eventually risking complete and total intolerance. This same naive, circular illogic also underlies our self-centered, egomaniacal fear and refusal to admit wrongdoing and validate the feelings and experiences of others, believing they will exploit our tolerance for their own selfish ends, and is not even remotely concerned with tolerance. Just as I was raised to be nice and identified as a nice person but was not in reality very nice, our conception of ourselves is often entirely delusional from how we actually behave, justifying our neuroses, fears, and lack of effective coping and interpersonal skills through emotional rationalization. The tolerance paradox does not exist, because although its authors use the word tolerance what they are actually describing in this so-called 'paradox' is not tolerance, but *permissiveness*. Like most factors of social structures, tolerance is not a personal, segregated behavior but a social contract which, to even exist, requires the participation of more than one entity. If the Earth had only one inhabitant it would not be possible for them to be tolerant because there would be no one else they must tolerate. Saying there is a tolerance paradox is a contradiction in terms, like saying there is a war paradox. War has both subject and object and requires both to satisfy its concept. It is not possible to wage literal war against oneself. Just like war, or marriage, or friendships, or business, tolerance is a two-way contract in which both parties agree to be tolerant just like two nations agree not to war with each other. If one party transgresses that agreement then there is war, even if one side refuses to fight back, and so it is with tolerance, which is no longer tolerance as soon as the contract is broken. The supposed absolute tolerance in the tolerance paradox is using a *helper* type of enabling argument in which people attempt to duplicitously enable behavior which in turn enables and sustains conflict. Wars are the most banal theater for the Karpman model, with entire nations acting as as persecutor, victim, and the helper who does nothing but wag a finger. Tolerating someone walking over you is not the same as the tolerance of others, there is an insufficiency in language exploited by helpers behaving as debate perverts and wannabe philosophers to castrate the practice of healthy boundaries and self-care behavior in service of philosophy and ego. In refusing to make amends (the fear of not being tolerated) we become victim to the fanciful delusion that there is no contract and we must take control of the actions of others, to create justification for our pain, disappointment, and frustration. But this leaves us as vulnerable and ignorant as those we try to control because they also are driven by trauma and mental illness and base animal instincts for survival which madly drive us away from loss, pain, and rejection in service of nature and the survival of the species at our individual expense. Allowing our ego to dictate the course of our behavior is acting the pawn in the game of biology, where having compassion for ourselves and learning how to accept responsibility for our behavior is revolutionary and enlightened, and that allows us to act in spite of our instincts and to control only that which we actually can, which is our behavior which, unlike those enslaved to their ego, makes us quite powerful indeed.

But since we are also adults and do not have access to parents who can teach us how to make a proper amends we must do this for ourselves, and we can and should do this for ourselves because, as an adult, nobody but us has the ability to do it. Beginning with entries made in the inventory which involve any untoward or hurtful actions against others we *must* then make an amends for that behavior or we will continue to be burdened with guilt and shame for our wrongs and the accompanying liability to our self-esteem. Of course, if it is difficult to even do any inventories because of fear of letting go of control we cannot even arrive at any productive understanding of our behavior nor the events which have shaped our lives, which is a convenient excuse to avoid taking responsibility for our behavior and giving in to our fear of it. If the prospect of doing inventory or making apologies generates fear and anxiety *that too can and should first be inventoried.* Inventorying the inventory or inventorying a resentment against having to apologize, or of fears of apologizing, or recrimination, or shame for our behavior, or fear of giving control to others or being vulnerable, or fear of letting go of control can teach us how to overcome those fears and resentments and thus empower ourselves not only with the courage to properly make amends to those we have hurt but also to do it in a way which is actually effective and avoid the pithy, egotistical strategizing which usually ruin an apology, and thus the strength required to care for such intimidating personal needs. This is how we teach ourselves new skills, by exploring them on paper through this structured practice we become the teacher and the student at once, no longer needing to rely on others for guidance and direction but giving ourselves that which would otherwise have come from effective parents, and all it requires is time, compassion, and paper.

Fearing exploitation by others when we attempt an apology is justifiable. Others can and do take advantage of weaknesses and exploit vulnerability for their own gain at our expense so they too can feel in control of their environment. Just as is the case in writing *a better way* in the fear inventory it is not useful to delude ourselves to reality and a possibility of recrimination and exploitation. But the nuance here is that it is not our job to control others and prevent them from hurting us. That is what we have been doing and exactly why we are ineffective. Others are responsible for their behavior the way we are responsible for our own. It is impossible to control others, and trying to do so is wasteful, distracting, and demoralizing. But we are also only vulnerable to this kind of exploitation in the first place because we lack confidence and self-esteem. In fact, many people profusely apologize because it plays into our identity as a weak and vulnerable person, and the solicitation of pity makes us feel seen and important and oftentimes apologies are made for things that should not be apologized for. Fear too of admitting and thus exposing our weaknesses is a reason many refuse to fix the problems we have caused, because our mistakes and weaknesses were used in childhood as an excuse to hurt us. But we are no longer children and when we refuse to face our weaknesses they in turn wield great power over us and make us infinitely more vulnerable to predators and opportunists because we do not even know our weaknesses. There is great power in understanding ourselves, including our weaknesses, because it allows us to change them into strengths, and clarity over our actions and behaviors can come from thoroughly inventorying everything in our lives before making any amends, which will also bring more confidence and peace in the face of making an apology. If a person does exploit our vulnerability when it is freely offered (which actually does not happen too often as most people actually resent conflict) they are manipulative and probably just as traumatized as ourselves, and it is not our concern. Only our behavior is our concern.

Very often when we offend others we begin to withdraw from them because their presence reminds us of our wrongs. For instance I have two siblings who in the past have stolen from me and both of them in turn withdrew from a relationship with me afterward, having never apologized nor made restitution for their offense, because they find my presence to remind them of those wrongs they feel incapable of making right, and not only cause me further harm but also deprive themselves of a relationship with their older brother who loves and cares for them. I myself did things in my youth which were embarrassing or harmful to others and not being empowered with skills to amend my mistakes instead withdrew from those relationships which I desperately needed because the feelings of shame and guilt I felt in their presence were too strong to bear (like one time abandoning a friendship after they witnessed me driving home intoxicated). Apologizing in truth increases our power because it resolves conflict with those on whom we rely for nurture, support, companionship, income, safety and security, and even social status. It is an act which, contrary to what our ego tells us, cares for our own wellbeing. It also relieves us of the burden of guilt, regret, shame, and unresolved conflict which influence our actions and ability to be effective in our lives. If we hurt someone, no matter the reason, we will still be burdened by the guilt of our choice even if we do the writing practice, and so we must approach them and make an honest amends without any concern for our own ego.

Making an amends is a specific process which must follow certain rules in order to be effective and to not cause more pain and problems (and thus more inventory!). Before making an amends it is important to make a lot of progress in the inventory, especially if the offense is very severe or egregious, because the unconscious and unresolved defense mechanisms will interfere with our efforts, even when we mean well or try very hard, and it will not be effective and thus undermine our confidence rather than nurture it. Remember that confidence comes from positive experiences, which can occur even if an apology does not go well in that we actually did something we might have been afraid of, or refrained from acting the way we used to, learning a new skill which thus imparts new confidence. But if we act with the same selfish defense mechanisms nothing will have changed and thus an opportunity to grow in confidence will have been lost (but if this happens there will be more opportunities in the future). For this reason too an amends should never be made with intent for our needs or desires. If we go into an amends with idea that it will save a relationship we value but it does not this will then cause us more demoralization, and such expectations are unreasonable anyway since we do not control others and there are often consequences to our own behavior (or things happen in spite of our best efforts). Inventorying specific resentment and fears in regards to required amends before making them can prepare us to fully understand ourselves and thus be more effectively prepared before engaging in such an encounter.

Never make amends when doing so would cause more harm. For instance, because I harassed an old boyfriend after he ghosted on me I would *not* go to him and apologize or contact him in any way because the harm I caused was not to leave him alone in the first place when he ended our relationship, and my presence would cause him yet more stress, not less, and would be more concerned for my own benefit, not his, where all amends should be entirely focused on the benefit of the recipient and not ourselves. Likewise, we would not approach the partners of those with whom we have cheated or been unfaithful, or in person to those whom we have physically harmed (a letter might be okay, maybe), and to honor any request to otherwise refrain from contact or behavior which upsets others. We also do not detail every instance of infidelity when we have been unfaithful or dishonest, but instead only sticking to the fact that it happened, to spare our victims more suffering and obsession. Often it is even appropriate not to confess to offenses if it would cause the other person pain, such as a former partner, so long as in doing so we are not potentially also causing them more harm, always concerned with the wellbeing of others over our own when we have done something to harm them.

In making an amends we also *only* address *our* behavior and *never* that of the other person. This is why it is important to wait until we have finished our entire inventory before making amends because addressing the behavior of others in an amends is always a manipulation. Making an amends prematurely we may still be controlled by insecurities and fears and in the middle of an apology become defensive or even more hurtful as we again try to justify our behavior. I once snapped at my mother when she was being particularly manipulative to one of my sisters and made her cry (to be fair my mother does use crying as a manipulation). My egoist instincts were that she deserved it and the old me would have never addressed the encounter again and just moved on and pretended I hadn't hurt my own mother. But having these new tools I pulled her aside the next day. "I'm sorry I hurt you yesterday, I was rude and shouldn't have talked to you like that." "Oh, it's okay" she began to reply, trivializing her experience in order to move past it, "I was being impatient…" "No," I shook my head, "I shouldn't have talked to you like that. It was wrong and I'm very sorry." She didn't reply, as she probably wasn't used to any of our family members doing that, and smiled knowingly and gave me a hug. It was not my job to make my mother treat anyone the way I thought she should, and even if I had tried to make an amends before having learned these tools it would certainly have contained dialogue from me about her behavior. If we are to make an effective amends we must be clear of prejudice against the other person and understand fully our own accountability, which is accomplished by identifying *my part* in the inventory practice, and it is only the *my part* which we are thus concerned during the amends process. Most of us operate with the assumption that we are entitled to our behavior just as others are entitled to theirs. But this is not true. If someone runs up to us on the street and stabs us and we die they are guilty of murder. But if we stab them back and they die we will *also* have killed someone, even if it was in self defense (and also we're dead but that's not the point). If a spouse insults us, do we not bear responsibility for our actions when we insult them back? Are we justified in calling our partner or siblings an asshole because they acted like one? Are we justified in threatening sole custody of children because our partner cheated, using children as leverage and a weapon to get what we feel entitled? Are we justified in hitting our children because they hit someone else? The answer to all of these is *no*, which is why we in fact carry guilt and shame around with us even when we feel justified in our actions. There is an absolute separation between our feelings and the actions we take in response to them, and blurring that line does not absolve us of the consequences. But our coping mechanisms try to do this, which is why resolving them first is important so that we may properly repair the damage we have done and effectively amend our wrongs. Including phrases like '*you don't ever take out the trash,*' or '*I'm sorry but,*' or '*you need to be more responsible,*' in an apology are truly egomaniacal control mechanisms which will only result in more hurt and more offenses of which to feel ashamed. Only when we are capable of taking responsibly for *our* actions alone is it appropriate to make an amends.

    For an amends to be completed requires a commitment to never do again that for which we are apologizing. This may seem self evident but we avoid doing this either because we don't really want to let go of control in such a way or we do not sufficiently value the wellbeing of the other person and therefore are not truthful in our attempt to apologize. This step is not really important for the words we say but simply that we are willing to say it, to give up a control mechanism and communicate that we recognize the harm it has caused. That my old boyfriend never once actually said he would not cheat on me again was an admission that he never intended to stop, and I willfully accepted his insufficient apologies because I so badly wanted to believe he loved me (which are both great examples of not recognizing there is never anything wrong with want, only in how we go about getting it, such as wanting to be treated with respect and empathy in a relationship, or getting to have as much sex as we want with a variety of partners). Often we do not want to make such a commitment because doing so gives power to the other person. If you do not want to make such a commitment you should not be making an apology, and must do more inventory on your behavior and the fears which underlie an unwillingness to stop behaviors which are harmful to others, and when you do come to this understanding it is easy to make such a commitment. Obviously in amends with those whom we no longer have have relationships, such as an ex, it's not relevant to commit to never cheating on them again. Such semantics are not the point—in such a case it can be that you hurt them, and can commit to never doing that again. Similarly, if the amends is to someone who wants to maintain a relationship but you do not, you can preface the amends by being clear you do not want a relationship—not, *I don't think a relationship between us would work*, or *you're better off without me*, as such refusal to be clear is also a manipulation because we fear being perceived as 'the bad guy.' But when we are ending a relationship we are 'the bad guy,' to them, and there is no getting around that fact nor that we will hurt people in the process, and doing sufficient inventory to recognize these control behaviors will help the amends be successful.

While making amends is a requirement for finding resolution of trauma, the flip-side of amends is the notion of *forgiveness*, which is not. Forgiveness as a concept is most often used as a control mechanism by abusers and manipulators as a way to further perpetuate abuse, control, and exploit vulnerability by implicitly demanding we excuse trespassers their transgressions even when forgiveness has never been petitioned. Many people will state they forgive someone as if we have explicit control over our emotions and feelings, as if saying we forgive those who murdered our child or abused us as children will somehow remove or lessen the pain we feel. I have oft been reprimanded to forgive those actively engaged in abuse and harm to me or my brothers and sisters who are also LGBTQI+, or whom have different skin color or commit violence against marginalized groups, purposefully mischaracterizing advocacy for those who are oppressed as a refusal to forgive because doing so helps those responsible for oppression avoid accountability for their actions and thus sustains conflict. In fact that is the primary purpose of forgiveness as a concept—unearned absolution of responsibility—and forgiveness is a tool created by abusers for the very purpose of avoiding responsibility and is not altruistic or useful in the resolution of trauma. Forgiveness is truly a vile and underhanded manipulation and promotes the most ghastly of crimes against humanity. A young woman once approached me because she had been molested by her older cousin while they were both children, he being about ten years her senior, because she felt awful for being unable to forgive him and had been counseled by many in her life to do so even though he had never asked for it nor attempted to make amends for the harm he had caused. One of the reasons forgiving people is difficult is that we are still possessed of human instincts for emotional security within our families, communities, and society which is facilitated through the acknowledgement, documentation, and resolution of offenses and administration of justice, and if those who have caused such wrongs are not conciliatory or held to account that safety is never achieved and so we remain aware of the continued potential threat from those who value their own needs over those of others. It is very wrong to tell people who have been harmed that they should forgive those who harmed them, especially when nothing has been done to heal those wrongs, because it robs us of our autonomy, self-determination, and support which underlie emotional security and self-esteem at the core of our identity and purpose as a human being.

Similarly, being unwilling to forgive those who have harmed us may be a reason we avoid making amends to them if we have also harmed them, because we mistakenly believe that making an amends when they will not implies we forgive them, which we don't because they have not asked for it. But this defensive mechanism is also a control mechanism and we are *never* responsible for the behavior of others and needn't design our own to effect such ends. Failing to make amends for this reason robs us of the pleasure and satisfaction of taking responsibility for our own behavior and condemns us to the same fate as those we resent. After a sufficient quantity of inventories have been completed it will be easy to recognize that we do not need to concern ourselves with the behavior of others, especially that which prevents us from taking care of ourselves such as through the making of amends. Those who have harmed us are compelled, like us, to wallow in the consequences of their own unresolved harms and mistakes. We know what it is like to have guilt gnaw at the back of our mind and those who have done us harm will have to live every waking moment with that while we will bask in that freedom as under the light of the sun unhidden in a cloudless sky. There is no need to forgive anyone of anything, but instead taking time to learn self-care and self-compassion for our past can bring results into our lives which forgiveness ostensibly promises but so often fails to deliver—which are personal peace, acceptance of life, self-love, and resolution of fear and resentment, without ever needing to give offenders the freedom they so unfairly and undeservedly desire. If someone asks for forgiveness and takes the steps required to amend wrongs it can then be done, but otherwise forgiveness is usually a tool for manipulation that can be discarded as such, where peace instead is found through resolution of trauma such as the inventory facilitates.

It's okay to wait until we feel strong enough and emotionally capable of handling the responsibility of a proper amends. But many people purposefully avoid the practice of inventory to avoid making amends, and this too must also be inventoried! Resenting having to make amends is also a resentment, because it is a condition of life which is unpleasant and painful, and cowardice as a character weakness is a self-preservation coping mechanism learned in youth when we were small and tormented and abused and demonstrates an absence of compassion for our experiences and understanding of our inherent self-worth. Continuing to inventory all parts of our lives and not just that which is convenient or easy can continue helping us to resolve our fears and insecurities, to become the most effective person we can become which in turn makes life more rich and rewarding, to reach heights of transcendence we never thought possible.

When we are ready and we do approach someone to repair the past (even and especially children), it should also never be done with an outcome in mind. The point of amends is absolutely *not* to repair a relationship or to receive benefits for ourselves. That is an underhanded, manipulative, and selfish coping mechanism which will also only result in yet more problems. Engaging in an amends is never about what we get. It is only about what we can give, and if you enter into an amends with the goal of securing a relationship or getting something for yourself it will fail and the relationship will be further undermined. This is still a desire for control, which must be abandoned entirely. It is up to the other person what occurs afterward and you must be willing to accept the consequences of your behavior, whatever they may be.

When we hurt people they might also not be ready to forgive us, and may use the opportunity to berate us or continue the conflict. Not once in my amends process did this actually happen, though, even though I was very afraid of it, because most people hate conflict and just want everything to be okay, but even if it does happen it's fine because just as we are responsible for our behavior we are also not responsible for the behavior of others. Becoming defensive, remember, is a control mechanism, and having done the inventory we probably are now aware of our tendency for self-defensive behavior. But negative reactions are typically avoided by communicating that we recognize not only that we did hurt someone but exactly, *how* we hurt them. Normally people become contemptuous when we apologize because we aren't actually apologizing. *"I'm sorry you got hurt"* is an incredibly deceptive and manipulative refusal both to accept responsibility for our actions and failure to repair the damage we caused, which is the entire point of an amends. A family member once tried to apologize to me but spent the entire time saying how sorry they were I got hurt because of the difficult time they were having. But I did not *get* hurt. *They* hurt me. There is a big difference and it is a destructive defense mechanism to obfuscate that fact and refuse responsibility for our behavior. *"I'm sorry I yelled at you, it was wrong of me to do." "I'm sorry I cheated on you, it was wrong and I regret the pain I caused you." "I'm sorry I stole from you, it was wrong and I was wrong to do it,"* accepts responsibility for our behavior, acknowledges the pain we have caused, and demonstrates that we understand exactly what it was we did that was the problem, which is usually all that our victims wanted in the first place.

An amends is also never complete without actually making reparations for the past. *"How can I make it better?"* or *"What can I do to fix what I've done?"* must always accompany and close an amends, unless it is so obvious what you should to do make reparations and you do it without needing a prompt (but still ask after anyway just to make sure). Avoiding the question so you don't have to reimburse stolen money, or correct lies, or reveal embarrassment, or lose a job or even go to jail is a liability that will weigh down the soul until you find the courage to do so. Sometimes the things we do to others are so egregious is would require forfeit of our freedom to make amends, but even then the inventory practice can help us find courage and value in doing that for those we have harmed and in so doing find some peace for ourselves over the things we did to cause pain and heartache. If we are unwilling to fix the past we have not fully resolved our fears and insecurities and must continue inventory therapy until this is the case. The fear of validating our fears by admitting our wrongs and taking responsibility for them is why murderous despots die in prison having never repented of their crimes, or why spouses would rather divorce and destroy their family rather than admit culpability, or why children who have grown into adults try desperately to prove what great parents they are by yelling at their children and siblings and parents who dare confront us about our poor choices and bad behavior. Fixing the past is as important as the words we use to address it, and making amends for our wrongs will finally put to rest all the demons which have for so long tormented us.

Sometimes it is best if relationships are discarded. It is okay to let those people go and to set healthy boundaries and make new connections and relationships with people who have our best interests in mind. Being empowered to make amends without concern for the outcome can also empower us to cut ties with people who are abusive and do not respect boundaries, without further compromising our own behavior and morals, skills which will become more clear as more inventory is accomplished.

Saying sorry is largely a very difficult task only because we take ourselves and life far too seriously. Most often the things we have done to hurt others are in fact quite ridiculous and hardly warrant the level of vitriol and animosity which accompany them. Regardless of the outcome, making real amends is the most empowering skill that any person can possess, and teaching ourselves this skill will also empower us to teach it to our children so their lives can be more productive and effective.

15

Pseudoempathy and the Duality of Control Mechanisms

The English language has a lot of deficiencies when it comes to language needs of humans to effectively interact, communicate, and handle life. As discussed frequently throughout this book, despite our best intentions and even with those possessed of expansive vocabularies and talented communication skills there can be deficits in communication due to biases, miscommunication, or cognitive hurdles which disconnect intent with outcome no matter our intent or purpose. When dealing with psychological trauma there exists a very distinct deficiency in the categorizing, describing, and treating of a very particular problem of psychological emotional stress which is not distinctly recognized by the medical and psychological establishment and perpetuated precisely because a word does not exist to describe it.

Normally this psychological problem is incorrectly described as *empathy*. As mentioned in the chapter on inventory therapy, taking on the feelings of others is most distinctly *not* what empathy is. Empathy is the ability to understand what other people are feeling, not the experience of actually feeling those feelings ourselves. Feeling compassion for someone who is going through something difficult is empathy, but actually taking on the feelings from experiences of others is a control mechanism closely related to narcissism, where an absence of emotional fulfillment as a child conditioned some of us to adopt other coping strategies for validation. This categorically distinct experience different from true empathy is not recognized because many psychological health professionals also experience it and do not recognize it as a distinctly different experience to empathy, thinking that what they are experiencing is empathy. Taking on the feelings of others is a unique psychological pathology which results from experiences of trauma, and functions to opportunistically subsume attention and generate a sense of validation from the experiences of others.

In order to distinguish between this experience and empathy there needs then be a word to describe it. I tried several terms but I think *pseudoempathy* works best since the experience of subsuming the emotions of others objectively demonstrates an inability to have sympathy for those from whom we are coopting emotions, since the act of taking in such a manner is an inherently narcissistic and self-centered behavior. Because pseudoempathy has heretofore been called empathy it is consequently excused, trivialized, justified, or even praised though it always is used as a means for control, manipulation, attention seeking, or to otherwise reinforce unproductive or destructive coping mechanisms. It can be especially prevalent within romantic and personal relationships and is especially destructive within a parent-child relationship. When a person actually feels the emotions being felt by another our ability to effectively navigate those relationships becomes impaired. For instance, if as a parent we feel a sense of sadness when our children feel sadness it often leads to us prioritizing our experience or reprimanding them instead of demonstrating both support and healthy coping behaviors. Because women are stereotypically regarded as the emotional gender the manifestation of pseudoempathy is often defended or praised in women though it makes us unstable, unreliable, and even volatile, not to mention the inherent vulnerability to our environment and relationships it causes since we do not possess healthy skills to otherwise handle interpersonal relationships.

Men are every bit as emotional as women, every bit as petty, selfish, histrionic, volatile, but also empathetic, kind, and compassionate. The only difference is that men are trained not to *show* their feelings, where women are taught not only to frequently show emotions but also to use them as a method to control and manipulate others. Although it is very clearly the case, many of us for some reason believe that failure to show or demonstrate emotion also means an absence of feeling those emotions. As a young man I actively demanded that partners reveal their emotions, because I was insecure in my own value and the security of my relationships, not understanding that anyone simply showing up and choosing to be part of my life was itself a demonstration of emotion and commitment. The desire to force people to talk about their emotions is a control behavior, very manipulative and destructive, and using emotions or the excuse of emotions to affect others is the same. Having emotions is healthy and good, but using those emotions to evoke or control behavior in others is narcissistic and self-centered and needs to be inventoried so we can be more effective in our personal relationships and life goals, as well as to empower children with healthy life skills.

Pseudoempathy is a particularly destructive behavior within relationships because it is used as a way to dominate the emotional dynamics of intimacy, to force others to accommodate our feelings and desires no matter how disruptive, self-centered, or destructive this can be while also excusing us from giving back to those from whom we take. The young man I dated who was sexually abused by his uncle in his youth suffered from pseudoempathy because he assumed the emotions I felt and therefore could not handle being in a relationship with me, and so he shut down as soon as things started to get emotionally intimate, even though he did not use his emotions to control me directly he used them to control his environment and personal experience and in the process destroyed what was playing out as an exciting and fulfilling love affair. Very often in men, pseudoempathy presents as feeling insecure when others, especially our partner, demonstrate insecurity. Being big and masculine we feel we must be impervious to insecurity, so when someone does something embarrassing or experiences failure we are not capable of having compassion for them and instead regard them with contempt or indifference which thus in turn distances ourselves from the person with whom we are in a relationship. Having some tendencies for pseudoempathy myself I often regarded erratic or emotional behavior in my partners with disdain which immediately cut off compassion for them and thus an ability to feel attracted. Demanding that potential romantic partners demonstrate confidence, stability, have money, or other narcissistic qualities is a direct manifestation of pseudoempathy because these are control behaviors attempting to prevent pseudoempathetic feelings. But since we cannot control our own emotions, which instead must be inventoried, these qualities never succeed in satisfying relationships because no person on Earth is entirely secure, stable, and invulnerable to loss and failure.

Being conditioned to believe the pseudoempathetic subsumption of others' emotions is an acceptable behavior causes severe chaos as a parent, because the lack of real empathy impairs bonding and effective parenting by obscuring real understanding of the experiences of children. It also actively causes ourselves immense emotional stress by compounding the stress already inherent of normal life, which is already sufficient without adding more on top of it. Since it is inherently a narcissistic behavior, pseudoempathy prevents us from meeting the needs of children because our purpose during any encounter is to first neutralize the pseudoempathy by controlling the encounter, rather than addressing the needs of the child, thus perpetuating abuse and trauma through our inability to effectively handle this responsibility.

While the emphasis in this book on self-care has been largely toward behaviors to relieve us of the stresses of adulthood, life, and parenting, the most important self-care skills are those which are cognitive, mental, and emotional, and it is the lack of such intangible and esoteric skills that we adopt pseudoempathy as a control behavior in the first place, unable to mentally and emotionally handle life thusly adapt to it through such unproductive coping mechanisms as pseudoempathy, self-contempt, self-pity, and contempt for others the effect their behavior has on our lives. The ability to deal with stress by making ourselves a really yummy grilled sandwich or taking time out of our day to do some introspective work is facilitated first by a mental ability to recognize problems and to formulate ideas for dealing with them. Most people think of self-care skills as something we do in the physical world, but if you are not even aware of a problem or possible solutions it is not even possible to make choices in the real world to then have material effects on our experiences. Those of us with alcoholism and addiction severely lack such cognitive self-care skills so that when confronted by real world stress such as disappointment, rejection, loss, loneliness, failure, mistakes, or powerlessness we are then unable to mentally handle that stress because we were never taught the cognitive and coping skills required. Then discovering drugs and alcohol, which are effective chemical treatments for the stress hormones by stress, become the only self-care skill of which we are cognizant and thus our dependency on them.

Having pseudoempathy is a distracting coping mechanism which prevents us from learning effective cognitive self-care skills because instead of learning new emotional skills for coping with experiences or people which are stressful we simply entertain and empower our destructive coping and control strategies which in turn reinforces defensive behavior which then makes us more vulnerable to the environment, not less. As in other chapters, resolving the condition of pseudoempathy does not come from exerting willpower, determination, control, but instead taking time to practice inventory therapy, specifically on those people, situations, or experiences in which we feel strong emotions or subsume the emotions from others' experiences. Similarly, other distractions in our lives often serve the purpose of helping us handle uncomfortable emotions caused by unresolved trauma from our past. While social media, pornography, and eating all serve as effective self-soothing behaviors and are inherently useful and beneficial, their excessive use, especially to deal with emotions such as boredom, insecurity, loneliness, and depression can hint at underlying and deeply traumatic conceptions of our self worth. Many of us try to handle these problems by willpower or discipline, but the reason we continue to struggle with them in spite of our best efforts is a fundamental absence of self-care and the skills which facilitate it. A great anecdote to demonstrate this principle would be comparing the relationship between two proverbial dog owners and their dogs. One owner has given their dog a bed in their own bedroom, another in the living room, or next to their desk in the office, is taken for walks daily, has plenty of toys, other dog friends, and is fed other foods besides just kibble. The other dog owner keeps their dog mostly locked in a cage, is rarely walked, fed nothing but standard kibble, is yelled at or even beaten when they make a mistake, and doesn't ever have interaction with other dogs because they are so neglected. How would the relationship of each owner to their dog be characterized? One clearly loves their dog. The other does not. We, as adult humans, are both the proverbial dog *and* the owner. Do we actionably demonstrate love toward ourself? Or do we discipline, scold, and neglect? Many people attempt inventory to resolve what we perceive as lack of discipline or other character issues—watching porn, not waking up on time, procrastinating deadlines, or not being productive—but this still demonstrates an absence of empathy and love for ourselves and is born purely of fear, insecurity, and self-hatred, and the problem is not that we watch porn, wake up late, or avoid responsibility but the trauma which makes us hate ourselves and thus unable to care for our needs just like the neglectful dog owner to their dog. If as a child our character was scolded for mistakes rather than our actions we were conditioned to see ourselves as the problem and thus fundamentally incapable of succeeding. *"Why is this wet towel on the ground? I've told you a million times not to leave the towels on the ground,"* is the very kind of abuse which teaches us to hate ourselves and withhold empathy for our shortcomings and vulnerabilities which in turn promote avoidance behaviors as an adult. *"Nope! Pick that up and put it where it belongs,"* is the kind of healthy discipline that does not cause abuse but which many of us were not lucky enough to receive and thus why we have such a hard time recognizing our own self-loathing and the source of our inability to meet our own expectations.

Pseudoempathy and self pity are at their core a failure to demonstrate compassion for *our* needs and feelings, because we find them so difficult to endure, so we adopt those of others in order to distract ourselves from our own emotions, pain, and absence of self-compassion. We will even pretend to have feelings we think we should have in situations when we don't experience them, because we are so dissociated by our trauma it is impossible to feel genuinely. Although inventory therapy can and does result in new tangible behaviors and skills which help us affect our material experience, its primary benefit is to increase our cognitive and emotional skills, which give us a greater capacity to handle life, endure stress, and the confidence to accept the indefatigable changeableness that is reality. Many respond to the prospect of inventory therapy by doggedly holding on to control behaviors and defense mechanisms because it helps us feel a sense of power over our environment, but in reality we are always at its mercy. Being able not only to accept that but to embrace it is one of the great results of dedicated inventory therapy practice, and the increase in emotional intelligence which results teaches the very self-care skills we lack. When we become thusly empowered it is possible to recognize that our own feelings are enough. They do not need to be justified, explained, or exaggerated.

One year in High School I discovered yet again that a friend had been hanging out with other people and did not invite me along. This had happened enough that it seemed like they were purposefully avoiding me (which they probably were). Hurt and depressed, I withdrew from the relationship entirely, as I had others, and refused to associate with them any longer—A preemptive rejection for the fear of being rejected, as ghosts of destructive behavior live within us all, those voices in our heads which motivate us to act in ways which we don't really want to, watching in horror as if behind a one-way mirror as we do something we know will get us the opposite of what we truly want, such as refusing to hang out with people you actually want to hang out with, yelling at a loved one when the relationship already sits on a knife's edge, or making unnecessary purchases when your bank account is so close to death, befuddled by our seeming inability to change course.

Self-defeating behaviors like this was for me most evident in romantic relationships in the shaming, blaming, and argument with men from whom I wanted love but seemed powerless to get it. Wanting peace and harmony I went about shouting and arguing until the only peace came from their departure. Similarly we may fear financial hardship but go to great lengths to empty our bank accounts, living paycheck to paycheck though frugality would easily provide the stability we crave and instead live in instability. Loathing disloyalty or fearing loneliness we hurry on our way to hurt romantic partners or alienate friends and family. Worried of falling out of love we eagerly pass the opportunity to put down our cellphone and hang out with those we love. Afraid we are not fit we pull up to the McDonald's drive-through and order hamburgers and French fries, or embark on destructive diets and starve and injure our bodies and end up making ourselves sick. Swearing we will not become our parents we become every bit as controlling and unreasonable with our own offspring.

Therapy as it is often practiced today usually consists of speaking about experiences and feelings to a professional listener who may or may not maintain a degree of impartiality and objective observation, and the net effect is always to reinforce the very behaviors we wish to be rid of because in the very act of listening the therapist is actually enabling the heretofore unrecognized dual nature of control and coping mechanisms (called character weaknesses in the inventory practice) which, motivated by fear, is the real root of personal discord which cannot be untethered one from the other without first identifying the origin of their shared motivation. I once had a partner who in therapy was contrite, helpful, and willingly capitulated to destructive habits and was an exemplary patient, but when we arrived home he instantly became defiant and even further entrenched in those behaviors eschewed in the doctor's office. When I was working on my own inventory therapy I was struck by how many of my identified character problems were actually complimentary counter-balances of others, and realized why we so often fail when trying to better ourselves. For instance, I had never considered myself a perfectionist because I often avoided even attempting certain tasks or engaging in life. It was pointed out to me by my sponsor in a recovery program that perfectionists also avoid doing something out of fear of not being able to do it perfectly in the first place. It was eye-opening, as I had never even considered I could be a perfectionist (which is a character weakness, not a strength as many people delusionally believe). Instead of sticking to task until it was 'perfect' I instead became unmotivated, fearing failure, having the dual character weaknesses perfectionism and avoidance which served to impair my effectiveness. Lacking self-esteem I also developed a talent for egotism in order to counterbalance feelings of worthlessness. Feeling entitled to success I was ungrateful for what I had achieved. Insecure about being wrong I argued to be right. Feeling inferior I thought myself better-than. Being unsympathetic I judged those who needed sympathy. Fearing loss, I isolated.

Once this tethering of character defects is recognized it is easily seen in the general population. In places like social media users are quick to assert their uniqueness, achievements, looks, wealth, or engage in antagonistic behavior as a reflex to deeper feelings of inadequacy, want, desire, or need, who lash out at others from fears of secret personal perceived failings, or in those who pile on the public mistakes of others because they secretly fear their own vulnerability and fallibility. Politicians who are corrupt drone on and on about corruption, those who have offended women and children prostrate themselves as family men with traditional values, closeted gay men harass and attack those who live openly (which is why we are never surprised when anti-gay politicians are found out to be one of us, we've known this happens for some time). In our personal lives the duality of character defects are one coping mechanism compensating for the problems caused by another, both causing us to act and lead our lives in ways we don't really want and which prevent us from meeting our goals and achieving real success, whether it be in personal relationships, business, health, creative pursuits, or even just enjoying life, because they are simply ways of coping with trauma and the absence of more effective life skills. Pseudoempathy for example is a coping mechanism which compensates for the problems caused by the coping mechanism of apathy, motivated by the fear of true emotional vulnerability which can be exploited by opportunistic partners, friends, family members, and even strangers we cut ourselves off from feeling real empathy for others, but this then makes our emotional life dull and dissatisfying, and replacing real empathy with pseudoempathy redirects emotional energy to ourselves rather than those who are actually affected by the problems at issue thus exploiting such situations to satisfy our desire for control, including of the problems caused by our own trauma and behavior in the first place.

Buried in every each set of codependent weaknesses is a judgment about ourself which is then instinctively reacted to by creating an apparent opposite, what appears to the unconscious mind as a complimentary strength but is usually just a reactive adaptation and more often takes the form of something potentially destructive. Insecurity is a self judgement that we are insufficient as we are and must justify our existence, desires, and needs, and then assume the response to insecurity is to be confident, but it is not possible to willingly adopt confidence which is instead a product of positive, lived experiences and so become arrogant or egoistic. Similarly, concern about financial status is a judgement that we are not capable of meeting our own needs and caring for ourselves (including the collecting and maintaining of relationships) and then assume the antidote is to appear wealthy, or we become braggarts or gaudy about the things we do have, or even completely lie about it, which obviously does nothing to satiate the actual fear of material insufficiency. I once went on a date with someone I was enjoying immensely until he spent the remainder of the date talking about recently having had a stalker. He even invited himself up to my apartment where we spent hours together naked, and when I called him several days later to follow up about a future date he snidely remarked that I was also stalking him, so I did not call again because he was clearly looking for someone to stalk him, to give him a sense of importance and excitement, and not a boyfriend, though he probably thought otherwise, his fear of control and judgement of his vulnerability controlled in turn by pushing others away. The man I briefly dated who was abused as a child spent half a decade working with a specialist to recover from it, but because the tendency for therapy is to only address one side of the tethering of character weaknesses he was not relieved of his self-defeating behavior, to cling to his trauma as a defensive anticipation of future harm, even though he was a fully grown man, and soon into our relationship began turning it into a reenactment of his abuse, avoiding certain sexual activities with me (like oral sex) even though we were both fully-grown, consenting adults. His fear of powerlessness which resulted from the abuse was not addressed during therapy and so neither were the outward control issues which prevented him from finding real and satisfying intimacy with other adults, and as is the subtle and nuanced nature of this aspect of human psychology, inadvertently assumed the opposite of being powerless was to assert power. In reality we are all powerless, which is why bad things happen to all of us, and such behavior only continues to make us even more powerless, destroying relationships, intimacy, and friendship and getting us the exact opposite of what we truly yearn, which is to heal and find fulfillment in life.

Practicing personal inventory and fear inventory analysis of the self properly illuminates these tricky devices of self-defense which end up causing us so much unnecessary heartache and frustration and stalls development into a healthy, balanced adult. Professional therapists who earnestly and consistently practice inventory themselves will be endowed with an uncanny ability to intuitively understand the entirety of the human psyche, because similarly most therapists also avoid confronting these control and coping mechanisms in themselves, never having been taught truly effective tools for resolving experiences of trauma and the resulting fear and coping mechanisms. In the case of the abused chid, doing inventory highlights our responsibility as an adult for continuing to ruminate on the trauma and anticipate potential future harm which no one but ourselves is actually capable of addressing, but which can also free us of misplaced sense of responsibility or contribution to the harm we did actually experience which, if we do feel that way, is merely a coping mechanism trying to exert control over such horrible things by believing we can somehow do something about it. It is not a hand-holding, overly-sentimental approach to suffering but is instead an effective and compassionate way to truly sever the cause and effect of suffering, as the adult victim of child abuse does not escape suffering until we can accept the reality of our own character weaknesses and coping and control mechanisms which continue to facilitate fear, anxiety, and self-destructive behavior, which is a condition that every single one of us must at some point accept that is not unique only to victims of abuse. If only we were like dogs and could quickly shrug off offenses to our person life would be much simpler. But we are not, and the human condition requires thoughtful searching and analysis of our inner selves in order to come to terms with who we are as a person and what conditions life has set for us. Only then can we operate realistically within the bounds of mortality and successfully meet the challenges of everyday life.

This dual nature of human control mechanisms is responsible for many of our oldest self-defeating behaviors, such as war, political conflict, child abuse, and the exploitation of our natural world to such a degree as to threaten our very existence as a species on this Earth. It is the fault of our ancestors that we no longer have some of the incredible species which used to roam this earth, even though they had been on the earth for millions of years while scientist naively say, 'well we really can't know what killed them,' after finding ample evidence of human predation and overexploitation which fueled our spread across the globe because we fear our own inherited nature of selfishness and so adopt willful naivety to cope with realities we find uncomfortable or which challenge our noble but delusional self-image. The catastrophic extinction of our prey species in turn forced us as humans to rely more on agriculture than we had previously, and in some regions of the world like North America endeared people with more respect for nature and traditions that held sacred the species which remained, a collective regret for wiping out our own natural resources and imperiling the lives of our progeny. Human peril arrives most often from our inability to recognize the contradictory nature of our coping mechanisms, and each of us are doomed to continue living in frustration until we recognize this self-defeating, coping behavior in our own lives through such practices as inventory therapy which can effectively illuminate the unconscious mind. For instance, we as humans often fail to recognize being ungrateful as a coping mechanism because our struggles often seem so overwhelming and absolute. But that is only a function of our biological psychology and even when I had absolutely no friends or family I was grateful for the warm bed and good food I have almost always had, not because of a willing change in attitude or mindset but because I sat down and practiced inventory therapy to resolve the unresolved experiences of trauma which motivated ungratefulness as a coping mechanism to cope with fears of financial insecurity. No matter how bad things are they can in fact always get worse, and being unable to recognize the ways in which our lives are working well is not a moral problem—it makes us ineffective because we only recognize those resources we do not have as opposed to those we do which can assist us in our efforts to survive and be more effective in our own lives. Manipulative people use forgiveness or gratefulness as a way to paper over the wrongs and harms they cause, but properly separating the things which happen to us in opposition of the things we do and choose such as the structured practice facilitates makes for the most effective psychological adaptation to these conditions of life.

One day in the office a therapist who was also the vice-president of a school of psychology at UCLA I realized after twelve sessions of therapy he was still rehashing the events of my last breakup even though I had expressed a desire to learn tools to heal and move on. Brought to tears again by yet another retelling of my heartache but not instructed with any tools to deal with my life I knew I was not going to get anything from him but an empty bank account. It wasn't until years later after I learned how to do inventory therapy that I was truly freed from these issues with my psyche, loss, and fear, and it is the most effective therapy for uncovering the secrets of the inner human mind that I have ever found. The median between these tethered character weaknesses all lie within accepting our faults, perceived or real, a process which is facilitated by seeing them written on paper before us. I was utterly blown away by how effective a simple worksheet was at helping to relieve my pain and self-destruction compared to the long hours and expensive sessions with trained professionals. Such convoluted, twisted problems did not seem like they should be so easy to solve, especially not without significant financial cost. In the case of a breakup I was confounded by a feeling of betrayal, of being abandoned, and yes I was legitimately hurt, but this also fed into a sense that I was in danger or that my life was destroyed, which wasn't really true but was nonetheless terribly painful. Those feelings were not a result of the breakup but because I had been deluded to the permanence of life by previous conditioning and experiences by other humans who also feared death and loss above all else. My character defect of having unrealistic expectations—that everything lasts—was jarringly rebuffed by lived experiences, and it was the alarm of having unmet expectations which caused the greater portion of my suffering rather than the actual separation which, while still painful and heartbreaking, would have been much easier and more successful if I'd known recognized and accepted that life is inherently ever-changing, but most importantly that this is not something to fear and is instead handled by more greatly appreciating the experiences we do have, especially since I knew I would in fact be better off without that kind of person in my life.

Our existence is also enough, and does not need to be justified, explained, or exaggerated. But, feeling the opposite, we think that we must instead compensate through coping mechanisms like pseudoempathy in order to feel in control, validated, or seen, and that act of controlling is the very act of withholding self-compassion which also prevents us from truly appreciating the specialness that is life. The opposite behavior, sitting down to do practice inventory on encounters which trigger pseudoempathy and other control and coping mechanisms is the act of having self-compassion, by acknowledging our needs and vulnerability and taking responsibility for our own behavior teaches empowerment which is the antidote to control behaviors. The ability to let things be the way they are is a cognitive skill that must be learned, but unlike other skills in life those which are required to find empowerment can be self-taught simply through the act of practicing inventory. Using this practice to understand why we have and use coping and control behaviors will resolve them and thus make space for us to experience real empathy both for others as well as ourselves which, unlike pseudoempathy, is not debilitating or intimidating but wonderful and validating. Likewise, apathy or blaming are other control mechanisms which, like pseudoempathy, appear when we dislike how the emotions or experiences of others make us feel, and instead of experiencing empathy attempt to control our environment to avoid the experience altogether. These are all very destructive, especially within interpersonal relationships and the parenting experience, so don't avoid doing inventory if these problems affect you, because a life which never experiences true empathy is severely myopic. Having real empathy is empowering because it increases our emotional intelligence and ability to effectively navigate personal relationships, especially those with our own children. Real empathy is also a very spiritual experience through which we can experience the true depths of humanity, and if pseudoempathy, apathy, or blaming are getting in the way of this experience resolve it as fast as possible through dedicated inventory practice, because it would be a shame to live all of life without every knowing how incredible an experience it can truly be.

Fear of Death is the ultimate forge of dualistic character weaknesses. Fearing our own mortality we concoct many schemes with which to divert our attention from something so alarming—the disfigurement of our faces with plastic surgery, obsession with health and fitness, even leaving those who love us when their own struggles force us to confront our fear of mortality. None of those behaviors actually resolve this fear, which will never truly resolve until we accept our limits and acknowledge the conditions of reality over which we are powerless. This can never be done by willfully restraining our attitudes, and must instead be done by thoughtfully putting pen to paper in structured practice, and in so doing we become aware of those weaknesses which are motivated by fear, cease striving to bury them with self-defeating behaviors, and later find them replaced by strengths. "He was always a rather stupidly optimistic man," goes one of my favorite lines from the movie Clue, "I'm afraid it came as a great shock to him when he died."

16

No

When I was eight or nine years old my brother and I were playing with Lincoln Logs, LEGOS, and Construx in our basement when suddenly our mother shouted for us from upstairs. Her voice was strained and panicked, so we went running as fast as we could. Reaching the living room we were horrified to see our mother standing with one of our sisters tightly grasped in one hand, in the other a large kitchen knife. "If you EVER tell me *NO* again I will CUT your tongue out with this knife. Do you hear me?" We nodded obediently.

While none of us ever actually had our tongues cut out, my mother was so stressed by the first decade of motherhood that, without more effective parenting tools and burdened with her own unresolved childhood pain and trauma, such desperate displays of aggression were very common. One of my little sisters once contracted ring worm, and my mother blamed me for it, claiming I had allowing her to touch a cat even though I had never been told what ringworm was nor that we weren't allowed to pet cats nor had even seen my sister touching a cat, never mind the fact that I am not as an eight-year-old boy capable of nor responsible for preventing the parasitic infection of other children.

Children who grow up in healthy home environments are able to form positive conceptions of themselves. Seemingly little acts like collecting music, finding a favorite hair style, and growing long-term friendships are in fact how we as children form personal identities. Those of us who instead grow up in abusive homes must spend all our time navigating our abusive parents. Instead of learning what music we like we learn what messes will trigger our Mom or what personal revelations might trigger our Dad. Growing up in such an environment then conditions us to live our life oriented toward everything that happens around us rather than what happens within us, then we enter adulthood without the tools to care for our own real needs and instead focus on those superficial things which we think are necessary for our wellbeing but which in fact are only priorities because our parents told us they were. A child raised by a mother who believed her own self worth was based in what she looks like or how clean her house is then becomes an adult with no conception of her inherent worth as a person, and because she has no concept of true self worth in turn is unable to show her own daughter or sons what self worth really means, and they too grow up thinking their self worth is entirely based on their physical appearance or how clean their house is.

Many of us adopt self-conceptions based on how others treat us because that is how our parents showed us that relationships work and where to look for self-esteem. If our husband or wife doesn't pay us proper attention we in turn believe they don't love us, so then we try attempting to make them do things the way we think they should but end up shaming our loved ones and driving them away. Or we see money or status or professional or religious success as the bar which must be reached, but because our inherent self worth is not based on any of this, never find the satisfaction we seek and spend our entire lives in conflict. Life simply can be stressful, and if we are not adequately prepared to deal with the fact that things often do not go our way we are instead doomed to suffer immeasurably. In this regard, *"no,"* is probably the most infuriating word in the English language and the one most reviled by all members of a family, but especially parents and their children. Because we rely on other human beings for many of our needs, spouses and offspring often become apoplectic when confronted by the obstinance of others, because in turn it means that we cannot get the things we need, or think we need.

For such a little word, *no* hardly warrants the amount of emotion which it inspires in its targets. Little children especially can fall absolutely to pieces when the word no is flung back at them, because no is very often exactly how our development as a child is denied, being continually blocked when trying to find out who we are as a person through life experiences. But parents too can be broadsided and enraged when their tiny, little children refuse them with as much determination as any grown, independent adult. Hearing the word *no* more than any other method of communication carries with it enormous amounts of psychological baggage. In truth, a parent's revulsion at being told *no* when asking their children to clean up their rooms or eat their dinner has very little to do with the moment at hand and everything to do with rejection from our childhood. We are not hearing the single word *no* said in the moment, which in reality is probably not a big deal, but instead all of the times we have ever been told *no* throughout our entire lifetime, and our accumulated struggle against all of humanity to survive, be seen, and included. When we feel uncomfortable feelings at hearing *no* from our children it reveals unresolved trauma at being limited most especially in our childhood. Remember that children are entirely incapable of caring for themselves, a request to a parent for opportunity, provisions, or love cannot be achieved without not only the consent of the parent but also their active participation and assistance. So the word *no* to a child is not just an inability to have what they want but in reality an inability to get the very thinks that a human being needs for survival. Being thusly stifled in our early and instinctual drive to live, the word *no* carries a much more primal and visceral context than what parents are aware when they use it with children, while also themselves suffering from their own trauma surrounding the word which originated in their own childhoods when it is flung back at them from little kids. Many of us as adults are hurt when our partners show indifference or apathy to our needs. Maybe we want our partner to watch a movie with us but they are more interested or preoccupied with work. Or maybe we feel they don't compliment us or notice what we do for them, or they spend time on their phone instead of with us, even when we point out that they are neglecting us. The act of rejection is especially painful when our conception of ourselves is based on acceptance, and being told no in its various forms as an adult is often just as painful as it was when we were children, sometimes even more painful since we have accumulated so many experiences of rejection it can sometimes feel difficult to even breathe.

Human nature is inherently and biologically one which is rebellious. This is morally and ethically legitimate, however, because unlike the way we are often portrayed, rebellion is an animal's way of acquiring the means for survival without which we suffer and die. A teenager trapped in a conservative family who causes depression and mental illness from their abuse will naturally attempt to distance themselves as much as they are able without compromising their access to the support both materialistically and emotionally that a family would normally provide, and their right and opportunity for mating and procreation being limited might also be inspired to act out sexually, especially since (as discussed in my other book) stress activates metabolic pathways which increase the sex drive and stimulates compulsive sexual behavior in order to increase the chance of procreation within a stressed animal, since in evolutionary terms that kind of stress normally came with an increased risk of expiration from famine, predation, or conflict. As adults we react with anger and resentment when our partners, friends, siblings, or bosses tell us no. Asking to be seen, to be included, to be loved is met with sometimes callous and summary rejection, and we respond in turn by trying to fight that rejection. Very few human beings will just stand by and allow others to oppress them. Those who do are probably too depressed and ill to respond to the natural inclination to fight barriers to access and opportunity, but most fathers and mothers would not watch their children starve and not try to do something about it, even if their only access to resources is through theft and criminal activity. So do we then lash out at our children when they tell us no, because as an adult our needs often become interrupted when children also insist on theirs. This propensity for rebellion at the perception of denial is so primal that it is one of the very first things children learn to do, and if an adult is at all sensitive to the word *no* it immediately catalyzes the struggle for control and dominance which then ruins most parent-child relationships, and can even spread between romantic couples who are stressed by the dynamics of control and manipulation which they employ and or are also affected by. In reality, there is actually nothing wrong with a child saying *no*. In fact, it's fucking hilarious. Children have absolutely no real say in the matter or ability to enforce their desires, and a little kid telling a grown adult *no* is situational comedy at its finest. The only reason it's a problem at all is because of an adult's own sensitivity surrounding the word and the dynamics of control and dominance we feel compelled to replicate. Reacting offended and angry at hearing *no* we actually act just like a child rather than an adult, insisting through sheer obstinance that we get our way and using our size advantage to force our desires on humans who are magnitudes smaller and more helpless rather than using maturity, intellect, and compassion to realize our needs. But we also, ironically, undermine our own position and authority by betraying to children our particular sensitivities and weaknesses through such undisciplined displays of emotional volatility, and as such empower them with the ability, information, and indeed obligation to manipulate us in return. A parent who is actually in control does not find the word *no* to elicit any emotionally negative reaction, because they have confidence in their position. Without allowing children to control the relationship, a parent should be proud of and amused by their child's instinctual drive at self-preservation. It's inspiring, admirable, and demonstrates an ability to carve out a space for themselves in a world which will put up much resistance. By virtue of our position, parents are in control and nothing the child can do can change that, only the parent, yet many parents feel out of control simply because of their unresolved psychological trauma and not because of any reality of parent-child relationship dynamics. Children are tiny. Parents are large. Parents possess the money, time, and resources to limit a child's power in the relationship. Ceding that power by falling apart and becoming emotional, volatile parents who react poorly to hearing the word *no* or their children's resistance to hearing it actively abdicate that control by losing control of themselves.

One of the major purposes of religion besides providing cathartic mythology to explain harsh realities of life is to control children, spouses, and other social relationships. Often during childhood religious ideologies are leveraged to effect behavioral control in children, where parents ill equipped to guide and instruct our children use the threat of hell and damnation as a powerful but desperate and destructive control strategy. If we do not possess effective parenting skills, a child who is throwing a tantrum or refusing to obey can be extremely upsetting, especially when their behavior triggers our own unresolved trauma, and having never known compassion for ourselves in turn frighten our children with terrifying threats to their eternal soul or inclusion within the family. Because the threat of abandonment is so terrifying to children they may comply but such threats and fearmongering always causes trauma since we have also damaged their trust and demonstrated ourselves unwilling to protect them or even a very source of danger and instability. Because we also waste time and emotions by frequently telling children *no* to even little things like when they want to help make dinner or play legos because it will make a mess we think we have to clean up because we don't also insist they clean up their own messes, saying *no* when they become a teenager and want to date at age thirteen or try smoking does not work because we have fully diluted the meaning and effectiveness of *no*, and then feel the only way to stay in control is resorting to extreme emotional conflict and religious harassment.

This same purpose of religion is also why adherents lie more often than politicians, because membership, not faith or belief, is the paramount purpose of religion, offering a group and place to belong in which to feel safe but with the costly price of forfeiting personal autonomy. Growing up I was instructed by my family and religious leaders to lie about being gay. My cousin was told by his mother to lie and even participate in religious ceremonies which were forbidden to those like us. Grown men rape women and children but the church covers it up and protects offenders from consequences, and young women who are made pregnant either willingly or by force are made to get abortions and keep it secret. If religion was about faith our position among adherents would not be jeopardized by admitting weaknesses or mistakes, and the very act of lying to protect that membership betrays the real purpose of religion for the control of our environment and personal gratification. This is also why members of religions so often turn on each other, such as the Salem witch trials or the people in my own community who lied to others about my parents, because inclusion in such groups is a way to feel in control our own lives and personal fears, but any threat of expulsion then subverts that sense of control and vilifying others in turn reinforces our own position, the institutional use of no to control people's behaviors and exactly why using no for purposes of control is so destructive.

Attempting to control our environment by controlling our children and our partners using the refusal of needs for the purpose of control only ever serves to destroy those relationships. If a relationship has been marred by conflict and one begins to withdraw from the other say by spending more time apart or not doing things or having conversations and experiences which draw us close, we often respond by trying in turn to make them tell us yes to the things we want by pointing out the disparity, behavior, or the effect it has on us. For instance, in wanting to spend more time with our partner we may say something like, *"I feel distant from you."* This may be something which appears politic or even what a therapist might encourage us to say, but is in reality extremely manipulative because it implies blame in several ways for the other person for our own feelings. By stating that we feel distant we are implying both that they are part of the cause, that their behavior is also required for the solution, and also that they are responsible for our emotional wellbeing. Others are not, in fact, responsible for our emotional wellbeing. Believing this is a result of parenting in which our parents controlled our very emotions as a parenting strategy, to demand that we feel certain ways to appease them, never being allowed to have our own emotions when we were upset, angry, frustrated, or often even when we were happy when jealous parents resented our joy and lashed out to hurt us and ruin it. Having been shown by our own parents that others are responsible for how we feel, we then enter adult relationships trying to make our partners responsible for our feelings.

This is not the same thing as passivity. When people do things to hurt us it is natural that we would feel hurt, disappointed, embarrassed, sad, etc. There is nothing wrong with how we feel—it is instead how we act in response to those feelings and attempt to control our environment which is the problem, to make others behave as we desire to control how we feel, because when we try to make others responsible for how we feel we end up hurting them too, drive them away, or fail to engender deep emotional bonds, including with our own children, still conceiving our personal identity as a function of our environment and other people instead of who we are inherently as an individual.

For the longest time I usually had anxiety whenever I had any obligations, both social and professional, and the day and night before coaching sessions, visits from family, or going out with friends I would feel slightly anxious, enough to distract me and ruin my day or evening, and like most of us try to cope by just ignoring it or pep talk myself into feeling better, which is also a form of avoidance. We approach problems in this way because when we don't have better tools to handle such anxieties and trauma, but the act of inventory therapy actively teaches new tools which are more effective because we directly confront our fears and anxieties instead of trying to ignore them. But sometimes we have trauma which is so deeply buried or burned into our identity that inventory does not immediately illuminate the real problem—After many years of practicing inventory, being very good at it, and having resolved most of my life's trauma I still had a few problems which popped up regularly such as this anxiety toward obligations, even when they were fun or positive, and it didn't make any sense. Coming back from a weekend the thought of my coaching obligations, even though I liked my clients, would inexplicably give me anxiety. The day before a fateful lunch date too with a potential new friend my mind would not relax, even if I was just watching a streamer and baking a cake. Through inventory I finally realized I had never uncovered an unconscious compulsion or feeling of obligation to control any and all encounters with people, having been raised in a controlling and fearful environment of our family's religious beliefs was conditioned to believe I not only should be defensive during any and all potential conflict, but also that I *could*, and since it is other people whom are always the source of conflict was actually afraid of my own behavior, should any conflict occur, and my inability to control others. An identity formed from trauma is so anchored to the actions of others that any conflict is unbearable, because we truly cannot control others but believing it is our job to do so become frustrated both by other people and ourselves. Ultimately, conflict is the act of being told *no*, to be opposed, to have our will and thus our perception of safety and security threatened, and if we think it is our job to make people do what we want being told *no* in any form is devastating, especially by tiny children a fraction our size whom we mistakenly think ourselves their master. If instead our identity comes from within and we let go of control and realize our job is not to control outcomes or people but to show up for opportunity and to do our best, being told no is no big deal.

Spite is a close relative of *no*, and a common tool in the human interpersonal arsenal. Spite is often discussed with disdain, and while it can be unsavory spite is actually an evolutionary behavioral adaptation to control and manage social creatures in their interactions one with another. There is a famous clip of a research scientist feeding grapes to two caged monkeys. One monkey gets more grapes than the other, and the one who was cheated absolutely loses their mind over the injustice. Spite is a tool we use as humans to try and level our playing field, because deprivation of resources can be a cause of our own demise, and demanding our fair share by voice or by action is an evolutionary survival strategy. Of course, spite can be used for self-centered purposes, but it exists in the human species because it helped us survive collectively. Spite is a more advanced version of *no*, and within a dysfunctional family it can cause severe destruction and emotional trauma, especially if it is wielded as a parenting tool. I have frequently witnessed parents making fun of or harassing their own children when they do things that the parents dislike, and because this kind of spite creates a clear chasm between interfamilial bonds it is one of the most effective ways to make children feel alone within their own families. Because spite is modeled as an acceptable behavior by the parents, the children then duplicate this behavior in their own lives, further stressing parent/child relationships and sabotaging a child's ability to have healthy adult relationships.

Political conflict is the most dominant destructive force in human society, dividing communities and harming society, economy, and families. But such conflict is often taken at its surface, one side against the other for various ideological beliefs and convictions, and perpetuates discord and unrest as all sides, equally convinced of their legitimacy, persecute the other in attempts to gain advantage. Debates then rage between opposing views, and progress and consensus seem increasingly scarce, and leaders and supporters alike behave as if the problem is their opponents and the issues being discussed and not deeply buried human biological psychology. Patterns of evidence of the true nature of geopolitical conflict are plainly visible in human society, and so simple it seems astounding that these dynamics have not previously been recognized. Any political map will generally show that progressive, liberal powers become concentrated in large population centers, especially those which have international travel and trade, while conservative political ideology is strongest in smaller communities further away from centers of population and power. If political dynamics were a function of conviction and ideology there would not be this kind of predictable geographical distribution, and ideological patterns would be more random and unpredictable, without such correlations. Political conflict is in reality *spite* functioning in a broader, geopolitical system, where those who perceive a relative lack of power because they are separate from larger centers of population and political concentration behave spitefully to control their own lives and the fate of their communities. This is also why beliefs and morals are inconsistent and change in political dynamics to whatever is convenient, such as how my parents actively supported a rapist, adulterer, and liar in opposition to their supposed religious ideology, because they perceived that candidate as the one who could satisfy their spite. Indeed this is also why many religious leaders use Us versus Them rhetoric and dogma to gain power, demonizing population centers and other disparate groups, actively exploiting the fears and insecurities which generate spite. When I first moved to Los Angeles from Utah I was most surprised by how much more lovely, warm, and wonderful its population was than Utahns, who are largely suspicious and resentful, because I had been told it was the opposite and that people outside of our religious isolation were terrible and unhappy. To coexist with millions of other people requires far more magnanimous behavior of every single person, because of the dynamics of spite, else such insanely dense population centers would rapidly descend into total chaos. Driving in Los Angeles is always a lesson in the better nature of humankind, because the overwhelming majority of millions and millions of commuters is typically considerate and patient. Twelve-million people in the Los Angeles area live in high rates of peace and harmony because the majority of all human beings are cooperative, loving, and compassionate. But because dense concentrations of human beings inherently hold more power both economic and political than those of less populous regions, those in smaller communities instinctually adopt more spiteful behavior in order to force larger population centers and government institutions to pay attention to them, exactly the way a younger, smaller child may do in a larger family when they feel ignored or slighted, even if the cost to do so is their own moral integrity, or their very humanity, because it is never about beliefs or morals, but survival.

In reality, there is no conflict between conservative and progressive political ideology, but between the spiteful and the spited, a struggle to control our environment against those we perceive to have more power than ourselves. Collectively, conservative populations find strength in numbers through like-minded ideological fellowship, because they are not physically proximate to each other, while those in large population centers get it simply from being near so many other humans, which is also why disparate ethnic and social groups can and do easily find cooperation within larger population centers in spite of differing needs, beliefs, backgrounds, and insecurities. Those who are more traumatized by their personal life experiences also feel more intense stress from situations of disparity, conflict, and powerlessness, and as such are those who act with greater extremes within spiteful dynamics. This is also why people will often support or side with leaders and movements which demonstrably do not have their best interests in mind, such as poor and working class voters supporting policies and politicians which cut government social programs and taxes that fund public services, working against their own ostensible interests because the interest which motivates their cause is not lower taxes, better education, or increased economic opportunities but the satisfaction of their spite.

This failure to recognize spite as the reason for political divides is the reason why any political force fails to maintain leadership, because by acting selfishly and promoting Us versus Them ideology actively draw to themselves spiteful opposition, regardless of policies or systemic effects, although those are the mechanisms by which conflict can be engendered. Many times there have been instances where spite was effectively neutralized, such as the 2008 presidential election, because leaders such as Governor Howard Dean effectively addressed and engaged everyone in spite of political affiliation, because political affiliation in truth has nothing to do with politics. But because spite can be effectively exploited for personal power (at the expense of universal stability) such inclusive political strategies are often abandoned by those who fear losing control.

The power that spite can have is the same reason we fear it, and why it can drive families apart and ruin interpersonal relationships. When used manipulatively and for dishonest reasons, spite will always imperil those who wield it, because fueling further divisions will always result in fewer benefits and less stability, not more, regardless of your reasons, beliefs, or personal affiliations. Spite and other behaviors of rebellion are usually also meant to hurt someone to get what we need or want, thereby effectively taking from us as much as it gives by perpetuating interpersonal conflict and destroying relationships. But especially within parent-child relationships this can be extremely destructive, and while spite can be productive when used effectively and responsibly (such as to purposefully sever relationships with abusive or manipulative persons), its wider use in interpersonal relationships usually causes more problems that it solves. Awareness and understanding of rebellious behaviors like spite and its purpose as an interpersonal tool can instead help neutralize destructive behaviors, within ourselves as well as our children, and healthier strategies can be learned to help us feel more empowered and effective in our lives and interpersonal relationships.

Since we are no longer children and have no parent to teach or show us how to create healthy personal identities which are not dependent on our environment, from whom do we learn? Although children are often taught by the behavior of their parents, children who grow up in healthy homes do not actually learn healthy identities from their parents. *They teach themselves*. That's the entire point. The very act of discovering their own personalities, their likes and dislikes, tastes, interests, by developing friendships, having experiences, is the very process by which a healthy identity is created, the only difference is they are allowed the space to develop it, where the rest of us were not, and the same process can be repeated for us as adults through the practice of inventory therapy, making the space for ourselves to go through this same process, to set aside time to do the work and to care for our own needs. By doing this practice we become our own teachers, keeping with the theme of healthy personal identity in not relying on or needing others to do for us what we can do for ourselves. Because we have never done this before it may seem a foreign or intimidating prospect, but such is any novel undertaking. The new and unfamiliar is always scary, but sitting down and writing is not. The very act of doing it is creating space for us to develop and grow, and by understanding through the practice how our life experiences have shaped us we then learn how future experiences and choices will too, and thus become empowered to learn for ourselves new lessons, skills, and insights into who we are as a person and what our life experiences and do to support ourselves, requiring no other but ourselves to facilitate this growth.

Being a parent is not about being an authority. Our job is not to wield control and power over children (or our spouses). Doing so is simply an instinct to control our environment and our own deeply seeded fears as demonstrated for us by our own insecure parents, and as such the desperate struggle for control over a few, tiny members of humanity is pathetic and ineffective. The role of parent is firstly as guardian, to protect children and to help them learn how to protect themselves. *No*, is often a useful tool to accomplish this, the refusal to allow neglect of sleep, diet, responsibly, preventing harm to others, undisciplined expenditure of money and indulgence in material obsession, dishonesty, disobedience, or even the premature use of sex or substance use actually can protect children from mistakes they might make in ignorance which can materially affect their future wellbeing. But when the word *no* is used as an expression of unresolved emotional and mental trauma its use is adulterated from a tool which protects children into one which actively endangers them by triggering instincts for self-preservation caused by the inappropriate and irresponsible use of *no*. Being constantly told *no* about everything, including things which are actually good for them because the adult uses the word as an expression of their emotional instability and prejudices rather than what is good for the child then renders it an active obstacle to the things a child feels are instinctually required for their very survival, and thus its use as a way to protect and save them is diminished. Because my own parents used the word *no* at a drop of a hat if I so much as frowned at them or failed to comply with enthusiasm, as I neared the end of my teenage years I entirely stopped complying, because when a child finally reaches the point when they realize they don't actually have to obey their parents the word *no* having never been used with the child's interests in mind but only for the convenience of the parents the effectiveness of the word will never again be useful, since it was never used with responsibility or respect in the first place.

Fundamentally, the ineffective use of the word *no* is a shortcut for parents to set boundaries between themselves and children which should be established through other, healthier strategies. When a parent says *no* we are usually responding through instinct to our failure to practice self-care, and the word *no* is the only way we have left to spare ourselves stress and create some autonomy within a relationship which does not have clearly established boundaries and consistent rules and expectations, because we have not learned how our conception of self is not dependent on what happens around us. *No* can be used effectively to provide ourselves with self-care when used responsibly. For instance, after one of my sisters finally began setting boundaries and practicing self care without justifying herself to her children her daughter one day came running into the kitchen while my sister was doing the dishes and listening to Celine Dion on their smart speaker (if you haven't picked up on the hint yet, Celine is great parenting music). Without asking, her daughter reached for the speaker and meant to unplug it. Normally my sister would have let her just take the speaker to avoid uncomfortable outbursts and the stress of conflict, and simply resent her children in secret, but my sister instead said, "What are you doing?"

"Can I take this upstairs?" asked my niece.

"*No*, I'm listening to it," replied my sister. My niece did not even protest, and just ran back upstairs, and my sister got to continue listening to her music while finishing chores as she deserved and without doing any harm to her relationship with her daughter, in fact strengthening that bond by demonstrating for her daughter what healthy personal boundaries look like. When we no longer hold others responsible for our own wellbeing because we have done the work facilitated by inventory therapy we ironically can more easily get those things we want for ourselves, because our choices and behavior are no longer controlled by coping mechanisms which hurt others. Because I have an iron will tempered by compassion and empowered by confidence because of the practice of inventory therapy I no longer feel the need to explain myself to others when I make decisions or mistakes, to justify my existence, and neither am I bothered by resistance or the needs of others or unable to make amends and repair relationships when required. Compassion (both for myself and for others) prevents me from exercising my will where it is ineffective or inappropriate, and as such I also do not wield it irresponsibly. This in turn narrows the scope of my energies which in turn makes them also more effective. Parents whose conception of *no* is one associated with trauma, frustration, and experiences which hurt our self worth then do not use or respond to the word *no* or its like in an effective manner, are then less effective in our role as parent and in turn resort to more control and coping mechanisms in order to rectify the stress and disappointment which accompanies the need to justify and assert ourselves, wasting precious physical and emotional energy on situations which do not at all call for it, actively destroying family bonds and engendering stress between siblings as well as between the parents themselves. When we instead learn through acts of self-care such as practicing inventory therapy whenever experiences show us emotional conflict we are instead empowered to care for ourselves by caring for our relationships in ways which build rather than destroy.

As such it is not the actual use of a silly, two-letter word which is the problem, but the emotion and intent behind rejection in all its complex forms which is the real problem facing parents—is it responsible and effective or emotional and manipulative? Do we try to control our partners and our children by making them responsible for our own wellbeing or do we take responsibility for that and allow others the same? If our response to hearing *no* or children responding unfavorably to hearing it triggers uncomfortable emotions in us, it isn't at all about the word *no* but instead our own deep and unresolved insecurities, pain, and trauma triggered by the situation of rejection, which must be thusly addressed to resolve this conflict. Feelings of poor self-worth, of ineffectiveness, worthlessness, self-esteem, shame, lack of pride, confidence, or feeling loved and wanted, or painful memories of rejection and abuse are what really occur at these intersections of parent-child and parent-parent interpersonal conflict which have nothing to do with the other except what their presence triggers within us, and we risks permanently damaging our relationships and ability to parent effectively by projecting this unresolved trauma onto others and into the power dynamics of relationships instead of resolving our own experiences of insecurity and pain in a healthy and responsible way, learning who we are as a person and developing our own inherent sense of self. Most parents just haven't done this already since we simply lack the skills and tools by which to do so, because our own parents also did not have them and as such could not teach us, which is why it is so important that we do this now, for ourselves, so that we can stop the cycle of pain, trauma, and destruction of families and win for ourselves the kind of stability and love we deserve.

When the use of the word *no* becomes ineffective because of its irresponsible and inconsistent use, and parents begin to feel ineffective we then resort to those strategies and tactics which in turn ask children for permission to parent them. *"No, we don't do that in this family. If you hit them again you're going to go to your room. You didn't have a nap earlier and you were cranky. I'm counting to ten. One. Two. Three...Do you want to go to bed without dinner? Test my patience. I tell you all the time not to do that."* Explaining to children why they should obey us betrays an absence of confidence and destabilizes the parent-child relationship. *"Stop," "No,"* or *"Uh-uh"* and a single look should accomplish what many of us achieve with elaborate speeches and beseeching. But this occurs because we feel unconfident, insecure, or ineffective because we have not yet learned through inventory therapy the tools which empower us, and we then betray our insecurity through negotiation, explanation, and attempts to justify our position to people whose age can be counted on one hand and are no more than fifty-pounds soaking wet. It would be really funny if it weren't also so sad and indicative of the deep pain and remorse we carry into our adulthood. But we have arrived in this position because of how our unresolved pain and trauma biases our perception of our self-worth and relationship to others and to life itself. Misunderstanding the intrinsic value inherent of our lives and experiences and accustomed to making excuses for our existence and having to justify our feelings to others we continue this pattern in our role as parents even though it is no longer necessary and in fact counterproductive. The power of *no* for a parent comes from the confidence and compassion behind it. If we are not effective we don't have either of those things, but we can find them simply by practicing self-care and self-compassion by practicing inventory therapy. Children who say *no* are actually extremely cute and funny, and it's only because we have empowered them to rebel through our ineffective use of the word *no* with our undisciplined emotional volatility that they even do it in the first place. Parenting is not as hard as we make it out to be, and a lot of our inability to experience peace and harmony in our relationships comes simply from our unwillingness to address our own unresolved pain and trauma. Children are naturally and persistently obedient, helpful, kind, compassionate, considerate, funny, charming, and unconditionally loving, but parents, seeing the trauma of their youth reflected back at them in their children instead corrupt the experience and see shadows of conflict where there is actually only light and joy and love. If the word *no* causes stress, look past the superficiality of these moments using the tools in this book to the origins of our feelings, and the answers which can save our marriage and our relationships with our children will be found. Parenting will then transform from a frustrating exercise in control, dominance, and self-will into one which is endlessly rewarding and uplifting.

17

Teenagers

My first ever date was with a beautiful girl who asked me out to a school dance. She had long been a friend and while I think she might have had some attraction to me, I think she was one of those who could instinctually tell that my romantic interests were for my own gender (she was on the dance team, after all). We had a really fun time and she is someone I still admire to this day. Then one of her friends from another school asked me to a formal dance (I must have come highly recommended). It was my first time having to get a tuxedo and flowers. I looked dashing and my date, six-foot herself, was stunning in a glittery blue gown and her dark brown hair piled high. If I had been straight I would have fallen in love. Regardless, we also had a great time, and when I walked in the door at two in the morning I was surprised to see my parents still up, with all the lights in the house turned on.

"Have we ever discussed curfew with you?" asked my Mom.

"Oh," I replied, also realizing how strange it was that they had not. "No."

"Well, it's fine that you were out late tonight, but from now on you have to be home by one."

All of my friends were from conservative, religious families, and we had spent the last few hours after the dance at one of the older boys' homes with their parents talking and playing video games. I was not yet out, but was so obviously gay that my parent's supposed displeasure at me being out late with a girl was clearly misplaced and wreaked of other motives. "We were just hanging out," I replied. "But I'll obey curfew, sure."

The absence of even establishing a curfew in the first place was a demonstration of what an absolutely well-behaved son I actually was. Most homosexuals instinctually overcompensate for the insecurity they feel being differently-gendered in bigoted and homophobic homes in order to increase the security of their position should they ever be discovered. A great deal of gays and lesbians are their school's valedictorian, prom kings and queens, student leaders, or team captains simply because they want to minimize the potential harm to themselves should their sexuality ever be discovered. I was no exception, and had for my entire childhood labored to endear myself to volatile and discriminating parents by being a consummate son. But instead of appreciating and lauding my responsible and adherent behavior, they instead leapt at the opportunity to berate and harass me. Around the time I turned seventeen my curfew was inexplicably reduced from 1 a.m. on Fridays and 10 p.m. on weeknights to 12 a.m. and 9 p.m., respectively, even though I was captain of my swimming team, got (and still have) the best grades in my entire family, and had never otherwise failed to meet curfew. My mother's rage at my unwillingness to submit to the a stricter schedule even as I got older was pure insanity. She took away the keys to my car just for refusing to agree, before any infraction actually occurred. But since they took my keys away if I so much as frowned it had no effect on my compliance, and since I could no longer then shuttle my siblings to school and other extracurricular events I got them back forthwith anyway. As a compromise I proposed to tell my mother always where I would go, when I would be home, and stick to my commitment. My proposal was soundly rejected as she doubled down on her impulse to dominate and control. Frustrated by her obstinance and unreasonable self-righteousness I gave up and refused to stick to any curfew at all and to never tell her where I was going. This in turn was met by a few occasions of frenzied phone inquiries to parents of my various friends searching for me and demanding I come home, but which was more embarrassing to her and as such short-lived. Eventually in her desperation my mother reached out to her own father for advice on how to force me to comply, and he told her to lay off me (thanks Grandpa!), and finally without any reinforcement, not even from my father, relented finally to accept that I was growing into an adult.

While it's true that teenagers can be difficult, it is typically the parent's refusal to relinquish some of the responsibility for their children's lives that is at the true heart of such conflicts. My mother's entire identity over the last two decades was only as a mother and wife, and the impending end of this role and her fears for herself and her child played a larger factor in her desire to prevent my adulthood than my noncompliance. The time to prepare a child for success is during their formative years, not when they are about to leave the house. If we as a parent have failed to engender responsibly, intelligence, and resourcefulness in a child when they are nearing the end of their teenage years we have already missed the opportunity to do so. From the time that a child is around fifteen and the rest of their lives, our role as a parent evolves from guardian to mentor. All we can do at this point is to demonstrate our own admirable adult behavior, to model an example for them to be inspired, and to be there for advice and assistance as needed. Using teenagers as a way to assert control over our environment is just asking for a volatile and unproductive relationship as young people begin to discover their own autonomy.

When I was nearly sixteen we went on a trip to Lake Powell, which is a very, very large reservoir at the southern end of Utah which dams the Colorado River just before it transitions into the Grand Canyon. We rented a houseboat with family friends and traveled up the enormous lake until we found a nice, secluded canyon in which to drop anchor. Being all red sandstone, there are no real beaches at Lake Powell, but the towering red and brown cliffs reflected in the dark, nearly black waters is a surreal experience. Days at Lake Powell are spent almost entirely waterskiing or wakeboarding and turning a toasting brown color, eating good food and sleeping out under the stars on the top of the houseboat as cute little bats swoop overhead to catch insects in the moonlight.

One of my best friends was with us on this vacation, but my awareness of my sexuality kept me from ever truly letting down my guard around other boys (or anyone for that matter). So one night I was completely surprised when he quietly whispered to me that we go skinny dipping. It had been a few years now that I was showering in the locker room, having transitioned into High School I was a bit more used to being naked around other people. But the thought of doing it for fun was something I had never even considered. I had a small crush on my friend, mostly because I loved him as a person, and the thought of being naked around him was at first something of which I was wary. But, longing for new life experiences to grow beyond the suffocating bounds of my religion-addled life I determined that another opportunity like this might not come along again. "Okay," I said with a smile.

When it was dark and everyone had gone to bed and we were still talking, we slowly snuck out of our sleeping bags and tiptoed down the houseboat stairs and onto the hard sandstone shore. The ground was still hot from the daytime sun and radiated heat upward to keep us warm even though the night air was on the chilly side. We ascended the low hill and onto the other side and the other small bay by the one where we had parked, fully clear of any view of the houseboat. The moon danced across the enormous lake and moon shadows descended from the dark cliffs, changing the landscape into something entirely ethereal, the tiny sounds of the water gently lapping against the shore the only sound other than the plodding of our bare feet.

"Have you ever done this before?" He asked as we reached the water and he pulled off his shirt.

"Nope!" I said, following his lead. His shorts came off and for the first time during the span of our friendship I finally knew what his butt looked like.

I also removed my clothes and slipped into the water, which was also still warm, like descending into a newly drawn bath. I could feel myself float around in the water between my legs, a foreign experiencing having only ever been in water wearing swimming shorts or briefs. The thought of a predatory fish swimming up and biting off my penis flashed through my head. "This is fun!" said my friend.

"Yeah it is," I agreed, feeling a rush of testosterone course through me at being so near another naked boy, alone, together. If only it were someone I was in love with.

"Let's play evolution!" he said.

"Ha. What's that?"

"You creep up out of the water like you're the first creature to walk on land."

I laughed.

"I'll go first," he said, then slowly crawled up the shallow beach before standing and lumbering up the shore, giving me an entirely unobstructed view of his naked body as he went, and his entire, beautiful front as he laughed and turned around to come back to the water. "Your turn."

I gaily repeated the trick, knowing full well that my return to the water was his opportunity to see me in all my young glory, but I couldn't dampen my nerves and didn't linger too long out of the water.

Swimming around for a little while I began to grow more confident about being naked. "Let's go for a walk," I proposed. We both got up out of the water and and headed off down the long shore deeper into the lake. The moon created a ring of silver around the towering sandstone pillars which seemed to keep a voyeuristic vigil for us. I don't at all remember what we talked about on the walk because my mind focused only on his naked body and floppy cock as we walked, trying not to be too obvious in my indulgence of his nudity. We walked for so long our bodies became completely dry. Reaching the end of the peninsula and a football field's length from our clothes decided to sit down and take in the magnificent view. But sitting made it easier for my erection to stiffen, and realizing my predicament hid it between my legs which were drawn up under my arms and tried to stop fantasizing about having my first kiss, naked, under the moonlight in this place.

After a while he decided we should get back. Thankfully my stiffness had subsided enough not to be aroused but filled me up pretty well to be impressive. But I noticed as we walked that he purposefully drifted behind me, out of view of my peripheral, to also take in the sight of me. If he had been interested in me, I missed one of the most special experiences of my childhood. But without anyone to have advised me on such matters, I was too frightened and ignorant even about other gay boys to have done anything about it, and even though I did not have my first kiss, I did come away with one of my first coming of age experiences and a small sense of promised adulthood.

While a teenager is not yet an adult, our minds and bodies are preparing to become adults, and that requires some separation from the parent in order that they may transition to adulthood, but this is more exaggerated if the parent has been excessive in their control and parenting, where a healthy parent-child relationship will never truly ever end. One day when I was seventeen, a few months before my encounter with the police at the waterpark, I was rummaging through my closet and was horrified to realize that all but two of my twenty or so shirts were some shade of green.

"Mom?" I asked. "Why are all my shirts green?"

"I think it's a really nice color on you," she said.

"Yeah, but they're, like, *all* green."

"Well, maybe we can get you some blue ones?"

"The only two that aren't green *are* blue."

My parents controlled everything in my life, I realized, even down to what clothes I wore and what haircut I had. I had *no* autonomy at all except what I could find in secret. My experiences of being a teenager though gave me small tastes of independence, and the more I realized what control my parents had over my life the more I resented them and the less inclined I felt to do what they wanted, and my small attempts at healthy independence such as staying out late on the weekends, making my own plans and communicating with my parents being rejected, I felt no choice but to resist their control if I was ever to become an adult myself.

Teenagers need space, but it does not need to mean separation from the family any more than it does for our partner our ourselves, each autonomous and independent adults. In truth, fear of losing teenagers and of our children growing up are also based on our own insecurities and conception of our self worth, our excessive and unhealthy identities as a parent, but trying to hold on to our children as if they are still little and helpless (or oppositely to overcompensate by neglecting your relationship with them and giving too much space) will only alarm them and trigger the kind of rebelliousness which is meant to prepare them for the autonomy of adulthood.

Our conception of ourselves as a fully grown person forms during the teenage years. Increased metabolic activity by the thyroid starts to change growth from a quantitative phase of increasing mass and size to that of qualitative phase responsible for the secondary characteristics of adult human beings. Because our identity formalizes when we are a teenager many adults never really grow beyond this state, acting like spoilt children well into their adult years (especially if they are burdened with alcoholism and addiction issues, which interfere with the function of a neurochemical called acetylcholine responsible for learning and memory). Even the oldest among us has a difficult time comprehending themselves as a person other than someone who is young, because while there can be much personal growth as an adult our biological psychology finalizes its development when we are a teenager, and thus it is this formative identity from which the rest of our life experience follows.

Many adults have a difficult time growing old, not only because it portends our eventual death but also that it becomes less easy to make friends and be part of life in the way which comes so naturally to the young. Watching children grow and seeing them experience many firsts, the freedom of youth (not least of all physical freedom), and the naivety of inexperience can be unmooring for adults who wistfully remember or grieve our lost youths, energy, and ignorance. How amazing would it be to go back to elementary school and do it all again knowing I can love myself and don't have to be afraid of people or the future. But the danger of this unresolved resentment for our lost youths is then burdening our children or spouses with our resentments for aging and envy of youth, even though we already had ours, and in so doing damage our relationships, especially with our children who are no more responsible for their being alive than we are of ourselves. I once had a friend who, having also grown up in our oppressive religious community, was so resentful of never having had sex with other young women in his youth than his future wife that he had entirely withdrawn from his wife and children though they were some of the loveliest people I have ever met. When I was seventeen and quit the swimming team due to depression and metabolic illness (of which I was unaware) I wanted to try other sports and went to my father with a plant to go out for track or wrestling. Instead of encouraging me he promptly said I was not fast enough for track nor tough enough for wrestling. Already saddled with suicidal depression I lost all interest in sports and would spend the rest of my time in high school just waiting for graduation.

My father acted out every one of his life's disappointments through me, especially when I started to become a man and triggered in him memories of every regret he had of his own youth, and in so doing cut off any possibility for a relationship with his own son. If instead of spending his time lost in the mythology of his religious beliefs he had learned tools to deal with his own personal disappointments and insecurities not only would he actually have had relationships with any of his six children, the unceasing tumult that was his life would calm and many of his unreachable dreams become realized since our control mechanisms always sabotage our lives. It is often said that we drive people away by our own behavior, but in truth our resentments drive ourselves away from those who love us, because their presence triggers every insecurity we may harbor, and without compassion for ourselves and our past experiences do not conceive of our loved ones for who they are but phantoms of our worst fears and expectations. It is imperative to resolve through inventory these experiences of regret, remorse, and resentment for things of the past which cause us to feel jealousy or insecurity by stimuli such as our teenagers else we risk solidifying those emotional boundaries which separate ourselves from them, forcing them to grow up to adulthood without anything but superficial access to their own parent. The loneliness of teenage years is always a result of emotionally unavailable parents, realizing that we are destined to navigate life on our own without any experience or resources to guide us. For though parents may reprimand their teenagers over their behavior or pressure them to excel, teenagers have never actually done anything and have no experience or knowledge from which to draw strength, so they then become preoccupied also with fear and insecurity which in turn imperils their effectiveness in their own lives.

A major preoccupation with the young is trying to find their identity, to set themselves apart from the crowd and to view themselves as a unique individual. This is a simple coping instinct to develop self-esteem (or self-pity, if depression is severe), to find justification for our own existence, because many times in our youth there seems to be no justification for our being here nor reason to stay. But uniqueness does not come from our tastes and style, nor our appearance, name, or identity. Instead, uniqueness is simply a product of our experience, which can never be replicated in all the eons which have existed or will exist. Though there be nearly eight billion human beings on the Earth, nobody has our particular brother or sister, or parents, or the events which occur to us individually or in various combinations collectively. Each of us grows up in a specific technological era, and are exposed to life experiences which are a product of the specific environment in which we live. It is this life experience which gives each of us individuality separate from the life experiences of everyone else, and using inventory therapy to pay respect to our experience and fearlessly confronting and resolving our past can grow and deepen our identity and build experiences into strengths and bring incredible satisfaction for our life no matter the circumstances. There is nothing wrong with longing, but resentment of and pain from unfilled youth can poison our personal relationships and cause us to miss out on our current life, even though we may be old are not as old as we will be in the future, and this runs the risk of continuously looking back on the past regretting our behavior but never learning how to be present. During one visit home when I was in my late thirties my father expressed regret for not having spent more time with my brother and I, and then continued to ignore us and work even though he had at least twenty or thirty years of life remaining. Just as self-compassion is not a feeling or emotion, but action, being present is also found in action, first by practicing inventory to resolve those emotional and psychological barriers which distract us from the current moment and burden us with preoccupation of the past and future. Only when we have bravely completed the resolution of all our past experiences can we expect to be fulfilled by the present and able to engage in it fully.

Complicating the matter of teenagers is that it also tends to coincide with a time that romance and attraction in our own relationship has probably waned. Not because this is inevitable, as it absolutely is not inevitable, but only because most of us live our lives on autopilot and follow biases and prejudices and mistaken ideas of life to ruin love and attraction and the bonds of our relationships. It often takes until we are even into our forties or fifties, if at all, to realize we are no longer children and that the world is no longer centered around us (or that it never actually was). Some of us persist even into old age insisting the world bend to our needs. But by the time that children are teenagers, adults have often transitioned into or are nearing middle age and the weight of life and the limitations of mortality are finally making themselves too obvious to ignore. So on top of losing our youth and vitality we are at this time also staring down the beginning of the end of our time with our precious little innocents for which we have also only now come to realize how much we love or need them. This in turn causes parents to dump all of our frustration with life and love into a teenager as if the teenager is the one responsible for our frustration and disappointment and not our own life choices and the inevitability of fate. Unlike many other aspects of life, having a child is not something that happens to us but is mostly something we choose, whether or not we are willing to accept it. This unfortunately also comes with all of the consequences of that decision, the heartache and pain and frustration when things go wrong, even loss. This is the point of being a parent, to experience the abyssal void of helplessness which results from loving something so helpless, so utterly and fully loving and precious. Teenagers still need boundaries and guidance, and protection from those whom would do them harm, but how can we expect to fulfill that role if we are also dumping every one of our frustrations into their lap? The purpose of life is to experience it, and being a parent is one of the most profound experiences we can have in life, and it is not the fault of our teenagers that they are there, inexperienced, and fearful of the life to come. That is our doing, and using tools like inventory we can be the strong, stable, and mature adult they need us to be.

This is why the answers to big questions like why are we here, where have we come from, and where are we going seem so elusive, because the answer is so simple—simply to experience it—that most of us think it cannot possibly be the answer. But to experience life also means that we must experience *everything* that is life, which includes loss, pain, trauma, and heartache as well as love, joy, and happiness. Without knowing the full breadth of experiences we would not actually experience life at all, just a dull facsimile, so horrible things must happen to us, especially since we would also not willingly submit ourselves to such experiences. No greater is the potential for pain and heartache than in being a parent, to willingly bring such a precious, innocent little child into a world such as this, fully understanding the horrors they will know, the pain of heartbreak that will come, bodies broken and consumed by mortality, and our own pain witnessing their suffering. But in turn parents often become the very source of such pain and horrors of life. While I have had some awful experiences at the hands of others, and experienced cancer and disease and rejection, my greatest pain and suffering came at the hands of my own family, which is by many magnitudes greater than what the rest of my life has brought. Humans often engineer the very things of which we are terrified, because of the special way in which our psychology operates, and when unresolved trauma, disappointment, and fear are what drive and motivate parenting then parents are doomed to become their children's tormentors, and without tools to resolve the destruction which has been heaped upon ourselves children commit upon their own children the very things which were done to them, and the cycle repeats itself without end. Teenagers are a harbinger of the indefatigable impermanence which is life, and our struggles with raising them is in truth our struggle with life itself, but not anything inherently difficult about teenagers.

18

Replicating Tribal Structures

When my Nana died in 2016 most of my aunts and uncles had demonstrated varying degrees of animosity toward me for being gay, even ones whom I had thought were on my side such as an aunt in whom I had first confided my sexuality before any other extended family, whom was a professed ally until her own son came out and then turned on me and forbade me from talking to him (which I had already been doing for several years after he first came out to me, lol). So though I was heartbroken I did not attend my Nana's funeral, nor my Granddad's when he also passed about a year later, and even though I was their firstborn Grandson (my Nana had a previous marriage to an abusive man and children by him).

When we were teenagers and one year gathered for a family reunion some of my other cousins who were my age snuck in marijuana and smoked out together. I did not even know about pot at the time and as an insecure and self-righteous little gay boy would most likely have tattled on them, but they got caught anyway and the story is now a staple of family lore. Our family reunions were joyous occasions, not least of all for the naivety we each had of the abuse being committed in nearly every family, and our cousins all more or less are wonderful people whom I loved dearly and without reservation. I desperately wanted to be like and friends with my older female cousins, who were all possessed of the same strength of character and determination as our Nana, who presided over her family at these gatherings with her characteristic poise, wry charisma, and jet-black bouffant, the rest of us engaged in games and fun not normally possible in our detached, separate lifestyles, and we exploited every last moment together.

My cousins more or less all experienced the same kinds of emotional trauma and abuse at the hands of the troubled baby-boom generation, and our pain and heartache was made immeasurably worse by the absence of our biological friends whom would have otherwise provided the sense of security, love, and acceptance of which our parents were incapable, and all of us in turn struggled with debilitating depression, anxiety, self-hatred, and substance abuse. By some miracle none of us actually died, in spite of our attempts, and as much as I loved my Nana and Granddad, the people responsible for our torment were their own children, and their failure to provide the kind of intimate family bonds which are required for human families to survive had consequences which have rippled now through literally hundreds of lives.

My family today can hardly stand to talk to each other for more than a few minutes. Just as our family growing up was mostly alone and separated from the rest, my siblings repeat this self-imposed separation, only visiting or talking with other members on occasion, because a primary consequence of unresolved childhood trauma is to distance ourselves from any reminder of that trauma, which includes our own siblings, even though they were as much victims as we and undeserving of separation, although we often can and do adopt destructive control mechanisms in response to that abuse which makes relationships difficult. My extended family with histories of abuse who do stay in contact with their families are also burdened with extreme codependency dysfunction and secret alcoholism or addiction, infidelity, and an abundance of child abuse as they try to cope with the consequences of abuse and lack of effective life skills to manage pain and trauma that no human being on Earth is equipped to cope, perpetuating abuse and condemning many hundreds or even thousands of progeny to suffer just as they have.

When our family structures fail or we are imposed upon to uproot and start over in a new location many of us establish new relationships, finding chosen family which replace those which are biological. But even when a family is not burdened by emotionally unstable parents and even when parents work hard to enmesh themselves in a community there still exists in contemporary societies a deficiency of connectedness with other human beings which tears at the foundations of human civilization and births many plagues of social dissatisfaction and conflict which in turn diminishes fulfillment, productivity, confidence, and even income and economic prosperity because we no longer live within the protective and nurturing family structures which are required for the successful functioning of human family groups. This also in turn puts enormous pressure on parents who are then required to fulfill the entirety of social dynamics what would normally be performed by many other grown adults in a variety of roles as well as entire social institutions, who are also not equipped in the first place to perform even normal healthy parenting roles, which leads in turn to the kinds of parenting failures experienced generally by the baby-boom and other generations.

One day while perusing social media I saw a post in which someone rightly condemned several examples of cultural appropriation. But, while well-meaning, one of these examples demonstrated an unfortunate misunderstanding of the human condition which very directly causes this failure to support family structures and parenting which is *not* a cultural construct but in truth a biological need required for the fulfillment of all human life. *"Use of the word Tribe,"* they proclaimed, *"is only for native cultures."* This is not even remotely true, though Western civilization and other contemporary societies have long abandoned the overt tribal structure as a system of social organization it is still very much a part of who we are biologically as social creatures and our unique need as humans to be fulfilled within those structures. No human can very well survive on our own. Even the most insulated and isolating of humans is still supported by infrastructure, social institutions, and other human beings. The hermit who lives alone in the woods has the privilege of living there because of policies and choices made by other humans which prevent destruction or privatization of that wilderness in which they live, and other humans who fight and stand up for our rights to exist peacefully, and even most hermits have possessions which were actually made by other human beings on which they still depend for their survival. Though they may hardly ever come into actual contact their lives are very much directly influenced by other humans, and their isolation is nothing more than a convenient illusion. The moneyed loners in crowded places like New York or San Francisco is possible only because other humans bought things from their company and helped build their success, and cities are managed and operated by yet other humans who willingly cooperate to provide water, electricity, trash removal, and other services, and even the peace and order which allows their lavish lifestyle to even exist. To believe that any of us can survive without our fellow man is merely a wish to be rid of our dependency on each other, feeling shame and resentment for the limitations of mortality and our dependence one upon another, and is in truth no realistic appraisal of our condition.

Refusal to acknowledge our shared need for one another and impairments to the kinds of social structures which support parenting is one of the most debilitating obstacles which burden our role as parents. The only time during my childhood that my parents were not completely stressed out and emotionally insane was when they had my Aunt or strangers nannying for them. None of us can do our job alone, even alone as a couple, or even with the help of a few other adults, and the expectation that we succeed as parents on our own without the support of social structures causes immense emotional, material, and logistical stress as we try to fulfill needs which in truth require entire social systems and dynamics normally afforded by the many members and roles which occur within tribal structures. The absence of these structures imperil us with depression, loneliness, and helplessness as we struggle on our own in a world overflowing with people. Often some of us are driven so mad from despair we resort to drugs and alcohol and other destructive coping mechanisms, only later may we stumble upon a refuge in recovery programs, which incidentally model some traditional tribal structures through group support and the passing of knowledge and sharing of support. When I first became part of alcoholics anonymous I was overjoyed having, for the first time in my life, a place to belong and people who actually cared about my wellbeing (though there were some predators in those groups), who freely gave me access and connection with others. When they leave, members of the military often have a profound sense of withdrawal and isolation, having tasted what it means to be human and to be with other humans, no less potent than that from drug abuse or alcoholism because such institutions often facilitate the camaraderie and closeness which should come from our families and society, and without it our soul begins to wither, shamed for our needs by others who will not admit our dependence one upon another refrain, in turn, from giving it.

Our instinct to form tribes is buried deep within our biology, and our contemporary societies not only fail to provide for this need but also often actively inhibit their creation and thus leave us feeling ineffective and acting ineffectively, and seeking those needs in other institutions such as the workplace, religion, politics, or even social media. We instinctually look forward to visits from family members even when we don't particularly like them because their very presence satisfies biological instincts for other adult human beings and their role as tribal members which is every bit as instinctual as eating, speaking, cooking, fighting, or having sex. Because we are social animals who instinctually form family relationships and social bonds and need them to survive and function we cannot help but naturally create tribes—they form organically in every aspect of our existence, from work to school to governments or within groups of friends, with humans naturally filling hierarchal roles of varying degrees of dominance or submission not because of cultural constructs but for our innate and instinctual and unconscious human biological characteristics which purposefully design such behavioral and social constructs specifically to fulfill tribal dynamics.

When my maternal great-grandfather, Royal was a child his mother died of tuberculosis. His father, an unreliable daydreamer, abandoned the family for promises of gold prospecting and gave up his kids to other people. Royal was sent to live with an aunt and uncle, but they shortly died in the Spanish Flu outbreak of 1918 when he was only seven. The next uncle he was handed to was extremely abusive, and after being beaten more times than he cared (for offenses like driving the new Model-T without permission) he left to live with neighbors and work for a living at only twelve-years of age. As a teenager he set out to travel the country looking for work, riding trains as a vagabond. Eventually he ended up in Arizona where he trained as a crop dusting and acrobatic pilot before meeting my great-grandma Rose. Grandpa Roy was one of the most wonderful people I have ever met, in spite of his childhood trauma, and when we went to visit them he would play his harmonica while their poodle, Charlie Boy would sing along. They spoke to us directly, generous in their kindness and more warm than anyone else in my family. I think his profound experience of loss as a child and the instability caused by fractured family ties and likely consequences it had for his own parenting experience made him deeply cherish family bonds. But the kind of trauma he experienced as a child was made worse by the absence of traditional tribal structures, families left to fend for themselves in isolation of one another which facilitated abuse of children, high mortality, and widespread impoverishment, and he was one of only a few of his siblings who actually survived childhood.

All of our primate relatives form tribal structures, and animals which don't form tribal structures tend to have larger, herd-like or flock-like behaviors as seen in bovines, birds, or even some species of snakes, where though animals congregate in large numbers their role within that group is still rather autonomous and individual, without instincts for distinct and cohesive family groups and individuation of social roles (incidentally, the pejorative use of the word "tribalism" is a relic of colonialism, its application inherently racist and prejudiced, and should not be used as such). Other animals without biological tribal structures are more isolated, such as how most raptors live simply in pairs, fully separate from adult groups and capable of providing for all social needs of their offspring independently from the rest of their species. Humans found a niche within our world precisely because of our biological design for forming tribal structures, which increases our potential for protection and resource gathering within our environment since we are not possessed of other tools like claws, speed, or strength, because the tribal structure in turn facilitated social and creative problem solving skills in turn not available to other species. Delegating roles is one of the functions which occurs naturally in the tribal structure, with duties and obligations being apportioned according to skill and ability which in turn advantages each individual more than what is otherwise possible and thus propagation of the entire species greater in proportion than what our individual abilities as a human animal is capable.

    Over the intervening centuries between our natural tribal structures and the advent of contemporary society, the tribal structure evolved from an obvious, micro dynamic of human life to one which was cannibalized by larger and larger tribal institutions which in turn coalesced into formal institutions such as government and religion. Religion originally evolved in family and tribal structures as a way for parents and grandparents to explain to vulnerable and frightened children (and themselves) the hardships of life and warn against potential dangers of life to their offspring, to provide comfort and guidance in a world which took inexplicably as much or more than it gave, a world in which wild animals snatched children in the night and mysterious, horrifying diseases came out of nowhere to rob us of loved ones and happiness, to make sense of violence and exploitation committed by other humans against us, and to find some reprieve from calamity and the unpredictability of nature.

    But what was meant as a guide to avoid injury, disease, and disappointment was over time usurped by opportunistic institutions and power-hungry humans, facilitating dominion over increasingly larger and larger populations of humanity, each advance in technology and social progression spreading influence and control and which ultimately supplanted our natural familial tribal structures and traditions and in turn subverting the function of tribal structures and thus successful interpersonal skills for cooperation, knowledge of food and our environment, and opportunity for personal human growth and development replaced with useless condemnations of human nature and sexuality but promotes highly destructive immoral behavior such as dishonesty, fear, bigotry, xenophobia, and absolution of personal responsibility. Worse, the delusion of control facilitated by religion brings some calm to turbulent, traumatized minds which then mistake the intermittent sense of power as spirituality, when it is in fact nothing of the sort.

Humans are naturally peaceful, not combative, as evident by the general tendency for harmony and prosperity in a world of nearly eight billion, and the deeds of conquerors both old and new never seem so great after realizing their heinous victories are not a testament to power and cunning but of the murder and displacement of those who are kind, embrace pacifism, and love of family and community. The elimination of our traditional tribal structures did not likewise eliminate our need for them, because this need originates from our very biology and inherent dependence on others of our species for both survival and satisfaction. Work hierarchy is a very obvious but artificial replication of organic tribal structures, with bosses and leaders attempting to function as tribal leaders, even leveraging subconscious psychological needs for tribal structure as tools to control and manage those beneath them. But since it does not truly satisfy the dynamics of genuine tribal structure, artificially replacing that which should be organic, altruistic, holistic, and loving it usually fails, most consequentially for the absence of actually wise, older humans which would normally enlighten younger members to the perils of self-defeating behaviors, and without this knowledge leaders fall into ethical and criminal wrongs as they pursue self-centered and narrow definitions of success at the expense of other tribal members for which they would have otherwise been rebuffed or enlightened by more experienced senior members. Other manifestations of our need for tribes reveal themselves in the organization of sport, which intimately replicates the bonds of tribal members working together for common goals, which also parodies conflict with other tribes in non-violent competition. Ball culture provide havens for those who are outcast and fulfills both the mentorship, support, and camaraderie using tribal hierarchical structures. Even alcoholics anonymous functions as a surrogate tribe for people who have none since not having the kind of emotional support that normally comes from tribal structures is part of the etiology of alcoholism.

Gangs, police, the military, and even terrorist organizations are also organic realizations of our need for tribal structures, borne from a necessity for emotional support, membership of a group, protection, and resource acquisition. When we do not provide these needs for our children they will instinctually be attracted to sources of it in their environment, since these groups can provide that which is not otherwise available. Ideology is not the driving influence of such groups, but instead membership, fulfillment, and connection to other human beings. The tribal structure is such an instinctual and necessary part of the human experience that this need causes it to manifest organically in every aspects of our lives, and when children are not provided fulfillment of these needs nor taught healthy skills for handling life they can be seduced away by promises of power and control. This is one of the reasons why so many police groups become violent and oppress the groups in which they operate, because fear and trauma as a child motivated them as an adult to forcefully try and control their environment, to become more powerful than the things of which they are afraid, but since as an adult there are many things and people to be afraid of, they lose control, become militarized, and transform into the very force of evil and corruption they initially opposed.

For the entire history of humankind before the modern era, children were always within constant closeness to parents or other familial and tribal adult caretakers, and were never apart from them the way we are separated now in contemporary societies. Sons and daughters accompanied mothers and fathers or aunts and uncles nearly every moment of every day, and their learning was accomplished by the close, intimate association with their progenitors and access to their example, whose demonstration of successful survival strategies and purposed or incidental instruction on everything from how to obtain food to skills required for the maintenance of successful interpersonal relationships. Now, children are ushered off to school, assembling in groups of mostly only other children with only one or two adults responsible for the rearing and education of large numbers of naive and unsupervised children. School as it is structured today is only marginally better than the plot of *Lord of the Flies*, with children having to navigate obscene and emotionally violent gangs and cliques of other ignorant and self-preservationist children. It's no wonder that bullying and harassment occurs so frequently since children are left to their own devices to survive and navigate the world without the watchful guidance of familial adults, which is made even worse when the primary adults in a child's life are also those incapable of parenting successfully. While bullying and harassment can be psychologically damaging to victims, the children who are really at a disadvantage are bullies themselves, whom because of this insufficient isolation and lack of access to healthy tribal adult structures never acquire skills required to live happily and effectively. Victims of bullying can learn empathy and compassion through their experience, but aggressors, having a temporary advantage, never see the true disadvantage of their position and thus continue their behavior far into adulthood, mistaking domination for success, acquiring much success from predatory behavior but become emotionally isolated pariahs who cause themselves and everyone around them amazing amounts of unnecessary pain and chaos and eventually self-destruct spectacularly. More commonly, children are simply abandoned to transition into adulthood having very little confidence or ability to solve their problems, left alone to navigate life without the support of our natural human family structures, and spend the first ten or twenty years of adulthood learning by making and recovering from mistakes which would otherwise be avoided in the first place or remedied more quickly within tribal support, and since we often become parents during this time of navigating life with a deficiency of wisdom and resources caused by the absence of tribal fulfillment inevitably raise children during our most unstable years and so perpetuate the failure of parenting across many generations.

As such, the absence of tribal structures forces entire generations to start over every time, the failure to pass on valuable life lessons which are learned from experience and demonstrated subconsciously by behavior and tradition rather than oral or conscious communication means each generation begins with a deficit of wisdom and resources. The function of a tribal leader is to provide access to knowledge and wisdom from a well-lived life, compounding the accumulation of collective knowledge and experience of generations, and benefit from their contribution in turn by the enlightenment of younger and able-bodied humans. Elephants pass on knowledge of water and food items and patterns of rainfall and location of verdant environments, as well as strategies for guarding against predators and demonstrating behaviors which strengthen bonds between family members. When the matriarchs of Elephant families are killed this knowledge is lost, and entire Elephant families are destroyed as a result. Humans also demonstrate and benefit from the same kind of intergenerational exchange of experience, but because we now usually live entirely separate from other generations we no longer benefit from the experience and wisdom accumulated by the past.

Many of us are lucky to have deficits of information and experience supplemented by access to books, reading, art, music, and now the internet, but there are aspects of the demonstration of human experience through behavior which cannot be replicated by intellectual learning. When I interviewed my Granddad for my school report and he told me about visiting a gay bar by accident I learned though his example and experience with those who are differently gendered (including with his niece and his brother's experience with having a gay child) that being gay was not as dire as I had been otherwise led to believe. If we had a more regular and close relationship as what would be facilitated through tribal family structures he might have altogether saved me from my attempt at suicide. My own parents, not having had any such experience and without the support of intergenerational wisdom and experience were miserably unequipped to do what was right when confronted with their bigotry and biases toward their own son.

Generations of humans which pass on material wealth demonstrate some of the strengths of tribal structures, albeit through stifling and prejudiced social norms and expectations, but whom nonetheless provide their progeny with access to the kinds of emotional, intellectual, and material inheritance and protection of an actual tribal structure enabled or compelled by wealth and social status, where elders of prosperous families maintain their positions through their material status by which they incidentally organize their families and associations into actual tribal structures, and this in turn coalesces financial resources and access to wisdom, friends, family, counsel, and opportunity for all members of the tribe, where the financial resources are not actually the cause of such successes but is instead caused by the mobilization and motivation of members to organize. The material wealth only incidentally facilitates the mindset which is required to achieve tribal family structures, which can be achieved entirely without it, especially access to and retention of senior family members and their breadth of emotional, logistical, and intellectual wisdom and the inclusion and support for and from other grown family members and chosen family members. Both sets of my grandparents were calmer and more rational and loving as they aged, but my family and most of my aunts and uncles moved far away or otherwise isolated from other family due to abuse and psychological trauma, and thus their own children were subjected to the same abuse and trauma perpetuated by their grandparents since the grandparents were no longer around to fulfill the role provided by wiser, more experienced adult humans. Even as insufficient and troubled as they are, my parents' accumulated life experience full of mistakes, regret, and remorse, and even if defiantly obtuse and unrepentant can't help but increase the social support and life skills for their own grandchildren and slowed by age and regret their behavior is far more helpful and beneficial. Instead of putting hot sauce on the finger of their grandchild who still sucked their fingers, my parents instead offered to buy them their first bicycle if they stopped, still misguided and unnecessary but nonetheless an improvement. We not only benefit from tribal structures, we require them to find success as a member of humanity, and their absence fails us individually and as a species.

Another way in which families are burdened by the absence of tribal structures which directly burdens the parenting experience is simply through the logistics of child rearing. In a normal tribal structure older grandparents would provide child care while the younger, more able-bodied adults spent their time obtaining food or producing products and developing skills which alleviated the stresses of living and acquiring and gathering resources. But today mothers are often left on their own, without time or freedom to function effectively as a human adult, because parents throughout human history were not in fact the ones only providing direct child-supervision which in turn allowed them time and energy to accomplish the other important tasks required of parents, our only freedom from childcare now coming in the form of daycare or hiring unrelated and inexperienced babysitters. Some families are able to form relationships with other parents and their own parents and do distribute some childcare responsibilities, but restricted by social norms these moments of sharing child-rearing burdens is still formal and limited and as such do not affect much benefit for human families and society, and parents are still stifled by the limitations of excessive and overwhelming responsibilities. No parents can successfully provide for all the needs of human children, and burdened by our inability to replace the function of tribal structure in human development parents then become stressed and even less effective, and those with psychological and metabolic illnesses or traumatized from their own childhoods perpetuate trauma on their own offspring, in addition to failing them with a lack of skills which would otherwise facilitate their success as an adult.

Social media is serving to supplement many of the benefits to children which would have otherwise come from healthy tribal structures, providing access to generational knowledge, support from a broader range of age groups and experiences, and access to a wide group of peers. This access has been responsible for steep declines in crime and other anti-social behaviors since children are finding that which their parents and society has heretofore been unable to provide, and it can serve a valuable roll in restoring many of the deficiencies which came from the elimination of traditional tribal structures.

One of the most harmful behaviors that parents practice which destroys tribal association is to discourage demonstrations of affection between children. Horrifyingly, men in Western civilizations are loathe to hold hands, embrace, or kiss one another due to homophobic insecurities and taboos surrounding both public displays of affection and displays of affection between those not involved romantically. But even countries where affection between men is abundant there still exists even more severe anti-homosexual bigotry, demonstrating that these attitudes are mutually exclusive and wholly arbitrary social constructs which, for the West, both robs us of our humanity *and* limits emotional fulfillment in relationships. The exploitative use of homophobia by romantic partners, most commonly women to control and manipulate the behavior of their companions underlies the origination of this castration of interpersonal human intimacy, and children observing such malign behavior adopt toxic attitudes which inhibit their own expression of love and endearment to their own friends, which in turn diminishes their position and emotional security since above all we depend on others for success in life. When I was twenty-one, before my suicide attempt, my mother saw a white rose displayed in my apartment which had been given to me by a dear friend for my birthday. When told from whence it originated, she proclaimed to me that "men don't give each other flowers," which is an absurd, sorry, and especially lonely conception of life. But even for someone like me who *is* homosexual and ostensibly comfortable with displays of affection within genders I found it impossible to establish good friendships with straight men for my own limitations and insecurities about friendship and intimacy imposed by such malicious exploitation of love and affection which corrupts humanity.

Because anti-social behaviors such as homophobia, racism, and other forms of prejudice do not also facilitate professional success, many young people find themselves constrained to responsible and kind personal behavior if they wish to succeed in the new mediums of social media, every word and behavior on display for the whole world, which in turn forces them to admit their own need for other humans and our shared dependence on each other, and millions of young humans are growing up with mutual admiration for each other. When our political leaders tried to ignite military conflicts with Iran, young men in the West and the East complained that they did not want to go to war with boys with whom they had been playing video games and sharing joy and love for the entirety of their childhood, becoming more immune to the corruption of bigotry and xenophobic political actors try to engender fear and hatred for their own profit. Many prominent male social media personalities confidently express love for their friends in ways which neutralize homophobia and other forms of bigotry, in turn making space for other children to find the kinds of love and acceptance we all need, which previous generations have been denied.

This condemnation of love between friends and family members is rooted in overly ideological conceptions of gender, as demonstrated by a sibling and her husband who one Christmas screamed in horror when their son wanted to join his female cousins in dressing like Elsa from the Disney movie *Frozen* (and he wasn't even one of the gay ones). Such children who grow up feeling that their safety within the family unit depends on adhering to gender conformity react instinctually to improve their position through censorship of their need for love and affection, and thus parents actively destroy their own children's ability to form healthy, intimate connections and strong friendships which underlie family and tribal bonds. In tribal structures the recognition of emotional bonds as the strength of a tribe is reinforced by tradition and ritual, and interaction and demonstration of affection between children is actively encouraged through the same behavior in adult members demonstrating affection for one another. Being empowered by social media younger generations are more and more discarding the self-hatred, isolation, and shame which burdened our parents, organically acknowledging and restoring the demonstrative need we have for each other and rejecting the plagues of misogyny, homophobia, and racism which underlie these deficiencies.

When I was almost seventeen our scout group also went on a trip to Lake Powell. Normally scouting trips were built around merit badges and scouting activities, but our adult leaders (including my father) decided that a trip meant just for fun would be a great idea, and instead used Scouts as an excuse for all the men and boys in our church group to get away for a time from normal life. By this time I had been friends with most of the other boys for many years, so the thought of going to this kind of getaway was thrilling. When we arrived at the lake we beat the other cars by several hours, so my Dad proposed we pass the time by getting in some skiing. We loaded up the boat and put out into the large bay. Some of us had a turn, but then one of the older boys wanted to ski, but his bag was in one of the other cars, so he decided to go waterskiing in nothing but his underwear.

I couldn't believe it. I had had a desperate crush on him for several years, incredibly intimidated by his manliness and rebelliousness I don't think I ever exchanged a single word with him. Once when I was fifteen he had come walking along out of nowhere accompanied by a girl his age one day when my friends and I went for a swim in a pond outside of town. He saw us, stripped off his shirt, and dove in the pond while still wearing his jeans, then emerged to continue, wet and shirtless, down the dirt road with his girl. Now he was eighteen, and even more grown and muscular, and though he had aged out of scouts was included in the trip because he had been struggling with church attendance and so had been invited as a way to keep him involved. But here we were with him about twenty feet behind the boat with his enormous dick plastered against his wet, transparent, white briefs and an enormous smile plastered across his handsome face.

The rest of the trip was not so momentous, but it was one of the most fun things I did as a kid, getting to spend five entire days with nobody but my closest friends and many other boys I both looked up to and greatly admired and envied. I had never had older boys in my life, no older cousins, or friends, or acquaintances from whom to learn or observe, which was probably a large reason for my childhood shyness and subsequent lack of confidence as an adult. Because children learn by observing we need all varieties of other people to observe, to see what life holds for us just over the horizon that we may prepare ourselves and learn the skills we need to successfully navigate the transition.

A more conscious restoration of tribal hierarchies will be more effective in providing not only for our offspring but also for ourselves. As I discuss in my book, *Fuck Portion Control*, the depression, anxiety, and post-traumatic stress disorders experienced by soldiers returning to civilian life is often described or even derided as a mental illness, when in truth these men and women have experienced the human condition more fully, replicated in a tribal structure in which we are actually allowed to thrive, with brothers and comrades living together in a hierarchy in cooperation for our collective safety, wellbeing, and fulfillment, who are then thrust back into isolation of unstructured society which requires every person to look out only for themselves in violation of normal human behavior find the loneliness and isolation even more exaggerated and despairing having known now what it really means to live as a human being, and part of overcoming that stress and despair is to actively restructure our families and communities into more organic tribal structures which similarly ally men and women to each other in common purpose, humility, and vulnerability. This need for intimate human contact and interdependence is the very reason through which cults form and thrive—facilitating a more connected experience by which members are more able to access the interpersonal intimacy which our biology requires.

It becomes clear in cult structures that although the charismatic leader or authoritarian hierarchy serves to catalyze a cult group it is the closeness with other members which perpetuates their association, even in spite of the leader or leaders where cults are often subsumed by their followers or displace their own leaders to perpetuate the closeness and cohesion that such a group desires. While cults have a well-earned reputation of being harmful the motivations of cult members are basic human instincts to belong, to have close, intimate relationships and to be protected by collective which is very often denied by our contemporary social isolation and widespread child abuse. Raising children in a home without the ready availability of love (frequent eye contact, hugs, kisses, time) leaves children aching for the satisfaction of safety and closeness with others, but when there is also fearmongering or some other catalyst which causes children fear and anxiety the combination of safety and closeness offered by groups like cults becomes extremely difficult for them to avoid since human instincts for safety and closeness are so powerful and only cult-like groups then satisfy our innate biological needs. It is indeed dangerous to raise children without providing them access to the affirming love and closeness which should define a family (which can include chosen family) which is facilitated by a natural tribal structure, because that same need can then be exploited by people who are not concerned with a child's best interests.

Conscious and healthy satisfaction of tribal structures will provide a greater sense of belonging and wellbeing for its members, as well as provide access to a broader range of knowledge, life experiences, resources, and opportunity not only for children but also parents. Organizing our lives into healthy tribal structures is a form of self-care, by designing access to friends, peers, associates, and opportunities and the support and safety and intimacy of a structured family group. Of course, the function of the tribe can sometimes be limiting, such as practices of arranged marriages, the ostracization of members which do not comply with bigoted notions of social behavior, or isolating groups which practice cult-like behavior, but all of these are failings of human behavior in general and not problems inherent of tribal structures, religions, cults, or other institutions which are instead avenues for the exercise of harmful human behavior. Even in abusive and exploitive constructs any institution can still provide incidental benefit for vulnerable members simply through the abundance of relationships it provides. A young man who feels and is alone and unsupported is more likely to engage in criminal activity, not only for the lack of role models but also the instinctual fear of insufficiency both of material resources as well as social support. Conversely, one who is supported not only by friends and brothers but also older males who have learned hard lessons about life can be directed and supported in directions which help him to avoid those mistakes, and feeling supported even if lacking in material resources is not so insecure as to then risk their own wellbeing with anti-social behavior. Young men and women, fulfilled by intimate and strong social bonds both with peers and role models feel less compulsion to enter into premature sexual activity, which can be supported too by healthy attitudes and education about sex, and are also better protected from sexual abuse and assault which occurs when children and predators are isolated from tribal structures such as what our current familial and social organization promotes.

When people become members of a cult or cult-like group it is always borne of a desire to find belonging, because their lives do not currently offer that benefit, and the human desire to be loved, to be safe, and to belong is one of our strongest survival instincts. The error in handling and dealing with those who belong to extreme or isolated cult-like groups is the attacking or addressing of beliefs and ideology at the center of such groups, but members do not belong to cults because of its beliefs, they hold those beliefs because it enables membership. This is why it can be so hard to rescue people from cults or other harmful group associations because it's not about the beliefs at all. The beliefs are simply the entrance passkey for membership among others who similarly need and crave safety and a sense of belonging, and are simply an excuse to spend time with each other, to focus on a common goal or objective which gives their association purpose, and members willingly and enthusiastically espouse those ideas because doing so satisfies their fears of loneliness and abandonment. Instead, rescuing those who are captured by harmful group associations requires the construction of a satisfying alternative option wherein they can be promised that same fulfillment. The problem is that the family structures of such individuals is not that and very likely the reason they have gone in search of a cult in the first place. If a child is possessed of self-care skills to manage fear and anxiety such as the chapter on inventory therapy teaches (because the parent taught them) they do not feel the kind of fear which motivates membership in harmful groups in the first place. But such skills cannot be taught to a grown adult coping with those fears through self-destructive behaviors, so it instead must be done by rehabilitating the family of origination (even if that is chosen family). While many deprogramming strategies can be harmful they also convey to cult-indoctrinated persons the degree to which the family cares about them, which prior to their entry into a cult was demonstrably lacking, so when they are successful it is because that effort more clearly communicates to a child or family member that they are actually important to the family. This process would be far more successful if the family members (i.e. those in charge such as parents but can include siblings and friends as well) first resolve their own control and coping mechanisms and fear as taught through inventory therapy so they can begin to provide those needs which have not previously been fulfilled. Whenever I teach anyone inventory therapy it is never because I offered to teach them—it is because those people have seen the effect it had on my life and asked for help because they wanted the same benefit for themselves. As is the case for most aspects of life we can best help others by first helping ourselves, to teach ourselves those skills we lack and to take care of our own trauma first, and thereafter will be empowered to do the same for others. We cannot, after all, give what we do not have, so how can any parent expect to rescue a child from a cult or other group when we refuse to first rehabilitate our own lives?

Forming a tribe is not about appropriating traditions from other cultures. Instead, a tribe is composed of members which span the full age range and experience of humans, from the very young all the way through the very old, which is lead by a cohesive coalition of competent senior members whom make themselves available both emotionally and materialistically to younger generations, who are also supported in their activities by younger adult members. Families already supply the members necessary to build such structures. Carting parents off to retirement homes instead of keeping them close by is one way in which the tribal structure is destroyed. Parents spending excessive hours at work is another, or jetting off to live independently after retirement, filling their dissatisfaction with trips and vacations and accumulation of material belongings to fill the void which would otherwise be filled by mentoring younger members of a tribe. The schooling experience of children can and should change to incorporate more adults and even older children actively engaged in the facilitation and supervision of education, mothers and fathers whose parents also assist in family life can in turn be actively incorporated into education systems and helping to guide the experience of children instead of turning them loose to fend amongst each other. Access to more senior members and tribal support in turn facilitates an increased ability for young adults to take chances on their own life path, since they are better supported during the event of failure and thus more able to handle life challenges, which in turn will bring an increase in material and social support to senior members whom as they age become increasingly unable to provide for themselves, and in turn reduce their own burden on society by having prepared their own progeny adequately to take up that responsibility. Associating with other aged individuals who share common life experiences in a way that facilitates integration of familial and social obligations and functions can quickly generate a tribal structure from which all of immediate society can benefit, delegating responsibility downward through a chain of offspring and associated family members and chosen family, reducing stress and narrowing responsibility for each member by spreading it amongst the group according to status, ability, and skill. Such tribal groups do not even need to use language which designates such structures, as it is the association and logistical coordination which provides the benefit rather than the trappings of identity. Supporting other tribal leaders instead of engaging in interpersonal conflict will also facilitate the success of a tribe—for which the point is to become brothers, sisters, and family and not simply leaders for the sake of leadership, domination, or control, which would only undermine the function of a tribal structure by undermining the bonds between leadership and members and engendering animosity, resentment, and distrust, where love, affection, and cooperation instead engineers a tribe.

Impairment of normal, healthy family structures is also a direct consequence of car and automobile-centric societies in developed countries. Yes, having a vehicle is great, but infrastructure which is built to accommodate only vehicular transportation also removes the ease of connection between both current and potential family members and friends. Even though the Los Angeles region has a population of twelve-million people, I went for years without meeting a single potential romantic partner because nearly all of my travel and interaction was at work or with the few friends I already knew, or at bars which are not a good place to meet people. Even those who were heterosexual who had far more potential options also found it extremely difficult to meet people. This does not occur in places like New York City, where when I visit it is not uncommon to meet ten times as many people over a given amount of time as I would in car-centric Los Angeles. In small towns where reduced populations provide a quieter quality of life, people can be even more removed from their friends and family because every single trip anywhere requires getting in the car.

When our infrastructure is designed to facilitate walking, biking, and other more conventional modes of human transportation it also facilitates more human interaction, which includes friends and family and the formation of better social, tribal, and community interaction which in turn facilitates and increased abundance of relationships both for adults and for their children who absolutely require such opportunities. One of the primary reasons that the baby boomer generation is so miserable is precisely because of the disparate, disconnected communities in which they grew up where normal human interaction and activities were castrated by the modern automobile. When I was a child, going anywhere and doing anything required my mother or father to transport me, and since I had five siblings and my parents were burdened with extreme and unresolved childhood trauma themselves this was not a task they were ever very willing to fulfill. The only time in my childhood when I had active friendships whom I saw regularly was when we lived in Salt Lake City, because I would walk to my friends' homes even if they lived many blocks away, or when I was a teenager and finally had my own car. Biking even in some of the small towns we lived in was extremely dangerous, and like many American children we were confined to our homes because of infrastructure built only for the automobile.

Thankfully, many of my generation and those after have come to recognize this deficiency of contemporary life, and have begun to make those changes, although sometimes boomers still have a stranglehold on politics and walkable communities become a car-destination which people have to first drive to. But getting involved in your community, actively working toward and changing things so that we can have places to live in which we can walk freely and safely amongst our friends and neighbors is an act of self-care, by asking for and working with others toward common goals of improving our quality of life and the community around us we invariably come to get those rewards and benefits for ourselves. Building societies in which our children can walk or bike to school, soccer games, and friends' houses which in turn removes the requirement for us to shuttle them around everywhere frees up hours and hours of time in which we can instead spend on our own needs, pursuing hobbies and interests, staring new businesses, and developing and maintaining our own adult relationships. Unlike financially insolvent and decaying car-centric communities, those which promote walkable and bikeable infrastructure are also more financially stable, producing taxable revenue from small and medium businesses which support the maintenance and upkeep of a community's infrastructure, improving and sustaining the quality of life for ourselves as well as access to opportunity and stability for our children, whom in car-centric communities after one or two generations find them falling apart and abandoned. Until our communities are no longer amenity-short, social deserts which prioritize cars over people, it will be difficult but not impossible to set up the kind of life which can be so rewarding. Moving to places which are set up like this can free parents of the time required to play chauffeur for their children, or getting involved in local government, running for office, and setting up or being part of active advocacy groups can change things very quickly.

The formation of tribal structures is not about competition. It is about providing for the needs of members and the development of new generations. This is why many of the groups of Native Americans lived cooperatively with each other before the invasion of White Europeans. Providing for the needs within a group removes stress between groups which thus facilitates more peaceful and cooperative institutions. Tribes on the European continent before the advent of larger religious and imperial institutions inherently created larger tribes with hierarchies descending from regional chiefs to local leaders which later evolved into Kingdoms which later evolved into countries, governments, and international religious bodies, and conflict only increased as these structures grew greater and lost the inherent purpose of tribal structures, which changed the purpose of leadership from wise and experienced senior family members to power-hungry, contentious, and opportunistic psychopaths seeking to assert absolute control over life.

The handsome older boy on whom I had a crush, the one who went waterskiing in his underwear, committed suicide just a few years later. I found out about his death through a schoolmate my age who also came out after High School. He had also been gay, and was struggling with severe depression and drug abuse, and decided to end it all with an overdose. Not only could I have probably acted on my crush with him, another missed opportunity for a first kiss and romance, but a community which would have facilitated such encounters between young gay men as they did young heterosexuals would probably also have helped spare his life. What other lives could be saved if instead of supporting bigoted, authoritarian, esoteric and theological conceptions of existence our families and friends gathered to support and love us simply for being a member of the family and community. A traditional tribal social structure can achieve such outcomes, to support everyone through the institution of tribes since it is impossible for us as parents to provide all these needs on our own anyway. The purpose of a tribe should always be to provide for the needs of all members, through access to older, more experienced adults and larger groups of peers and romantic and platonic opportunity. All that is required for the restoration of these important and necessary social constructs of tribal organization and the benefits they provide is the conscious and purposeful establishment of bonds by and between senior members of likeminded family groups, making ourselves available to other family members both logistically and emotionally, especially as we age, and treating the children of our friends and siblings as family and not as distant, disparate members who happen to be biologically related. The mere act of senior members facilitating and coordinating togetherness and inclusivity will naturally and effortlessly cause other members to organize and function emulatively into a tribal structure. Individual egoistic needs may interfere, but such can easily be overcome by practicing empathy for others as well as ourselves, and abandoning self-centered obstinance in favor of cooperation and love. When parents organize themselves and their children into cohesive tribal structures the job of a parent will finally be restored to its natural function, simultaneously becoming less difficult and more successful, spreading the responsibility for childhood growth, development, and fulfillment across the entirety of a social group as is required for our human biology, to create well-developed and empowered new generations of human beings.

19

Education

When I was eight and nine my family lived in a small dusty town in Northern Utah with very little services and amenities, but luckily we had a mobile library service called the *"Bookmobile"* which visited our little cul-de-sac weekly, and the regular visitation of a mobile library was nothing short of magical, showing up early one morning as if having appeared out of nowhere. Even though we also had a *Nintendo* to compete for our attention, the *Bookmobile* was by far the most thrilling part of our week, nearly rivaling even holidays like Christmas and Halloween.

Reading was not an explicitly intellectual focus of our childhood, but was instead used as a tactic to placate and occupy our time. But consequently as I and my siblings grew and our reading skills improved my parents began practicing daily family scripture study. This most especially impacted our younger siblings who were regularly exposed to the higher reading levels of such archaic (and violent!) books. My little sisters developed reading skills many grades above their own, even better than mine and the other older siblings when we were their age, but which benefitted all of us generally in our schoolwork, education, and professional pursuits in spite of exposing us to themes of incest, murder, and genocide.

Because of my debilitating mental and physical illnesses I found it impossible to attend college, but the skills I developed from reading as a child afforded me others which advantaged me more than those who spent four years and tens of thousands of dollars pursuing higher learning. Able to grasp technical concepts and read documentation for complicated software I taught myself the skills necessary to advance in my career simply by reading the help menus and tutorials for that software and skillset. Later when my health imploded and answers to my health problems proved nearly impossible to solve I found that comprehending scientific literature and complex medical studies came naturally and soon was discovering information for myself to solve not just my complicated health problems but in turn many of those which have plagued mankind for millennia. While there are lots of factors which determine intelligence, it is most of all the ability not only to read but also to *enjoy* reading which advantaged my life more than any other skill. When I began to delve into video game design and needed to refresh my comprehension of calculus I was able with the help of a fat textbook re-learn the concepts I had forgotten in adulthood and construct complicated algorithms to achieve technical systems in my games, all because I simply developed a reading comprehension level that facilitates such accomplishment, having no other formal education or experience in any of those areas.

Part of my heightened intellectual development in spite of a limited formal education came directly as a result of being homosexual in a conservative home, because the constant presence of fear caused me to turn inward and develop skills of imagination and abstract thought, and to spend my leisure time playing video games, drawing, or reading. I first read the *Hobbit* at the age of twelve when my father gifted me his childhood set of *Lord of the Rings*. I read *Moby Dick* at age fifteen and attempted *The Silmarillion* (but that was pushing it just a bit). My ability to read helped me perform well in advanced placement classes for Literature and English studies for a student who never studied and didn't place any special effort toward achieving high in academics (imagine if I *had* studied), and even though I didn't go to a single day of college significant cognitive ability.

Insecure adults are often embarrassed by their lack of knowledge or intelligence, and will even ridicule or harass people they perceive to be more intelligent than they are. I have family members who are hostile to my work because the big words make them feel stupid. This is a result of insecure parents misunderstanding what it means to be smart, and it has nothing to do with big words or the accumulation of facts and information, but through their own insecure behavior in turn teach children they should be embarrassed by making mistakes or being ignorant to something. I remember once raising my hand to answer a question in elementary school, and said the word bologna wrong. The kids in my grade actually laughed at me, because who the fuck would think the word bologna is actually pronounced ba-lone-ee. Yeah— how dumb of me not to know that. But I never again raised my hand to answer a question in school, ever. This wasn't the fault of those kids, though. Mispronouncing bologna is actually funny, and most people laugh because they also found out the hard way how to pronounce it. But in my family we were taught to be insecure about ignorance, which is an extremely ignorant thing to believe.

I love dumb people, they are so much fun and bring a lot more joy and levity to life, and if I had been able to be less serious and more relaxed as a child I would have made a lot more progress in my life and had many more friends and positive experiences. Nobody needs to smart, and nobody can ever know even most things there are to know, and shame about being ignorant is really just a lack of self compassion. In reality, hostility toward those who are intelligent by those who *think* they are not is just another form of spite, the self-centered, preservationist, instinctual human reaction we feel toward those who have that which we do not. We evolved this instinct in order to compete with others within our own species, because in an evolutionary sense how could a cognitively challenged human compete with another who is more intelligent if not also possessed of other tools at their disposal? The instinct recognizes the disadvantage and thus inspires contempt for those who possess anything more that we, including that which is intangible.

The truest measure of intelligence is curiosity. What success I've achieved in life, even without any special access to opportunity and marginal education, was curiosity in turn satisfied and fulfilled in my ability and *desire* to read. The latter is the more important part of education, because even though many people can read well it is our reluctance to read which impedes our personal progress. Indeed those who hold bigoted and fearful ideas of the world and of others are simply incurious, and purposefully decline the pursuit of knowledge and insight which would otherwise relieve them of their ignorance. Though my mother has an exceptional reading level she never reads any books, not even the ones I write which would help her with her health and emotional problems simply because she does not want to spend time reading (and there is only so much I can do to help people who won't spend time and effort helping themselves). It is this point about reading education which is the most crucial for children to achieve—that simply being able to read is not sufficient for the empowerment of success, but the *desire* to read is what must be achieved. Most early education simply seeks to achieve a barely functioning reading level for children, then immediately progresses to math and science, content only that children can functionally read regardless of proficiency.

To accomplish a desire to read is rather simple, but specific achievements must be made at certain points in a child's life. Children are highly motivated to learn and to emulate older humans if they are not abused to the point of being shut down about it. My mother's reluctance to read originates from her own mother's failure to engender confidence and self-esteem in her daughter, and fear of self-reflection and self-improvement such as is often perpetuated within religious communities. But this curiosity is built into our biology, and children need absolutely no encouragement from parents or caretakers to develop it, only the space to do so. It is during this time that reading *must* be introduced. If too much time is wasted or children are abused and harassed during this crucial time and not enough focus on reading practiced before a child is much older (probably before age ten) then the natural energy required to achieve a love of reading will be lost in favor of a shift toward interpersonal survival and social coping and development, and the window for easily empowering reading skills will have passed.

Instilling a desire to read also has the incidental benefit of making a parent's job much easier, because a child needs to be guided into a love of reading *on their own*, rather than listening to others read, so as soon as it is accomplished children will spend hours devouring books on their own thus bringing more frequent periods of quiet and repose for tired parents, but also beginning the process of empowering children to educate themselves instead of always relying on others to facilitate education. Practical problem solving due to the ability to read and comprehend information can enable a child to do anything to provide for themselves as they age and begin to have their own families. I was once harassed by an employer who stole wages from me, who preemptively filed a lawsuit in an attempt to intimidate me into giving up the wages I had earned for my labor. Stressed and ignorant I solicited advice from my father, who told me to ignore it and it would go away (which in hindsight is *never* good legal advice). I listened to him, and my harasser nearly won a default judgment against me. When I realized the error I quickly got to work learning how to protect myself and the steps required to respond to the lawsuit and successfully resolved the situation. Reading came to my rescue even (and especially) when my parents could not.

Since education is an important part of our development which should occupy the entire first quarter or more of our life, it is made much more effective and effortless if a child is first and foremost empowered with the ability and desire to read. Because our education system does not actually facilitate even sufficient reading skills in many children it is imperative that parents empower their children to read before and during their early years of education. Most parents, however, think that this looks in practice like nightly or daily reading to their children. Though this can introduce children to reading it in fact is not helpful if the goal is to accomplish a child's independence in reading. In order to become not only skilled at reading but to also develop a desire to read (which, again, all children have a natural inclination and motivation to do) a child must actually read themselves. A great strategy to begin doing this is transitioning family reading time where children sit and listen to the parent read to that in which everyone chooses their own book to read together but on their own, near parents and other family but engaged in a book of their choice. This demonstration of the capacity for reading individually as is accomplished by reading *with* children transitions the act of reading from something we do for the child to something the child does for themselves. It is important that parents join their children in this practice, though, and not just corral their children and force them to read while we go off and watch TV or read on our phone, because doing so will communicate to children through our behavior that reading is not, in fact, important and that there are more rewarding activities, which there really are not. Of course, not all parents like to read, but since you are reading this book you are probably not one of them. If you don't like to read, it's good that you are doing this for your children, and as soon as their love of reading becomes stronger and more independent then we no longer have to practice this (although doing so will become a cherished memory for children).

Though not nearly as much a problem as it used to be, access to books can be a hurdle for many families, in which case it is important to visit libraries, borrow, or establish book exchanges within the community. If such resources do not exist, make them. Organize, ask for help, and look for programs which assist in providing books. Dolly Parton, for instance, has a program which mails free books to children from birth until they begin school. Options and opportunities exist. If you are someone with means, helping to provide access to literature and reading programs for others who do not have access to such opportunities will help to create populations of adults who possess empowering skills which they can use to care for themselves instead of revolting and rioting against you when they grow up and find oppressive political and economic barriers and a paucity of opportunity. Reading and a love of reading is absolutely the most important skill that children can learn, and is really the only skill which we absolutely must learn, since it alone can empower us to achieve everything else that must be discovered in life.

Schools should be reoriented to focus primarily on reading for the first several years of education. It doesn't matter if a kid can count or add if they can't even read the damn math problem, where a child proficient in reading can learn any new skill at any period of their lives. Because so much of social media requires reading and typing, these skills are now more naturally and commonly practiced by children. Before she could even properly read, my first niece learned to operate the DVD player and remote, because the shows she watched also taught her reading basics, and children are naturally interested in facilitating their own access to information and experience. Turning on captions while children watch television or internet programs and films will also help to increase familiarity with reading and writing. But this merely facilitates the superficial act of communication, where the love and desire to actually read is the more important skill and requires books in order to achieve. Like my mother, many people's ability to solve their own problems originates from an unwillingness to solve their own problems through the acquisition of knowledge, even though it is on the face of it one of the most simple and accessible solutions possible.

Making matters worse is that reading and writing only in order to participate in social media makes people vulnerable to the kinds of misinformation and manipulation that makes them vulnerable to exploitation, becoming unwitting victims of fraud, scams, and political, commercial, and social chicanery. When I was in my early twenties my mother in a passing conversation mentioned the new "business venture" that one of my siblings had gotten started. The details sounded very suspicious, so I promptly inquired directly of them the details. A schoolmate of ours had recruited them into a multi-level marketing pyramid scheme, selling them a "web storefront" which promised to make them thousands of dollars a month, never mind that my sibling had no products to actually sell. The induction was *six-hundred dollars* (at the turn of the millennium), which had probably taken my sibling several months to save up. I immediately urged them to put a stop payment on the check, even though that would cost them about thirty-dollars, because they would never again see that six-hundred they were about to lose. Thankfully they listened to me and that person was not able to take advantage of them. But this sibling took more after our mother with their attitude toward reading, and was throughout their life roped into other schemes such as laser hair removal subscriptions and oppressive credit-card debt because their ability to comprehend information was not developed through many years of reading from which I benefitted.

No parent wants their child to be someone who is taken advantage of, robbed, or misled from truth, and yet enormous populations of those whom one might believe to be intelligent enough to protect themselves from deception become fully entrenched in it. Better still that our children not become the very criminals seeking to harm others since they will also be empowered with life skills which are better suited for success. The ability not only to read but to also comprehend what is being read and to discern truth from misinformation and lies is a skill acquired *only* by reading prolifically—the conceptualization of what words actually mean, and to distinguish motivations and intentions behind the composers of works whether they are books or twitter posts is developed only by thorough exposure to written works from a variety of authors and backgrounds. You must remember that perfectly ordinary, well adjusted and intelligent human beings are capable of committing the systematic extermination of others if they even think it will advantage them in the slightest. Recognizing the animal in other humans but not in ourselves deludes us about our own individual nature and the things of which we are all capable, though also in the most magnanimous terms as well as the vile. The person who would choose an eugenic model of letting coronavirus run rampant and take those it will for the sake of markets and livelihood is the very same who would smile at prisoners as they shut the gas chamber door, or continue about their lives as millions of people are exterminated a few miles from their local shopping mall. The only difference between people who dismiss the suffering of others and those who engineer it is a society which merely restrains the more heinous, until it doesn't, but make no mistake—it is a short walk from bystander to participant, and all such self-preservation instincts no matter how apparently benign originate from only one source—the belief that the Other, rather than Self, is an impediment to fulfillment.

The atrocities of the past were not borne of their time but is an ever constant trait of humanity, alive and well, which survives in the darkness of willful naivety even as it plays out unashamed at this very moment! If you ever wondered whom among you would become the murderous Nazi or how such horrors ever come to be look no further than your parents or siblings, friends and neighbors who value their own comfort over the meekest of human lives, hesitate to empathize with those for whom mortality calls, or excuses base callousness as pretended intellectualism. Unknown to them a trick of nature has selected them too for a population control mechanism which is built into the human race, which sacrifices itself during perceptions of burdensome competition, erupting not only into wars and brutal conflict and oppressive political strife but also attitudes which sacrifice others and, just like the Nazis who died under the very bombs and guns they thought themselves too superior, those whom are stupid enough to believe in their own moral and deserving superiority over others also offer themselves unconsciously into a mass-suicide pact every bit as instinctual and pathetic as suicidal lemmings, and maybe as they die alone and abandoned in a nursing home, robbed by their own children who were just doing as they were taught, may finally concede some small amount of regret for their narrow-minded and compassionless self-serving labors. But privately. In their mind. So not to admit their wrongs. Those who rage against authoritarianism instead of helping their fellows are simply mad they do not wield such power themselves, because the desire for authoritarianism is a desire to control and subvert those things which cause us fear, and such conceptions of personal worth and power which in turn catalyze sociopolitical conflict are rooted in ignorance to the realities of mortality which are otherwise learned through exposure to human stories. When people have very little experience with reading and writing they are more likely to take information at face-value, beholden to fear, and accept information without questioning it, to become both victim and persecutor, seeking conflict to solve their problems rather than enlightenment, and if the origination of encounters comes from those whom are malign and scheming our children at best will always become victims, at worst criminals if they are not adequately empowered to consume, create, and wield information effectively.

Fear is all that prevents us from self-improvement. The fear that we will fail. The fear that we cannot do what we want to achieve. The fear that we are every bit the loser, the fake, the weak imbecile that our abusive parents or other adults wielded as their excuse. Like belief, which is just a feeling of want, failure is an artificial concept which does not actually exist. Does a sun fail when it finally burns through its trillions of pounds of hydrogen over a span of time unfathomable to the human mind? No. Even then a sun will continue to participate in the physics of the Universe and become part of other stars and planets and black holes to do and be incredible things in an endless cycle of reality. The concept of failure is simply a manipulative tool designed by opportunistic humans to win advantage one over another, parents over their children or spouse, or peers over their friends, or country against country. Stories end but human lives persist in their entirety, and what we perceive as failure are simply moments of insecurity and doubt we encounter during moments of challenge, difficulty, mistakes, frustration, or loss when life reminds us that we are not the ones in control. Failure must be the natural course of behaviors and choices which do not bear out logical consequences. To live in reality is to be bound by rules. If consequences did not match with causes there would be no logic nor order to the Universe and thus we would not be here. To persist in ignorance is to live at the mercy of life and have little control over what consequences we must encounter, but to find enlightenment is to be part of it and thus understand what consequences we must endure.

Religion is by and large an enormous exercise in this kind of fear, and indeed all those who subscribe to religion are afraid of life. We are borne of instinct to survive, to fear that which can impair this survival, and the fear of abandoning abusive and hateful traditions is just a fear of getting in trouble, of authority such as our parents or what we are told is God telling us once again we have failed and as such are undeserving of the love, safety, and companionship we need to thrive in life. All religions fixate on fear—death, disease, retribution, or failure because the exploitation of fear is a potent method to manipulate others, and offer anecdotal conceptions like salvation, nirvana, or resurrection as the antidote. But because fear is exploited to effect adherence fear can never actually be subverted, and so believers persist the entirety of their lives preoccupied with death and loss, driven insane by the constant fear of failure, always in a state of limbo and missing out on everything happening around them only at the end to recognize their lives as unfulfilling and empty.

Our ancestors used to observe the Easter holiday as a celebration of Spring and the Goddess Ēostre before Romans forced them under threat of death to adopt Christianity and co-opted the holiday to consolidate political power. Lithuania was one of the last countries to be converted to that religion in 1387, and as such retains more of their pagan traditions than other Western civilizations. But even after thousands of years we still host egg hunts, paint Easter eggs, and revel in bunnies, food, flowers, and candy without even taking the time to learn why such obvious symbolism persists in our traditions in obvious antagonism to religion which currently hosts Easter because of the fear of what those answers mean. Even black Americans who were forced into Christianity by slavery will enthusiastically endorse the religion of their ancestors' slavers because our willingness as humans to perpetuate tradition is rooted in biological instincts to survive, even when they are clearly harmful to our personal wellbeing, the instinct to belong and fear of getting in trouble even as we are grown and free to do as we will can keep us chained to injurious behavior. Overcoming fear through inventory therapy liberates us from the burden of instinct and that fear which prevents self-improvement, learning, and having lives which are productive, peaceful, and satisfying, and removes the concept of failure altogether.

More than access to education or curriculum, however, is the influence also that diet has on a child's ability to learn. Many studies have been performed which show how children's capacity for learning is affected by nutrition, and those who are malnourished always perform poorly, which is why children must start each day with a good breakfast that provides ample and generous nutrition and calories. But some studies are also misleading, and concepts of nutrition and the effect that specific nutrients have on our health are woefully misunderstood. As I discuss at length in *Fuck Portion Control*, sugar is actually a necessary requirement for human health, being animals which have evolved to subsist with fruit and specifically both glucose and fructose as major sources of chemical energy. It is why children so often *crave* sugar, not because it is addictive nor are they spoiled or hedonistic, but because our biology communicates to their brain that it is required to for our metabolically demanding brains, growth, and development. Sugar directly promotes one of the most important pathways in the human body called the *kynurenine pathway*, the end result of which is a product called *nicotinamide adenine dinucleotide* which in turn functions to pass electrons (and thus energy) from the point of acquiring them from food to that of their use in systems which use energy. There is direct causation between the amount of NAD a body has and how well our brains are able to function. Stable saturated fats like coconut oil, butter and other dairy fat, or ruminant fat such as beef tallow along with dietary sources of vitamin C and B vitamins also promote successful kynurenine pathway activity (which come naturally from food and supplements should not typically be given to children unless they have specific metabolic problems which are addressed in my other book). Inflammatory foods like gluten from common varieties of wheat directly suppress the kynurenine pathway, as does a deficiency of sugar. The absence of sugar also happens to stop the kynurenine pathway at the exact enzymatic step which results in the production of a toxic neurostimulant called *quinolinic acid*. The function of this failure in the kynurenine pathway is meant by the body to actually increase cognitive ability through the strongly stimulating effect of quinolinic acid, to facilitate an increase in cognitive problem solving ability in an organism under nutritional stress to help resolve their dietary deficiencies by stimulating novel investigation and exploration and thus increase their chances of resolving their predicament. But because quinolinic acid is so destructive it also causes extreme restlessness and agitation, which in a natural animal motivates them to move, explore, and otherwise occupy their energies to search and acquire new resources. Lack of sunshine also impairs the kynurenine pathway, and failure of the kynurenine pathway also results in male-pattern baldness as addressed in my other book (and female hair loss too if women get very ill), which is why there is a strong association of hair loss with intellectual occupations. Some studies have shown omega-3 fatty acids and essential fatty acids to promote cognitive ability in children, and as a result many products including infant formula, milk, cereals, and lunch products and snacks now contain added omega-3s and so-called essential fatty acids. But these fats also *directly* inhibit the kynurenine pathway at the very same point that fructose deficiency does also, even if fructose is present, resulting in heightened quinolinic acid production and thus stimulating cognitive capacity through neurological stress. Because it also causes a deficiency in NAD, failure of the kynurenine pathway prevents tissues from resisting the excitotoxic effects of quinolate, and this in turn leads to mental health deterioration, presenting first as an increase in irritability, agitation, and restlessness, but which quickly progresses to conditions like ADHD and childhood depression, and later more severe psychoses like schizophrenia, sociopathy, psychopathy, violence, and even cancer as cells and tissues can no longer handle the stress of excessive cellular excitation caused by quinolate and the failure of the kynurenine pathway.

    True, healthy mental cognition is achieved through a complete diet which is free of inflammatory foods and full of generous nutrients as discussed in *Fuck Portion Control*, and which also includes amble amounts of sun exposure. Truly healthy children and adults are, in truth, possessed of a more balanced mental *and* physical development due to the absence of quinolate excess and excessive neurological excitation, which in turn facilitates more physical growth and development. It is in fact this function or deficit of the kynurenine pathway, NAD, and quinolinic acid which incidentally accounts for the stereotypical disparities between those who are athletically or intellectual gifted, where the presence of quinolate, though performing an evolutionarily useful purpose, favors mental development over physical, where a healthy diet replete in nutrients, calories, and sugar low in quinolate favors healthy and robust physical development. A good diet will accomplish both. To be clear, when I refer to sugar I am talking about sugar as a chemical form of energy storage and not processed junk food which is too often colloquially referred to as sugar, rife with chemicals, gums, emulsifiers, and inferior ingredients, but those which satisfy the nutritional needs of a human being.

As a young athlete my nutritional needs were astronomical, but inexplicably ignored and neglected even by my coach and other adults who should have known to promote access to the kinds of nutrition required for extreme and demanding physical activity. During the height of my swimming achievements some practice days totaled nearly four hours a day swimming and lifting weights, as much as college level athletes even though as children our bodies were still developing and so also going through the stresses and increased nutritional requirements of adolescence. It is a miracle that I or my other teammates didn't actually die from aneurysm or sudden cardiovascular episodes, so extreme was our training without proper nutritional support. The only increase in nutrition for myself during this time was due to my own instinctual response to hunger and fatigue in the form of a plate of spaghetti and sauce when I would get home from practice. I had somewhere a deficit in the range of one or two thousand calories every day from what this level of activity required, let alone the quality and quantity of specific required micronutrients, and my failure at the sport and plunge into suicidal depression, thyroid disease, and eventual cancer begun specifically because of this inattention to the nutritional needs not only of a growing child but one also engaged in demanding mental and physical activity. If attention had been directed at my nutritional needs I would have been able to continue in the sport I loved and achieve notable success which in turn would have opened other opportunities, including those of an emotional and social nature and not simply the superficial titles, awards, and academic excellence, since the fallout also affected my morale and ability to make and keep friendships and alliances and ability to provide for my own emotional wellbeing.

That day in second grade when my exhausted and ill-tempered teacher forced me to piss myself in public was one of the most humiliating events of my childhood, even though not a single person actually noticed it. The experience was less about actually wetting myself, which is kind of funny, but in the absolute psychological control that authoritarian woman wielded to will me to sit in place and willingly urinate on myself rather than protest and stick up for my own wellbeing. In truth, my attitude and propensity for it was being the son of a mother who did the same and had already psychologically subjugated me into little more than a drone of a human being. Because children are naturally inclined to promote and pursue their own education and learning, it is not required of adults to motivate or coerce them and doing so will only facilitate damage to children's natural propensity for education. Insulting, antagonizing, and controlling children to do what we think is best for them will always also destroy their ability to do it on their own, and will in turn make it more difficult and stressful for us to facilitate learning and education in the future. This is why many experimental and preeminent educational programs which facilitate student-led and initiated learning rather than teacher-led learning produce not only better academic success but also broad social and professional achievement as well. Prominent achievers are also always self-led in the pursuit of knowledge and achievement, often in spite of a parent's failures, but which needn't be difficult to facilitate in a child, requiring only the promotion of our natural instincts for learning rather than their inhibition by abuse. Being empowered by the knowledge that we can facilitate learning for ourselves, such as when my mother unintentionally helped me learn to draw instead of doing it for me, children find more success than they would otherwise because the motivation for learning is so powerful and natural and does not need coercion, doubt, and scheming but merely encouragement and opportunity, and also happens to make a parent's responsibly much lighter in turn.

Many people do not think that wonder and amazement exist all around us, and pine for the novelty of fantasy or history and bemoan the relatively boring state of our world compared to that contained in books and fossil records, how neat it would be if dinosaurs still roamed the Earth or we could ride on the backs of fantastical flying alien creatures and swim in enormous waterfalls which cascade from gravitationally suspended floating rocks. This pessimistic characterization of our world is a quality of traumatized human psyche, not reality, and if our world was teeming with incredible dinosaurs we would think the Tyrannosaurus rex every bit as uninteresting as a lion or bear. There are absolutely incredible animals which live in our world today, such as the Pleistocene plains bison, the tapirs and ratites of South America, the elephant and rhino, and the mighty wild horses which defy domestication and have reconquered their evolutionary homeland of North America. As humans we naturally project our own sorry opinion of ourselves onto the world around us, including the people and things in it, and if we think we are boring or have low self-esteem it seems impossible that wonderful things should exist all around us, so we consider the world with the same unhappy attitude we have for ourselves and miss out on the incredible wonders of the here and now. There is nothing wrong with fantasy and imagination, they fuel human creativity and technological progress, but the same experiences of abuse and trauma which cause us to adapt destructive coping mechanisms and impair our sense of self worth biases us against reality and impairs our ability to learn, observe, and experience. It must be inventoried and our low conception of ourselves, our families, and our world enlightened in order that our eyes be opened to the reality of the Universe and so benefit more directly from what is.

Reading and writing is an uniquely human trait which our very biology has evolved to accommodate. It is not an artificial construct of society or civilization, but a very real part of our physiological and genetic nature as a human animal. Like all known historical firsts, the first known written language, Sumerian, cannot have actually been the first written language as it demonstrates elements of written communication far more complex than what a first written language could actually accomplish. The consistent appearance of specific symbols and pictographs in ancient cave art tens of thousands of years old as identified by paleoanthropologists like Genevieve von Petzinger demonstrate that elements of written language have existed for much more of human history than we have realized, where only the more complex systems of writing executed in more permanent mediums which actually persist through history began to develop from others already established when societies were more agrarian and did not in fact simply materialize alongside the development of agriculture and trade but which were themselves facilitated through our already developed ability to communicate through written language, even if it was as primitive as merely a handful of symbols, though it is obviously more likely to have encompassed more. The ability to read and write is so innately human and so deeply ingrained in our DNA that cultivating these skills is one of the only skills that humans require in order to flourish, and conversely its deficiency also deprives us of the very nature of our species and impairs our ability to succeed. Failing to empower children sufficiently through reading skills fails them through the entirety of their lives, and as such the focus of education should always first and foremost be centered on the development of reading and the love for and desire to read. Especially since this empowers children to facilitate their own further learning and education when developed sufficiently and as such remove much of the stress and responsibility for education from parents, the priority for education above all must be reading.

20

Systems of Failure

"Nathan," my mother said one day as she walked into my room. "I want to talk to you." I was seventeen-years old and it was summertime between my Junior and Senior years of High School. I was co-captain of my High School swimming team, one the fastest in our entire school and potentially the entire State even though I had only been swimming for two years. I'd been to an early-morning workout that day and spent the afternoon taking a nap to recover before my second workout later in the day and a Student Council meeting after that, since I had won the position of Student Body Technical Director at the end of the previous school year. I was also studying to take the ACT for the first time in preparation for college admissions, and was very near becoming an Eagle Scout, which required the planing and execution of a large-scale community service project. I was also working two days a week at an internship for a company which made 3D special-effects for major Hollywood films. Several days before this I had fought my father about going to work on his construction site. From the time I was eleven or twelve I had been working construction with him throughout the summers and on weekends. We worked mostly cleaning up his sites, picking up leftover chunks of two-by-fours, sweeping sawdust, loading old shingles and hundred-year-old insulation into dumpsters, or raking the grounds of detritus. A few weeks previous I had gotten a second-degree sunburn after being forced to lay sod in the very middle of the day instead of the cooler hours, and even after my skin began to boil and blister with first degree burns was forced to go back the next day in the afternoon and continue, in the middle of the day, being supplied with nothing but some Solarcaine. It took weeks for my skin to heal. Working for my father was demoralizing. No matter how much we worked it was never enough, he never taught us construction skills or let us work alongside him, and any protest of our treatment was met with insults and harassment. I had finally had enough and, exhausted by my other commitments, my depression, and my anxiety surrounding my sexuality and fed up with his abuse I had finally outright refused to accompany him to work in spite of the threats and berating. It seemed pointless and fruitless to be exhausting myself for such a miserable, abusive and neglectful man, especially when doing so meant neglecting my other obligations, commitments, and personal development.

My mom shut the door to my room and sat at the side of the bed, looking at me with an expression of total disappointment. "I'm afraid you're not going to be able to provide for a family when you grow up," she said.

An overwhelming sense of hatred washed over me. I was well past shame by this point in our relationship, no longer surprised that my own parents were adversaries in my life. I mentioned earlier my achievements and obligations for a sense of context, to illustrate the inanity of the moment, but at the time fully believed them and listened to her words, having absolutely no appreciation for the exceptionally committed, talented, hardworking, and special kid I was. In that moment I wasn't Captain of the swimming team. I wasn't an academically achieving honor student. I wasn't a member of Student government nor on my way to earning my Eagle Scout, even though I was. Neither was I someone who had secured a prized internship at a special effects company learning 3D software, nor had I spent my childhood working in occupations and conditions in violation of child labor laws.

Children are a mirror, but not one from which we can choose to look away—they are strapped and padlocked to the front of our face and we must stare every moment of every day to face the depths of our deepest fears and insecurities. Because we experience life, parenting, and children through the filter of our own experience, our experience is what informs our anticipation of our children's future rather than reality, since reality has not yet occurred in terms of our children's future. Our past disappointments and trauma make us hyper aware of those things we experienced which were painful, which in turn focuses our self-preservation instincts to those areas. This in turn causes us to project our fears and insecurities onto the lives of our children since those are the things to which we are most sensitive. For instance, if our access to opportunity as a child was impaired by insufficient material resources we may then identify material sufficiency as a key to success in life and thus anticipate failure to achieve material wealth as a barrier for our children's fulfillment. Or, if we were body-shamed by our parents, friends, or romantic targets we may identify being fat or simply failing to be a physical specimen as a source of rejection and pain. If we were embarrassed or shamed by our parents for being silly and childish we may identify levity and joy as as a vulnerability which exposes us to pain and in turn see those qualities in our children also as liabilities. Because these experiences were our personal experiences of pain and trauma, seeing their equivalents in our children also reminds us of that pain and trauma, increasing our emotional reaction to their observation.

If we do not possess the skills to resolve our own pain and trauma we then try to redirect our attention from those uncomfortable realities and instead neutralize the source which triggered the emotions, which in this case is our loving children. One would assume that overweight mothers would be sympathetic to their daughters' struggles with weight and body image, and inspire sympathetic concepts of self-worth learned from their own experiences of rejection and disappointment. But having experienced weight as an apparent source of pain and rejection which also reinforced poor estimation of self-worth they instead reflect upon the child their own paucity of self-esteem, seeing in the mirror of their children the aspects of their own life they most hate. Fathers who feel like failures because they have not yet become financially rich could teach their children how to be happy no matter their financial status, but because they connect their own self worth and personal disappointment to monetary status and a lack of obscene wealth see in their helpless and immature little children who also lack material wealth the very embodiment of that which they believe has prevented their happiness.

This tendency to see our insecurities reflected in children is why parents insist on abusing and destroying their innocence and unconditional love, heaving upon them the burdens of adulthood long before they even have their first kiss or earn their first dollar. When we have unresolved pain and trauma from our own childhoods our own children then become receptacles for our self-hatred, all our resentments and disappointments, since by being little versions of us force us to face things we have spent our entire lives trying to ignore. Then mothers who have been rejected and harassed by husbands and boyfriends for their weight turn instead upon their own daughters, and even fathers who have achieved degrees of material wealth turn upon their children who constantly remind them of their personal disappointment which has never actually been resolved by success as they expected.

We often exhaust much energy when children are mean or misbehaved in attempts to correct that behavior. One mother I was helping had a child who was quick to ridicule and harass their siblings. The mother felt overwhelming frustration and embarrassment trying to convince, motivate, or coerce their child to treat his siblings with love and respect, yelling at him to stop yelling at their siblings, even punishing him with time out or banishment to their room when they offended another child, as most parents might expect is reasonable and responsible. But it was completely lost upon this mother that their behavior was, in reality, the exact behavior that the child was demonstrating—Someone does something to offend me. I react by lashing out in anger. In her persistent disciplining of him for actions which she disapproved she was modeling for him the very behavior she took offense. We as parents do this in many ways and in many contexts. Parents who value material wealth and financial success spend their money and acquire many possessions in excess of what we really need as humans, then turn around and blame their children for being financially irresponsible even though we have modeled for them the accumulation of obscene amounts of shit as the way they should live their lives. Parents who value physical fitness and wellness abuse our bodies and treat them as a thing to be ashamed and controlled, then act surprised when our children grow up fat and struggle with confidence as if we hadn't spent their entire lives telling them to abuse and feel shame for their body. This kind of incongruity of our actions and what we want of our child, demonstrating the very same behaviors and traits we actually despise in our children is a major consternation for parents, because we are unaware to what extent hypocrisy pervades our life because of the way in which trauma obfuscates self-awareness and self-compassion. We then mistake our emotional instability triggered by children as authority rather than the insecurity and abdication of authority it truly is. We have not matured and are not at all a functioning adult, being led instead by emotional self-centeredness and reactivity to being hungry, tired, or sad every bit as unrestrained and indulgent as the children we are trying to empower.

We also do this when interacting with our significant others or other adults—teachers, coworkers, bosses, government, employees, and friends—because disappointment and loss can be so painful and our life experiences have taught us to anticipate uncomfortable experiences before they occur and maybe we can head them off before they cause us more pain and more heartache. But in reality we can never really do that, and often through our own machinations bring upon ourselves the very pain and heartache we expect. For instance, many women I know persist in relationships where their husbands shame them for their weight or appearance. This is a heinous behavior on the part of men (although women do it too), but in reality there is nothing actually stopping people us leaving partners who treat us poorly. Like myself who stayed in a previous relationship even though he treated me terribly and cheated on me repeatedly. We often do not actually want to be with someone better because that would actually deprive us of the ammunition used to control our relationship or partner. My mother never actually wanted my Dad to be nice to her, because then she could not use his meanness against him during their conflicts. If she had, there was more than ample opportunity to leave. Especially when they got divorced for three months and could have stayed separated and begun new lives but in reality felt more comfortable with each other since each fulfilled the control mechanisms in the other, which is also why I did not leave my partner either.

This type of insecurity also leads us into dangerous conspiratorial or fantastical thinking which renders us unable to understand life and live effectively. The instability of the world and its geopolitics and socioeconomic forces are a source of significant stress for most people since they are forces which are larger than we can often cope and sometimes even comprehend. Most of us cope with such enormous systems by trying to ignore it and carry on as best we can (people who 'aren't into politics' are a great example). But our inability to interface with fear, insecurity, and disappointment can also lead us to feel very alone, as if our lives and those lives for which we are responsible are only up to us, and lacking god-like powers which can actually control fate we become so afraid of other people, disease, loss, and death we end up compromising not only our own wellbeing but also that of others as we act irrationally. In the early part of the coronavirus pandemic a woman approached me with an offer for a television show on a very popular streaming service. After having lived in Los Angeles for fifteen years I immediately knew her as a predator trying to glean free assistance for her health problems, which was especially funny because I help people for free all the time and all she had to do was ask, but people like her are so traumatized they feel unable to ask for help and instead invent unnecessary schemes trying to get the help they need but will not ask for. Instead of directly addressing this and to avoid embarrassment I made the mistake of indulging her desperation, although it would have been better if I hadn't, and tried to help her a little in spite of the situation. I was quickly alarmed to hear her then start rambling about her expansive collection of conspiratorial ideology and realized she was beyond help, as someone with that kind of trauma will refuse to do even simple things like self-education through reading my book, and seeks my assistance for the emotional support and validation of already held beliefs, not gleaning of new information, and in spite of giving her my time and books did nothing beyond buy and take a few supplements which is not at all reflective of my work and advice. Sadly, because of her and her partner's incorrect understanding about vaccines (which do have side effects as discussed in my other book but are usually still useful to prevent severe illness), her partner of several decades died from contracting coronavirus, which I know because she later used that fact in yet another attempt to solicit free counseling which I had already given which she wasn't following anyway, and became a tragic victim of her inability to confront reality.

If in reading that story you had the thought you are not subjected to such delusions I can assure you that you are, and the entire problem behind this flaw in human psychology is the inability to recognize it in ourselves when it is happening, which is why people like this woman or yourself who might believe incorrect ideas about dieting, health, or child rearing think they are legitimate because you think them and not because they are true. Many professionals and so-called experts in psychology or sociology have proposed reasons for why people, even those who might be considered intelligent, fall into such self-destructive patterns of behavior like entertaining conspiracies or being preyed upon by grifters to lose money, time, and even important relationships or even trigger legal jeopardy, but most of them are not only inaccurate they are also not even reasons but simply further depictions of symptoms, for instance one expert suggesting this is caused by 'losing identity,' which is exceptionally vague and illogically assumes without supporting evidence there was a differing 'identity' to begin with. An easy way to tell if a supposed expert truly understands any such problem in humans is whether they demonstrate contempt for those they are describing, as contempt for human weaknesses betrays their own personal insecurity which is triggered by the problem and thus presents a conflict of interest which prevents the empathy required for effective understanding. Closely related to conspiracy thinking is sycophantic behavior in which those who are insecure obsequiously debase themselves in service to charismatic and powerful figures in authority. When asked what they want to be when they grow up no child ever answers 'an acolyte of a predatory grifter,' but many people sacrifice their integrity, freedom, money, time, and even important personal relationships to serve even the most transparent and inelegant of predators while we look on in bewilderment. One day while watching some supposed experts incorrectly discuss this problem on social media (in which their discourse was dripping with contempt) I realized that, like most of our problems it is fear which primarily motivates these weaknesses of character which make us vulnerable to conspiracies and exploitation, but that this kind of *alignment* even to that which is obviously exploitative or dangerous is motivated specifically by an intense sense of powerlessness associated with a feeling of personal danger due to the absence of effective tools required to otherwise cope with concepts of mortality and powerlessness, and alignment occurs to the thing which is polar opposite of that danger, even if that opposite is fantastical, because it assuages the fearful mind of that feeling of powerlessness imposed against our will upon our person. At the very beginning of the pandemic I wrote an article about why a vaccine would not be an effective way to control the coronavirus since coronaviruses behave much like the flu which requires not a single vaccine but multiples, and it was illogical to expect the entire population of all countries to be vaccinated multiple times in perpetuity in order to control this disease. As the pandemic progressed I watched prophetically as people who consider themselves immune to conspiratorial alignment blindly regurgitate government propaganda for efficacy of a single vaccine to then unquestioningly support the necessity of multiple vaccines and then to 'well the multiple vaccines don't prevent illness at all but just make death less likely' as if their unctuous, servile capitulation to government propaganda was any less desperate than the antagonistic behavior they viewed with contempt. During the pandemic too the conspiracists got ahold of the antiparasitic, ivermectin and claimed it to be an alternative to the vaccine which garnered even more ridicule from supposed intellectuals and intelligent, rational people—but as I discovered through my work on immunity parasites are a primary inhibitor of the immune system so even though they were crazy for taking ivermectin without guidance since it is also a powerful pharmaceutical made by the pharmaceutical industry it could have helped save some people from coronavirus by resolving parasitism and thus improving the immune reaction.

 While the source of any danger which triggers alignment is an important factor, it is the feeling of utter powerlessness which primarily motivates alignment to a particular conspiracy, ideology, authority, etc., and those of us who do find ourselves in alignment often have a vague feeling of knowing the risks of our position or behavior but which is relatively less jeopardizing when weighed against powerlessness. For instance while many people getting the vaccine put on a brave face in support of science and government we always feel a sense of trepidation when it comes to disease and mortality because nothing is ever certain and we know and understand that exploitation, malfeasance, and incompetence exist. When weighed against our fear of danger imposed upon us by unmitigating circumstances the lesser of two bad options, at least to our reasoning, is the one to which we align and when those two choices are literal death or something like our relationship with our children the mind which lacks tools to effectively cope with the concept of death will instead align itself with ideology that claims to master it, as this then relieves the mind of the feeling of utter powerlessness, even if it is not real but which is also not okay even if it is real. While the concept of vaccination might on the surface promise the control and protection from death, those who ridiculed anti-vaxxers during the coronavirus pandemic promulgated government propaganda as if the government hasn't a long history of doing abject evil like the forcible sterilization of minorities and the mentally ill or massacring millions of foreigners for capitalist gain and propping up and enabling an amoral and predatory pharmaceutical industry that feels no guilt letting diabetics die if they can't afford the thousands of dollars they were charging for insulin they were gifted for a single dollar and are equally as ridiculous as conspiracy theorists because we do not recognize how we are doing the very thing we accuse them of doing—which is alignment to anything perceived as alleviating fear.

The reason we devolve into conflict and constantly act as if disaster is imminent either with ourselves, our partner, our job, children, government, political adversaries, etc., is simply because we do not possess better tools to handle life and to behave and operate effectively, which is the entire point of inventory therapy and what it easily accomplishes which is to teach us new skills and generate new insights which then empower us to actually care for ourselves and be effective in our own lives instead of expecting the world to do it for us. The burden also of anxiety for the future, for pain, for disappointment, for calamity is often worse than those things we actually fear, and definitely dominate our lives and supplants peace and harmony. Most relationships are destroyed simply from the stress of anticipating problems rather than actual problems, with husbands and wives thinking that everything is wrong even when nothing is. This can be most difficult for people who grew up in very abusive homes, when there was a problem occurring every moment of every single day without end, and being a stranger to peace cannot even abide its presence and feel uncomfortable without conflict. The worst part of anticipating failure is that we can permanently damage our children, and doom them also to a life wracked with anxiety, hypervigilance, pessimistic and fearful ideas of life, and self-defeating and destructive relationship control behaviors. Instead of trying to control life and those in it, we must instead resolve our past pain and trauma and understand our own personal worth as a human being. If the formula going on in your head is: if _____ happens then I will be _____ then we are operating already on insecurity and control mechanisms, and instead of directing this formula at your partner or your children, it must be analyzed in the inventory practice, remembering that all problems we have are based on underlying fears, which can be identified by what is entered in the personal inventory, and must also be entered into the fear portion, to understand what it is we are afraid of that makes us behave the way we do. Sometimes fears keep popping up and must be inventoried many times before we can fully understand them, but like any practice becomes easy and every effective the more we practice.

There is a very intuitive rule to live by which can help us easily understand this self-defeating behavior, which is to turn the golden rule on its head and rather than doing unto others what you want done to you, do unto *yourself* what you would do to others. Many of us treat others with far more kindness and patience than we do to ourselves, and those of us who don't treat others well need to take a dose of our own medicine. When I was fifteen and got my learner's-permit to begin driving lessons my father took me and my brother out for a drive. I had been driving for about a year at this point, but only ever on country roads or within our immediate neighborhood. We drove through our town and to the neighboring city, much larger and with more traffic than I was accustomed, but I knew the roads well after having lived here for the last several years, and it was going well until we reached an intersection with a major road—State Street, which ran parallel with the city and was crossed by many stoplights and other major roads. The street at which we had arrived was only managed by a stop-sign. "Put on your blinker, then pull out and turn right," said my Dad. I put on my blinker and began to pull forward. "Right!" he shouted angrily, even though I *was* going right. I continued to pull out into the road but, now being yelled at, began to hesitate and reconsider my decision, which in turn meant accidentally slowing down. "Right!" he shouted again. I was confused. I was turning right, but he was yelling at me while I was trying to pull out into a busy road and avoid getting hit. The approaching traffic in both directions once far away were now rapidly nearing as I reached the median. "TURN RIGHT!" he screamed, grabbing the wheel. I suddenly realized that I had in fact been turning left, in my confusion and anxiety just assumed I was going in the correct direction to our destination and thus uninterested in whether that was actually left or right. His interference in my trajectory made us stop in the middle of the road, and the approaching cars in the far lane moved to the side to go around our truck. "TURN RIGHT," he yelled once more, even though that was now impossible to do without actually running into other cars and traveling in the wrong direction. "STOP YELLING AT ME," I screamed in return. I righted the car, turned into the turning lane and made a U-turn. "I could have made a U-turn. You shouting at me only made me more confused!"

My father was embarrassed by my mistake because he is embarrassed whenever he makes a mistake instead of having compassion for his own limitations as a human being thus does not have it for others but would if he did for himself. Many of us have this burden because such coping behaviors are a characteristic of human biological psychology and how we are designed to cope with adversity and trauma to promote the survival of the species at the expense of the individual. Anticipating failure in our children is always an instinct borne of our own fear and insecurity, and we can never actually empower our children with true skills for success until we also address and resolve our fears and insecurity, which means first practicing self-care and compassion for our own shameful experiences. We all have insecurities which originate from failure. The disparity between what we think we should be and what we actually are induces strong feelings of regret and shame, and without skills to effectively resolve this trauma feel powerless and in turn project our energies onto our environment in misguided attempts to supposedly help spare our children from the same remorse by making them aware of the shortcomings and weaknesses we are hyperaware. But by turning away from ourselves and instead toward our children we are trying to avoid responsibility for our own behavior and mistakes by distracting ourselves with pretended concern for the wellbeing of our children, who have not actually experienced any of these failures since they are children and entirely dependent on us as parents and incapable of the kind of autonomy which facilitates personal responsibility. The day my mother chided me for refusing to work with my abusive father and conveniently marginalize my other obligations and accomplishments she was actually seeking to resolve the sense of shame she felt at being powerless, financially insecure, and the insecurity of tying her own self worth to materialism and inability to win a man who provided generously for her wants and needs. It took until the age of thirty-eight for me to realize that *I don't actually give a shit about money!* And that all the people around me who have ever tried to shame me about my own financial status, even when I was experiencing material success, in fact worship and revere money and covet material status and fear financial insecurity. But instead of seeing the strengths in her child—one who was exceptionally talented and ambitious—just not for money—she simply saw reflected in me all the basest insecurities which imprisoned her in her own life, seeking to liberate herself through her child.

When we as parents preemptively insist our children behave a certain way *"or else,"* we are communicating to the child that we do not believe in them (just like we do not believe in ourselves). Statements such as *"Be good or there's no dessert tonight,"* tells children we expect them to misbehave. Even if this is true, betraying our obsession with it simply draws the child's focus to it as well, effectively causing them to adopt the very identity we ostensibly wish to be rid of. If we tell a child they are shy and need to be more outgoing, the child will believe they are shy. If we tell a child they are lazy, the child will believe they are lazy. If we tell a child they are misbehaved, the child will believe they are misbehaved! After all, we must be these things if our parent, whom we love and trust with all our being, says it is so. Because our evaluation of our children is also filtered through the lens of our prejudices and biases our estimation of them is often wrong, and we can rest assured if we have a strong estimation of our child which is negative, we are absolutely not only wrong about them but also the catalyst for the problem in the first place.

We also do this to children because it gives us a sense of control over them and life in general. Insecure about our position in life and seeking ways to feel powerful, the supervision and correction of a devious and mischievous little hellion suddenly gives us purpose and control which in turn can distract us from our own problems, fears, and personal insecurities. It is a convenient control and coping mechanism meant to make ourselves feel better at the expense of our children and not their betterment. Once when I lived in Palm Springs, California my brother and his wife came to visit us with their amazing young daughters. They drove all the way from LAX after flying in from Hawaii and though it was already late they still wanted to go out to dinner with us. We sat around a large table at one of our favorite Mexican restaurants. We were having a great dinner, catching up and laughing and joking even though my brother and his wife were exhausted by traveling. One of my nieces was preoccupied with an iPad and the other was joyfully coloring while we waited for our food, but suddenly in the middle of the conversation my brother announced there was going to be trouble between them, though his girls had not moved or even looked up from what they were doing. I was confused, as if maybe I had missed some conflict which had occurred between them. But they continued to enjoy their respective activities, even seeming unaware of the other. "They seem fine," I said. But he still appeared preoccupied with them, then got up from the table and made each of the girls switch places at the table. Immediately they began to cry and fall apart. My brother perhaps viewed his actions as vindicated, since there had in fact been emotional conflict following his actions. But in reality he caused the very problem he anticipated by treating his children as if they were sources of trouble when they absolutely were not.

This tendency for self-sabotage on the part of parents interrupts our quality of life and ambitions for ourselves. When I was a teenager and suddenly and quickly began catching up to my father's height he suddenly realized I was going to be tall and as such could realize his unrealized dreams of being a professional basketball star. Suddenly conscripted into an activity I was not good at nor wanted to participate and carrying the weight of an adults unrealized dreams and absence of self-worth, basketball rapidly changed from a fun game to something I absolutely dreaded, to the point of becoming physically ill from the stress. My father's merciless and incessant berating of my performance and lack of desire was never intended to help me become a good ball player but so that *his* hopes and dreams could be realized. Even so I patiently and willingly participated in this abuse for the sense of obligation I felt toward my parents and adopted for myself the very characterizations they made of me, not believing I was athletic or driven even as I demonstrated those attributes in other areas of my life. It wasn't until I was in the middle of my thirties that I realized my love of and talents in other sports had been actively subverted by my own parents through their manipulative abuse and harassment. If instead of projecting his fears and insecurities onto me my father had compassion for his own experiences of disappointment and failure and practiced self-care for his own needs he might have actually recognized my natural talents and strengths and ironically actually have realized the success for me he claimed to want.

Children who are inclined to hurt their siblings or act out in disruptive ways are likewise *not* misbehaving. They are performing exactly as we as parents have instructed them to. Children are often regarded as empty vessels in need of moulding and guidance, but this is absolutely not true. Children observe actions, intent, and attitudes about life and not the content of our words. They see body language and our reactions to life and people in it. Looking for skills to help them navigate and survive life, if a parent focuses their energy and attention on what they view as problems in the child it thus informs the child to what they are and not what they should change. If that day in my room my mother had come in and talked to me about how proud she was of me for taking on so much responsibility and that she understood that I was stressed out and taking on more than I could actually handle as a teenager I would have felt proud of myself instead of ashamed, I would also have felt supported and protected which would have given me more confidence to meet my obligations. The irony of her imposition in terms of my sexuality, of which she was also fully aware, further engineered a rift between us, and not only did she fail to inspire in me a desire to pursue the material wealth and success she wanted (which would have failed regardless), she also precipitated the abuse which would ultimately undermine our relationship altogether.

This kind of negative reinforcement can be very difficult to identify, because as a parent we should help our children learn not to do things which hurt others or themselves. But in so doing we can also be the source of negative self esteem in our own children, even when we only mean to help them be good. No matter how bad a child behaves, a parent should *never* focus on the flaws of a child. Even if a kid behaves horribly, preoccupation with a child's negative behaviors is exactly the kind of sign that indicates a parent is providing negative reinforcement. Because we are preoccupied with their behavior we in turn draw attention to it, both directly and because of our attitude about it, which in turn draws the child's attention to that as well and since their identity is forming at this stage of their life it sets the foundation of their self conception around those negative qualities, even if our intention is to be helpful and help our children to be good, because life does not care one iota about our intentions. This does not also mean ignoring negativity, and the opposite behavior of ignoring mistakes and being pathologically optimistic is also a control mechanism, just the opposite of pessimism, and if mistakes and problems occur or persist they must be addressed. Specifically, we as parents tend to focus on the negative because of larger life themes and control mechanisms such as what are addressed by inventory therapy which we in turn see reflected in our children, who are not personally responsible for the failings of humanity or the ills of society. First we must address why we become preoccupied with our children's mistakes, specifically addressing the sensitivities and themes presented during conflict. Without first understanding our own biases and sensitivities we cannot hope to relieve our children of them. If for instance you feel that your child is overly mean to siblings or friends, your opinion of this may be colored by your past and the conditioning from your own parents. Your child may in fact simply be a tease, or themselves insecure about their own self worth and themes of failure and disappointment, but you will not be able to see this if you do not understand it in yourself. Secondly, addressing behavior from a motivation of anticipation of failure will often inadvertently cause a parent to characterize their child in such a way that communicates they are their mistakes—mean, selfish, lazy, etc., which then assumes the responsibility of forming the child's identity for them, and is a consequence of parents seeing a child as a product of their choices rather than who they are as a person. This practically occurs through the act of negotiation, oration, opining, and grandstanding on the part of parents, because we also feel insecure about our effectiveness as a parent, unconsciously motivated to justify our role as a parent to the children whose care we are charged. Explaining to a child why we don't do certain things or enjoining them to behave in certain ways is the act of negotiating and thus cheapens our role as a parent since it essentially asks children for permission to parent. Instead, we just say

"That is not acceptable behavior." When behavior requires an abundance of emotional time and energy from parents it communicates insecurity toward and about the child. When we are direct and concise, it instead communicates confidence. It is also unambiguous in its expectations, where long diatribes and admonishment are vague and nebulous—Is the child responsible for the entire ethical behavior of society? Or should they just not call people names?

Most "problems" which parents identify are in fact merely the anticipation of problems fabricated through our own personal biases and trauma, filtered through the experiences of many thousands of people in societies overly concerned with universal themes of morality and human frailty reflected in individual persons who may or may not be capable of understanding, let alone atoning for the sins of every human who has ever lived, and as such we actively create the very problems we are afraid of having through our own unwitting insecurity and fear-motivated behavior. Life is difficult enough without having our own parents betting against us. We as parents we need to be on the side of our children, to be their supporters and protectors and not their adversaries, to anticipate self-empathy, joy, happiness, love, and personal success.

In the middle of my Junior year of High School when my depression began to take a serious toll on my health and what I would later recognize as the beginnings of my struggle with thyroid and metabolic disease I made the difficult decision to quit swimming. I had been on course to being one of the fastest swimmers in the State, but was terrified of the things which were happening to me and feeling powerless to resolve them on my own. When I approached my parents to inform them of my plan to quit, to my surprise instead of demeaning me for quitting or insisting I stick with it, they said "Okay."

"Really?" I asked, confused.

"Yeah, that's fine," they said. "We didn't think you would stick with it this long in the first place."

Ah. That made more sense. My heart sank into my chest. My father had only ever come to a portion of one swimming meet, and my mother had only come to two. They didn't *want* me to swim because *they* didn't like swimming as a sport. The people who were supposed to believe in me not only didn't believe in me, they weren't even interested in my wellbeing or personal development. I would rejoin the team the next Summer when my break from the swimming pool inadvertently helped me get a little better, but once I joined a second time and without anyone to advocate for my wellbeing succumbed yet again to the effects of chlorine intoxication and excessive exercise unsupported by sufficient nutrition. I was possessed every bit of the kind of ambition and desire to achieve that both my parents claimed me to be lacking. But because my parents could only see their insecurities reflected in me I did not get access to the kind of support which would have enabled me to excel in all the areas in which I was talented. When I took the ACT it was after a grueling swimming workout, without even eating beforehand. Still, I got impressive scores in the reading, science, and English sections, but when I got to the math section I was so exhausted and undernourished my brain forgot the stupid fucking Pythagorean theorem even though math was my best subject in school, bringing my final score down to 28, which is still highly respectable and on its own would have gotten me into most Universities in the country. But had I been rested, fed, and actually studied for it would likely otherwise scored much higher and gotten myself a scholarship to any school in the country. My parents were aware of none of this, because they regarded me as an ambitionless failure, being only able see who I was through the lens of their own personal disappointments, fears, and insecurity.

Our children do not need to be shaped or moulded, but as parents we do decide what our children are going to be through the effect we have on their lives. Will that be a problem child, a lazy one, sexualized, depressed, ill, or lacking self-confidence? If we tell children that's what they are then that is exactly what they will be. The opposite is not to artificially inflate a child's potential with exaggerated estimations of their talents and self-worth. That is still a manipulation and motivated from our insecurities and not the best interests of our child, which they would still find overwhelming and stressful anyway. If instead we treat our children as the unique individuals we love for who they are, capable of achieving so much in their lives independently of ourselves and supporting them in their endeavors then they will always grow up to be the kind of well-adjusted, talented, and accomplished adults we desire for them to be. It can be difficult to do this as a parent because parenthood brings with it so many overwhelming fears and insecurities, which is why we must find the space for self-compassion and self-care first for ourselves and understand the origins of our pain, trauma, and insecurity. Developing and practicing self-care and finding self-compassion through introspective therapy like doing inventory will in turn empower us to do the same for our children. No longer controlled by fear and doubt we will instead see their natural strengths and talents.

What exactly encompasses personal development, education, and success in the first place is also one of the problems facing parents and our ability or inability to empower our children with the skills and talents they will need to live successfully. Largely, our education systems and priorities are designed to promote material, social, and professional success only within the system of *capitalism*, which is generally an effective financial system which has lifted untold masses out of poverty and desperation which was the human existence for much of the preceding several thousand years, but which also only prepares children to serve a monetary system and worship wealth and power rather than their inherent value as a human being. Many anti-capitalists cringe at any praise of capitalism, but capitalism is in fact not the system which pervades developed Western countries today which ostensibly operate under capitalism. Put immoderately, the system of economy in which we currently find ourselves as defined by its material effects and not simply words and labels is a blend of capitalism, oligarchy, and corporate and elitist socialism where our government spends the bulk of its energy, resources, and treasure rescuing untalented and inept businesspeople from the consequences of malfeasance, crime, exploitation, and suppress productivity through policies which benefit the upper class, redistribute wealth to the wealthy through subsidies and corrupt tax breaks and loopholes, and design institutions with the singular goal of amassing market value for the monied class who estimate products and productivity purely on stock price rather than other measurable profits like quality and economic stability, and to sustain impossible supply chains through colonialist exploitation of foreign nations. Many people discuss economic systems as if the words and labels matter more than tangible effects and consequences of policy and behavior, and many of the evils which anti-capitalists or anti-socialists attribute to economic systems are in fact not traits of any system at all but that of innate human nature and our response to unresolved trauma and control behaviors, and the understandable desire to resolve inequality is misdirected toward intellectual concepts, academic posturing, and rigid adherence to lexicon rather than practical, applicable, positive, and relevant change in the real world.

Many of us who advocate for economic equality believe we must wait for institutional change in order to resolve poverty, hunger, and economic instability. But even with its shortcomings, failures, and vulnerabilities, capitalism does or can actually provide for the wellbeing of all members of society in effective and equitable means every bit as can socialism if we in our personal lives exploit its benefits rather than waiting for institutional change, especially since institutional change is often too difficult to achieve within any one lifetime. One of the reasons capitalism has prevailed for so long as the predominant economic system is that it naturally leverages humanity's worst actors against each other, to mostly neutralize those weaknesses and thus spare the majority of people from even worse exploitation and oppression. Other economic and government systems ostensibly designed to provide for everyone such as socialism and communism have typically failed because they are usually facilitated by authoritarian forces possessed of singular intent to dominate political and economic machines for control rather than to implement ideals of egalitarianism. I have occasionally seen proponents of such systems ostensibly promoting equality advocate for the killing and murder of opponents, and there is nothing less egalitarian than taking a life as what occurred in several major world events changing to systems of socialism and communism using the very same kind of violence employed by capitalism. This occurs because basic human conflict nature is to view adversaries as Other, and so in turn exploit the power of institution to achieve their own desires and subvert their own fears, or even to enrich themselves, which is why these systems have failed, not because there is anything inherently wrong with seeking equality for all but because the singular purpose of socialist institutions are ironically immeasurably easier to exploit by corrupt actors when governments and economic machines are consolidated and vertically integrated, which is why countries dominated by these systems typically continue to experience poverty, corruption, social stagnation, and exploitation of shared resources rather than success and prosperity, not because socialism or communism are bad but because they are prized targets for authoritarian narcissists who seek to capture and exploit the wealth and power they centralize, and catalyze imbalance and disparity even when they are supposedly erected to achieve the opposite and, like China, eventually transition to capitalism because although their words and definitions are different the human desire for control to protect their personal interests and subvert personal fears and insecurities is exactly the same as their opponents'.

No matter the organization of economies and governments it is more difficult to provide for the needs of people than to empower people to care for themselves, and the problem with any institution is whether it and its members seek to impose authoritarian control, even if their intent is well-meaning, because it is always subjective and assumes an impossible degree of responsibility. Many austerity movements such as those enacted by cruel and stupid British ideologues in the 1980s claim this kind of motivation but in practice robbed many people of the ability to do that by taking from them state services paid for by the people's taxes and labor, and there is a big difference between actually accomplishing empowerment and simply blaming people for being unable to help themselves, where the former requires action and policy and the latter only employs words and speech. Many of us who seek to improve society seek to do so by running for office or gaining power in some way, but in reality no person can ever do for another what they must do for themselves, and the greatest way to effect change is instead to empower people with skills and knowledge so they can care for themselves. This happens to also be the most effective parenting strategy, and the aim of any political or social reform should be the decentralization of authoritarian power and empowering others with skills and knowledge, because when there are many different empowered groups and institutions it is harder for any one authoritarian force to dominate systems and exploit power inherent within institution. When power is distributed across not only government but also private companies and individuals such as typically occurs in a capitalist system there are far fewer points of exploitation through which power-hungry authoritarians can gain power and control, which is exactly why dictatorial leaders often try to eliminate lawyers, journalists, educators, and other members of unrelated institutions.

Because a truly capitalist system requires a large degree of autonomy for participants to actually participate in a capitalist system business leaders cannot allow other leaders to cheat, lie, steal, or exploit consumers, even if they do it themselves and are also amoral, otherwise their chance of loss increases precipitously, so everyone, even the most depraved and corrupt must compete within the set of rules and consequences to affect some degree of restraint and ethical behavior which is unnatural to exploitative and abusive human beings. As such those with power, means, and access form coalitions to promote as much a fair playing field as possible which in turn incidentally protects the common man from much of the exploitation and oppression enabled by singularly minded and empowered systems, thereby ironically exploiting mankind's general tendency for self-destruction to also neutralize it. Capitalism also requires an educated and well-funded middle class to sustain the cycle of consumerism as well as the relative peace and stability required for commerce, and so its very interests also align with the majority welfare of the population because a population which is sick, unhappy, or stupid cannot participate in consumerism so elites which might otherwise be disinterested in the welfare of the proletariat are forced by the very system to at least somewhat support the interests of the proletariat to a degree greater than would otherwise be the case. A great example of this is the Great Rail Workers Strike of 1877 in the United States in which workers went on strike after having their wages cut three times in a single year. Railroad companies and Governors amorally used militias, the National Guard, and federal troops to put down the strikers and killed 100 people in the conflict. Because the railroads were private entities they suffered extreme financial losses in the strike and in the years after finally began giving increased benefits to their workers, including pensions and some health care, even though they ostensibly won. Unionization of laborers also increased significantly after this time as workers became more cognizant of their collective power, and through the intervening century eventually won the various rights and benefits such as overtime pay, holidays, weekends, minimum wage, etc. which has led to the incredible degree of relative prosperity we enjoy today.

Because of this self-regulating dynamic much effort is made collectively to maintain rules and promote lawfulness, compliance, and equality amongst a species which is highly motivated to self-centeredness, exploitation, and violence. When one business does break the law or runs afoul of the populace it is often opportunistically antagonized by competitors (not only business competitors but also politicians, lawyers, etc.) for their own gain but which in turn establishes expectations of moral accountability even though such antagonism is not altruistic, where such competition is not even allowed in other systems. For another example, in the late twentieth century a famous beer brand displayed distinctly homophobic behavior toward the LGBTQI+ community but a competing brand acted in opposition and proactively embraced the LGBTQI+ community. Their support was opportunistic and motivated by money, as they still fund anti-LGBTQI+ politicians, but the effect was to both lift up and support the gay community and to entrench their brand into thousands of bars and millions of beer glasses across the country. In a socialist or communist system which assumes responsibility for entire economic systems there is no such competition because there is no free market and thus no self-interests within business and government which effect these ends, which instead orient themselves toward supporting the government rather than consumers, which is why homophobia and persecution of minorities also occurs so rampantly in those supposedly egalitarian systems though they are supposed to be concerned with the welfare of the common man. To this day it is less common to find the former brand in any gay bar in the entire country even though most bar-goers and even their employees and patrons are no longer aware of why we have such loyalty to the latter. Even the retelling of this tale is a consequence for the former and their despicable behavior and failure to act with social responsibility permanently cost them a sizable chunk of the market from which they have never really recovered. Such lessons persist in capitalist systems because of the market consequences to profit which in turn benefits all of society. Even a giant online retail company which currently exploits poor and minority workers by paying painfully exploitive and insufficient compensation for exhaustive, dangerous work felt compelled to run socially-minded ads on their streaming service, while refusing to actually improve the lives of marginalized populations by paying them a living wage, indirectly bringing attention to and supporting the very people they have tried to oppress, and at time of publishing of this book are struggling to staff their warehouses, having churned through the workforce and cemented a reputation for exploitation and abuse. Such market pressures precipitously and permanently alter social and political landscapes in favor of progress, and the very companies practicing their cynical and hypocritical behavior are eventually held accountable by their own reluctant participation in and reliance on market forces and consumer attitudes.

There is a simple reason why systems of socialism, which is morally superior to capitalism, has not had the traction that capitalism has had in the modern world, and it has nothing to do with war and corruption which is usually the cited reason. Instead, like a young child learning to navigate life, people simply do not want to be told what to do, and so they view systems of Marxism, communism, and socialism as authoritarian limits on their potential rather than systems which attempt to resolve economic inequality and provide for all. Many politicians, pundits, philosophers, and journalists currently feel perplexed by conservative voters, protestors, and conspiracy theorists who use terms like communism to describe capitalist organizations like the International Monetary Fund, and dismiss those people and their concerns as misunderstanding the difference or being delusional. In fact it is the people making this distinction who misunderstand what is occurring because we do not listen to and understand the motivation and purpose of those antagonists who cannot effectively articulate what they want and what they mean, and flippantly disregard the difficulty most humans have in using language and communicating. When people equate ideas like communism and the International Monetary Fund what they are protesting is authoritarianism and the practical effects that powerful ideas, movements, and institutions have on the real lives of people, and to those who are not academics or studied in political philosophy simply see the same effects of oppression and exploitation whether it was communist forces that subjugated populations in countries like the former Soviet Union or by capitalism in "undeveloped" places like the Congo who are purposefully exploited and kept undeveloped by capitalist institutions.

In reality those who equate communism and the IMF are more correct than those who point out the philosophical difference, because the former recognizes the real effects and actions by powerful, authoritarian institutions which are tangible and experienced, while the latter are more concerned with theory, words, and ideology. While exploitative, opportunistic, power hungry political actors purposefully mislead and obfuscate, most of their supporters simply want less taxes and oppression and more freedom of opportunity and quality of life, but dialogue is easily derailed by slogans, labels, ideology, and philosophy which are easily exploitable because they are words, not action, because words are relative and arbitrary to each person's individual experience, and it's often difficult to communicate, and unresolved trauma and difficult life experiences prejudice the meaning and use of words. Because of economic stress and political posturing most of us also tend to fixate on words and labels instead of context and reality, even to the point of supporting politicians and leaders who work against our best interests, and if you think you don't do this you are exactly someone who does, and so we get lost in Us versus Them conflict which always serves to undermine efforts to actually improve our lives because, as in an acrimonious marriage, such conflict always assumes winners and losers and because nobody wants to be the loser everyone fights each other rather than helping the other. In order to affect real change there must not be a system which inherently assumes some as losers, which works instead to care for the needs of all and without waiting for permission to do it to affect change such as the overhaul of government.

The real problem with our current form of capitalism is that it is a market and stock-centric capitalist system which bleeds profits from companies and workers simply to enrich executives and shareholders, which inevitably devolves into fascism when capitalism reaches the natural consequences of such systems of exploitation. It's a severely limiting and uninspired form of capitalism which can instead be evolved and transformed into a true capitalist system which is not obsessed with endless growth and such narrow definitions of value. *Cooperative Capitalism* instead focuses on goods and services rather than stock value and enables worker ownership rather than executive ownership, and seeks to achieve longevity and stability instead of rapid growth and short-term investment and can facilitate our basic human instincts for togetherness, cooperation, prosperity, and access to quality resources since such a system empowers workers with commensurate rather than exploitive compensation while retaining profit motives and requiring less time commitment for the same or more income that only executives and capital holders have previously enjoyed. Many people complain about the inequalities we suffer—the low wages, low benefits, poor job security, economic volatility, and income disparity, but willingly show up for work each day to support the very institutions which sustain this system as if our willing participation isn't required to actively keep it alive. While it's true that the working population is not so easily capable of change we can still refuse to be exploited. Stop working jobs which are demoralizing and exploitive. Move to a smaller house and less expensive town or city. Buy less crap, grow food, run our own businesses even if it means making less money. The desire for wealth is what drives exploitative capitalism in both the capital holder and the exploited worker. It must be given up not just by executives but also those they oppress. Cooperative capitalism can also be accomplished in a very short amount of time with relatively little effort, without having to wait for an overhaul of institutions, government, or political leaders as would be required by entire systems such as democratic socialism. If even just a few philanthropists, social activists, or workers organize and use their collective financial and social power to establish and run cooperative businesses to accomplish the positive aspects of socialism now without having to wait for systemic, glacial change it would rapidly outcompete market capitalism and destabilize conglomerate oligarchy which would be unable to compete with the quality and employment opportunities produced by cooperatives.

For example, during the course of writing these books I worked on my own creative concepts, writing, and art for video game projects and tried to recruit coders, sound designers, and composers to collaborate with me on several different projects. Nearly everyone I spoke with was unemployed but wanted to be paid for their work as if I were a corporation and not also a worker without capital, because we are so conditioned to feel dependent on the very system which exploits us willingly turn down the opportunity to become wealthy for the security of a steady paycheck. Any philanthropist of means or a mutual aid campaign could buy up struggling businesses and turn control over to employees, who are also the ones that actually do the work and know how their businesses run, able then to choose their directors and set wages while increasing productivity, quality, and profits for those doing the work. Professionals can abandon *all* companies which exploit them by not organizing as a cooperative from the very beginning, to instead band together and form their own cooperative operations, to be run by employees and not executives, without accepting venture funding and turning over their value to financial predators. Just a handful of major companies structured in this way would rapidly destabilize exploitive capitalism because cooperatives of this nature are more stable and produce better goods and services, since their workforce is not exploited by short-sighted opportunists, are invested in their own profits, better funded, less stressed, better staffed, and as such also able to more easily recruit better talent and valuable workers. There are hundreds and thousands of video game professionals out of work who can volunteer their time and work remotely with their own equipment to create their own companies to rival even the most established conglomerate with very little overhead and even more creativity and productivity. Nurses already armed with their education and experience could set up clinics to serve their community's general health needs using their own resources or small loans or donations, and even recruit doctors to participate in a cooperative. Restaurant workers can start their own restaurants instead of waiting for fancy investors and prestigious chefs to hire them. Farmers and smaller food producers can set up their own markets where they provide unbeatable, quality, organic foods and products for the same price as exploitive and substandard corporations. While a cooperative ride-sharing company would require the support of a philanthropist, it would also blow the others out of the water as drivers abandon the exploitative and abusive companies en mass. The services industries are even easier to organize since they so often only require human resources and very little overhead. The entire construction industry is nothing without its skilled laborers, who instead of scraping by from job to job could start their own construction cooperatives and promote job and market stability even in times of reduced demand.

Cooperative capitalism can also provide more part-time job opportunities for those who do not want or need a full-time job, and thus distribute economic opportunity to more people and thus increase productivity and economic prosperity. It will also generate more wealth created from less work which can in turn allow humans to spend more time focusing on families, living, and create more opportunity for entrepreneurs and facilitate more innovation and economic and technological progress. Because our system is not truly capitalism but a hybrid with corporate and elitist socialism, imbalance is entrenched in the system as beneficiaries of it exploit their advantage to skew government function further in their favor. Because this imbalances dynamics which would normally self-regulate in a truly capitalist system it has a destructive effect on the lives of everyday citizens in the form of waning opportunity and prosperity and constant risk of economic collapse which in turn catalyzes social discontent and disruption in the form of racist, nationalistic fervor as disenfranchised populations entreat the support of those usurping power to share it. Of course, such persons who are willing to cheat, lie, steal, and commit crime do not share, so once the populace's usefulness is spent the supporters of revolution are always discarded by the powers they installed, and long stretches of authoritarian oppression persist until the population is finally emboldened by dire enough circumstances to risk their lives taking it back. By empowering the working class, cooperative capitalism can instead stabilize markets, economies, and thus generations of families through just compensation of their talents, contributions, and sacrifice. This is already occurring all over the world. Mondragon Corporation in the Basque region of Spain is the largest cooperative corporation in the world with about 15 billion Euros in global sales, and employed 84,000 people during the 2012-2013 recession with no layoffs during a time when Spain's unemployment rate otherwise rose to 26%. There is no reason not to build these kinds of institutions for ourselves instead of supporting the systems which burden life and hand over our hard work and talents for pittance (as an aside, pensions are incredible burdens to institutions which should be done away in favor of personal and familial responsibility and universal guaranteed income to avoid burdening the future on the backs of our children).

When considering a child's potential as a human being in terms of personal, social, and professional development we fail to consider other areas of human life and human nature which need fulfillment which have nothing to do with money, and adults often only realize when we are much older, after already having raised our own children and even grandchildren, that none of the things we have spent our entire lives pursuing actually brought us fulfillment, and then we die having never actually experienced real happiness, peace, or satisfaction, nor empowered our children and their children with the skills and opportunities required to experience them. This happens because we do not know how or even what to instead spend our time and energy, and many aspects of human life and biological instinct remain unfulfilled in the worship of things and power, and the vague burden upon the psyche which results from living to work within materialist systems causes desperate and unfulfilled parents to misplace the source of their discontent to lack of monetary wealth, even when they have it, rather than the failure to satisfy all our biological purpose as human animals, instead focusing the entirety of our parenthood and conditioning of children to achieve only within such incomplete and dissatisfying artifices of human life.

More primal biological needs of the life of an *Homo sapiens* which largely remain unfulfilled in most of our lives, which are requirements for happiness and the full realization of human potential, are things such as farming, cooking, singing and dancing, reading and writing, and intimate social bonds with other humans. The feeling of dirt between our fingers, a book in our hands, expansion of minds, good food in our belly, the beauty of music, and the bonds established between altruistic friends, lovers, and children are all things that every human being needs in life which cannot be satisfied by money or material belongings. Societies which have been plagued by failings of economy are also those who abandon or lose their knowledge of such basic human purpose as farming, cooking, literacy, music, and cooperation. For somer reason it is ignored or taken for granted that we are a species of animal which actually makes harmonic vocalizations with our mouths, and evolved vocal cords and intellects designed specifically for singing. We are designed by our very biology to make music, to sing, to channel the spiritual and the inspirational energy of the Universe through our voices and musical instrument. The absence of singing in our lives is a travesty, where thankfully many of us do get to enjoy popular music and sing along with our favorite artists, but fail to understand just how novel, unique, and inherent song and music is to the human animal. Because of the adulteration of human life by religious, government, and academic institutions and the pathological pursuit of artificial replacements for our true needs as humans, children who are ill-prepared for adulthood through the limited focus on money and stuff are doomed to dissatisfaction in their lives and the frustration of meaningless existence if they are not also empowered to fulfill the other needs which all of us have as human beings.

As a species we have been engaged so long in the curation of nature that it is now literally a part of our biological makeup. A need to grow plants and animals, to secure our own wellbeing through the gardening of nature is so primal that most humans try to satisfy this need even by growing decorative plants in pots in apartments and on balconies. Many microbes which are active in our guts and members of our commensal microbiome can be found in soil and on the plants we eat, and farmers have traditionally been healthier than their city-dwelling counterparts simply from the exposure to beneficial microbes which are not readily available to us who live in cosmopolitan areas though now due to toxic chemicals used in commercial agriculture which kill the soil microbiome this is no longer the case, and farming is often a liability to the health of farmers since these chemicals also kill the microbiome in their own bodies. Additionally, gardening places us outside in the sunshine, which is absolutely required for healthy metabolic function and the promotion of robust cellular respiration, and people who acquire deficiency of sunlight due to excessive sequestration indoors causes the body to react as if it is always winter and in turn triggers weight gain, lethargy, and even hair loss (as discussed in my other book). Living in Palm Springs was the first time as an adult I had ever had access to ground on which I could garden. I had always wanted to grow plants—mostly ornamental but also some tomatoes, herbs, other simple staples which are easy to cultivate and productive in a home garden. The stress of my health and relationship problems was beginning to take a severe toll on my life, and as a side effect I spent a great deal of time gardening to distract myself from my problems, but I was surprised how profoundly cathartic the act of gardening was on my life, because I was inadvertently fulfilling a biological need as a human animal to organize nature for my own benefit, which to that point in my life had never been fulfilled.

Rearing children to empower their fulfillment through natural human potential and biological needs rather than that which is singularly monetary, superficial, and expedient will in turn facilitate a more wholesome, satisfying, and successful life experience. The happiest children on the earth, according to studies, are children in the Netherlands. This happens because children in the Netherlands still ride their bikes to school, go to friends houses, and participate in other activities without needing their parents to facilitate their activities. The Netherlands is built to accommodate more normal human activities where most of the rest of the world is built to accommodate the automobile. Neighborhoods, towns, and cities in the Netherlands facilitate walking, biking, and access to the outdoors and nature where ours actively inhibits it. This community design also increases safety through the presence of many other humans, where ours removes human beings from the outdoors and thus increases danger. In the Netherlands, kids as young as six are allowed to go off on their own and with their friends without the need for supervision. This also means that parents spend up to 50% less time shuttling their children around and as such have more time for themselves. Access to the kinds of developmental and environmental needs of humans requires that our communities also be built to accommodate us rather than our stuff. Getting a robust education and working thirty-five hours a week to fund gardens, families, and creative and intellectual pursuits, being outdoors and congregating with others will shift the focus of life from endless and despairing monetary accumulation to a richly broad and fulfilling life experience. As humans we really only need good food, friends, and family to feel happy, which are all activities better fulfilled by gardening, reading, learning, singing, and dancing than endeavoring for financial success. I often use France as an example when entreating changes in dietary and environmental behaviors because as a country it has a achieved much in the way of the things which are required for a healthy and well-lived life. The French and some other European countries like Spain or the Netherlands spend as much of their days focused on the quality of food production and engagement in farming and agriculture as they do in professional success, not simply as a commodity to be profited but as a means to improve quality of life, and their governments are actively engaged in promoting more aspects of successful human existence than simply monetary valuation such as through generous holiday time, family leave, and strict standards of food production. Literacy and social life is richly abundant, leading to more empowered citizens and robust economies. Cooperative capitalism can, ironically, facilitate the basic requirements of human fulfillment because it empowers people to work for themselves, to apportion their time and energy as they desire, achieving self-actualization through a person's own effort and priorities and the stabilization of family life because they get paid equitably for their work and supported by all of society. The problem with Western capitalist market socialism is that it only focuses on corporate and elitist socialism in the form of generous tax breaks and subsidies for industry, business, and the upperclass who are allowed to hoard wealth they've taken from the workers who produce products and services and almost nothing for the working class and the poor. Resolving this problem is not one of revolution, but protest, by refusing any longer to engage the system which demands our lives and gives little in return. Empowering children to care for themselves and their future families and communities by establishing cooperative capitalism and fulfilling all our human needs by farming, gardening, producing quality foods in abundance and cooking and preparing good food alone and in collaboration with others, empowering academic achievement through accomplished literacy, and securing their social safety and welfare through effective interpersonal skills and activities and creative talents will help children achieve the kinds of success and joys in life which very few generations have ever enjoyed, and to avoid the mistakes and prejudices which have impaired previous generations from experiencing a fulfilling and satisfying life.

All children possess boundless potential for achieving the greatest heights of human enlightenment and experience. It is only because we mistake what those achievements actually are that we drift astray of what is possible during a human lifetime and burden ourselves with misery and regret. Lacking compassion for our own shortcomings, pain, and mistakes colors our ability to empower our children to avoid these pitfalls and sustains the cycle of abuse and failure engendered from parent to child from generation to generation. As such we must endeavor to learn compassion for our own mortality and weaknesses, practice self-care by taking action to improve our own quality of life, and in so doing empower our children to the same, redirecting their focus from the shallow and impermanent pursuit of monetary artifice for those aspects of life that money seeks to achieve, which can be had more easily without it. Because a human being requires also a proper physical environment we must also take into consideration our needs for sufficient exposure to sunlight, fresh air, clean water, and the kind of superb nutrition which cannot be met necessarily even by organic food but requires regenerative, holistic agriculture and the nurture of the soil microbiome. Grow food, cook good meals, share with friends, loved ones, and community. Read and write prolifically. Sing until the heart is content. Empower children that they may do the same. It is all we really require for happiness in this life.

21

Nutrition, Growth, and Maturation

It was in the midst of my suicidal turmoil that my family up and decided to move back to Hawaii. But the week before my mother and siblings were set to join my father there my mother had a moment of panicked realization that she was leaving me behind. In a desperate bid to ease her sadness she insisted on visiting with my siblings for Easter at my new apartment. She also kindly insisted on bringing food for the occasion, even though I had expressed an interest in contributing assured me she would get all of it. Growing up we had always eaten fairly lavishly, though not especially healthy, especially on holiday occasions and as a family had grown accustomed to roasts, elaborate pastas, and Kalua pig my father prepared regularly. Expecting our traditional ham, mashed potatoes, and other decadent Easter excesses I was more than disappointed when, bless her heart, my mother showed up with ham and reconstituted potatoes from a chain restaurant. Reconstituted mashed potatoes are always an abomination, but especially at Easter. My mother has a lot of great qualities as a person, and is known for her legendary chocolate torte, Christmas cookies, and lemon cake. But having a more cosmopolitan disposition, cooking was generally never an interest of hers (and neither for her mother nor her mother's mother). Most days of the week my mother prepared foods which were commonly accepted and promoted at the time such as boxed macaroni and cheese and peanut butter and jelly sandwiches, and the only regular fruit we ever really got besides jelly and jam was canned fruit salad or my father's apple pie.

Fuck Portion Control goes into great detail about how food, nutrition, food traditions, and the food industry affects our health, causes disease, and how to cure specific illnesses and avoid health and developmental problems rooted in our nutritional, behavioral, and social environments. But when it comes to children there are specific food behaviors which have severe consequences not only on the physical wellbeing and development of children, but also their mental and social health as well.

But first, there is nothing wrong with serving simple meals. Simple cooking can be every bit as nutritious as big, elaborate occasions. Sometimes even more healthful. Because as parents we do have limited time and energy, it's ridiculous to spend hours in the kitchen every day when there is no need for it. The generation before ours inherited the silly tradition of having several different courses all at once—a meat, a side dish or two, and a salad—which really has its roots in trying to emulate the rich and has no real basis in human nutritional needs, and many parents spend a lot of time constructing several different dishes every single meal. I will often make myself a large casserole dish of enchiladas because the effort will last me for several meals, and there is nothing wrong with having that kind of approach to our own family's nutritional needs because it cuts down on the time required for meal preparation but not necessarily access to great nutrition—which is more dependent on the quality of food rather than how much of it or what form in which we make it.

Bread and cheese used to be a sufficient dietary staple which parents could easily depend to provide sufficient nutrition for their growing families. Bread is traditionally pretty cheap, and if made properly can be full of healthful nutrition. Cheese too is typically dense with calories and nutrients, especially those which are required for growth of children such as ample protein, calcium, phosphorus, and B vitamins. But over the last several decades our food supply has been adulterated, and bread and cheese have evolved from foods which promote health to that which can actually destroy it. Bread, being made of common wheat, contains forms of gluten which are highly allergenic and promote inflammation. In my other book I relate a story how my younger sister developed inflammatory chronic ear infections as a child which is a specific reaction to the gluten in common wheat. Additionally, refined grain is typically fortified by law with extra iron which is highly reactive and promotes unrestrained oxidation of other nutrients and the growth of microbial pathogens. Common wheat consumption impairs growth and promotes thyroid illness in children, prolongs bedwetting, development problems, and can contribute to illnesses like depression, obesity, Autism, and alcohol and drug dependence if other factors agree.

My father drank bismuth solutions like a beverage at every meal when I was a child. So when I neared the end of my teenage years and began having debilitating stomachaches I didn't even consider that it was a problem with my diet, since my father simply accepted it as a condition of life and modeled for me the example of resisting change and self-improvement. Later when I discovered that my health problems were rooted in consumption of common wheat I found immediate relief from chronic and debilitating recurrent sinus infections from simply abstaining, as well as an increase in energy and feelings of wellness. I personally know parents of autistic spectrum children who actively feed wheat to their children despite knowing full well that it contributes to symptoms. My own siblings feed their children common wheat even though their children present with frequent and debilitating stomachaches at alarmingly younger and younger ages than what my family went through. One family even had a child shit himself in the car on the way home from a family event due to such stomach problems and they didn't even consider changing their diet, preferring rather to endure crying, miserable children and cleaning up shit to adjusting dietary traditions. Once when I suggested choosing fruit and cheese for lunches instead of sandwiches a sister shouted at me that it was too hard to make those changes, even though putting fruit and cheese on a plate is arguably *less* effort than constructing sandwiches. In truth it is hard but not because of the actual effort of preparing food, but to change who we are and our preconceptions about life, which includes food culture passed down to us from generation to generation and how our psychological development promotes bias and prejudice as a survival mechanism even when such behaviors are obviously in violation of our own wellbeing. For some of us, accepting that common wheat is bad doesn't simply mean avoiding wheat, it means changing our personal identities and entire worldview, which many of us are not willing to do, and so we persist in perpetuating our own metabolic illnesses and deficiencies in development and in turn that of our children.

One of the biggest consequences of feeding children inflammatory foods like common wheat gluten is disruptions to metabolic development. Ironically, inflammatory foods may promote increases in physical height due to the interference it has on thyroid function, because thyroid is what promotes cellular differentiation (which is the process by which cells mature and specialize), but this will also prevent the development of robust secondary sex characteristics as a child enters adolescence, since mature thyroid function is what children need to grow healthy breasts, penises, and muscular strength. The more wheat we feed our children the less fully formed adult they become. Muscle development, posture, physical beauty, and metabolic wellness are all inhibited by foods like common wheat. Children who have a more nutritious diet easily develop muscles, breasts, great eyesight, nice penises and vaginas, good dentition and strong jaws, and unending stamina, coordination, and intelligence when they reach young adulthood. Kids who have diets high in foods like common wheat and fortified iron are frail, weak, easily ill, with underdeveloped secondary sex characteristics, depressed, stupid, and even get severe acne since it is dietary iron excess which causes acne (also discussed in my other book). Such diets also increase the expression of stress hormones which in turn makes kids restless, distracted, and even angry and violent, since the body reacts to inflammation with stress hormones and stress hormones are what precipitate and motivate anger and violence.

Because of dietary trends toward organic and whole food eating, all of my siblings inadvertently ended up feeing their children far better diets that what was fed our generation. Instead of snacks composed of fake cheese, industrial bread, and shitty butter substitutes like margarine, all of which are extremely harmful for humans, my nieces and nephews have all had generous amounts of fruits and vegetables to snack on. Children actually instinctually crave and love fruits and vegetables as snacks, as I was surprised to learn such as when one toddler niece of mine developed a passion for snacking on cucumber, which is a potent source of the trace mineral molybdenum. Children develop obsessions for inferior and processed snacks only after their parents spend years already feeing these stupid foods to their children, out of convenience, then turn around and throw tantrums when their children won't eat their vegetables even though their children were already eating their vegetables before we purchased and provided mostly cheaper, crappy, processed replacements, as if such cheap, industrial shit is somehow not consequential to a child's development.

Yogurt absolutely should not be fed to adults, let alone children. An older study I found while researching *Fuck Portion Control* which was published before infant formula was widely available described a clinical trial where researchers attempted to make cow milk more digestible as a milk-replacement for children by adding either lactic or acetic acid. The children consuming cow milk with added acetic acid actually had a lower rate of mortality, but the children on the lactic-acid-fortified milk actually experienced an *increase* in mortality, and the study had to be stopped prematurely because of the deaths it caused. Lactic acid is the byproduct of yogurt manufacture and responsible for its sour taste, but it inhibits thyroid function and lowers metabolic rate and body temperature. The entire point of children's fat and metabolic function is to keep them warm, because human metabolism is facilitated through high body temperature, and consuming yogurt actively increases the risk of death and illness by lowering metabolic temperature. Children are less resilient to such insults than adults because of their smaller and immature physiology. The types of microbes in yogurt also supplant our actually healthy and natural species of bacteria, as the primary microbes used in yogurt manufacture are not actually natural residents of the human gut, and since they are high producers of lactic acid and consumers of vitamins and nutrients we need can sustain production of lactic acid in the gut indefinitely and cause deficiencies of important B vitamins, even during times that yogurt is not consumed, and catastrophic deficiencies in the short chain fatty acids. Yogurt is often used as baby food since it is cheap and convenient, but even ice cream is a better food for children than yogurt (as long as it doesn't contain gums, toxic carrageenan, and other additives) and would serve to promote sleep and calmness where yogurt and its excessive lactic acid content causes the reverse. Milk is excellent for children, and can be improved by adding a small amount of B12 to it. One tablet, for instance, dissolved in a gallon of milk can help promote the synthesis of short chain fatty acids from milk by our gut microbiome as well as promote a healthy microbiome. A drop of iodine in a gallon of milk can also help provide necessary iodine to children without causing overdose.

Some vegetables are not loved by children, because children are highly sensitive to anti-nutrients and inflammatory foods such as phytic acid, which occurs in many plants to promote the retention of minerals and elements within the plant, and has a distinctly bitter taste especially to children because our body knows it will bind and prevent absorption of nutrient. For instance, the skin of carrots contains phytic acid, and as such children will react with displeasure when tasting a carrot which has the skin on. Peeling a carrot (and purchasing ones which are actually sweet) will instead make a child *love* carrots. Some parents get around the inconvenience of peeling a carrot by purchasing "baby carrots," but these are treated with chlorine to prevent decay, and is a wasteful product anyway, and you can spend a few seconds peeling a carrot or, better yet, teach children to do it when they are sufficiently grown to operate a peeler safely. In some cases children will not even like simple foods such as potatoes, but which is also rooted in the nuances of biology and nature. A nephew of mine had a brain tumor as a child, which is a consequence of strongly anti-metabolic factors in the diet such as exposure to highly polyunsaturated fats or agrochemicals such as glyphosate, dioxins, pesticides, and synthetic fertilizers because these factors inhibit mitochondrial respiration. Because our mammalian, primate physiology also demands high intake of carbohydrates, especially sugar, a deficiency of fruit and other sweet food consumption exaggerates metabolic illness, since for instance sugar helps the body to balance calcium and phosphorus ratios, and without sugar we cannot absorb zinc. His illness in turn caused his nervous system to be highly sensitive to factors which agitate it and cause inflammation, and this in turn made him very sensitive to a chemical in potatoes called *solanine*, which is a potent neurological toxin meant to kill nematodes but which also aggravates our nervous system and which, I also discovered, underlies the development of neurological diseases like that which causes dependence on alcohol and drug addiction. This neurological sensitivity in turn made him despise potatoes, much to the frustration and ignorance of my sibling who assumed it to be willfulness, but which actually has its roots in the function of our biology and children's natural sensitivity to chemicals and compounds which have potentially deleterious effects on their vulnerable physiology. As a child I had a similar distaste for tomatoes, which are also part of the nightshade family and contains other similar glycoalkaloids, and was no surprise that I then grew up to have alcoholism. In the case of vegetables and food choices, parents should not waste much time or effort making children eat foods which are clearly distasteful to them. Doing so is simply fighting biology, not brattiness, which is something we cannot control anyway, and children will always win this struggle if their aversion to these compounds is sufficiently disturbing. Finding instead options they will eat which provide a broad range of nutrition is a far better strategy, and when children get older and their aversion to such compounds wanes their dietary options can expand.

    More than anything, children's behavior is influenced by diet. Because children are driven purely by instinct and inexperience they are driven by feelings, and feelings are actually hormones, and since the diet most strongly drives hormone balance, feeding children foods which are inflammatory and metabolically destructive in turn promotes profound expression of stress hormones, making children more susceptible to emotional instability and volatility. The world over, school lunches are so unacceptably poor in quality and nutrition, as if our children are not worth the cost of feeding high quality food, and this directly promotes poor academic and social performance since it impairs a child's metabolic health which in turn impairs cognitive and emotional wellness, but people are also usually misinformed to what is healthy and what is not, for instance chicken nuggets can be extremely healthy because using the entirety of a chicken including the bones and organs provides much better nutrition than only the meat, which is high in stress-associated amino acids and low in calcium and B vitamins, where the wheat and the bad fats in which it is cooked are the biggest problems. Tonsillitis is most definitely caused by exposure to unhealthy food like common wheat, but rather than fix our diets many parents would rather subject their children to traumatic surgeries and remove a valuable body part. The iron fortification of foods such as flour promotes bacterial pathogenic activity in the gut, producing stomachaches and high susceptibility to infections. When children reach puberty this iron also results in acne, and since acne can strongly affect a child's self esteem and is often treated with very harmful medicines that can have life-long consequences the avoidance of iron fortification is crucial for proper development. Oppositely, children who are fed generous calories from good fats, proteins, and plenty of carbohydrates and sugar from organic, healthy sources full of valuable nutritional quality produce far less stress hormones and are more resilient against the effects of stress and as such are calmer, happier, and more intelligent and productive. Fixing the food supply, especially for developing children when attending important institutions such as school, would do more for a child's academic and professional success than any effort to improve the actual curriculum or educational standards. A mentally impaired child damaged by toxic agricultural chemicals and deficiencies of minerals, protein, and carbohydrates and sugar and fat-soluble vitamins E, C, K, and D cannot effectively learn even when courses are perfected and teachers competent, but an ignorant child whose mind is healthy and hormones balanced due to healthful and generous nutrition can easily learn, even on their own, unassisted, and without much access to academic resources.

Fixing the diet does not mean depriving ourselves of options. Quite the opposite, the use of delicious foods like breads, mashed potatoes and gravy, sandwiches, pizza, doughnuts, steak, fries, and desserts can and should have a generous place in the diet, and only requires replacing harmful options with those which are safe, while not also neglecting the other requirements for a healthy diet as discussed in my other book. The metabolic, developmental, and emotional effect having fun with food can have on both our own and our children's wellness should not be underestimated. Treating the diet with severity and discipline is the antithesis of wellness and access to a broad range of nutrition. Pizza, for instance, if made with safe grains rather than common wheat, is actually a health food. The yeast which are required to raise dough produce an abundance of B vitamins and break down grain so we can digest it. Tomato sauce is a concentrated source of dietary potassium. Good cheese is a great source of calcium and other nutrients, and three slices of cheese pizza has nearly as much protein as half a chicken breast. Pizza made from a chain restaurant contains common wheat, bad fats, added iron, and likely toxic preservatives, pesticides, and other harmful chemicals and is harmful for our health. Homemade organic pizza is a health food. Grains can also be sprouted before being refined to increase the vitamin E content by more than double (though this doesn't exist yet as a product that I know of).

Children are, however, especially designed by nature to benefit from fruit (especially berries). I am always amused at seeing a small toddler wolf down more bananas and apples than I could stomach. Some parents misguidedly believe that sugar is a problem for children, and withhold fruit and sweet foods, believing that sugar causes cavities and restlessness (surprise—cavities are caused by pathogenic microbes, not sugar), even as their sugar-deprived children exhibit extreme emotional restlessness and mouths riddled with cavities, since that's not how any this works. French adolescent populations have *the lowest rates of periodontal disease in the entire world*, by a large margin, and yet French children consume ubiquitous daily sweets during the tradition of goûter, which is basically an indulgent after-school snack time. They are not consuming cheap, crappy, industrially produced junk food but traditional French chocolate, patisserie, fruit, preserves, and other confectionary. An inability to sleep in children is often a direct consequence of both calorie, carbohydrate, and sugar deficiency, which is why ice cream, as long as it does not contain allergenic and inflammatory additives like carrageenan or gums, can actually promote great sleeping patterns in children and in turn help adults get more sleep themselves. Many parents feel that they do not want to reward children who get up in the night or do not go to bed on time and so refrain from giving our children indulgent foods like ice cream. *But they are not awake because they're fucking disobedient.* Stress hormones rise swiftly during carbohydrate and fructose deficiency, and is the entire reason they are up at all, so children will then remain awake for several hours, completely depriving us too of sleep, where if instead we gave them some ice cream they would zonk out in thirty-minutes and we would be able to get to bed ourselves. Fruit also protects children's teeth, oral health, and general health due to nutrients like polyphenols and pectins in fruit which are naturally antibiotic and facilitate human resistance to pathogenic infection and modulate both oral and gastrointestinal microbiota. Children are so sensitive to fructose/glucose ratios in food that they will also not respond favorably to bread unless it has added sugar, because the excess of glucose relative to deficient fructose disrupts our body's ability to properly metabolize glucose, which is why adding sugar to bread makes children much more interested in it, because bread is otherwise nothing but pure glucose, which is actually stressful to our cells. Of course, children do need protein in order to thrive, but protein is also found in lots of sources besides meat and other animal products, which is why bread can be such a good food for children if it is homemade and made from safe flours such as spelt, einkorn, emmer, kamut, and other ancient grains. Real bread is especially healthful for children when made correctly and which contains sufficient sugar because the fermentation process breaks down the grain, making it more easily digested, and the microbial activity of yeasts and bacteria also produce a broad range of B vitamins, short chain fatty acids, and other nutrients which promote its effective digestion and nutritional benefit. Homemade bread can also dramatically help reduce our food bill as well, because real bread contains a special form of niacin which is more bioavailable than other sources of dietary niacin, it is far more satiating than other foods and is the primary reason we crave bread in the first place, not because of its high carbohydrate content which could be satisfied by any other starchy food source. Normally, niacin requires four enzymatic steps for the body to transform it into the metabolic cofactor NAD, which is required by our bodies to utilize energy obtained from food. The form produced by yeast in its action on bread is called *nicotinamide riboside* and only requires one enzymatic step for transformation into NAD. But commercial bread often skips the fermentation process which generates this form of niacin, raising bread with chemicals, which does not accomplish the breakdown of bread performed by yeast nor provides the other B vitamins, short chain fatty acids, nor nicotinamide riboside, which is not available from any other dietary source in nature. Sprouting grains too helps reduce anti-nutrients and also increases vitamin E content by more than 500%, and since vitamin E is required for healthy fatty acid metabolism and sufficient steroid production, neurological, and cardiovascular health, potent dietary sources of vitamin E such as sprouted spelt and other grains, almonds, or sunflower seeds can help children successfully transition into adolescence and promote the increase in steroidogenesis which occurs, with less stress and more healthful physical and mental development (however, children absolutely will not like or eat whole grains). Humans can live for long periods of time on only bread and water for these reasons (although it misses other required nutrients like vitamin K), so making bread, especially from sprouted flour, but which can still be refined, and teaching our children how to make bread, and storing grain (and a grain mill) and learning to soak and sprout grain as a healthful practice can be an extremely effective safeguard against food insecurity, nutritional stress, and times of disaster.

Fruit, especially berries due to compounds called anthocyanins, are the most important factor for good, long-term oral health and resistance to tooth decay and gum disease. I once helped a couple with their child who was exhibiting autistic symptoms, who fed their child a diet typical of "clean eating" and "healthy lifestyles" which consisted mostly of alternative nut-milks, lots of grains, some meat, and very little fruit and sugar. Fruits like grapes (or raisins), apricots, or watermelon are high in nutrients like boron and citrulline which participate in both the protection of teeth and gums from pathogenic microorganisms and the promotion of commensal microorganisms. As we age, such nutrients begin to be depleted from our body, and there is typically not sufficient amounts in our environment to support adult health, which is why we accumulate them as children and in fact why we are even children at all, to accumulate nutrients required for adulthood. Foods high in boron are things like grapes and raisins and apricots, and watermelon, cucumber, and squash are good sources of citrulline (in that order) so protecting children's long-term health by protecting their oral health mostly relies on generous consumption of fruit as available. Meat is an important source of necessary B12, but that can also be added to food using a supplement, such as to milk, which is often more effective too since muscle meat typically doesn't contain very large amounts. Safe, sprouted grains like sprouted oatmeal can be good but absolutely must be sprouted otherwise the high phytic acid content will cause tooth decay, stomachaches, and growth and emotional problems (and when oats are both organic and sprouted they are a really good food for humans).

Because diet so strongly affects a parent's experience and stress, it is ridiculous to continue parenting without leveraging nutrition in childhood development, and parents who obstinately insist on continuing dietary behaviors which are harmful to children out of convenience, tradition, familiarity, or an unwillingness to adapt to dietary and food supply realities is a parent doomed to continue suffering through the stress of stressed and malnourished children. Sugar is analgesic (dulls pain) and as such can help with childhood experiences like teething or injuries. It reduces stress hormones and promotes sleep and happiness. Parents who do not leverage food as a parenting tool are greatly stressed parents. Because making such changes is in reality a lot easier (and delicious) than we may assume, adopting the kind of diet which makes parenting easier has no real impediment other than willful ignorance and moralistic obstinance. Like I said previously, there is nothing wrong with paring down meals and being more simple in preparation. Rather than designing a traditional meat, sides, and salad dinner every night there is nothing wrong with making delicious real grilled-cheese sandwiches on good bread accompanied by tomato soup (since there are plentiful options of well-made pre-made tomato soup too). Or a delicious broccoli casserole with chicken that doesn't use crappy, pre-made food products. Soups are very delicious options and extremely healthy since they break down foods well and are easy to construct and can be made well in advance of dinner. Making homemade bread also doesn't actually require much time commitment either—it does take some time to learn, but once proficiency is reached it requires only a total of about thirty minutes active preparation, and provides far more food and satiation in relation to time commitment than other culinary projects.

The most important nutrient for kids is *potassium*, but most contemporary diets are actually quite deficient. For comparison, a cup of wheat flour contains only about 134 mg of potassium, where sweet potatoes have 448 mg and true yams have 1,224. Potassium is invaluable for the proper working of all cellular processes, as it is the most abundant element in intracellular fluid which plays an active role in cellular pH, homeostasis, water management, inflammation, chloride and sodium function, and energy production. Many of the health problems that most of our generation have experienced is rooted in diets which have replaced high potassium foods like root vegetables with foods poor in potassium like grain, and serving children root vegetables daily (rather than only special occasions like Sunday dinner or holidays) can help their bodies develop properly and avoid many of the metabolic diseases so common in contemporary industrialized societies. Fruit and other vegetables can also be good sources, but supplements like potassium chloride, which is sometimes used as a salt replacement, can actually cause potassium loss (because potassium helps counterbalance the effect of chloride on cells). While potatoes are the most common root vegetable high in potassium their high solanine content can actually promote alcoholism and addiction if eaten in excess, but more especially if accompanied by deficiency of saturated fats, sunlight, and affection. So potatoes should always be peeled and never used as a primary source of potassium, where yams, carrots, sweet potatoes, turnips, fruit, and leafy greens are safest. Yuca can also be useful although it contains cyanide (which we actually need in our diet) and should similarly not be used in excess.

Social and personal development are as important as nutritional and physical growth, but we often do not pay as much attention to these factors and instead simply run on instinct, indifference, and obsessive control mechanisms. As a child raised in an emotionally abusive and unstable home I never had the chance to explore ideas and concepts of who I was as an individual, what tastes were unique to my own experience and preference, and in turn how I related to others and the outside world to form a strong and well-developed personality. Specifically, in response to the tumultuous environment of my youth I developed a dissociative personality, which is where a person psychologically and emotionally detaches from the people and events in their lives in response to sustained emotional and environmental stress. When children are given the emotional space to develop they are more likely to establish a well-formed identity and sense of who they are as a person. Experiencing life, events, and other people they are able to consciously identify and meet their needs, wants, likes and dislikes, and personal interests which inform their sense of identity which in turn helps them develop the skills, knowledge, and experience needed to successfully navigate life and find and exploit opportunities for success. Children who are instead dominated or neglected by their parents spend their entire childhood simply trying to navigate their parents and threat to their wellbeing which in turn prevents any inward exploration and formation of identity. My art was one of the only things (probably the only thing) I developed as a child independently from my parents, because I never had any stability which afforded the establishment of close friendships or development of skills which were of interest to me, such was my identity forcibly entwined with frenetic and domineering adults. But I also actually practiced art because it was a source of praise and attention and one of the only sources of demonstrable affection I could find for myself, and so I practiced art not because I loved it but so that others would notice and value me. This in turn actually caused me stress and resentment associated with my art rather than pleasure and fulfillment and I eventually abandoned it altogether.

Many of us have similar developmental disappointments from our childhoods where skills and talents performed as sources of validation which were not otherwise forthcoming, and not being empowered to achieve a sense of self-worth and esteem for who we are as an individual found these skills and talents to also become as much a source of stress and pain as the rest of our lives. Opportunities for development should be forthcoming for a child's growth, but they should not be a replacement for their inherent sense of self and value simply for being who they are. Being a productive member of society is not the same thing as self-esteem, and parents and adults who think that children need to be shaped and formed and forced into successful and well-developed adults are also those who actively impair children's natural ability to actually accomplish it, corrupting a child to believe we do such things *because we have to* and not *because we can*.

Similarly, most ineffective parents parent simply because we do not want to be *perceived* as bad parents, which is not the same as actually being a good parent, which is exactly why we become defensive and hostile when we are criticized for our parenting, because we are not actually interested in the well-being of our children but our own ego and reputation, the same impetus for us who mercilessly harass our children about piano, academics, soccer, work, relationships, or other developmental activities and also why we may feel stress surrounding our own developmental activities when they are in fact supposed to be fun and rewarding. Whenever my father took us along to participate in basketball, skiing, or other activities he always bragged about how much better he was than us, his young children, and directly competed with us, like a sociopath, instead of playing *with* us, confusing criticism and egotistical domination with teaching, and predictably these occasions became a deterrent to our personal development and revulsion by activities which are meant to be fun and recreation since, again, they were only meant to indulge the desire to control and subvert adult fear and insecurity.

Many children also have conditions like ADHD, autism, learning disorders, or even anxiety and depression which complicate behavioral challenges and retard development, but are treated by the medical profession as incurable and managed only with medications which can further harm a child's development and physical health or cause even more problems later on in a child's life. In reality, ADHD is specifically caused by high stress hormones which result from diets high in inflammatory foods like wheat and those high in polyunsaturated fats like corn oil, canola oil, vegetable oil, or even fish oil, because these dietary fats are highly unstable and easily oxidize in human bodies. These foods generate high amounts of reactive oxygen species which cause irritation and agitation and in turn promote high stress hormones as the body tries to arrest the damage they cause. These high stress hormones then make children easily irritated, angry, and restless and inattentive. If you want to have the same experience as a child with ADHD, drink five or six espressos on an empty stomach and try to sit still and be productive for five hours. That is exactly the feeling that children with these issues have, and can hardly be expected to focus when their diets and environments illicit such extreme expression of stress hormones. Children are actually quite resilient to stress, and these conditions demonstrate just how severe the problem actually is.

Diets low in antioxidants like vitamin C or anthocyanin and carotene compounds from fruits also make a child's body (and an adults) far more susceptible to reactive oxygen species and compound the irritation and agitation caused by these diets. And emotionally volatile and unreliable domestic life and dissatisfying emotional relationships exaggerate and prolong the expression of stress hormones. Stress hormones also motivate humans to move, explore, and be active, which is why children with these problems cannot sit still or focus. A good diet free of inflammatory foods and high in natural, whole-foods high in antioxidants like vitamin C and fruit can rapidly resolve these underlying endocrinological issues, and resolving your emotional volatility and establishing a consistent, loving, and emotionally available home and empowering children with healthy coping skills such as trauma inventory facilitates (from the adult practicing it, not children although they can be taught as they grow older) can completely resolve conditions of ADHD, anxiety, and childhood depression. More serious conditions like Autism can also be resolved but require more specific intervention strategies in restoring the gut microbiome and immune system as discussed in my other book, Fuck Portion Control. These strategies can also even improve the quality of life for incurable conditions like Down's syndrome because many challenges faced by those with such conditions are caused by incidental dietary and environment insufficiencies like wheat consumption, gut dysbiosis, and sunlight deficiency.

Promoting childhood development, much like self-care, is also accomplished by focusing on *our own development* within the context of a family. Once an adult and finally had ample time and money (and mental energy), I undertook learning the guitar, which I had always wanted to do and greatly regretted never having had the opportunity. Having spent many years as pianist, the basics came rather easily, and during one trip home I brought my guitar along. Several of my nieces and nephews were immediately enraptured by it, even though I was absolutely terrible, and likewise desired to have a turn and play themselves. It piqued interest in several of them who now expectantly participate in guitar lessons. Because we are biologically programmed to desire more than anything to be like our parents and other adults, when children see us engaged in adult activities they are naturally drawn to and obsessed with them. Asking us to do it for them is really children asking us to *teach* them. If we take care of ourselves by spending time indulging our own interests and talents in view of and with family, not apart from them, we will naturally instill motivation and desire to achieve similar accomplishment in them, and since motivation is the hardest part of any endeavor easily guarantees that children will then develop the kinds of talents and skills which can enrich their life and promote success in adulthood. I mean, children are actually willing to do dishes and organize the pantry and cupboards. FOR FUN. Just because they see us doing it. Why wouldn't they also be interested in learning math, or the piano, or engineering, or amending relationships, or doing well in school, using the same methods of emulation? In which we also get to do what we want and need to take care of our own needs. All notable people who have achieved places of esteem through personal accomplishment always reference being inspired by the things their parents did. Dolly Parton talks endlessly about how her parents played instruments and cultivated music in their home, central to their family life. Albert Einstein's father was an engineer and inventor and his mother was well-educated and an accomplished musician herself, and Einstein credited music for much of his ability to advance scientific discovery. When I was a teenager I saw my father drawing architectural plans. They were amazing. I couldn't believe he was so talented, and that someone could actually draw plans and later turn it into a real, physical structure. I asked him to teach me architecture and he did, and to this day I continue drawing architecture with such skill that I could easily transition into the profession. But when we went to work on his construction projects, instead of leveraging our natural inspiration to be just like him and pass on those talents and skills he always just forced us to work as the cleanup crew apart from him, and thus never learn or develop in any appreciable way. Because personal development can also be rewarding for the adult, it is a far less stressful and more effective and efficient way to accomplish it in children to teach by example.

We as adults who do not do things like read, play the piano, practice cheffery, sing, invent, write, paint, or otherwise indulge ourselves in personal interests and personal development most likely were also harassed and traumatized by our own parents and childhoods regarding our own development, and avoid it in adulthood not because we are lazy or uninterested in personal development as our parents may have suggested but because our interests and ability were also obscured by traumatizing feelings and heartache which occurred in childhood! Some adults may believe we don't have the ability or resources to practice personal development, but in reality there are many things we can do even when our time and resources are limited (like reading!) and only don't do these things for ourselves because of deeply rooted personal trauma and unresolved pain and disappointment, poor self-esteem, and absence of compassion for ourselves and the child we once were, using our limited abilities and resources as a convenient excuse not to confront that which is often overwhelmingly painful. As such, first uncovering and exploring the origins of our pain and frustration, having compassion for ourselves and practicing self-care can help us find the space to explore, perhaps even for the first time, our own interests, priorities, and talents, which will in turn facilitate this naturally and effortlessly in our children.

Parents are often also obsessed with the physical growth of their children, placing emphasis on height, weight, and other markers of quantitative growth. Of course, physical growth is important, though not as much as many people influenced by inappropriate conceptions of self worth assume. Dietary factors strongly influence growth as mentioned previously, but parents are often mistaken about what growth is actually healthy, and often regard childhood physical development with prejudice. For instance, it is unknown to the general public that homosexual boys tend to begin puberty on the same timeline as heterosexual girls, around the ages of 11 to 13, and I think the reverse may be true for homosexual girls being on the same timeline as young men, from ages 13 to 16, with broad variations according to each child's individual gender composition. These physical and biological inconsistencies in development are conveniently ignored by bigoted religionists who wish to continue portraying those who are differently gendered as a lifestyle choice (as if membership in a religion isn't and as if anyone would willingly choose to give up their attraction to one gender of preference in exchange for an increase in harassment and danger to personal safety in the bigoted families and societies in which we were raised). This growth pattern is not entirely constant for all children, but it may help bring clarity to disparities between children's development even within the same families. For instance, I was alway tall and hit puberty very early, while my younger, heterosexual brother was always short and didn't begin puberty until several years after I had pretty much finished. He perhaps was insecure and envious of my apparent early and rapid ascent into manhood, but it was in fact a function of my hybrid gender which facilitated this and not in fact anything to do with manliness.

There is also a wide range of heights in my extended family. Though I am six-foot-seven some of my male cousins are well below six-foot, even though we all share the same genetics. Diet strongly affects growth, and healthy growth does not always mean substantial quantitative growth. Shorter stature often indicates a more timely and healthy differentiation of secondary sex characteristics, since the function of the thyroid, which increases at adolescence, slows quantitative growth in favor of qualitative. But consumption of generous amounts of high-calcium and protein foods such as milk and cheese can also promote increased growth, because calcium, being the mediator of bone growth, is itself a primary mediator of height, which is not really a function of genetics. Protein of course is also required for growth, but this tends to be more easily accomplished than in our evolutionary past, though what foods exactly contain protein is often misunderstood. While meat has protein, so does nearly all food, including milk, cheese, grains, and even fruits and vegetables. Much emphasis is placed on "complete proteins," which are protein sources which contain the full range of essential amino acids, but combining foods which may or may not contain the full range of amino acids will still provide the complete range of requirements, and while the amino acids in fruit and vegetables are not as abundant as other sources like grains and meat, they are often higher quality and promote stress reduction which in turn facilitates an increase in growth both of quantity *and* quality. Because fruit is one of the most important dietary requirements for human primates, when part of a broader range of food sources promotes the best growth and growth outcomes in children, improving sleep, hair, skin, mood and emotions, and later sexual function which can also help prevent sexual compulsion and emotional dissatisfaction which is itself promoted by excess stress both dietarily and environmentally. Height should not be an emphasized aspect of childhood development, but instead the quality of growth which is best facilitated by a diet which prevents inflammation and provides generous quantities of carbohydrates, good fats, sugar, protein, and micronutrients. If you are very enterprising, regenerative agriculture which nurtures the soil microbiome produces the most nutritive food, because soil microbes make environmental nutrients bioavailable for plants to then take up, something that is not even necessarily achieved in organic agriculture and which is completely absent from standard industrial farming which destroys the soil microbiome, and regenerative, no-dig farming and gardening practices can provide your family with nutrition that is easy to do but not available to the general public.

 Diet is first and foremost the origin of many problems and frustration with parenting, and many problems can be solved or avoided by providing a good, healthy diet, which is not at all based on socially accepted standards of eating and deprivation. Kids don't sleep? Feed them. Kids are cranky? Feed them. Kids are fighting? Feed them. Teenagers are brooding and moody? FEED THEM. Good food should be the first strategy to solve all of our parenting dilemmas (pretty much any problem in life, actually). Only after food fails to solve a problem should other options be explored.

22

Sexuality

    I must have seen a picture or someone on television wearing a thong, because I can't remember how I came up with the idea to make one of my own. I remember seeing the bands and seams on my underwear and thinking how it resembled one of those really tiny swimming suits that for some reason I knew I wouldn't be allowed to wear, let alone ask for. I was nine or ten years old, and even though we were in a new house mine and my brother's room was still in the basement, this time without even a window. One wall of the large basement space to which ours was adjacent was nothing but beveled mirrors, about a foot each in diameter, from floor to ceiling—a very 70's aesthetic.
    One day when I was alone I snuck into the basement bathroom and began ripping up an old pair of underwear into something much sexier. After some work I eventually had a tattered but skimpy alternative to my conservative and suffocating clothing standards which allowed no exploration of my own body and physical development, and though it was shoddy the barbarian aesthetic of tattered cloth actually added what I would later come to learn as an adult as erotica. I quickly ran out of the room to look at myself in the wall of mirrors to see that, yes, I was indeed sexy. Then fearfully ran right back into the bathroom and shut the door.
    But suddenly I realized there was no going back. In my hands I held the evidence of my crime. I daren't walk out of the bathroom with it in my hands for fear of being caught, so I hid it on the very top of the bathroom cabinets, somehow being completely ignorant to the full extent of my mother's obsessive cleaning standards. "Nathan!" came a tremendous scream from the bathroom

a few days later.
 In the bathroom my mother held the shame of my body curiosity with as few fingers possible as if holding dead roadkill rather than my runaway childhood imagination. "What is this?" she demanded.
 "I don't know." I lied.
 "Don't lie to me!" she shouted. My brother was there and had apparently been interrogated already, but his innocence was apparent .
 "It was already ripped," I lied, "and I just ripped it more and got carried away." The look on my mother's face was still dubious, but glad that I had not, in fact, been interested in anything sexual.
 Once when visiting a sister who is a mother to one of my gay nephews, she screamed at me for referring to him being gay. She had, in fact, earlier in the evening used the word *gay* to refer to him. *Oh good*, I thought. *We're finally acknowledging this.* During my visit he had expressed an obsession with people's butts. My sister asked why he was so interested in stuff like that. I explained to her first that he was at an age which children are intensely curious about their bodies. Perhaps it is a dawning awareness of the human form in preparation for coming adolescence. But I also made the mistake of humorously explaining that us gay boys are also very precocious, and take notice of everything. My sister's restrained homophobia was instantly and mercilessly unrestrained, screaming at me for "assigning a sexuality" to her eight-year old, and in direct hypocrisy to herself having used the word *gay* earlier in the day.
 When I was a teenager I confided in a religious leader that I was gay. I had not yet even kissed another person, not even a girl, but I knew I was not straight. Instead of counseling me with love and wisdom and helping me to navigate the complex world of adulthood and my precarious sexuality and protecting me from depression and ostracization from my very own community he condemned me, embarrassed me, and urged me to work on not being gay, whatever the hell that means. I find it hilarious that religions who claim being gay is wrong because God told them so do not also have instructions for fixing gay. Did they just forget to ask after he told them it was bad? I found out later that our religious counselor then accused my sister of being gay, since she had confided in him her deep disappointment at having never been asked out on a date (she was so beautiful no boys dared ask her), and because homosexuality was so demonized in our religion she then dealt in secret with even more shame and embarrassment at his smarmy, bigoted hands. Sexual abuse is so rampant in communities like the one in which I grew up that after years of complaints Mormon religious leaders were finally compelled to keep their doors open when meeting with women and children to avoid more lawsuits for sexual impropriety. But this also completely misses the fact that adult religious volunteers are not at all apt sexual and developmental counselors for young and vulnerable men and women. Having no specific training or knowledge to qualify them they typically do great harm to people who actually need genuine help, information, and protection. Utah has consistently had the highest rate of teen suicide in the United States, amongst a population which ostensibly cares about and focuses on the family, which is in truth meant to control people by leveraging membership in their family, which is collectively one of

the most pure and absolute needs of human beings, and such religious dogma serves in truth to fracture and destroy families as evidence by the hundreds of members of my immediate and extended family who are depressed, traumatized, and estranged.

The reason that sexual abuse, suicide, and the destruction of families is so rampant among conservative and religious communities is that, contrary to what they believe, religious people actively and aggressively sexualize children at a very young age during the act of indoctrination, with frequent discussions or exploration of sex under an excuse of religious instruction, and to a far greater extent than is understood do a great deal of harm to children's sexual development in the process. This obscene preoccupation with sex actively promotes sexual behavior and sexual abuse in developing children who are unable to understand they are being sexually abused and exploited. An adult who doesn't think about sexualizing a child doesn't concern themselves with a child's sexuality, because it is something which develops naturally and is a personal and private experience. But adults who do sexualize children become obsessed with children's sexual behavior, development, private parts, and romantic interests, even when those children haven't even reached adolescence. A common but nefarious behavior of sexualizing children is the constant and effusive praise of their physical appearance by adults. Occasionally telling a child they are handsome or pretty is not a problem, but very often it is done excessively and becomes one of the only sources of praise a child might receive, with grandparents, parents, or other friends and relations constantly talking about a child's physical appearance. This abuse transfer's a child's sense of worth from who they are as a person to that only of their body and commodifying it as a source of value to others. Adults who do this are often simply repeating the same behavior which was directed at them as children, but that is exactly how abuse is perpetuated, and is a manifestation of similarly unresolved trauma, shame, or pain from our own past. Abuse by older siblings of younger ones, especially young men to their younger sisters, is frighteningly common but expected in conservative communities which simultaneously sexualize children but deny them any healthy outlet for sexual behavior. Though they were religious, my grandparents bought my Dad playboys and allowed him to keep them under his bed. But he in turn strictly denied any exposure to sexualized material the entirety of my youth, which led to extreme and pathological frustration that ultimately culminated in attempt at suicide.

Some of the most brazen and heinous abusers of children, such as John Harvey Kellogg who practiced circumcision on both male and female children of all ages, even without anesthesia, as both a punishment and supposed deterrent to masturbation was regarded as a devout person of faith rather than the psychopathic eugenicist and child abuser he actually was, and is the primary reason that boys in Western civilizations are even circumcised to this day. Circumcision permanently damages the penis and ruins pair bonding as adults since the sexual function of the reproductive organs are meant to promote bonding between partners. Because sex is often a primary purpose of marriage and sexual union, permanently damaging the reproductive organs actually leads to sexual dissatisfaction within relationships, especially late in life when the body loses the ability to regenerate tissue which in turn causes circumcision scars to become fibrotic, dull, and especially to promote the condition called soft glans (the cure for which is discussed in *Fuck Portion Control*). Being then unable to find sexual satisfaction with their partner and constrained by ideological restrictions surrounding sexual activity, religious adherents who are circumcised find that only mental sexual stimulation from novel experiences remains operative, since the brain is the primary sex organ, and as such secretly indulge in pornography, fantasy, and even adultery because without the functional use of their reproductive organs their physical attachment to their romantic partner was never established, and being still yet driven by a need to mate and find intimacy can no longer achieve those ends with a partner to whom they have grown accustomed since the mechanism, physical sexual stimulus, was taken from them. The guilt of disloyalty and shame of perceived failure then actively promotes emotional distancing from their partner as their relationships begins to sag under the weight of impossible expectations and lack of compassion for our mortal human limitations, fighting each other for problems which are greater than any one person's role in a partnership, made worse by unresolved pain and trauma surrounding shame and sex from their own childhood. I was first taught about sexual behavior (not maturation) by adults in my family and religion when I was as young as seven or eight because, being centered around themes of sexuality, religion cannot help but expose children to sex at an inappropriately early age, especially in the context of shame and graphically illustrative sexual behavior and other very unhealthy attitudes about sex.

Sexual preoccupations, shame, predatory impulses, and problems with personal intimacy in romantic relationships are also effectively resolved by practicing inventory therapy surrounding those issues. For instance, many men feel ashamed of sex after ejaculating with a partner, even if they feel they are actually doing what it expected of them. This is because we are naturally designed as humans to experience extreme vulnerability after orgasm, in order to promote pair bonding. But if we were raised by sex shaming parents this vulnerability instead makes us acutely aware of our vulnerability and thus resent it and become susceptible to reliving feelings of shame about sex. This can severely limit intimacy with a partner since after sex we should be enjoying their presence, not replaying tapes of abuse in our head and distancing ourselves from it. By inventorying these shameful feelings as a resentment and exploring fears of rejection we can come to terms with our vulnerability, the pain of the past, and the harmful effects abuse had on our experience. Doing so will then result in acceptance of this stage of vulnerability and thereby promote the kind of intimacy which is both terrifying and wonderful.

Many sexual problems related to physical health such as erectile dysfunction, premature ejaculation, or absence of sex drive, and infertility can often be barriers to sexually fulfilling relationships. As I discuss in my book *Fuck Portion Control* there is no such thing, however, as sexual addiction, which instead is a sexual compulsion instinct motivated by our biology in response to poor metabolic health and environmental and emotional stress which requires intervention in diet and cultivation of a healthy environment and dietary behaviors. There is still psychological trauma at the root of sex compulsion which affects the body, endocrine system, and hormone functions which also must be addressed with inventory therapy to help us come to terms with realities of life and our own mortality. Sexual predation, abuse, and violence are always rooted in dysfunction of the endocrine system as a direct result of abuse experienced as a child which deranges the hormone balance maintained by structures of the brain such as the hypothalamus. But, psychologically, these destructive behaviors and impulses are at their core a desire to control our stress and stressful feelings and problems by in turn controlling others in our environment, especially by exploiting vulnerability, and none are more vulnerable than children.

People raised in abusive homes are especially at risk for sexual criminal activity or committing abuse themselves because the combination of emotional loneliness, psychological abuse and neglect, lack of effective mental and emotional skills, and the sexual compulsion stimulated by stress, poor diets, and sunlight deprivation can drive people insane and desperate for relief which unfortunately comes then at the expense of their victims as they try to control their own experiences through that of others. Men are stereotypically offenders of rape and sexual violence, but women can and are sexual predators every bit as much as men, since none of us are immune to the trauma of childhood abuse, where women having less size advantage typically channel their sexual trauma into sex abuse such as obsession with children's sexuality, genitals, often disguising this obsession in the bounds of religion, poorly disguising their abuse as morality or concern, but in reality constantly exposing theirs or others' children to sex discussion or engaging in pseudo-sexual abuses like spanking. Most of us are not taught effective coping skills to handle trauma, and most everyone on the planet is ignorant to its effects on biology and metabolic health because that is not something naturally built in to our human instincts, and many of us experience severe trauma as children which in turn destroys our sense of self and disrupts our ability to create and maintain healthy and fulfilling relationships, which then disturbs the function of the endocrine system and impairs intimate bonding with others to perpetuate our struggle and frustration as adults driven by sex hormones and instincts. All of us deserve wonderful, happy, and intimate relationships with other people to accept us for who we are, whom we in turn treat with the same kindness, care, and compassion desired for ourselves, and if we in any way are frustrated in finding such fulfillment this is the very manifestation of the very trauma which results in control and coping behaviors that impair romantic success which must be resolved through the kind of thorough, courageous, and introspective therapy such as inventory accomplishes.

Often as a child my parents would try to censor movies and television which showed any kind of erotica. In our family this took the form of my mother leaping up from the couch right before a sex scene to open her cardigan and block the television while shouting at my father to hit the mute button as she watched to surveil when it was passed. One particular movie which was a favorite of my parents was *Top Gun*, which we watched several times throughout my childhood, each time when Tom Cruise and Kelly McGillis came together in that dimly lit, blue tinted room as *Take My Breath Away* by Berlin began to play my mother would leap up to block the screen with her body. This in truth served only to heighten my interest in the scene and conjure wild imaginations of what state of undress Tom Cruise might be, imaging his taut, perfect butt thrusting and clenching or Kelly's hands running down the smooth curves of his strong back muscles. Though my parents thought they were censoring sex they were in fact exposing us to even more sex and sensuality by constantly obsessing over it, which was also a control behavior since they would have no one to chastise about sex if they did not also expose us to it, in the process promoting intense shame and emotional self-hatred surrounding sex by communicating that it was bad and wrong for us to see instead of simply keeping such content out of our lives altogether if they truly desired us not to be exposed to it. There was no reason that we needed to see *Top Gun* as six, seven, and eight year olds. That could have been reserved as a film for my parents and their own relationship, waiting until we were old enough to see sex for ourselves. But even as a late teenager my mother, like many religious women who were themselves victims of sex abuse, was still pathological in her obsession to prevent us from seeing sex. Their censorship of this scene and my resultant fantasy for Tom Cruise drove me insane with desire to see his butt I knew must be in the movie, why else would my mother give her very life before letting us see such steamy erotica. The day that my father picked me up from juvenile detention after my stunt at the water park and forced me to accompany them to the summer resort for the weekend I saw when I arrived that they had brought *Top Gun* along. I cunningly refused to go with them on a hike, then watched from the window as they ascended the mountain and, alone with the VHS tape of my dreams, took off my clothes and got a jar of Vaseline with which to realize my ultimate fantasy. I put in the tape, literally shaking with anticipation and fear, fast forwarding to the forbidden scene only to find a very disappointingly boring shot of the two actors kissing in silhouette from the shoulders up, not even descending to show a lower back or a hot piece of thigh. It was the most tame sex scene in cinematic history. The kissing scenes in Jaws and James Bond, the latter of which we had seen every one, were more explicit and erotic. By this time finally having seen my first pornography on the internet it was wholly disappointing to find that reality had not lived up to the fantasy playing in my head, planted ironically by my mother's insanity surrounding sex and thus betraying her own secret obsession with Tom Cruise, who was pretty good with his tongue, admittedly, which still was more than enough to get me off.

In spite of the name, and my last anecdote, homosexuality is not about sex. Homosexuality and other different sexual and gender orientations are more appropriately their own third gender, one which is any combination of male or female in varying degrees unique to each person. Our gender makes us unique and informs much of our experience and talents in life, things which are only occasionally related to sex but often related to gender. There are in fact six possible biological combinations of the X and Y chromosomes in human beings, so the idea that only two exist in nature is completely without scientific evidence, let alone anecdotal. Different genders are also not a result of any "imbalance" in the womb or other such negative conceptions of sexual and gender non-conforming individuals. Sperm carry options for determining the gender of a baby, they do not themselves decide, and a womb chooses from those options according to environmental stimuli which we have yet to fully understand but is clear from consistent quotas of males, females, and third-gender persons that biology knows about and even designed all of us to exist in proportion to others in our environment. Gender is also not a role to play that anyone is born into but is instead a vehicle through which we experience life, which is why it is ridiculous for others to insist on the gender of another person since their gender has nothing to do with you. Even though I am gay and have some similar experiences to women I will never know what it's like to actually live as a woman, and even though I am male and lived for a time pretending I was heterosexual I will also never know what is is like to live as a straight man because our underlying biology which creates gender, unlike our friends, family, and society, cannot be deceived.

Anyone with a little compassion can see that third-gender people play an integral role and function in our families and society, if they allow us, acting as a joyful glue and cheerleaders who help hold a family together. As a child I frequently brought all my siblings together in creative projects, making films, forts, and make-believe adventures and as a teenager tried my best to protect and care for my siblings. When I was almost forty years old I moved back near my home town in a misguided and naive attempt to restore my familial relationships, and after only a few days back was horrified to learn nobody had made plans to celebrate my mother's birthday, though a sister and her family also lived nearby. I immediately put together plans to for a birthday cake with my sister and nieces. It failed horribly and comically but the impromptu party turned out wonderful and for a moment I again, naively, thought things were going to be okay. But I still could not help feeling despair from a family torn apart by ideological and bigoted warfare, even among the heterosexuals who clung to their so-called traditional beliefs which separate even those who share membership and ideology and subscribe to the same dogma and traditions, because the subversion of humanity and denial of our shared need for one another which religious institutions indoctrinate engenders shame and insecurity even in those who subscribe to those very bigoted, homophobic, and racist ideologies and thus impair their ability to connect to everyone since their own humanity must be subverted to sustain such cruel and compassionless beliefs.

I was grateful to finally understand why we as third-genders exist, both biologically and karmically, since all my life I had mostly only heard of reasons we shouldn't. We whom are differently gendered is intended by nature to be non-reproducing adults which increase the ratio of caretakers to offspring, in order that rates of childhood mortality decrease. It is also why gays and lesbians are so attached to their own families and often find especially important roles in helping their siblings or nieces and nephews, if they are allowed, as we are literally a biological and evolutionary strategy designed save humanity it its darkest moments, to strengthen families and help children grow into better developed, capable adults and assist other parents in their obligations. Many animals in nature exhibit homosexuality for the same purposes, increasing the ratio of adults to offspring to increase odds of survival to adulthood. The increased emotional intelligence of third-genders incidentally also results in the creative and artistic contributions of those who, unburdened by the responsibility of actual parenthood, have time, energy, and intellectual resources to contribute intangible benefits to the human race, which is why so many outstanding human achievers throughout history have been disproportionately differently-gendered, such as the father of computers, Alan Turing, or Roman Emperor Hadrian, or even Sir Isaac Newton who was a tormented bachelor during an era when homosexuals were especially persecuted and threatened with death. Homosexuals clearly have more child-like orientations toward the world, to relationships, and to love and family to assist our siblings and nieces and nephews develop more successfully than we were able, to learn from the past and promote those lessons in the future though an increased capacity for emotional intelligence.

Many cultures have recognized the sensitivity to matters of the spirit and propensity for insight and counsel of those who are differently-gendered, and wherever homosexuals are allowed to exist there also exists a great abundance of wealth, prosperity, and progress, while societies which persecute us are also those inclined to prohibit education, art, and hoard wealth for oppressors and terrorize their citizens. It is also a myth that homosexuality is a recent phenomenon or only recently accepted. Roman Emperor Hadrian who "preferred to invest in the development of stable, defensible borders and the unification of the empire's disparate peoples" rather than continue expansionist and imperialist policies, was known for one of the greatest periods of the entire Roman empire and publicly and passionately courted Antinous whom tragically died after which Hadrian established a religious cult dedicated to him. As are many accounts of homosexuals of history, such relationships are excused away as an anomaly or rarity by bigoted and homophobic institutions, to invalidate our existence rather than recognize our place as constant members and contributors to the human race. The famous *Lovers of Modena* skeletons were revered and admired the world over and studied as a heterosexual affirmation of affection and marriage until it was discovered that both skeletons were actually male, which thereafter was homophobically excused as a fraternal connection even though that kind of burial tradition has never existed or been supported by any anthropological evidence in any culture. I mean, seriously, when have soldiers ever fucking been buried together in pairs, holding hands, even if they were close? The Greeks and Spartans revered homosexuality, which is why it occurs so often in Greek mythology and even in real life, such as the accounts of the *The Sacred Band of Thebes* which was an elite military force which consisted only of pairs of male lovers. Even graffiti from ancient Rome carved into its timeless stone hilariously describes joyful and homosexual debauchery and love.

This is not to say that heterosexuals alone are the persecutors of differently gendered people. In the same way that Patriarchy is supported and sustained also by women, we who are differently gendered have also participated in our own oppression throughout history as in contemporary times, such as homophobic politicians so frequently being caught living secret lives and harboring intense self hatred and delusion. The tradition of eschewing wives for clergymen in the Catholic Church was most certainly established by a gay man. A great mistake often made about humanity and our history is the assumption that we were very much different even not so long ago. Every society believes that the atrocities of the past and the crimes committed against humanity were a function of more primitive humans and olden standards and beliefs. Most people don't realize that during and immediately after the Salem witch trials other citizens of Massachusetts and even residents of Salem were well aware of the insanity of the crimes committed there, the murdering of innocent women, and in course petitioned and sued the government for redress. The religious fanatics of Salem were not some occultist anomaly which took place deep in the woods at the hands of barbarian puritans during a time long ago. It was a crime of hysteria committed by educated and intelligent bigots and fear-mongers bent on power and control of their society, to assuage their own fears and their own insecurities, the very same traits possessed by authors of the Holocaust and other genocides which by the way did not even occur one lifetime ago. Humanity has always been conscious of amorally repugnant behaviors, because our morals are created by our biology as the tools and skills which facilitate the lives of social animals. Cyrus the Great, the first king of ancient Persia, freed all slaves and declared that all people had the right to choose their own religion and established racial equality. In 500 B.C.E. It is only when we lose sense of our shared humanity and turn on each other that we are subjected to our darkest and most vile potential which is no less potent in us today as it was when man first discovered fire. Failing to care for the rest of humanity is what facilitates our darkest potential and retards progress and peace by triggering banal conflict and instincts for self-preservation at the heart of such conflicts. Young, differently-gendered children possess different strengths and abilities which help us to help our families and thus humanity itself, to relieve parents of their despair and promote familial bonds with siblings and other progeny, and our increased emotional and intellectual capacity to serve as more effective guides and guardians.

  One day when I was sixteen and out raking the dirt of one of my Dad's newly finished homes into which we had just moved, I saw my mother watching me from their upstairs window. She motioned to me to come up to her room. I put my shirt on and excused myself for a moment.

  "I want to talk to you," she said as she sat down on her bed with a yellow legal pad and pen.

  "Okay," I said.

  "Do you know how the vagina works?"

  Oh my god.

  They had not yet confirmed my homosexuality—and at this point I was still questioning it myself. But I suddenly wondered if my mother had caught me ogling one of the several older boys who worked for my Dad—their bulging construction muscles and sweat dripping down their skin, speckled with dirt and smelling of sawdust and perspiration at many times overpowered my self-awareness. Once when we were building the house and it was only just recently framed I went into the basement to retrieve an extension cord only to suddenly see out the basement window one of the adult men who worked for my Dad unzip his pants beneath the adjacent porch and pull out his absolutely enormous penis to take a piss, ignorant to the presence of a young, gobsmacked admirer. After hearing *vagina* I suddenly thought about that penis and how much I wanted that man to use me.

"I mean—yeah. I guess?" I said uncomfortably. To my embarrassment she then began drawing a diagram of the vaginal and perineum area of a woman. "A woman has three holes," she said, to my horror, drawing three different circles of various sizes. I couldn't believe this was happening. I learned about the vagina and its anatomy in fifth-grade. My Dad had the sex talk with me and my brother when I was thirteen. There was no way this was happening because she really thought I didn't know about vaginas. "Okay," I said again. She continued to explain what all the holes were for, and that sex is also pleasurable for women. I tried to hurry along this lesson in eroticism, thanked her, and then got back to the yard as quick as I could to take my mind off what happened through hard work and the sight of shirtless, sweaty construction boys.

Just as we do in other aspects of our lives, we teach children attitudes about sex not by our words but by our actions and unconscious attitudes. My mother, clearly pained and traumatized about sex herself, had no skills with which to deal with the fact that her children would grow up to be sexual beings too. Many parents selfishly (but understandably) want their children to remain children forever. For some this is a passing fantasy tempered by reality. Others actually commit to it by attempting to cut off all outlets for sexuality, or purposefully fail to empower children with skills needed in adulthood to manage sex and relationships until the child eventually has to forcefully break away from their parents in order to lead an adult life. My mother so engendered me with shame for my body and sexuality that once when we were very young a neighbor child and my siblings decided to show each other their genitals—a very common and not only harmless but empowering behavior which all children at some point participate—but I ran upstairs right away to tell on them, even though I myself had been engaged in my own secretive swimwear experiments. Freewheeling abandonment of parental duties also impairs a child's development due to ignorance, borne out of fear it communicates to children their curiosity shameful, even if unintended, but it also opens them up to more hurt and pain as a young adult through exploitation by opportunistic and predatory adults, never having been taught about how the world works or given tools with which to care for themselves.

In order to develop healthy sexual attitudes in our children we must first resolve our own insecurities and past trauma surrounding sex. If our parents berated us about sex and made us feel shame for our body it doesn't matter how much we try to act with neutrality about sex for our own children—we will subconsciously and inadvertently communicate these attitudes and thus engender and burden them upon our children. One mother I know harbors intense prejudice against men and penises, and her sons will likely grow up with the same kind of self shame and hatred surrounding sex as what burdened me. It might seem difficult to recognize when we are unconsciously communicating such biases or are hampered by unconscious and residual pain and trauma, but in reality there are some obvious and not-so subconscious ways to discern the difference. Someone who is controlled subconscious prejudice is both highly emotive and deliberate in strategy. If you have feelings when things happen—those feelings inform us to our attitudes about something. If we find our child cutting up a pair of underwear and become enraged instead of thinking it's one of the most funny and embarrassing things that a child could do, we clearly have unresolved issues which are controlling our effectiveness in life. If we also approach situations—especially conversations—thinking we must word them carefully to avoid causing problems it is actually a control behavior and attempts at manipulation, acting on insecurity and fear because deep down we know we cannot really control other people but are still spending much time and energy trying to do so. Many times in a relationship I would consider how I could phrase something I wanted to bring up with my partner so that he would not fly off the handle. The fact that I was *trying to manipulate him* by saying the right things to avoid his reaction is the very act of manipulation—trying to influence someone to behave as we desire. The thought, *"how can I phrase this so it doesn't offend them,"* is a warning sign that we shouldn't fucking say it at all, and instead need to explore why we are having those feelings in the first place.

But then of course, the reason we are doing this in the first place is because we ourselves have had painful and traumatic experiences which have taught us that we can't ask for what we need and as such feel that we must be manipulative in the way we get it, never mind the fact that offenses can always be repaired through the making of amends, so the excessive preoccupation over context and strategy is itself evidence of being unable or unwilling to apologize when we hurt others. Remaining silent in a partnership to avoid causing conflict is also a deceptive act of manipulation. We are not, in fact, being selfless but especially selfish, engineering an identity of ourselves as a sacrificial, giving, and dedicated partner whose only concern is for the wellbeing of others, an entire drama in three acts performed only on the stage of our brain, spanning the years of our life or marriage. But we cannot actually endure being silent forever, so our frustration likely erupts into anger, contempt, and emotional violence when we cannot take it anymore and some event, likely harmless, sets us off, the victims of our behavior likely those closest and most convenient who cannot fight back because of their very helplessness and dependence on us as parents.

The boy I dated many years ago who was himself the victim of familial sexual abuse by an uncle was himself unable to resolve the trauma of his past. At first it inspired in me feelings of pity and compassion, this boy with whom I was falling in love, so handsome and talented and amazing, and I wanted to protect the child that was now the adult by loving him unconditionally, loyally, and nonjudgmentally. So when he began acting out in our sex life—acting as if certain sexual activities reminded him of his past, I endured it willingly, changed activities, and regarded it with patience and compassion. What I didn't realize at the time was that he was reenacting his abuse with me, a person who was absolutely not his abuser, and how unfair and manipulative it actually was for him to turn me, a consenting adult who loved him, from whom he had also solicited romance and intimacy, into an effigy of his abuser. I was not his abuser.

I was my own person, with my own interests, pain, loves, and life experience and not just a shell on which to dump all of his hopes and fears. To him I served only as a vehicle with which to understand his own painful experiences. But that's *exactly* what abusers to do children, or their wives, or their husbands, to revisit their pain upon someone else, feeling motivated and justified by our feelings seek relief from them not by confronting our pain but by acting on it. When this relationship ended I did not behave admirably either, engaging in harassment after he ghosted on me with no explanation for his disengagement or closure for our relationship, and my own inability to confront the trauma of my own past experiences consumed me in turn. I would certainly have been a poor parent if I'd had the occasion to be a father when I was young, because I did not possess any of the tools which are required to deal with life, let alone the complicated dynamics and responsibilities of parenthood. Like the oxygen mask allegory I made earlier in this book, we are often expected to perform as if we are already successful in the role of parenting despite having never been taught how to do it nor empowered with the skills which are most effective, in addition to dealing with tremendous burdens of trauma, abuse, neglect, disappointment, and frustration. Pouring all of this into the sexual education of our children, you can see why so many parents utterly fail.

Because religious institutions do not educate people about how their bodies work or how to deal with problems of a sexual nature other than imploring for divine assistance, people with unresolved sexual shame or trauma or even those burdened by taboo sexual compulsions and potential to cause harm to others never actually find resolution, and instead the only relief from their stress is to project their pain, trauma, and insecurity onto the world around them, which unfortunately usually includes children or others vulnerable to abuse. We often view such evidence of such trauma incorrectly as the failure of some to control their sexuality, rather than the result of a cycle of pain and retribution which passes from generation to generation because of ignorance, abuse, and an absence of compassion for our own weaknesses and shortcomings. Because of the work I did not only with inventory trauma therapy but also my health, wellness, and nutrition in resolving the underlying metabolic illnesses which make it difficult to deal with anger, disappointment, depression, anxiety, and other mental health issues the trauma of my past no longer affects me nor colors my perception of life. This in turn provides space for my brain to act from a place of calm, insight, compassion, and wisdom, for myself and in turn others, and these are also the tools required when teaching children about sex and their bodies. When issues of our past are sufficiently resolved, speech turns naturally helpful, compassionate, engaging, insightful, and effective without trying to be that way, and motivations are genuine and no longer in pretense since we gain access to our real feelings and no longer inhibited by a need to hide our pain, because we have cleared away all the wreckage, found forgiveness, and there is now space for compassion, love, meditation, and inspiration, which naturally leads to wisdom, or at least patience and self-compassion for when we make mistakes, empowering us to set healthy boundaries and have new experiences and learn new skills to effect our children in better ways and in turn empower them also to improve their own lives.

In working with adult survivors of childhood sexual abuse (or general abuse as well) I have seen a common theme emerge from those for whom it is still fresh and relevant or burdensome. Abusers always try (and often succeed) to convince us that we bear responsibility for our abuse. This manipulation in turn empowers an abuser to more easily commit abuse but also misleads their victim into accepting responsibility for something of which they bear none. Some people might believe that by having their door open at night they somehow participated in what was so clearly abuse by a parent or other adult, or that by not saying *no* when it occurred that they failed to prevent it, or that even by feeling pleasurable sexual feelings they are somehow in the wrong or complicit in the abuse. The later is often the most confusing because sexual activity can feel good even when it is abuse, which in turn confuses survivors about their role in the abuse. I often fantasized about older men as a teenager, and to me the thought of having a sexual encounter with one would have been incredible. If such abuse were to have happened to me, I might have thought that because I fantasized about it or maybe enjoyed parts of it that I was complicit and therefore as bad or as deviant as my abuser. This is not at all the reality surrounding abuse, however. Adults are adults because they possess the ability to care and provide for *themselves*. No matter how seemingly mature, children lack not only the means but also the experience, wisdom, and insight with which to provide for and protect themselves, including their emotional needs, and adults who are predators *specifically exploit this vulnerability for their own benefit*, and being unable to care for ourselves not just physically and materially but also intellectually and emotionally, abusers often succeed in convincing us it is our fault they abused us.

Children are incapable of giving consent, because they do not have any autonomy to do so. That is why consent is so important but also so special when adults play together sexually, because the act of giving oneself freely to the encounter, of willfully offering oneself to such vulnerability and not compelled or coerced into it is what engenders intimacy between adults, or conversely causes pain and trauma in those who do not or cannot give consent. When I was a brand new young man older men exploited my ignorance and naivety to take advantage of me, but because I was no longer officially a child it wasn't considered criminal abuse—but it was still abuse, and I was still traumatized by their behavior and thought I had borne responsibility because I let them get me drunk or failed to more forcefully communicate *no*. Newly grown children are still psychologically children, having never actually lived in an adult body we have not yet gained the wisdom and insight to effectively care for and protect ourselves (which is also why we suck at parenting or why moving into a dorm can be so fractious as we expect the world to continue indulging our self-importance). Sometimes abusers convincing us of our complicity is not even overt—an abusive parent who sex-shames us and expends much time and emotion surrounding sex behavior implies that we are naturally deviant and as such deserving of abuse, punishment, and harassment, but not love, when in fact we are not in the slightest bit culpable and no one but the parent responsible. But as we transition from childhood to adulthood our mistakes are entirely our own, and this includes our ability to abuse those as vulnerable and helpless as we once were, since we are, in reality, no longer helpless, even if we feel helpless. But we nonetheless carry our shame, regret, pain, and trauma into adulthood and this includes the maleficent harm committed upon us as children, our natural curiosity and interest in the human body exploited by opportunistic and self-hating adults seeking salvation from their own emotional maelstrom.

There is nothing we could have done as children to protect ourselves from those who were supposed to be our protectors. The only reason we believe we should have is because adults manipulate us to have greater control and to excuse themselves of the responsibility and consequences of their behavior and condition us to accept abuse. Helplessness is the very point of childhood—it is intended by nature to facilitate development, learning, and growth, but which also causes us to be vulnerable to such unfortunate intersections in life. We do not decide for nor facilitate that vulnerability, and when making inventories about such trauma it is very helpful to recognize this in the relevant entries which can in turn fully relieve us carrying those burdens. Abuse is always something that happens *to* us, and never something we chose. Parents are supposed to protect, but often can't, or make mistakes, or are in fact our very tormentors. It's a harsh reality of life but it also does not condemn our fate as an adult, and though our childhood experience may mislead us to believe otherwise life is actually full of joy, happiness, and peace. When we are grown the continued suffering of abuse from the past occurs only because we either have not yet learned the tools by which we can excise the past or we are unwilling to do so. Often, knowing only one reality we are loathe to move on, even if we know we can or should, because what we know is more comfortable that the unknown, even when feeling unworthy of love and peace or frightened of letting go for the absence of control it might appear, pretending we are as helpless as we were as children even though that is no longer the case, because the world seems a frightening and uncontrollable place, but which is exactly how our own abusers felt when they acted on those feelings and committed the abuse in the first place, the endless cycle of parents and adults harming their children who go on to become traumatized adults who harm their children and so on and so on and so on.

But moving on is not something into which we can will ourselves—no amount of discipline or dedication or determination can do what must be done through purposeful practice, making time and sitting down to do inventory therapy, and making an entry on every single thing we can possible think until it is "done," to care for ourselves through action and through this learn compassion for ourselves. Facing the past, accepting that our helplessness was not something that caused us harm, that it is okay that we have happened upon pain and heartache, and that we are valuable as a person not in spite of our experiences but for the intrinsic value inherent of life. Bad things happen to us that we might know fully what it means to be alive, the full breadth of experience from which our soul can experience both love and pain, a meaning which would be very small indeed if, as Dory says in the Disney film, *Finding Nemo*, nothing ever happened to us. Sadly trauma is much more horrible than what is portrayed in Disney films, and in truth real atrocities occur in the world at a regular clip. But our ability to protect our children from such horrors comes not from promoting ignorance nor a firm grip, but instead empowering them with tools which can save them from a lifetime of pain and trauma when bad things do happen to them too, tools we can teach them by first learning ourselves.

The way conservative, prudish, or authoritarian people consider sex is a perverted desecration of a sacred and special part of human nature. While they may use words like *sacred* to describe their behavior, in that context it really means shame, and sex is usually considered embarrassing, or bad. How could something sacred be embarrassing? How could something special be bad? And yet they are often unable to handle sex not only in their own lives but also the sexual nature of others. Once when I was very grown, at the age of 41 and had many past boyfriends and even a fiancé whom my mother met I was one day regaling her with an extremely tame and censored version of a romantic affair I'd had with the extremely hot son of an extremely hot and famous film and TV actor from her generation. I didn't tell her how he would come over to my apartment and we would suck each other off. Or how I didn't even know his name until several years after our liaisons. I only told her that I had a love affair with a young man I should have married, but didn't think about it at the time because we only just hooked up. She completely checked out of the conversation and told me she didn't want to hear about it, further castrating our already difficult and distant relationship.

Even though I was a freewheeling gay boy I still settled into a relationship with someone with whom I had been formally dating, and predictably it imploded spectacularly with him cheating and relapsing into a cocaine addiction. If instead of him I had dated one of the several boys I met regularly just for hot, fun sex we would likely be married and happy because there was never any dishonesty, and only the residue of prudishness impeded the potential for a relationship based on sex, which is the entire point of a romantic relationship (or should be). Misunderstanding what sex is, the ideology of sexual purity pervades religious groups whom are then ironically obsessed with the carnal act of physical penetration but completely naive to its true spiritual purpose since they never get to experience it. Many religious adherents wait until after marriage because they want to save themselves, thinking that doing so will make sex special (i.e., having been told). But then we enter into such relationships and after the novelty of sex wears off find ourselves emotionally abandoned by our partner, lonely, and resenting them and our imprisonment. Having never known what sex really is we wrongly understand issues with sex to mean things like sexual preferences, tastes, or physical compatibility. In reality sex is not a performance or collection of sexual preferences but a deeply thrilling connection of souls through the act of giving ourselves utterly and without reservation. Choosing to be so vulnerable with others and willingly exposing ourselves to potential hurt is so intensely frightening most of us erect emotional walls to prevent even our marriage partners from ever really getting to know us, so the mind wanders and erections subside and satisfaction becomes elusive. Because sexual dissatisfaction in a relationship comes not from a lack of physical compatibility but an absence of emotional vulernability, religious people don't know this until many years into a relationship, thinking of sex in mundane, carnal, inane terms of penetration, ejaculation, and copulation and never consider what can be accessed through the act of sex, a spiritual experience which transcends the physical world which cannot be replicated in a restaurant or movie theater (well, I mean it can but you're probably not that adventurous). When two persons are so enamoured with each other they are willing to strip off not just their clothes but also their emotional armor it does not matter what positions or techniques are used, the mere touch of a loved one is enough to fulfill a thousand lifetimes.

But after you've married and gotten past the novelty of sex and squeezed out several children to find that either we or our partner is unable to bond during sex is suddenly not worth any of that abstinence, and many adults realize only late in life the silly mistakes made in youth from the idealization of sex and compliance with institutional and authoritarian ideology. Relationships which become stale and require sexual adventure are in truth a boredom of emotional loneliness, one or both partners unwilling to share their true selves with the other and thus requiring other stimulants to generate satisfaction. Finding someone who is compatible in such a deep and meaningful way cannot be done by simply holding hands and gazing into each other's eyes during dinner dates. It requires fucking. Hard, fun, satisfying exploration of each other's bodies, and is precisely why so many marriages end in misery, resentment, and animosity, because these truths and walls, especially for those who are prudish and naive, are not discovered until *after* sexual intimacy. If that does not occur until after entering into marriage it's just that much harder to find fulfillment and compatibility, and many of us spend nearly the entirety of our lives trapped in a partnership with someone we don't even know, and probably even despise.

What religious, prudish, and self-hating people often don't understand is that rewarding sexual intimacy can occur even from casual sex or one-night-stands if all parties involved are honest and behave with care for one another and appreciation for what is being offered (and are not also burdened by self-hatred and sex shame), nor that sex in a committed relationship bounded by morals and ideology can, and often is, disturbing and shameful for abuse, control, manipulation, and callous disregard for one's partner. The institution of marriage itself is benign. It imparts no qualities to a commitment simply by its nature. The ideology and dogma that accompanies religious marriage is in truth meant to control people and strengthen their convictions toward theocratic institutions than provide a stable framework from which to grow a family or relationship, which instead comes from the emotional skillsets of participating adults and whether there is any unresolved trauma. Most of us mete out our past trauma and disappointment onto our partners within the confines of a relationship, reenacting the very dynamics responsible for our torment and frustration as children in a futile effort to exorcise it from our soul at the expense of others (usually our spouse and children). It is no wonder marriages fail, when mostly they serve as a vessel for acting out fears and controlling insecurity. Of course, responsible sexual behavior is paramount to a fulfilling sex life, but such behavior must come from a personal desire to care for our own wellbeing, not adherence to an institution. The act of waiting until after marriage to engage in sex is demonstrably without compassion for ourselves, denying ourselves the opportunity to learn, grow, and provide for ourselves a satisfying, safe, and productive relationship simply to pacify authoritarian control freaks and the power of the group. Often we lack the skills required to care for our needs in the first place, especially when it comes to sex, and so feel powerless to make choices, or even to know what to do. This is where inventory therapy can help tremendously, by clarifying our needs and what needs or wants we have adopted at the behest of others or institutions who may or may not actually be concerned with our personal wellbeing.

Oppositely, the freewheeling and careless exploitation of others for sexual gratification or control is equally disturbing and harmful and originates also from the same sense of insecurity and desire for control every bit as those pathologically adhered to theology. Just because we want something does not mean it's okay to get it at any cost. There is also no need to be dishonest or opportunistic anyway. Many men (and women) do not realize that women are every bit as horny and desirous for sex as men stereotypically are, and that wanting to fuck someone just for the fun of it is not carnal nor shameful but fun and exciting if everyone involved willingly gives themselves to the experience. Because of these misconceptions which are often established in childhood by fearful and hypocritical adults we can grow up without tools to responsibly and effectively get sexual intimacy, so men grow up to be liars thinking we must trick women into bed, or women think we must hide behind the pretense of commitment and marriage to get that vitamin D inside us. Dishonesty not only destroys relationships, it also prevents us from actually getting what we want, which is to be touched by someone as if it means everything to them, and there is nothing wrong with wanting or getting that. Inventorying attitudes and experiences with sex, from childhood to adulthood, consensual or not, wholesome or wrong can help us come to terms with human sexuality, and in the future we will be more effective, confident, and fulfilled.

Having healthy attitudes about sex is absolutely necessary to empower our children and protect them from abuse, exploitation, and codependent relationships. Unfortunately, heartache is never something we can guard against, but healthy attitudes about sex can empower ourselves and our children to deal with rejection in healthy and productive ways. But this is impossible to do if we have not first addressed our own trauma, frustration, shame, and disappointing experiences with sex. We only experience trouble in handling this tricky stage of development in our children when we lack compassion for our own experiences, insecurities, and weaknesses with sex and our bodies. Finding compassion for ourselves by practicing self-care through inventory therapy can empower us with the skills and confidence to successfully handle such personal and parenting challenges and pass those skill to our own children who can then do the same for themselves.

23

Friendship, Bullying, and Other Social Challenges

I cried the first day of school nearly every year of my childhood. Because I was a little bed-wetting gay boy loathed by his father, who hated sports (or so I was told) and construction and interpersonal conflict and was afraid of most everyone it just seemed a natural thing for a wimpy boy to do.

My fourth-grade year I had made some wonderful friends, one of whom was the first to teach me to draw cartoons, but my parents yet again uprooted us and set off for an entirely new locale, this time the burgeoning metropolis of Salt Lake City. There was little more than a month remaining till the end of the school year and, traumatized by the instability and losing my friends, I was nearly motionless my first day of class and did my best to keep my tears hidden from my classmates. But being the newest thing at the end of a long school year proved irresistible to bored and restless fourth-graders and before the day was out I got a note from two pretty girls asking if I wanted to walk home with them.

"Check no!" whispered one of the boys who had congregated around me. "They'll pull you into their house on the way home *and have sex with you!*"

This was an especially horrifying thought for a gay eleven-year-old. I imagined the two girls cornering me against a wall and forcibly removing my clothes as their wet, shiny mouths pressed aggressively against mine, their hands groping my penis. Then I imagined them assaulting the handsome boy eager to assist me and found the fantasy much more tasteful. Everyone involved seemed overly dramatic, so I was intensely grateful the next day when a more calm and collected boy near me in class struck up a conversation, whom later outright asked if I would be his friend.

We hung out a few times that summer, but it was really after the next full school year that we became inseparable, roaming the neighborhood almost daily, visiting the local convenience store, playing *Nintendo* at my house or *Sega* at his, having sleepovers, watching his mom make her giant vat of homemade marinara sauce, and discovering a copy of *The Joy Of Sex* in his parent's basement. The safety and support of his companionship also helped me during this time to venture into other precarious relationships of early adolescence as I grew and matured, until that day that my unreliable parents yet again uprooted our family and hauled us off to yet another new and unfamiliar town.

One day in sixth grade I was walking along the pavement over hopscotch and tetherball courts near the grass field of our school's playground, watching a horde of boys playing touch football, secretly wishing I could join them. It had not occurred to me that I was a head taller than every one of them and appeared outwardly every bit as able to join such a group. I had only been at this school less than a year, and while I had made a few friends I had not yet learned how to be a friend, and in my mind I was an outsider, different than those balling boys who seemed to show no fear of each other.

"Hey, wanna play?" said one of the boys as a group of them slowed when they noticed me standing on the sidelines. My heart jumped into my throat. Too frightened and excited to say anything, I nodded and walked onto the field. Someone had not only seen me, they regarded me as a potential peer. I couldn't believe my luck! They pointed out my team and I stood to the side, sure that none of them would throw the ball to me. In fact that would be preferable, as I could quietly integrate myself just being near them.

The ball was snapped. I ran to the side of the defense, feeling the freedom of the wind across my skin, running among my peers. I was part of them at last. I could pretend to fit in.

But again I underestimated my presence. The quarterback saw me unguarded on the field. He threw the ball. In my direction. I stopped in my tracks. Only at that moment did I realize I had no idea how to play football. I had been in T-ball as a young child and played baseball for a year until my parents birthed too many children to support me in individual activities. When I was ten I begged my mother to let me play soccer after seeing a group of boys running down the field under the summer sunshine kicking a ball. She relented, but not two weeks into the season I broke my arm falling from the monkey bars. My Dad loved basketball and had taught me how to shoot hoops, and though football often appeared on our television I think my Dad perhaps never considered that a wispy, effeminate boy such as myself would ever set foot on a field.

I caught the ball. It was only around the age of thirty that I realized I had actually spent the better part of my life an athlete, not only competitive but also talented. I had always listened to the despairing voices which told me otherwise, and that just because I didn't like basketball didn't mean I wasn't athletic. But there on the field the fact that I had no problem catching a football was entirely lost on me, too frightened trying to figure out what to do next. I had seen people run with the ball after catching it. I decided to run.

I made it quite a distance before a few boys sprinted to cut me off. No one objected to my decision, so I must have been doing it right. But the opposing team drew nearer and nearer. I began to panic. What was I supposed to do next? Afraid that I would get tagged and fail, I threw the ball.

The boys stopped, staring in disbelief. I had messed up. Having no idea how the world worked I assumed they were angry at me. "You can't throw the ball once you've caught it," said one of the boys. He wasn't mad, it was a kind gesture, but I could not hear it. I had also never learned to ask for help, or admit that I didn't know something. I could have said "I don't really know how to play, can you teach me?" They wouldn't have hesitated to be my friend. But I was so overcome by fear and embarrassment it was impossible to see. I ran off the field. No doubt those boys were very confused by my behavior. Here they saw a tall, capable boy who had every reason to participate. They had no idea the tumult of confusion and uncertainty which tore at my insides. I could have made a host of new friends and been an active participant in life and the world around me. But it was not to be.

Though it had been demonstrated to me by boys and girls such as he that friendship can be established as simply as asking someone to be my friend it was never a lesson that sank in very deeply, because of my dissociative and guarded personality, and throughout my entire life until my middle-thirties I always waited for other people to ask me to be their friend instead of doing it myself. When I was new to Los Angeles I ventured once to a bar alone in the daytime to see if I could attract any attention. Because I have always been tall and handsome I have never had trouble drawing people to me. Unaware of why this occurred I more often attracted romantic rather than plutonic friendship, and wasn't even able to recognize the presence of a potentially good friend when they were right next to me. At the bar in Los Angeles, also wearing a ridiculous leather cowboy hat I had brought with me from Utah, I was approached by a devastatingly handsome, tall boy named Andrew who wasted no time in making my acquaintance. He asked me out but from the beginning of our association it felt plutonic. Further confusing me he cuddled up close while we rewatched *X-Men* cartoons from the early nineties for which we discovered a shared appreciation, but turned away when I moved in to kiss him. I did not yet know that friends could share intimate contact, nor that failed romances could make excellent friendships, and misunderstanding the situation as a romantic loss I left that relationship behind. Andrew went on to become one of the most revered people in West Hollywood because of his integrity, kindness, and joy that he brought everywhere with him, and was exactly the kind of person I longed to have as a friend, and the two of us, young and lost in that big city could have been the kind of inseparable friendship I so desperately needed.

I did make some good friends for several years in Los Angeles, and we got into a lot of fun such as making an entire day out of a concert outing complete with picnics and wine or dressing up in themed costume for disco nights and holidays. One Halloween I dressed as a steampunk aviator with bronze pained aviator goggles, art deco wings, and a bronze painted nerf gun and holster complete with striped pants and brown leather boots with white buckled spats and little bronze wings on each ankle like a steampunk Mercury. Of course it was a shirtless costume, though, and my friends and I went on a 'liquor-treat' tour of West Hollywood going from house to house imbibing far more than what is responsible.

Toward the middle of the night at one apartment which either lacked furniture or had moved it to make room for the thirty or forty guests gaily chattering and parading in Hollywood quality Halloween designs (it was gay Hollywood, after all), I was talking to some new people when suddenly an anonymous assailant snuck up behind me and nonconsensually grabbed my ass. This kind of thing happened occasionally in West Hollywood and other places, but he was also probably drunk and uncoordinated and his hands went fully up my butt crack, startling me more than would normally be the case. It just so happened I was standing with all my weight on just one leg—the one injured during ninth-grade basketball tryouts so many years ago, and when I jerked around at the assault my kneecap popped right off, inactivating my leg as if it were powered by a battery which suddenly run out of power, and my leg fully gave out, sending me straight to the ground like one enormous, drunk rag doll.

It also happened that I was standing next to a folding table holding all the red cups, liquor, and a giant chocolate fountain (not all gays have taste), and my giant, six-foot seven-inches and two-hundred thirty pounds crashed into on my way down, sending most of the cups flying and some of the liquor bottles tumbling in a great ruckus. Luckily the chocolate fountain and folding table were far sturdier than they appeared, although my friends later said they saw the fountain go straight up several inches and come right back down into place and only splashed a little chocolate, but my fall drew the attention of everyone gathered whom I'm sure all assumed me to just be enormously drunk and not suddenly and inexplicably crippled. The face of the boy who had molested me was completely white with shock, wondering just how in the hell the target of his lust had literally crashed to the ground in front of him like a pile of bricks just from a single touch.

My friends immediately gathered around and attempted to hoist me up, but my kneecap was still out of place, so I had to push them off and exclaim that no, I wasn't actually drunk and embarrassing, it was an old sports injury that had suddenly imperiled my ability to stay upright. My kneecap had dislocated a few times since the injury, so I wasn't entirely surprised by it, but this time I had to push it back in place which was not very pleasant, and sat for a while in my steampunk Mercury costume hoping the throbbing pain would stop and that I wouldn't have ruined everyone's night. It didn't get better, and though it was only around midnight, hardly close to the end of the night, my friends took me home and against my protestations stayed with me instead of going back out to finish the night, like good friends do. While I had some years of dear friendships the instability of my youth and paucity of interpersonal skills for the making and sustaining of friends I couldn't even recognize a true friendship when it was cuddled up next to me or sacrificing their own comforts or desires to be a friend. Though they may not understand or appreciate it, those who have grown up in the same place all their lives and have people who've known them since childhood are the luckiest of people on Earth. There really is nothing in life but our connections to one another. Most of us think the point of going to work is to be productive and to make money, but the only purpose of work is an excuse to be around and engage with other human beings. Earning money and being productive is just part of the illusion. Of course, many people use their professions as a way to control their environment and the people in it, but that is still just using work as an excuse to be with other humans. Having such connections from the very spring of life thus makes such people rich in every way that matters, and if we are burdened by trauma which makes us resent coworkers, working, responsibility, failure, judgment, rejection, authority, or powerlessness we can instead misunderstand the point of career and work, misuse our authority or resent coworkers and bosses and miss out on opportunities for friendship and connection or get into situations which imperil our wellbeing.

The reality is that life often takes us away from those whom we love and who love us, so to adequately prepare children (and ourselves) to succeed in life is to truly understand that we need friends and learn how to make and sustain friendships. I never understood that it was within my power to establish friendships. Because of the particular way in which I was raised, wherein my parents demonstrated by example that other people are to be surveilled, judged, and mistrusted I never even considered that I could reach out and just ask someone to be my friend. Then my life experience of finding success by waiting for friends to approach me further solidified this misconception of life. I once saw a random text on Twitter by a person bemoaning the withdrawal of their friends, and offered some advice about it being okay and that new ones would come along, and that I too had found it difficult to secure friends throughout my life. They promptly informed me they were fourteen and not to ever talk to them again, completely unaware of the irony of their behavior.

Familiarity begets friendship, a simple truth I did not understand until after four decades of life, especially since my entire childhood was characterized by moving from home to home and hardly spending more than several years in any one place never had the opportunity to experience this reality. Because I also did not understand the value of friendships nor our collective need for one another, and because attracting superficial friends was ridiculously easy, I also did not value friendships nor make myself emotionally available to those who wished to be involved in my life. Through my insecurity I also wasted much time and energy as an adult on friendships of convenience and power dynamics, choosing people who found me physically attractive for the apparent security it seemed to imply, but which in turn opened me up to be preyed upon by predatory and opportunistic individuals. But friendship firstly and most importantly *requires* vulnerability. It is why my best friend in fourth, fifth, and sixth grade was precious to me, because *he* felt no hesitation in sharing his vulnerability with me. Eventually our friendship weakened, though, because I did not offer the same kind of vulnerability in return.

Most higher order of animals on this planet require friends in order to survive. Lions coalesce into small but strong groups of tightly bonded friendships. Horses, giraffe, elephants, gorillas, and even sharks have friendships. While the bonds of friendship are deeply emotional and altruistic, the applicable relevance of friendship to survival is not. Friendship is an evolutionary necessity which promotes the success of groups of animals. Without friendship, animals (including humans) are far less likely to flourish and much more vulnerable to expiration. This is why even insufferable and evil people have friendships, because it is a requirement demanded by our biology and position in life and not because it's a luxury which can be taken for granted. Lacking friends directly destabilizes a person's position in human society. It imperils access to opportunity and to resources, potential mates, employment, education, and the development of valuable interpersonal skills. Part of the reason my parents moved so often was a subconscious desire to purposefully castrate their children's social development, to remove outside social support and access to other sources of emotional connection to thus engineer our increased interdependence on them. But in reality all children grow, and the damage done by interfering with this crucial aspect of human development caused their children to be ineffective in personal relationships and to waste much time as adults making and learning from unnecessary mistakes.

In practice, making friends requires demonstration of qualities which sustain friendships. Many children are lucky enough to have access to a breadth of adult influence from which they can observe such qualities and thence adopt or experiment with, and friendship is actually more common in the world than otherwise. But parents are often an active barrier to a child's ability to find and establish good friendships because of the parent-child dynamic and mistaken ideas about social dynamics. In Junior High School I was still extremely shy, but being very tall caused me to stand out and be noticed by everyone, which included potential bullies. Once in Geography class I had apparently zoned out, and two enormous boys on the football team threw a broken piece of pencil at me. When it hit me in the face it was startling, but I looked up to see them laughing. There are several options for how a person can respond in this kind of a situation—Most parents might prepare their child for such interactions by warning them against bullies, by instructing them to inform teachers or other authority figures, or to ignore them or even maybe to fight back. My height had made me very naive to the kind of harassment which other children can experience, although I was subjected to some, and my general nature as a child was by default to think well of and like anyone until they gave me a real reason not to. Looking up and seeing these handsome and athletic boys actually paying attention to me made me instinctively smile and genuinely laugh. My reaction actually endeared them to me, because I did not actually recognize it as an act of bullying and thus did not provide them with the annoyed or fearful response which would in turn have made them feel powerful, and as such they too laughed and turned their attention to someone else in the class.

A bully is just someone who wants love and attention but is aggressive in how they try to find it. Homophobic boys and girls who harass those of us who are LGBTQI+ are very deeply touched by the idea of sharing such intimacy with someone of their same gender, because this need for such desperately close bonds with our friends and brothers goes unfulfilled in a society which artificially destroys true human nature in favor of sterile and guarded distance from others, usually made worse or established in the first place by the absence of emotional intimacy with their own family members, especially parents. Realizing they can never have what we do they strike out in jealously. Most bullying is, however, simply testing others within their environment to find out whom among them can be the kinds of friends they are searching for—those who are fun, strong, confident enough to take teasing as the demonstration of affection that it actually is, who aren't so serious and as such will become faster and more intimate friends in opposition to those whom are less emotionally available, scared, and uptight. Of course, it can get out of hand and there are other dynamics of self-worth and abuse which also play out through such relationships, but at its heart the vulnerability of friendship also requires the ability to let others tease and cajole us which in turn demonstrates commitment and dedication to the other, by permitting a degree of antagonism at the expense of ourselves. It is an offering to the friendship, a sacrifice, a demonstration of our commitment to the other by enduring ridicule and discomfort. Those who take themselves too seriously to allow friendship in are then discarded, because they are not willing nor emotionally available for the depths of intimacy which such a friendship requires, and not in spite of but because they are better behaved, ironically find themselves more often alone and friendless.

When I was fifteen my mother kindly gifted me a week at summer camp for art students at our local University. It was a stayover camp in which we slept in the dorms on campus, and as art had been an important part of my young life I was thrilled to be going. But having no skills required to make friends (of which I was unaware) I was also extremely nervous, especially since my past experiences at scout camp had been so demoralizing. Spending all day learning art and creating was amazing, but I also somehow ended up without a roommate, and felt extremely lonely and unable to approach any of the other camp-mates. After several nights I felt so alone and sad I didn't even go down to dinner and instead ate a bag of Skittles alone in my room, choosing painful hunger over the stress of being alone in a group.

Even when I was an older teenager and had many experiences to easily make friends it never materialized because I never had occasion to learn how. When I was elected to student council we went to a summer training day camp with the student councils of other schools and a group of kids with whom I was paired took such a liking to me they started calling me by a nickname (it was "Chief"). Another potential friend at a religious camp took to calling me Kareem (because I was so tall). It would have been so easy to get their numbers and probably make some real friends for the first time in my life, but not even that option crossed my mind and I would, sadly, spend my entire adult life waiting for people to come to me instead of proactively forming my own relationships. If my parents had been able to teach me to make and sustain friendships my life would not have been so desperately lonely, but they likewise lacked those skills and also had no friends (as do none of their siblings), especially since they rely on spouses and religious affiliations to artificially substitute the function normally filled through real friendships.

Likewise and perhaps more important than being emotionally available for friendship is the ability to sustain them. Because teasing is so often a part of friendship this also results in many harms or offenses which can potentially impair a relationship, in addition to the simple tendency for human beings to make mistakes. When I was a teenager I was best friends with a boy who was also an artist and I thought we had much in common—but when our interests began to diverge and I grew increasingly self-aware of my homosexuality I began to feel danger with my friend whom I did not for one second believe would love me if I came out to him (I also demonstrated homophobic behavior myself in a misguided attempt to distract people from my own—which also goes to show that bullying, especially of this variety, originates from such insecurities, and anti-gay bullies are in large part nearly always also homosexual). During a summer camp this friend discussed a girl whom had affections for me for whom I did not reciprocate (since, you know, I was gay). He characterized her in a way which objectified her as a possession, and it infuriated me. It was the last straw in the disparity between what I wanted for my life and what our friendship was offering, so I ended it. Normally when friendships are challenged by such interpersonal conflict they can be remedied by communication, the resolution of conflict, and the amending of wrongs. But this particular friend was the son of some interesting and controlling adults whom then took to discussing our friendship in not-so-subtle allegories during church lessons. They then called my parents to discuss our relationship and to force me to make amends. Thankfully, my parents recognized that the relationship was my responsibility and did not get involved. But because this power-dynamic removed his autonomy within the friendship and ability to demonstrate his commitment to our relationship by voluntarily engaging in communication and resolution of our problems it effectively ended any possible reconciliation. If instead my friend had come to me and said that our friendship meant everything to him and wanted to understand why I was angry I would have exploded into confession about my sexuality and fear and anger over being unable to tell him. But neither of us got that opportunity because of his parent's insistence on intervening in matters which had nothing to do with them. Several years later his father was arrested and jailed for sexual assault of female colleagues, which put my friend's malign opinion of women in a different light, but also more clearly illuminated why the end of our friendship unfolded as it had, since neither of us had parents who were capable of demonstrating healthy interpersonal relationship skills and effective conflict resolution.

Sometimes it seems that maintaining friendships is difficult or impossible, and that even when options for friendships are plentiful our success in them is not. But in truth, any friendship can be maintained forever through use of the simple words *"I'm sorry."* Using these words is not always so simple for people, however, which is why they are so infrequently used. Too often the use of these words is mistaken as forfeiting power within a relationship. In reality, it secures power by communicating to our friends how much they actually mean to us, that we are willing even to lay down our ego if it means keeping them in our lives. *I'm sorry* must always be genuine and unsolicited, however. During an argument with a family member over their inappropriate preoccupation and harassment about my personal finances and career choices in which they hurled insults and personal attacks they eventually screamed "I'm sorry" at me, which is exactly the kind of example how not to use it. "I'm sorry" is a tool by which we can repair damage we have done to our relationships. If the intent is not to repair the damage but instead to save face and insist on positions which cause harm to our friends and relatives it is instead a weapon to control and coerce, which always serves to undermine, destabilize, or even destroy bonds of intimacy. But there is almost nothing that cannot be amended in relationships. Most people love each other so much that even egregious wrongs can be forgiven, and only require our willingness to demonstrate commitment to the relationship by employing the use of these words properly and without manipulation. An ex of mine effectively employed the effusive use of flowers, cards, and words to maintain our relationship whenever he did something wrong (which was often egregious), but he never actually said that he was sorry for what he did, nor that he would never do it again. Typically the apology was oriented toward me finding out or having a problem with what he did, but because I was so desperately in love with him and burdened by intense insecurities I found it impossible to extract myself from the relationship though it was obviously bad for me. But while his actions served to distract me from the problems in our relationship, his apologies still only served to undermine it in the long-term because there was never a genuine interest or ability on his part to actually repair the damage he caused, which is the real point of apology, and eventually we devolved into a state of toxic resentment and the relationship predictably dissolved. Friendships are no different than romantic relationships. If we do not understand how to sustain and demonstrate healthy interpersonal relationship skills like the employment of *I'm sorry* and an ability to open ourselves up to vulnerability, our children also will not learn how to establish truly healthy friendships which can empower and protect them throughout their own lives.

 Toward the end of High School I one day found myself somehow hanging out with a group of popular girls whom I had long envied and admired. These girls weren't stereotypical popular, bratty cheerleaders. At our school the popular girls were mostly members of the soccer team or other athletics and actually pretty great people. Most of them were charismatic and fun and absolutely beautiful and I had long watched them from a distance, secretly desiring to be just like them but never considering I could actually be friends with them. I still don't remember exactly why I was there that day, and even though I was the only boy and clearly welcomed I didn't understand that I could have just continued those connections and built on that catalyst to achieve the kinds of friendships I always wanted, and that day simply passed into oblivion though opportunity was again right in front of me.

 Parents tend to either obsessively monitor and manage their children's friendships, involving themselves inappropriately in their child's personal issues and relationships or to detach themselves altogether from the process, leaving it up to the child to navigate the complexities of interpersonal relationships while also having no experience or insight for doing so. The only time my parents ever inquired about my friendships was when I fell apart at being denied the opportunity to finish a present for my best friend and my mother asked if the reason I was upset was because I was *attracted* to him. Even if I was, which by the way would have been perfectly fine (I wasn't, just FYI), their simultaneous manipulative control and absence from my personal relationships was debilitating toward my effectiveness in maintaining relationships both as a child and as an adult, having never been taught how to maintain healthy relationships, since they too had no such skills to teach me and were similarly failed by their own parents, so on and so on. Every time we moved my parents never brought up or discussed friends, except for the unreasonable standards of bigotry and conservatism by which they expected us to choose them. In reality, children need parents to be involved in their friendships and relationships but in ways which empower a child and not those which control them. If at any time my parents had asked me as a child if I was finding fulfillment through my friendships, able to make friends with those whom I wanted to be friends or felt included and loved by those with whom I was involved they may have been able to help me overcome the insecurities which prevented me from establishing the kinds of friendships I desired instead of those which were convenient and saved myself a great deal of insecurity and heartache. I, like many children, was not aware that everyone wanted friends as badly as I did (at least, as children) and often felt as insecure about friendships and exposing oneself to vulnerability. Talking to children about their friendship ambitions, failures, and fulfillment, what they desire to gain from such relationships, how they can contribute to them, and what kinds of people they desire to associate with and why can help to empower a child with the wisdom we have gained through our own life experience (which is the fucking point of parenthood). Of course, if we also find friendships difficult it would be helpful for us to also evaluate our position, opinion, and successes and failures in friendship and our own needs and desires and mistakes that we may in turn be better empowered to help our children. But we do not need to have experienced success to effectively empower children. Relating our own mistakes and disappointments (where appropriate) in the very least can help children to understand that we all go through such things and that they are not alone in their experience, thus lessening their stress and instincts to control and manipulate or otherwise act on insecurities and in turn more likely to experience success in friendship.

Many of the coping mechanisms we develop in childhood to navigate relationships are actually used later to inform other humans how we expect to be treated. Just as learning experiences for children are unconscious and involve psychological processes of which we are neither aware nor in control, when we present ourselves to the world, to friends, acquaintances, and strangers we actively but unconsciously instruct them how to treat us, and those people in turn also respond unconsciously to the cues, signals, tone, and body language which are instinctually read and demonstrated to facilitate human interactions one with another. One of the most obvious examples of how this functions is with those who are shy. Shyness is an overt communication of our opinion of ourselves and other people, with those who are shy feeling that they are less powerful than other human beings, perhaps less worthy of attention and affection, and as such the world treats us who are shy exactly the way we want to be treated, to be ignored, alone, and forgotten. Of course, we probably do not consciously want to be alone, and probably long more than anything to be loved and included. But our past experiences have taught us that we can be hurt by other people, and we protect ourselves from that hurt or embarrassment by becoming shy. Then, after practicing this behavior for many years find it nearly impossible to extract ourselves from this identity or to adopt behaviors which are more confident and extroverted which may instead win us the affection and belonging we desire. Of course, there is nothing wrong with being shy or an introvert (I myself am extremely introverted), but it does communicate to other people how we expect to be treated, and others will treat us as such, just as is every other human identity. Oppositely, those who are arrogant or confident may project outgoing and aggressive behaviors which in turn communicate to others how they expect to be treated, and we in turn respond to our psychological programming and treat them as such. This unconscious aspect of human behavior can even get us in trouble—for instance whenever we ruminate over how to phrase something we want to bring up with a loved one or friend and end up causing the very conflict we wished to avoid, because we can never actually subvert the subconscious, and our intent and attitude is conveyed by unconscious signals of tone, body language, and demeanor which directly inform the other person regardless of our chosen words. Because these coping mechanisms are formed in childhood they become an engrained and inextricable part of our identities, and cannot be understood nor resolved without significant internal retrospection and self-evaluation. But in so doing we not only begin to understand how we affect our environment, we also empower ourselves as parents to avoid burdening our children with unconscious behaviors developed in response to abuse and neglect which in turn cause them more difficulty navigating life outside our families and into adulthood.

Children begin life with natural inclinations toward friendship, not because of any cultural or social factors but because it is an evolutionary, biological survival strategy characteristic of all human beings which naturally strengthens our chances of survival as social mammals. This natural talent for making friends only becomes corrupted as we grow up, when our life experience and trauma begin to accumulate and more visceral concepts of fear, and our natural inclinations toward helpfulness, unconditional love, and conception of equality become subverted by social and cultural traditions and coping and control mechanisms. If religion was truly useful for humanity it would naturally promote and empower our instincts for friendship rather than division, suspicion, and distrust. I am always horrified when socializing with people whom by default I assume to share commonality of purpose and brotherhood and potential for friendship, since you know, they are also other human beings, to be suddenly maneuvered against and suspected as *not one of them* as if I were actually an adversary simply because I do not belong to their religious institution and not because of anything I've done to demonstrate anything other than an interest in friendship. Human instinct by default is to regard others with inclusion, love, and companionship, which is why children are so naturally pure and full of love and desire for emotional integration, and then why those who become ostracized from bigoted communities largely and consistently move into agnosticism rather than other religions, instinctually recognizing how dogmatic ideological fear impairs the realization of connection with other human beings we all so desperately need. Religious leaders prognosticate about divinity even as they suffer the emotional and social isolation from the rest of humanity which their ideals engineer, telling others they can be happy in sharing their beliefs even as they foment in anger and hatred toward their fellow human beings, destroy their families, friendships, and other human relationships, further isolating themselves from the kind of emotional vulnerability and love which engenders friendship and thus satisfies our instinctual human needs for the safety of intimate bonds.

When this natural desire to be part of humanity becomes subverted by abuse it is then replaced by the adoption of the fears and insecurities of the adult, and humanity then begins to develop its most heinous potential in forces of racism, prejudice, and political conflict. In 2016 in the midst of the Presidential election a friend commented on a social media post of mine that he was voting for the disastrous conservative candidate. My friend was also homosexual, and I was so incensed by his position that I quickly blocked him in anger. I could not understand how someone could so callously vote against their own and others wellbeing. Not to mention all the little homosexual, transgender, and intersexual kids who would and were greatly harmed by such a man at the head of our country. It was and still is, to me, morally wrong. But the political opposition was also in disarray, unable to come to a satisfactory union surrounding any one particular candidate, and in the end settled for someone who was also the architect of a great many policies at the root of our current problems of inequality and unrest, who refused to extend compassion and access to the common man, the poor, and the oppressed. After several years under that administration I began to realize why people like my friend voted against their own interests in the first place—they were acting as agents of disruption, purposefully supporting someone who was inept and dangerous in order to force change since their usual party of choice would not do it actively (and in that sense were successful).

But often lost in such conflicts is an appreciation or understanding of the larger forces at work during such times. There is a cycle not only in the American election process but in all struggles for power and governance which repeats itself over and over and over and over through time ad nauseam. Opposing powers of ideology emerge in every society, no matter how broad or narrow the collective breadth. The conflict within Ireland during the last century is an excellent example of this, where people actually *killed* each other mostly because of which sect of Christianity to which they belonged. The whole conflict between Iran and Saudi Arabia literally originated from a conflict about which person should succeed leadership of the exact same religion to which they all belong, men who have been dead for over a thousand years (obviously there has been a great deal of aggression and retaliation over the centuries which complicate such struggles, and money is actually at the core of the conflict too, with idealogical differences conveniently used as divisions for such interests—but the point remains). It would be like if all the Mormons in Utah eventually started fighting with and killing fundamental Mormons who live on the Arizona/Utah border.

Or if a sect of Evangelicals began killing other Christian religions. They all literally believe in the very same religion, ideology, and way of life except for some very, very trivial differences, and yet it has exploded into an international, intergenerational, geopolitical drama (Middle-Eastern conflicts, not Mormons). This also brings up the point that if you remove descriptors and characters, Islam and Christianity are for all intents and purposes the very same religion, though their adherents relentlessly lock horns as if the Other is not entirely motivated by the same desires, fears, and beliefs as their supposed opponent. This is the reason why the Founders of the United States enshrined separation of Church and State in the Constitution—because people get petty as fuck, and will even kill each other if allowed to engage in such pedantry, for the psychological forces of the human mind which above all seeks self-preservation.

When I was in seventh grade and had only one friend, he and I decided one day to go to the arcade at the mall. We walked from our homes in the Avenues of Salt Lake City, Utah all the way to downtown. It was a warm summer day and not being allowed to play video games very often at home I was more than excited to spend a few hours away from my family having fun. But my joy was short lived as I walked into the arcade, suddenly surprised when a black boy several years older than I walked up and immediately got in my face and began threatening me. He spoke angrily and I couldn't even understand what he was saying since he was using heavy jargon and slang. My little white-boy country background had never encountered someone like this—I hadn't done anything, not even looked at him until he was invading my personal space, and I could not understand what I had done to solicit such an aggressive and unwarranted confrontation, most especially since he wasn't communicating in a way that I could understand.

My friend had lived in the city much longer than I, and when I looked to him with confusion and fear for my safety he simply said— "just say: '*it's cool man.*'" I didn't immediately follow, because I couldn't understand how such a little phrase could resolve such an intense situation. The boy got closer to my face and even more intense in his aggression. Surely I had done something more egregious which required a more thoughtful response that just, *"it's cool, man."* That phrase was a common one of the nineties, common on every sitcom we were watching at the time. I also couldn't understand why the guy didn't just hear my friend and respond in kind. My friend repeated his advice

"It's cool, man," I said while looking at him directly. The boy stopped berating me, then walked away as if nothing had ever happened, leaving me shaky, distressed, but most of all confused.

I would later learn as an adult that many men are intimidated by other men who are just taller than they are, and would spontaneously pick fights with me just because I towered over them, even if I'd not done anything at all to antagonize them, like a little Chihuahua barking at a Great Dane just because the Great Dane is big, and not because it's done anything to actually threaten them (and also the history of oppression and geopolitical conflict which set the stage for such a confrontation). This incident was in all likelihood just that, this boy not understanding that I was a nice twelve-year-old gay boy who was terrified of everything even though I looked like a big, straight, sixteen-year-old, and irrationally directed his own insecurities and feelings of powerlessness onto me, when in fact we could have probably become friends had he instead said *"hello,"* or if I had ever been taught effective interpersonal skills. I will admit that this encounter engendered no small amount of anxiety for a while whenever encountering solitary black men, since I lived in a largely white society, irrationally fearing that they too might see me as a threat and preemptively harass me, since nobody else had ever acted toward me that way in my entire life. But soon most encounters with all straight men in general became a source of anxiety, regardless of their skin color, since it is from them that some of my most unpleasant experiences came, such as the time a predatory white businessman who ran a scam of an apartment-hunting service screamed at me in front of all the other customers to get out of his office or he would call the police after I asked for my money to be refunded, without any discussion and with such vitriol as to belie an intense fear of my towering stature. Or the one who conned me into working for him for free and then threatened to sue me when I demanded to be paid for my work. Or the many straight white men who condemned me for my sexuality and demanded that I adhere to their religion which had robbed me of my family and driven me insane with suicidal depression.

I once shouted obscenities angrily at two police officers in downtown Los Angeles who cited me for walking in the gutter of the street on Thanksgiving morning in my pajamas, when the only other car on the road was the police cruiser itself, pottying my dogs in the gutter as requested by the city to avoid dirtying the sidewalks. But not only was I not tasered or body-slammed or put into a chokehold for my behavior, the officers stood there and took the berating even as I made them call up their superior and wait for him to arrive and waste their time over their unethical harassment. Yet again I was targeted by an insecure male regarding my height, and when these officers saw my boyfriend emerge from the building, sleepy-eyed to ask what was wrong and realized I was gay entirely changed their tone and posture toward me. It's insane to think that things like racism and prejudice really exist, especially to the degree where people are straight up murdered for their differences, such as the murder of Tamir Rice, George Floyd, Breonna Taylor, Trayvon Martin, Eric Garner, Ahmaud Arbery, Botham Jean, Stephon Clark—and countless others—or the persecution and murder of gay men and boys or transgender women in many countries of the world—including the United States. It can make one feel the kind of despair and hopelessness for humanity that makes it difficult to breathe.

Racism and prejudice in general has existed in some form or another throughout the entirety of human existence, and has been the source of an unfathomable amount of human suffering, the prelude to incredible horrors like the enslavement of humans in America by white Europeans, the extermination of indigenous Americans by the same group, the Holocaust, the Rwandan Genocide, or the killing of Rohingya people or enslavement of Uyghur in China which continues to this day, and other of the most vile of human atrocities. But I am also lucky to live in a time and place where homosexuals are no longer targeted the way we even so very recently were, which still occurs in places like Kazakhstan, Iran, and Russia. Mankind is capable of great, great evil and hatred toward one another, but nowhere is it more apparent than in conflicts between those who exhibit different physical characteristics.

The reason we seem unable to get rid of racism and prejudice altogether is because we do not correctly understand its source of origin. The most basic part of racist and prejudiced thought and action is the failure of humans to understand that we are actually an animal, and not some divine gift to the Earth which is exempt from animalistic behavior. Those who believe otherwise are, ironically, condemned to behave as animals since they are unaware of and seek to deny and ignore our animalistic instincts rather than accept and understand them. This also leads to the erroneous idea that travesties of the past were merely of their time, rather than exactly the way all humans can and do continue to behave, and so they repeat in the future since humans have pretended it was a problem of the past, of unenlightened and more primitive humans. Murder, rape, child sexual abuse, racism, theft, and war are all behaviors that other animal species also commit upon each other. For instance, do you know that ducks commit rape? Or that monkeys commit infanticide? Have you ever seen the video of a male Zebra literally trying to murder a baby? The way in which the Zebra understands that the baby cannot breathe under water and then uses his limited dexterity with purpose and violent intent to consciously drown a helpless and vulnerable infant is often a shock to people who like to believe that life is not as harsh and violent as it really is, or that animals are more stupid and unintelligent than we which thus means we cannot share their most awful instincts. But of course we can, and of course humans are racist. We are some of the most violent and murderous creatures to have ever existed, extinguishing other life wherever we go, even that of our own species and our own families. Hell, the very reason we are spread across the entire Earth and no longer have Mastodons and Mammoths is because our ancestors used those large mammals as a food source and subsequently wiped them out. A mother zebra and others of her community do not feel any less fear and revulsion at the calculated and murderous rampage than any of us might feel when the same is done by our own species.

Our misunderstanding of the origins of these behaviors comes from also misunderstanding the origin of morality. Social and moral feelings and ideas and institutions are not a special trait bestowed upon humankind to rule over the earth but are instead a tool developed by evolution to promote and maintain systems of social animals, to help species succeed in the struggle for life. Similarly the vile and repulsive, self-centered behaviors like murder, rape, theft, and other crimes are also part of this system. This does not make such behavior legitimate or which come without consequence for the perpetrator of such actions, but they are nonetheless part of the arsenal of strategies that nature devised to keep species alive in the harshest of conditions, with the individual being sacrificed for the good of the whole, the individual being sacrificed *not* the victim of such individuals but the criminal itself. Driven by animalistic instincts to act in ways which compromise its moral fitness and thus integration into the group, their own personal wellbeing and relationship to others, on which we are all abjectly dependent, sacrificed on the altar of nature to continue the line of genetic and progenitorial inheritance at the expense of that individual not for one moment even suspecting it, so driven are they by instinct.

The stresses which cause such anti-social, violent, and amoral behavior which results in racism but also other crimes against humanity originate from the perception of competition and availability of resources. Viewing life as a struggle where everyone must fend for themselves, where the acquisition of basic needs like food, shelter, community, romantic opportunity, or even medicine come with uncertainty and competition creates within individuals the sense that they must win the things they need in order to survive. Real human nature is to be cooperative, to work together to achieve common goals and thus through the power of the many provide for each individual. Derangements to this system break down our naturally cooperative and compassionate nature to instead elicit those basic and animalistic instincts to survive, which then activate increased alertness to potential conflict and competition, feeling unsupported by society and the group which would normally provide it.

An individual human being who is relatively powerless and inept then feels overwhelming fear, distrust, and insecurity when the things they require for their survival are not forthcoming from the group. If this person is then also raised in an environment where they are taught that other human beings are the cause of this struggle rather than their own lack of empowerment, that person becomes hyper-aware of who is and who is not potential competition. The easiest denominator for our weak and ineffectual human brains to identify competitors are then those who appear physically different than us, thus the origin of racism, but which also extends to other forms of bigotry and prejudice such as inter-religious, xenophobia, or transphobia and homophobia.

But even if every human being were the same color, sexual orientation, followed the same religion, ate the same food, had the same amount of money, and worked the same job we would still find things with which to be in conflict—if we were so homogenous the smaller differences would stand out all the greater, and might be things like whether or not you wore your hair long, or if some people had moles and those without, or if others got sick and you did not. Conflicts are never about the things which they appear. An ideological divide such as between religions, political groups, socioeconomic backgrounds, or even countries and nationalities is an illusion, a trick of optics. Other humans are more often barriers to our fulfillment and safety and security than anything else in life, so ideological divides are nothing more than a litmus test, a shortcut to determine whether you are with me against me—a threat or an ally. I am fearful and stupid and cannot be bothered to learn about you, so a quick affiliation check will suffice.

All my life from my parents and church I heard platitudes about honesty, morality, the importance of fidelity and the evils of adultery, fornication, dishonesty, and theft, only watch in horror as every one of them abandoned every last shred of integrity and threw in politically with what to me appears the antagonist of everything they ever held sacred and holy. Because political struggles are never about the content of words, but which team you are on, and the power to protect us from them no matter the cost. The content is merely the ball being passed between teammates as they dribble around you to score. This unceasing struggle for power is merely the flux in the karmic forces of life, the powers of good and evil, dark versus light, optimism versus fear, the needs of the individual versus the needs of the many, us against them, balancing each other as they have throughout the entire history of man, except the dichotomy of good and evil is really a misnomer and more aptly represented as forces of antagonism and those of agonism. But the goals of every person on this planet are *always* the same no matter their political alignment, background, position, socioeconomic status, or tactics, which is to secure their own fulfillment as a human being.

Because racism is such an instinctual human behavior we don't even recognize it when it appears in culture and art. I love the game Minecraft, but it is an outright racist game. The villains are all one skin color separate from the peaceful ones (no surprise since its creator has publicly demonstrated racist and homophobic sentiments)—the villains also alarmingly have darker skin color too—if there were any doubts to the subliminal influence racism has on our daily lives since this game is the best selling of all time, with players of all skin colors being completely unaware of their own instinctual acceptance of prejudicial bias. Beloved works of fiction such as the *Mice of Redwall* blatantly host racist ideals in the form of the rats being presented as ubiquitously evil and mice universally good, which is ludicrous since rodents don't inherently have human nature and as such is entirely a construct of human prejudicial orientation toward conflict and competition. Even *Star Trek*, which took great strides to include racial diversity in its casting and storytelling portrayed entire species such as Klingons as a collective threat, and I can think of no greater manifestation of the subliminal influence of our biological fears of competition which fuel the fires of prejudice (an alternative would have appeared as a politically aligned sect or force within the species, rather than the entire species as a whole, which I think the writers began to realize this with the introduction of Worf, but you could probably write an entire book about the subtleties of racism in regard to this—including Worf's casting, the characterization of the species in general as dimwitted, and that the character was raised by humans thus suggesting racial superiority, etc.). In the real world, our own ignorance to our own racist and prejudiced natures can be seen in events such as those surrounding the murder of black Americans, where professed allies and even those who work to end racism still sent armed forces of police to monitor and harass protestors and tear gassed peaceful demonstrations which in turn led predictably to more violence, because fear of the Other is so strong that it prejudices us even against our better and more compassionate natures. Or the disparity of the violent and disgusting treatment of Native Americans protesting the XL Keystone Pipeline which the President of the United States did not even try to stop, with those who believe they are not at all racist actually acting it very much in practice.

Racism will *never* be entirely extinguished from the human race, because it is built into our psychological biology as a potential resource to fuel interpersonal conflict and aggressive competition for resources, and the idea that racism is borne solely out of rearing is part of the reason why we have had such a difficult time stamping it out. Believing that only select groups of people can be racist, that we aren't like that or capable of it is itself prejudice and precisely what keeps racism alive. In order for social conflicts like racism and prejudice to be resolved, individual human beings *must* be empowered to understand that we are each individually and equally capable of providing for *ourselves* and securing the resources each of us needs not just to survive, but to thrive, such as this book seeks to accomplish. This requires the teaching of life skills such as literacy, civics, financial responsibility, but most importantly interpersonal and social skills such as how to make and keep friendships, how to parent effectively, how to resolve the trauma of childhood abuse, how to resolve the disease which causes alcoholism and addiction, and the ability to apologize and amend interpersonal conflicts. But because racism is rooted in competition or the perception of competition, this also requires that our societies are arranged in ways which provide sufficiently for everyone. This is the benefit that most white Americans have received from Democracy and capitalism, but for which other groups have been systematically denied access to this system through policies such as red-lining, which legally impaired access to financial and commercial services to neighborhoods occupied by those of homogenous minority groups, especially Jewish and black neighborhoods in recent decades but which were also directed at even white groups such as the Irish at other times, or voter disenfranchisement laws which currently seek to accomplish the same. The authors of such policies view minority groups as competition for resources of wealth and prosperity, insecure in their own self-worth and ability to succeed at life, who erroneously seek to increase their chances of success through limiting competition. The reality is that we can create as much wealth, opportunity, and prosperity as we want. Why is there a limit? We can do anything we set our minds to. There is no reason for competition other than what is arbitrarily concocted by fearful and feeble minds and the most base of human instincts. While racism exists across all of humanity it has its origins in the failure of human societies to support those in our own communities who are vulnerable to abuse, exploitation, poverty, and neglect, and it can be easily extinguished if we engineer our institutions and traditions to better empower the individual, and to provide opportunity and access to success so that illusions and fears of competition and scarcity of resources are eliminated, with compassion for those we normally consider opponents, recognizing that antagonism always arises from abuse and neglect.

If there is truly any test in life it is to humble ourselves to the absence of control. Sometimes religion and spiritual disciplines have recognized this or sought to promote it, but mostly religion serves only to comfort and support people in their attempts to subvert fear and wrest control from life and destiny and validate control mechanisms we adopt in response to the pain and trauma which life can bring. *Feeling* in control does not actually mean we are in control, and the disparity between our actions and experience cause people to lose even more control and who then try to entreat God to serve *them*. Religion is in truth a pitfall of psychological and emotional self-comfort to excuse our mistakes rather than demand accountability. This in turn stymies the course of human life since we must take responsibility for our actions and amend our wrongs in order to sustain human relationships, the failure to do so interrupts our journey toward enlightenment and grace. It is a trap to snare those who are not yet ready to transcend the limitations of human mortality. Abandoning our responsibility to and connection with other humans by selfishly retreating to the safety of our ideological harbors ironically retards a person's spiritual progress. Teaching and learning how to truly establish and care for real friendships instead helps satisfy our spiritual needs in addition to our material and emotional needs because it is through our shared mortality that we can find the strength and wisdom to accept vulnerability and the terror of powerlessness over life and through that knowledge the key to transcendence.

When I was an adult and finally began extracting all the trauma and abuse of my life I finally realized one day that the reason I always cried the first day of school was because I started all of those years *without any friends*. In reality I was not a wimp at all as a child. I was brave and acted in spite of my fears, placing myself in situations which opened me up to extreme vulnerability, subjected to an intense amount of neglect and abuse that no child should have to endure, and without the strong, guiding hand of loving parents was right to feel so frightened and alone in the world. Especially compared to my own parents, who grew up with consistent friends throughout the entirety of their own childhood and never had to endure the kind of abuse to which I was subjected, was in reality courageous in the face of adversity. Many of us have similar experiences which failed to help us develop into healthy adults, and all of us have trauma and pain from our pasts which cause us to act in ways which are not only detrimental to our own wellbeing, but also for those whom we are charged to care. The ability to say *"I'm sorry"* lies in recognizing that it is okay that we have made a mistake, having compassion for ourselves in our imperfection and practicing the self-care of resolving our mistakes. Because our survival most of all depends on other humans, the most important thing a parent can do for their child is to empower them in the making and sustaining of friendships, not by doing it for them but by teaching them the skills with which they may achieve such connectedness on their own. Tell your children just to ask people to be their friend, and to keep asking until they find success. Show them they can ask for what they need, that failures do not define their value as a person, and that any wrongs which undermine relationships can be corrected easily with the earnest making of amends. With these skills our children will be safe throughout their lifetime, even after we are no longer here to protect them, because the skills we gave them to seek out and sustain friendships with other humans will be there instead.

24

Problem Children

"I hate you," said my friend's kid as I sat on the couch across from him. Even though I was sitting he didn't come up to more than my chest. But I was completely devastated. "I don't hate you," I lied. He was mean, obnoxious, and frankly kind of stupid. I was babysitting him in turn for my friends allowing me to sleep on their couch after my fiancé of four years decided he loved cocaine and infidelity more than me and my increasingly serious health problems. Already vulnerable in one of the most profound ways a person can be, being invalidated by a little six-year-old was the last straw, and as soon as he went to bed I spent the rest of the night crying into the couch pillows.

My friends had adopted this boy knowing he had emotional problems, and were frankly doing a *really* good job with him as much as could be expected. Neither of them had experience being parented by good parents, let alone the skills needed to care for an emotionally troubled child, but there were still glaring problems and a lack of parenting skills which not only failed to resolve those issues but sustained and fertilized them.

Many parents, including some of my siblings, have children which are deemed 'problematic,' and blamed for their behavior as if they are every bit as conniving and scheming as the parents who raise them, as if they have a lifetime of frustration and malice which informs their choices instead of being the helpless, little children who have only been alive for a handful of years and have no idea how to consciously navigate life or adults other than what is built into their instinctual human biology and modeled for them by their own parents (are you getting as tired of hearing this as I am of saying it?). One of my darling nieces was given to frequent tantrums and outbursts of emotion, causing my sister no small amount of consternation. Exhausted by the unceasing tug of war and feeling increasingly powerless she finally broke down, swallowed her ego, and asked me, the single, childless homosexual for help. "I don't know what to do," she said. "I try everything—I try to be patient, but that doesn't work, I try punishments, those seem to make it worse—"

"Of course it does," I interrupted and then attempted to help her calm down and feel better about herself, because in truth she was doing the best she knew how with the tools available to her. Then when she felt better we began to have a more earnest conversation, and I asked, "What do you think is going through her head when this occurs?" My sister's instinct was to condemn her daughter as selfish and combative, but stating it as such she knew she sounded unkind, which she was reluctant to betray, so she struggled to actually discern what might be going on in the mind of her daughter. "Tell me the times of day that you interact with her," I said, "and what you are doing." She proceeded to inventory their interactions over the last few days. Then I pointed out something which was not obvious to her, that every single interaction for the last several days was either a conflict or attempts to avoid conflict. Not a single encounter was an occasion for love or affectionate interaction. "The problem parents encounter when facing what they see as problem children," I began, "is that the majority or even all of our interaction with a child is negative. Parents get very exhausted being parents, and our goal each day becomes focused on when we will get some alone time, or relief from the stress of parenthood, and to avoid the uncomfortable moments of conflict with children. Their screaming, whining, complaining, and fighting. We begin to resent our children, because they take up so much of our time and we never get to relax. So we start to actually ignore them outright, except for those moments when we absolutely must interface with them, which increasingly become those times they are acting out and must be reprimanded, so then our interactions with children become only ever negative, because we are otherwise disengaging from our children and the only time we are forced to engage is when they do something which needs correction, and the only quality of our interaction is during conflict. Our children need us. They need love. They need touch. They need time. We withhold it from them and so the only way they can then get our attention is by acting out. They essentially do this because we don't actually love them. Not really."

My sister found this very difficult to hear, because it's painful to fully realize how much trauma we are actually causing our little children through our self-centered behavior, which also makes us more conscious of our own pain in the process. But she internalized my advice and began to make serious efforts at reforming and improving her relationship with her children. Likewise, another sister complained to me that her six-year-old son was still sucking his fingers, and they began to engage in abusive strategies to dissuade him. This too was met by rebellion and even greater dependence on finger sucking, because parents do not want to believe that children who continue to suck their fingers far into childhood do it as a substitute for the dearth of physical affection from us, because that would mean we are failing. But failing to embrace and kiss and gaze at children deprives them of the necessary reassurance of love and connectedness they need for their instincts to tell them they are safe, and having no other resources to fill this need they in turn provide it for themselves, through self-pleasuring activities like finger sucking, or acting out to force parents to pay attention to them. Parents time and again refuse to acknowledge their utter failure at parenting and wish desperately for it to be the fault of the child, who has only been alive for a handful of years and has no knowledge, no experience, no means by which they may devise such behavior except that which is instinctual and designed for self preservation. If we ignore and neglect our children nature will make sure we pay attention. If we do it willingly we will receive unconditional love in return. If nature had not designed children to be insistent that they be cared for they would die, because parents would lose track of them, misplace them, forget about them, even well-meaning and good parents. The cries of a newborn baby are designed by nature to draw the attention of the parent, to make it care for their offspring. Demonstrable love from a parent is reassurance that the child will be cared for, which is why sufficient physical closeness inactivates a child's self-preservation response and in turn makes room to allow more magnanimous, generous behavior.

One evening with my parents my sister's child was behaving particularly possessive of her favorite blanket. She had accidentally gotten a toy car stuck in her hair and my sister had spent the better part of the last hour carefully prying it out. Freed, we finally set the table on the patio for a delicious steak dinner, but my very young niece would not let go of her blanket. I gently suggested that she be allowed to keep it, as it wasn't actually a problem and she had just gone through a tiny traumatic episode and was feeling vulnerable. But suddenly the issue again became control and dominance, and my sister, falling back into her old coping mechanisms from being around my parents jumped in to try and wrest the blanket from her with my parents cheering her on. I lost my patience and told them to stop, and my sister realized her error (or the futility of resisting me) and dropped it. I thought it was over. "Such a nasty girl," my mother uttered from the table not more than three feet away from her. About a toddler. About her granddaughter.

Not a single one of my nieces and nephews are actually problem children, though a few of their parents might tell you otherwise. Typically children are actually justified in the way they are responding to their parents, the constant harassment, derision, and conflict directed their way that no other adult on earth would also appreciate. For all the emphasis that religions place on family they tend to more often foster an environment where accusations of contention and family division are the norm rather than close emotional bonds. All growing up my parents and siblings flung labels of *"contention"* as regularly as other families share hugs and kisses, and though I never tried alcohol, drugs, underage sex, skipped school (until I was a senior), missed church, let my grades slip, or refused to help out around the house my parents would without a moment's hesitation label me a problem child simply because I resented the indifferent, loveless treatment to which we were subjected.

It is true that children can be frustrating and obstinate, but so are all human beings whom are harassed and oppressed. So-called problem children are *always* a result of parenting, no matter how much parents loathe to admit their own responsibility, which is most often simply a lack of empowerment and not really personal failings, since we cannot effectively solve problems without the tools required, since hardly any of us are empowered with effective parenting skills until *after* we encounter problems with parenting. My sister had no idea she was withholding sufficient physical affection from her children because she was parenting exactly the way in which it had been modeled for her, which was the only parenting she knew.

More insidious are parents who explicitly (and instinctually) leverage the dependence of a child against them, manipulating feelings of helplessness and vulnerability to dominate children. Parenting is *not* about control. We are not actually here to dominate our children, to be their boss and authority, which is what the adults were doing over my niece's desire to keep her blanket since there was in fact no problem that she needed to feel comforted in that moment. We are only here to be their protector and provider, and often that means even protecting them from ourselves.

The most fundamental reason children repeatedly misbehave or act with great emotional volatility is that they do not actually feel safe and secure at home, with you. For instance, a child who is constantly afraid of going to school and experiences anxiety at night before they go to bed or after a long weekend (Mondays, right?) feels that anxiety and fear because their life with you is not a safe place, in which they are not only NOT protected and nurtured by adults in their lives but actively persecuted and harassed, where other children instead receive the confidence of their loving parents which in turn empowers them to brave the risk taking which venturing out into the world as a vulnerable young child requires, because they know they have a safe harbor to return should any harm come to them and powerful, large adults who have their safety foremost in mind and, more importantly, who believe in them. Having our own unresolved emotional trauma we being insecure about our children's insecurities, fears, and behavior then become one of their primary adversaries, constantly berating them, withholding love and emotional intimacy, and demanding they fulfill our dreams or desires and use them as a receptacle for our own personal frustrations and disappointments while expecting these stressed little children to be emotionally stable when we as a full grown adult are not even capable of it? This is a particularly insane and cruel approach to parenting and fundamental refusal to accept responsibility for our own personal behavior. Imagine how you would feel if the only place you had to live was with enemies and adversaries who constantly harassed you, shamed you for mistakes and weaknesses, and exploited your needs and desires while also refusing to give you the emotional support and unconditional love you needed and expected you to go into the world a naive, frightened young child without any emotional support. In truth, you probably grew up in such a household, but now as an adult are doing the very same thing to your own children, and thus are not blameless and have become the very abuser you so resented when you were young.

Inescapable stress begets anxious, fearful, depressed and angry children and drug and alcohol addicted adults and there is no excuse as a parent to turn your children into adversaries other than our own petty inability to stop acting like a child. That we, a capable adult able to make our own life decisions and the emotional and material resources which enable freedom should treat a child as if they have the same is a vile and detestable act, a purposed lie used as an excuse to hurt and abuse those who are dependent on us, precisely because they are dependent on us, to callously and cruelly use them as an outlet for our inability to deal with our own problems. For a child to be obedient and agreeable they must first know that they are safe and supported at home and that means changing our behavior, not theirs, by resolving our unresolved experiences of abuse, fear, and trauma such as inventory therapy can and does accomplish.

The desire or motivation to control our children in the first place through manipulating their dependence on us originates also from the fear of not being in control in our own lives, such as when we are limited in our freedoms and ability to get what we need from our spouse, work, social life, family, or institutions, and the misconception that we are supposed to be in control of things which we absolutely are not. For instance, try as we might we can never eliminate the possibility of our children dying. Or ourselves dying and leaving them without a parent. Such fear in turn causes parents to anticipate death and engage even in behaviors which do nothing to really improve our odds and in some cases actually increasing the chances of early departure by engaging in abuse of our bodies or our children. The development of alcoholism and addiction is a direct consequence of treating children as if they are a problem, because our biology responds to the emotional volatility and emotional absence from parents as an indication of environmental insufficiency, increasing stress hormones and the activity of the parasympathetic nervous system to empower children to more deftly navigate their dangerous childhood but which in turn saddles them with debilitating neurological damage as an adult. In *Fuck Portion Control* I also discuss so-called "sexual addiction," which is not actually an addiction at all, but a biological function motivated by an excess of nitric oxide due to environmental and dietary stress which our biology perceives as an increased risk of expiration which in turn motivates promiscuity and sexual compulsion in order to increase chances for mating before the portended expiration of the animal. Using control and manipulation techniques and fighting with children communicates to them an unstable and unreliable family environment and in response creates children whose susceptibility to the effects of stress hormones increases dramatically. These stress hormones (such as adrenaline and cortisol) create children which are restless and easily agitated, made worse especially when fed an insufficient diet lacking in sufficient calories, carbohydrates, sugar, vitamins and minerals, sunlight, or high in allergenic factors like wheat gluten, agrochemicals, and harmful polyunsaturated fats which further increase susceptibility to stress hormones. This is one of the reasons why children get so cranky when they are not fed, being less resilient to the effects of stress hormones since they have smaller bodies with less stored nutrition, but also because being hungry in a child signifies parents who are neglecting their children's wellbeing, and the response is naturally, in turn, an emotional outburst designed by nature to get the parents attention such that they are strongly motivated to do something about it. Parents who are incapable of successfully addressing such parental challenges due to our own insufficient upbringing and dearth of parenting skills who revert to subterfuge, shame, manipulation, and coercion and blame the child for their needs rather than providing are thereby exploiting a child's very helplessness and merely adding to the difficulty of parenting because our biological response to neglect and abuse is an increase in protestation or acting out to draw even more awareness to increase our chances of getting that which we need and thus a cycle of conflict and recrimination which ends only in substance abuse, suicide, or separation.

Parents who engage in such abuse of their children must first address why they are motivated to act this way in the first place. A lack of effective parenting skills is often part of the problem. But instead of condemning ourself or our own parents for the lack of such skills (or resentment of children for requiring care), have compassion for yourself and your own suffering and trauma. Imagine a football coach sending in a young, novice athlete to play quarterback during State finals. We are parents who are being asked to play quarterback even though we have never even played football—only watched it from the sidelines—yet for some reason we are expected (or expect ourselves) to jump into this role and not make mistakes, to do perfectly, and hate ourselves and hate others when we inevitably fail. As such this problem is fundamentally not an absence of compassion for our children, but compassion for ourselves. Admitting our only skills as a parent are manipulation and coercion empowers us to recognize the need for help, for instruction, for support, for growth and self-care, which can then allow space for us to actually seek out and acquire these things. Like my brother who was offended at receiving parenting advice from someone who was not a parent (because it also identified and acknowledged his shortcomings), refusal to admit our weaknesses and mistakes serves only to perpetuate our frustration and exhaustion, to compound our problems and mistakes, where our helpless children are only trying to survive, same as us.

This resistance to emotional vulnerability occurs between adult siblings, friends, other relatives, and associates, through the unconscious practice of defensive mechanisms to prevent the development of intimate bonds and connection. Simply never texting, calling, or visiting brothers, sisters, cousins, and aunts and uncles is the most obvious of these behaviors. Because the terror and horror of our childhoods included them we may even feel fear at the thought of contact, and chose to simply avoid further involvement with those who remind us of our pain, even if they were also victims. More subtle control mechanisms seek to sustain relationships but only so far as to avoid the perception of indifference. Have you ever been on a phone call with a family member and found yourself suddenly preoccupied with anything other than listening to the person on the other side? Thoughts of picking up a child after school, or that work assignment or that you need to go fold laundry? All the while your friend, brother, or even wife are talking away as if you're listening but you're not actually paying attention? Growing bored, because we aren't actually listening to them, then make an excuse to end the encounter rather quickly even though we haven't actually even talked to them in a while. This problem happens to many people and you are not alone in this experience because while we may think it is our thoughts and choices to be distracted and disinterested this is actually a reflexive defensive mechanism used by our subconscious mind to prevent the development of close relations with others and risk the chance of further heartache and pain which that kind of vulnerability can expose us. Having experienced much trauma and disappointment in our past the mind has been conditioned to fear intimacy and to dissociate from attachment, so when intimacy presents itself the mind flees toward anything else than risk being present. Since the conscious mind cannot understand the conscious we then find ourselves emotionally cutoff from the people in our lives, or even without anyone in our lives because our defensive mechanisms such as dissociating is are very, very effective at preventing intimate relations and being ill equipped to handle them instead actively prevent relationships from advancing beyond the superficial.

Many people recognize these problems in their lives and crave true intimacy, but because we are normally limited in our toolset we try to cope with silly strategies like trying to be present, or consciously choosing to engage or participate. This never works because the reflex is a function of the subconscious which, by definition, we can never be conscious of, so in spite of our best efforts we still find ourselves zoning out or interrupting encounters again and again. This also robs us of the support and companionship we need from other adults, even those whom by their very biological relationship to us would otherwise make it extremely easy to establish and sustain the kinds of relationships we need. This problem is even more complicated amongst siblings and those who have been friends since childhood because association with them, such as what occurred with my siblings, is a constant reminder of the abuse and trauma we experienced as children, so while we might love them and desire to have relationships with them our mind experiences rather intense anxiety, panic, resentment, and fear in their presence, even when they were just as much a victim of abuse as ourselves, because our primary defensive mechanism to handle trauma from the past is to put it out of our mind or try to forget about it, and the presence of those whom were also victims of abuse and present during ours entirely sabotages that coping mechanism. So we withdraw emotionally from those relationships even when those people are the only ones in the entire world that can fully empathize with our experience, because they lived it too, and thus abuse continues to harm us well into the future.

This also robs us of the support and companionship we need from other adults, even those whom by their very biological relationship to us would otherwise make it extremely easy to establish and sustain the kinds of relationships we need. This problem is even more complicated amongst siblings and those who have been friends since childhood because association with them, such as what occurred with my siblings, is a constant reminder of the abuse and trauma we experienced as children, so while we might love them and desire to have relationships with them our mind experiences rather intense anxiety, panic, resentment, and fear in their presence, even when they were just as much a victim of abuse as ourselves, because our primary defensive mechanism to handle trauma from the past is to put it out of our mind or try to forget about it, and the presence of those whom were also victims of abuse and present during ours entirely sabotages that coping mechanism. So we withdraw emotionally from those relationships even when those people are the only ones in the entire world that can fully empathize with our experience, because they lived it too, and thus abuse continues to harm us well into the future.

Many of us anticipate the emotions of those with whom we are interacting, ever vigilant for potential conflict and disappointment. In phone conversations some of my siblings will wind it down pretty quickly then outright lie about calling me in a day to two when they have downtime. We both know they won't call and they are lying, and this control mechanism is a result of mind-reading and future-tripping, trying to manage a fear of conflict by managing another's expectations. Once at the end of a three-hour phone call with a sister I do have a relationship with she still had the impulse to proffer a lie. I stopped her and assured her that I was done talking to her too and wanted to go play a video game. We do not need to manage the feelings of others, and the impulse to take responsibility for such things only serves to corrupt our own perception of our relationship to others and imagine responsibilities which are burdensome and tiring, thus limiting our interaction with people who trigger our own trauma simply from their mere presence which in turn deprives us of love and relationships. Real intimacy lies on the other side of uncomfortable silence, that pause in conversation when we suddenly come up with an excuse to end the phone call or say goodbye to visitors because we have nothing left to say and our ego begins to threaten us with consequences. We get close to lovers because the desire for sex compels us to persist beyond that discomfort when we first begin to grow close, overpowering our instinct to avoid intimate relationships. But with plutonic relationships there is no compelling instinct to mate to overpower our self-destructive boundaries, and we unknowingly deprive ourselves of healthy and fulfilling relationships without even realizing what is happening. When there is no more superficiality to be said only then can our true desires and vulnerability be shared with others and accepted in return. But when we are insecure, distrustful, or resentful, suddenly we announce that our children will be home from school in twenty minutes and we should get ready and hang up the phone as if it was a visit from the fucking Pope and not just other members of the family whom I also loved dearly. Failing to return or prioritize texts, phone calls, and other communication from family members, ending visits just because we can't think of anything else to say, or only calling loved ones while we're in the car and bored but not really paying attention anyway is a not-so-subtle message which says, *'fuck you, you're not important to me.'* Establishing unhealthy boundaries in this manner motivated by insecurity and a desire to control our environment through manipulation and indirect aggression, for the prevention of emotional dependence one upon another which in practice engenders indifference and erodes those family bonds we need which results in the separation of siblings, cousins, aunts, uncles, nieces, nephews, and friends and acquaintances to engineer our isolation from the world and increases stress and responsibility and thence the perpetuation of intergenerational trauma.

These subtleties of control and manipulation which actively interfere with our ability to find support both emotionally and materially can only be resolved through purposed self-reflection and resolution of unresolved pain and trauma. By practicing self-care and compassion for the child we were by practicing inventory and resolving trauma can enlighten our subconscious to the ways in which we actively undermine and interfere with our own best interests and begin recognizing and meeting our real needs. Instead of trying to force yourself to pay attention to others in your lives, which never works because of the function of subconscious defensive mechanisms, inventorying the resentment of having phone calls or conversations with others, because they bore you, or because you have so many other priorities and recognizing the fears associated with those resentments will enlighten the unconscious mind to this debilitating behavior and thus facilitate new, more effective behaviors without any further effort or trying. I know this because I used to zone out all the time during phone calls with siblings and I hated it but was unable to fix it, until I realized I could use inventory therapy to resolve it, which it did, and for the first time in my entire life was able to be consciously present and enjoy the company of my friends and siblings. Once when working with someone I was teaching the inventory they would often zone out or dissociate from our conversation and even start fiddling on their computer or with their guitar. Since it was my job as their coach to help them resolve psychological trauma I pointed out this behavior and told them to inventory how boring it was to talk to me, which they did, and not once during any other session did they ever zone out again.

These problems are not a result of poor willpower but of a traumatized subconscious and can never be resolved consciously nor through willpower. They can only ever be resolved through effective introspection such as what is accomplished by inventory therapy which empowers us to effectively care for our own needs. Problem children are the direct result of unconscious dynamics which separate and prevent true emotional intimacy between parents, other adults, and thus also children, resulting from coping and control mechanisms meant to protect the ego but which in turn protect us from the vulnerability required to experience the true depths of love and affection required in parent-child relationships. If we do not have the capacity to give such emotional vulnerability to our children we *must* address the trauma and fears we have which prevent it. Crying to our children about how terrible our husband is or complaining how demanding our wife is absolutely not vulnerability. Vulnerability is opening ourselves willingly to occasion and relationships which can cause us hurt in the first place, not the actual experience of being hurt. Adult children who were not held in our childhoods are unable to hold our own children because the sensation of physical intimacy brings up feelings and vulnerability which are foreign, intense, and frightening. To be vulnerable in this instance is holding the child in spite of the terror we feel at being close and the discomfort which torments our mind. A parent must grow up and make the journey through our own past and psyche first to discern the origins of our unresolved pain and trauma, and not require our children or other relatives and relationships to do it for us. Only when this is resolved can we effectively create the space to give to our own children without prejudice that which was denied to us.

When physical love and emotional availability is given to children it reinforces feelings of safety and eliminates a child's instinct to draw attention to themselves, facilitating personal development and promoting growth and self-sufficiency which in turn relieves the parent of much of the potential stress of parenthood, because physical intimacy communicates safety, love, and inclusion and thus reduces stress in the child which in turn allows them the luxury of acting from a place of confidence and security rather than insecurity and rebellion. If this seems a vague task to accomplish, purposefully doubling or tripling hugs, kisses, cuddling, back scratches, and eye contact is a simple strategy which can powerfully accomplish such a reduction in stress behavior. When children fall apart or have emotional problems our goal should absolutely *never* be to make it stop. Fixating on a desired outcome is exactly the opposite of empathy, and there is a big difference between wanting a child to feel safe and wanting them to just stop crying. When our actions and reactions are designed to get a child to stop screaming or to stop crying we actively withhold empathy, because we are in truth only thinking of ourselves. Empathy is the ability to listen, to understand, and that can only be done when we forget our own needs in such moments and make ourselves emotionally available. This task can be difficult for those of us for whom empathy was never shown when we were children, being unfamiliar with the face of love, but this inability to show empathy to our children is also an inability to find it for ourselves. But empathy is a natural human instinct which needs not be taught, and instead of trying to make a situation reach an outcome we desire can instead be practiced by the simple act of listening. Learning to resolve the trauma of our past and recognize how we fail to have empathy for ourselves will in turn make this task more natural and easy.

In an episode of This American Life titled "Unconditional Love," host Ira Glass interviews a young man and his adopted mother who had an extremely difficult time getting along when he was young. Their life was marked by a struggle for belonging until one day a doctor named Ronald Federici suggested that the mother treat her son, who was now thirteen, like he was an infant. To spend most of the day with him, never more than 3 feet apart, and to even spoon feed him dinner, and ice cream. Mothers usually bond deeply with their children shortly after birth, because infants are incapable of moving a mother or other parent or caretaker must constantly hold and cradle the baby and feed them, and instinctually gaze into the baby's eyes for hours and hours of their developing life. The act of providing food and love in this intense manner is what creates the intimate bond between parents and their children, or oppositely prevents it if fathers or mothers can't or won't fill this responsibility. Because this young man had been adopted as a toddler and his mother was never forced by circumstance to create such intimate eye contact they had never truly bonded, and the young man's aggressive behavior was a reaction to never having felt truly loved. During this therapy the young man was even punished by having to sit and receive hugs from his mother. The family relates that after eight weeks of this intensive love therapy the young man one day suddenly realized that his mother did love him, and felt love, and his violent outbursts completely stopped and never returned.

The couple in this story relate how 'weird' it felt to cradle their thirteen-year old son, or to spoon feed him ice cream, but that feeling of weirdness surrounding familial intimacy is exactly what prevents it, because it is vulnerable and makes us attached to others where usually we would prefer not to be emotionally obliged to other humans who can die, leave us, or hurt our feelings. It is that vulnerability, choosing to open ourselves up to such potential heartbreak which creates love, which is love. In romantic relationships the lure of sex compels us past this daunting barrier, the instinct to mate so strong as to distract our minds from the discomfort of developing intimacy. But in relationships where sex is not a motivating factor such as in parenting or between siblings or even friends it can be very difficult to let down our ego and show love for those in our lives who deserve it, so most of us don't, even to our own children, and grandiose protestation and reactionary behavior becomes our compensation.

Growing up with undiagnosed autism, making eye contact with others was an excruciating experience that continued well into my adulthood. At about my mid-twenties I realized specifically that I avoided eye contact entirely with strangers, after having heard a story of two husbands who met on the street in New York City simply making eye contact as they passed one another. Analyzing my own behavior I realized that I never made eye contact with anyone unless I already knew them which likely cost me the attention of many potential, high quality romantic partners. Even during obvious opportunities to make eye contact, such as in a job interview or conversing with friends at dinner I became painfully aware of just how much I continued to avoid it, unless I was blasted drunk which then helped tremendously. Behaviors like avoiding eye contact occurs because avoiding eye contact is an instinctual human response to fear, and in those with metabolic disorders the hormones which mediate fear are greatly exaggerated and so in turn greatly exaggerate the human instinctual response to fear and the environmental stimuli which triggers it. The psycho therapy of inventory practice is especially useful for those of us with intense fear and anxiety because the entirety of the endocrine, psychological, and neurological response to fear or anxiety stimuli is mediated through the mind and our perception of threats to our wellbeing are learned both from direct instruction such as religious fearmongering or from past lived experiences with trauma. Being such an effective tool to access the psyche it can and does help us learn new ways of perceiving threats to our wellbeing, which in truth are actually far less than our past experience has led us believe. Resolving the health problems which underly autism and other metabolic illness nearly eliminated my anxiety, while the psychological therapy of inventory empowered me to better handle fear and insecurity and opened an entire new world of human interaction and self-confidence I had never before experienced.

Many of us likewise absorb the emotions and energies which surround us, but being empathic does not mean absorbing the emotions of other people. Quite the opposite, soaking up the emotions which surround us is a characteristic of codependence, being unable and unwilling to construct healthy boundaries between ourselves and the world around us. This problem is one of abundant self-pity, not empathy, as pity denies our own personal responsibility where empathy acknowledges it. This problem is created through the anticipation of failure by parents as discussed in that chapter, which is one of the best ways to create problem children, by insisting that our children are talentless, ambitionless, disobedient, disagreeable, combative, promiscuous, or selfish when in fact they have not at all committed any of these offenses and which are in reality psychosomatic anxieties perpetuated by a parent. The act of intruding on a child's identity and defining it through our anxieties impairs our ability as children to create healthy boundaries. In truth, many parents think children are far more misbehaved than they actually are, because we are so preoccupied with anticipating problems and avoiding pain and inconvenience we begin to actually believe it is reality and our children miserable miscreants, creating the very reality we ostensibly detest. While we can influence outcomes and must act responsibly as parents, we are not ever actually in any capacity or purpose able to determine the outcomes of life. We are only required to show up for opportunity and to do our best. The delusion that we have control over life is what causes us to expend so much fruitless energy on behaviors which actually damage our children and destroy our personal relationships. Since we cannot determine outcomes, when we obsess about outcomes and not our own behavior and personal responsibility we become ironically more ineffective. Believing it is our job to raise distinguished and accomplished members of society we embark on quests to bend the course of life and fate and force our little children to subvert our fears. We cannot protect children indefinitely. We cannot force them to become who we want them to be. Indeed it is not even our responsibility to do so. Our only requirement is provide security, love, and guidance, and to empower them with the tools required to live well as an adult.

This tendency to act on the anticipation of fear and sabotage our children's potential also denies their own capacity for self determination and personal responsibility, which every one of us has. We are all able and required to decide what kind of person we want to be and will be, what activities we undertake and what life choices we make. Parents, feeling insecure about who we are as a person and powerless in life, will instead adopt a child's decisions for our own, robbing the child of the opportunity and capacity for self-determination and self-care, and in so doing decrease our children's chances of succeeding in life since we have robbed them of the chance to learn such skills for themselves. Parenting more than any other activity in life is truly an exercise in futility, and failing to recognize just how powerless we are and how capable and amazing even little children can be we exhaust ourselves with pointless displays of emotional volatility and control, express self-will and in turn hurt those whom on us are most reliant.

Several years ago there was a sensational story in the news about a young man who was forcibly disappeared by his family to a remote disciplinary camp. His parents had accused him of being violent, but family friends who knew the boy believed it to be a lie and searched desperately to save him, but could not find where he was and he was tortured and abused and subjected to inhumane practices and punishments. Several other children actually died at the camp before it was shut down, and eventually the young man returned to his community, but continued to be rejected by his own parents who obstinately accused him of willfulness and disobedience. It turns out he broke a window during a fight with his parents and they were severe religionists who sought total control and domination of children. A cousin of mine from a Mormon family in a tightly knit Mormon community developed a serious heroin habit. He began stealing from his parents in order to support his addiction. His parents responded by locking him out of the house, forcing him to be homeless even though he wasn't violent. Drug and alcohol addiction are a neurological disorder caused by an excessively stressful childhood, where the instability and emotional torture at the hands of unstable and even mentally ill parents cause children's developing brains to be constantly exposed to hormones of the *fight or flight* response which in turn damages their neurological development. This condition does have dietary factors as discussed in my other book, but is primarily the fault of parents themselves in failing to provide healthy and fulfilling emotional connection and stability. By the time addiction problems occur, it is far too late for the parents to prevent it, obviously, and doing things like locking our children out of the house or sending them to troubled-teen camps will only further sever our relationship with them and continue to make the disease worse since it is rooted in the trauma of instability and absence of intimate emotional support. My aunt and uncle who drugged their children were unable to handle their own personal trauma and emotional volatility, and chose instead to cowardly and criminally drug their children throughout their entire childhoods, to avoid the consequences of their own behavior which caused severe amounts of suffering for their whole family. The cure for alcoholism and addiction involves using specific tools to relieve an alcoholic and addict of their neurological illness, which is also something they cannot do on their own due to the same cognitive impairment which causes the disease, and as such require assistance from family, friends, and society to help them, which also requires practice of the trauma therapy discussed in the upcoming chapter, because its successful practice helps the brain to live new learning experiences which replace the old psychological lessons of trauma and despair. But a parent who is themselves volatile and unstable who tend to react in anger and frustration cannot help their children whom they have hurt until we also have become empowered by this same therapy—so helping children by first helping ourselves is the only way to begin this process, though it can be started very quickly, limited only by our willingness to make it a priority. Substance abuse problems can be avoided in the first place through a diet which promotes healthy neurological function as described in my other book in addition to practicing this trauma therapy for ourselves which will in turn help us discard that traumatizing behavior which in the first place damages normal neurological development in our children. Empowering ourselves to address our own pain and trauma of the past gives us the tools to resolve our problems and thus empowered to take responsibility for our actions and in turn the ability to help others.

There is in reality no such thing as problem children. It is only through the subversion of love and the abuse of children and absence of skills to care for our own emotional and spiritual wellness that we as parents fail to empower and protect our children, even or especially from ourselves that any child's life path advances down roads which are described as problems, which are always rescuable and preventable if those of us responsible for such children can recognize and resolve our role in creating the problem. Unfortunately for many of us this never happens, and we enter our adulthoods traumatized by our experience and operating from ruined and inaccurate assessments of our true self-worth and value as a human being. I once listened to a brilliant episode of *This American Life* which told about a mother and her adopted son who experienced extreme emotional and interpersonal turmoil until one particularly insightful therapist asked them to sit and spoon feed ice cream to their son, who was now thirteen-years old. Parents normally spend many hours simply gazing into the eyes of their newborns and feeding them, which in turn establishes strong emotional bonds, but having been adopted by parents who were emotionally unable to replicate this connection and avoided such intimate and vulnerable interactions, eye contact, touch, etc., they failed to engender a real parent-child relationship. We can avoid these problems by resolving the pain and trauma of our pasts which prevent us from being so emotionally available for our children. Conflict does not have to be our fate, and only occurs because of the dynamics of human instincts and psychology, which can be subverted by working with our our minds and souls, to practice the kind of self-care and compassion that was denied us as children, what our parents would not do for us, to learn who we truly are and what we really want out of life and not the conceptions with which they burdened us. Learning the tools they were unable to teach can give us these strengths and skills (without much effort too!), and thus bring with it confidence and self-love which we did not before think ourselves capable. Because our tendency to interact with children only during negative and disciplinary encounters increases the busier we become, such as when school starts or if we work a demanding job, it is even more important to purposefully make time to interact with children in positive, affirming, and emotionally and physically intimate capacities, if we expect them not to act out in defiance at our refusal of love. But even the act of discipline should not disrupt the love between a parent-child relationship nor the self-esteem and validation of a child. If it is, we are surely operating too much of our life from fear and desires for control. If we are the parent of a child we consider problematic, we must analyze and reflect on our own childhood experiences and identify how we have created the problem and have compassion for the child that is us who was damaged in such a way as to perpetuate the same kind of harm upon our own children. Obstinate refusal to accept responsibility, probably the very thing we are accusing our own child of doing and thus demonstrating for them the very behavior we are unwilling also to change, will only make things worse and possibly cost us our relationship with them. Honestly confronting, admitting, and taking responsibility for our own role in the situation will instead resolve it entirely.

25

Our Other Half

Parenting can be extremely difficult when our struggles with our partner adds stress to parenting rather than helping to relieve and distribute that stress, as parents fight not only their children but also their spouse, who may or may not be disrespectful, unhelpful, absent, ungrateful, absent-minded, neglectful, antagonistic, inept, or as is too often the case actually violent and dangerous. Making matters more complicated is the role of sex in our partnerships as a source either of stress-relief or struggle for control and domination and a tool to manipulate and coerce. The more years spent together as adults and the more accumulated personal history, conflict, and resentments the more dysfunctional and destructive the relationship, which in turn can prevent us from finding success as parents, or at the very least make the job lonely and stressful.
 When we first fall in love (or lust) with a partner we come from a place where we as an individual were probably working on ourselves with at least some degree of effectiveness. Having only ourselves to worry about and no distractions to dilute our energies we perhaps were to some degree fulfilled and hopeful for ourselves and our future. Then comes along that beautiful face which fills us with desire and frustration and absolutely makes us lose our minds as we become entranced by their presence in our lives. To entice them further in we typically censor not only our own behavior but also our evaluation of them in return, since either could potentially jeopardize our chances of securing a relationship. We put the toilet seat down, or we jump up from dinner to help with dishes, show up with flowers, or rub their back before bedtime. A lot of the behaviors we employ during courtship are actually manipulative behaviors. All human interaction is manipulative, actually—

being nice to someone is intended for them to like us. Or we show up for work because we want to keep our job and get paid. Much of the manipulation we practice in daily life is actually good and useful. But when we enter into relationships we typically mistake many of the things we do for ourselves and the object of our desire as selfless or altruistic when in fact it is some of the most deluded and self-centered manipulation we can devise. An ex of mine won my heart by constantly delivering little presents of personalized cards, presents, and even flowers. I had never had anyone lavish attention on me this way and it absolutely won my undivided adoration. In reality I wanted to believe that I was so special as to deserve this kind of fairytale attention, since I had always suffered from such overwhelming and despairing depression and absence of self-worth. *Of course I would be vulnerable to such adulation.* Women are not the only ones who get placed on a pedestal, but it is more common for their experience to be told how beautiful they are, how enraptured their partners, and the lure of equating our self-worth with the way we look and the response it evokes in others is intoxicatingly overpowering, and the eroticism of giving in to a conqueror enshrines our delusion. As we grow older and the attention of our pursuers begin to wane, as we always feared it might, the insecurities we harbor which led us into the trap in the first place now refuse to let us out, and we start to fight the manifestation of truth by entering into a war of endless recrimination in an attempt to control and keep our better halves since we can no longer leverage our youth, looks, and novelty. Men are not the only ones to desire autonomy, virility, and self-esteem through conquest and freedom, but having once been fulfilled by victory and ravished by such a prize whom no longer provides the sense of self-worth we gleaned from our youthful games, and our body begins to sag and hair to grey the panic of aging and impending mortality changes us from noble warriors of love we once believed ourselves into the true, validation-craving, craven monsters we always were.

Each believing the other to be the problem standing in the way of our own fulfillment we then spend as much or more energy than parenting in attempts to neutralize this new threat which is our partner. But because the problem actually comes from internal valuation of self-worth and our perception of identity, war rages on until everyone loses, even to the destruction of what was once such incapacitating attraction and awe-inspiring love, until couples become nothing more than spiteful little miscreants, withered shells of human beings whose sole purpose each day is to hurt the person they once promised to honor and love, or finally give up and move on just to finally put an end to the suffering.

Our problems which are revealed within the dynamics of romantic affairs originate from the same insecurities and unresolved trauma of our childhoods, created by the coping and control mechanisms we developed in response to that pain and experience and then employ with abandon to manage and maintain people in our lives. Some relationships are able to persist in spite of even some significant problems, not because the relationship is good or works but because both partners have complimentary control mechanisms and insecurities which fit together like puzzle pieces. A healthy, well-developed human man will not end up with a despairing, manipulative woman because her behavior will scare him away. Fast. A beautiful, daring, lovely woman will never fall for a self-defeating abuser of a man because she has too much self respect and compassion for others to take on such a burden. Our individual coping mechanisms, fears, and insecurities even prevent interaction or chances to meet with those we desire in the first place. For instance, someone who is despondent and tormented by the horrors of our past may gravitate instead toward certain friend groups which are cathartic for our experiences and conception of self but which then remove us from populations of healthy people and thus romantic options we truly desire, and thus exposed only to those options for whom we settle, or cathartic environments and comfortable activities rather than those which might contain more desirable romantic options, or maybe we adopt certain clothing styles, tastes in music, or even the kinds of jobs we take or venues we visit which wall us off from the partner of our dreams. A man who grew up in a home where he believed his sense of value as a man to originate in the domination of others, especially women, will go actively seek those women who can be dominated rather than a woman who is self-confident and emotionally available, which would in turn make him feel vulnerable, which above all he despises. Myself only feeling a sense of security in a relationship from the demonstration of affection I responded only to potential romantic partners who presented obvious and flamboyant displays affection, or likewise despaired when they didn't and mistook the absence of overt displays of affection as the absence of affection itself, and so I never wound up with the strong, silent type I actually fantasized about, the boy who would show his love for me simply through his presence, his tender touch, his soft voice asking me to share the goddamned covers, nor even the light-hearted fun type of guy since his freewheeling and confident demeanor meant also that he didn't *need* me in the way which made me feel safe (but not actually safe). Because I also had fears about my own self-worth and value as a person I also only responded to men who effused over my appearance and person, but only narcissistic romantic partners do that because they see in another's beauty validation of their own, which above all they most desire, and is in truth the motivation for their fevered worship and not because they in truth care for us as a person, otherwise they would also show adulation for our personality, our intellect, our mistakes and shortcomings, and spend time getting to know who we actually are. It is quite common (especially for men) to lift our partner onto a pedestal and leave them there, ceasing emotional intimacy once the relationship is established for fear of interrupting the fantasy we have concocted because the entire point of the relationship was to subdue fears about our self-worth and not because we actually love or even know the other person. They serve a function in our life to separate us from our insecurities and fears, but because our partner is not a lifeless mannequin but a living person with their own needs and desires and because life is ever changing and mortality eventually comes to collect what's due this cannot persist indefinitely, and finally confronted by the reality of life and the end of our delusional buffer we lash out at our partners for failing to defy death and illness and stay young forever, or demanding that we pay attention to their needs as much as we do our own.

When we find ourselves in a relationship plagued by conflict and disharmony it is because we, not our partner, have been unable to resolve our past and our trauma which inform our various control mechanisms used to navigate relationships. Many individuals I work with believe whole-heartedly that their partner is only interested in their misery and heartache rather than someone trying also to hold on desperately to the person they actually love but also possess no useful tools through which to handle their insecurity. Being hurt so many times and not having the means or the skills to heal that pain and to resolve interpersonal conflict we are left with nothing but behavior which actively undermines our relationships and gets us exactly the opposite of what we really want, and believing ourselves without options withdraw from the relationship as our only remaining defensive mechanism. After that, infidelity or separation are inevitable. Some of us possess so much trauma and such profound defensive mechanisms we never even really get to know the person we supposedly love, from the very beginning construct over them a shadow of our darker selves and see in them everything we hate in us.

At the core of this, still, is the unwillingness to practice compassion for ourselves. Believing we must justify our experience we barrel into our partners exclaiming how they have hurt us and what pain and heartache they have caused and how terrible they are for having done it. Although our partner may in fact do things which antagonize us, we also blatantly characterize them as an adversary so that we might have someone to fight with, and their mistakes or bad behaviors serves conveniently to support this. To ourselves we are merely defending our experience and standing up for our own wellbeing, but in reality we are tearing down the person who more than anything in the world wants to hear that they everything to us, whom they love. No man wants to hear that the love of his life believes him to be an underachiever, a lazy fuck who won't do enough to provide for his family. No woman wants to hear from the man of her dreams that she is fat and unattractive. And yet we do these things to our partners in attempts to change them, to make them take responsibility for our insecurities, to blame them for the insecurities which are our own and manipulate and control them as if we are justified in hurting people just because they disappoint us or don't meet our expectations, then act surprised when the day comes they no longer love us because in reality we never desired them to change but simply to use them and the relationship as an anchor for control of our environment and those fears we refuse to confront.

A fundamental problem in most relationships is that choosing a partner for most people is not much different than picking out a new car. We tour the lot, look at options, and choose the flashiest, most impressive we can afford. When romantic partners are chosen as a commodity to embellish our self-esteem relationships are built on inherently unsound foundations of superficiality, and then because a partner is their own person with their own personality, interests, wants, needs, and desires we are caught off guard when our prize suddenly has a mind of its own. This is a problem which especially plagues the young, not having had the life experience which wakes us up to this disparity conjure superficial answers like tall, sexy, or fit when asked what we are looking for in a partner. In relationships we do not live with a body, its hair color, or its fat. There is a person inside that body and when we have unresolved childhood trauma and lack effective self-care and relationship skills we are unable to cope with the presence of others and their differences and relationships implode in spectacular shows of petty self-centeredness. Of course we want to be attracted to our partner, but physical attraction is (should be) only one small part of romance and when choosing someone with whom to share our lives the priority should be someone we thoroughly enjoy. When physical attraction dominates a relationship, not attraction to who they are (and who they really are, not who we think they are), it is due to emotional defensive mechanisms and the inability to understand who we are and what we really want, since defensive mechanisms protect us from remembering painful trauma or discovering we are every bit as awful as our parents made us out to be. While emotional walls may serve to deaden pain and obscure loss they are also a massive liability since they also obscure reality and cause us to be delusional, unrealistic, and unkind, so we act ineffectively, make poor decisions, and hurt others while also creating significant consequences we also cannot handle for the same reasons we made these choices in the first place.

There is never anything wrong with what we feel or what we want—it is the going about the getting of those things which cause problems in our lives, but because our very emotions and desires were used against us as children we doubt ourselves and instinctually hide our dreams, desires, and insecurities. Every person on Earth seeks only safety, to feel love and attain intimacy, and because of the way were raised many of us think the only way to get it is through subterfuge, cunning, or even force when in fact everyone else also wants those things and all we must do is be kind and find compassion, first for ourselves by resolving trauma, fear, and insecurity and then for others which will come simply from the work we do on ourselves. Relationship stress can actually affect our biological health, so it is important for our physical wellbeing that we resolve our control and coping mechanisms and set healthy boundaries with others. Very often it can be observed that one or both partners in volatile relationships gains weight or struggles with their physical health. Besides exposure to communicable infectious microorganisms such as those which cause oral disease, or eating disorders which compel people to diet and abuse their bodies in order to please others, human are dependent on one another for a sense of safety and inclusion and experience significant psychological stress in unstable and volatile interpersonal relationships. In such relationships our instinctual psyche understands that we cannot rely on our significant others for emotional safety, and their antagonism to our wellbeing and exploitation of our bodies puts us in an untenable and unpredictable position in which they could, at any moment, abandon us entirely. The stress of such unreliable relationships puts us into a heightened state of vigilance mediated by elevated stress hormones which in turn downregulates the metabolism, impairs the immune system, and promotes weight gain because, in evolutionary terms, abandonment by other humans means certain death if we are left to fend for ourselves, and the body prepares for such inevitability by lowering the metabolic rate and packing on the pounds.

Ironically, those who make demands of their partners and control and manipulate and exploit vulnerabilities and weaknesses directly contribute to expanding waistlines and metabolic illness through their very behavior, because this sets the psyche of our partner into a defensive position which triggers these changes in the endocrine system which promotes such metabolic changes. Those of us who are victimized by the narcissistic and antagonistic demands of those with whom we are involved are in turn vulnerable to this manipulation and abuse not because of their behavior but because of our own unresolved experiences of trauma, especially from our childhood, which made us believe we are less powerful than others. But those who are charismatic and narcissistic can also experience this psychological isolation from the rest of humanity which triggers changes to the endocrine system and imperils the immune system and metabolism as we ruin every relationship in our lives and thus feel unconscious jeopardy in every interaction and every relationship.

Because sex is part of our biological nature and such an important part of pair bonding, problems with sex can also become enormous vectors for stress in a relationship which can and does add to the stress of being a parent. Because intimacy is often a need just like eating, sleeping, and having plutonic relationships it can also be used as a source of control within a relationship, using sex as a means to force behavioral changes or to feel a sense of control in a partnership which, by its very nature of intimacy, makes us feel vulnerable in the first place. But using sex as a control mechanism is one of the fastest ways to destroy love and intimacy. This does not mean we should give sex when we don't feel like it nor to compromise our own standards, boundaries, and behavior for the sake a relationship—that too is also nothing more than control, in the sense of still trying to make others do or feel what we want. Being manipulative can occur in directions of positivity (or presumed positivity) as much as it can in the negative. The problem with sex is that our reticence to relent control is exactly what prevents intimacy. Cheating is often regarded as a partner destroying a relationship or acting selfishly, which it may very well be, but the cause of most infidelity is an absence of emotional intimacy which is the result of unhealthy boundaries and control and defensive mechanisms which keep romantic partners from ever really getting close to us. Sleeping next to someone who won't let you get emotionally close is extremely demoralizing, so we try to force their behavior to resolve this, but control and manipulation further assaults insecurity and only drives them further away. Feeling unfulfilled and lonely while part of a romantic relationship is even more stressful than being alone and single, so eventually one or both partners will begin to seek emotional intimacy elsewhere. But even if we aren't able to find real emotional intimacy elsewhere, the novelty of cheating or the thrill of getting to know someone new can feel like intimacy and thus lure us out of an unfulfilling dead end.

Many couples reach a point in their relationship when sex stops or is very infrequent, but persist in those sexless relationships in order to maintain a facade or support the institution of marriage. But the only reason we get into that spot in the first place is not because we get old or fat or stop being attracted to our partners, but because the only motivation for being in the relationship in the first place was attraction, and in fact never loved them for who they are because we never actually got to know them or become intimately close. So when sexual attraction wanes there is no other motivation to be in the relationship.

Defensive mechanisms like demanding behavior, criticizing a partner's appearance, indulging pseudoempathy, dissociating from a partnership, or hyper-focusing on children or other obligations are convenient distractions and defense mechanisms meant to prevent the vulnerability of real intimacy, and because many of these defense mechanisms are even admired or respected in our moralizing, productivity obsessed cultures these defense mechanisms can be nurtured and emboldened and thus persist for years and decades and rob us of ever really knowing the soul-tearing love that comes from letting go of control. True intimate vulnerability is also not something most people are courageous enough to experience, because it requires a degree of ego subversion and acting in spite of fear that we with coping and control mechanisms are unwilling to do. During one relationship a particular position my partner liked made me feel extremely uncomfortable and vulnerable. It wasn't abusive or disrespectful at all, it simply made me feel like I was not in control, and so I would hardly ever let him do it. Some of us even refrain from pleasing our partners indulgently because experiences of sex shame in childhood make us feel uncomfortable about swallowing a cock or eating out a vagina. In reality there was no problem with the position I disliked, it's actually really fun and intimate and it was only my own experiences of embarrassment, humiliation, and insecurity with close emotional intimacy and desire to control by which I used sex to deny myself and my partner the kind of emotionally spiritual connections which sex can create and thus persist in frustration and loneliness even while being with someone.

The ability to truly bond intimately with another person in ways which transcends the physical body is entirely reliant on our ability to subvert our ego and desire for control. Excessive fixation on body type, fitness, and sexual tastes are all control mechanisms meant to help us with fears and insecurities, so when relationships are built on control mechanisms it is impossible to experience real vulnerability. Resolving barriers to intimacy cannot be done through willpower, purpose, or intent. It is why most relationship counseling fails or is unproductive, because the goal in seeking couples therapy is usually to make the other person behave the way we want, not to experience them for who they are. The only way to know true intimacy with another person is to resolve our own experiences of trauma through inventory therapy. The reason this practice is successful is because the act of doing it is the very action of having compassion for ourselves, where the opposite—not doing the practice and trying to ignore our wounds—is the act of withholding self-compassion. Being unable to experience intimacy is ultimately being unable to have compassion for another because we do not in turn have it for ourselves. So, exercising compassion by doing inventory in turn opens the ability to have compassion for others and thus experience them as they really are, which is what intimacy is.

I once went to bed with someone I had met only earlier that day, and the next morning he told me I needed to be careful with his heart, so I didn't call him again. Not once had I represented an interest in dating. It had only been six months since my fiancé had left, and I did not have the capacity to care for another person, let alone someone who was needy and controlling, and the last thing I wanted to do was take care of another adult baby who used their emotions to manipulate and hurt others. Adults are only responsible for their actions, not the feelings of others, and when we foist our own insecurities onto potential romantic interests it is a defensive wall meant to control others rather than facilitate intimacy. Entering into a romantic relationship is a risk and we must be brave and smart enough to accept that responsibility for our decision. We are not responsible for the actions of others any more than they are responsible for ours. The ability to truly bond intimately with another person in ways which transcends the physical body is entirely reliant on our ability to subvert our ego and desire for control, especially that of trying to make a partner do what we want, including staying and being faithful to us. That is not our job nor in our responsibility. Having a discussion about expectations such as fidelity or polyamory is not the same as telling someone they need to make us happy and fulfilled, which nobody can actually do but ourselves. Other excessive fixations on things like body type, fitness, and sexual tastes are all control mechanisms meant to help us with fears and insecurities, so when relationships are built on control mechanisms it is impossible to experience real vulnerability. Resolving barriers to intimacy cannot be done through willpower, purpose, or intent. It is why most relationship counseling fails or is unproductive, because the goal in seeking couples therapy is usually to make the other person behave the way we want, not to experience them for who they are. The only way to know true intimacy with another person is to resolve our own experiences of trauma through inventory therapy. The reason this practice is successful is because the act of doing it is the very action of having compassion for ourselves, where the opposite—not doing the practice and trying to ignore our wounds—is the act of withholding self-compassion. Being unable to experience intimacy is ultimately being unable to have compassion for another because we do not in turn have it for ourselves. So, exercising compassion by doing inventory in turn opens the ability to have compassion for others and thus experience them as they really are, which is what intimacy is.

We do not need to justify our experience to anyone, least of all our romantic partners even though our defensive mechanisms drive us to do that. It is nothing more than a control mechanism. Trying to control how someone regards us. We cannot, ever, control what people think about us. But we do need to learn compassion for ourselves, spending time in self-reflection such as the inventory facilitates is the first step, recognizing that our experiences do cause us pain and frustration without needing to justify or explain our pain and frustration. When we are young and desirous of a relationship it is enough that we want to be loved and be in a relationship. It does not need to be a demonstration of or in refutation to our ideas of self-worth and desires. When a partner leaves us or cheats on us it is enough that the experience was painful without making a judgment on ourselves or the other person or seeking to justify our pain to the world and those around us. When a partner fails to take care of their responsibilities and it makes us feel more stressed out it is enough that the experience caused us stress, and does not need to be an exercise in self-righteousness, contempt, and control or dominance. When we do not practice self-compassion and seek instead to defend and justify our position we also end up missing and denying our own culpability and become ineffective which increases our frustration. We are not justified in returning insults upon our partner just because they did the same. We are just as guilty and just as much responsible for our actions as they are theirs, no matter your excuse or feelings or beliefs. Because the act of control and nature of coping mechanisms attempts to assume control of other people's behaviors it means we abandon the personal responsibility we have for our own, and in so doing actively engineer the destruction of our relationships even though we want to believe it's the other person's fault because of our already low estimation of self-worth.

Instead, we justify our experiences to *ourselves* through the practice of inventory. For many of us, feelings are not real unless we act on them. This is an instinct leftover from childhood which wills us to turn our feelings into our experiences in order to increase our chances of survival. But feelings do not actually have any real connection to our actions, and acting on feelings is the very act of self-hatred. Hurt by a partner we respond in self defense because some part of us believes they are right, and hating that part of us we react defensively in agreement with their assessment. In a previous relationship I was unambitious and unmotivated to work. I had not yet come to understand that I did not care about money and instead valued creative and intellectual fulfillment and valued my time *more* than money (and was also burdened with cancer, thyroid disease, and alcoholism). My partner attacked my lack of ambition for monetary success, and because I was insecure of and resented that part of myself because of the expectations of other people I defended myself in return by making excuses and justifying my situation while also exploiting his personal failings for ammunition with which to defend myself. I did not have compassion for myself and my perceived weaknesses or shortcomings, so when confronted by criticism instead of saying, *"yeah, you're right. I don't care about money"* I instead lashed out in recrimination and hurt him in return. I see many couples exchange barbs when one of them hurts the other and when the recipient makes their offense known, instead of saying *"sorry I hurt you,"* we instead try to justify our behavior. This can even be so petty as once when making cookies with a couple the wife messed up a recipe due to a very simple mistake that could have been avoided by reading the directions. The husband, instead of having compassion for his disappointment and the unpredictability of life (and humor of the situation), instead chose to insult and berate her. The wife, instead of having compassion for herself in making a mistake and saying sorry, became defensive and defiant. Over cookies.

Making an inventory of every single uncomfortable thought and experience surrounding our self worth, relationship history, and relationship desires both platonic, familial, and romantic can help us come to discover how truly capable and self sufficient each of us can actually be, because our perception of life, other people, and our own personal effectiveness are entirely imagined and conditioned by our past and childhood conditioning, which includes thinking we are responsible for things which in truth we have no control, such as the behavior of our loved ones or being desired by romantic interests. In fact, believing we not only can but should control our romantic partners leads to pronounced psychological and endocrinological stress which changes even our very physical body, because we can never actually control others, and the mind is aware of this even if we desire control and the very orientation toward control impulses drives us insane even if we get what we desire, as reality can never actually be subverted no matter how much we desire it.

One of my most favorite books in the whole world is *The Missing Piece* by Shel Silverstein. It is a beautiful story with endearing illustrations and a sweet, happy message, and seeing the copy sitting on my bookshelves reminds me of the blissful joy and hope I experienced as a child when reading Shel Silverstein.

The Missing Piece is also total bullshit. The message it communicates is that we must be whole to find or be worthy of love, that having flaws makes us less desirable and that we should work on them rather than relying on other people. My experience has proven this idea to not only be completely and utterly and absolutely wrong in every single possible way, but also to have led me down the very life paths such conceptions of self-worth promise to help us avoid. This mindset was not instilled in me by Shel Silverstein, who in truth was one of the most inspiring parts of my childhood, but instead by the society in which I was raised and the people around me who were unable to teach me the kinds of skills which actually lead to a fulfilling and successful life. Like most queer people (and a good many heterosexuals too) I did not have the support of social groups which tend to coalesce around young people and new families to support, validate, and increase the success of pair bonding, structures which are direct repudiations of this idea that we do not or should not need others to compliment our own strengths and weaknesses. Burdened also by trauma from my abusive childhood and saddled with toxic ideas of self worth, I was left to my own inadequate devices, without role models or support structures, spending most of my adult life trying to make sense of and undoing the wreckage of my earlier life, trying to eek out an existence in a world which is often hostile and opportunistic. As a child and a young man I always assumed that I would be married with children by at least thirty. But I have been single for more years than I have been loved, and as a weepy Libra this fact came as quite a hard pill to swallow as I swiftly approached the waning end of my fourth decade, alone and without any family of my own.

In spite of my detours and heartbreaks, I love my life. I wake up nearly every morning with excitement and enjoy immensely the mundaneness of the every day, even though I have very little and life has not met any of my expectations for it. This is a result of the process and tools of inventory therapy and solutions to health problems as discussed in my other book. In my earlier life, whenever I was in a relationship I constantly wondered if I actually loved those with whom I was lucky enough to spend some time or whether my feelings were simply just a codependent needed for them. Queer people and women have long histories of being attacked for our mental health, justified or no, and as a result it was difficult to move through life without questioning whether or not the things I felt were really legitimate or just a result of the trauma through which I had navigated. Most people who had input into my life, from family to friends to boyfriends and even therapists all suggested in varying degrees that having mental hangups made a person less desirable and less worthy of love, even when they too possessed the same mental illnesses I did. It wasn't until the end of an important relationship (during which I was engaged to be married) that I finally realized the truth of my reality—that I was both codependent *and* in love. Never in all my life, with all the therapy and self help and unsolicited advice had anyone suggested that codependence and love are not mutually exclusive, nor that I was valuable and worthy of love even though I was mentally ill, and I could also be capable of real love in spite of my hardships and difficulties and that my love for someone was not cheapened by own shortcomings or weaknesses.

Feelings for other people are not only not bad, they are what make us human and are part of our experience, even and especially when they are overwhelming—it is instead behavior that can be bad, and feelings do not and do not need to equate to behavior. The ex with whom I separated who disparaged me to our friends about how devastated I was at the demise of our relationship also professed to be a romantic and to want love and an intensely passionate relationship—but how can anyone expect to find love with another who would also *not* be intensely hurt when you leave them? Such feelings and desires are mutually exclusive, and emotional devastation is the price of real love. Many people who also focus excessively on sex or the mundane, mechanical aspects of it such as creative positions, exploration, "freedom," variety, control, shame, or the heightening effect of drug or alcohol use have never actually experienced the most devastating type of sex, which is that which occurs during real emotional vulnerability. Most of us are far too terrified to ever allow this, and instead focus on the physical sensations which may be heightened by such preoccupations with sex, which can never even come close to what occurs when offering oneself to another during a state of real emotional vulnerability. This truly transcendent state of sexual intimacy can never be achieved when we are burdened by desires or impulses for manipulation, control, attempted subversion of fear, or preoccupation with superficial aspects of sex, and is instead facilitated by such practices as inventory therapy, because it relieves us of our desires and machinations for control and our delusions of realty which in turn reveals to our mind the absolute insignificance of our lives, a frightening realization of just how little power we have and the true magnitude of control that others have on us—their charm, their lovely spirit, their incomparable otherness and our complete inability to live without them, and the emotionally suicidal experience of willingly allowing ourselves to participate in experiences which can and will rend our souls and tear out our hearts. Such truly intimate experiences show to both partners just how truly fleeting and fragile our lives really are, how insignificant our lives and how vast the Universe, and also how rare and special such are moments of existence.

In a culture which sheds our wounded we are constantly reminded of how we fall short. Social media can be the worst place that this rears its head, with countless memes about being a whole person, about loving yourself first, and lists of features to identify the right person instead of *being* the right person. There's one meme with a Pokemon Squirtle throwing flowers, the text exclaiming the author to be a complete and interesting person and thus it's okay to be alone. Yes, it's okay to be alone, but it's laughable that anyone thinks they are a complete person, and interesting is highly subjective. I'm so boring I often bore myself. This meme was made precisely because not one of us is complete and this fact sits sourly with those who dislike our own flaws. Being human means a reliance on others, that none of us is complete nor whole, that we each have our own weaknesses and flaws, and a culture which denies that is in truth crafted by those who wish not to be so reliant on others, nor to acknowledge reality or mortality, which is entirely understandable but a rejection of who we are as a species and as individuals. Many of us delude ourselves into thinking there is nothing wrong with us, when in fact there may even be a great deal wrong, because a lack of tools to get well or fix our own problems and little social support which are also required to do so leaves us feeling helpless, the only method of coping then being self-delusion.

Ignoring our own problems and shortcomings or pretending we are fine or whole is exactly the opposite of acceptance. If we seek harmony with ourselves and with the world we must first come to *accept* our flaws and weaknesses—which every single one of us has. This sounds great in practice, but what exactly is acceptance? This has bugged me for a very long time since the word acceptance is thrown around by lay persons and mental health professionals alike as if any of them really know what it means. A raging, adulterous, cocaine addicted ex once told me that a person had to first be whole to find success in relationships. So of course they did not. The people who make these kinds of memes, books, and advice are simply trying to handle their own inability to cope with the challenges of being human, and is in reality a tormented soul trying to make sense of the pain and frustration that life can bring, and because ideas of acceptance are misinformed, most people are unable to actually practice it.

Acceptance, first of all, is *not* a mindset. We are often powerless over our emotions. You wouldn't be expected to stay calm and happy if someone came into your house and murdered you, right? But why do we expect ourselves to try and feel good when other bad things happen to us? If a partner insults us or our day at work doesn't go well or we are ravenously hungry why would we expect ourselves to feel anything other than unhappy? Trying to change our mindset when things are going poorly or we are under stress is called *denial*—It is a toxic way to approach life that trains the mind to ignore reality, which itself is a behavior that later comes with very serious consequences and causes one to live life in every aspect but the present. Most methamphetamine addicts I know have done or were encouraged to make gratitude lists while in recovery, and guess how many of them achieved the kind of happiness that I in my cynicism have achieved? Such practices deny us the right to feel bad, and so when we do feel bad are instead taught to try to change our feelings through action, which does not work, and as such only leave us running in circles. No—acceptance is not changing our attitude or mindset, which is why trying to do that so often fails to change our lives and only leads to more and constant frustration and insanity.

Instead, acceptance is the simple act of *inaction*. Specifically, choosing not to do the thing in response to our feelings we would otherwise is what acceptance looks like in practice. We feel bad, but we don't act on it, which includes outward actions like not shouting or taking pills or hitting someone, even the act of defending ourselves is often the opposite of acceptance, since this behavior focuses on others instead of ourselves, and is more precisely the act of not trying desperately to change or control things. Instead, trying to understand our feelings—why we have it, where it came from, and what it tells us about life and ourself as a person, to show ourselves compassion for our experience rather than leaping into conflict with others. This kind of introspection into who we are in relation to our life experience and not focusing on the people and events around us is the act of acceptance, of practicing self-compassion. When our partner says we're fat or we didn't do the dishes right, and our blood boils and eyes narrow as feelings of anger and humiliation rise within us, the person who does not accept our own flaws and weaknesses and has no compassion for ourselves will choose to jump to our own defense, to in turn attack our adversary and point out their flaws and inconsistencies in return, where the act of acceptance allows the other person the responsibility of their actions, not taking it upon ourselves, and having compassion for our flaws even and when it means that they are right. Maybe we are fat. So what. Maybe we didn't do the dishes right. So what, we will try better next time. Feeling it's not okay to be flawed we then react to being told we are flawed and in turn become hurtful ourselves and thus give more power to our shortcomings, not less, while simultaneously destroying relationships and engendering resentment. Reacting to our insecurities and the things we view to be deficient within us actively seeks to ignore why these things exist in the first place, by trying to change reality through denial and resistance, without proper understanding of why they are there in the first place, and then we are ineffective and exist in a ceaseless cycle of self-incrimination and interpersonal conflict and dissatisfaction. When someone says we're fat, responding by telling them they are mean is the exact same behavior, each of us pointing out a flaw in the other and each of us failing to practice self-compassion by focusing instead on the flaws of others.

It is not only true that we all have flaws and shortcomings, it is *okay* and desirable that we do. It is the entire point of life to have a variety of characteristics, some good and some unhelpful or even down right bad. Life would be nothing without this variation, indeed we would not even exist. If I was instead an accomplished lawyer with a big house and lots of money and not someone who nearly died from suicide and alcoholism I would not have come to find the cure for alcoholism nor other things like baldness and depression. There must be a balance in the creative and destructive forces of the Universe in order for us to even be here, for us to be interesting and desirable, and because we too are a part of this balanced Universe we must also reflect that balance. Though you or your partner (or both) may exhaust much of the day complaining about the other and all their little flaws and shortcomings, the reality is that those very things you complain about are also the very things you will desperately miss when that person is gone (notice I said *when* and not *if*). It is good, right, and proper that we all fall short in the stereotypical measure of human beings, and the interestingness and adventure of life exists within the borders of what is good and what is not and our journey between them, the growth that develops, and the life experience we accrue. So you can stop feeling bad about your shortcomings, including the things you want and the feelings you have and what other people say you should be.

You should, however, feel *very* badly about the things you've done (while still practicing compassion for yourself). There is an enormous difference between having feelings and acting on them. Because acceptance brings us peace, the opposite, which is not accepting and as such acting on feelings brings us the opposite of peace, which cannot be resolved until our actions are as well. If our partner constantly criticizes us, insults us, and fights with us, are we any different when we do the same in return? Of course not—Because we are justified by our feelings, right? This is exactly how our partner (or adversary) feels too—slighted, annoyed, offended—and they too justify their actions by their feelings. If everyone does this, when does the madness end? Feeling insecure and vulnerable because of our flaws, we act on them, and when everyone does this our worlds erupt into chaos and conflict. Instead of demanding that others meet our expectations in a relationship, work on meeting your own. The idea that we are not okay for having feelings makes us demand that others satisfy our insecurities for us, and we act on them to justify our feelings instead of seeking to understand ourselves and find compassion for our experiences and our place in the Universe.

Actions are *never* justified by emotions, and failing to separate the two is what gets us into trouble and is the opposite of acceptance. The act of acceptance is simply choosing not to act on our emotions, which includes trying to change them. When I was codependent with a partner the proper advice I should have received was that it was perfectly fine for me to feel the overwhelming feelings I had for them, my fears of being abandoned, and my desire to be near them. These feelings originated from my past experiences of rejection and abuse, and it was only natural to have these kinds of feelings as a result, and finding compassion for myself and for these feelings would have instead diminished their influence over me, being replaced instead with self-compassion. Instead of trying to control those feelings by being overly concerned with my partner's actions or desperately trying to find some way to satisfy them, I could instead have let my partner do what they wish and spend time trying to understand why my feelings existed in the first place and what they had to say about myself, my experience, and the nature of living. Getting to know why and how we work on our own terms through practices like inventory therapy and not in relation to others is what the act of acceptance accomplishes. I did not understand this until I was well into the later half of my fourth decade, and much of the hardship and suffering of my life and failure to find emotionally healthy and desirable partners was a direct result of my unwillingness to accept that I was flawed and had serious shortcomings, where instead if I had accepted them and come to terms with the pain and trauma which I had experienced would instead have found great success.

Surprisingly, I also found that most of that which I viewed as flaws such as being sensitive, permissive, homosexual, horny, or obstinate were not actually even flaws or shortcomings but were instead what society, religion, and opportunistic and abusive individuals told me were flaws and shortcomings in order that they could control me, and it wasn't until I spent time actively accepting what I perceived to be my flaws that I even realized many of them were not even flaws! Instead of fighting our husband, our wife, boyfriend, girlfriend, or friends or family or political climate we can discover our true strengths through inventory therapy to learn how to accept our own flaws and insecurities, and in turn discover how to live the kind of life we truly want and not the one other people have chosen for us.

This also cannot be done simply through will, attitude, or commitment. The inability to see reality as it is and not that which is filtered through our experiences of abuse and trauma causes the great majority of relationship turmoil, and our conscious mind is not capable of changing the subconscious without such a structured practice as inventory therapy provides, because we are not even aware of it. Once toward what would be the end of a significant relationship my partner was on a business trip for several days. I missed him greatly and the day he was to return I spent hours cleaning up the entire house, prepared a large dinner, cut my hair, shaved, and got dressed in some of my best date clothes. When he pulled up in the driveway I opened the door to greet him and our dogs ran out of the house to do the same. When he stepped inside he seemed to be in a foul mood. Concerned that something happened on his way home, I asked what was the matter?

"It was really nice to be somewhere I am actually appreciated," he said.

My partner was a public personality, and had likely had many fans fawning over him during his trip, but I couldn't believe my ears, and thought there had been some misunderstanding. Was my presence and effort not apparent? I sort of ignored the comment because it hurt so badly, and said I had been cooking dinner for us, pointing to the very clean kitchen and the table already set and wine decanting, completely gutted at his behavior toward me after I had spent the entire day doing nothing but preparing a welcome for him, and even after eating he continued to be cold and spiteful.

Likewise a woman to whom I taught inventory therapy used to greatly resent her husband, and viewed him as lazy, complaining, and miserly. After many weeks helping her it became clear that most of her negative conception of him was entirely in her head and were in truth control mechanisms meant to manipulate him, a result of her own self-hatred and shame and prejudices. In reality he was a very kind and loving person and a really good husband and father. Although mildly neurotic (from his own childhood traumas), he had none of the qualities which she projected onto him, which were all in truth anxieties and fears originating from her childhood by which her ego attempted to protect her, by seeking for them in others, and the absence of compassion for his uniqueness and eccentricities which she lacked also for herself. For many of us entire lives play out in our heads completely separate from reality because our fears and traumas so deeply disturb and dominate our perception of ourselves. No doubt my partner also saw me and our lives together through similar filters of trauma which were the representation of everything he feared about himself, which kept him from being able to see the loving, handsome man waiting at home for him, and not even a warm embrace and unconditional love was sufficient to break through that self-hatred. In fact, I cooked or prepared nearly every single breakfast, lunch, and dinner not eaten at a restaurant during the entirety of our four and a half year relationship, and it was only half a dozen months after it ended that he finally realized (after he had to start cooking for himself) how much I actually took care of him.

 No person is whole. We are all equally strong and weak in different areas of our lives, and listening to garbage self help about how we need to be different than we are for reasons which seek to cover up our wounds rather than accept them only prevents our ability to grow as a person. Recognizing this now has also allowed me to give love to those who fall short, where before I also withheld it due to the incorrect notions I had been taught about who did and did not deserve love. Everyone deserves love. Real growth comes from accepting our weaknesses and flaws and understanding the true parameters of our individual worth, and that we are desirable not in spite of our flaws and shortcomings, but because of them. Failure to do this can keep us trapped within endless cycles of conflict as we focus on our flaws reflected from the mirror that is our partner, never seeing them for who they really are and thus being dissatisfied and resentful over nothing more than our own deeply rooted delusions.

 Very often our attraction to others can prevent us from seeing their true natures, or at least admitting to ourselves what is plainly true. I knew an ex of mine was a serial cheater even before he ever cheated on me, because he told me. During our early courtship he mentioned he cheated on at least two past partners, it was an enormous red flag which his charm made short work of, and because I was so lonely and desirous of companionship (and not overly concerned with monogamy) I willingly ignored obviously problems with loyalty which would have been more clear had I already been empowered by inventory therapy to recognize my own weaknesses and trauma. There is an easy shortcut, however, to evaluate whether a potential romantic partner is a good choice, if we feel unsure of our own emotions. It is simply evaluating whether or not we like our love interest's *friends*. Not a single narcissist, abusive asshole I dated had friends I actually liked. Because we as human beings tend only to coalesce with those who compliment our own control and coping mechanisms, a potential romantic interest is just like their friends, but editing themselves during the process of courtship to a version which they think will be more attractive to us. Not only this, our potential partner also finds acceptable the qualities we dislike, which speaks volumes of their true character which they may be concealing (but not that well, usually, as we are more victim to our own trauma than to deception). That same ex kept liars, cocaine addicts, gossips, and enablers and miscreants as friends. I thought or rationalized it as him being compassionate to them, until the day he relapsed into cocaine addiction himself, after having first disparaged me to all his friends and relatives who refused to help, and left.

 I later realized he kept those friends because they were every bit as shallow, cruel, and disloyal as he was, and so felt comfortable being his true self in their presence. If cocaine addiction sounds like an unrelatable or extreme example, every one of us possesses the same set of self destructive and abusive survival instincts which are embedded into our human biology, which underly all untoward, dishonest, and nefarious behavior, on which abused and traumatized people rely because they lack effective self-care and interpersonal relationship skills which then imperils relationships no matter how extreme or trivial, and if we are unable to be honest with ourself about whether a potential or current love interest is good for us, evaluating whether or not we actually like their friends can be helpful, especially when analyzing this information in the context of inventory therapy.

When relationships do become acrimonious or lonely it only takes one person practicing inventory therapy to put and end to cycles of offense and recrimination which dominate romantic partnerships. Very often this can also lead to helping a partner, since after all our conflicts always result from an absence of effective interpersonal relationship and self-care skills. One sister who did begin to change her life after seeing what these tools provided to my life helped restore the quality of her relationship back to the thrill and excitement of first getting together. Her days went from hair-pulling exercises in futility, acrimony, and exhaustion to ones which are endlessly satisfying and full of love and excitement, all while having even more kids than she had before. Once, when standing in line at the DMV with her large family after moving to a new town due to a job transfer a random woman approached her in line and whispered, "Excuse me, but I just wanted to say I have never seen a husband look at his wife the way yours looks at you." My sister is now one of the happiest people I know, not because anything in her life materially changed but because, like me, she finally learned how to resolve her past experiences of pain and trauma and find true self-worth and compassion for herself through the self-reflective practice of inventory therapy.

Divorce is an unfortunate reality of life, and even happens to couples who do everything right and is not necessarily a failure, although often it is. My old partner said he liked to think of our separation not as a failure but as just a step in a better direction. This is total bullshit and was meant simply to subvert insecurity and deny personal responsibility. Yes, there is not really such thing as failure, as we are always on a continual path of progress and development. But of course we fail. All the time. That's the way life works. Rather than delusionally denying failure, accepting that it's *okay* to fail and having compassion for our failures recognizes the true limitations of mortality and thus empowers us to be more effective in the future. Those who deny failure and thus the limitations of mortality are condemned to continue making the same mistakes over and over and over again, such as him jumping right into several rebound relationships and relapsing into cocaine addiction where I stayed single and got sober and turned my life around. Constantly berating a partner for their mistakes is not "fixing the relationship." It is merely an exercise in self-will and domination and control, turning our partner into an adversary purposefully so we can feel a sense of control. If a partner really does cheat on us and it's a problem, leave. If a partner's lack of ambition really is a problem, leave. Do not threaten to leave, just like the act of threatening a child this kind of behavior is merely a manipulative tactic to frighten and control rather than care for our own wellbeing, feeling powerless to do so without effective interpersonal tools. A resentment against our spouse or partner which might be entered into the inventory practice for instance would include in *my part* the fact that we chose to enter into a relationship with them, and choose to continue being in a relationship with them. Being loyal is not a standard that must be established in a relationship, and if a person needs that spelled out for them their problem is a lot more serious than we realize and doesn't actually have anything to do with our behavior other than choosing to participate.

All failed relationships are a failure of intimacy, to be emotionally available and to find emotional availability, and having chained ourselves to someone to whom we either cannot get or will not give emotional connection we or they become trapped in a sterile, impersonal prison in which we go through the motions expected of commitment while not receiving any of the benefits, obligated to someone who seems a barrier to that which we thought such a relationship is actually supposed to bring and then, over time, grow to resent them and the absence of love we all want so much. Being then unable to kindle true intimacy with a partner, we fixate on sex as a source of intimacy, since such experiences can bring us intense feelings but which are in reality simply a distraction from our lack of real emotional connection, and if the dearth of emotional intimacy is great enough will naturally be tempted away toward other sources of it, which in many cases requires separation or cheating in order to find.

Many of us feel stupidly entitled to intimacy from someone even though we have been disloyal to them or treat them with much antagonism and contempt. No woman would feel like being intimate with a man who criticizes her appearance, but will turn right around and hurt their husband then still selfishly expect to be caressed and cradled in spite of our cruel and terrible behavior. A husband who wants his wife to overlook his mistakes and shortcomings and give him a satisfying sex life while also hurting her with underhanded comments and disconnecting from a relationship is an idiot who will always experience rejection. Being completely and entirely delusional to the nature of personal responsibility and the immutable laws of cause and consequence, unable to share intimacy in return for fear of accidentally revealing our crimes or insecurity we can never, ever get what we also will not give. Nowhere in life is the phrase "two wrongs do not make a right" more appropriate than within the bonds of a relationship, feeling that because our partner hurt us we are entitled to do so in return makes you every bit as cruel and bad as they. Their behavior does not absolve you of yours, and doing things to hurt other people we also carry that guilt and shame which makes us even more insecure and more volatile and unloveable. The inability for both parties of an unfulfilling relationship to fully share themselves because of the limitations imposed by our unresolved childhood trauma can only ever result in either separation or at best a lifetime of loneliness, even while another person yet sleeps in our bed and we see and talk to them every day, then wonder stupidly why our partner doesn't want to spend time with us, because we are awful to them.

Having a slutty, carnal, sexual encounter even with a stranger for only a night has more honesty in it than an entire lifetime of marriage plagued by manipulation, distrust, recrimination, and suspicion, because both persons in such a raw encounter are being honest in their needs and rational in their expectations of one another, and thus ironically finding far more intimacy, which is borne of honesty, than couples who have spent thousands of dollars on therapy or dedicated decades of their life to each other.

There is never any reason to hurt others. Doing so is on our head, regardless of what is done to us. But being raised by spiteful, vindictive, self-hating people we get taught that this kind of behavior is okay, even while watching their relationships explode and seeing the consequences of incongruent behavior. Conflict can actually be productive, and avoid hurting others even when we need to talk about important things. The only reason it is ever acrimonious is because of the insecurity and fear through which our trauma operates, to obfuscate the reality that to get what we want does not require that others lose.

Being ill equipped to deal with impossible burdens of mortality, intergenerational abuse, and the limits of human ability during such unfulfilling relationships we in turn try to make others responsible for those realities of life we feel incapable of handling, and in so doing burden them with the fears and insecurities we are unwilling to face, then after unloading this burden on a person who only wanted to love us somehow expect our relationship to be a beacon of love and sensuality? It is heinously stupid. How can we, in all our humanity, expect a person to sleep next to us night after night while never letting them close to the person we really are, and expect them not to stray in their search for fulfillment? Though we have not been unfaithful we have also been their jailor, their warden, constantly withholding that which above all they desire of life, which is to find love in the arms of another, unconditional acceptance which might assuage them of their wretched self hatred. Or enter into a relationship demanding that a partner fulfill our needs without complaint or concern for theirs like a telepathic personal sex slave and expect the relationship not to be affected by such self-centered cruelty? Straying from the bonds of commitment, betraying trust and loyalty, and berating and shaming our partner for their fears or the conditions of their mortal body and expect them not to notice the change in our affection, though we speak nothing of our betrayal and are Herculean in our machinations for deception think they will not feel our bonds callously severed?

Though such betrayals and disappointment are very personal, their root lies in our inability to care for our real needs in the first place, to set boundaries, find partners who fulfill our true expectations and not those we pretend to have, or to settle for those we know are not what we want for the sake of loneliness, acceptance, expectation, prejudice, approval, etc. If you don't want to date someone who will cheat on you, don't date someone who will cheat on you! Or, if you don't want to date someone for whom sex is not a priority, then don't date someone disinterested in sex! It is much easier to conceptualize than to actualize as anyone who has experienced such turbulence may attest, and this failure to protect ourselves or to ask and get what we need and want in relationships fail because trauma drives human behavior so powerfully that it is impossible to recognize or, more importantly, do anything about when we are not possessed of tools required to do so, tools such as what inventory therapy empowers by resolving trauma. Lacking skills to care for ourselves and to ask for what we need in turn motivates our tendency to pretend, to deny, to excuse, to conform, to ignore, and to lie because we think it expedient, and to paper over those warning signs which are all so plainly obvious, and to in turn make the consequences of our choices so much more devastating because that too we lack the skills to cope.

We are limited not only by our deluded attempts to control our partner and life in general but also the reality of our value as a person and inherent self worth, believing ourselves to be the very scum that our parents treated us rather than the delightful and wonderful child we actually were, which can only be discovered by uncovering the truth of our past and the reality of life. But the removal of this self-conception can make people lose the very thing from which they derive a sense of self-importance, the victim or the persecutor or the helper, and as such meet inventory and improving our relationships and our daily life with resistance. The stress of divorce and separation can instead be immensely improved by this practice because the pain of such failure is often mostly from the apparent validity it gives our fears and insecurities rather than reality, and insight and wisdom for solutions to interpersonal conflict become more forthcoming and effective when we are informed by compassion and empathy for others and more importantly, ourselves, which also can happen to help prevent divorce and separation since we finally begin to resolve our problems without the need for others to do it for us.

The reality is that other humans, including our own parents, also exploit the vulnerabilities of others on purpose for personal gain. It is one of the reasons why we have such a hard time letting go of control, because others will use our vulnerability as leverage for their own ends, often at our expense. We were told lies told by our parents, explicitly or otherwise, that we were misbehaved, incapable, shy, a failure, unkind, stupid, or other maleficent and cruel characterizations of us as individuals. But because we were children we believed them and thought they were true evaluations of who we are (or afraid they were true), never able to recognize the opportunistic exploitation of our vulnerabilities meant to shore up their emotional control at our expense. With strangers and in more mundane settings humans do this with alarming frequency, exploiting mistakes or vulnerabilities in others such as being overweight, having different skin color, economic status, possessions, sexuality or gender, beliefs, political affiliations, etc. But we as adults turn around and practice this very behavior with our own children and partners. When a husband fails to take out the trash it's a perfect opportunity to excoriate him and dominate the relationship. Or a wife accidentally flirting with another man or who fails to clean up the kitchen it is a perfect opportunity to exploit them to our advantage, never really concerned about the behavior but really about our control over life and those in it, then wonder stupidly what went wrong as we go to bed hating our partner or cry during disingenuous therapy sessions, pretending our own egotistical and fearful behavior bore no destructive consequences. Exploiting the mistakes, weaknesses, or vulnerabilities of others is not self-care, it is harmful both to the relationship and our own sense of confidence and security and emotional resources by driving away those we need to in turn care for us, severing emotional ties and condemning ourselves to abject and unnecessary loneliness. Opportunistically preying upon our loved ones undermines emotional connections and is never justified, no matter how you feel, the time of the month, or what was done to you. It is always possible and required to resolve conflicts without hurting others, and the how and why can be elucidated by inventorying all acrimonious encounters, to enlighten our subconscious to the reasons we felt that way and how we acted, to understand what parts are our responsibility and which are not, and in so doing be empowered to form healthy boundaries, build emotional intimacy, and care for our own needs as well as those we love.

Even supposed acts of kindness can be attempts to manipulate and control which undermine a relationship. For instance, once when my parents visited me for Thanksgiving (which was a very lovely occasion) my mother saw my bare-bones inventory of housewares and proclaimed that I needed to have a full set of certain items for entertaining. I had just purchased several nice, expensive, and high-quality items such as stoneware plates for the occasion, and told her emphatically that I did not want more items, that I had limited my collection because I had to move apartments soon and did not want the burden of packing and hauling more belongings with me, since I had to do it all on my own. After she returned home and in spite of my protestations she ordered more stoneware plates, bowls, and serving utensils to my house, and I was then obligated to find more boxes for packing and effort moving the heavy items while still recovering from cancer, without any help. She had not purchased them out of a concern for my wellbeing or even as a gift to improve my life but because her idea of success and a proper kitchen was not met by my substandard collection, which made her in turn feel insecure, and because it was done not only without concern for me but in spite of my protestations it engendered resentment, not appreciation, and convinced me more of my own mother's indifference to my wellbeing rather than the opposite. I once knew of a wife who gave their husband an expensive, weeks long tropical vacation as a birthday present even though he had expressed a desire not to get any such gift, and when he told her he could not go on the trip she completely lost her mind and the pair argued for days. I know of more than one husband who has given their wife an appliance for a birthday or holiday, and even if they say thank you and accept it such gifts are also a test of a partner, to see how poorly we can treat them without retaliation and as such an act of control, when if we really cared for their wellbeing even something as small as handmade cookies would show more affection.

I heard it said once that we listen to others so that we can respond, which is also a form of deceptive giving, not actually being interested in what others say we only give our attention so we then get the opportunity to indulge our own wants, and zone out during conversations or talk over those we supposedly want to keep in our lives and dominate conversations and relationships. Helping others because our insecurities demand it we become ineffective in our efforts, and attempts to help or be useful are instead met with animosity and distrust, because our actions belie our ulterior and self-centered motives which obfuscate the real needs of those on whom we foist our insecurities, then double down on the pain and inconvenience we cause by insisting they are the ones at fault for not graciously accepting our generosity when our actions hurt them, and in turn hurt them even more. This dynamic of pretended giving occurs plenty between romantic partners when one becomes emotionally despondent or even vindictive when the machinations of our self-centered scheming and booby-trapped generosity fails to produce the manipulation we desired and expected. Since the purpose of such gestures is in truth meant to secure and strengthen our position with regard to our target the failure of it is then doubly alarming to our precarious sense of insecurity, and so we fall back onto yet even more manipulation meant to control and coerce, but in so doing sow intense feelings of resentment and hostility as we selfishly use our loved-one's feelings of obligation against them.

As I discussed in earlier chapters, our tendency to only interact with our children during times of stress and conflict due to our desire to avoid conflict and failure to care for our own-wellbeing also occurs within our romantic relationships. As the grind of daily life goes on, being unempowered with the skillset to properly handle our stress and our personal needs, interactions between couples become increasingly sterile or even outright acrimonious as we try to sustain pockets of self-care we feel can only be had apart from our family and not with them. This tendency to avoid our partner originates from a fear of conflict, which for instance would be an entry into most people's fear inventory, and thus fearing conflict and our partner or children being a major source of conflict will in turn distance ourselves from them not only materially but also emotionally in order to reduce our chances of stimulating this fear. But since we cannot avoid people entirely, especially those whom we need and with whom we are in a relationship, our interactions with them thus become largely negative since confrontations force us to interact, but since these encounters are negative only serve to reinforce our avoidant behavior until we no longer even like our significant other and resent our relationship, because all of our time has been spent in conflict or neglect. Getting to the root of why we behave the way we do, through the inventory practice, such as what can be done about a fear of confrontation can enlighten us to the unconscious ways in which we both fail to care for ourselves and also how we harm those we love. Once this fear is resolved through the inventory practice we can then take steps to proactively interact with our loved ones in ways which affirm love rather than only those of obligation and stress and thus restore bonds of affection, even if the other person does not respond right away to our renewal. No longer at war and needing to defend ourselves we also stop collecting ammunition, which creates emotional space and literally more time and energy we can spend doing things which care for ourselves and our relationship.

Manipulative I statements are a common strategy we use to control our partners under the guise of communication. A husband who checks out of a relationship emotionally who is then told that *you feel hurt when he does so* is not taking care of our needs, because the act of making him the warden of your heart is an act of taking without also giving, and being responsible for the emotional welfare of another adult, especially one burdened by a lifetime of trauma, is a task that no adult wants to carry. Likewise, a wife who is angry or vindictive and told that she is such is not setting healthy boundaries, only boundaries, because it entirely lacks empathy for the reasons she behaves as such, which is unresolved childhood trauma, which you would know if you did inventory and found empathy for your own painful experiences. Telling our partners that they are responsible for our feelings is a selfish act of control which seeks to arbitrate the course of life and prevent uncomfortable and painful experiences at the expense of others, and since every adult has their own burdens of pain and trauma this becomes an impossible task. Since we also can never prevent painful life experiences this strategy never works but instead actively undermines the strength of emotional bonds and ruins families and other important relationships. We who use control mechanisms in this way immediately think the other option is to then allow harmful behavior and let ourselves be taken advantage of, which some of us do anyway since we do not know how to take care of our own needs, but this binary, reactive, and myopic view of life is precisely the type of problem which results from trauma and the bad education we received, or oppositely those of us who are exploitive and narcissistic will condemn the needs of our partner because we feel insecure about lacking empathy for their experiences. The fear of losing governs our perspective of self worth and personal power and thus limits our ability to act effectively, to get what we need and to care for ourselves, which never requires that someone else should lose, least of all our beloved.

The impulse to blame someone else for the way we feel is often a direct result of parents demonstrating that we should be vigilant for opportunities to assert ourselves over our environment and exploit the mistakes and vulnerabilities of others. Others do affect the way we feel, but instead of having compassion for our experience we instead try to neutralize those threats, the act of which withholds compassion for ourselves and actively antagonizes those on whom we rely for emotional and material support. *"I feel lonely, can we hang out?"* Is far and away a better response to feelings of want within a relationship than *"I don't like that you spend so much time on your phone"* (or work, friends, etc.). The former takes responsibility for our emotional needs and gives our partner autonomy and the ability to choose to help and be our savior, where the latter seeks to force this result upon them while also refusing to state our needs, and even though it is phrased as a fucking "I" statement still blames them for our feelings, which are in fact not their responsibility, but ours. The idea that we are responsible for our feelings can also seem overwhelming and frightening, but this is only because we were never taught the skills required to care for ourselves and our needs in ways which are both effective and healthy, and so instead rely on others to do it for us. Writing inventories for these fears, resentments, and disappointments will teach us how to care for our needs and in turn remove the need for others to do it, which will lead to a significant reduction in stress in both our life and those within it, and help us feel empowered and to see the love which in truth exists all around us.

As discussed in earlier chapters, our ability to form any relationship with any human being, especially those which are romantic, is entirely limited to those who share complimentary psychological coping states and control mechanisms, and the decisions we make based on our trauma, fears, and insecurities not only dictate where we go and what we choose to do with our time, money, and person but also whom we find attractive and what qualities draw our interest. The charisma of my past boyfriends was a tempting lure because of my personal insecurity and poor sense of self-worth because of the trauma I experienced in childhood. In reality all I really wanted was to find someone who would be kind and really love me for who I was, but we cannot access people who have those traits we truly desire in a partner (or friend, business partner, and even employees) if our decisions and interests are informed by trauma, fear, and insecurity. Failing to resolve trauma and practice inventory fully thus limits romantic options to those who have complimentary control mechanisms to our own, but practicing inventory and learning compassion for ourselves, our needs, and our past experiences oppositely makes us available to those who are also unburdened by control mechanisms, who practice kindness to themselves and others, which leads to deeper, richer experiences since there are no longer walls preventing us from experiencing others.

 Practicing inventory should cover every aspect of life, but specifically in regard to our better-halves it will help us learn compassion for ourselves and in return also for the person to whom we have made a commitment. Truthfully, when we are insecure and have low feelings of self worth we cannot but help also despise those involved with us, because how could someone love another so undesirable, unless they too are also a loser? When through this practice we finally learn empathy for ourselves we in turn find it for our partners, and in turn give them the space to make the same kinds of changes to their lives. It then becomes easy to be genuine, to enjoy altruism, to give for the sake of giving. To listen not to respond but simply to listen. But most of all it can remove the burden of stress which before depended on things going well, which never really happens, and thus removes unnecessary stress which may encumber our responsibilities of parenthood. There are many parents out there who are single. It should be entirely possible for every parent to do the job alone, as such parents so often demonstrate. After all, that is the definition of adulthood—to be able to provide generally for one's own material and emotional fulfillment, which by definition does not actually require another adult to realize. It is only because we heap stress upon stress onto our lives by ignoring our insecurities that another person even seems necessary to parent successfully, engineering all sorts of ways to complicate our responsibliities and distract ourselves from unresolved pain and trauma which, when finally resolved, free up an incredible amount of time, energy, and resources we did not even know we had. Of course, the presence of a partner can just make things better, and if they too are empowered by such tools (not by force), the job of parenting can be the kind of transcendent experience it is meant to be.

26

The End

My mother, prone to loneliness, despair, and indulgent self-pity characterized my expulsion from the house at eighteen as something that was happening to *her*. She did help me find and set up my first apartment (which was in close proximity to aforementioned University), but seemed completely unaware that the entirety of the situation and the end of my childhood was hers and my father's choice alone, and the conflicts raised ostensibly as an excuse to abandon me originated solely from their own unresolved trauma and fears about life and drive to dominate their children and nothing really to do with my behavior or wellbeing. Crying and expending much emotion about the beginning of the end of her time as a parent she completely abandoned me to the world, welcomed home only every few weeks or so even though I lived just a short distance away.

One day my father phoned to tell me he was coming for a visit. Overjoyed, I was immediately heartbroken to see a stack of anti-homosexual volumes in his hand as thick and heavy as any college course curriculum. His visit was brief. I felt like a patient in a psychiatric ward instead of a young man newly loosed on the world. After he left I looked through the books. Though they were all homophobic and anti-gay, but half of them were written for the *family* of homosexuals. He hadn't even bothered to look at them. I tried to read some anyway but found them full of self-hatred, despair, and hopelessness.

A few girlfriends from High School found out that I was still around, took pity on me and welcomed me into their small group, and for the next several months I had a few people to support me as I planned my next move—another in yet a long list of little moments God was looking out for me when the rest of the the world would not.

In reality it was a blessing that I didn't go on a mission. Many of my friends who did had even more psychological distress from the experience. One friend tried to commit suicide after having an intimate encounter with another handsome missionary, and his mother came home to find her son in the bathtub with both of his wrists slit open in a pool of his own blood (the story of which informed me to use the same method when I tried to commit suicide a few years later). You'd think such an experience might help parents recognize the pain they cause their own children but to this day that mother refuses to have a relationship with *both* of their sons who are gay, who now have families of their own, even though they belong to a religious group ostensibly concerned about the family. Shortly after this time as my other siblings matured and began to leave home my mother fell absolutely to pieces at "losing her children," which in reality was just another in an endless stream of excuses to vent her emotional volatility and indulge self-pity at the expense of others, because of her own paucity of hope and self-compassion and abundant unresolved trauma. In reality every single child except me was back home within two years, and the only reason I wasn't there was because they kicked me out for refusing to lie and pretend I was heterosexual. Children never really grow up, and they never lose their love or need of parents, even when their parents have spent decades rejecting and abusing them. The convenient ignorance to a second generation of coming children when our own in turn have theirs and thus a second chance at parenting is also somehow a surprise to woeful parents even though it has been repeated every single generation throughout the entirety of history. Once begun, the responsibility, pleasures, and joys of parenting never really end except when we abdicate our responsibility or destroy relationships. It is a blessing which can endure the remainder of our entire lives if we take steps to secure and promote bonds of intimacy which are achieved through the resolution of our personal pain and trauma and taking responsibility for and amending our mistakes.

One pitfall of parenthood though which affects us in our later years is that tendency to unwittingly and demonstrably instruct our children exactly how and what to hate about us. Because children expose us to our deepest fears and insecurities and because we then react to those insecurities by attempting to control and extinguish them, our children are then instructed exactly how to hurt, hate, judge, and despise the very things we are ourselves, since in life our insecurities originate from our personal weaknesses. Through her actions and choices as a parent my mother taught her children to revile neediness and emotional intimacy, to resent weakness and dependence on others, to worship money and stuff and belongings and value a person on their monetary and supposed moral worth. All of these provisions originated from her own fears about who she was as a person, her estimate of self-worth, and her role and value within society, relationships, and parenthood. Because she was in fact, needy, lonely, emotional, and desirous of connection her children then shunned and judged her for the very reasons she taught them, and when they became adults showed callousness and indifference when she needed help, and laughed and scorned them for their financial mistakes and miscalculations because thats exactly how we were taught by our parents to treat them. This particular pitfall of parenthood and instincts to actively and subconsciously undermine the stability of our future through our own children is such an unconscious part of parenting that it cannot be subverted through willpower or discipline, and even good parents will ultimately engineer their own undoing in some degree because of the unconscious nature of the parent-child relationship. The only way we can avoid this fate of parenthood is to become conscious and compassionate not only of our own struggles as a human being but also that of others, through practices such as inventory therapy, and in so doing teach our children to have compassion for themselves as they grow which will also result in compassion for us when they finally discover that we are not the all-knowing, perfect, and all-powerful humans they believed us to be.

We will as parents also cause harm and abuse to our children even when we don't do anything wrong. Because of the complexities of human language and how our brains learn to communicate, we will unwittingly cause harm to our children simply through personal sensitivities, assumptions, and translation which interfere with our interaction with the world. I don't doubt that my parents thought the movie *Gremlins* would be a fun and entertaining film to show their eight-year-old son, and I am constantly surprised by the kinds of films kids these days can see and not be traumatized (probably because they're not very good and don't suck us in emotionally). But *Gremlins* was terrifying, and I had nightmares about it for months. It's now one of my favorite films. But they also showed us *Ghostbusters*, and the images of those hellhounds and Slavitza Jovan as *Zuul* absolutely made me piss myself. Literally. Sometimes we may say things to children they hear differently than what was said, or they might not understand the context of what we say or do and in turn find hurt where we did not intentionally commit harm. Most adults handle such encounters defending their position rather than helping fix the harm our actions caused. The only recourse to help our children in turn is to empower them with these tools to resolve childhood trauma that we demonstrate to them through our behavior, since we cannot anyway protect them in perpetuity, even from ourselves.

When I was eleven-years old I went down into the dirt cellar of our vintage victorian home and latest restoration project to retrieve some canned peaches for my mother. In the middle of all the brown cardboard boxes was a tan, pink, and sea-green Hot Wheels bike decorated with decals of Ariel and Flounder from Disney's *The Little Mermaid*. I thought it strange that such a beautiful prize would just be sitting in a dark and dirty cellar. A few weeks later at Christmastime when I walked in to see the same *Little Mermaid* bike beneath the tree with a note ascribing it *from Santa* I finally realized I had been lied to every holiday season for my entire life. It was devastating not because my parents lied to me nor the accidental realization of the falsity of Santa but because I suddenly became aware of all the other sources of deception and manipulation being committed against me by people who were supposed to love and care for us and provide for my wellbeing. Suddenly I was conscious of my vulnerability and danger within a family burdened by lies and abuse, which

I would have eventually become aware anyway (to be clear there is nothing wrong with Santa or the Easter Bunny except the manipulations with which they are associated).

Parents begin missing out on our children's lives as soon as they are born, before they are even a year old start complaining of how quickly they are growing and that they will never have any more, sometimes in jest and awe of children but often in presupposition to defeatist and despairing conceptions of life, unable to live in the present for the presence of pain and insecurity, to check out and distract ourselves with obsessions over self-improvement, gain, profession, success, and interpersonal conflict. When we resolve our insecurities and come to terms with our mistakes and our trauma this impulse to avoid life vanishes and we in turn become capable of existing in every moment, being able to sit still, to be satisfied by the mundaneness of everyday life and filled by the beauty and serenity which surrounds us. Being a parent is not just a one-time job that begins and ends with our own offspring. We can all be parents to everyone in our lives, including ourselves, to our nieces and nephews, to children of friends and associates, to those without parents and even to grown children who still need guidance, love, and protection. Offering our homes, our cooking, our insight, and companionship as an older and experienced adult with emotional and material resources is what a parent is and does. The only reason we hoard and conserve our love and access to our own, immediate biological children originates from the very same kinds of fearful and selfishly limiting views of humanity that causes our own familial conflicts in the first place. Service to all is a desperately instinctual aspect of humans as social creatures, driven by our biology to cooperate and be useful we turn into raging monsters of endless consumption and dissatisfaction when we neglect our need to be of use to others and to succeed in cooperation and helpfulness. The narrow-minded isolation of families from one another and the destruction of intergenerational bonds and fellowship is a tragedy of previous generations, torn apart by war and conflict and selfishness and materialism we have forgotten what it means to cook, to eat well, to associate, to love and to be loved, and can never as a species feel satisfied and fulfilled until we address our shared need of one another, help those who are less fortunate, promote policies and governance which facilitates equality and fairness, and help those who are burdened by the trauma of the past to find healing and relief.

A few months before my parents kicked me out of the house my Dad one day asked if I had ever had sushi. "No," I laughed. He would know, since they had been buying all our meals and restaurant visits over the last two decades.

"Would you like to go have sushi with me?"

I was honestly grossed out. The idea of having raw fish sounded completely and utterly disgusting. Once when I was much older and took a date to a sushi restaurant and had been having sushi for many years I still gagged when we were presented with toro, which is the expensive and prized fatty underbelly of tuna, as well as my first time trying uni (sea urchin), thinking the orange goo was a sauce on top of the uni but was in fact the slimy, revolting mucus that is sea urchin flesh. But I was desperate to have a relationship with my own father. I couldn't believe he actually wanted to hang out with me. So I didn't even hesitate in making a decision.

"Sure!"

We drove to a small sushi shop which had opened recently in our small Utah town, just the two of us, and it was not lost on me the ridiculousness of having sushi in a tiny interior Western American town one-thousand miles from any ocean. My Dad greeted the chef with the ease which accompanies familiarity. "Have you been coming here?" I asked. "At least a few days a week since it opened," he said. I didn't even know he liked sushi.

"I don't know what to order," I said as I leafed through the menu.

"I'll order for you. You'll love it," he said.

The chef brought us several large dishes as we sat at the bar chatting. "This is wasabi," said my Dad, who then demonstrated how to mix it into the soy sauce. "It's hot, so only try a little bit first."

I separated my chopsticks and clumsily retrieved a piece of salmon and avocado sushi, then dunked it lightly into the wasabi soy mix. I was utterly romanced by the sweet flesh of raw fish and the cold heat of the wasabi, the earthy saltiness of the soy jumping out to envelop the whole bite. I had never had such flavors in my mouth.

"Holy crap," I said as the wasabi began to make my eyes water.

"Told you," said my father.

We continued to eat, but I had in truth expected this occasion to be one for lecturing or reprimanding me for something. We had, in fact, never been alone on an activity in my entire life. Every outing, every meal at a restaurant, movie, or camping had always included other family members, if not all of them. So it only seemed natural that this was some ploy to disarm me and launch an attack. But to my surprise we simply chatted about life. He told me stories about his youth I had never heard before, such as when he drove home drunk for the first and only time as a teenager on an empty country road and was so frightened by the experience he never again picked up a drink (well, he did but won't admit it). We went home without a single cross word said or hurt feeling between us. For a moment I thought my life with them was salvageable, that maybe they really did love me and had my best interests in mind. But only a few months later they were escorting me to a different city for the sole purpose of living apart from them, the beginning of the end of our journey together.

Parenting is not as hard as it often is, and like all things in life we typically are the authors of our own misery. Life can be devastating, and loss can bring us the kind of despair which robs us of the very will to live. Our mortality can be frail and our limitations infuriating. I recognized that the disparity between my Grandparents more loving relationships with us came because of the regret and pain of failure and mistakes they learned through their own experience of being thrust headlong into parenthood without many useful tools to succeed and burdened by the pain and trauma of their own childhoods, without compassion for their own mistakes and mortal limitations. I am grateful for my nieces' and nephews' same naive belief in their Grandparent's facade of benevolence just as I did mine. In truth all this suffering comes *only* because we refuse to live by the laws of reality and instead persist in fear and isolation. We can reach for the stars but Heaven and its angels are here on Earth, because life is more rich and wonderful than most of us even realize. We are more special and amazing and good than our religious backflips and creativity can accurately estimate. The true accounting of self-worth and the value of our experience is found in the simple practice of sitting down with ourselves and spending time to inventory our lives through which we can become empowered to realize our true nature, skills, ability, and humanity. It only takes a pen, some paper, and willingness. Being a good parent is not in reality about being a parent. It's about being who we really are and learning to forgive not just the past but also ourselves as we navigate this complex and ever-changing world in which we live.

All children are perfect. Yes, even the one which you used to be and in many ways still are. You didn't need to read this book to know that, but life and human nature has a way of forgetting obvious truths and complicating simple realities. All the pain and suffering and disappointment of our childhoods came only because our parents did not also have compassion for their own experiences nor the skills and tools to resolve the pain and trauma and abuse which has been the cycle of the human parent-child relationship since the dawn of man. We can spare our own children this fate and heal our own wounds and spend the rest of our lives in happiness and joy no matter where life decides to take us, if only we spend the time to care for ourselves. Life is actually *full* of joy, and there are far more moments of love and peace and happiness than we have been taught to recognize. We are capable as adults of so much more than our parents ever realized was possible, and each of us has the power to correct the past and heal the present, to give to ourselves the love, friendship, and care that we are due that nobody else needs to give us. That is what it means to be an adult. Grow up. Take care of yourself. That you may in turn care for those who need you.

For more information on health, wellness, and living in harmony with the human condition, recipes and food ideas, and to stay up to date on my latest work or follow me on social media, please visit *fuckportioncontrol.com*.

www.ingramcontent.com/pod-product-compliance
Lightning Source LLC
Chambersburg PA
CBHW071952290426
44109CB00018B/1999